alt.culture

alt.culture

an a-to-z guide to the '90s—
underground, online,
and over-the-counter

nathaniel wice and steven daly

HarperPerennial
A Division of HarperCollinsPublishers

HarperCollins books may be purchased for educational, business, or sales promotional use. For information please write: Special Markets Department, HarperCollins Publishers, Inc., 10 East 53rd Street, New York, NY 10022.

FIRST EDITION

Designed by Nancy Singer

Library of Congress Cataloging-in-Publication Data

Wice, Nathaniel.
Alt. culture : an a-to-z guide to the '90s—underground, online, and over-the-counter / Nathaniel Wice and Steven Daly. — 1st ed.
p.   cm.
ISBN 0-06-273383-4
1. Subculture — Computer networks.   2. Life style — Computer networks.
I. Daly, Steven, 1960–   .   II. Title.
HQ2042.W53   1995
025.06'3061—dc20   95-47432

95 96 97 98 99 ❖/RRD 10 9 8 7 6 5 4 3 2 1

concerning the online addresses

alt.culture is one of the first non-computer reference books to assume a degree of knowl-edge about the Internet. Most of the entries in the book end with Internet addresses where you can go for online information and discussions about the subjects, from the Beastie Boys and Hello Kitty to snowboarding and veganism. As we were planning the book, the Internet was proving to be instrumental both as a research tool and in the development of the culture we were writing about. (As we were writing it, email addresses became a familiar sight in the letters pages of magazines and newspapers, then in their entertainment and news sections; by the time we finished, Web addresses were appearing in movie and even car ads on TV.)

There are two problems, though:

First, some of the addresses in *alt.culture* already don't work. The enthusiast who puts on a Web site devoted to a band, for instance, might switch allegiance when that band either becomes popular or falls from sight. This informality of electronic commu-nication is at odds with the process of preparing, printing, and distributing a book. (Since 1994 the computer sections of bookstores have been filled with online guides that don't acknowledge this simple fact of their subject matter.) Our solution is to publish updates to the online addresses, *online*. If you find that an address doesn't work, you are online and able to get the update. Our online home is printed on the back cover:

web **http://www.altculture.com/** email **info@altculture.com**

alt.culture

Second, what do all these addresses mean? What follows is a brief guide to online access and the addresses in this book.

online addresses & access

There are eight different kinds of Internet addresses in this book, and each is explained below. Which of these addresses tends to be accessible from which online services follows afterwards.

online addresses

WEB

World Wide Web, a collection of millions of interconnected "pages" stored on Internet-joined computers around the world. The World Wide Web makes it possible to graphically navigate the Internet by pointing and clicking on links embedded in the text and images of Web pages. The links are programmed with the addresses of other Web pages, but you can also jump to a Web Site by manually entering a web address (or URL—for Uniform Resource Locators—as they are also known). URL's typically begin with "http://" as in "http://www.hyperreal.com/".

GOPHER

Text-only version of the World Wide Web. "Gopher space," as it is often known, is separate from the Web, although most Web access also makes it possible to browse Gopher information. Gopher addresses in *alt.culture*—like the ACLU's files on campus speech codes at gopher://aclu.org:6601/—are formatted to work for someone coming from the World Wide Web. To get the "Gopher space" address itself, drop the "gopher://" prefix (e.g. aclu.org:6601).

FTP

File Transfer Protocol, another format standard for storing and retrieving files over the Internet, usually used for archives. FTP access requires an account name and password, but public access is often offered as "anonymous FTP" (where the username is "anonymous" and you are asked to voluntarily enter your email address as a password). FTP addresses in *alt.culture*—like the Prince lyrics stored at ftp://math.montana.edu/pub/carlson/pltt/—are formatted to work for someone coming from the World Wide Web. To get the FTP address itself, drop the "ftp://" prefix (e.g. math.montana.edu/pub/carlson/pltt).

EMAIL

Electronic version of a postal address. (The slower, physical version is often dismissed online as snail mail.) Some email addresses—like info@altculture.com—are set-up to function as outgoing answering machine messages, automatically replying with basic information that often includes more methods of contact. Internet email addresses are easily recognized by the "@" ("at sign") dividing the user's name (user i.d.) from the user's affiliation (domain name).

USENET

Collection of more than 10,000 separate "newsgroup" discussions. Conversation is conducted via messages posted to newsgroups, with replies to previously posted message creating message "threads." Some newsgroups are moderated, which means that you or your message has to be approved before you can post.

MAIL LIST

Like a Usenet newsgroup, except messages are distributed via email. This tends to make mail list discussions more intimate, and discussions are often more focused because they require a proactive act of subscribing and are less vulnerable to drive-by contributors. At the same time, mail lists are also more accessible than newsgroups—while many small online services do not carry full newsfeeds (and some large ones censor or do not offer any Usenet access at all), Internet email is the basic currency of Internet access. Some mail lists, like some newsgroups, are moderated, while others are intended for announcements only.

Instructions for subscribing to a mail list include a subscription address to which a specific message usually must be sent in the subject or body of the subscription request. To subscribe to the PJ Harvey mail list, for example, you would send a piece of email to the address majordomo@homer.louisville.edu with the message "subscribe pjh" in the body of the letter.

IRC

Live online discussion via typed messages. IRC (Internet Relay Chat) channels are easy to recognize because they always begin with a # sign (usually pronounced "pound" or "hash"), as in #wicca. Well-established channels like #hottub can attract dozens of people at pre-arranged times, but—since anyone can create a channel—most channels form and disappear by the hour.

TELNET

Direct login to another computer on the Internet. Telnet is one of the earliest Internet functions and—though many of its functions are being incorporated into the World Wide Web—still usually the connection of choice when one wants to run a program on another computer, as in MUD participation. Telnet addresses in *alt.culture*—like the FurryMUCK MUD at telnet://furry.org 8888/—are formatted to work for someone coming from the World Wide Web. To get the telnet address itself, drop the "telnet://" prefix (e.g. furry.org 8888).

online access

Here's a rundown of what to expect from online accounts, and more explanation of the questions you can ask to compare them (e.g. does the connection include an email account, Web access, a full Usenet newsfeed?). There are four main kinds of Internet connections, none of which guarantees (or, in most cases, precludes) access to all the addresses in this book.

EMAIL GATEWAY

Connection most common in educational and corporate settings, where an in-house computer network is upgraded to handle email (and nothing else) in- and out-bound over the Internet.

BBS

Bulletin Board System. This type of service was the dominant form of consumer computer networking in the '80s, run over phone lines, often out of the basement of a hobbyist (though many of the largest BBS concerns have grown into Internet Service Providers or "indie" commercial online services). In the late '80s BBSs began to form their own networks for forwarding mail and their own version of Usenet discussions (sometimes called "echoes"); in the mid '90s many have added Internet email and limited selection of Usenet newsgroups. The typical BBS is homey, with users who chose the local color over a more industrial Internet "on-ramp." Accounts tend to be cheap, flat-rate monthly fees.

COMMERCIAL ONLINE SERVICE

Generally recognized term for America Online, CompuServe, Prodigy, Microsoft Network (MSN), and the other big guns of mass-market, nationwide online access.

Before 1994 the commercial online services were competing to build the best self-contained theme park—even sending and receiving email outside the services was an iffy proposition. In 1995, though, they scrambled to offer Internet access (buying up many independent Internet providers), first to Usenet, later to the World Wide Web. Commercial services tend to be easier to use than straight Internet accounts but, since they use their own proprietary software (for Web browsing and the like), the Internet access tends to be less flexible. Most offer free trial periods and charge by the hour beyond a monthly minimum.

INTERNET SERVICE PROVIDER

Internet version of the phone company, providing the Internet equivalent of a dial-tone (static or dynamic "IP number") and often not much else. Once the purview of hardcore techies operating local services, Internet access started getting better, easier-to-use packaging in 1995. With your own "IP number" and a SLIP or PPP phone connection, your computer isn't just connected to the Internet, it's actually part of it. This enables the widest and most up-to-date choice of Internet software, from enhanced Web browsers and audio-on-demand to crude videoconferencing and encrypted phone calls. Local service providers (look in newspaper ads, ask around, or get a list from online [there's a good one at http://thelist.com/]) tend to charge a flat monthly rate that's much cheaper than regularly using a commercial online service.

NETWORK CONNECTION

Versatile, high-speed connection most commonly found in educational and corporate settings. Network hook-ups work the same as IP connections over phone-lines from an Internet Service Provider, but they usually run at much higher speeds. Where the typical phone connection runs at 14,400 or 28,800 baud, a typical network connection over Ethernet could ideally clock ten million bits per second, but tends to be limited by the ability of the computers at each end to serve and swallow that fast. Cable companies hope to bring network connections to the masses via so-called "cable modems," while digital phone (ISDN) service over standard phone lines can also soup up the speed of Internet connections.

editorial

SENIOR CONTRIBUTORS
Ted Friedman, Richard Gehr, Ben Greenman, Daniel Radosh

ASSOCIATE CONTRIBUTORS
Jennifer Baumgartner, Jennifer Bretan, Suzy Coue, Sarah Ferguson, Simson Garfinkel, Susan Kelly, Joseph Malgarini, Suzanne McElfresh, Artie Nelson, Nilou Panahpour, Tracey Pepper, Alison Powell, Marny Requa, David Shenk, Kip Shives, Christina Wayne, David Williams, Jeff Yang

ESSAYS
Nicole Arthur, Erik Davis, Mark Ehrman, Jim Farber, Rob Kenner, Eric Konigsberg, Leslie Savan, Alexander Star

RESEARCH EDITOR
Tracey Pepper

Associate
Luke Dempsey

ONLINE RESEARCH EDITOR
John Zacharias Grace

Associates
Parisa Jaffer, David Williams

Photos

PHOTO EDITORS
Alexandra Flood, Nancy Iacoi

PHOTOGRAPHERS
Bill Bytsura, David Corio, Cheryl Dunn, Sue Kwon, Linda Rosier, Tina Paul, Sandra-Lee Phipps, Natsuko Utsumi, Brooke Williams

Internet Services

Digital Telemedia Inc.

Compiling an "a-z of '90s America" might seem a doomed proposition, what with the decade barely half over, but these past five years have arrived practically pre-packaged for Zeitgeist-watchers. Cultural currents from Birkenstocks to heroin have been presented, with some justification, as a salutary reaction against— yes!—the Go-Go '80s. In youth-culture terms the transformation could hardly have been more swift or certain: as early as 1991, Nirvana, Lollapalooza, the movie *Slacker*, and— yes!—the novel *Generation X* countered the previous decade's onslaught of MTV production values, baby-boomer nostalgia, and big shoulder pads.

With the notable exception of hip-hop, no major youth movement emerged during the '80s—in hindsight, the backlash looks inevitable. It came in the shape of a generation of musicians, designers, film- and other culture-makers who in large part defined themselves against the prevailing ethos, just as the original punks were galvanized by the rockstar excesses of the '70s. Comparisons were frequently made to America's last youth culture boom, in the 1960s, but chief among many differences was the fact that where hippie culture organized itself around rockstar iconography, the '90s were a pantheistic throwdown of self-expression and consumer choice. Instead of waiting around for the next Dylan album or Lennon interview, you could be watching a video of a Hong Kong action classic, surfing cable channels or the Internet, or mountain-biking in city traffic. (Youth politics have likewise been transformed by the new lifestyle options and lack of defining heroes and causes.) If there was any commonality among the tribe dubbed— along with millions of salaried peers—Generation X, it was a distrust of celebrity culture in all its forms, from rock mythmaking to infotainment gushing.

The word *alternative,* descended from '80s college rock, became a handy description for the milieu, but it was soon reduced by overuse to just a cooler way of saying "cool." ("You're so alternative" was an ironic taunt long before radio commercials in 1994 touted Bud Dry as the "alternative beer.") Even spread this thin, alternative—with its roots in white, middle-class rock—couldn't describe American youth culture in all its fragmented glory: what about Snoop Doggy Dogg or Nike or Mortal Kombat or *Melrose Place*? Our own use of "alt" in alt.culture isn't, then, to be taken as a straight abbreviation—it's also a reference to that consummate "alternative" outlet of the '90s, the Internet, where "alt" is a prefix for a bewildering number of "alternate" discussion newsgroups ("alt.culture.us.1970s," etc.), many of which appear after the entries in the book.

> *A few months ago I went to Martin Luther King Day at my old junior*
> *high in Eugene [Oregon], which used to be an ass-kicking, Led Zeppelin,*
> *evil, stoner high school ... Now all the girls are like* Sassy *readers with*
> *Nirvana shirts and little dreadlocks and nose rings.*
> —Courtney Love, *Los Angeles Times*, August 1992

In early-'90s America, MTV News beamed new scenes (queercore, spoken word, "college" rap) across the country within months of their advent. Urban Outfitters quickly stocked its nationwide chain of stores with the styles of New York and L.A. club-goers (baby T-shirts, poleclimber boots, thigh-high stockings); a couple of months later the Gap pumped the same fashions into every mall in the country. Suburbs were, for the first time, home to the majority of voters—trickle-down hip had become a downpour.

The marketplace itself has perversely been remade in the image of America's youth-culture renaissance; lifestyle corporations have developed an alarming capacity for absorbing fresh styles and attitudes, whether licensing them from their makers, or putting them to work selling soft drinks, cars, and sneakers. This conformity of non-con-formity looks like it will set the tone for the rest of the decade. "My God!" Courtney Love went on to exclaim to the *L.A. Times*, "If the charts were just and fair and the Pixies and Nirvana and Hole were the most [popular bands] ... I'd probably start listening to Poison. I don't want utopia, I want cacophony."

This good-taste epidemic is marketed by conglomerates that are absorbing each other and their boutique-sized competitors on an hourly basis. Every culture-maker ("content provider") worth his or her salt faces the imminent prospect of being owned by one of several global brand names desperate to have a piece of the latest software (in old-world language: music, film, etc.). Muscular and efficient, these brands will further blur distinctions between their news and entertainment divisions, while locking-in new forms of cross-promotion that make a movie project worthwhile only if it can also be spun-off as an indie-rock soundtrack, theme park ride, *and* fast-food cup series.

The '90s consolidation of culture corporations has paradoxically arrived at the same time that access and choice have led to cultural Balkanization, flourishing subcults, and esoteric micro-niches. (TV channels proliferate, for example, but they are owned by fewer, larger companies.) In the past two years, the Internet—an open-ended global network of computer networks controlled by no one—has emerged at the center of these contradictory trends. The Internet's driving metaphor, hypertext, epitomizes the age's excess of access, making it possible to surf, skim, point-and-click through oceans of words, sounds, and pictures stored (published) on Internet-connected computers. The global reach also nurtures communities of interest which exist outside the marketplace, whether surrounding pot libertarianism or feminist Wicca rites. And yet, the Internet's promise has become a central justification for legalizing monopoly control of the media. If small-time entrepreneurs and consumers have open-access to Internet "broadcasting," the argument goes, then there's no longer any need to protect citizens from the likelihood that a single corporation (Time Warner, for instance, or News Corp., the parent to *alt.culture*'s publisher) will move to control a region's newspapers, phone system, and cable, radio, and TV outlets.

Disney, which is also gearing up for an invasion of the Internet, is a prime example of the new corporate paradigm. Mickey can be in bed with indie-film superpower Miramax—the company responsible for Larry Clark's scandal-ridden *Kids* and (partly) for Quentin Tarantino's venture into the advertising business—at the same time as it builds vast, ultra-secure family compounds in Florida, takes on ownership of the ABC network, and begins calculating the multi-billions to be made setting and selling curricula standards for the nation's schools. By the end of America's fifth youth culture decade, companies like this could conceivably subsume all of the signifiers on Courtney Love's anthropological checklist. You know, like, *everything*.

As for our own anthropological checklist, the world-view might seem random once you get beyond the likes of Liz Phair, Karl Kani, snowboarders, and ACT-UP, but there is a clear logic hidden in here somewhere. O.J. houseguest Kato Kaelin is catalogued as a model of '90s virtual stardom, but O.J. himself is deprived of his own entry. No tabloid stories, then, except Amy Fisher, who was, after all, played by Drew Barrymore in a TV movie. (John Wayne Bobbitt is here for the record-breaking sales of his porn tape; poor Tonya Harding only to help define white trash.) We did Chelsea Clinton but not Bill. *The New Yorker* is included as an example of pretension (our own). Music-wise, we sought out stylistic innovations and aberrant personalities; worthy alterna-troopers like Soundgarden and Belly would, we reasoned, be well-covered in rock consumer guides. Why isn't karaoke in the book? Because we forgot. Why the Baldwins and not the Arquettes? Because we think the Baldwins are funnier. That's why it's *an* a-z of the '90s, not *the* a-z of the '90s.

Steven Daly and Nathaniel Wice
New York City, September '95

Abortion clinic violence "If you believe it's murder, act like it," was one motto of anti-abortion activist and OPERATION RESCUE founder Randall Terry. In 1993, blockade, harassment, death threat, phony malpractice suits, and even firebombing tactics against abortion clinics escalated to actual incidents of murder. Shouting "stop killing babies," "pro-life" activist Michael Griffin shot dead Dr. David Gunn in March of that year outside the Pensacola, Florida, clinic where he worked. Subsequent precautions included bullet-proof vests and armed escorts, but another doctor, John Bayard Britton, and a volunteer, James H. Barrett, were fatally shot in July, 1994—also in Pensacola—by ex-minister Paul Hill. That December, beauty school student and zealot John Salvi killed two clinic workers, Shannon Lowney and Leeann Nichols, at a Planned Parenthood in Brookline, Massachusetts. Despite the network of violence, the FBI had concluded as of spring 1995 that it would not be possible to bring conspiracy charges against any anti-abortion leaders or groups.

WEB **Violence at Abortion Clinics** http://www.matisse.net/ politics/caral/violencepage.html ✦ WEB **National Right to Life College Outreach Program** http://www.cencom.net/ ~jen/life/ertelt/nsl2.html ✦ WEB **Abortion & Reproductive Rights Internet Resources** http://www.matisse.net/ politics/caral/abortion.html ✦ USENET **talk.abortion** WEB **Refuse & Resist! Abortion Rights** http://www.calyx.com/ ~refuse/ab/index.html ✦ USENET talk.abortion

Absolutely Fabulous Scabrous British fashion-world sitcom, first shown in the U.S. in July 1994. *Absolutely Fabulous* (U.K. debut November 1992) is written by actress-comedienne Jennifer Saunders, who stars as a fashion-victim publicist (reportedly based on a London publicist-acquaintance, Lynne Franks) whose cavortings with a dipso-nympho gal pal put her at loggerheads with a POLITICALLY CORRECT daughter. Swooning U.S. critics of *Ab Fab* (as it became known) commended cable channel COMEDY CENTRAL for its bravery in carrying a series with levels of sex and drugs that reportedly daunted potential purchaser PBS. It's also possible that the latter network was put off by the show's opaque cultural references and unwaveringly shrill pitch. In late 1994, with *Ab fab* enjoying a vocal cult audience (many gay, many via videotape) in the U.S., Roseanne Barr acquired the rights to create an American version of the series.

WEB **Absolutely Fabulous Home Page** http:// src.doc.ic.ac.uk/media/tv/collections/tardis/uk/comedy/ AbsolutelyFabulous/ ✦ WEB **Edina** http://edina.mothership.com/ ✦ USENET **alt.tv.absolutely_fabulous**

Abu-Jamal, Mumia (b. Wesley Cook, 1954) Radio reporter sentenced to death for the fatal December 1981 shooting of a Philadelphia police officer who had stopped Abu-Jamal's brother for driving the wrong way down a one-way street. A former official in the local BLACK PANTHER chapter and an outspoken critic of the city's prosecution of a radical black group called MOVE, Abu-Jamal was hired in 1994 by National Public Radio to do a series of monthly three-minute commentaries about life behind bars for the respected *All Things Considered* nightly news program. (The reports were not to discuss his case, a rallying issue for the left.) When police groups and the slain officer's widow protested, NPR withdrew the assignment and Abu-Jamal's case became a cause célèbre among death penalty opponents. The canceled commentaries formed the basis of Abu-Jamal's book *Live From Death Row*, published in May 1995 with an introduction by novelist John Edgar Wideman and a jacket blurb from Alice Walker. In June, the Pennsylvania governor signed Abu-Jamal's death warrant, but owing to mounting international pressure a stay of execution was granted mere weeks before the August 17, '95 execution date.

WEB **Free Mumia Abu-Jamal** http://huizen.dds.nl/ ~tank/mumia002.htm ✦ WEB **Refuse & Resist!** http:// www.calyx.com/~refuse/ ✦ USENET **alt.activism.death-penalty**

acid house Originally an experimental offshoot of Chicago HOUSE music (Phuture's 1986 *Acid Trax* was one influential example), acid house came to denote a sensibility that radically altered club culture worldwide. After the ECSTASY-fueled summer of 1987 on the Spanish holiday island of Ibiza, several influential British DJs used acid house as a jumping-off point for a new eclecticism. The status-conscious dress codes of '80s clubbing dissolved in all-night RAVES where the fashion statement consisted of baggy jeans and hooded tops with garishly blithe logos, and faceless, home-made recordings topped the charts with little radio play or media attention. (Some critics anointed acid the "new PUNK," pointing to its egalitarian, anti-fashion, experimental, anti-star elements; others called it mindless and apolitical.) The acid house aesthetic was central to California's nascent rave scene in 1990–91, joining the tradition of American black music that has been exported to Europe, customized, then imported back in a more acceptable form.

WEB **streetsound on-line** http://www.phantom.com/~street/

acid jazz Music genre nurtured by London's Talkin' Loud label in the late 1980s (and named as an oblique reference to the dominant dancefloor form of the time, ACID HOUSE). Original British proponents like Galliano and the Young Disciples married vintage jazz samples and live instrumentation with DJ-friendly HIP-HOP break-beats. America's acid jazz wellspring was New York's peripatetic Giant Step club (founded 1990), where live pairings of rappers and jazz musicians inspired several HIP-HOP projects (notably the Brand New Heavies' 1992 multi-rapper *Heavy Rhyme Experience: Vol.1*, and 1993's *Jazzamatazz* collaboration between Gang Starr leader Guru and jazz great Donald Byrd). The club's unusually MULTICULTURAL clientele were fashion leaders, with STÜSSY the dominant label and "old skool" ADIDAS and PUMA sneakers *de rigueur*. The next wave of acid jazz-influenced acts—including the Digable Planets and US3—achieved success in America with hits that became the perfect soundtrack for TV fashion shows, stylish bars, and URBAN OUTFITTERS stores. Some detractors have dubbed the music "flaccid jazz," arguing that it waters down an authentic form for a trend-hungry mass market.

WEB **AcidJazz** http://www.cmd.uu.se/AcidJazz/ ✦

WEB **Psycho Friend's NETwork (Moonshine Records)** http://www.moonshine.com/ ✦ WEB **streetsound on-line** http://www.phantom.com/~street/ ✦ MAIL LIST **Acid Jazz List** email listserv@ucsd.edu

ACT-UP AIDS Coalition to Unleash Power, direct-action protest group formed to agitate for a concentrated response to the AIDS crisis from the Federal government, and by default the single loudest voice of opposition to Republican social policies from housing to health care. A "wake-up call" speech by playwright-author Larry Kramer galvanized the first of a series of Monday night meetings in New York, March, 1987. Impassioned, polemical, chaotic, informative, and sometimes entertaining, ACT-UP meetings brought together an impressive coalition, though the group's roster tended to be filled with white, gay males (among other things, meetings once functioned as a booming pick-up scene).

ACT-UP is best known for its guerrilla-style demonstrations, "die-in's," and "zaps." In 1989, ACT-UP protesters infiltrated the New York Stock Exchange and brought trading to a halt, embarrassing pharmaceutical giant Burroughs Wellcome into dropping the price ($10,000 per year) of its new antiretroviral drug, AZT. ACT-UP also persuaded the FDA to "fast track" two experimental drugs, gangiclover and DDI. By the early '90s, ACT-UP boasted over 100 chapters worldwide from Seattle to Paris. T-shirts and buttons bearing the group's emblem, the pink triangle of Nazi persecution

ACT-UP protestors at George Bush's vacation home, September 1991.

inverted in a disavowal of victimhood, and variations of its "Silence = Death" slogan became ubiquitous. ACT-UP has also had its share of failures; a notorious 1990 storming of Saint Patrick's Cathedral, in which a communion wafer was reportedly destroyed by a protestor, enraged right-wing critics. ACT-UP has also endured internal feuding over its focus, leading to such splinter groups as QUEER NATION. Although attendance has dwindled in recent years—partly owing to the deaths of many integral members, and the assumption that a "more sympathetic" President in office had made the group obsolete (the Washington D.C. branch shut its doors in 1993)—ACT-UP meetings continue on Monday evenings in most major cities.
mail list **act-up list** email act-up-request@world.std.com ✦
USENET **misc.aids.health, sci.med.aids**

Adbusters   Vancouver-based leftist quarterly which parodies and critiques "mental pollution" ad campaigns to get its own social justice, health, and environmental messages across. *Adbusters'* "subvertising" has included "American Excess: Leave Home Without It," "Absolut Nonsense," and "Buy Nothing Day"; the organization's activist shell, the Media Foundation, helps activists place the ad parodies in local markets.
EMAIL adbuster@wimsey.com GOPHER **WELL Cyberpunk & Postmodern Culture** gopher://gopher.well.sf.ca.us/ 00/cyberpunk/cultjam.txt ✦ USENET **alt.tv.commercials** ✦WEB **Media Watchdog** http://theory.lcs.mit.edu/ ~mernst/media

Adidas   Sportswear company formed in 1948 by German athlete Alfred "Adi" Dassler (b. 1901, d. 1978). Adidas' trademark triple-striped track and field gear was much prized among American high school students throughout the '70s; in 1983 rappers Run-D.M.C. hymned the company's shell-toed sneakers in "My Adidas." The street popularity of Adidas faded as newer, more aggressive and innovative companies like NIKE and Reebok dominated the sportswear market. However, English style warriors revived "old skool" suede Adidas sneakers (and their PUMA counterparts) in 1990–91, and U.S.

style-mongers like the BEASTIE BOYS and the Digable Planets soon joined in. Increased demand spurred Adidas to re-manufacture its older styles; by 1992–93 the Gazelle model was standard-issue among LOLLAPALOOZA aesthetes, with the shell-toed classic also prized. The three stripes soon exerted a powerful influence over fashion collections: in 1993 LAURA WHITCOMB's Label company issued an Adidas-sanctioned collection of long, stretch-fabric dresses; ANNA SUI, Katharine Hamnett, and Donna Karan were among those who offered their own variations on three-stripe couture. Knock-off versions reached overkill proportions on urban streets by 1994.
WEB **Adidas** http://www.adidas.de/

BEASTIE BOY protégées Luscious Jackson model LAURA WHITCOMB's Adidas-chic, 1993.

Adult Album Alternative   Rock radio format aimed at affluent, college-educated listeners who grew up in the '70s. AAA, which emerged in late 1993 most successfully at San Francisco's KFOG-FM and Seattle's KMTT-FM, aims for larger, "smarter" playlists that are familiar but less obvious than classic rock or pop, that still rock but not as hard as metal. The format typically mixes one-third rock hits from the mildly edgy likes of Tom Petty, Sheryl Crow, or Hootie and the Blowfish, with the rest comprising some of the less-threadbare classic rock album tracks. In 1995 one of the biggest AAA syndicators, Radio One, switched its emphasis to the "commercial alternative" rock format heard on some 65 stations around the country because, the company explained to *Billboard*, "we did a good bit of research, and it looked like alternative rock is really gaining in popularity faster."

Adventures of Pete and Pete, The

Knowing, surreal children's program equally popular with kids and rock fans. A product of the NICKELODEON cable network, *Pete and Pete* points a warped lens at the trivial (but compelling) travails of two brothers (both named Pete) and the adults who afflict them in the mystical suburban enclave of Wellsville. Originally a series of short segments in 1989, this whimsical show grew to half hour specials before acquiring a regular slot in November 1993. *Pete and Pete*'s word-of-mouth following was bolstered by guest appearances from the likes of R.E.M.'s Michael Stipe, Iggy Pop, TARANTINO alumnus Steve Buscemi, CHRIS ELLIOTT, JANEANE GAROFALO, and a hipper-than-tomorrow INDIE-ROCK soundtrack.

WEB **The Web Site of Pete & Pete**

http://www.cs.indiana.edu/entertainment/pete-and-pete/

Aeon Flux

Hyperkinetic, ultraviolent spy vs. spy CYBERPUNK animation. *AF* first aired on the June 1991 debut of MTV's *LIQUID TELEVISION* show, and was created by Peter Chung, the Korean-born head of animation for *Liquid Television*'s production company. The show boasts one of the highest body counts per minute of any set of images ever committed to film, condensing the gun-propelled physicality and action sequences of an entire JOHN WOO feature into an animated short, more than a few times involving the death of the svelte heroine-assassin herself. In the second half of 1995 MTV gave the heroine a voice and spun off a separate *Aeon Flux* show, videogame, and book. Chung's second series, "Phantom 2040," was a futuristic adaptation of comic hero The Phantom, first offered through syndication in 1994.

WEB **AEon Flux Homepage** http://www.expanse.com/ aflux/index.html ✦ WEB **mtv.com** http://www.mtv.com/ ✦ WEB **MTV Animation** http://mtvoddities.viacom.com/ animate.html

Aerosmith

1970s Rolling Stones copyists whose career was revived by a 1986 re-make of their funky-rock oldie "Walk This Way" by HIP-HOP pioneers Run-D.M.C. The song was a Top 10 hit that helped Run-D.M.C. (and rap generally) cross over to a white audience, and introduced Aerosmith to a new generation of record buyers. Reinvigorated, the band (led by ageless, rubber-limbed singer Steven Tyler [b. Steven Tallarico, 1948]) cranked out a string of polished, lascivious hits (among them 1989's "Love In An Elevator," "Dude [Looks Like a Lady]") that put them squarely back on the charts and on MTV. Even as Aerosmith's music has grown stale and formulaic in the '90s, they've continued to manipulate the channel expertly, particularly with a trio of clips ("Crazy," "Amazin'," and "Cryin'"—memorably satirized by *Saturday Night Live*'s ADAM SANDLER) which showcased video nymphet ALICIA SILVERSTONE (and, in "Crazy," singer Steven Tyler's toothsome daughter Liv). In 1992 Aerosmith signed a reported $35 million deal with Sony, to take effect sometime after Tyler's 47th birthday.

WEB **Joe's Aerosmith Tribute** http://coos.dartmouth.edu/ ~joeh/

Afrocentrism

School of thought which argues that African-American identity must be rooted in the African origins of black people. Afrocentrism's principal theorist is Molefi Kete Asante (b. 1942), director of Temple's African-American Studies program and author of 1987's *The Afrocentric Idea*. Afrocentrism builds on the black nationalism of the 1960s, when protests on college campuses led to the creation of Afro-American Studies departments in universities and the "black is beautiful" movement first popularized African-derived fashions (KENTE CLOTH) and new cultural institutions (the holiday of Kwanzaa). While scholars in the '70s and '80s worked to lay the foundations for the new discipline's critique of "Eurocentrism," it wasn't until the explosion of politicized HIP-HOP in the late '80s that Afrocentric ideas gained broader popular exposure through the music of artists like KRS-One and X-Clan. (At the same time, education reforms sought to revise high school and elementary school curricula.)

Opponents of Afrocentrism have been largely successful in identifying the point of view with its least-lettered and most intolerant proponents, such as CUNY's Leonard Jeffries, who has blamed Jews for the slave trade and argued that blacks, as "sun people," are biologically superior to whites, or "ice people."

WEB **AfriNET Home Page** http://www.afrinet.net:80/afrinet/
◆ WEB **The Universal Black Pages** http://www.gatech.edu/bgsa/blackpages.html

AIDS Quilt Folk-art project commemorating people who have died of AIDS-related diseases. The National AIDS Quilt comprises thousands of homemade 3 X 6-foot panels (sewn by volunteers into 12 X 12-foot sections), created by the loved ones of the deceased; panel designs range from simple crayon drawings on sheets to those more elaborately festooned with personal items, photographs, and poems. Conceived by gay activist Cleve Jones (b. 1964) in 1986, and developed by The Names Project in San Francisco, the Quilt is intended to be symbolic of healing, comfort, and warmth. When it was first unveiled in October 1987 on the Capitol Mall in Washington, the Quilt included 1,920 panels. The Names Project has since arranged partial displays around the country to raise money for AIDS organizations. With the exposure came the addition of more panels which, as of mid–1995, number over 28,000 (among more than 270,000 AIDS deaths), and weigh a collective 34 tons.

WEB **The Names Project: The AIDS memorial quilt** http://ecosys.drdr.virginia.edu/namesproj.html/

Albini, Steve (b. 1962) Founder of the seminal '80s noise-rock band Big Black, now known as a prolific producer and fanatical arbiter of musical integrity. Albini's hallmark—in his own music, his production for other bands, and his simultaneously pedantic and vitriolic ZINE writings—is an unflinching dedication to "independence, self-determination, absolute total honesty and common sense." (Albini's common sense apparently went AWOL in 1988 when he named a short-lived band Rapeman, after a Japanese MANGA charac-

ter.) What the music sounds like is apparently less important than its ethical stance; the producer's deep-seated loathing of anything that suggests sellout resonates across the INDIE-ROCK world. Though he mostly records independent bands, Albini has worked for a few major label artists, including The Breeders, PJ HARVEY, and NIRVANA, whose *In Utero* album he recorded for Geffen Records. The project ended with recriminations, accusations, and remixes, cementing Albini's reputation for being difficult. In 1993 he formed a new band, Shellac, that answers to no one.

WEB **Steve Albini on SonicNet** http://199.170.0.76/albini.html

alien abduction Experience or near-experience reported by five million Americans, according to a 1994 poll reported in *Time* magazine. This hardy perennial of supermarket tabloid headlines burst into full mainstream flower in the early '90s. The current fascination can be traced back to horror author Whitley Strieber (*The Hunger*, 1981), who published a chronicle of his own spirited-away experience with almond-eyed aliens in 1987 (*Communion*). The success of mini-series like *Fire in the Sky*, the 1993 movie adaptation of an Arizona logger's E.T. kidnapping memoir, set the stage for the X-FILES series ("The truth is out there"). In 1994 John Mack, a Pulitzer Prize-winning Harvard professor of psychiatry, published a book of abduction memories recalled under his therapeutic guidance, and added that his patients' consistent accounts suggested that the stories of alien anal probes and environmental warnings were true. (Mack's material echoed larger therapeutic trends in recovered stories of childhood abuse and SATANIC rituals that often turned out to be the product of the therapist's own suggestive questions.) [See also SETI.]

WEB **The Ultimate UFO Page** http://www.interaccess.com/users/newman/ ◆ USENET **alt.alien.visitors**

all-climax porn Directly reflecting the power of technology to transform media, the biggest adult-video development of the late '80s and early '90s was all-climax pornography. With names like

Raunch-O-Rama and *Colossal Combos*, these compilation tapes of narrative-free copulation allowed porn distributors with large libraries to repackage their material for budget-oriented connoisseurs. Fans of a single adult-vid star, like Amber Lynn or Debi Diamond, could purchase "greatest hits" anthologies of their works; those seeking a particular kink (e.g. black-on-white, oral, anal, or "watersports") could buy tapes containing nothing but choice fantasy fodder. Like the K-Tel albums of yore, all-climax tapes tend to be price-pointed at rock-bottom rates like $14.99 and $24.99, which, as much as their convenience, contributes to their popularity.

WEB **alt.sex.movies Home Page** http://www.xmission.com/ ~legalize/asm/ ✦ usenet alt.sex.movies

alpha-hydroxy acids   As the key ingredient in a new generation of anti-aging skin care products launched in 1992, AHAs have a fervent following among women both old and young. These acids, derived from fruits (and sometimes augmented by lactic acid from milk), work by removing the skin's damaged upper layer, usually after an overnight application. (This is basically a lighter version of a face peel.) AHAs have the combined effects of revealing younger-looking skin underneath and hastening cell renewal; unlike the sometimes troublesome '80s skin-care "miracle product" retin-A, the only known side effect of AHAs is mild skin irritation in some users; reportedly they can be used indefinitely without harm, or stopped without deterioration of skin condition—leading to the moniker "PROZAC for the exterior."

WEB **Skin Treatment Page** http://www.cyber-hawaii.com/ health/skintrea.html/

alt.binaries.pictures.erotica   Main porn conduit on the INTERNET. A daily flow of scanned photos, video grabs, and even videoclips are anonymously posted to separate USENET newsgroups including "ANIME" and "cartoons," "bestiality" and "tasteless," "blondes" and "Asians," "bondage" and "fetish," "male" and "female." Learning how to reassemble the GIF, JPEG, and MPEG files is a

CYBERSEX rite of passage. The files would be much easier to browse, download, and decode if they were stored at fixed addresses instead of being broken up for broadcast over discussion groups, but the traffic brought on by experiments with semi-permanent porn archives has brought some of the most powerful computers on the Internet to their knees within days of word leaking out. Besides testing the reach of local obscenity and intellectual property laws in cyberspace, another a.b.p.e cultural contribution is the "frankenstein," the head of a celebrity like Christina Applegate or Al Gore seamlessly grafted onto Miss (or Mr.) February using the latest photo-retouching software.

USENET **alt.binaries.pictures.erotica.**

alternative   '90s term for counterculture, often of a non-oppositional nature. Current use of "alternative" in the music/youth culture world originated in the late '70s/early '80s, when it described the strain of post-PUNK music cultivated by a growing, informal network of college radio stations. The word "alternative" already had a meaning as related to culture: commonly associated with the independent, oppositional press of the late hippie era, this counterculture label also came to denote any lifestyle outside of the mainstream. As college-rock favorites like R.E.M. and U2 became chart and stadium fixtures in the second half of the '80s, successive waves of newer, rawer bands inherited the "alternative" mantle. However, NIRVANA's meteoric rise to the top of the charts in 1991–92 disrupted the ecosystem: suddenly alternative was a musical category as lucrative as HIP-HOP or metal, as were its country associated fashions. Record companies, radio, and MTV embraced the "new" form, the LOLLAPALOOZA tours enshrined it, and marketers used it as youth-bait to

The BAFFLER
Number Five
ALTERNATIVE TO WHAT?
Rock 'n' Roll is the Health of the State, page 5
TOWARD A RETRO APOCALYPSE
The Nostalgia Gap, page 152
CONSOLIDATED DEVIANCE, INC.
Youth Culture Fabrication Specialists, page 159
Plus new writing by Janice Radus, Robert Nedelkoff, and Steve Albini
"The Journal That Blunts the Cutting Edge"

Chicago's *BAFFLER* magazine asks the big question of the day.

sell everything from cars to soft drinks to movies. For those who wrangled with the question "what is alternative?" there was no satisfactory answer—the term was now in the public domain, and dissent from the mainstream was rewarded within a fragmenting mass culture.

USENET **alt.music.alternative, alt.music.alternative.female**

alternative medicine   General term for medical treatments not traditionally administered or sanctioned by a physician, ranging from acupuncture to HOMEOPATHY to visualization therapy. In 1990, according to *The New England Journal of Medicine*, the number of visits to alternative practitioners outstripped the number of visits to primary-care doctors. While the shift toward holistic wellness and prevention contains a strong dose of patient independence and self-care, the medical establishment itself has begun incorporating alternative practices—most dramatically in 1992 when the National Institutes of Health established the Office of Alternative Medicine. [See also: VITAMIN LABELING SCARE, SPIRITUALITY.]

WEB **Homeopathy Homepage** http://www.dungeon.com/ ~cam/homeo.html ✦ USENET **misc.health.alternative** gopher **Exploratory Centers for Alternative Medicine Research** gopher://gopher.nih.gov:70/00/res/nih-guide/rfa-files/RFA-OD–94–004 ✦ USENET **misc.health.alternative**

amateur porn   Thanks to the camcorder revolution, there were by 1991 more than 50 companies (most successfully, Homegrown Videos of San Diego) buying up homemade sex tapes from would-be porn stars (many of whom, apparently, favor shag carpeting). The material, bought for between $250 and $2,500, is resold in a business estimated at $3 billion. Celebrating the phenomenon in *The New York Times*, CAMILLE PAGLIA declared, "I think amateur adult videos are very positive because people are not letting the priests, the feminists, the therapists tell them what sex should be." The new amateur video market spun off its own stars (including a Kentucky lawyer who debuted with two carpenters in "Mary Lou the Stud Finder"), a series of slickly produced amateur magazines (and

expanded amateur photo sections in established porn mags), and a new subgenre of semi-pro tapes playing off the video-virgin mystique of "real people."

WEB **Video Alternatives** http://www.videoalt.com/ ✦ USENET **alt.sex.movies**

ambient   Term coined circa 1978 by BRIAN ENO to describe his forays into drifting instrumental composition. Beginning with the 1975 album *Discreet Music*, Eno began producing a series of records partially influenced by the piano music of early-century French composer Erik Satie; intended as background music, the disks highlighted tape loops and "treated sounds." The combination of fast-paced electronic dance music and ECSTASY that began to dominate clubs worldwide in the late '80s paradoxically created an appetite for soothing sounds and still surroundings. Ambient music made an ideal soundtrack for "chill-out" rooms in clubs; the word became a catch-all label for spacey variations on numerous established forms, including HOUSE, TECHNO, and DUB. The "textural soundscapes" and "rich timbral explorations" (they bring out the worst in rock critics) of name-brand groups like the Orb and Aphex Twin rework the socially acceptable elements of PROGRESSIVE rock (no solos, please) for the RAVE generation, and for proprietors of NEW AGE-y restaurants and boutiques.

WEB **Epsilon: The Ambient Music Information Archive** http://www.hyperreal.com:/ambient/ ✦ USENET **rec. musicambient** ✦ WEB **streetsound online** http://www. phantom.com:80/~street/ ✦ USENET **rec.music.ambient**

America Online   Largest of the so-called commercial online services. Launched in 1990 after the Sears-IBM Prodigy network and H&R Block CompuServe already had more than a million subscribers between them, AOL steadily gained ground on the strength of a simpler, more colorful user interface. Where Prodigy experimented with advertisements and CompuServe loaded up with added-cost games and news databases, AOL focused on social chat rooms that ended up accounting for most of the network's revenue (AOL still protested when the mainstream press praised it for the best gay chat). Though it suffers from its vaguely jingoistic name and the censorship instincts of a mall manager, AOL was the first major online service to see the INTERNET writing on the wall, and in 1994 began marketing its access to NEWSGROUPS as Internet-made-easy and—more significantly—buying up Internet service and software companies. AOL also benefited greatly as the first stepping stone for newspapers, magazines, record labels, and TV networks going online before the WORLD WIDE WEB's commercial advent in late 1994. America Online led the charge in accusing Microsoft of monopolistic tactics for its plans to build Microsoft Network software into the massively distributed Windows 95 operating system.

WEB **America Online** http://www.aol.com ✦ USENET **alt.online-service.america-online**, **alt.aol-sucks**

Amis, Martin (b. 1949)   British novelist who made international publishing waves with *The Information* (1995), a hyperbolic tale of literary envy. In a real-world scenario worthy of an Amis meta-fiction, the author was mauled in the British press for leaving his wife and firing the agent wife of his friend novelist Julian Barnes on the way to an unseemly advance of almost $800,000, some of which was controversially spent on American dental work. (Amis's new agent, one Andrew Wylie, reportedly obtained an even greater sum for SALMAN RUSHDIE's incendiary 1988 novel, *The Satanic Verses*.)

Amis, the son of misanthropic novelist Kingsley, published his award-winning first novel, *The Rachel Papers* (1973), at age 24. Inspired considerably by Saul Bellow and Vladimir Nabokov, Amis *fils* developed a cruelly comic take on *fin de siècle* doom and venality that reached its most fevered pitch in 1984's *Money*. ("Banalities delivered with tremendous force," said one critic—Amis heartily concurred.) As well as a collectible book about VIDEOGAMES, and collections of journalism and short stories, Amis has one screenwriting credit, the Farrah Fawcett science fiction vehicle *Saturn*

Three (1980). (In 1992 he was reported to be writing another sci-fi film for the producer of *RoboCop*.)

Amnesty International   First human rights group (founded 1961) to systematically catalogue human rights abuses around the world. Based in London, Amnesty became a household name in the '80s through major concert tours such as the 1986 Conspiracy of Hope (including U2, Peter Gabriel, Lou Reed, Joan Baez, Bryan Adams, and the Police) and the 1988 Human Rights Now tour (including Bruce Springsteen, Gabriel, Sting, Tracy Chapman, and Youssou N'Dour). Such celebrity-endorsed events (and massive direct-mail campaigns) multiplied the group's membership in the U.S. tenfold from some 40,000 members at the start of the '80s.

In addition to being well respected in the rights field for its annual *Report on Torture and Political Persecution Around the World* (which typically include harsh criticism of the U.S. prison system), AI can point to dozens of political prisoners freed through letter-writing drives carried out by its grassroots membership. Amnesty's own definition of human rights has evolved over the years to incorporate a range of economic, environmental, and social issues including rape and the persecution of homosexuals. Although AI rules prevent—in an effort to remain non-partisan—local chapters from working on cases within their own country, U.S. branches have been at the forefront of death penalty protests in America.

In late 1993 the AI board pushed out its high-profile executive director Jack Healey, who had engineered most of the group's connections to the rock world. The membership levels are said to have been hurt since; in 1995 Healey announced plans to stage another gargantuan rock festival in 1998, this time under the auspices of his own group Human Rights Action Center, to coincide with the 50th anniversary of the United Nations' Universal Declaration of Human Rights.

WEB **The Amnesty International Page** http://www.traveller.com/~hrweb/ai/ai.html

Amok Books "Sourcebook of the Extremes of Information in Print," which started as a mail-order operation in 1985, and then went retail in 1987 in L.A. Along with its stock of Burroughs, Bowles, and Bataille, Amok stocks intriguing tomes like *The Sniper's Handbook*, *The Color Atlas of Oral Cancers*, and *Physical Interrogation Techniques*, plus videos ranging from autopsies to Hitler speeches—anything, in fact, to *épater le bourgeoisie*. The store added to its notoriety in 1989 by organizing an exhibition of then-convicted SERIAL KILLER John Wayne Gacy's chillingly innocent "Pogo the Clown" paintings and BOB FLANAGAN's "Nailed" show. The Amok formula has recently affected the mainstream book world, most notably TOWER Books' Tower Outpost, which boasts a somewhat similar inventory. [See also TRANSGRESSIVE FICTION.]

Amos, Tori (b. 1963)   Flame-haired daughter of a Baltimore, MD, minister who, at age five, became the youngest-ever student at the city's Peabody Conservatory. Amos launched her rock career in 1988, fronting the short-lived, little-heard rock band Y Kant Tori Read; after retreating to London she re-emerged with a new, piano-based style (heavily influenced by Kate Bush and Joni Mitchell) and a set of new songs, many of which were harrowingly personal in lyrical content. Notable among them was "Me and a Gun," a narrative about Amos' experience as a rape victim; the album which contained that song, *Little Earthquakes* (1992), went platinum, as did the follow-up *Under the Pink*. Amos' febrile, piano-stool-straddling live performances, her unhinged persona, and her bluntly sexual lyrics overshadow the innate conservatism of her music. Her 1992 piano cover of NIRVANA's "Smells Like Teen Spirit" brought her INDIE-ROCK credibility that was burnished by a duet with R.E.M.'s Michael Stipe on the SOUNDTRACK of *Empire* (1995).

WEB **Tori Amos Page** http://hubcap.clemson.edu/
~watts/tori.html ✦ WEB **Tori Amos French**
WWW Pages http://olympe.polytechnique.fr/
Tori/rec.music.tori-amos

Anarchic Adjustment   San Jose-based purveyors of "digital WORKWEAR." Founded in 1988 by a trio of English expatriates, Anarchic Adjustment took as its trademark a cleaned-up version of the PUNK A-in-circle "anarchy" symbol. The Anarchic sensibility, though, was logocentric, baggy SKATEwear that evolved into a range of clothes in hi-tech-looking fabrics. These are sometimes decorated with ANIME characters and pseudo-political slogans like "Mankind could make this world a heaven, or he could make it hell." Anarchic Adjustment has benefited from the patronage of entertainers like TIMOTHY LEARY and DEEE-LITE; and the company experienced success in Japan after a well-known DJ wore an A.A. T-shirt in a magazine. Europe and the U.S. are now voracious markets (annual turnover is over $2 million), but Japan remains an Anarchic stronghold—the company opened its own store there in 1994, and it designed a T-shirt for Sega Japan's *Pulseman* VIDEOGAME.

Anarchists' Cookbook, The   Cult classic on how to cook hash brownies and bombs. Although most bookstores have refused to carry *The Cookbook* since its 1971 release, it is one of the most successful mail-order books ever, with sales passing two million in 1993. Many acts of violence have been blamed on the book: DAVID KORESH, for example, consulted it to make his hand grenades.

William Powell, the book's then–21-year-old author, has since relinquished royalty rights and now lives somewhere in Asia. *The Cookbook* has inspired a whole industry of criminal manuals, such as "How to Launder Money," "Successful Armed Robbery," and "Complete Guide to Lock Picking," distributed by fringe-culture mail-order dealers like AMOK and LOOMPANICS (Loompanics actually dropped *The Cookbook* because of recipe errors that can lead to unexpected detonations). While the book itself has always been protected by the First Amendment, in 1993 BBS operator Michael Elansky was arrested in Connecticut for distributing an e-ZINE called "Anarchy for Fun and Profit" that contained similar material. Charges were later dropped.

WEB **Spunk Press-Anarchist Cookbook** http://www.cwi.nl/
cwi/people/Jack.Jansen/spunk/cookbook.html
✦ WEB **rec.pyrotechnics FAQ** http://www.cis.ohio-
state.edu/hypertext/faq/usenet/pyrotechnics-faq/faq.html
✦ WEB **Spunk Press-Anarchist Resources**
http://www.cwi.nl/cwi/people/Jack.Jansen/spunk/Spunk_
Resources.html

Anders, Allison (b. 1954)   Although a
UCLA film school graduate, this writer-director is
no sheltered movie brat: at 15 she fled to L.A. with
her mother and sister to evade an abusive stepfather;
there were then a series of psychiatric wards, foster
homes, jails, and a commune; by the time Allison
Anders was 22, she had two daughters by different
fathers. Before enrolling at UCLA she had an odd
variety of part-time jobs, and even after graduating
with an industry fellowship, Anders languished on
welfare before making her writing-directing debut,
Gas, Food, Lodging (1992). This trailer-park tale did
well enough to make possible *Mi Vida Loca* (1993),
Anders' gritty saga about the girl gangs in her Echo
Park, L.A., neighborhood. *Mi Vida Loca*'s cast
included local gang members. (The movie's premiere funded a community center and scholarship
program in the neighborhood.) In 1995 Anders
filmed a segment of *Four Rooms*, alongside
QUENTIN TARANTINO and ROBERT RODRIGUEZ.

Animal Liberation Front   Loose organization of radical animal rights activists that targets science labs, slaughterhouses, fur farms, and retail fur
stores. Founded in England in the mid-'70s, the
Animal Liberation Front is best known in Britain
for reputedly bombing the Harrods department
store, and in America for planting battery and paper
bag incendiary devices in Chicago outlets of Saks,
Neiman Marcus, and Marshall Field's during the
1993 Christmas shopping season. The Animal
Liberation Front is affiliated with PETA, which pub-
licizes ALF actions. A 1993 study from the Justice
and Agriculture departments reported that the FBI
was considering classifying the ALF as a terrorist
organization, and listed dozens of other, smaller animal rights groups that "claim to have perpetrated
acts of extremism."

WEB **Animal Rights Resource Site** http://envirolink.
org/arrs/index.html ✦ USENET **talk.politics.animals, alt.
animals, clari.news.interest.animals, talk.environment**

anime   Casually sexy and stylishly violent "Japanimation" which
accounts for one of the fastest-grow-
ing American video markets. Usually
adapted from popular MANGA
COMIC books, Japan's billion-dollar
adult-animation industry churned
out, according to a June 1995
Variety count, between thirty and
forty anime (pronounced AH-NEE-
may) TV shows and features (several
containing graphic sexuality) to theaters and video in 1994. The U.S.
anime cult can be traced to producer
Carl Macek, who in 1985 success-

Tekaneda's @anime!
(http://pc207.media.uvs
c.edu/tekaneda.html)
celebrates *Ranma 1/2*,
a martial arts comedy
by Rumiko Takahashi.

fully packaged three unrelated Japanese anime
shows into a series syndicated on U.S. television
called *Robotech*. In the following years an informal
but elaborate underground tape-trading network
developed, first on BBS networks and then over the
INTERNET, where U.S. anime purists proudly pro-
claim themselves "OTAKU." By the early-'90s,
spurred in part by the Macek's 1989 art-house theatrical release of *Akira*, new anime releases were
finding their way into American hands within days,
illegally copied, and subtitled with English transla-
tions. In 1995, prompted by the show's merchandising success in Japan, the Fox network debuted
SAILOR MOON. Anime's foremost creator is Hayao
Miyazaki, whose canon includes the children's classics *My Neighbor Totoro* (1988), *Kiki's Delivery
Service* (1989), and *Nausicaa of the Valley of the
Wind* (1982). Anime's influence is far-ranging,
manifested from Disney's *The Lion King* (1994) to
Michael Jackson's 1995 "Scream" video. The SCI-FI
CHANNEL has also emerged as an outlet for anime
imports.

WEB **Anime FAQ** http://www.cis.ohio-state.edu/

hypertext/faq/ ✦ usenet/anime/faq/faq.html ✦ USENET
rec.arts.anime, **alt.binaries.pictures.anime**, **alt.binaries.**
pictures.erotica.anime ✦ WEB **Anime Server** http://
web.mit.edu/afs/athena/user/o/m/omv/Anime/default.html

anti-gay rights initiatives   State referenda
to block local ordinances which prohibit discrimination against homosexuals. In the November 1992
elections, Colorado's voters approved Amendment
2—spearheaded by the Board of Colorado for
FAMILY VALUES—to deny gays the "special privileges"
of Denver, Aspen, and Boulder laws guaranteeing
civil rights for homosexuals in matters of employment and housing. (In Oregon, a similar initiative,
Ballot Measure 9, was pushed by the religious
Oregon Citizens Alliance but defeated after heavy
campaigning on both sides.) Gay and civil rights
groups nationwide launched a boycott of Colorado
to protest the law (an abundant snowfall, however,
led to a booming tourist season); later in 1993, the
state Supreme Court declared Amendment 2 uncon-
stitutional. In 1994, petition drives by the religious
right failed to put similar measures on the popular
ballot in Arizona, Florida, Idaho, Maine, Michigan,
Missouri, Nevada, Ohio, and Washington. By election time, only Oregon (Measure 13) and Idaho
(Proposition 1) actually voted on such initiatives,
and both were defeated. The Idaho measure
included provisions to bar teachers in the public
schools from discussing homosexuality as an acceptable lifestyle.
WEB **Gay & Lesbian Web Alliance** http://emanate.com/glwa/
✦ MAIL LIST **Anti-Idaho Citizens Alliance** email LIST-
SERV@idbsu.edu with "SUB Freedom [My Name]" in message body

anti-folk   Lower East Side, Manhattan, scene
created by young PUNK-influenced songwriters
emerging during the mid-'80s in opposition to the
folk establishment. Named after the Akira
Kurosawa film *The Hidden Fortress*, the Fort was
opened in 1987 by the singer known as Lach. The
venue gave stage time to mainly white, middle-class
performers like Brenda Kahn, Cindy Lee Berryhill,

Paleface, Michelle Shocked, cartoonist David
Chelsea, King Missile's John S. Hall, and Beck.
When police closed the Fort in 1989, Lach moved a
few blocks north to Sophie's (now the Sidewalk
Cafe), where Bob Dylan made a brief yet fabled
appearance. The latest aggressive folkie to warrant
the label is Buffalo-born Ani Difranco (b. 1970), a
charismatic, witty feminist with a burgeoning
national audience.
WEB **The Ani DiFranco Home Page** http://
www.columbia.edu/~marg/ani/

Antioch   In June 1992, under pressure to deal
with campus DATE RAPE, the board of this Ohio college passed an amendment to the school's sexual
offense policy. Thenceforth, if two people were
becoming physically intimate, one participant had
to ask the other for consent each time he or she
wanted to go to a "new level of physical and/or sexual contact/conduct." Widely cited at the time as
one of the great follies of POLITICAL CORRECTNESS.
WEB **Antioch's Home Page** http://college.antioch.edu/

Araki, Gregg (b. 1961)   Independent L.A.
filmmaker whose 1992 picture *The Living End* was
widely described as a "gay *Thelma and Louise.*" One
of the two leads in Araki's freewheeling road-movie
was an HIV-positive man whose defiantly anti-
social demeanor enraged many gays; the writer-
director may have had a premonition of this controversy when he coined the subtitle "An Irresponsible
Movie by Gregg Araki." *The Living End*'s modest
success enabled Araki, a USC film school graduate
and festival-circuit veteran, to complete his earlier
low-budget film Totally *F***ed Up* (asterisks director's own). In this first part of Araki's intended
"teenager trilogy," half a dozen bored Angeleno
teens flail around between jump-cuts in search of
love and identity. The film's alt-rock SOUNDTRACK
(MINISTRY, This Mortal Coil) would do a studio
marketing man proud; the same marketing man,
perhaps, who came up with the title for Araki's
1995 follow-up—*The Doom Generation* (shown at
LOLLAPALOOZA's movie tent that year).

Arnet   In 1992 designer Greg Arnette left sunglasses giant OAKLEY to set up his own operation, Arnet Optic Illusions, catering chiefly to the SNOWBOARDING community. The new company, based in San Clemente, California, astutely stoked interest in its lines by doling them out in limited-edition variations. This marketing strategy paid big dividends in 1994 with the Ravens line of wraparound shades; originally produced in silver, then withdrawn after sales of only 4,000, the glasses (retail price $80) re-appeared in gold, transforming the originals into a sought-after commodity—especially after they'd been seen on the high-profile *visages* of the BEASTIE BOYS (on the cover of *DETAILS*) and MADONNA.

Art Club 2000   Group of six (sometimes seven) early-'90s graduates of New York City's Cooper Union Art School assembled by SoHo art dealer Colin de Land. Photos of the comely gang wearing identical GAP outfits, shot with the care of an advertising campaign, hit a neo-WARHOLIAN chord in the 1993 art world by mocking the uniformity and cliqueishness of youth fashion marketing. That first project, entitled "Commingle," also targeted the clothing chain itself: Art Clubbers displayed staff assessments and unrecycled cardboard boxes found in Gap garbage, and tested the "no hassle" exchange policy by returning dirtied clothes that had been used in the photo shoots.

Art Club 2000's 1994 "Untitled (Cooper Union I)" from the "Clear" exhibition.

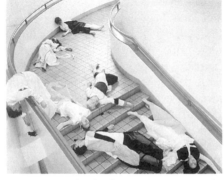

Courtesy American Fine Arts, Co.

artificial life   Computers programmed to mimic, rather than analyze, the basic processes and systems of living, evolving beings. A 1987 Los Alamos, California, conference helped formalize the discipline of AL (or "Alife"); bio-imitating computer models now influence game theory, medicine, robotics, artificial intelligence, FUZZY LOGIC, and NANOTECHNOLOGY. AL has also become, like fractal art before it, a defining artifact of computer kitsch: variations of John Conway's seminal *Life* program exist free on the INTERNET for every kind of personal computer; Rudy Rucker's 1994 *Boppers* program enables users to tinker with the DNA and sexual habits of creature colonies. Journalist Steven Levy's 1992 book *Artificial Life* colorfully traced the field's own evolution, from the "cellular automata" of founding computer scientist John von Neumann to John Holland's Darwinian experiments in the '60s getting programs to mutate and self-select. *WIRED* editor Kevin Kelly further explored the meaning of COMPUTER VIRUSES and AL metaphors such as the "hive mind" in his 1994 *Out of Control: The Rise of Neo-Biological Civilization*, arguing that computers should be seen as part of human evolution.

WEB **Artificial Life** http://www.wi.LeidenUniv.nl/home/mvdweg/alife.html ✦ WEB **Life Page** http://alife.santafe.edu/ ✦ USENET **comp.ai.alife**

artist directors   Having mastered the mercurial patrons and fly-by-night financing of SoHo in the go-go '80s, only to watch the art market bubble burst in the early '90s, several stars of the art world followed the trail of money and celebrity to Hollywood, trading galleries for screening rooms. Robert Longo (b. 1953) parlayed his giant multimedia pop-culture panels and short stints making rock videos for R.E.M. and MEGADETH into directing KEANU REEVES and HENRY ROLLINS in 1995's $27 million, youth-targeted adaptation of WILLIAM GIBSON's "Johnny Mnemonic" CYBERPUNK short story (critics said the bomb *looked* good). David Salle (b. 1952), another neo-Expressionist star of '80s painting, also released his small budget *Search*

& Destroy that spring, executive produced by Martin Scorsese. (The adaptation of Howard Korder's 1990 anti-yuppie play concerns a Florida hustler who is obsessed with making a movie; in Salle's adaptation, the crook is sympathetic.) Another high-profile artist-directed project was a biopic of painter Jean-Michel Basquiat by Julian Schnabel (b. 1951).

Athey, Ron (b. 1961)   California performance art veteran; intensively PIERCED and TATTOOED *L.A. Weekly* editorial assistant; prominent NEA target. In March 1994 Athey was presenting the autobiographical, typically harrowing piece *4 Scenes in a Harsh Life* at a Minneapolis nightclub sponsored by a local, NEA-funded arts center. One act, entitled "The Human Printing Press," involved Athey cutting the flesh of one fellow-performer, then having another hang some blood-soaked tissues over part of the audience. When one outraged patron contacted local health authorities to complain (wrongly) that the audience had being exposed to the H.I.V. virus, the story went national, soon reaching the ears of moral watchdog Senator Jesse Helms. Athey, a former junkie who is himself H.I.V.-positive, made the perfect political football for Helms and his fellow NEA opponents.
WEB **American Arts Alliance** http://www.tmn.com /Oh/Artswire/www.aaa/other.html

Attention Deficit Disorder   Just as chronic fatigue syndrome (yuppie flu) was the diagnosis *du jour* of the '80s, ADD has captivated the abridged attention spans of the channel-hopping, INTERNET-browsing, interrupt-driven '90s. The childhood version, marked by hyperactivity, is a decades-old DSM classification called Attention Deficit and Hyperactivity Disorder (ADHD), commonly treated with Ritalin, now threatening to become another personality-tuning pill like PROZAC. (Overprescription of Ritalin is nothing new—it was widely misused by elementary schools in the '70s to subdue rowdy kids.)
USENET **alt.support.attn-deficit** FTP **ADD Archives** ftp://ftp.

netcom.com:/pub/lds/add/ ✦ WEB **Attention Deficit Disorder Archive** http://www.seas.upenn.edu/~mengwong/add/

Audio Home Recording Act   1992 U.S. law which imposes a 2 percent surcharge on sales of DAT, DCC, and MINIDISC recorders, and a 3 per cent tax on blank digital tape, disks, and cartridges. The tax funds a royalty pool which is intended to compensate songwriters, performers, record companies, and publishers for sales lost to piracy—providing an automatic windfall for entertainment corporations even when the new digital recording technology is used for non-pirating purposes (such as recording a car tape or storing computer data). The precedent-setting law can be seen as the product of the late '80s mergers of hardware and software companies (Sony bought CBS Records, Matsushita bought MCA)—before those acquisitions, equipment makers had been the proposed law's most active opponents.

Austin   Host to Texas' largest bohemian enclave, fed by the nearly 100,000 students who live in Austin, half of whom attend the University of Texas. A center of cyber-literacy and CYBERPUNK, Austin's youth makeover began in 1991 with the release of RICHARD LINKLATER's independent film *Slacker.* The story of one day amidst the town's burnout aesthetes, anarchists, would-be rock stars, and amateur philosophers, the film was languid, liquid, and plotless—much like Austin itself—and became a solid art-house hit. In the wake of *Slacker,* Austin began to draw film and television production crews; Linklater's follow-up, 1993's *Dazed and Confused,* was shot there, as was *What's Eating Gilbert Grape* (1993). Long known as a mecca of live roots-and-blues music, Austin is also home to the annual spring new-rock festival, SXSW. As of 1995, several trendy retailers—from URBAN OUTFITTERS to Starbuck's to Barnes & Noble—had either recently opened stores or anounced plans to open them shortly.
WEB **Austin Axis** http://www.awpi.com/AustinAxis/index.html
✦ WEB **SXSW** http://monsterbit.com/sxsw.html

Avedon, Richard (b. 1923)   Former Merchant Marine who survived World War II to become arguably the world's most influential modern fashion photographer. After the war, at *Harper's Bazaar* (1946–65), Avedon introduced a more naturalistic style of fashion photography in which models broke out of frozen poses to run, jump, and even laugh. (Sports photographer Martin Munkacsi, a contemporary at *Harper's* under legendary art director Alexei Brodovich, is credited as an influence.) Such was Avedon's renown that the 1957 fashion-world movie satire *Funny Face* used him as a "Special Visual Consultant" and featured a character based on him and played by Fred Astaire. Uncomfortable with his role as fashion photographer, Avedon moved into portraiture, producing stark, icon-making, black and white images of the great and the good and the powerful, and also of anonymous weathered faces from America's heartland. Full-page Avedon pictures are a signature of the reformulated *NEW YORKER*, which appointed him its first-ever staff photographer in 1992.

B-Boys Male HIP-HOP fans—the "B" is short for beat or break-beat—usually styled in some variation or derivative of rap music's distinctive, early '80s crystallization in New York (which also included '70s breakdancers). With their gold chains, "ghetto blaster" stereos, and pricey (ADIDAS) sneakers, Run-D.M.C. (and their 1985 smash *King of Rock*) defined B-Boy style for both urban and suburban audiences. The white BEASTIE BOYS, wearing baseball caps turned backwards, made chart-topping, beer-sodden anthems out of B-Boy manner with *Licensed to Ill* (1986). (Female B-Boys are flygirls.) In the '90s, the term has come to describe hardcore hip-hop fans through a succession of street styles.
USENET **alt.fan.run-dmc**

baby boomers American citizens born in the post-War baby boom, usually defined as 1946–1960. Having largely invented youth culture as we know it in the '60s, baby boomers are now characterized by an inability to relinquish their grip on it—thus their tendency to institutionalize the culture of their youth, as in the ROCK AND ROLL HALL OF FAME. The peak of the boomers' power as culture-makers came in the '80s, when their middle-aged economic clout made them an attractive audience (see also *ROLLING STONE*); films like *The Big Chill* (1983) and TV series like *The Wonder Years* (1988) and *thirtysomething* (1987) profitably echoed the clash of nostalgia with their adult concerns. The baby boomers' idyll was brought to an abrupt halt with the advent of so-called GENERATION X. It was supposedly an article of faith among this new group to hate "boomers" for their economically cushioned passage through youth, and their insistence on prolonging it. The new, media-sanctioned generation gap had arrived.

baby doll dresses High-waisted, diaphanous frocks reclaimed from the sex industry in the '90s as an ambivalent statement by young women about fashion and gender roles. The origination of the baby-doll look became the subject of an unseemly public dispute between Kat Bjelland of Babes In Toyland and Hole's COURTNEY LOVE, who called her own slut/infant fashion combo "kinderwhore." As with so many other examples of thrift-store chic, baby doll dresses were quickly co-opted by the fashion business, surfacing in ANNA SUI and Isaac Mizrahi collections shown in 1993.

Baffler, The Infrequently published, ascetic journal of cultural criticism (founded in 1988 by University of Chicago undergraduates Keith White and Tom Frank) that tackles the big questions weighing on the minds of INDIE-ROCK intellectuals. Defiant, anti-commerce *Baffler* mottoes include "Accessorize Your Dissent," "The Journal That Blunts the Cutting Edge," and on the back of the official T-shirt, "Your Lifestyle Sucks." Each issue sneers at the hip-seeking excesses of the corporate culture-business. The early 1994 "ALTERNATIVE to What?" issue mocked the post-NIRVANA commodification of insolence (or, in *Baffler* parlance, "consolidated deviance") thusly: "'rebellion' continues to perform its traditional function of justifying the economy's ever-accelerating cycles of obsolescence with admirable efficiency . . . 'anti-establishment' [is] the vocabulary by which we are taught to cast off our old possessions and buy whatever they have decided to offer this year." Most widely known for reporting THE GREAT GRUNGE HOAX of 1992.

Bagge, Peter (b. 1957) Former editor of R. CRUMB'S *Weirdo* anthology who set a new standard for the comics of social cruelty. Bagge's signature flourish consisted in having his cartoon creations run an emotional gamut of mildly annoyed to *totally enraged* in three panels or less. *Hate* (formerly *Neat Stuff*) features the trials and tribulations of aging protoslacker Buddy Bradley, who languishes in low-life scumhood, a slave to cultural marginalia. Buddy's a weasel, but as one of his girlfriends tells him, at least he doesn't pretend not to be. Like R. Crumb (who called Bagge "one of the great cartoonists of the post-Crumb generation"), Bagge derives much of his cachet from his association with an audience he himself holds in bemused con-

Tonio Roque's *Comix Reviews*
(http://www.umich.edu/~troq/Comix/) tackles Buddy Bradley's frequent "freak outs."

tempt—in this case, the INDIE-ROCK world. Bagge has created album art for the SUB POP label; his take on the SEATTLE GRUNGE scene ("I scream, you scream, we all scream for HEROIN"), was turned into a popular T-shirt.

WEB **Hate** http://www.umich.edu/~troq/Comix/hate.html

Baldwin brothers, the   Long Island, New York, handsome-actor siblings. Most renowned of the four is the sardonic hunk Alec (b. 1958), whose marriage with troubled actress Kim Basinger is as headline-prone as his political activity (voluble animal rights buff, Democrat) or his reasonably solid career (*Glengarry Glen Ross* [1992], *Malice* [1993]). Former CALVIN KLEIN model William (b. 1963) did not, alas, inherit his older brother's self-deprecating charm; he can be relied upon to be insufferably smug, as in the Sharon Stone dud *Sliver* (1993). Stephen (b. 1967), the pup of the litter, is also a former Klein mannequin, but is only sporadically employed as an actor (he graced 1994's BISEXUALITY dud *Threesome*). Last in looks, but not in talent, is Daniel (b. 1961), a stoic cast member of the gutsy TV drama *Homicide* for three seasons until he left in June 1995.

Ballard, J. G. (b. 1930)   Specialist in apocalyptic fiction, enormously influential on the CYBER-PUNK movement. Ballard writes "Myths of the Near Future" (as one of his short stories is titled), believing that all contemporary writing is essentially science fiction. Some of Ballard's best-known works— *Crash* (1973), *The Drought* (1965), *The Crystal World* (1968)—present apocalyptic visions of the earth destroyed by technology, nature, and hubris. Born in Shanghai, Ballard recounted the amazing story of his survival under the Japanese occupation in *Empire of the Sun* (1984), filmed by Steven Spielberg in 1987. In 1994 RE/SEARCH introduced to a new generation this aficionado of the "invisible literature" that surrounds us (e.g. advertising, instruction manuals, travel brochures). Ballard's most recent novels take a bemused look at fashionable ideologies.

WEB **J. G. Ballard** http://www.simons-rock.edu/~craigs/ballard.html ✦ USENET **rec.arts.sf.written**

Barbie art   In recent years, artists have begun reclaiming the type of Barbie-doll deconstruction usually associated with young, bored kids (e.g. dressing the icon of California girlhood in boy's clothes, posing her in rude positions). The collection *Mondo Barbie* (1993) brought together poems and short stories on Barbie and Ken, while M.G. Lord's *Forever Barbie* (1994) and Erica Rand's *Barbie's Queer Accessories* (1995) survey the highlights of Barbie appropriation. Mattel has responded by suing when they can (director TODD HAYNES was forced to destroy all copies of *Superstar*, his 1987 Barbie-acted film about '70s singer Karen Carpenter), and by sponsoring the much tamer *The Art of Barbie* (1994), featuring paintings by the likes of Leroy Neiman. In Christmas 1993 the New York–based Barbie Liberation Organization, which described itself as a "loose network of artists, parents, feminists and anti-war activists," made headlines by switching the voiceboxes of 300 "Talking Duke" G.I. Joe and "Teen Talk" Barbie dolls and placing the tampered toys back on store shelves. Deep-voiced Barbies inveighed "Dead men tell no lies," while sweet-sounding Joes worried, "Will we ever have enough clothes?" Perhaps the most impressive piece of Barbie performance art is the work of Cindy Jackson: over 20 years and 19 operations, she's managed to transform herself into a living Barbie clone. [See also QUEER KEN].

WEB **Hacker Barbie Dream Basement Apartment**
http://www.catalog.com/mrm/barbe/barbe.html/

Barkley, Charles (b. 1963)   Volatile, outspoken, outlandishly gifted basketball player. Despite his improbable (6'4 3/4", 250 pounds) physique, the Alabama-born Barkley was one of the best, most versatile pro-ballers of the '80s and early '90s (first at the Philadelphia 76ers, then the Phoenix Suns). What won him attention, though, were his hard-charging, powerhouse moves—in 1990, for example, Barkley's fouls cost him $35,950 in fines. Frequently, his game-style didn't stop with the game: in 1991 Barkley punched a fan on the street, threw water at hecklers, spat on an 8-year-old girl (aiming for another heckler), attacked his coach in his autobiography (later claiming he was misquoted) and, in his defense, declared, "I'm a '90s NIGGER." In the 1992 Olympics, Barkely created an international furor by elbowing a lanky Angolan player to the floor and then claiming he thought the man might be "carrying a spear." (The following year, in a multi-million dollar TV campaign for NIKE, he declared, "I am not a role model. I am not paid to be a role model.") In 1994 "Sir Charles" declared an interest in entering Republican politics, possibly as candidate for Governor of Alabama. He spoke up after seeking the counsel of RUSH LIMBAUGH and former Vice President Dan Quayle.

Barney, Matthew (b. 1967)   Artist celebrated for sculpture and video explorations of his own body. On the eve of his precocious 1991 New York debut, he scaled the walls and ceiling of the gallery naked, engaging in a number of disciplined exertions that included lowering himself into a refrigerated chamber where sporting equipment coated with Vaseline was waiting for his various orifices. At the gallery opening the next day, all that greeted visitors were the climbing marks, leftover greasy equipment, and a monitor playing a videotape of the previous night's SoHo spelunking. The Yale grad (where he was recruited to play football

from high school in Boise, Idaho) went on to enjoy a starring role in the 1993 WHITNEY BIENNIAL and embark on a three-year "Cremaster" project, the title of which refers to the set of "thermometer" muscles that retract the male sex organs when the temperature drops.

WEB **Whitney Museum** http://www.uky.edu/Artsource/whitneyhome.html

Courtesy of Barbara Gladstone Gallery, photo by L. Lame

Artist MATTHEW BARNEY, hanging around in SoHo, New York, as documented in the *Blind Perineum* video.

barrettes   Hair clips worn with middle-parted hair or with pig-tails as part of the "baby femme" style, with color-rimmed tight baby T-shirts or BABY-DOLL DRESSES and Mary Jane shoes. Barettes are commonly blue, yellow and pink in color, made of plastic with butterfly or daisy decorations; they can be bought at low-end retailers like Walgreen's or K-Mart. This post-RIOT GRRRL, almost pedophilic look sprung from the club and RAVE scene in mid–1993; it complements the worship of anything child-like, including lunch boxes and wide-eyed coy facial expressions (see INFANTILIZATION). It was popularized by COURTNEY LOVE of Hole, singer BJÖRK, and DEEE-LITE's Lady Miss Kier; in 1994, barrettes spread to fashion-show runways via designers like ANNA SUI and X-GIRL and to the television characters of Tori Spelling on *BEVERLY HILLS 90210* and Nicole Eggert on *BAYWATCH*; the hair accessories also showed up on gay male urbanites and even GREEN DAY drummer Tré Cool.

Barrymore, Drew (b. 1975)   Scion of the Hollywood-royalty Barrymore family who first acted at 11 months-old in a TV commercial; at 7, Barrymore was starring in box-office record-breaker *E.T.* (1982). The flip side of child stardom was revealed when she dropped out of school at 14 and published her co-written autobiography, *Little Girl Lost* (1990): drinking at 9, dope-smoking at 10, and coke-snorting at 12 were some of the stops on Barrymore's descent. After a string of roles in little-seen movies, Barrymore played an amoral teen seductress in *Poison Ivy* (1992); the role brought her minor-icon status that was cemented by an Ellen von Unwerth-shot Guess? jeans ad campaign which highlighted her WHITE TRASH sex appeal. Barrymore tends to fare best in high-spirited, low-class projects like *The AMY FISHER Story* (TV movie, 1993), *Guncrazy* (1992), and the short-lived twentysomething soap *2000 Malibu Road* (1992), rather than in mid-budget Hollywood fodder like *Bad Girls* (1994), *Boys on the Side* (1995), and *Mad Love* (1995). Less than two months after her March 1994 marriage to an L.A. bar owner, Barrymore filed for divorce; she subsequently became involved with Hole guitarist Eric Erlandson, whose praises she invariably sang on her many TV talk show appearances.

WEB **Miss Barrymore** http://ftp.macweek.ziff.com/peopl e/doy/drew.page/drew.first.html

Barthelme, Frederick (b. 1943) Sympathetic satirist of suburban America. In his novels and short-story collections (including *Moon Deluxe* [1983], *Chroma* [1987], *Natural Selection* [1990], and *The Brother* [1993]), the younger brother of the late post-modernist Donald Barthelme has mined his stories from a rich Southern vein, writing of brand names, cable TV, and middle-aged men disoriented by sexual and cultural confusion. While this is the same ground tread by realists like John Updike and Philip Roth, Barthelme treats the subject with a highly distinctive comic control, relying on brightly colored images, poetic compression, and an elevation of the inanimate that is both alienating and endearing. Often grouped with such writers as Ann Beattie, Mary Robison, and Raymond Carver,

Barthelme more accurately belongs with such faux naif comedians as film director HAL HARTLEY.

Bayer, Sam (b. 1964) Music video director who, in 1991, launched MTV's grunge revolution with his video for NIRVANA's "Smells Like Teen Spirit." The clip's sickly tones, anomic, moshing kids, and TATTOOED cheerleaders that accompanied Kurt Cobain's anthem announced the beginning of the end for the station's promotion of high-gloss pop-METAL clips. Bayer, who began his career as a director of photography for renowned video director Matt Mahurin, continues to do his own camerawork, sometimes borrowing Mahurin's trademark use of Vaseline smeared on the lens to create a blurry effect around the edges of the frame. (A memorable example of this was Blind Melon's 1992 bee-girl hit "No Rain.") In 1994 Bayer directed Hole's "Doll Parts," in which COURTNEY LOVE controversially cavorted with a child manqué for Kurt Cobain.
USENET **rec.music.video**

Baywatch When *Baywatch* was first shown on NBC in 1990 it was canceled after a single season. Revived in off-network syndication it became the most popular TV show on the planet, with an estimated one billion viewers in 150 countries. The world apparently can't get enough of this sun-kissed vision of an America in which David Hasselhoff (former star of '80s talking-car show *Knight Rider* and pop legend in Germany) presides over a group of male and female Malibu lifeguards of formidable pulchritude and questionable acting ability. Stretching their swimwear to near-bursting point, these bathing beauties (including *Playboy* Playmates Pamela Anderson Lee and Erika Eleniak) drift frictionlessly through sexless, usually moralistic plots. The "*Babewatch*" formula looks unstoppable: co-executive producer Hasselhoff and partners were able to spin-off detective show *Baywatch Nights*, and possibly a cartoon show called *Baywatch Kids*, as well a legion of licensed products that include a planned series of THEME RESTAURANTS starting in New York.

WEB **Babewatch Hot Links** http://www.netter.is/~pesi/
baywatch.html

BBS Electronic "Bulletin Board System" that
runs on a computer set to respond to modem
phone calls from other computer users wishing to
exchange messages and files. In the decade before
the INTERNET became a household word, BBB's
(often run from the basement of hobbyists and
small entrepreneurs) defined the horizons of cyberspace for the average modem dabbler, with tens of
thousands of separate computers around the world
reflecting a similar diversity of interests as is now
found in USENET newsgroups. Unlike the Internet,
most BBS's were self-contained islands, incapable of
connecting with any other BBS to forward or
receive messages. This situation began to change in
the late '80s with the advent of shoe-string networks like FidoNet in which participating BBS's
were programmed to exchange files during off-peak
phone times; though immensely successful given
their modest infrastructure, such BBS networks
have largely been absorbed into the INTERNET in
recent years.

USENET **alt.bbs**, **comp.bbs** ✦ WEB **Bulletin Board Systems**
http://www.dsv.su.se/~mats.bjo/bbslists.html

Beastie Boys Hardcore/funk/rap group and
style-arbiters of ALTERNATIVE culture. Formed as a
PUNK band in New York City in 1981 by Adam
Yauch (b. 1964, aka MCA) and Mike Diamond
(b. 1965, aka Mike D). Adam Horovitz (b. 1966,
aka King Ad-Rock) joined in 1983, and the band
began experimenting with HIP-HOP, recording the
jokey phone-prank rap "Cookie Puss." Teamed with
Def Jam house producer RICK RUBIN in 1986, the
Beasties released their debut album *Licensed To Ill*,
melding heavy metal guitar with hip-hop beats and
bratty rhymes; fueled by the frat boy anthem "(You
Gotta) Fight For Your Right (To Party)" and vulgar
live shows (which included a 20-foot inflatable
penis), *Licensed To Ill* became the first rap album to
top the pop charts.

After a financial dispute with Def Jam, the
band relocated to Los Angeles and re-defined
themselves with 1989's *Paul's Boutique*; although a
relative financial failure, the album built the Beastie
Boys' critical reputation with a complex, funky
weave of eclectic sample-collages and catch-it-if-
you-can torrents of cultural references. (Enduring
Beastie obsessions tend to involve, in dizzying combination, New York sports figures, the '70s,
Jewishness, blaxploitation, high culture, and low-
brow TV.) For their next two albums *Check Your
Head* (1992) and *Ill Communication* (1994) the
band picked up instruments for the first time since
their early days, revisiting their punk roots, dab-
bling in ACID JAZZ grooves, and creditably repro-
ducing the type of funk they once sampled. Both
records were certified platinum, and 1994's
LOLLAPALOOZA tour confirmed the Beasties' place
in the affections of the alternative rock crowd.
Perhaps more than their music, the Beastie Boys
are appreciated for their impeccable SKATER/HIP-
HOP taste, but their self-determined lifestyle is the
true art form. Horovitz, who is married to actress
Ione Skye, occasionally takes modest movie roles;
Diamond, who is married to director TAMRA
DAVIS, is a partner in X-LARGE; Yauch, who is an
avid SNOWBOARDER, studied Buddhism in Tibet.
The Beastie Boys propagate their world-view from
a self-created scene that revolves around their
Grand Royal studio (complete with basketball
court) and record label, which is home to the likes
of female band Luscious Jackson (featuring early-
'80s Beasties drummer Kate Schellenbach) and

Photo by Brooke Williams

Lifestyle as an artform–the Beastie Boys v. the New
York Knicks' Anthony Mason, LOLLAPALOOZA '94.

teenage Australian songwriter Ben Lee; the meticulous, infrequent house magazine *Grand Royal* magazine serves as the *Martha Stewart Living* of the HANG TEN set.

WEB **Music Kitchen: Grand Royal** http://www.nando.net /music/gm/GrandRoyal/Magazine/ ✦ USENET **alt.music.beastie-boys** ✦ mail list **The Beastielist** email majordomo@world.std.com with "subscribe beastielist" in the body of the message

Beats, The Community of writers (chiefly Jack Kerouac, Allen Ginsberg, Neal Cassady, William Burroughs) who in turning their lives into art passed along an intimate and transparent portrait of a literary generation in the wake of WWII and Korea. Beats (or beatniks) were often invoked in the early '90s as an influence on contemporary youth culture; superficial similarities between the decades included fashion statements like baggy pants, sneakers, crewcuts, and GOATEES; SPOKEN WORD and COFFEE BAR culture; and chatty, spontaneously composed jazz-HIP-HOP. There was a modest spate of associated culture-products, such as re-issued books, a RHINO RECORDS CD compilation, and a Francis Ford Coppola movie of Kerouac's 1957 book *On the Road,* which attracted thousands of "wannabeats" to an open casting call in New York. Meanwhile, THE GAP, Cappio iced coffee, and even Wendy's hamburgers were invoking the Beat aesthetic in the name of commerce. All of which bespeak a cultural time warp if not, as Ginsberg puts it, "the intergenerational transmission of sympathy."

WEB **Literary Kicks** http://www.charm.net/ ~brooklyn/LitKicks.html ✦ WEB **A Jack Kerouac ROMnibus** http://www.penguin.com/usa/electronic/titles/kerouac/ ✦ USENET **alt.books.beatgeneration**

Beavis and Butt-head MTV cartoon variously regarded as the nadir of idiot comedy or the apex of pop-culture meta-criticism. Beavis and Butt-head were created by former musician Mike Judge (b. 1963), who supervises the show's production and does most of the voices (it is written principally by *National Lampoon* alumni Sam Johnson and Chris Marcil). The characters are two hapless adolescent metalheads who alternate between Freudian deconstructions of pop videos and aimlessly nihilistic hi-jinks. An example of the latter was *Frog Baseball*, their September 1992 debut on *LIQUID TELEVISION*; by March 1993 B&B had their own show. Seven months later, an Ohio mother said the pyromaniacal pair caused her 5-year-old son to burn down their trailer home, killing his 2-year-old sister. The ensuing attention, coming just before Senate hearings on TV violence, led MTV to give the show a late-night timeslot, a disclaimer, and the banishing of references to fire; but it also catapulted the duo to stardom. (So much so that favorable mentions from Beavis and Butt-head are credited with boosting the record sales of struggling acts like White Zombie and Corrosion of Conformity; unfavorable mentions tend to be reserved for retired videos.) As MTV's signature show and its most popular, B&B earned the channel over $15 million in ad revenue in 1994; the 500,000 sales of both B&B books convinced Paramount to create an MTV publishing imprint; a feature film was in the planning stages in 1995.

WEB **Beavis and Butthead Episode Guide** http://calvin. hsc.colorado.edu/episodes.html/ ✦ USENET **alt.tv.beavis-n-butthead**

beepers In 1993 alone, the number of beepers (more officially, "pagers") in use in the U.S. increased by nearly 50 percent—from 15 million to 22 million—the largest increase coming among users aged 18 to 25. ("Back in the days when I was a teenager / before I had status / and before I had a pager," rapped A Tribe Called Quest on 1991's *The Low End Theory*.) This rapid proliferation was due in part to '80s telecommunications deregulation, principally the auctioning off of vast amounts of wireless frequency by the FCC. Pagers were originally the province of doctors and drug dealers, but as prices dropped they began, like answering machines before them, to affect familial and romantic relationships: "beeper babies" replaced "latchkey kids" as working parents gave their unsupervised offspring pagers, and the item became the ultimate intimate gift between teens going steady. (Future

enhancements may emulate the Bandai toy company's combination infrared palmtop communicator and PERSONAL DIGITAL ASSISTANT that has taken school-age Japan by storm.)

WEB **Motorola Paging Products**

http://www.mot.com/MIMS/PPG/

Ben & Jerry's Superpremium, socially conscious ice cream. Founded in 1978 by Ben (Bennett R.) Cohen (b. 1950) and Jerry Greenfield (b. 1951), who started their empire in a vacant Vermont gas station with $12,000 investment and the resolution to stay in business one year. Their first franchise opened in 1981, with distribution outside Vermont beginning in 1983. After going public in 1984, Ben & Jerry's Homemade Inc. sales grew to 1994 annual revenue of some $150 million worth of Cherry Garcia, Wavy Gravy, maple walnut, White Russian, and numerous other flavors in grocery stores, delis, and its approximately 100 "scoop shops." It thus equals Häagen-Dazs in superpremium ice cream market share. In 1995 the Waterbury, VT-based company chose a new CEO—not from among the 22,500 candidates who submitted essays to its "Yo! I'm Your C.E.O." contest, but through an established corporate headhunting firm. Meanwhile, the company continues to donate 7.5 percent of pretax income to the charity-serving Ben & Jerry's Foundation.

WEB **Ben & Jerry's Homemade Inc.**

http://www.benjerry.com/

Ben Davis San Francisco-based utility clothing firm which entered a new phase of popularity during the '90s WORKWEAR trend. Company founder Benjamin Franklin Davis (b. 1914) had excellent design credentials when he set up shop in 1935: his father was Jacob Davis, a Latvian immigrant who invented the pocket rivet for Levi's. Ben Davis' baggy, hardwearing "coarse clothing," with its smiling-ape logo, changed little between that time and the point almost 60 years later when West Coast rappers adopted it. Ben Davis was one of the handful of brands carried initially in X-LARGE clothing stores; it also inspired many other young design start-ups.

Benetton Although it has been eclipsed in America by the inexorable ascent of THE GAP, Benetton continues to flourish in Europe under the stewardship of Italian fashion magnate Luciano Benetton. Founded in 1965 near Venice, Italy, the company maximizes its profits through a unique system that restricts its role to dyeing, labeling, and shipping clothing items made by independent subcontractors; the merchandise is sent to independently owned boutiques in amounts determined by a complex computer network that helped pioneer "just-in-time production."

The one area Benetton lavishly invests in is public image: in 1993, the company spent $50 million on advertising, largely supervised by creative director/photographer Oliviero Toscani (b. 1942). Toscani's forte is conceptual, often controversial ads that pass over Benetton clothing in favor of stylized visual metaphors—a priest and a nun kissing, a black woman nursing a white baby—and harshly realistic pictures of contemporary tragedy. (In 1991, Benetton launched *Colors*, a stylish magazine chiefly devoted to the same MULTICULTURAL messages that have made the company's "United Colors of Benetton" a sometime byword for racial tokenism.)

In 1994, a Toscani ad showing a human arm tattooed with the words "HIV POSITIVE" led to widespread protests. A group of French PWAs (Persons With AIDS) successfully sued the company for defamation—the court stated that the campaign "evoked Nazi barbarity." (When Toscani made public a threat to quit rather than sacrifice his artistic freedom, Benetton's stock immediately

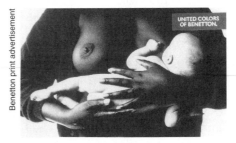

Benetton print advertisement

A 1992 example of BENETTON'S MULTICULTURAL marketing.

dropped by over 6 percent.) In July 1995, a German court banned the "HIV POSITIVE" ad and others in the campaign (including child laborers and a bloody soldier's uniform), decreeing that "anyone who exploits feelings of pity in such an intense way for commercial interests violates competition law." Two weeks later Toscani came to New York to unveil advertising for the "Benetton Sportsystem": a climbing boot was juxtaposed with the Crucifixion; a rollerblade with a student-tank face-off in China. "We strongly believe there is the right balance between the innovation and what is needed to explain the sporting-goods products," one Benetton executive told the *New York Times*.

WEB **Made In Italy: Benetton** http://www.flashnet.it/fashion/bene/bene.htm/

Bernhard, Sandra (b. 1955)   Difficult-to-categorize entertainer and sometime media provocateur. As a manicurist/stand-up comedian in late-'70s L.A., Bernhard plied a ferociously negative, heavily referential shtick that gained her entree to several different media worlds, none of which she has ever quite fit into. In her time Bernhard has been an acidly comedic, underutilized film actress (*King of Comedy* [1983], *Hudson Hawk* [1991]), piquant author (*Confessions of a Pretty Lady* [1988], *Love, Love, and Love* [1993]), one-woman show (*Without You I'm Nothing* [1988, movie version 1990]), magazine writer, and chanteuse (*Excuses for Bad Behavior Part 1* [1994]). In 1992 Bernhard joined the cast of *Roseanne* as a randy lesbian; her aggressively ambiguous sexuality was apparently becoming less so.

WEB **Sandra Bernhard's Excuses for Bad Behavior**
http://www.music.sony.com/Music/ArtistInfo/SandraBernhard.html

Beverly Hills, 90210   Nighttime soap opera about well-heeled high schoolers in America's most enviable ZIP code. Although it floundered on its October 1990 launch, *90210* survived to become a major hit among both star struck teens and slumming camp-followers. *Beverly Hills, 90210* made pin-up idols of its toothsome male leads, alleged bad boy Luke Perry (as Dylan McKay) and overly empathetic Jason Priestley (Brandon Walsh); and an anti-star of SHANNEN DOHERTY (Brenda Walsh). And by reeling in the elusive under-30 demographic *90210* inspired a mini-"youthquake" of shows, among them *The Heights*, *2000 Malibu Road*, MELROSE PLACE, *Freshman Dorm*, and *Class of '96*. Only the last two didn't involve *90210* co-producer Aaron Spelling, and only MELROSE PLACE (by *90210* creator/producer Darren Star) outlived its first season. Meanwhile, most of *90210*'s maturing cast made the transition to the fictional California University, where they wrestled bravely with the campus "issues" of the day.

MAIL LIST **90210 List** email Majordomo@top.com with "subscribe 90210" in the message ✦ USENET **alt.tv.90210** FTP ftp.tcp.com/pub/90210 ✦ WEB **90210 Central** http://wwwcip.informatik.uni-erlangen.de/tree/misc/bh90210/

bike messengers   Although messengers have carried packages by bicycle for more than a century, the bike messenger as cultural icon is a phenomenon of the 1980s and '90s. With its combination of high risk and low payoff, bike messengering is the quintessential youth culture job; the urban anti-hero overtones and sleek fashions (such as Lycra shorts and rugged shoulder-satchels) of bike messengers were memorably invoked in one Clinton '92 campaign ad (which echoed the 1986 movie *Quicksilver*, starring Kevin Bacon). Commission-based compensation encourages risk-taking among messengers, who are unencumbered by medical benefits or job security. (Only in 1994 did the Teamster's Union begin an uphill drive to organize messengers.) In the '90s, fax machines and modems have cut into the bike messenger business. Manhattan, for example, had 2,000 messengers in 1994, down from 7,000 in the mid-'80s; average earnings reportedly fell from $600 to $300 a week. Although the 1994 CBS sitcom *Double Rush* flopped in double-quick time, MTV's hit series *The Real World: San Francisco*, was bolstered by the presence of the compellingly repulsive messenger Puck, who went on to find modest fame as a VJ and a CALVIN KLEIN model. In 1995, one of the first interactive movies released was the messenger-themed *Ride For Your Life*.

WEB **Biking Page** http://www.gorp.com/gorp/activity/biking. htm ✦ USENET **rec.bicycle**

binge drinking   Public health term for the "work hard, play hard" alcohol credo, defined as five drinks in a row (four for women). In spite of a general decline in drinking among college students, a shift towards more safety- and health-conscious attitudes, and the virtual campus prohibition brought about by 21 MINIMUM DRINKING AGE laws, a December 1994 Harvard School of Public Health survey of some 140 colleges found that many of those still drinking are hard-core practitioners. Nearly half (44 percent) of undergraduates engage in binge drinking, and of those, nearly half (19 percent of total) do it often. The fraternity figures are even higher (86 percent of residents). A follow-up survey of 13 "party schools," released in April 1995, found that nearly half of college frosh binge drink in their first week of college. The Harvard studies also connected heavy drinking (often from drinking games) with unsafe sex and DATE RAPE.

WEB **National Clearinghouse for Alcohol and Drug Information** http://www.health.org/

binocular dysphoria   Health problem associated with VIRTUAL REALITY headsets that can cause depth perception difficulties to linger for hours after disengaging from computer-generated visuals. VR headgear simulates 3D by creating a separate image for each eye—apparently the brain can somehow distinguish between this illusion and the effect of two eyes seeing a single image from different perspectives. [See also CARPAL TUNNEL SYNDROME.]

bio-engineered groceries   The first genetically engineered food, the MacGregor Flavr Savr tomato, was introduced in 1994. By scrambling the gene for the enzyme that makes a tomato mushy, producers were able not so much to improve the tomato's taste as lengthen its shelf life. The rBST and rBGH hormones fed to cows to increase their milk output had similar, obvious economic benefits, but in an effort to protect small dairy farmers from corporate overproduction the state of Vermont passed a 1994 law which required the labeling of rBGH dairy products. (Always correct, BEN & JERRY'S introduced a slashed circle over the letters "rBST/rBGH" on the lids of its ice cream.) Another hi-tech food controversy concerned the irradiation of meat, spices, and farm produce—while the FDA had approved the X-raying of many foods as a way of reducing disease-causing micro-organisms (not unlike the homogenization of milk), in 1994 all but a few producers of herbs and fruits were avoiding the process for fear of consumer boycotts over the "radiolytic" transformation of nuked food.

WEB **GBH In Milk Cows** http://lablinks.com/ sumeria/anim/bgh.html

Biosphere 2   Three-acre, glass-enclosed human terrarium located in the Arizona desert. In September 1991 four men and four women decked out in jumpsuits smiled for cameras and entered the 'sphere, embarking on a two-year experiment in recycling their air, food, water, and waste to gain a greater understanding of Earth's own ecological balance. (The Earth itself being "Biosphere 1" in the parlance of the parent company, Space Biosphere Ventures.) The project was widely hailed as the greatest scientific adventure since NASA's moon landing; compared with NASA's recent Space Station mishaps, the fact that the $150 million venture was privately funded by the maverick NEW AGE heir to the Bass Texas oil fortune was taken as evidence of private enterprise's superiority to government bureaucracy. But then *Village Voice* investigative journalist Marc Cooper practically blew the glass lid off the project, revealing not only that the supposedly self-sustaining environment was outfitted with air vents and a carbon dioxide scrubber (apparently the greenhouse suffered from greenhouse effect), but that the experiment was conceived and administered as an extension of a '60s cult dedicated to the colonization of Mars, where a select group of super men and women would breed the evolutionary successors to human beings.

WEB **Space Settlement Archive** http://www.nas.nasa. gov/NAS/SpaceSettlement/Archive

Birkenstock Unsightly orthopedic sandals invented in 1965 when Karl Birkenstock, the scion of a German footwear dynasty, combined his company's molded sole with a suede-lined cork footbed and straps. Birkenstocks were first distributed in the U.S. in 1967, and were favored mainly by DEAD-HEADS and CRUNCHY types (health-food stores were one outlet) until the early '90s. They then went overground with a vengeance, appearing on the feet of designers, celebrities (most famously those of MADONNA and KEANU REEVES), and runway models who were swept along with fashion's supposed swing to NEW AGE values. The *New York Times* reported that the Birkenstock company sold more shoes between 1992 and 1994 than it had over the previous 20 years. [See also DR. SCHOLL'S.]

WEB **Birkenstock Express** http://www.footwise.com/

bisexuality Sexual non-preference of the '90s for those who take romantic or sexual partners regardless of gender. Scorned in the recent past as a "queer" variant by straight society and disliked as much in the gay world, where people assumed that bi's were either too timid to "fully" come out

Newsweek magazine, July 17, 1995

Bisexuality as GAP ad, via *Newsweek*, 1995.

or, worse, to be heterosexuals drawn to the "exoticism" of gay sex. The term itself gained wide circulation in the '80s from AIDS epidemiologists, who labeled male bisexuals as "vectors of disease" along with blood transfusions and needle-sharing. This helped set the stage—in conjunction with ANTI-GAY RIGHTS INI-TIATIVES that also included bisexuals—for broadening the Gay Rights Movement.

At the same time, the successes of the gay rights movement broadened the spectrum of sexuality in the popular culture, creating new bisexual role models: MADONNA flaunted her relationship with SANDRA BERNHARD in 1988; R.E.M.'s Michael Stipe, DREW BARRYMORE, Sophie B. Hawkins, model Rachel Williams, and others openly discussed their bisexual relationships; there were even wanna-bi's, most notably Kurt Cobain and COURTNEY LOVE, who said that although they had never had a same-sex experience, they still considered themselves bisexual. In 1995 Harvard Shakespeare professor Marjorie Garber made the academic case for bisexuality with her 600-page *Vice Versa: Bisexuality and the Eroticism of Everyday Life*, in which she argued that most people would be bisexual if not for "repression, religion, repugnance, denial . . . premature specialization." In July '95 *Newsweek* worried in a cover story that "to a social order based on monogamy, bisexuality looms as a potent threat," suggesting that bisexuality somehow poses a special danger to stable relationships.

WEB **soc.bi Home Page** http://sun1.bham.ac. uk/J.W.Harley/soc-bi.html ✦ USENET **soc.bi** ✦ WEB **Bisexual Resource List** http://www.qrd.org/QRD/www/BRC/brl-toc.html ✦ WEB **The #Bisex Home Page** http://www.interac cess.com/maggy/bisex/index.htm/ ✦ MAIL LIST **Bisexu-L** email listserv@brownvm.brown.edu with "SUBSCRIBE BISEXU-L your_full_name" in the text/body of the message ✦ IRC #bisex

Björk (b. Björk Gudmundsdottir, 1965) Impish Icelandic songstress whose original band, the Sugarcubes, won over the British press in 1988 with sinewy grooves and her spiraling vocals. When the band's willful obscurity failed to expand their cult following after three albums, Bjork left the group and aligned herself with such cosmopolitan talents as photographer-turned-video-maker Stephan Sednaoui, designer JEAN-PAUL GAULTIER, and former Soul II Soul lynchpin Nellee Hooper, who produced her 1993 *Debut* album. (Björk's previous two solo albums, in 1977 and 1990, had been of Icelandic traditional music, and jazz.) This folksy futurist became an MTV staple, club fixture, respected ALTERNATIVE act, and a gold-selling solo artist; she even co-wrote "Bedtime Story" for MADONNA's 1994 album *Bedtime Stories*. 1995's glossy, hyper-eclectic *Post* album confirmed Björk as one of the more avant-garde ideas-merchants in the pop marketplace.

WEB **Won's Astro Bjork Page** http://www.netwave.net/ members/wtchoi/bjork/bjork.html ◆ WEB **Bjork Net Resources** http://pages.prodigy.com/OH/poliki/bjork.html ◆ WEB **Bjork Gudundsdottir** ttp://www.infosys.tuwien.ac.at/ Entertainment/Bjoerk_Gudmundsdottir/Bjoerk.html ◆ WEB **Björk's Web Sense** http://www.centrum/is/bjork

Black Death vodka   Belgian-made vodka first imported into the U.S. in 1991 by Cabo Distributing Co. of California. The following year Black Death was banned by the Bureau of Alcohol, Tobacco, and Firearms, which asserted that the liquor's name and label—featuring a sinister image of a grinning skull in black top hat—created "the misleading impression of bubonic plague and poison." (This impression was furthered by Black Death's product endorsement by Slash, the sinister, black top-hatted guitarist of pop-metal bad boys Guns 'N Roses.) In October 1992 Cabo won its appeal against the ban in a Federal district court in San Francisco, emerging from the case with its rock 'n' roll outlaw credentials in good order.

Black Dog   Logo from the well-weathered restaurant on the New England resort island of Martha's Vineyard; faded-color T-shirts bearing the understated Labrador silhouette have become a kind of Hard Rock Café insignia for the upper classes. Most versions of the shirts state the year of vintage in antique type on the back, the better to separate *ancien* from *nouveau*; earliest models date from 1980, with a large mail-order business started in the early '90s through classified ads in the likes of *ROLLING STONE*. In 1992 Vineyard residents Helen and Paul Hall successfully defended their right to sell "Dead Dog" parodies (originally picturing an upside-down dog), which led to a spate of other knock-offs, including a dread-locked "Black Dawg"

and, to celebrate President's Clinton's 1993 vacation on "The Vineyard," a Clinton-headed canine.

Black Panthers   Radical black nationalist political party from the late '60s, co-founded in Oakland by Huey Newton (b. 1942, d. 1989) and Bobby Seale (b. 1936), that marked the high-water mark of the black power movement. Police were "pigs" to be resisted with armed "self-defense" patrols; black people had to help themselves with free breakfast programs, health clinics, and political campaigns like the one that helped elect Lionel Wilson mayor of Oakland. The Panthers faltered in the early '70s from their own unsustainable rhetoric and constant FBI harassment (one FBI report made public in 1976 detailed the Cointelpro division's illegal wiretaps, false arrests, and fomenting of violent confrontations with the police). SPIKE LEE blames the FBI for the NATION OF ISLAM's murder of MALCOLM X, but it was Panther leader Fred Hampton who was shot dead in his sleep by Chicago police during a pre-dawn 1969 raid. Panther imagery persisted in the '90s through HIP-HOP, self-proclaimed New Black Panther neighborhood patrols in Dallas and other cities, and an embarrassing, historically fanciful 1995 Mario Van Peebles movie.

WEB **Peter's E-Text** http://cs.oberlin.edu/ students/pjaques/etext/home.html ◆ WEB **The Black Panther Coloring Book** http://www.cybergate.com/~jonco/bpcb.html

Black Rock Coalition   Founded in New York City in 1985 by music critic Greg Tate, artist manager Konda Mason, and Living Colour guitarist Vernon Reid, the Black Rock Coalition attempts to remove the barriers African-American bands encounter acquiring gigs, record deals, and black audiences for rock music. A Los Angeles chapter followed in 1988. The ghost of Jimi Hendrix looms over the BRC, whose members include the bands Afro-D-Ziak, Admiral Ball-Z, Civil Rite, and Total Eclipse. The group has issued a number of compilation albums, including *A History of Our Future* (1991) and *Blacker Than That* (1993)—the latter was put out on BRC Records, which the group launched in 1993. In the age of GANGSTA RAP, the BRC has fostered forums and debate about the "ghettocentric" imagery of black popular culture.

WEB **BRC Home Page** http://www.phantom.com/ ~giant/brc/brc.html

Black, Shane (b. 1962)

Role model for the hundreds of aspiring screenwriters hoping to cash in on Hollywood's mania for potential blockbuster scripts. At age 25, UCLA graduate Black wrote and sold for $250,000 the spec script (written without assignment) to *Lethal Weapon* (1987), the wise-cracking shoot-'em-up that made him an A-list scenarist. In April 1990, while operating from the semi-legendary, communal "Pad O' Guys" apartment in Hollywood, Black was paid $1.75 million for the NOIR-tinged action movie *The Last Boy Scout* (made in 1991, starring Bruce Willis). Although the movie bombed spectacularly, it did not dent Black's reputation—he was paid $1 million for a re-write on the quip-heavy Arnold Schwarzenegger flop *The Last Action Hero* (1993). In July 1994 New Line paid Black a record $4 million for *The Long Kiss Goodnight*. (This spec script, dubbed *The Last Girl Scout* by *Variety*, overhauled the previous record-holder, Joe Eszterhas' $3 million *Basic Instinct*.)

WEB **Internet Screenwriter's Network** http://www. screenwriters.com/hn/writing/swdesk/board.html

FRANCESCA LIA BLOCK, creator of Weetzie Bat.

Block, Francesca Lia (b. 1962)

"The reason Weetzie Bat hated high school," begins *Weetzie Bat* (1989), the first in this Los Angeles novelist's remarkable series of beautiful and bizarre paeans to growing up weird on the West Coast, "was because no one understood. They didn't even know where they were living." Weetzie lives in a fairy-tale L.A. in which commodities and fetish objects cohabitate shamelessly—a lyrical land of sunshine and shamanism. Block's four Weetzie Bat novels address adolescent fears and passions with a sassy brand of magical realism and private language.

Bobbitt, John Wayne (b. 1967)

Protagonist of the fastest selling porn tape ever, *John Wayne Bobbitt Uncut* (1994). The video graphically displays the handiwork of Virginia surgeons who reattached the penis that Bobbitt's Venezuelan-born immigrant wife Lorena, after years of abuse, cut off with a 12-inch kitchen knife and threw in a field. ("It never did me any good," she later explained about the organ. She was acquitted of all charges.) Bobbitt leveraged other spin-offs from the case's 1993 tabloid coverage, including strip club gigs, a line of penis protectors, and a featured appearance on HOWARD STERN's notorious 1994 New Year's Eve pay-per-view special.

Body Shop, The

Retail cosmetics chain specializing in wholesome beauty products and political causes. Anita Roddick (b. 1942), the co-founder and public face of the company, cultivates her reputation as a cross between Estée Lauder and Indiana Jones, scouring the Third World for age-old beauty tips and returning with better-world, better-skin knickknacks such as the Mexican cactus supposedly used by peasants there as body scrubs. The Body Shop's image of virtuous commerce, dating back to the first 1976 store in Brighton, England, went down well in American malls—by 1994 there were some 300 outlets in North America. The company has lately been plagued by accusations of hypocrisy and heavy-handed dealing with critics. Notable disputes include the company's 1989 fudge of its animal-rights stance by changing product labels from "Not Tested On Animals" to "Against Animal Testing"; and a stock-damaging October '94 article in an obscure American magazine (*Business Ethics*) critical of the company's "Trade Not Aid" dealings with the Kayapo tribe of Brazil.

WEB **Body Language** http://www.the-body-shop.com/

bodyboarding

Water sport regarded by surfers as an inferior form of their own practice; bodyboarders skim along the waves lying on boards under four feet long, usually made of soft foam. According to its many detractors, bodyboarding is a beginners' pastime, a horizontal cop-out from the risk-fraught thrills of surfing. Clashes between groups of rival waveriders are not uncommon on the beaches of Southern California—sometimes physical, but usually restricted to name-calling. Surfers' most egregious insult for their rivals is "Boogie boarders," after the foam board marketed in 1971. Bodyboarders, however, have had their own pro circuit since the mid-'80s; the sport even has its own magazine, *Bodyboarding* (from the publishers of *Surfing*), and body board sales, at half a million in 1993, far exceed those of surf boards.

WEB **Drop In! (Bodyboarding Info)**
http://www.sd.monash.edu.au/~jasonl/dropin.html

Boiled Angel Violent, anti-religious, and scatological self-published COMIC book found "obscene" by a Florida jury in March, 1994, turning the artist, a 24-year-old convenience store clerk named Mike Diana (b. 1969), into a free speech poster boy for the underground publishing world. A show at Chicago's Goat Gallery ensued, along with a twentyfold increase in sales of the "obscene" issues, *Boiled Angel 7* and *Boiled Angel Ate*. In a typical story line, a child goes to church looking for a priest, only to have a giant penis squirt semen in his face. Traumatized, he grows up taking drugs and sodomizing himself with a crucifix. Held in a maximum security prison while awaiting sentencing, Diana is the only cartoonist in U.S. history to be imprisoned on an obscenity charge.

WEB **Alternative Comics: The Mike Diana Story**
http://bronze.ucs.indiana.edu/~mfragass/diana_obscure.html

bootleg fashion "A Fendi bag and a bad attitude / that's all I need to get me in a good mood," rapped L.L. Cool J in 1991's "Round the Way Girl"—chances are, he wasn't talking about one of the Italian designer's $150-plus originals, but one of the thousands of knock-offs that were appearing on New York streets. There has always been fashion counterfeiting, but the status-obsessed '80s saw a booming interest in high-end, hard-to-afford European labels like Fendi, Chanel, Louis Vuitton, Gucci, and MCM that was manna to bootleggers. These easily-recognizable logos were quickly plastered on items both authentic-looking and absurd (Gucci BEEPER covers?). As bootleggers grew sensitive to market trends, American sportswear designers such as RALPH LAUREN, Tommy Hilfiger, Guess?, and Nautica saw accurate, computer-detailed reproductions of their lines selling on the street (beside $15 Rolex and Tag Hauer watches) for a quarter of the original's price. Even street-wear labels like STÜSSY and KARL KANI are not immune—the latter responded by attaching to their gear a small, hard-to-reproduce brass plaque.

Bosnia-Herzegovina Central European nation which has weathered some of the bloodiest fighting in history since declaring its independence from what remained of Yugoslavia on April 5, 1992. On that day, former Yugoslav country-mates Serbia and Croatia, predominantly Christian, each attacked the mostly Muslim Bosnia using the heavy arms left over from the dissolved country. A U.N. arms embargo that was supposed to maintain the peace ironically prevented Bosnia from defending itself against the "ethnic cleansing" proclaimed by Serbian militias. The international anti-fascist left rallied to the cause of cosmopolitan, polyglot Sarajevo—one enduring image is Susan Sontag directing *Waiting for Godot* against the background rattle of sniper fire—while Western democracies set-up and abandoned safe havens. (The women's movement was also active, protesting the use of rape by Serbian soldiers as a terror tactic, as documented by feminist author Catherine MacKinnon and others.) By 1994, more journalists had been killed in the Balkan wars than in Lebanon and Vietnam combined. Commenting in 1995 on the failure of the Western democracies to stop slaughters taking place in the heart of modern Europe, writer Christopher Hitchens observed "As we become more civilized, we seem to find the pain of others easier and easier to bear."

USENET **misc.news.bosnia**, **soc.culture.bosna-herzgvna**
✦ WEB **Sarajevo Online Messages** http://MediaFilter

.org/MFF/SJform.html/ ✦ WEB **GeoPolitics in Yugoslavia, Bosnia and Hercegovina** http://civil.colorado.edu/~jeremic/geopolitics.html/

Bowers v. Hardwick 1986 Supreme Court decision holding that the privacy rights of married and unmarried people to have consensual sex in private (affirmed in the landmark 1965 Griswold decision striking down Connecticut's ban of contraceptives) do not exist if the people are of the same sex. The defendant Michael Hardwick was interrupted in his own bedroom, in flagrante, by an Atlanta police officer enforcing the state's anti-sodomy law. Although the Georgia prohibitions, like those of many Southern states, apply to any anal and oral sex between consenting adults, the Supreme Court effectively ignored the heterosexual permutations and ruled that there is no constitutional right to practice homosexuality. Many gay rights activists regard the case as the 20th century version of *Plessy v. Ferguson*, the infamous 1896 "separate but equal" decision used to justify six more decades of legal segregation of the races.
WEB **Supreme Court Decisions** http://www.law.cornell.edu/supct ✦ WEB **Queer Infoservers** http://www.infoqueer.org/queer/qis/email.html ✦ USENET **alt.politics.homosexuality, alt.politics.sex**

Box, The Miami-based music-video channel founded in 1985 on interactive-TV principles: from an on-screen menu, viewers order videos that add $2 to $3 each to their phone bill. After a shaky beginning as Video Music Box, the channel has grown to a $20 million per annum cash cow with over 6 million customers. Thriving on a populist diet of rap, metal, and street R&B, The Box (motto: "Music Television You Control") often screens more risqué versions of videos than its competitor MTV, without having to program Top 40 filler. The Box's ability to break acts (it takes credit for platinum R&B crooners R. Kelly and Mary J. Blige) makes its 160 custom-programmed outposts a target for record companies, who often employ workers to sit and order high-priority clips. No one is more aware of The Box's power than the station

itself: it created "The Great Playola Scheme of '94," a system whereby record companies can buy pre-set slots for their acts (along with disclaimer).
USENET **rec.music.video**

Brady Bunch, The Flat vintage sitcom (1969–1974) which came to life as an after-school hit in late-'70s syndication. With its premise of two broken families made whole, the show resonated with a latchkey generation experiencing a fifty percent divorce rate; the six Brady children of varying ages gave most boys and girls viewers a sympathetic character with which to identify. The show's status as an underground totem was tapped in June 1990 by an independent Chicago theater group which began performing *Brady Bunch* scripts; *The Real Live Brady Bunch* became a cult hit, and concert promoter Ron Delsener put together a touring version (with CONAN O'BRIEN sidekick Andy Richter debuting as Mike Brady) that received extensive media coverage. Brady interest was heightened by 1992's salacious, incest-hinting literary hit *Growing Up Brady* by son Greg (actor Barry Williams; co-written by BEAVIS AND BUTT-HEAD scribe Chris Kreski). In February 1995, the aging '70S FASHION revival proved combustible at the multiplex when *The Brady Bunch Movie* (which posited the Bradys as, to quote TV critic Rod Dreher, "wholesome, clueless anachronisms grooving their way blithely through the angry, brutal youth culture of the 1990s") spent two weeks as the country's top-grossing film. (Meanwhile, X-rated tales of unwholesome Brady couplings circulated on the INTERNET.)
WEB **Unofficial Brady Bunch Homepage** http://www.teleport.com/~btucker/bradys.htm ✦ WEB **Encyclopedia Brady** http://www.primenet.com/~dbrady/ ✦ USENET **alt.tv.brady-bunch**

branding The rarest and most extreme form of body manipulation and decoration, in which an image is burned into the skin with hot metal, not unlike the branding of cattle. A hazing rite in black fraternities since at least the 1930s (most commonly the horseshoe-shaped scar of Omega Psi Phi or the

"K" of Kappa Alpha Psi), branding surfaced along with SCARIFICATION in the left coast's MODERN PRIMITIVE culture in the early '90s as TATTOOS and PIERCING went mainstream via SUPERMODELS and pop stars. Typical designs such as Celtic runes are by necessity simpler than tattoos, but they can still take 7–15 strikes of cut sheet metal heated with a blow torch. Although modern medicine has come a long way in TATTOO REMOVAL, the keloid welts and whitish scar tissue markings of branding are considered permanent. In some S/M subcultures the sizzling ritualistic act, often videotaped before a group of witnesses, is seen as collective journey from pain to pleasure.

WEB **BME Scarification, Branding, Cutting**
http://www.io.org/~bme/bme-scar.html ✦ USENET
rec.arts.bodyart

breast implants $30 million "bigger is better" industry. Only one third of the million-odd women who received implants between 1990 and 1995 got them after mastectomies; defending the majority opting for cosmetic enlargement, actress Cher told *People* magazine in 1992, "You know if I want to put tits on my back, they're mine." Plastic surgery was routinized as an everyday medical procedure in the mid '80s; in spite of disputed evidence about dangerous side effects from tissue inflammation and loss of sensation to rheumatoid arthritis and fatal autoimmune diseases like lupus, body modification has become a kind of business expense for models and actresses in the '90s. Real-life BARBIE Pamela Anderson Lee told *TV Guide*, in a May 1995 cover story, "Everybody says I'm plastic from head to toe . . . Can't stand next to a radiator or I'll melt . . . I had [breast] implants, but so has every single person in Los Angeles." In 1992 the FDA called for a voluntary ban of the silicone-filled pouches—they reportedly are more harmful when they leak than the saline-filled version—and further study of current users. In the mid-'90s, manufacturers and the American Society of Plastic and Reconstructive Surgeons looked to tort reform and new evidence of the implants' safety to preserve their revenue stream in the face of mounting lawsuits.

WEB **Plastic Surgery Information Services** http://nysernet.org/bcic/numbers/psis.html

bridge lines As the market for designer-label clothes has waned in recent years, designers have begun to covet the young customers lining up at tasteful, lower-priced stores such as THE GAP and Banana Republic. Thus, "bridge lines": priced well below a designer's signature collection (but well above the Gap), these cash cow spin-offs make elite designer goods more affordable to younger and less affluent customers, paradoxically bringing exclusivity to the masses. Bridge lines (in Europe, "diffusion lines") had been doing healthy business since the early '80s, but a new era dawned in 1989 when Donna Karan launched her eclectic, street-inspired DKNY; ultra-tasteful Italian designer Giorgio Armani opened his utilitarian A/X chain in December 1991; CALVIN KLEIN unveiled its new bridge line CK Calvin Klein in 1992, and proceeded to churn out enormous collections marked by their maximum hype to minimum design ratio; RALPH LAUREN first presented his classically styled youth-centric Ralph line in October 1993. In addition to providing "styled" versions of what are often essentially generic clothes, bridge lines help designers to indoctrinate young customers, seducing them into brand loyalty at an early age.

Bright, Susie (b. 1958) "Sex is fun" feminist lecturer and author who became a successful mainstream libertine personality with her 1992 essay collection, *Susie Bright's Sexual Reality: A Virtual Sex World Reader.* The BISEXUAL single mom from San Francisco is frankly pro-libido, -porn, and -vibrator, most comfortable defining herself against the bourgeois decorum she attributes to "middle-class feminism." From the 1984 launch of *On Our Backs* magazine Bright wrote an Ann Landers-type sex advice column for the lesbian readership; in 1987 she became *Penthouse*'s first female reviewer of porn movies. Other published works include *Susie Sexpert's Lesbian Sex World* (1990) and edited collections of *Best American Erotica* and women-written *Herotica* (1988–). She is closely allied with LISA

PALAC, founder of *Future Sex,* and had a public falling out in 1992 with CAMILLE PAGLIA, who called Bright an "anti-intellectual who doesn't want any deep thinking." Bright also co-wrote the *Let's Talk About Sex* (1995) PHONE SEX screenplay with filmmaker Lizzie Borden.

Bristol West-of-England town whose tradition of Jamaican DJ sound systems helped foster a trio of influential '90s bands. The first Bristol outfit to achieve international recognition was Massive Attack, a group of three former DJs whose 1991 debut album *Blue Lines* marked something of a quantum leap forward for dance music. Using their laconic tag-team rhyming as a foundation, Massive Attack incorporated satellite rappers and vocalists, simmering beats, DUB bass and string arrangements into a groundbreaking, if modestly successful, vision. Bristol's easygoing pace meant that Massive Attack sophomore album *Protection* (with re-configured guest line-up) didn't arrive until late 1994. Shortly afterwards came *Dummy,* the debut album from Portishead (featuring a former Massive cohort), which brought torch-singing and '60s film-score arrangements into the equation. When Massive Attack guest rapper Tricky (b. Adrian Thaws, 1968) released *his* sullen debut, *Maxinquaye* (recorded with a singer-partner), trend-spotters dusted-off the occasionally coined epithet "trip-hop" to label the Bristol sound.

WEB **Massive Attack—Rolling Daydreams** http://www .vmg.co.uk/massive/index.html ◆ WEB **Portishead** http://www.godiscs.co.uk/godiscs/porthead.html

Gothic author
POPPY Z. BRITE.

Brite, Poppy Z. (b. 1967) Former GOTH/stripper/artist's model whose first novel *Lost Souls* (1992) earned her a reputation as an ANNE RICE for swingers. (Like Rice, she lives in New Orleans.) Brite's stories are typically steeped in decadent, doomed romanticism, her characters practicing BISEXUALITY and vampirism, as well as an unsettling familiarity with the lyrics of The Cure. Her cult following grew through her second book *Drawing Blood* (1993), the short story collection *Swamp Foetus* (1993), and 1995's *Exquisite Corpse.* A frank interviewee, Brite has said that she considers herself "a gay man who happens to be born in a female body." (The gay characters in *Lost Souls* got Brite nominated for the prestigious Lambda Award for gay fiction.) Brite has also freely discussed an unusual domestic arrangement that has doubtless informed her work: she lives, she has said, in a stable *ménage à trois* with two men.

WEB **WeaselBoy and Friends Index Page** http://www. cascade.net/~weasel/ **MOJO Press** http://www.eden.com/ comics/mojo.html

Brown, Chester (b. 1960) Part of the Drawn & Quarterly Comics triumvirate that also includes Joe Matt and Seth, this Canadian cartoonist employs a deceptively simple and sensitive style to render momentous, shocking, and emotionally charged concepts. The issues of Brown's *Yummy Fur* comic collected as *Ed the Happy Clown* (1989) took readers on a jaw-droppingly uncensored politico-religious odyssey through a universe of humiliations and mutilations—in one memorable scene the miniaturized head of President Reagan becomes affixed to the end of the title character's penis. In the back half of the book Brown worked through his illustrated versions of Biblical gospels. *Yummy Fur* next went autobiographical with stories about Chester's youthful sexual awakening. In 1994 he began a new story, "Underwater," in a new comic bearing the same name.

Brown, James (b. 1928) Godfather of Soul and HIP-HOP's most-SAMPLED artist. In the mid-'60s Brown practically invented funk with his band, the JBs, and hits such as "Papa's Got a Brand New Bag," "Sex Machine," and "Cold Sweat." In contrast to Motown's assimilationist soul, Brown's funk was insistently African-American—musical statements such as "Say It Loud (I'm Black and I'm Proud)" made him a symbol of Black Power. SAMPLING reintroduced Brown to a new generation of fans in the '80s, as the riffs, rhythms, and shrieks of

Brown productions powered rap standards such as Eric B. & Rakim's "Paid in Full" and Rob Base & DJ Easy-Rock's "It Takes Two." Brown saw no royalties until his legal fights helped institute the current system of sample-clearing. He enjoyed a brief comeback with the soundtrack hit "Living in America" in 1986, but in 1988 he was jailed on assault and weapons charges after leading police in a high-speed interstate chase. Foreshadowing later celebrity criminal-cases such as MIKE TYSON and O.J. Simpson, charges of racism produced a swell of "Free James Brown" sentiment. In 1994 Brown was again arrested after his third wife charged him with criminal domestic assault.

USENET **rec.music.funky**, **alt.funk-you**, **alt.music.soul**

bungee jumping   Early '90s EXTREME SPORT fad which involved jumping off a bridge with an industrial strength elastic cord tied to one's ankles. The fear-conquering pastime first arrived in California and the Pacific Northwest from Australia. At its height in 1992 there were two deaths and some 200 jump operators charging an average of $50 per plunge at state fairs, amusement parks, and roadside sites nationwide. Most operators used construction cranes to hoist metal cages for the several-hundred-foot jumps, though hot-air balloons and platforms were also common. Bungee apocrypha has it that the sport originated on Pentecost Island in the South Pacific, where vines are supposedly used in an ancient rite of passage for boys. (The greatest thrill of the typical 30-second jump is said to be the weightless "boing" recoil.) In 1990, Reebok ran a TV ad featuring a pair of bungee jumpers that was hastily yanked after parent complaints (the jumper wearing Reebok Pumps bounces back into view while his buddy's empty NIKES sway at the end of a cord).

UESNET **alt.sport.bungee**

Burns, Charles (b. 1955)   An early contributor to ART SPIEGELMAN's *Raw*, artist Charles Burns is a hard-edged, high-contrast cartoonist with an affinity for the spooky and surreal. His work has been collected in *Hard-Boiled Defective Stories*

(1988), *Skin Deep* (1992), and *Blood Club* (1992), and he collaborated with GARY PANTER on the flip book *Facetasm* (1993). Burns' signature characters include the Mexican wrestler/private dick El Borbah, suburban mutant Big Baby, and the half-canine Dog Boy, who was adapted for MTV's LIQUID TELEVISION series; side projects include work for OK SODA and the set design for choreographer MARK MORRIS's update of Tchaikovsky's ballet *The Nutcracker*, *Hard Nut*. Burns's most ambitious series, *Black Hole* comics (launched 1995), strives to capture the emotionally off-kilter aura of the hormonally charged early-teen years.

Burton, Tim (b. 1958)   Burbank, California-born GOTH-humorist filmmaker. After graduating from high school, Burton took a job as an animator at Walt Disney Studios, where he made his first movie, the six-minute animated film *Vincent* (1982, featuring the voice of Burton's mentor, horror-movie veteran Vincent Price). Burton's short, grim follow-up, *Frankenweenie* (1984), was at the time deemed unsuitable for release by Disney but led to his first feature, the lurid *Pee-Wee's Big Adventure* (1985, starring PAUL REUBENS), and his first collaboration with composer Danny Elfman, formerly of L.A. new-wavers Oingo Boingo. The campy sleeper-hit ghost story *Beetlejuice* (1988), starring WINONA RYDER and Michael Keaton, was the first of several special-effects laden Burton films resembling live-action cartoons. In *Edward Scissorhands* (1990) and *Ed Wood* (1994), Burton cast JOHNNY DEPP as dark yet ultimately sympathetic characters. The director preceded each of these relatively small, personal films with megabudgeted and megamarketed blockbusters, his brooding *Batman* (1989) and *Batman Returns* (1992), both also scored by Elfman. Burton also produced and wrote the macabre *The Nightmare Before Christmas* (1993), Disney's first stop-motion animated release.

WEB **The (surprisingly popular) Tim Burton Page**
http://www.magi.com/~gray/burton.html ✦ USENET
alt.movies.tim-burton

Butler, Judith (b. 1956)   UC Berkeley philosophy professor and one of the founders of the acade-

Judy! fanzine

"Miss Spentyouth"'s fabulous fanzine tribute to Prof. JUDITH BUTLER.

mic field of Queer Theory. As an "anti-essentialist," Butler argues that gender roles are not functions of "nature," but rather are cultural constructs, continually reinscribed and reworked through their daily repetition. Taking the title of her dense, difficult book *Gender Trouble* (1990) from JOHN WATERS' camp classic *Female Trouble* (1975), Butler claims DRAG as a model for how gender is *always* "performed": "[T]here is no original or primary gender that drag imitates, but gender is a kind of imitation for which there is no original." Like ANDREW ROSS and CORNEL WEST, Butler is one of the "superstars" of '90s academia, with a devoted following of grad students nationwide. This cult status was enhanced in 1993 with the appearance of *Judy!*, a fanzine devoted to Butler.

WEB **Feminism and Women's Studies** http://english-www.hss.cmu.edu/Feminism.html

Butthole Surfers AUSTIN· Texas-based band renowned for scatological humor, stomach-churning back-projections on stage at gigs, and high-octane psychedelic noodling. As decade-long ALTERNATIVE favorites and players on the first LOLLAPALOOZA tour, the Butthole Surfers must have looked promising to Capitol Records, who signed the band to a substantial deal in 1991. Former Led Zeppelin bassist John Paul Jones was drafted in to produce *Independent Worm Saloon* (1993), but the band's lack of radio-friendly material consigned them to the margins. With guitarist Paul Leary (b. circa 1958) concentrating on outside production jobs and singer Gibby Haynes (b. circa 1957) widely rumored to be riddled with personal problems (as well as guesting with JOHNNY DEPP's band P), the Butthole Surfers failed to capitalize on the cultural shift they helped effect.

WEB **Butthole Surfers Home Page** http://www.peak.org/~zogwarg/bands/butt/main.html ✦ USENET **alt.music.butthole.surfers**

Caesar haircut Forward-combed, close-cropped style revived from ancient Rome (and the 1960s) as the definitive gay male cut of the late '80s. Reminiscent of retro-fashion icon Steve McQueen and the '60s MOD look, the Caesar crossed over from gay club staple to straight men daring a gay look to hipsters worldwide. The coif, which works well with a widow's peak, was taken mainstream by musicians like DEEE-LITE DJ Towa Tei and George Michael (who defiantly hailed Caesar throughout his court battles with Sony), and actors Harrison Ford (*Presumed Innocent*, 1990), Kevin Costner (the object of tonsorial ridicule in 1992's *The Bodyguard*), and TV late-comers George Clooney (*ER*) and David Schwimmer (*Friends*).

call waiting Call-interrupting service which gives an answerable beeping sound to a call-receiver already on the phone. This replacement for the busy signal has created a new phone-etiquette vocabulary ranging from the straightforward "let me get that" and "I'm on the other" to the more oblique "where are you" (implying "can I call you back?"). Call waiting undoubtedly also contributed to the increased time that people spend on the phone, removing any doubt about missing a call because of an in-use line. First introduced by local phone companies in the mid-'70s, call-waiting was not prevalent enough to merit social commentary from Miss Manners, Dave Barry, and Dear Abby until the late '80s, when each bemoaned the "last-come-first-served" innovation. This in spite of phone company commercials showing Dad getting through to Mom even when there's a phone-addicted teen at home. (Deadly to most modem and fax connections, call waiting can be disabled by beginning calls with the increasingly familiar "*70" sequence.)

CamNet L.A.-based documentary news show found on the fringes of cable TV, and drawn from the off-beat, counterculture contributions of amateur Hi–8 videographers around the world. CamNet rose in 1992 from the ashes of the can-celed PBS series *The '90s*; its roots go back to Videofreex, a radical video group from the '60s. Notable show segments include coverage of *High Times* magazine's 1994 Cannabis Cup in Amsterdam and a report on the life of New York City squatters.

USENET **alt.tv-public-access**

Capriati, Jennifer (b. 1976) Tennis-prodigy-turned-fallen-angel. 13 year-old Capriati went pro in March 1990 when the Women's Tennis Council bent its minimum age requirement for her—she was a women's top 10 player before year's end. In July 1992, with career earnings of over $1 mil-

Photo by Coral Gables, Florida, Police Department

JENNIFER CAPRIATI, fallen angel of the baseline.

lion, she won an Olympic gold medal in Barcelona. Capriati's tender age was all too apparent when she stormed off the tennis circuit after a first-round defeat in the 1993 U.S. Open. She was then arrested in December 1993 for shoplifting a ring in Tampa Bay; the case was dismissed, but Capriati was forced to undergo psychiatric evaluation. At a May 16, 1994, party in a Coral Gables, Florida motel room, police arrived to find traces of MARIJUANA in her backpack. The ensuing mug shot told of the journey from corn-fed mall-rat to nose- (and navel-) ringed rebel, bestowing upon Capriati unsuspected ALTER-NATIVE credibility. (The *New York Times* revealed that she was a fan of Pantera and Jane's Addiction.) Capriati emerged from rehab with no conviction and returned to professional tennis at the Virginia Slims tournament in Philadelphia, November '94.

Carhartt Michigan-based apparel company (established 1889) which supplied blue-collar workers with rough-hewn, easy-fitting canvas jackets, pants and overalls long before the early-'90s WORK-WEAR boom. Fashion demand for Carhartt was stoked when its "chain gang" blue jackets were sported in 1989 by L.A. GANGSTA rappers N.W.A; on

the East Coast its blanket-lined mustard brown jackets were (as noted by the *New York Times* in late 1992) popular among CRACK-dealers, whose business requires being outdoors in winter. Another significant factor in the company's record sales (almost $92 million by 1990) was exposure in the video clips of rap acts like N.W.A., House of Pain, and Naughty By Nature. The latter's record label Tommy Boy distributed hundreds of promotional Carhartt jackets, embroidered with the company's logo, to HIP-HOP cognoscenti.

carjacking   Crime in which the victim is ordered out of his or her car at knife- or gunpoint and the stolen vehicle is driven off. Notable victims include German tourist Barbara Meller-Jensen, who took a wrong turn in Miami (and was beaten, robbed, and run over in front of her six-year old son); Mark Rayner, the 255-pound National Golden Gloves heavyweight champ who was killed for his Jeep Grand Cherokee in Detroit in 1993; and Pamela Bastu, who was killed in November 1992 after being dragged for two miles outside her car. In October 1994 in Union County, South Carolina, Susan Smith claimed her two toddlers had been kidnapped when she was carjacked by a black man. (After a 9-day manhunt, Smith confessed to drowning the children in a nearby lake.) In July 1995, rapper QUEEN LATIFAH had her BMW stolen while parked curbside in Harlem, New York.

carpal tunnel syndrome   Potentially crippling computer-related injury caused by too much typing, in which inflamed muscles pinch the nerves that run through the wrists and fingers. CTS is only one of many repetitive strain injuries (aka OOS, Occupational Overuse Syndromes; CTD, Cumulative Trauma Disorders; and WRULD, Work-Related Upper Limb Disorders) associated with extended computer use. Both CTS-inspired lawsuits and ergonomic design emerged as cottage industries in the early '90s, with exotic new keyboards, wrist pads, gloves, and OSHA regulations.
WEB **Computer Related Repetitive Strain Injury** http://engr-www.unl.edu/ee/eeshop/rsi.html ✦ WEB **Typing**

Injury FAQ Archive http://www.cis.ohio-state.edu/hypertext/faq/usenet/typing-injury-faq/top.html ✦ WEB **OSHA** http://www.osha.gov

Carrey, Jim (b.1962)   Elastic-featured former stand-up comic who came to prominence in 1990 on the largely black Fox-TV ensemble series *In Living Color*. Carrey's loser white-guy characters (such as the horribly disfigured pyromaniac Fire Marshall Bill) made it clear that he was eager to humiliate himself in the pursuit of humor. This came in useful in the low-budget *Ace Ventura, Pet Detective* (1994), a critically reviled blockbuster that led to a star turn in *The Mask*, which was based on a comic book about a MORPHING loser white guy (with a digitally enhanced elastic face). Carrey's next movie was *Dumb and Dumber* (1994), hailed as a new low in lowbrow humor. All three of Carrey's hits have raked in over $100 million domestic box office, ensuring him endless sequel opportunities and a spot in the screen pantheon (and upper tax stratum) alongside body-conscious types like Schwarzenegger, Stallone, and Stone; this status was confirmed with a reported $7 million fee for Carrey's appearance in *Batman Forever* (1995) and $20 million for *The Cable Guy*.
WEB **Jim Carrey: A Tribute** http://www.en.com/users/bbulson/jim.html **The Temple of Jim Carrey** http://metro.turnpike.net/L/lloyd/tojc.htm **New/Improved Jim Carrey Page** http://www.halcyon.com/browner/

Carrot Top (b. Scott Thompson, 1967) Freakish-looking red-headed comedian renowned for his ability to produce outlandish sight gags on stage from both everyday objects and elaborately constructed props. With an ingenuity that's sometimes ascribed to having a NASA engineer father with a home lab, Carrot Top devises props like the one described by the *Los Angeles Times* as "a paper-cup-and-string phone with a third cup for CALL WAITING." Carrot Top's tireless touring of colleges earned him a following that was recognized with awards from the National Association of Campus Activities. From this platform the comic was able to develop a sitcom and procure a three-movie deal with non-highbrow Trimark Pictures.

Carson, David (b. 1956) California designer who defined the look of early-'90s magazines. Carson made his mark with the six issues of *Beach Culture* magazine in 1990–91; he was then hired for the 1992 launch of *Ray Gun*, where his freewheeling designs provided a handy counterpoint to the magazine's unremarkable rock journalism. Carson pushed computer graphic-style to its logical conclusion, digitally manipulating the text in a frenzy of stretched, layered, and distressed type. (Many of Carson's fonts come from California's influential EMIGRE company.) This much-discussed former world-class surfer has many detractors, but his kinetic layout experiments at *Ray Gun* have shaped contemporary advertising, magazines, and TV graphics. "Advertisers seem to feel that [he] has that nihilistic slacker approach nailed down," one industry insider told the *New York Times* in 1994, explaining Carson's many print-ad commissions for youth-hungry corporations like NIKE and Pepsi.

CBGBs Legendary, claustrophobic New York rock venue, now enjoying at least its third lease of life. When Hilly Kristal (b. 1931) established CBGBs in late 1973 its Bowery location was mainly known for being a wino haunt; under Kristal's stewardship this dive (whose initials stood for Country Blue Grass & Blues) became the New York PUNK equivalent of Liverpool's Cavern Club. CBGBs' first glory days were in 1975, when the club hosted luminaries like Television, the Ramones, Talking Heads, Blondie, and Patti Smith—progenitors of the PUNK movement who would tighten up the sagging jowls of rock 'n' roll. The club's second heyday came in the mid-'80s, when the underage children of punk cavorted at its fabled afternoon HARDCORE shows. And even when that scene passed, CBGBs kept enough cachet to play host to late-'80s/early-'90s bands on their way up the ALTERNATIVE food chain.

CD Plus Enhanced format for including CD-ROM text, graphics, computer programs, and even video on a standard audio CD. While one still needs a CD-ROM drive to access the multimedia files, the disc plays fine on a regular CD player. The format, the subject of a patent dispute with the CD developer Philips Electronics, hopes to make good on the broken promises of the CD+Graphics format which bombed in the late '80s. It's possible to see CD Plus as multimedia for the masses, a new medium rivaling MTV as a venue for music videos and competing with music magazines as a publicity outlet. The first consumer titles were released March 1995 with elaborate electronic liner notes and prices lower than most CD-ROM's, but still at a $10 premium over a standard audio CD.
WEB **Microsoft CD Plus** http://www.eden.com/cdplus/

CD-ROM Computer-linked medium capable of storing information equivalent to around 500,000 pages of text (one gigabyte). The CD-ROM format's most useful application so far is as repository of bulky reference materials, such as encyclopedias, law libraries, and corporate data. As a multimedia phenomenon, the format's potential was hinted at in 1994, when, according to Dataquest Inc., nearly eight million PCs with CD-ROM drives were sold to consumers—quadruple the number sold the previous year. *Myst*, the first CD-ROM entertainment hit, was released in 1993 by Cyan Inc. Created by brothers Rand and Robyn Miller, this atmospheric quest on a lonely island had sold more than a million copies by the end of 1994. A handful of CD-ROM magazines, including *Medio*, *Blender*, *Go Digital*, and *Trouble & Attitude* showed how the format could easily preview music, film, and video to consumers, and offered the seductive lure of interactive advertising, such as Dewars commercials disguised as a videogame. The spread of high-speed INTERNET connections in the mid-'90s prompted many long-term computer observers to speak of the CD-ROM as a transitional technology. [See also CD-PLUS.]
WEB **CD ROM Standards and MPC** http://www.a1.com/cdrom/About_CD-ROM_Standards_&_MPC.txt/ ◆ USENET **alt.cd-rom**, **comp.publish.cdrom**

celebutots As late-century media proliferate, celebrity entrance qualifications get lower, and the star-maker machinery is grateful for anything with a modicum of name recognition. Thus, American culture is presently awash with star-spawn, of varying degrees of accomplishment. Among the upper echelons of '90s "celebutots" are Beach Boy daughter Carnie Wilson, a pop star-turned-talk show host; Jill-of-all trades Sofia Coppola, her video director brother Roman, and friends like Zoe Cassavettes and Donovan Leitch (respectively the daughter of legendary filmmaker John and son of '60s folk-singer Donovan); Rebecca Walker, founder of THIRD WAVE and daughter of novelist Alice. In the middling ranks are FRANK ZAPPA's amusingly named children Moon Unit and Dweezil; E! CHANNEL hostess Eleanor Mondale, daughter of former Vice-President Walter; and television presenter Katie Wagner (daughter of Natalie Wood and Robert Wagner). Occupying the less appetizing end of the celebutot food chain are model-royalty Daniel and Lucie de la Falaise, and non-specific entities like Josh Evans (son of '70s film star/'90s INFOMERCIAL star Ali McGraw), Ethan Browne (son of mellow rocker Jackson), and lesbian activist Chastity Bono (offspring of occasional singer Cher and her sidekick-turned-Congressman ex-husband Sonny Bono).

cellular phone Radio telephone for making and receiving calls over a computer-coordinated system of local transmitters organized into cells. Once redolent of Dick Tracy and bulky car phones, by the late '80s pocket-sized "cell phones" could be had for less than $500. A 1993 panic that the phones cause brain cancer (see EMF RADIATION) came just as the phones began to be commonplace upgrades for BEEPERS in American business, legal and otherwise; it briefly sent Motorola stock tumbling. Shorthand in urban conversation for "yuppie asshole," the phones approached social acceptability as the price of monthly service fell to the levels of basic cable TV. The flimsy security on cellular calls—anyone with a radio scanner can listen in—led in the late '80s/early '90s to several high-profile tabloid incidents (Governor Douglas Wilder of Virginia and the Prince and Princess of Wales were notable vic-

tims) and an epidemic of "clone phone" cellular piracy.
USENET **alt.cellular**

Chan, Jackie (b. Chen Gang-shen, 1954) Top star of HONG KONG ACTION MOVIES; arguably the most physically agile action film actor of all time. Originally touted as the next Bruce Lee in a series of undistinguished '70s kung fu flicks (one directed by a young JOHN WOO), Chan did not make a name for himself in HK movies until he introduced hammy double-takes and Chaplinesque wit into the fighting of *Drunken Master* (1978). In the '80s Chan perfected the kung fu comedy in period pieces (*Project A*), adventures (*Armor of God*), and *policiers* (*Super Cop*). He also forged his own legend—his Chinese screen name Sing Lung translates as "becoming the dragon"—through death-defying stuntwork, the bloody outtakes of which are featured under his films' closing credits. Burned by several Hollywood

JACKIE CHAN, 41, accepts Lifetime Achievement honor, MTV Movie Awards 1995.

cross-over attempts (most egregiously in 1984's *Protector* with Danny Aiello), Chan became in 1995 the first HK talent to sign a mainstream U.S. distribution deal for his Chinese language films. The U.S. marketing of Chan began in earnest in June 1995 when a beaming QUENTIN TARANTINO presented him with a Lifetime Achievement Award at MTV's Movie Awards special.
WEB **The Jackie Chan Gossip and Trivia Page** http://www.ios.com/~sahpngyi/dinying2.html ✦ WEB **Project A: An Unofficial Jackie Chan Web Site** http://weber.u. washington.edu/~magritte/chan.html ✦ WEB **Jackie Chan's Home Page** http://www.hk.super.net/~zero/rock/jackie.html ✦ WEB **Hong Kong Movies Homepage** http://www.mdstud. chalmers.se/hkmovie/ ✦ USENET **alt.asian-movies**

Channel One 12-minute news show (including two minutes of ads) directed at junior and senior high-school students. When it was introduced in

1990, Channel One gave new meaning to captive audience—the program is shown during class-time; in exchange for using it, schools get to keep the supplied TV, satellite, and video equipment. Launched by the flashy publishing entrepreneur Chris Whittle, Channel One was in 12,000 schools (reaching some eight million students in 350,000 classrooms) in 1994 when Whittle's empire collapsed (in part depleted by Project Edison, his plan to privatize schools by using computers to augment a pared-down teaching staff). The program, which continues under the ownership of publishing giant K-III, has faced opposition from many school boards, scattered pockets of students, and an Oakland-group called UNPLUG which released a 1993 study showing that Channel One is most common in schools that serve poor and African-American students.

WEB **Channel One Home Page** http://www.sonetis.com/

Chapel Hill North Carolina college town much scoured in 1992 by record company scouts eager to find, post-NIRVANA, the next SEATTLE. With an economic base of 15,000 University of North Carolina students, Chapel Hill sustained an INDIE-ROCK "scene" of impressive size, if not scope. As far as it went, the Chapel Hill sound—alternately described as "Seattle on PROZAC" and "SONIC YOUTH Youth"—was equal parts snarling feedback and naive buoyancy; another defining aesthetic reported back from media forays to North Carolina was thrift-store Levi's corduroys, cutoff as Bermuda shorts. Superchunk, led by Columbia University history-major Mac McCaughan and his photogenic bassist girlfriend, Laura Ballance, were local heroes; the two formed their own label, Merge. No band from their coterie—Polvo, Finger, Erectus Monotone, and Picasso Trigger—ever actually signed a major-label deal. For many, Chapel Hill's defining moment was Superchunk's abiding mini-anthem "Slack Motherfucker" (1990), a song written about working in a 24-hour Kinko's copyshop.

WEB **D.I.Y. with IndieWeb** http://www.forfood.com/ ~indieweb/diy/diy.html ✦ WEB **here with Superchunk** http://www.umich.edu/~mransfrd/superchunk/index.html ✦ USENET **alt.music.chapel-hill**

cheongsam Form-fitting, traditional Chinese dress that has endured in Western fashion as svelte evening wear. Usually made from lustrous, flower-patterned silks, cheongsams are sealed in the front by "frog" closures, and topped by a round Mandarin collar. Thanks to its simple, flattering lines the garment was easily knocked off in Spring 1995 by designers with a renewed interest in *chinoiserie*, such as JEAN-PAUL GAULTIER. Street-fashion princess Sofia Coppola had introduced a youthful version when she debuted her Milk Fed line in late 1994, while German designer Jil Sander interpreted the classic siren's habit in stern black; MADONNA sported one in deep red at the Grammy Awards in March 1995. That following summer, trend-facilitating, New York-based department store chain Barney's was selling authentic, Chinese-made cheongsams alongside designer versions.

child stars of the '70s, fallen The post-fame lives of child stars are often fraught with tribulation, none more so than those from the '70s. Danny Bonaduce, the *The Partridge Family*'s resident redhead nuisance, navigated drug abuse, low-budget martial art flicks, borderline bankruptcy, and a well-publicized run-in with a transvestite before finding a talk-show gig on Chicago's WLUP-FM that led to memory-enhancement INFOMERCIALS and, in 1995, his own syndicated talk-show, *Danny!* Perhaps hardest hit were the young cast-members of *Diff'rent Strokes*. Todd Bridges beat an attempted murder rap; Dana Plato posed for *Playboy* and held up a Vegas video store. (The clerk reportedly identified her to police as "the girl who played Kimberly Drummond on television.") And Gary Coleman, who once seemed poised on the brink of superstardom, was left with so little money by his family that he was reduced to selling cars to pay for his dialysis, sometimes insisting that he was researching a role. The child star problem even spawned its own support group, A Minor Consideration, founded in 1990 by Paul Petersen, who played the son on the '50s sitcom *The Donna Reed Show*.

Children's Television Act of 1990   Law passed by a Democratic Congress attempting to reverse Reagan-era deregulation. The Act ordered the FCC to require educational programming for children as part of the public-service component of all TV station licenses. Gray areas remained— within weeks of the law's passage the Bush-appointed FCC ruled that toy-based shows such as *G.I. Joe: Real American Hero*, *Smurfs*, and *Thundercats* did not constitute "program-length commercials" that would run afoul of the CTA's limit on twelve minutes of advertising per hour of children's programming. In 1993 the Clinton FCC reformulated the enforcement of the law after advocacy groups caught local stations claiming, in an echo of the '80s "ketchup-is-a-vegetable" school lunch argument, that reruns of *The Jetsons* teach children about life in the 21st Century.

WEB **Federal Communications Law Journal: Children's Hour Revisited** http://www.law.indiana.edu/fclj/v46/no2/hayes.html

Chilton, Alex (b. 1950)   Former frontman of '60s blue-eyed soul prodigies the Boxtops who in 1970 formed Big Star, a seminal influence on '90s INDIE-ROCK. (Their renaissance was presaged by The Replacements' 1987 tribute song "Alex Chilton.") Derided in their time as British-invasion copyists, this Memphis four piece (which debuted with 1972's *#1 Record*) broke up after recording just three albums: the first two spare, harmony-laden pop-rock, the third one of the most emotionally harrowing song-sets in rock. Chilton went on—reportedly thanks to a drinking problem—to have an emotionally harrowing solo career, with recordings and performances that did little justice to his writing talents. He re-formed the band (with original drummer, plus hired hands) for an April 1993 University of Missouri concert that was later released as an album.

Cho, Margaret (b. Moran Cho, 1968)   Brash and brassy San Francisco-born, pop-culture-

addicted comic who became in 1994 the first Asian-American to break out of the regional comedy club circuit (primarily college campuses, in her case) into national acclaim. That year she had her own half-hour HBO special and, riding the crest of the post-Jerry Seinfeld stand-up migration to prime-time, got her own ABC sitcom, *All-American Girl*. Cho starred as a savvy, pop-culture-addicted girl named Margaret who is trapped between her Korean immigrant parents and her stereotypical GENERATION X pals. Many Korean-Americans found the program culturally spurious, and mediocre ratings led to its 1995 cancellation (despite a *Pulp Fiction*-parodying cameo from QUENTIN TARANTINO). Cho lives with the gay comedian Scott Silverman, whom she calls her "partner in life."

choker   Tight-fitting necklace, evocative of both Victorian chastity and the hippie fetish for pre-modern styles. Out-of-fashion for some twenty years, chokers experienced a renaissance in the early 1990s. DEEE-LITE's Lady Miss Kier was one early adapter—a 1990 *New York Times* article on "accessory fetishes" described how the retro diva was forced to make her own chokers to satisfy her craving. MADONNA's enthusiasm for chokers convinced two of her admirers, the designers Dolce and Gabbana, to incorporate them—wide velvet ribbons with oversized cameos—in their spring 1993 collection. Other haute couture designers soon followed suit. At the same time, minimalist silk- and leather-cord variations became ubiquitous signifiers of femme GRUNGE, in both rock clubs and *Beverly Hills 90210* episodes. By mid–1993, the mass-market passion for chokers drove the necklace market up 25 percent that year, but choker chic was '90s nostalgia by year's end.

Chomsky, Noam (b. 1928)   Massachusetts Institute of Technology professor whose contributions to the field of linguistics elicit comparisons to Freud and Einstein, while his radical political critiques make him the party pooper of American capitalism. Already famous within the fields of philosophy and cognitive psychology after the publication of a set of 1957 lecture notes, Chomsky took a public stand against the Kennedy build-up and Johnson prosecution of the Vietnam War years before the War became unpopular. Chomsky's relentless criticism often centers on the complicity of intellectuals and corporate news organizations in imperial escapades from El Salvador to East Timor, helping explain perhaps why his voice is rarely heard in major newspapers or on network news. Such themes were explored in an ardent 1993 documentary on Chomsky, *Manufacturing Consent*. [See also OPEN MAGAZINE.]

USENET **alt.fan.noam-chomsky** ✦ WEB **The Noam Chomsky Archive** http://www.contrib.andrew.cmu.edu/usr/tp0x/chomsky.html

Christian Coalition   Main political organization of the religious right, founded by TV preacher and media magnate Pat Robertson after his 1988 presidential bid. The group, which claimed 1.5 million members after the 1994 election, is anti-abortion, pro-school prayer, and opposed to "special rights" for homosexuals. Evangelical conservatives were briefly thought to be a liability for the Republican party after the 1987 televangelist scandals, the collapse of Jerry Falwell's Moral Majority, and the truculent "family values" night at the Republicans' 1992 convention. But by methodically organizing at the local precinct level—stocking local school-boards and G.O.P committee meetings—the CC had by 1994 actually taken over the state caucuses of the Republican party in five states, including Texas and Virginia, and become a major player in another dozen. Consequently, boyish, born-again executive director Ralph Reed (b. 1961) has figured prominently in the selection of a Republican candidate to oppose Bill Clinton in the

Photo by Sandra-Lee Phipps

The CHRISTIAN COALITION founder Pat Robertson, 1994.

1996 presidential election. A May 1995 *Time* magazine cover proclaimed Reed the "Right Hand of God."

WEB **Christian Coalition** http://www.cc.org/

Christian rap   Minor musical trend in which hopeful musicians attach wholesome messages to potent beats. Christian rap's one notable success is DC Talk, a squeaky-clean trio that emerged from Liberty University (home of Moral Majority founder and televangelist Jerry Falwell) and sold over 500,000 copies of each of their three albums. On the fringes of Christian rap are such strangers to *Billboard* as the S.S. MOB (Soul Serving Ministers On Board), T-Bone, and the Gospel Gangstas, an ensemble of former L. A. gang members who adapt GANGSTA rap posturing to the Lord's message. This story was reported nationally in *Newsweek*, November 1994, and subsequently disseminated in sources as diverse as *VIBE* and British *Vogue*. (A bible using HIP-HOP vernacular, *Black Bible Chronicles: a Survival Manual for the Streets* [1993], also surfaced in the national press.)

Church of Christ   High pressure, fast-growing evangelical quasi-cult successful on college campuses. The Church was founded in 1979 when the then–25-year-old Kip McKean took over a mainstream Church of Christ ministry in Lexington, Massachusetts. The two organizations should not be confused—the mainstream movement links 18,000 autonomous congregations, whereas the cult is made up of some 160 ministries around the world collected under the name International Churches of Christ and tightly managed from the largest chapter in Boston. COC college groups often go under the name Campus Advance. Though McKean is not regarded as a charismatic guru, the group uses other common cult tactics such as "disciplers" who shepherd the thoughts and movements of new members and conduct marathon Bible study sessions that isolate prospective members from friends, family, school, and work. In 1994, tabloid television show *Inside Edition* reported that the Boston COC keeps a computer database of sins confessed by members.

Estimates of the remarkably heterogeneous 1995 membership range from 40,000 to 70,000.

Church of the SubGenius   Spoof-religion formed in 1980 by Ivan Stang (b. circa 1953), a conspiracy-minded Texas filmmaker, and a rock musician friend, Philo Drummond. The Church of the SubGenius was first manifested in a series of mysteriously worded pamphlets whose central tenet was "slack," a commodity Stang has translated as "perfect luck, effortless achievement." The SubGenius icon is J.R. "Bob" Dobbs, a handsome, pipe-smoking cartoon character drawn in the style of 1950s advertising—aliens (X-ists) and a "Space God" (Jehovah–1) also figure prominently. (The self-explanatory "Normals" are considered enemies.) Ministers of the Church (who have mailed the Church $30) reportedly number over 6,000, and tens of thousands more have read the scripture or participated in the live "devivals" staged around the nation. The SubGenius literary canon began with *Book of the SubGenius* (1983), the first of four books; there is now an occasional magazine, *The Stark Fist of Removal,* as well as a syndicated radio show, *The Hour of Slack.*
WEB **SubSITE** http://sunsite.unc.edu/subgenius/ ✦ USENET **alt.slack** ✦ MAIL LIST email slack@ncsu.or ✦ FTP ftp://ftp.etext.org /Publications

Citadel, The   State-supported Charleston, S.C., military academy that bitterly but unsuccessfully fought to maintain its 152-year-old policy against admitting female cadets. An earlier policy against admitting blacks had fallen a generation earlier (as portrayed in alumnus Pat Conroy's novel *The Lords of Discipline* [1980] and movie [1983]). A young woman named Shannon Faulkner (b. 1975) was accepted in 1993 after omitting references to her sex in the application; the acceptance was rescinded when the school discovered her secret. After Faulkner sued, a Federal judge order her admission but let stand the school's traditional "knob cut" HAZING for all new cadets. In 1994 "Shave Shannon" bumper stickers proliferated in South Carolina and in neighboring Virginia (home of the country's only other all-male military academy, the similarly embattled Virginia Military Institute). Faulkner was finally admitted in August '95, but—like 30 fellow male cadets—dropped out after a few days. Word of her departure was greeted by cheers from remaining students, who celebrated with "mattress surfing, victory push-ups, and rebel yells."
WEB **The Citadel Home Page** http://www.citadel.edu/

Citrosonic   Los Angeles club that moved RAVE indoors to minimize police and media attention. Started February 1992, Citrosonic was held on Wednesday nights at The Probe in Hollywood until June 1993. The crowd was young and racially diverse; HOUSE and TECHNO were the music of choice; the original DJs were Barry Weaver and Doc Marten.

Clark, Larry (b. 1943)   Legendary photographer who in 1963 began documenting the squalid, violent lives of speed freaks in his native Tulsa. The resulting book, *Tulsa* (1971), was a disturbingly graphic, sometimes first-person work that established Clark's reputation despite a tiny print run. Work on his second book, fueled by an NEA grant, was delayed by a 19-month jail sentence in 1976 for a parole violation: *Teenage Lust* (1983), was even more unsparing than the first, this time depicting teenage runaways; Clark's accompanying text (and, again, pictures of himself) hinted strongly at autobiography. (In 1993 a scrappy collection of Clark photographs, *The Perfect Childhood,* was published

LARRY CLARK's controversial *Kids.*

in Britain.) A greater notoriety beckoned for Clark, however: his directorial debut *Kids* was a *succès de scandale* at the 1995 SUNDANCE festival, where festival-goers gazed slack jawed at the movie's elegant depiction of anomic, sexually ravenous New York teens. Ironically, distribution rights were secured, sight unseen, by the Disney-owned indie-film giant MIRAMAX. (Released by the specially created Miramax company Excalibur the film was an art house hit.)

clear products   Early-'90's marketing phenomenon that saw companies rushing—hot on the cresting bottled water craze—to release a wave of "pure" product alternatives untainted by caramel colorings and FD&C blues and yellows. From Amoco Crystal Clear motor oil to Ban Clear deodorant to Ivory Clear soap to Clear Tab cola, clear products were transparent in more than one way: not only were the items themselves see-through, so were the advertising schemes that sought to posit them as NEW AGE novelties. The most visible example of the phenomenon came with the introduction of Crystal Pepsi in April 1992—the only notable difference was the absence of chemical colorant and roughly 27 calories. In 1993 NPR's *All Things Considered* opined that advertisers were simply "playing mind games with the American public." The clear trend, however, did not proceed invisibly: one 1993 *SATURDAY NIGHT LIVE* commercial spoof touted "Crystal Gravy: Lighter, cleaner, more transparent. . . . I don't see any lumps!"

Clinton, Chelsea Victoria (b. 1980) America's First Adolescent, complete with frizzy hair, braces (later removed), and a public persona marked by mute shyness. Awareness of young Clinton (and of the more sophisticated, pretty daughters of Vice President Al Gore) was manifested early in the new administration when she was welcomed at MTV's 1993 Inaugural Ball with chants of "Chelsea, Chelsea," and soon thereafter featured on the cover of the prominent ZINE *Ben is Dead*. Chelsea (named after the 1969 Judy Collins hit

song "Chelsea Morning," originally written by Joni Mitchell) has also been the subject of a particularly oafish RUSH LIMBAUGH attack (calling her the "White House dog"). In December 1994 *New York Press* writer Tom Gogola reviewed and quoted lyrics from *Are You There God? It's Me Chelsea*, a tape she supposedly recorded "because [her parents] refused to let her go to WOODSTOCK '94, canceled her subscription to *SASSY*, and didn't invite LIZ PHAIR to the White House . . ." Gogola answered an NBC request for a tape by recording some material with a singer friend; the songs survived for several months as a minor media prank known as Chelseagate.
WEB **White House First Family** http://www.whitehouse. gov/White_House/Family/html/First_Family.html

Clinton, George (b. 1941)   Through his bands Parliament and Funkadelic, as well as innumerable offshoots and solo projects, George Clinton has created a utopian vision which combines Black Nationalism, psychedelic hedonism, and sci-fi lunacy. "P-Funk"'s music—blending rubbery bass, trippy synths, rich horn charts, and skewed multi-layered vocals—is a model of the anarchic harmony envisioned in songs like "One Nation Under a Groove" (1978). Clinton's influence waned after the 1983 solo hit "Atomic Dog," as James Brown's more minimal groove came to dominate HIP-HOP SAMPLING. But in 1989, the bizarrely attired bandleader was embraced by a new generation of rappers, beginning with DE LA SOUL's sample of "(Not Just) Knee Deep" in "Me, Myself, and I" (1989). Today, Clinton's influence is widespread, primarily disseminated by DR. DRE's appropriated "G-Funk"; this was acknowledged by Clinton's inclusion in the 1994 LOLLAPALOOZA tour. (To make things easier for the next generation of disciples, Clinton himself has issued a best-of collection called *Sample Some of Dis, Sample Some of Dat*, which includes mail-in legal forms for sample clearance.)
WEB **Welcome to the Motherpage** http://www. duke.edu/~eja/pfunk.html ✦ USENET **rec.music.funky**

Clowes, Daniel (b. 1961)   Chicago cartoonist who debuted in 1986 with *Lloyd Llewellyn*, a will-

fully unrealistic comic that reveled in fabulous-'50s retrosnazz. *Eightball*, his 1989 follow-up, is a hodgepodge of exquisitely drafted stories reflecting Clowes's unremitting misanthropy. "Like a Velvet Glove Cast in Iron" (from *Eightball*) was a sado-masochistic nightmare combining Pynchonesque paranoia with fast, furious, and elliptical scene changes. Clowes mocked the legit comics trade (as well as *Raw*'s coffee table chic) in stories about superhero hack artist Dan Pussey, and assaulted the world at large in such rants as "I Hate You Deeply." Along with PETER BAGGE, Clowes is ALTERNATIVE comics' angriest (and most successful: see OK SODA) no-longer-young man.

WEB **WraithSpace – Comixographies – Dan Clowes**
http://www.digimark.net/wraith/Bibliographies/HTML/Dan-Clowes.html ✦ USENET **rec.arts.comics.alternative**

club kids   Outrageously dressed, aggressively whimsical, attention-seeking young nightlife denizens. The epithet "club kids" gained currency in 1988, when a *New York* magazine cover story featured a posse of young nightcrawlers who managed to parlay their exhibitionist antics and fondness for glitzy, flamboyant getups into budding careers. Paid by promoters just to show up and be ogled by the less-fabulous clubgoers, the most enterprising of the bunch—Michael Alig, Julie Jewels, Michael Tronn, Mathu, Zaldy, Keoki, among others—were taken under the wing of clubowners, earning as much as $1,000 per party. Outlandishness was the only common denominator in a look that incorporated glitter and androgyny (false eyelashes, bright red lipstick on men), with a heavy dose of theatricality (faces painted to clownish or ghoulish effect). The club kids' patron saint is the late Leigh Bowery, a London-based Australian who used his impressive bulk as an artwork in London from the early '80s until his death on New Year's Eve, 1994.

New York's original club kids have moved on to greater glory within the downtown nexus: Julie Jewels edits the clubland monthly *Project X*; Mathu and Zaldy design costumes for RU PAUL; Keoki DJ's and Michael Alig hosts Disco 2000 at the Limelight. "Club kid" now refers less to the original crowd, than to their many replicants nationwide—a tribe that is also a reliable standby for desperate talk-show bookers. Couture for this new generation of club kids runs from outer space WORK-WEAR to Muppet Chic, with *Sesame Street*'s Elmo a frequent mascot.

CLUB KIDS parade outside Patricia Fields store, New York, April 1994.

Cocktail Nation   Seeking relief from GRUNGE overkill, the SUB POP band Combustible Edison included the "First Manifesto of the Cocktail Nation" with its 1994 debut, *I, Swinger*. Exhorting "Be Fabulous!" the band declared its allegiance to a new-old, suave aesthetic embodied by highballs, banquettes, ascots, matching tuxedo outfits, and hard-to-find "exotica" LPs recorded by Martin Denny or obscure Fellini soundtrack by Nino Rota. Fellow-travelers like the Cocktails, the Millionaires, and Kentucky's acerbic Love Jones had all independently reached the same conclusion. The group Black Velvet Flag did "mellow angst" covers of punk classics while URGE OVERKILL's pop-metal was lounge on steroids, and Japanese trio Pizzicato Five offered a jet-set variation. At the same time, record companies raised their hopes for kitsch-lite revivals in the careers of oldveau crooners like Tony Bennett and Tom Jones, and country legend Johnny Cash.

While journalists obliged the micro-movement with breathless prose, RE/SEARCH PUBLICATIONS, Rhino Records, and Hoboken, NJ's Bar/None Records each put out lounge act reissues (Bar/None's anthology of "avant-Muzak compositions" by Juan Garcia Esquivel, was a popular favorite). Regular C-Nation haunts were clubs like The Fez in New York (Loser's Lounge), the Green Mill in Chicago, the Green Street Grille, in Cambridge, Nye's in Minneapolis, Café Deluxe in San Francisco, and even L.A.'s VIPER ROOM (Mr. Phat's Royal Martini Room). As a PUNK phenomenon, cocktail is an old joke, of course: the Circle Jerks did an easy listening version of their "When the Shit Hits the Fan" in 1984's *Repo Man*; before that, Sid Vicious's swan song was a cover of Frank Sinatra's "My Way."

WEB **Combustible Edison Home Page** http://www.subpop .com/bios/comed/index.htm/ ◆ WEB **Tony Bennett** http:// www.music.sony.com/Music/ArtistInfo/TonyBennett.html/

Coed Naked Vaguely absurd "attitude" T-shirts such as "Coed Naked Lacrosse" were familiar on college campuses during the '80s, often tailored to the particular school or local geography. "Surf the Schuylkill" at the University of Pennsylvania, for instance, referred nonsensically to the waveless, polluted Schuylkill River flowing nearby. In 1990 two University of New Hampshire grads bought the Coed Naked trademark and unleashed it on teens. By the 1993-'94 school year the shirts (and even cruder latecomers like "Big Johnson" and "Butt Naked") reached fad proportions and were the subject of dozens of ACLU lawsuits across the country as schools deemed inappropriate the proliferating double entendres like "Coed Naked Band. Do It To The Rhythm" and "Coed Naked Billiards. Get Felt on the Table!" [See also NO FEAR.]

coffee bars Europeanization of U.S. coffee culture via SEATTLE, where Starbucks, the largest of the coffee-bar chains, began opening retail outlets for its upscale coffee in 1987. By 1995 there were some 4,500 coffee-bars nationwide (500 of which were Starbucks), caffeinating both overworked yuppies and underemployed wanna-BEATS. The latter typically show with laptops and literary publications (*Java Times*, *Literary Latte*), and stay for hours. The public's widespread willingness to pay hefty premiums for labor-intensive, speciality versions of what had once been simply "a coffee" is prime evidence for marketers' LITTLE LUXURIES hypothesizing. Coffee-bar contributions to American civilization also include the popularization of specially designed plastic cup lids that protect cappuccino foam on take-out orders and the substitution of the words "tall" and "grande" for large. Coffee-ordering etiquette has become a staple source of mild humor for mid-'90s TV sitcoms like *Frasier* and *Friends*. [See also CYBERCAFÉS.]

USENET **alt.coffee, alt.food.coffee, alt.pub.coffeehouse, rec.food.drink.coffee, alt.drugs.caffeine**

Cole, David (b. 1962; d. 1995) Tennessee-born New York club DJ turned producer/musician/remixer, best known for his work with the pop-dance group C+C Music Factory. Cole and his partner Robert Clivilles wrote and produced hits for Mariah Carey, Aretha Franklin, and Whitney Houston; as C+C Music Factory the pair brought underground club rhythms to the mainstream with hard-driving hits like the Grammy-nominated 1991 singles "Gonna Make You Sweat" and "Things That Make You Go Hmmm." Clivilles and Cole's work, and that of their imitators, pushed Top 40 radio toward a dance-dominated format. Cole died in January 1995 due to complications from spinal meningitis.

WEB **The Producer's Archive** http://www.dsi.unimi.it/Users/ Students/barbieri/awrrng.htm

Coleman, Joe (b. 1955) New York-based artist who is one of the prime exponent of SERIAL-KILLER CHIC: Coleman's often-horrific body of work includes portraits of convicted killers CHARLES MANSON, Henry Lee Lucas (as in the movie *Henry, Portrait of a Serial Killer* 1990), and Carl Panzram, a sadistic 21-time murderer who received the death penalty in 1930. This art was collected in *The Infernal Art of Joe Coleman* (co-published by FANTAGRAPHICS, 1992), which boasted a jacket blurb by Manson himself. Coleman (who was raised by a drunken, abusive father) blandly explained his artistic impulse to an *L.A. Times* reporter in 1993: "I need to find empathy for those who are least understood."

college rap Several stylistically and geographically diverse HIP-HOP acts came to the fore in 1992, all sharing the chimerical quality of "ALTER-NATIVE-ness." That is, each group deviated enough from the accepted strictures of JEEP music that they were marketed to the mainly white college radio audience. Nashville-based Me Phi Me had an almost folksy approach; Washington, D.C.'s Basehead were laid back, with garage-rock overtones; while San Francisco's Disposable Heroes of Hiphopcracy took political stridency further than

comics

For more than 40 years, superhero comics have supplied a sexually deprived, mostly male audience with an endless stream of masterfully marketed four-color disempowerment. The super-stud books turn their readership on with a nonstop orgy of bulging muscles, pneumatic breasts, phallic weaponry, orgasmic explosions, ecstatic flight fantasies, brutally sadomasochistic confrontations, and guilt-ridden identity crises between hyperpotent superselves and less-than-adequate everyday cover.

Superheroes survive as the Big Macs of comics culture, but the menu was expanded in the late '60s with the advent of underground comics (a.k.a. "comix"). R. CRUMB, S. CLAY WILSON, ROBERT WILLIAMS, Kim Deitch, Spain Rodriguez, and the other Zap Comix artists proved comics could do just about anything: explore social mores, *épater le bourgeois*, perform drug-inspired visual experiments, touch on radical politics, and put a bulge in a young man's pants. The comix form took on new life in the late '70s/early '80s as the PUNK do-it-yourself aesthetic trickled down to a new wave of independent creators and publishers (DAVE SIM's 1978 epic-to-be *Cerebus* being one notable example).

The medium was enriched by small-circulation black-and-white titles that were marketed directly to comics shops rather than to the wider retail universe of drug and grocery stores. At the same time, independent publishers were attracting imaginative young talents by allowing them to retain the rights to their characters. In response, Marvel and DC later issued numerous "collectors editions" aimed at obsessive fans and speculators, damaging many smaller publishers. As chronicled in *The Comics Journal*, a highly opin-ionated yet comprehensive insiders' monthly, the indie comics explosion introduced such highly crafted and individually voiced writer/artists as the HERNANDEZ BROTHERS (*Love and Rockets*), PETER BAGGE (*Real Stuff, Hate*), DANIEL CLOWES (*Lloyd Llewellyn, Eightball*), and dozens of others.

The indie comics boom's biggest influence, however, was on the numerous artists who bared their souls in the sort of autobiographical comics pioneered by Crumb, Justin Green (*Binky Brown Meets the Holy Virgin Mary*) and Harvey Pekar (*American Splendor*). By the early '90s there were more than a dozen series devoted to the cult of personality–that is, the personality of their authors. Titles like *Real Life* (Dennis Eichorn), *Lowlife* (Ed Brukbaker), *Slutburger* (MARY FLEENER), *Jizz* (Scott Russo), and *Dangle* (Lloyd Dangle) suggested an artistic smorgasbord of low-rent emotional drama, sincerity with a snarl or a shrug. Whether

Sadomasochistic nightmares and Pynchonesque paranoia by DANIEL CLOWES.

scratched out by youngish victims of underemployment, or by disappointed middle-aged neurotics wondering why their second marriage fell apart, these autobio-graphics provided unflinching confirmation that things really *are* that bad.

Cartooning emerged as the perfect, marginal medium for existential meandering. These cartoonists

PUBLIC ENEMY and had a musical approach more INDUSTRIAL than funky. Among this new mini-generation only Arrested Development and PM Dawn flourished: the former, a 1993 LOLLAPALOOZA inclusion, had a 1992 hit with "Tennessee," while the latter (dismissed by rap purists because they sang) reached the Top 10 with 1991's "Set Adrift On Memory Bliss" (based on a sample from British vid-pop band Spandau Ballet). Neither was able to withstand the imminent GANGSTA rap onslaught that captured the suburban market in 1993–94. (In 1995, Dionne Farris, who sang on "Tennessee," reached the top of the charts with "I Know.")

WEB **Basehead Home Page** http://skexix.europa.com/~basehead/

---

were, to varying degrees, protoslackers, dilettantes, and autodidacts, attracted to the art's open, doodling forms, flexible relationships between language and graphics, and a spectrum of representational strategies ranging from stark realism to wacky modernist abstraction.

ART SPIEGELMAN and wife Francoise Mouly's *Raw* ("The graphix magazine that overestimates the taste of the American public") introduced America to the more artistic European comics styles of artists like Bruno Richard, Pascal Doury, and Joost Swarte. American artists who fell between the cracks of underground cartooning and commercial art–like GARY PANTER, Chris Ware, Mark Newgarden, and Ben Katchor–also found their way into Spiegelman's high-design playground. (Panter, Swarte, and fellow *Raw* alum Kim Deitch followed Mouly when she joined Tina Brown's *NEW YORKER* in 1992.)

The early '90s also saw an unexpected deluge of sexually oriented comics, some witty and affecting, some as mundane as low-end top-shelf porn. "There's an air of irrespectability to publishing erotic comics that I rather like," said publisher Gary Groth, who started the Eros line in 1989 as a way to finance the "serious" FANTAGRAPHICS titles. Some of Eros's higher quality smut included Dori Seda's *Lonely Nights Comics*, Craig Maynard's *Up From Bondage*, Dennis Eichhorn's autobiographical *Real Smut*, and punky BOB FINGERMAN's *Skinheads in Love*.

Even though the contemporary underground offered sarcastic and smutty alternatives to the world of comic superheroes, these alternatives were still overwhelmingly male. In the '80s Aline Kominsky-Crumb, Robert Crumb's cartoonist wife, built up the influential *Weirdo* anthology as an outlet for women artists. By the '90s, there was a significant audience for the growing network of women cartoonists; prominent names included JULIE DOUCET, Roberta Gregory, and the aforementioned Mary Fleener. There also emerged distinct lesbian and gay comics, notably the syndicated, anthologized strips by Howard Cruse (*Wendel*) and Alison Bechdel (*Dykes to Watch Out For*).

Such fringe activity had little influence in the corridors of Marvel, one of the two companies that continued to dominate the lucrative superhero market. Apart from exploiting, early on, the genius of artists like Jack Kirby and Steve Ditko, Marvel largely hewed to its original "universe" (excepting FRANK MILLER's NOIR-influenced, late-'70s *Daredevil* issues). DC, on the other hand, responded to independent, '80s-launched, high-end superhero shops like Dark Horse and Malibu (later Image and Valiant [renamed Acclaim]) by investing in an impressive stream of writing talent coming out of Britain. ALAN MOORE rethought the very nature of superhero comics with his revisionist *Swamp Thing* ; inaugurated in the early '90s, DC's Vertigo line introduced America to such talented U.K. writers as NEIL GAIMAN, GRANT MORRISON, Jamie Delano (*Hellblazer*), and Peter Milligan (*Shade the Changing Man*). DC acknowledge the real-world force of MULTICULTURALISM when it struck a distribution deal with Milestone Media, now the leading publisher in the growing area of multi-ethnic superhero comics.–*Richard Gehr*

WEB **The Comics Hotlist** http://www.uta.fi/yhteydet/sarjikset. html ✦ WEB **Alternative Comics WWW Guide** http://bronze. ucs.indiana.edu/~mfragass/altcom.html ✦ WEB **The Comic Book Legal Defense Fund** http://www.insv.com/cbldf/ ✦ USENET **alt.comics.alternative, rec.arts.comics** ✦ WEB **Eden Matrix: Comics** http://www.eden.com/comics/comics.html

combat boots Cheap, unisex military footwear valued in PUNK and INDIE-ROCK culture throughout the late 1970s and '80s for its aggressive overtones, and also in gay culture as a WORKWEAR variant. Madonna wore combat boots in a 1990 MTV "ROCK THE VOTE" ad, flanked by similarly shod male dancers and controversially wrapped in the American flag. Three years later combat boots (usually around $60 at Army-Navy stores) were identified as part of the perma-fashion labeled GRUNGE and were absorbed by the fashion mainstream, as designers like CALVIN KLEIN and Donna Karan used them in runway shows with (echoing street fashion) floral print and satin dresses. Not everyone was enamored with the look, however: designer Isaac Mizrahi complained to the *International Herald Tribune* in 1993, "If I see another baggy dress with heavy boots, I'm going to . . ." The following year DREW BARRYMORE got married wearing a white SLIP DRESS and combat boots.

Combs, Sean "Puff Daddy" (b. 1970) HIP-HOP promoter-turned-entrepreneur/producer who, as a teenage Vice President at ANDRE HARRELL's Uptown Records, took SMOOTHED-OUT R&B merchants Jodeci and NEW JILL SWING chanteuse Mary J. Blige double-platinum. Combs' Midas touch deserted him on December 28th, 1991, when a charity basketball game he organized at New York's City College ended in a stampede in which nine people died. (The subsequent official investigation found Combs' security and insurance provisions wanting.) Combs parted ways from Uptown in 1993, licensing his Bad Boy label to Arista; his platinum and gold co-productions of street-rappers Notorious BIG (aka Biggie Smalls) and Craig Mack (as well as Mary J. Blige and others) proved that he had lost none of his formidable instinct for a hit. In June 1995 the former's "One More Chance" debuted at No. 5 on the Billboard Hot 100, matching the previous week's record-setting performance by the forcefully marketed "Scream" by Janet and Michael Jackson (on whose 1995 *HIStory* album BIG guested).

comics See page 44.

Communications Decency Act 1995 bill proposed by Senator Jim Exon, Democrat of Nebraska, to effectively outlaw CYBERSEX. The law—actually an amendment tacked on to the Senate Commerce Committee's version of the first major reform of U.S. communications law since the advent of network television—included fines as high as $100,000 and prison terms of up to two years for transmitting material that is "obscene, lewd, lascivious, filthy, or indecent." The CDA drew an anti-censorship howl on the INTERNET and mockery from those acquainted with the impossibility of enforcing such restrictions. A "dial-a-porn" PHONE SEX law with similarly broad language was judged an infringement on free speech by the Supreme Court in 1989. Exon explained the CDA to the *New York Times*, saying, "The first thing I was concerned with was kids being able to pull up pornography on their machines." Online companies responded with a slew of filtering products that most kids will have to explain to their parents.

WEB **Stop the 1995 Communications Decency Act** http://anansi.panix.com:80/vtw/exon/ GOPHER **Department of Justice** gopher://gopher.panix.com:70/0/vtw/exon/media/ doj-leahy/ ✦ WEB **New Age Comstockery (The Cato Institute)** http://www.cato.org/main/pa232.html/

computer adaptive testing The computerization of standardized tests, said to minimize the anxiety associated with the rite of passage by adjusting the difficulty of a test while it is being taken (get an easy question right and the computer gives you a harder one; get a harder one wrong and the test gets easier). But when Education Testings Services—administer of the country's largest multiple choice tester, the SAT—proudly introduced in November 1993 its silicon substitute for the proctor, No. 2 pencil, rigid test dates, and two-month wait for score results, the result was decidedly low percentile. Because ETS did not develop a large pool of questions, test takers were able to memorize portions and retake it, tell their friends, or post answers on the INTERNET. ETS curtailed most of the computerized testing in December 1994 after the largest test-prep company, Stanley Kaplan, presented it with evidence of how easy it was to cheat. Nevertheless, it is probably inevitable that the hundred million standardized tests taken every year in America as part of everything from driver's license to law school applications will migrate to the computer.

computer virus First postulated by computer science researcher Fred Cohen in the 1970s, computer viruses are small programs that propagate by attaching copies of themselves to other programs. (Early versions spread into the U.S. by two Pakistani brothers who hid their virus in pirated software that they sold to American tourists.) Well-known viruses include the Jerusalem virus, and Michelangelo (programmed to wipe out a computer's hard disk on March 6, Michelangelo's birthday). Although virus scares—with the attendant AIDS metaphors—regularly make headlines, no large-scale outbreaks have yet taken place. (*U.S. News & World Report* launched its own media virus during the Gulf War, claiming—nonsensically—that the U.S. had disabled Iraqi air defense systems with a computer virus.) The "Peace virus"—the first to be unwittingly distributed with a commercial program—took command of thousands of MACINTOSH computers on March 2, 1988, greeting surprised users with a "universal message of peace," and then erasing itself. Other major outbreaks have included the Christmas Tree virus, which clogged IBM's 350,000-terminal network in December, 1987, and Robert T. Morris's INTERNET Worm, which accidentally infected thousands of computers and crashed the INTERNET in November 1988. Increased exchange of files over computer networks has fueled a handsome side-business in virus protection software.

WEB **Anti-Virus Reference Center** http://www.symantec.com/virus/virus.html

Conal, Robbie (b. 1944) Guerrilla artist known for satirical street posters of right-wing polit-

ical figures that have been plastered in urban America since the late '80s. An abstract expressionist painter by training, Conal first hit the lampposts and construction sites of L.A. in 1986 after galleries rejected his original swirling, monstrous paintings of Ronald and Nancy Reagan. Other targets, many collected in the 1992 book *Art Attack*, have included Jesse Helms, Dan Quayle ("damage" was lettered over his head, "control" over his mouth), Clarence Thomas, George Bush, former L.A. police chief DARYL GATES, and "Newtwit" Gingrich. The Gates poster, which appeared shortly after the RODNEY KING video, had a shooting-gallery target over the face, along with a Gates quote, "Casual Drugs Users Should Be Taken Out and Shot," with "Shot" crossed out and replaced by "Beaten."

Photo by Sandra-Lee Phipps

ROBBIE CONAL'S art in action at a pro-choice rally, 1992.

condoms Time-tested form of sexual protection whose use has gained new currency in the age of AIDS. The 1987 endorsement of condoms by Surgeon General C. Everett Koop launched a prophylactic boom, leading to the growth of niche products like glow-in-the-dark condoms, all-condom stores like the Condomania chain, and condoms specifically marketed to women. (The more recent development of the FEMALE CONDOM provides women with a new degree of control.)

By the late '80s, condom commercials were finally airing on cable TV, attempting to destigmatize that classic bashful-teenager-at-the-pharmacist confrontation; in 1991, Fox became the first network to allow the ads. Meanwhile, some porn producers attempted to help overcome male resistance to condom use (oft-likened to "taking a shower with a raincoat on") by eroticizing the whole procedure, treating the prophylactic like another rubberized sex toy. Public health officials attempted the opposite approach, attempting (and failing) to divert controversy by demonstrating proper application techniques on bananas, cucumbers, and other phallic produce.

The real outcry, though, has been raised over the distribution of condoms in public high schools, as concerned parents appear to equate schools' prevention of unsafe sex with the defilement of their teenagers. Despite such public health efforts, condom use in the '90s appears to have plateaued; a 1994 survey found that only 48 percent of sexually active teens claim to use condoms, and in the heat of passion the real figures may even be lower. Also of concern is the unreliability of many of the most-used devices; a 1995 *Consumer Reports* ranking of condoms by "burst index" found seven major brands (including six manufactured by industry leader Trojan) to be unsafe at any speed. (*Consumer Reports* also noted the folly of using a petroleum or mineral-oil lubricant; it dissolves the latex.)

WEB **The Sheath File** http://www.lanminds.com/explore/ sheath.html ✦ WEB **Condoms & Latex** http://www.cmpharm .ucsf.edu/~troyer/safesex/condoms.html

Converse   With early-'90s sneaker sales of less than 20 percent those of NIKE and Reebok, Converse set out to build on the underground success of PUMA and Vans and corner the alterna-sneaker market. The nonsports division of the North Reading, Massachusetts, company began tracking counterculture styles and relaunching discontinued sports footwear from the '70s: the spread of thrift store and GRUNGE aesthetics led to the reintroduction of the colorful version of the Chuck Taylor All Stars (originals introduced 1917); in 1993, suede low-top One Stars returned (the popularity of hiking boots and outdoorswear later prompted a "chunk" All Star); and CLUB KID experiments also led in the same year to an All Star PLAT-FORM SNEAKER. Most prized, however, were the company's super-basic Jack Purcell canvas low-tops,

which came to define, by 1994, the sneaker's simple elegance for both Kurt Cobain and *Vogue*.

WEB **Charlie's Sneaker Pages** http://www.neosoft. com/users/s/sneakers/ ✦ USENET **alt.clothing.sneakers**

Cooper, Dennis (b. 1953)   Purveyor of anomic gay fiction. Ever since Cooper's first novel *Closer* (1989), he has been notorious for sparsely written tales of lost teenagers and predatory adults laced with sexual explicitness and unnerving morbidity. The questionable taste of the Cooper *corpus* has provoked some violent reactions (including a death threat from some QUEER NATION members), but not at the expense of his literary reputation. British journalist Elizabeth Young was moved to describe Cooper as "Georges Bataille trapped in Disneyland," while novelist Edmund White weighed in with the opinion that "Dennis Cooper is reciting Aeschylus with a mouthful of bubble-gum." In 1995, Cooper's 1991 book *Frisk* was adapted into a film starring art-house superstar Parker Posey.

Cooper, Douglas (b. 1960)   This Toronto-born writer is a publishing pioneer of sorts: his sophomore book *Delirium* (following 1992's well-reviewed *Amnesia*) was one of the first novels from a major publisher to be serialized on the INTERNET as it was being written. Laden with HYPERTEXT links to other material and illustrated by "cyber artist" Barry Deck, Cooper's tricksy *Delirium* (published on paper by Hyperion, 1995) was a futuristic curio.

WEB **Literary Links** http://www.mnsfld.edu/~library/lit.html ✦ WEB **Delirum** http://www.pathfinder.com/.com/twep/ Features/Delirium/DelTitle.html

Corbijn, Anton (b. 1955)   Dutch photographer/video maker born of the British post-PUNK era. As a contributor to English music paper *New Musical Express* in the early '80s, Corbijn established his trademark style—dense black and white pictures of doomed romantics like Joy Division and Echo and the Bunnymen. His unassuming personality and empathy with his subjects helped Corbijn forge alliances with some of future *éminences grises* of the ALTERNATIVE world: MORRISSEY, Depeche Mode (for whom Corbijn also designs stage sets), U2, and R.E.M. have all, at one time or another, sworn fealty to him, sometimes insisting on sanctioned Corbijn photos in place of commissioned shoots. As a video-maker from the mid-'80s on, Corbijn has revealed an affinity for religious imagery and off-the-wall humor. "A mixture between Tati and Tarkovsky," he remarked to London's *Guardian* in 1994. One of Corbijn's rare forays into color was NIRVANA's memorably lurid "Heart-Shaped Box," the band's last video.

WEB **The Photographic Works of Anton Corbijn**

http://yar.cs.wisc.edu/~wonko/anton/

Coupland, Douglas (b. 1961) Vancouver, Canada, native whose writing career began with a respectable advance of $22,500 for what was supposed to be a nonfiction book about his generation. Instead he delivered *Generation X* (1991), a well-observed, marginalia-heavy novel that limned the lives of three ironic underachievers adrift in the retirement hamlet of Palm Springs. By 1995, the book—subtitled *Tales for an Accelerated Culture*—had grown from early word-of-mouth cult to cultural phenomenon, selling nearly 400,000 copies and naming a new youth culture era (see GENERATION X). Coupland cultivated his cachet with modest, consistently clever Zeitgeist lists for outlets like *The New Republic*, and honed his minimal prose-style in the low-concept *Shampoo Planet*

Post-ironic author DOUGLAS COUPLAND, in "Close Personal Friend," a short promotional film.

(1992) and *Life After God* (accompanied by MTV vignettes; declared one of 1994's ten worst books by *People* magazine). In 1995 Coupland published the more ambitious novel *Microserfs* (1995), which originated as a *WIRED* magazine cover story about six preselected Microsoft employees. With a keen eye for peripheral detail, and a heightened radar for colorful cultural MEMES (especially those derived from growing up watching '70s television), Coupland confirmed his talent for imbuing background cultural radiation with human resonance. A half-hour video occasioned by the promotion of *Microserfs, Close Personal Friend*, is prime Coupland: a breezy media adept for the post-ironic age.

WEB **A Hotel in San Felipe** http://weber.u.washington.edu/milhous/Coupland.html

cowrie shells Sea-borne jewelry originally used as currency in pre-Christian times. Cowrie shells, which are found in the Indian Ocean region, began their most recent incarnation on the tables of African-American street vendors who offered them sewn on to leather bracelets and necklaces. The shells are also purchased individually—usually for under a dollar each—and sewn into garments and dreadlocks. Increasingly associated, like KENTE CLOTH, with AFROCENTRIC fashion, the small, white shells became an easy, MULTICULTURAL fashion statement among early-'90s pop stars and celebrities.

Cox, Patrick (b. 1963) Canadian-born, British-based shoe designer responsible for one of the significant footwear fads of the mid-'90s. Although Cox has designed footwear for Vivienne Westwood and ANNA SUI runway shows since he entered the business in 1985, he is now known for his own Wannabe collection—in particular for the square-toed loafers first marketed in London in late 1993. Produced in fake crocodile skin and various shades of patent leather (among other fabrics), the Patrick Cox loafer (which sells in the US for $170) was instantly established worldwide as an object of desire among club-goers and fashion insiders. Reports of waiting lists for the shoes, and the necessity of a security guard outside his modest London store, stoked demand; in March 1994 Cox opened a New York store.

crack Form of smokable cocaine that condensed the cost and experience of getting high into a more marketable product. The name comes from the crackling sound that the lumpy off-white chips make when burned; its other appellation, base, refers to the rocky alkaloidal crack residue that is hardened from boiling cocaine powder in water and then cooling it in cold water. Before crack's advent in the '80s, cocaine was an expensive drug associated with upper-income bracket or nightclub use, but between 1980 and 1992 the South American acreage devoted to coca crops doubled, the street price of cocaine dropped four-fold, and the purity tripled.

Drug users had long rolled an oily version of the residue called "con-con" in cigarettes and MARIJUANA joints or sprinkled cocaine over bong hits (called "snow caps"), but in the '80s it became economical to enjoy the more intense but less efficient high of "freebasing" (smoking) the rock itself. Drug gangs soon democratized freebasing and cocaine addiction by packaging crack in clear plastic vials that began selling on the street for as little as two dollars a piece. The vials were a smash hit in the inner city, with basing galleries and crack houses flourishing in New York by 1985. (Crack's advent in Harlem is the historical setting for the film *New Jack City* [1991]; in-depth treatments include anthropologist Terry Williams' two multi-year studies, *The Cocaine Kids* [1989] and *Crackhouse* [1992].) By the late '80s the crack trade was sometimes described as the single largest employer of minority youth in America and, owing to territorial gunbattles over retail profits, the largest killer. The dramatic decrease in New York City's 1995 murder rate was interpreted by some experts as evidence (and the result) of crack use burning out.

WEB **crack.info** http://hyperreal.com/drugs/stimulants/crack.info

credit-card cinema Originally intended as a source of short-term financing for emergencies or impulse purchases, credit cards have opened the door to capital funding for young entrepreneurs (thanks in part to the nonexistent credit history requirements of UNDERGRADUATE CREDIT CARD OFFERS). The motion-picture industry in particular has seen an explosion of low-budget credit-card projects, many helmed by unlikely or nontraditional directors. Among the first to publicly celebrate multiple-card capitalization were black directors SPIKE LEE and Robert Townshend, who had sleeper hits with, respectively, *She's Gotta Have It* (1986) and *Hollywood Shuffle* (1987). In 1992 19-year-old Matty Rich scored a special jury award at SUNDANCE with his maxed-out *Straight Out of Brooklyn*; in 1994 Sundance again rewarded the TRW-baiting genre when KEVIN SMITH's slacker opus *Clerks*, produced with cash-advance dollars, also won a Sundance prize and a major-distribution deal. According to one survey, more than a quarter of all small and midsized businesses used plastic capital to meet cash needs in 1994—at a time when the average card interest rate was 17.75 percent, or more than twice that of the average home mortgage or business loan.

Cross Colours Los Angeles streetwear firm that claimed sales of over $15 million within a year of its October 1990 launch. Owners Thomas "T.J." Walker (b. 1959) and Carl Jones (b. 1954) touched a nerve in the HIP-HOP clothing market with their distinctive use of the AFROCENTRIC red-black-green color combination and KENTE cloth linings; this self-proclaimed "Clothing Without Prejudice" was also adorned with vague, feel-good political messages like "Increase the Peace," "Educate 2 Elevate," and "Stop D Violence." (Cross Colours—named after Walker and Jones' desire to end Crip/Blood gang warfare—funded the nonprofit Common Ground Foundation, run by a former Crip, to promote education over gang membership.) At its height, Cross Colours had an impressive following among black celebrities; its parent company Threads 4 Life was distributing the burgeoning KARL KANI line; and the *Los Angeles Times* reported that the company left the 1992 MAGIC (men's apparel) show in Las Vegas with a phenomenal $40 million in orders. The company's 1994 demise was blamed on several factors, from BOOTLEGGERS to sloppy management practices. Miscalculation of popular taste also figured: at MAGIC 1993, Cross Colours unveiled a collection heavy with earth tones; "I call the new look ACID JAZZ" Jones told *Women's Wear Daily* of the catastrophic change in direction. He and Walker downsized to a design company in 1994.

Crumb, R. (b. 1943)   The cantankerous, misogynistic godfather of underground COMIX, Robert Crumb began his career as a sexually obsessed misanthropic loner under the influence of *Mad* magazine and Bruegel. One of the seminal San Francisco underground cartoonists responsible for Zap Comix, Crumb introduced such characters as Fritz the Cat, Schuman the Human, Mr. Natural, and Angelfood McSpade into hippie iconography, as well as such irritating catch phrases as "Keep on truckin'." The increasingly bitter, acerbic Crumb remains the most brutally honest autobiographical cartoonist (having influenced an entire generation of same); Crumb and his wife, Aline Kominsky-Crumb, provided a no-holds-barred account of their relationship in the pages of *Dirty Laundry*. FANTAGRAPHICS BOOKS has released more than ten volumes of *The Complete Crumb Comics*. *Crumb,* Terry Zwigoff's 1995 prize-winning documentary on the cartoonist and his dysfunctional family, enshrined Crumb as a national treasure.

USENET **alt.comics.alternative, rec.arts.comics.alternative**

crunchy   All-purpose adjective for that which is earth-toned, organically grown, and recycled. When applied to people, "crunchy" (and its synonymic source, "granola") implies environmentalist politics and an absence of deodorant. Not all eco-culture counts as "crunchy"—THE BODY SHOP, for instance, repackages rain forest products as bright and shiny consumables.

CU-SeeMe   Video-telephone software developed by Tim Dorcey at Cornell University (CU) and,

beginning in 1994, distributed free of charge over the INTERNET. There, CU-SeeMe (pronounced "see you, see me") soon spawned video "reflectors" that could support broadcasts (including news videofeeds, concerts, and movie premieres), conference calls, or a dozen-odd users with fast network connections from around the world making faces at each other at a few frames per second. Public reflectors have also spawned a few streaker myths; more real are the early 1995 cyber-brothel experiments of Brandy's Babes and the two-way, $4.95 per minute NetMate (aka ScrewU-ScrewMe). Grassroots videoconferencing would have been much more limited were it not for the appearance of the Connectix QuickCam, a $99 golfball-sized black and white camera. The CU-SeeMe software has been licensed for a commercial version from White Pine and inspired a host of commercial followers, including Internet Phone and Apple's QuickTime Conferencing.

WEB **CU-SeeMe FAQ** http://www.jungle.com/msattler/sci-tech/comp/CU-SeeMe/ mail list **Cu-SeeMe Events** email list-admin@www.indstate.edu with "subscribe CUSM-Events firstname lastname" in body ✦ WEB **NetMate** http://www.soc.com/sysreq.html/

"Hey, New York." CUSEEME, video conferencing with total strangers.

Cultural Studies   Academic field focused on the politics of popular culture, from MADONNA videos to *STAR TREK* ZINES to NIKE commercials. Cultural Studies' own image in popular culture has been colored by reports of KEANU REEVES seminars and *BRADY BUNCH* dissertations. While study of such subjects within the academy was formerly the province of a still-extant backwater called Popular Culture Studies, in the late '80s the interdisciplinary term "Cultural Studies" arrived from Britain via the high road of continental theory (Frankfurt School, French literary theory, Italian Marxism). Though the "cult studs" field faces fierce, sustained academic resistance from defenders of "the best that's been thought and said," it is now commonplace at major schools to also find study of "what's been thought and said by the most people." Concerned less with the qualities of texts in themselves than with those texts' effects on the world, cultural studies scholars, most of whom are TV-reared BABY BOOMERS, attempt to chart how audiences make sense of mass media—be it MTV, the INTERNET, or even Shakespeare (who still commands a large captive audience in U.S. high schools). One of the biggest debates within Cultural Studies is between MULTI-CULTURALISTS, who want to expand the canon to include authors like Zora Neale Hurston or Willa Cather, and populists who want to scrap it altogether.

WEB **Critical Approaches to Cultural Studies**
http://polestar.facl.mcgill.ca/burnett/englishhome.html

Culture Babes   All-female "old boys network" for New York media professionals; founded as a series of SoHo cocktail parties by feminist authors NAOMI WOLF and Amrutha Slee in 1993. "This is not yuppie networking women from hell or a consciousness-raising group," declared Wolf in *New York* magazine while promoting her "power feminism" manual, *Fire with Fire*. "It's an experiment in the kind of thing we need to do in the '90s—combining resource activism with material support." Over time the group has evolved from its original core of invited participants into a more egalitarian, albeit less chic, organization principally defined by its popularity with magazine interns.

EMAIL hannael@aol.com

Cusack, John (b. 1966)   Modest, self-deprecating romantic lead of movie touchstones for '80s teens like *The Sure Thing* (1985, co-starring Daphne Zuniga, later of *MELROSE PLACE*) and *Say Anything* (1989). Both followed Cusack's quixotic pursuit of barely attainable women (Ione Skye in the latter); in *Say Anything*'s "I don't want to sell

anything, buy anything, or process anything" dinner table speech, Cusack made one of the definitive cinematic statements of his generation's anti-commercialism. Cusack himself has turned down roles in blockbusters (*Indecent Proposal* [1993], *White Men Can't Jump* [1992], and *Sleeping With the Enemy* [1991]) in order to work with directors like John Sayles, Stephen Frears, and Woody Allen. A Chicago native, Cusack began acting in a local repertory company at age nine, along with his brothers and sisters; his sister Joan is a successful character actress, nominated for an Academy Award for her *Working Girl* role in 1988. With the stated goal of getting rock fans into live theater, Cusack founded the New Criminals theater group in Chicago, producing unusual plays such as a 1991 adaptation of Hunter S. Thompson's *Fear and Loathing In Las Vegas*. In 1995, MGM began production of a Cusack-penned screenplay, *Gross Pointe Blank*.

custom-fit Levi's   In 1994 America's favorite jeans-maker introduced a futuristic system of custom-tailoring: measurements for the waist, inseam, hips and rise (waistband-to-waistband, under the crotch) could be taken at Levi's own stores—initially in Cincinnati and New York—and sent online to a Levi's factory in Tennessee. Assembled automatically to match one of several thousand combinations, the trousers are then sent to the customer (initially women only) within three weeks. At a relatively affordable surcharge of $10 over standard Levi's, the custom-fit jeans was seen by many as a glimpse of the anticipated revolution in mass-customization, when centrally manufactured goods can be fit to individual tastes.

WEB **Levi Strauss & Co.** http://www.levi.com

cybercafés   High-concept COFFEE BARS that combine the '90s craze for high-end java with burgeoning INTERNET fever. Icon Byte Bar & Grill in San Francisco, which opened in 1991, claims to be the first café to have installed computer terminals and modem linkups that allow customers to surf cyberspace while sipping a cappuccino. As of mid–1995, a London-based WORLD WIDE WEB site devoted to cybercafés cited more than 80 world-wide, with dozens more in the works. They range from high-tech emporia like Cybersmith in Cambridge, Massachusetts (with 53 terminals available at hourly rates) to mom-and-pop cafés in towns like Boise, Idaho, and Plano, Texas, where oftentimes mystified owners have given into clamoring regulars and installed a single terminal (sometimes coin-operated). While the thought of hanging out around computer screens may seem oppressive even to those accustomed to socializing through computer networks, cybercafés add a social dimension to what is typically a solitary pastime, and provide one of the few public spaces where the uninitiated can explore the Internet.

WEB **Cyber Café Guide** http://www.easynet.co.uk/ pages/cafe/ccafe.htm ✦ USENET **alt.cybercafes** WEB **SF NET Coffee House Connection** http://www.slip.net/~wgregori/

cyberpunk Literary movement characterized by science fiction that combines flashy hardboiled narrative with an interest in mind and body invasions, technology, and boundary-displacing "interzones" whether on- or offline. The new form found its ideological nexus in BRUCE STERLING's *Cheap Truth* fanzine (1982–1986, published under the pseudonym "Vincent Omniaveritas"); the term itself was first employed in the early '80s by *Isaac Asimov's Science Fiction Magazine* editor Gardner Dozois, who may or may not have cribbed it from the title of a Bruce Bethke short story. In addition to stars Sterling and WILLIAM GIBSON, other writers identified with "the Movement," as it was known in *Cheap Truth*, include NEAL STEPHENSON, Tom Maddox, Pat Cadigan, Rudy Rucker, Marc Laidlaw, Lewis Shiner, John Shirley, and Lucius Shepard. (Cyberpunk also spawned the Victorian imaginings of STEAMPUNK.) As a subculture and '90s media label, cyberpunk connotes the doings of HACKERS, PHONE PHREAKS, and cryptography-concerned CYPHERPUNKS. Cyberpunk-oriented magazines include *MONDO 2000*, *bOING-bOING*, and *FRINGEWARE Review*.

GOPHER **Well Cyberpunk Archive** gopher://gopher.well.sf

.ca.us:70/11/cyberpunk ✦ WEB **Cheap Truth Archive** http://bush.cs.tamu.edu:80/!erich/cheaptruth/ ✦ USENET **alt.fan.cyberpunk**

cybersex Computer-enhanced masturbation or -simulated copulation. Always instrumental in the consumer acceptance of new technologies, sex contributed mightily to the early '90s boom in the INTERNET and online services, as well as CD-ROM. Although the subject of VIRTUAL REALITY hucksterism, CYBERPUNK sci-fi (one famous early example is WILLIAM GIBSON's *Neuromancer*), and tabloid headlines such as the *New York Post's* 1994 "Computer Sickos Target Your Kids," actual netsex tended simply to involve picture downloads (see ALT.BINARIES. PICTURES.EROTICA) and textual flirtation by one-handed typists. Some of the best examples are found in the gay chat rooms on AMERICA ONLINE, crowded IRC chat channels such as #wetsex where cross-dressing males run rampant under assumed names like Bambi, and in Internet MUD's such as FurryMUCK. (The latter is famous for the TinySex—"speed-writing interactive erotica"—that users engage through role-playing as furry animals. FurryMUCK was also the site of a much discussed 1993 "cyber-rape.")

Cybersex has also been a boon for magazines. *DETAILS*, for example, writes about futuristic "long-distance love-making machines" that produce tiny electrical shocks in the inner thigh of a partner over telephone lines. The subject lured *Time* out on a shaky limb in June 1995 when the magazine ran a scare-mongering "Cyber Porn" cover story that, it transpired, was premised on the shoddy scholarship of a student who had previously been a consultant to purveyors of BBS ultra-porn.

TELNET **FurryMUCK** telnet://furry.org 8888/ ✦ IRC **#hotsex** ✦ USENET **alt.sex**

cypherpunks Loose network of computer privacy freaks, mainly based in Silicon Valley, committed to the development and dissemination of public key cryptography (see PGP) that makes it possible to conduct electronic correspondence and business transactions with near perfect privacy. Police, fearful that the spread of this technology will make it impossible to trace transactions, conduct wiretaps, or execute search warrants, are attempting to criminalize its use. "DIGITAL CASH," a possible consequence of widespread encryption use, portends the breakdown of nation-states unable to collect taxes. This notion became a basic assumption in CYBERPUNK storytelling circa 1995 (e.g. BRUCE STERLING'S *Heavy Weather*, NEAL STEPHENSON'S *Diamond Age*). Cypherpunks also support the use of "anonymous remailers" that make it possible to send and post anonymous computer messages. Other cypher-activists include EFF.

WEB **The Cypherpunks Home Page** http://snyside. sunnyside.com/pub/cypherpunks/ **Pointers to Cypherpunks Sites** http://www.uic.edu/~varun/sites.html ✦ USENET **talk.politics.crypto** ✦ FTP **Cypherpunk Archive** ftp://soda.berkeley.edu/pub/cypherpunks/Home.html

Cypress Hill Mexican-American, Cuban, and Italian-American rap trio—named for a tough Latino L.A. neighborhood—whose self-titled major label debut showed one idiosyncratic way out of GANGSTA clichés. Band leader/producer DJ Muggs (b. Lawrence Muggerud, circa 1970), whose whiny,

hectoring style is among rap's most distinctive, subverted the hip-hop norm by placing an almost ska-style emphasis on the "off" beat. Cypress Hill's rhythm, and its accompanying stiff-kneed dance, quickly became a standard part of the hip-hop vocabulary (Muggs also produced House of Pain's 1992 hit "Jump Around"). Lyrically, Cypress Hill's GANGSTA leanings ("Hand on the Pump," "How I Could Just Kill A Man") were accompanied by an obsession with pot culture ("Light Another") that was perfectly aligned with the Zeitgeist (see MARIJUANA CHIC). This was a rap band that even DEADHEADS and GRUNGE kids could embrace. On their second album, *Black Sunday* (1993), these tireless proponents of marijuana use and legalization married drug-inspired lyrics with doomy sentiment and heavy metal skull-and-dagger imagery; the record entered the charts at #1 on the strength of "Insane in the Brain" and the band, by now official spokespeople for NORML (National Organization for the Reform of Marijuana Laws), set off on the summer's LOLLAPALOOZA tour.

WEB **Cypress Hill** http://www.brad.ac.uk/~ctttaylo/lyrics/ cypress.hill/cypress.html ✦ WEB **Sony Records** http://www.sony.com/Music/ArtistInfo/CypressHill.html

Daisy Dukes Denim cut-off shorts as worn by Daisy Duke, the lead female character in late-'70s/early-'80s TV show *The Dukes of Hazzard.* These ultra-short, buttock-cleaving trews enjoyed a revival in 1992–93 and, under the quirkily spelled name "Dazzey Duks," even spawned a hit single by one-hit wonders Duice. The brisk, bass-heavy two million-seller was released by Bellmark, the same label which released the 1993 Tag Team version of the "Whoomp! (There It Is)" novelty anthem that also swept the country's sports stadia and afternoon talk shows.

dancehall See page 56.

EVAN DANDO, alterna-hunk.

Dando, Evan (b. 1967) Strikingly handsome, occasionally lucid singer-songwriter who, with his ever-changing band the Lemonheads, began his career with a string of snotty, poppy records on Boston's Taang! label. The indie world, though, was never quite comfortable with a performer as genetically gifted and suspiciously folk-pop-leaning as Dando, and it seemed his 1990 move to Atlantic Records would fulfill the Lemonheads' manifest Top 40 destiny. A punky, throwaway cover of Simon and Garfunkel's "Mrs. Robinson" was an easy score in 1992 (and one inspiration for cheap-shot fanzine *Die Evan Dando, Die*), but since then the flops have accumulated as quickly as Dando's magazine covers. Movies could yet deliver this KEANU REEVES of INDIE-ROCK from the limbo between success and credibility: he launched his acting career opposite Liv Tyler (model daughter of AEROSMITH's Steven) in 1995's *Heavy.*

WEB **Lemonheads Chords** http://comp.uark.edu/~cbray/lemon/lemon.html ✦ FTP **Discography** ftp://net.bio.net/pub/misc/music/lemonheads

Dartmouth Review The most infamous of hundreds of reactionary campus newspapers published at American universities in the heyday of Reagan youth, and bankrolled by various right-leaning foundations. Among its original staffers was Dinesh D'Souza (author of 1992's *Illiberal Education*); like D'Souza, the *Review* made its name with rabid baiting of liberals and minorities. Its most notorious pieces included "A Field Guide to the Poor" (1988), which included the line that poverty "is hardly prep," and a 1984 article effectively OUTING several students by quoting minutes from a meeting of a campus gay rights group. The *Review* got further attention for tearing down anti-apartheid shanties that stood on campus grounds in 1987, and for printing a line from *Mein Kampf* on the masthead of a 1990 issue. Once referred to in *SPY* magazine as "[*Family Ties'*] Alex P. Keatons without the charm or looks," the *Review*'s staff affected patrician poses as Dartmouth's aristocracy. Although the paper recruited members by way of pseudo-literary cocktail parties and promised a return to WASPier times, the still-extant *Dartmouth Review* derived much of its energy from middle-class Catholics from the heartland.

WEB **National Review** http://www.townhall.com/townhall/natreview/

DAT Available in Japan since 1987 and introduced to much controversy in America by Sony in 1990, DAT (Digital Audio Tape) offers digital sound on a tape smaller and lengthier than analog cassettes. DAT initially threatened the commercial potential of compact discs, which only provide recording capability for wholesale producers. The industry's fear of digitally "perfect" bootlegging ultimately resulted in the AUDIO HOME RECORDING ACT OF 1992, which forwards special consumer taxes collected on DAT tapes and players to the major recording companies. The medium, facing competition since 1992 from Philips DCC (digital compact cassette) and Sony's own sonically inferior MINIDISC, has struggled to win consumers at a relatively high price, but will likely survive as the high-end tape format even as CD's evolve to incorporate CD-PLUS and like formats. DAT's primary use is in computer network backups, high-end software piracy, recording studios, and among the fans of the GRATEFUL DEAD, PHISH, and other bands that condone audience tapers. A few labels have experimented unsuccessfully with distribution of major releases on DAT.

WEB **The dat-heads Mailing List Archive**
http://www.atd.ucar.edu/rdp/dat-heads/ **DAT WEB**
http://www.edge.net/ch/datweb.html

date rape   Forced sex by an acquaintance, accounting for more than 60 percent of reported rape cases. Although far from a new phenomenon,

---

dancehall

The term dancehall reggae (also known as ragga) has come to describe a hard-edged, up-tempo style of dance music that began to develop in urban Jamaica in the early '80s. Although it shares a set of musical and cultural associations with traditional "roots reggae," dancehall is a distinct genre on its own terms—its aggression and brazen artificiality are as far from the rural lilt of roots reggae as CRACK cocaine is from MARIJUANA.

Like American HIP-HOP, dancehall is usually created by a producer employing synthesizers and computers rather than players of instruments. Dancehall also shares hip-hop's tendency to deliver its lyrical content—whether girls, ganja, guns, or God—raw and uncut. (The two forms actually share some pre-history: one founding father of hip-hop was Kingston's Kool Herc, who brought his JA-style sound system to the South Bronx around 1970. And Jamaican "deejays" like King Stitt and U-Roy were "chatting" and rhyming over records a full decade before the release of the Sugar Hill Gang's groundbreaking 1979 hit "Rapper's Delight.")

In the years following Bob Marley's May 1981 death, the Jamaican music industry entered a new phase. Rather than creating original compositions from scratch, vocalists (whether singers or deejays) voiced the latest lyrical styles over pre-recorded rhythm tracks. Entire albums were released featuring a dozen versions of the same hit "riddim." (Old-school hold-outs included popular crooner-composers such as Gregory Isaacs and Barrington Levy.) Most of these popular instrumentals were played by well-known bands of studio musicians such as Roots Radix or the

Aggrovators (featuring drum and bass legends Sly Dunbar and Robbie Shakespeare). But in 1985, the legendary producer Prince Jammy and his engineer Bobby "Digital" Dixon put together Wayne Smith's "Under Me Sleng Teng," the song whose riddim changed everything.

Sleng Teng was originally constructed for a live sound clash between Jammy's and a rival system—not only did the new "digital" riddim win the clash, it revolutionized the sound of Jamaican popular music. The relentless, hypnotic, droning two-note bassline and the metallic, assaultive 4–4 drum beat were both programmed on a cheap Casio keyboard. Reggae producers had already been experimenting with digital bass and drum sounds, but Sleng Teng was a sonic breakthrough on a par with rapper Afrika Bambaata's appropriation of Kraftwerk for 1982's "Planet Rock"—edgy music for a brave new techno-topia. Combined with vocals like Johnnie Osborne's tongue-twisting sing-along "Budy-Bye," or Tenor Saw's haunting "Pumpkin Belly," or John Wayne's raspy-throated rap "Call the Police," Sleng Teng announced that a radical new sound had entered the world music arena.

Photo by David Corio

Dancehall deity SHABBA RANKS, *As Raw As Ever.*

Sleng Teng has since been endlessly recycled, thanks to the same streamlined digital production that made possible instant records about new slang terms and dance steps (and, in turn,

date rape first emerged as a high visibility issue on college campuses in the early–1980s as a feminist cause when Take Back the Night marches—at which women spoke out about their experiences—became common. At several colleges, anonymous lists of alleged rapists were posted in women's bathrooms. In 1983, Carleton College passed one of the nation's first sexual-harassment policies, and many other colleges and universities quickly followed, most famously ANTIOCH in Ohio. In the media the issue is more often portrayed as a conflict within feminism than as a social problem—in 1993 Princeton graduate student Katie Roiphe published *The Morning After*, arguing that "rape-crisis femi-

---

records which rapidly answered these originals). With producers like Dave Kelly, Bobby Digital, and Sly Dunbar incorporating sound and styles from electronic bloops and cartoon sound effects to Indian bhangra music and Henry Mancini movie themes, dancehall established itself as an effortlessly postmodern form.

Digital technology also meant that dancehall records could be made almost anywhere, even without a live band: cities with large West Indian populations like New York, London, and Miami became important dancehall nerve centers, and top artists like Tiger, Admiral Bailey, Yellowman, and Lt. Stitchie traveled throughout the network of reggae producers, creating new records as they went. New York City was an early dancehall stronghold, with black-radio jocks like Red Alert and Frankie Crocker mixing reggae records into their prime-time hip-hop mix shows. Many dancehall stars were Jamaican counterparts to American GANGSTA rappers: the likes of Ninjaman (who never left the island) and Cutty Ranks engaged in an arms race in their lyrics, striving to outdo each other with tales of extravagant firepower. (Ninjaman's GOLD TEETH are reputedly imprinted with images of guns.) As with gangsta, dancehall's verbal violence spilled over into real life: among the stars who have come to violent ends are Tenor Saw, Major Worries, and Nitty Gritty (who was actually killed–in self-defense, ruled the courts–by the "Don Dada" [Godfather] Super Cat in 1991).

Dancehall remained a parochial phenomenon without its own international superstar until SHABBA RANKS, a rangy Kingstonian baritone whose popularity swept neighborhoods in Kingston, New York, and London. In the late '80s his records dominated hip-hop parties and were among the first records to displace rap as JEEP music of choice on the streets of urban America. "The Jam," a duet with KRS-One on his first U.S. album, solidified the dancehall/hip-hop cross-pollination that Just-Ice, Masters of Ceremony, and Asher D & Daddy Freddy had hinted at years before, and that Patra (dancehall's First Lady), Mad Lion, Born Jamericans, and Willi One Blood carried into the mid-'90s.

Though rapid-fire ragamuffin interludes are now a familiar feature of hip-hop hits by artists from Method Man to Poor Righteous Teachers, many Americans first heard of dancehall in 1992 thanks to the homophobia of Buju Banton. The newcomer unleashed a wave of outrage with his single "Boom Bye Bye," a catchy number that bluntly advocated the slaying of gay men ("batty boys" in Jamaican parlance: "Faggots have to run / Or get a bullet in the head" ran one line, in translation). More legitimate inroads were made with hip-hop remixes like Super Cat's "Ghetto Red Hot" and Capleton's "Tour." Meanwhile, original, uncut Jamaican dancehall selections such as Chaka Demus & Pliers' "Murder She Wrote" and Terror Fabulous' "Action" have been embraced by listeners from Barcelona to Tokyo. In 1994–95 dancehall-inflected tunes like Ini Kamoze's "Here Comes the Hotsteppper" and "Boombastic" by Shaggy went to the top of the U.S. pop charts, providing further evidence that dancehall has graduated from exotic novelty to staple soundtrack of urban life in the '90s.–*Rob Kenner*

USENET **rec.music.reggae**

nism" perpetuated stereotypes of weak, asexual women.

WEB **Sexual Assault Information Page Index** http://www.cs .utk.edu/~bartley/saInfoPage.html ✦ WEB **Rape Prevention Education Program** http://pubweb.ucdavis.edu/ Documents/RPEP/rpep.htm ✦ WEB **False Rape, Abuse and Molest Reports-Index** http://www.vix.com/pub/men/falsereport/index.html ✦ USENET **talk.rape**

Davis, Mike (b. 1946) Premier social critic of L.A. and lecturer on urban theory at the Southern California Institute of Architecture. Davis' class-conscious *City of Quartz* (1990) eerily anticipated the RODNEY KING beating, L.A. RIOTS, and other forms of social breakdown with separate essays on the militarization of DARYL GATES' police force, South Central gang culture, the political economy of CRACK, and the de-industrialization of Southern California.

Davis, Tamra (b. 1963) Former Francis Coppola apprentice who graduated from the music-video world to features after working with credible acts such as N.W.A, Hüsker Dü, Black Flag, and SONIC YOUTH. After helming the stylish *Guncrazy* (a 1992 DREW BARRYMORE vehicle loosely fashioned after 1949's NOIR classic *Gun Crazy*) in three weeks for less than $1 million, Davis was hired to direct the "feminist" western *Bad Girls* (1994, also starring Barrymore). After initial shooting Twentieth Century Fox replaced her with Jonathan Kaplan and allocated a larger budget; the film still flopped. Davis' next project was *CB4*, the 1993 film billed as a rap SPINAL TAP. (Davis' husband is BEASTIE BOY Mike Diamond.) Although this suggested that comedy was not Davis' métier, she did enjoy fleeting success with *Billy Madison* (1995), a low-brow romp starring SATURDAY NIGHT LIVE's ADAM SANDLER.

Day Without Art 24 hours of shrouded statues, interrupted performances, empty picture hooks, dimmed theater lights, and other arts-related (non-) events to dramatize AIDS's toll on the artistic world. Organized since 1989 by Visual AIDS, a New York coalition of arts professionals also responsible for RED RIBBONS, as part of the annual December 1st observance of United Nations' World AIDS Day (aka International AIDS Day). By 1994, DWA reached thousands of arts institutions around the world.

WEB **AIDS and HIV—World Aids Day** http://www.ircam.fr/ solidarites/sida/1dec/index-e.html

De La Soul Long Island, New York, HIP-HOP trio whose 1989 debut, *3 Feet High and Rising*, was a benchmark for COLLEGE RAP. The new sound (whimsically called "The DAISY Age—Da Inner Sound Y'All") was based on sophomoric humor, progressive politics, and trippy aural collage which SAMPLED from sources as diverse as Liberace, Funkadelic, and Schoolhouse Rock. De La Soul—made up of Posdnuos (b. Kelvin Mercer, 1969), Trugoy the Dove (b. David Jolicoeur, 1968), and P.A. System (also "Pasemaster") Mase (b. Vincent Mason Jr., 1970)—had to settle out of court a suit from members of '60s pop group The Turtles for unauthorized use of their song "You Showed Me." The group's second LP, *De La Soul is Dead* (1991), with its shattered flowerpot cover, was a dyspeptic denunciation of the group's "hip-hop hippie" label, addressing darker issues such as drug abuse and incest. Neither fans nor critics were particularly impressed by the harder De La sound. After watching the likes of PM Dawn, Digable Planets, and Basehead garner attention with variations on their sound, De La Soul released *Buhloone Mindstate* (1993), a low-intensity nod to its newly marginal status (the title track explains, "it might blow up / but it won't go pop").

WEB **The Producer's Archive** http://www.dsi.unimi.it/Users/ Students/barbieri/awrrng.htm ✦ USENET **alt.rap**, **rec.music .hip-hop**

Deadheads With their Central American peasant clothing, lyric-marked and tie-dyed T-shirts, and occasional TRUSTAFARIAN DREADLOCKS, the recent hordes of young GRATEFUL DEAD tour-followers resemble stylized, highly codified versions of their 1960s hippie forebears. Somewhere between a psychic free-trade zone and a suburban bazaar, the parking lot scene at a Dead show is a synesthetic pit stop of finger-raising "miracle" ticket seekers, hissing NITROUS OXIDE tanks, bootlegged musical history, half-glimpsed psychedelic oddities, patchouli- and pot-scented breezes, and "kind" (neohippie for excellent) veggie burritos. Inside the hall or stadium, "tapers" (authorized bootleggers in a special section, often some 200 in number) coexist with "spinners" (twirling dancers), who might be found in the "Phil [Lesh] Zone," or the "Jerry [Garcia] Side." (There is a complex, well-established range of on-line activity to sustain "Netheads" between tours.)

Deadhead sociology took a hectic turn with the 1987 influx of "touchheads" (fans who joined after the MTV hit "Touch of Grey"), but maintained its precarious and subtle economy nevertheless. (The crux of the Grateful Dead experience was encapsulated in David Shenk and Steve Silberman's 1994 handbook *Skeleton Key: A Dictionary for Deadheads*.) 1995 saw Deadhead culture threatened by events both random and malicious. In June thousands of ticketless fans gate-crashed a Vermont show; later that month, three fans were struck by lightning at Washington, DC's RFK Stadium. The following week hundreds of fans showered Indiana police with rocks and bottles, then in Wentzville, Missouri, over 100 Deadheads were injured when a camping-ground pavilion collapsed during a storm. (Two other fans died separately in Missouri.) The Grateful Dead—whose leader Jerry Garcia had just received death threats—subsequently issued a letter asking people without tickets not to come to shows, and asking fans not to vend, for fear of attracting the ticketless element. The death of Jerry Garcia in August 1995, and the Dead's instant cancellation of their fall tour, cast doubt on the future of the Deadhead cult.

WEB **The Deadhead Home Page Index**

http://www.shore.net/~aiko/dead_html/index.html ◆ WEB

Skeleton Key: A Dictionary for Deadheads

http://www.bdd.com/newrl/bddnewrl.cgi?w=07–01–95&m=bd dprevu&p=bddnrp-skel&h=bddnrpskel1 ◆ WEB **America's Favorite Deadhead!** http://www.clark.net/pub/sinkers/ toons4.html ◆ USENET **alt.rap-gdead, rec.music.gdead**

Deal, Kim (b. 1961) Greasy-haired, afeminist icon of INDIE-ROCK cool. This former bass player has, with her own band The Breeders, garnered more attention with one MTV hit than had her previous outfit The Pixies after years of hard-won college-rock credibility. (Pixies leader Black Francis [b. 1965, Charles Michael Kitteridge Thompson] is now enjoying a modest solo career as Frank Black.) The Breeders were initially an informal Pixies side-project with Tanya Donnelly (Throwing Muses, later of Belly), who was replaced by Deal's twin sister Kelley, a former office worker. Together they created a shambling power-pop vehicle for Deal's reassuring, 40-a-day voice; they scored quickly with the MTV-propelled, hook-laden "Cannonball" (1993; video co-directed by SPIKE JONZE and SONIC YOUTH's Kim Gordon). In November 1994 Kelley was arrested in the Deals' hometown of Dayton for receiving an Emery Worldwide package containing three grams of HEROIN; she avoided jail and even a trial in part by entering a rehabilitation program at Minnesota's Hazelden Foundation. During the family difficulties, Kim Deal recorded her first solo album under the name Tammy and the Amps.

WEB **Music Kitchen: Breeders Home Page**

http://www.nando.net/music/gm/Breeders/ ◆ USENET **alt.music.alternative.female**

Photo by Brooke Williams

Chief Breeder Kim Deal, LOLLAPALOOZA '94.

Death Cigarettes Brand of otherwise-normal cigarettes launched in L.A. in 1991 (and subsequently more widely distributed) in a black package bearing a skull and crossbones logo reminiscent of the attention-getting BLACK DEATH VODKA brand.

Justifying this marketing gimmickry to the *New York Times*, Death Tobacco owner Charles Southwood said his product "disseminates an anti-smoking message directly to smokers." (In Britain, where the product is sold only by mail order, one ghoulish ad campaign for Death was banned from billboards.)

Debord, Guy (b. 1931; d. 1994) French essayist and filmmaker who helped found the Internationale Situationniste (Situationist International), an anti-art movement of café radicals that rose out of the ruins of surrealism in the '50s. On December 1, 1994, the reclusive Debord committed suicide by shooting himself at his country home. Subsequent obituaries noted that he "drank too much and wrote too little," but his slim critique of the alienation and commodification of consumer capitalism, *Society of the Spectacle* (1967), became the main text of the worldwide student-led cultural revolts in May 1968. (Situationist graffiti like "sous les pavés, la plage" ["under the paving stones, the beach"] appeared throughout Paris then). Nearly three decades later the book remains a *locus classicus* for CULTURAL STUDIES academics, anarchists, PUNKS, direct action activists, and more than a few late-century dilettantes—arguing that media and technology ("the spectacle") have reduced people to mere voyeurs of their own lives, all desires and relationships sold back as leisure products.

WEB **Situationists International** http://ernie.bgsu.edu/ ~swilbur/si.html ✦ WEB **We Go Round and Round In The Night and Are Consumed** http://english-server.hss.cmu. edu/ctheory/r-we_go_round.html/ ✦ WEB **Nothingness.Org** http://www.nothingness.org/ ✦ WEB **Situationist!** http://204.156.22.13/love/gate/debord.html

deconstruction (fashion) Mini-movement propagated by three 1980–81 graduates of the Royal Academy of Fine Arts in Antwerp, Belgium. Dries van Noten, Ann Demeulemeester and Martin Margiela took up a common style that, partly as a reaction against the designer overkill of the '80s, involved drab-colored clothes with their seams and linings left visible, and their edges often unfinished.

(Amy Spindler of the *New York Times* noted that these garments provided "a sort of asbestos suit against the bonfire of the vanities.") The deconstructionists' ideas were spread worldwide partly through shows underwritten by an export-seeking Belgian government; their influence reached its peak in the early '90s, with the designers insisting (somewhat justifiably) that the label ignored the majority of their work. According to British magazine *The Face*, Van Noten's newer, more sober designs enjoy a healthy following among style- and status-obsessed English soccer fans.

Deee-Lite Dance act whose 1990 debut single, "Groove is in the Heart," was an influential hit in both clubs and the mainstream. The record featured guest spots by Tribe Called Quest rapper Q-Tip and funk royalty Bootsy Collins and Maceo Parker alongside original Deee-Lite line-up Lady Miss Kier (b. Kierin Kirby, 1964), Super DJ Dmitry (b. Dimitri Brill, 1964), and Jungle DJ Towa Towa (b. Doug Wa-Chung, 1964). The band's crossover success with the *World Clique* album brought New York club culture overground, both musically and sartorially (Lady Miss Kier's DRAG-queen wigs, iridescent gowns, and FLUEVOG platform shoes helped further the '70S FASHION revival). After two further, less successful albums (the overtly political *Infinity Within* [1992] and the frankly sensual *Dewdrops in the Garden* [1994]), Towa Tei stopped touring with the band and released a solo album, *Future Listening* (1995).

MAIL LIST **DEEE-LITE** email majordomo@world.std.com with "subscribe deee-lite" in the message body

Deep Dish TV "The first national grassroots satellite network," a New York-based distribution network for videos of experimental art and community (usually left-leaning) reporting, set up in 1986 to take advantage of the country's disparate public access cable stations and the rising popularity of satellite dishes. Some of its biggest and most timely projects have made it to PBS. Born of Paper Tiger, a consortium of progressive TV producers, Deep Dish TV was cut off from NEA funds in 1991 after being red-baited for distributing speeches by Castro and Nicaragua's defeated Sandanista President, Daniel Ortega. In the mid '90s Deep Dish provides one of the most consistent national outlets for documentaries, broadcasting ground-zero interviews with New York CRACK addicts, Latino mental-health workers in Boston, and foot soldiers in the 1994 Chiapas uprising.

WEB **Paper Tiger TV** http://cyberwerks.com/1/flicker/orgs/papertiger ✦ USENET **alt.tv-public-access**

Def Comedy Jam Popular late-night HBO cable show created in 1992 by rap mogul RUSSELL SIMMONS. *Def Comedy Jam* stands out from the glut of televised comedy by virtue of its exclusive showcasing of black stand-ups, its near-undiluted stream of blue jokes, and the force with which they're delivered. Weekly, a series of raunchy turns whips the *Def Comedy Jam* audience into a burlesque frenzy with material that flies directly in the face of POLITICAL CORRECTNESS, and drives a wedge into African-American class and gender divides. *DCJ* apologists argue that the overwhelming number of pussy jokes from male comedians is redeemed by the quantity of dick jokes from the show's female stand-ups; black superstar Bill Cosby, on the other hand, called the program a "minstrel show," noting that "HBO tells African-Americans, 'You can't come on the show unless you undignify your Africanness.'"

Depo-Provera Synthetic hormone injection which prevents pregnancy for three months at a time. Although the contraceptive method had been used around the world by some 15 million women since the late '60s, FDA approval for the U.S. did not come until 1992. At $30 per injection, DP is cheaper in up-front costs than the $600, five-year implant NORPLANT, and it lacks the latter's telltale physical evidence. In March 1994 Surgeon General Joycelyn Elders accused DP's maker Upjohn and Norplant's maker Wyeth-Ayerst of profiteering at the expense of unwanted pregnancies: "the price of Norplant and Depo Provera is too high in this country for a large portion of working poor women

to realize contraceptive equality." India and Mexico have been experimenting for years with once-a-month injections—Cyclofem and Mesigyna—that tend to be less disruptive to the menstrual cycle. Depo-Provera, which is closely related to progesterone (a female hormone that can lower the sex drive), is also used to "chemically castrate" convicted sex offenders.

WEB **Contraception** http://www.cmpharm.ucsf.edu/~troyer/safesex/contraception.html

Depp, Johnny (b. 1963) Photogenic Hollywood enigma renowned for turning down commercial scripts. Depp came to Hollywood with his Florida rock band The Kids, but ended up becoming a teen idol via Fox TV's fluffy teen-detective drama *21 Jump Street* (1987). Exiting the series after nearly four years, he immediately teamed up with left-field filmmakers JOHN WATERS (*Cry-Baby*, 1990) and TIM BURTON (*Edward Scissorhands*, 1990). Depp continued to eschew mainstream Hollywood with offbeat, neurotic roles in 1993's *What's Eating Gilbert Grape* and *Benny & Joon*; and in Burton's *Ed Wood* (1994, a whimsical performance as the transvestite movie director).

Depp's penchant for high-profile romances is at odds with his oft-stated contempt for the media: while squiring WINONA RYDER, he famously had "Winona Forever" TATTOOED on his right bicep (later removed letter by letter). More recently Depp romanced model KATE MOSS; while staying with her at New York's Mark hotel in September 1994 he trashed $9,767 worth of furniture and was carted off before TV news cameras to spend a night in jail. (Damages paid for, no charges brought.) In 1995 Capitol Records signed Depp's musical side-project, P, also featuring the BUTTHOLE SURFERS' Gibby Haynes.

Details Originally a downtown New York style magazine, *Details* was bought in 1990 by publishing giant Condé Nast and re-launched as a young men's fashion magazine. After struggling to find an audience, the overhauled monthly hit pay dirt when it redefined itself as the GENERATION X manual.

Although *Details* has a foundation in fashion and celebrity culture, the magazine has most successfully used sex to define itself, as evidenced in an annual sex issue, highly charged photo shoots, and personal essays on the subject including those of the sex columnist and star writer ANKA RADAKOVICH.

DiCaprio, Leonardo (b. 1974) Lanky, puppy-ish actor whose performance as JOHNNY DEPP's backwards brother in the 1993 movie *What's Eating Gilbert Grape* earned him a Best Supporting Actor Oscar nomination. DiCaprio's potential has been announced by *This Boy's Life* (1993), in which he held his ground against a scenery-chewing Robert De Niro. A lull in productivity ended with his appearance in 1995 Sharon Stone Western bomb *The Quick and the Dead* (directed by SAM RAIMI). That same year DiCaprio grabbed two coveted roles: junkie/poet Jim Carroll (opposite underwear icon MARKY MARK) in the film of Carroll's book *The Basketball Diaries*, and French poet Arthur Rimbaud (opposite David Thewlis' Paul Verlaine) in *Total Eclipse*.

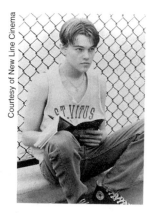

Courtesy of New Line Cinema

LEONARDO DICAPRIO in *The Basketball Diaries* (1995).

Dick, Philip K. (b. 1928, d. 1982) The spiritual godfather of CYBERPUNK science fiction, Philip K. Dick wrote more than forty novels and dozens of short stories that envisioned alternate worlds only barely held together by the plaster and greasepaint of quotidian reality. A prolific master of '50s pulp SF, Dick's first masterpiece was his award-winning alternative history of postwar America, *The Man in the High Castle* (1962). Propelled by scotch and speed, Dick's '60s work involved increasingly fantastic scenarios of looped time, nested hallucinations, unreliable memory, and paranoid despair. In 1974 the burned-out author experienced a revelatory "divine invasion" sent courtesy of a "Vast Active Living Intelligence System," or VALIS. Dick's novels *The Divine Invasions* (1981), *VALIS* (1981), and *The Transmigration of Timothy Archer* (1982) represent his subsequent attempts to reconcile radical ontological doubt with ethics based on human empathy. Some of Dick's more influential works include his 1968 novel *Do Androids Dream of Electric Sheep?* (adapted as the 1982 Ridley Scott film *Blade Runner*), and 1977's *A Scanner Darkly*, widely regarded as one of the best-ever novels about drugs. His short story "We Can Remember It For You Wholesale" inspired director Paul Verhoeven's 1990 Arnold Schwarzenegger vehicle, *Total Recall*.

USENET **alt.books.phil-k-dick** ✦ WEB **PKD FAQ**
http://www.interport.net/~regulus/pkd/pkd-int.html

digital cash Electronic exchange of money without coin or paper. The commercialization of the INTERNET has lent currency to the ideas of David Chaum, who is largely credited with devising a system of "digital coins" rendered difficult to steal or forge using public-key cryptography. Chaum envisions an extensive system of "micropayments," where users are charged page-by-page for penny access to online information. Consumers first experienced digital cash in the 1980s when mail-order companies began accepting credit card payment over the telephone without requiring written signatures, but Chaum's systems add anonymity—a fact that fills U.S. law enforcement officials with fears of untraceable bribery, money laundering, drug trafficking, and smuggling.

WEB **Digicash Home Page** http://www.digicash.com/
Network Payment Mechanisms and Digital Cash
http://ganges.cs.tcd.ie/mepeirce/project.html

digital TV satellite System for delivering crisp images and CD-quality sound to television viewers via a digital signal broadcast from space instead of cable. Also called DSS (Direct Satellite System), the satellite beams down a signal containing more than 140 television channels and 40 radio channels (although local programming is largely absent). Each television program and movie is coded with a digital title that includes the show's name, start & stop time, stars, and—shades of the V-CHIP—a rating. The first system was set aloft by a partnership between GM Hughes Electronics Corp. and Thomson Consumer Electronics, the parent company of RCA, in a $750 million venture called DirecTV that has paid off handsomely, with more than half a million people signing up within the first six months of operations. The Hughes satellite was launched in 1994 and started taking its first customers later that year. A competing system, Primestar, has the backing of the cable industry but uses older technology; a third, USSB, uses the same satellites as DirecTV but offers different programming. Cost to consumers: about $700 for the receiver, then a monthly fee between $6 and $60, depending on which programs are ordered.

USENET **alt.satellite.tv** ✦ WEB **Satellite TV Weekly**
http://www.wcs-online.com/sat-tv/

Dilbert Scott Adams (b. 1957) began drawing his daily comic strip about the rigors of modern corporate life in 1989 to kill time during boring meetings. And while he still attends boring meetings (he develops ISDN applications for Pacific Bell), his strip currently appears in some 400 papers. Adams's strip riffs on office politics, esoteric management strategies, technological snafus, and the generally demeaning experience of corporate environments. His title character resembles a mature Bart SIMPSON wearing a curiously erect necktie. Scott Adams suggests that corporate life is a sort of purgatory; hence the occasional appearance of Phil From Heck, the Prince of Insufficient Light, who takes care of business a little too insignificant for Hell. Adams, a self-confessed INTERNET junkie, acknowledges that most of his ideas originate as emailed suggestions. *Bring Me the Head of Willie the Mailboy* (1995) is a recent Dilbert collection.

EMAIL scottadams@aol.com ✦ WEB **Dilbert** http://www.rpi.edu/~tatnaa/dilbert/dilbert.html

Dinah Shore Golf Classic Palm Springs golf tournament named after the late talk show host (and former paramour of super-macho actor Burt Reynolds) that occasions the "biggest lesbian party of the year." Every March thousands of gay women converge on the town for a series of dances and balls loosely associated with the Nabisco-sponsored event. Palm Springs itself is something of a gay tourist Mecca: in the official visitor's guide, the Greek letter lambda identifies dozens of gay accommodations in the town.

Dinosaur Jr. Indolence has never been a recognized route to stardom, but that was the path taken by Dinosaur Jr.'s lank-haired frontman J Mascis (b. Joseph Mascis, 1965). From Dinosaur Jr.'s 1985 debut (with the then-eponymous *Dinosaur*) onwards, Mascis' high-decibel mood swings and near-catatonic public persona helped create the stereotype of the INDIE-ROCK loser-star. Bass player Lou Barlow departed acrimoniously in 1989 to pursue his prolific LO-FI project Sebadoh, and Mascis effectively went solo, taking almost three years to deliver his major label debut album *Green Mind*, the 1991 record that formalized Dinosaur Jr.'s signature of melodic pop songs sullied with noisy eruptions. So vigorous was the harvesting of callow ALTERNATIVE youth after NIRVANA's '91-'92 breakthrough that older acts with a shred of credibility and a workable back catalog were ushered into the pantheon. Rightly accredited as a seminal alt-rock influence, Mascis would soon grace daytime MTV in SPIKE JONZE's golfing-in-Manhattan video for 1994's "Feel the Pain."

WEB **IUMA: Dinosaur, Jr.** http://www.iuma.com/Warner/html/Dinosaur,_Jr..html

Photo by Brooke Williams

J Mascis of DINOSAUR JR. wields a drumstick

dis African-American slang for insult; short for "disrespect." When PUBLIC ENEMY's Chuck D. appeared on *Nightline* in January, 1992, he corrected his own speech, saying "as a black person [I have] been tired of being dis—respected," but most viewers already knew what "dis" meant. HIP-HOP had popularized and disseminated the term, making it part of the American vernacular. By 1995, even white-bread figures like former *Today Show* host Jane Pauley could use the term without pause or apology on CONAN O'BRIEN's talk show.

WEB **The Totally Unofficial Rap Dictionary** http://www.sci.kun.nl/thalia/rapdict/dict_en.html

Diseased Pariah News Brazenly morbid ZINE by and for people with AIDS (PWA's). Founded in 1991 by Silicon Valley computer freelancer Beowulf Thorne (b. 1964), the semi-regular publication paved the way for the literary *Art and Understanding* and glossier "positive" publications aimed at the one million infected Americans; these included the Chicago-based *Plus Voice* and New York-based *Poz*. The latter was financed when the founder, Sean Strube, used a VIATICAL SETTLEMENT to cash in his life insurance policy. *DPN* is still the cheekiest, with coverlines like "How To Tell if Your Loved One is Dead" ("increased sleeping during the day," "abrupt cessation of sarcasm," "relatives looting apartment") and essays such as "Get Your Fucking RED RIBBON out of My Face." One motto has it, "we don't care how you got HIV, as long as you're not a whining and hateful virgin about it."

DMT First isolated by V. L. Stromberg in 1954, DMT is a tryptamine psychedelic related to psilocybin. Known as the "businessman's trip" in the 1960s because of its very intense, short-acting properties, DMT was repopularized in recent years mainly by TERENCE MCKENNA, who touted it as the ultimate psychedelic. (It is also an active ingredient in ayahuasca, a ritual psychedelic used by South American tribes.) Described by British Zen philosopher Alan Watts as akin to "being shot out of an atomic cannon," DMT is usually smoked in freebase form in doses averaging between 30 to 60 milligrams. Within seconds of inhalation, consensus reality evaporates, a shrill carrier tone is heard, and the subject enters a disembodied hyperspace of bright, swirling colors that often leads to apparent contact with nonhuman intelligences, such as the "self-transforming mechanical elves" described by McKenna. The initial rush is over within minutes, with the user resuming quotidian existence within half an hour.

WEB **dmt.experience** http://hyperreal.com/drugs/psychedelics/mckenna/dmt.experience✦ USENET **alt.drugs.psychedelics** ✦ WEB **Hyperreal** http://www.hyperreal.com/

"do me" feminism "A new generation of women thinkers . . . are embracing sex (and men!). Call them 'do me' feminists," announced the February 1994 cover story of *Esquire* magazine. The magazine discovered feminists championing no-regret, no-guilt sexual liberation; and contrasted them with the supposedly prudish '70s feminists (who were themselves called "sluts" in their time). The article was illustrated with kittenish poses by NAOMI WOLF, THIRD WAVE leader Rebecca Walker, and a cross-section of young authors enjoying recent publishing successes such as *Future Sex*'s LISA PALAC, DATE RAPE skeptic Katie Roiphe, and self-styled "sex guru" SUSIE BRIGHT. As the flip term found media currency, Bright complained that *Esquire* had reduced the women's movement equal-pay and anti-discrimination causes to a "sexual beauty pageant," equating, in the words of columnist Anna Quindlen, "good feminism" with "great sex." An exasperated SUSAN FALUDI later suggested her own new catchphrase for revisionists: "pod feminists," after the sci-fi classic *Invasion of the Body Snatchers*.

"Don't Ask, Don't Tell" Popular paraphrase of the U.S. military's confusing policy towards its homosexuals. The policy was adopted in 1993 after President Bill Clinton—under strenuous pressure from those putatively worried about troop morale—backed away from his campaign promise to end government discrimination against gays and lesbians. (During the campaign gay activists had heavily invested in the symbolic value of lifting the military ban, likening it to Harry Truman's integration of blacks in the U.S. military after WWII.) The '93 policy, which was further elaborated to "Don't Ask, Don't Tell, Don't Pursue," actually left individual commanders with considerable discretion to "ask" and "pursue." Nevertheless, successive court decisions have tended to favor "don't care" by disallowing discharges under the prevailing anti-gay rules.

MAIL LIST **dont-tell** email dont-tell-request@choice. princeton.edu

Do Something Foundation Charity cofounded in 1994 by *MELROSE PLACE* heart-throb Andrew Shue to promote community projects among the young through seed grants for recycling, day-care, tutoring, and the like. Money is raised from sales of $15 T-shirts and corporate sponsors such as Guess?, MCI, Blockbuster, and *ROLLING STONE*. In Shue's hometown of Newark, New Jersey, it helps fund a program to reform kids who steal cars (see JOYRIDING) by teaching them auto repair. In Chicago, graffiti artists are hired to paint educational murals and in Florida, a GREEN TEEN group campaigns for clean water laws. Shue, who says he was inspired to "do something" by his exposure to Third World poverty while playing pro soccer in Zimbabwe, has been cut off trying to talk about the program in TV interviews.

WEB **Philanthropy Related Links** http://www.egr.duke.edu/ DOHP.philanthropy.html

do-rag Headgear so named because it is used to cover up the hairdo. Originally the provenance of older black women (as on Aunt Jemima product boxes), the do-rag is fashioned from a square of material (usually a patterned bandanna) which is folded, tied behind the head, and stretched over the forehead. Common among prison inmates, the do-rag acquired fashion currency in the late '80s/early '90s through its use as an insignia among feuding L.

A. gangs (Crips—blue, Bloods—red). Its outlaw cachet was appreciated by would-be macho types and hairdressers.

Doc Martens Footwear uniform of young individualists worldwide. Doc Martens shoes were invented in 1945 by Claus Maertens, a German doctor who needed a comfortable shoe after a skiing accident; Maertens formed a rubber sole from a tire and heat-sealed it to an upper, trapping a cushion of air. Patented two years later, the Maertens design found favor as an orthopedic shoe among older women; on April 1st, 1960, "Doc Martens" were first produced under license in England by R. Griggs & Co. The company's original, eight-eyelet, 1460 model boots—still a staple today—were adopted in the 1960s by English SKINHEADS, who coveted their potential for violence. PUNK rockers revived "Docs" in the 1970s, and the shoes have been youth-culture staples ever since, in ever-expanding forms and colors. With their simple utilitarian design, Doc Marten shoes and boots are the perfect anti-fashion statement. According to *Forbes* magazine in January 1995, the U.S. accounted for only 3 percent of 1990 sales for Doc Marten's export subsidiary Air Wear, and nearly 20 percent by 1994.

WEB **Stage Clothes Shoes & Boots** http://www.w2.com/ docs2/s/scdmhome.html

Doherty, Shannen (b. 1971) Actress whose 1991–1994 portrayal of Brenda Walsh on *BEVERLY HILLS 90210* brought her teenybopper fame that was later rivaled by notorious off-camera antics. Doherty, an actress since age 10, had an attitude that preceded her reputation; the crew of the seminal teen satire *Heathers* (1989) reportedly nicknamed her the BMW—Bitch and Moan Witch. Tantrums and tardiness on the set of *90210* made her a pariah with her fellow cast members, to the point where Luke Perry successfully pleaded for an end to his character's romance with Doherty. Meanwhile, Doherty became a tabloid staple via drunken diva fits, bar brawls, and bed checks.

Despite her non-FAMILY VALUES behavior, Doherty fancies herself a social and political conservative: she led the 1992 Republican National Convention in the Pledge of Allegiance, allegedly while "completely pickled." The latter revelation came from a RNC staffer's letter to *The I Hate Brenda Newsletter*, a 1992 spin-off from the L.A. ZINE *Ben Is Dead*.

In September 1993, Doherty tied the knot with suntan heir Ashley Hamilton (son of George), whom she'd known for a matter of weeks. They divorced after five months. In 1994, Doherty was dismissed from *90210*, reportedly because Aaron Spelling felt she was a bad influence on his daughter Tori. Doherty soon fell into a romance with hot young director ROB WEISS, and appeared in the 1995 film *Mallrats* by hot young director KEVIN SMITH.

Don't Panic Apparel company founded in 1990 by former stand-up comedian Skyler Thomas (b. 1963) after his "Nobody Knows I'm Gay" T-shirts became a hot seller at that year's L.A. Gay and Lesbian Pride Celebration. Thomas has since shown an aptitude for unleashing media viruses: "I Can't Even Think Straight" and "Closets are for Clothes" were hits in the gay world before he broadened out in early 1993 with "Leave Chelsea Alone." (This noble defense of beleaguered first daughter CHELSEA CLINTON reportedly prompted a note of thanks from the President himself.) Skyler has conceived the "Bad Hair Day" hat as well as jewelry, bed sheets, and a Christmas tree decoration with the RED RIBBON of AIDS awareness (a portion of the proceeds go to AIDS research). By 1995 Don't Panic had annual revenues of over $2 million, with six retail outlets in America and one in London.

Doom Gory, technically innovative 3D kill-'em-all computer game which defined the post-MORTAL KOMBAT look of arcade mayhem. Despite absurd features such as the ability to chainsaw enemies (and watch their bodies jerk in response), Doom escaped hand-wringing over VIDEOGAME violence because it first ran on business computers. Key to Doom's success—besides the vertiginous graphics—was its embrace of the computer network, both in the game's early-'90s shareware distribution over the INTERNET, and in the ability to blast up to three network-linked co-workers (the world's largest computer chip maker Intel famously banned the game after office productivity took a nose dive). The game was also highly customizable, leading to dozens of high-quality amateur adaptations that substituted the monster cast of *Aliens* or simply a gaggle of purple Barney dinosaurs as antagonists. Doom II, the sequel, sold more than 500,000 copies for Christmas 1994 according to its Texas-based creator id Software, which also has a movie deal with Ivan "*Ghostbusters*" Reitman. Quake, the company's next game, promises to link online an unlimited numbers of players, conjuring up images of cyberspace consumed in a virtual World War III.

WEB **DoomGate** http://doomgate.cs.buffalo.edu/ ✦ USENET **alt.games.doom, rec.games.computer.doom** ✦ MAIL LIST **Doom Editing Mailing List** email majordomo@nvg.unit.no with "subscribe doom-editing" in the message ✦ FTP ftp://wcarchive.cdrom.com

Dorff, Stephen (b. 1974) Prematurely jaded movie actor, sometime friend of R.E.M.'s Michael Stipe and a satellite of the culture-maker power-axis whose prominent members include SPIKE JONZE and CELEBUTOT Sofia Coppola. Dorff cut his teeth on sitcoms like *Empty Nest*, *Family Ties*, and *What a Dummy* before making his feature-film debut as a South African boxer in *The Power of One* (1992). As doomed Beatle Stu Sutcliffe in *Backbeat* (1994) Dorff garnered the kind of press reaction that often precedes a major breakthrough. He followed up with a role in the lamentable 1995 flick *S.F.W.* as generational spokesrebel Clifford Spab; the film's title (a naughty acronym for "So Fucking What") was intended as an outrageous statement, but it merely ended up as ammunition for its numerous critics.

Doucet, Julie (b. 1965) On the cover of the first issue of her sporadically released *Dirty Plotte* comic, this French Canadian artist pictured herself at a kitchen table full of books and bottles, her hair in tangles, underwear torn, with blood-red paint dripping from her nails and mouth. *Plotte* (Quebeçois slang for vagina) is Doucet's erotically charged vehicle for excitedly paranoid, self-lacerating meditations on sexuality, menstruation, claustrophobia, bestiality, alcoholism, and high-risk decadence. In 1993 *Drawn & Quarterly* published *Leve le Poisson* (*Lift Your Leg, My Fish Is Dead*), an anthology of Doucet's work. Doucet began including other artists in *Dirty Plotte*, but returned solo in 1995 with "A Fine School," a 23-page autobiographical tale about art school.

Dr. Dre (b. Andre Young, 1965) With the first release on his Death Row records this former N.W.A producer-rapper could claim to have changed the face of HIP-HOP. Dre's unanticipated 3-times platinum album *The Chronic* (1992) turned a clutch of funk classics into a new form dubbed "G-Funk" (as in GANGSTA funk). Juddering basslines lulled listeners into a mid-tempo stupor while high-end '70s synths wove a hypnotic top-end around implacable GANGSTA threats; three straight *Chronic* hits were accompanied by Dre-directed videos evoking an idyllic GANGSTA lifestyle (the title is an alias for MARIJUANA).

Dre, once a member of the obscure, effetely clad funk group World Class Wreckin' Cru, had earned respect as a producer during his N.W.A tenure, creating diverse hits for fellow band member EAZY-E, Texas rhymer the D.O.C., female rap trio J.J. Fad, and tiny-voiced R&B singer Michel'le. *The Chronic*, released on his (and his formidable partner Marion "Suge" Knight's) Death Row Records, confirmed him as an astute businessman: Dre used the album as a proving ground for Death Row artists, including SNOOP DOGGY DOGG and the Dogg Pound. The SOUNDTRACK to 1993's *Above the Rim* was another notable success for the label that was later to find itself at the center of the 1995 media firestorm over TIME WARNER's corporate responsibility.

In late 1994 Dre announced that he intended to further extend his franchise by reuniting with former bandmate ICE CUBE on an album to be titled *Helter Skelter*. The video for the "Natural Born Killaz" single expensively spoofed tabloid stories like the O.J. Simpson murder and the MENENDEZ BROTHERS case. In 1995 Dre found himself doing five months in Pasadena City Jail for parole violation (he broke a fellow record-producer's jaw in 1992). His prior offenses included assaulting TV host Dee Barnes in 1991 and hitting a police officer in a New Orleans hotel in 1992. "Suge" Knight plead no contest in February 1995 to assault with a deadly weapon on two rappers back in 1992. Eazy-E had previously accused the former football player of using duress to end Dr. Dre's contract with his Ruthless Records.

WEB **The Producer's Archive** http://www.dsi.unimi.it/Users/Students/barbieri/awrrng.htm ✦ USENET **alt.rap,** **rec.music.hip-hop**

Dr. Scholl's Exercise Sandals In 1992, like its frumpy health-slipper cousin the BIRKENSTOCK, the Dr. Scholl's Exercise Sandal was issued a new visa by fashion's immigration officials. The first example of orthopedic-chic, the shoe was invented by Dr. William Scholl in 1961 and marketed mainly through drugstores. The distinctive wooden-soled slip-on, with its single leather strap, promised, with the ingenious disciplinary action of the "toe grip," to tone leg muscles. Discontinued in 1985, but reintroduced in 1994, the plain, functional summer staple found a new life when designers Michael Kors and Isaac Mizrahi sent it clomping down the catwalk. (Some would say it takes models' legs to imbue Dr. Scholl's with sex appeal.) Couture cobbler Gucci spruced up the ergonomic mule with color and a shiny buckle, and the GAP proffered its take, with a dead-ringer at $18. Dr. Scholl's were also the perfect accessory at a time when street fashion clothes were mimicking cafeteria workers' and waitresses' uniforms.

draft registration Anachronistic Cold War leftover which requires young men to register for the draft within 30 days of their 18th birthday; a related enforcement effort denies federal jobs and college loans to nonregistrants. The pseudo-draft is the only surviving element of President Jimmy Carter's election-year response to the Soviet invasion of Afghanistan (the grain embargo and Olympic boycott having been consigned to "Carter Malaise" answers on *Jeopardy*). The Reagan administration, however, turned this Russian-baiting proclamation into a loyalty test for young Americans. A March 1994 Pentagon report argued that the $29 million Selective Service program could be safely scrapped "without irreparable damage to national security" (today's wars being too brief for conscription), but President Clinton renewed the program that September.

drag Formerly transgressive dress code which crossed over from gay culture in the early '90s. Drag queens—often treated as an embarrassment by the modern, post-Stonewall Gay Rights Movement of the '70s and '80s—first had to establish their place within the modern gay world. Instrumental was New York City's annual WIGSTOCK festival, started in 1984 by the Lady Bunny. Though drag performances are traditionally exercises in lip-synching, they have more recently become full-fledged performance art pieces featuring live singing and speaking. Old-time drag icons Judy (Garland), Liza (Minnelli) and Barbra (Streisand) have been supplemented with contemporaries like Taylor Dayne, RICKI LAKE, and Patsy and Edina of *ABSOLUTELY FABULOUS*. By 1995, there was also a small but growing contingent of female drag performers, or drag kings, such as L.A.'s Split Britches.

Drag has been a respectable part of mass entertainment since before Tony Curtis dragged up in 1959's *Some Like It Hot*, but the subculture itself was brought overground in 1991 by the VOGUING documentary *Paris is Burning*. Jaye Davidson's 1992 Oscar-nominated performance in *The Crying Game* was followed by a slew of cross-dressing films: *M. Butterfly* (1993), *Orlando* (1993), *Priscilla Queen of the Desert* (1994), 1995's *To Wong Foo, Thanks for Everything, Julie Newmar* and Wigstock documentary, and, in-production, a remake of French drag classic *La Cage aux Folles* (1978) starring Robin Williams. In 1993, singer RUPAUL became the first drag pop star and two years later was anointed the

official M.A.C. cosmetics girl. During that time, performers like EVAN DANDO, U2, NIRVANA, and Duran Duran also dabbled in drag. Fashion designers like TODD OLDHAM and Thierry Mugler began featuring cross-dressed models in their fashion shows. De-sexualized drag—comedians Robin Williams as Mrs. Doubtfire; Mike Myers as Linda Richman; and Martin Lawrence as Shenehneh, for example—made for even broader exposure.

Although drag queens are a big favorite of sex-thinker CAMILLE PAGLIA, there is a strain of resentment among many feminists, who see the fetishization of bitchiness, corsets and insanely high heels as inherently oppressive, rendering drag performances little more than minstrel shows.

WEB **Above and Beyond Gender Links** http://199.170.0.46/cb/tg/res.html

The Samuel Goldwyn Company

WIGSTOCK 1994–a decade of DRAG.

Dragonball ANIME import from Japan in the vein of *Star Blazers* and *Speed Racer*, but far more violent and profitably merchandised than either. Loosely based on the Chinese tale of the Monkey King, *Dragonball*, created by Akiya Toriyama, follows the story of Son Goku, an innocent martial artist from another planet, as he searches the Earth with a motley group of friends for the five mystical Dragonballs that can call forth the all-powerful Dragon God. Throughout Asia and parts of Europe, *Dragonball* has been a toy and accessory megahit, with best-selling items ranging from VIDEOGAMES to figurines to snack crackers. Christmas 1994 sales of *Dragonball* products in

Japan were second only to *Sailor Moon* and far ahead of *The Mighty Morphin Power Rangers*— a fact that must have figured in plans to option and Americanize *Dragonball* for Saturday morning syndication in the U.S. starting in fall 1995.

WEB **Dragon Ball/Dragon Ball Z** http://cent1.lancs.ac.uk/ TB/dragonball.html ✦ WEB **Dragonball Z** http://www.ccs.neu.edu/home/dquonjr/dragonball/

dreadlocks Hairstyle dating back to the 1920s and the founding of the Afro-Caribbean religion Rastafarianism. Rastas outlawed the combing or cutting of hair, citing the Biblical injunction of Leviticus 21:5: "They shall not make baldness upon their head . . ." The name dreadlocks was adopted to mock non-believers' aversion to the look; the term was popularized internationally by the 1975 Bob Marley song "Natty Dread" ("natty," in this case, meaning "knotty"). In the 1980s, significant numbers of non-Rastafarian blacks began wearing dreads as fashion, and by the early '90s, trend-conscious whites followed suit. Those unable to grow the right kind of hair can pay stylists to graft pre-made locks of real or synthetic hair onto their heads. The resulting pseudo-dreads, sometimes called "African" or "Nubian" locks, allow SNOW-BOARDERS, musicians, and models to sport an exotic look without the pain and mess of, say, body-PIERCING.

WEB **The Jammin Reggae Archives Home Page** http://orpheus.ucsd.edu/jammin/ ✦ WEB **The Marley Story Board** http://www.netaxs.com/~aaron/Marley/Bulletin.html ✦ WEB **Rasta/Patois Dictionary** http://www.willamette.edu/ ~tjones/languages/rasta-lang.html

dream pop Primarily British music movement based on the surrealistic and soporific combination of blurry, dreamy vocals and layers of white-noise guitar. With its roots in the AMBIENT experiments of Brian Eno and (more directly) Scotland's post-PUNK Cocteau Twins, dream pop was pioneered by the London quartet My Bloody Valentine, which rose to prominence on the strength of two dense, droning LPs (1988's *Isn't Anything,* 1991's *Loveless*)

and improbably loud live shows. MBV touched off a slew of derivative acts, including Slowdive, Ride, Swervedriver, Chapterhouse, Lush, Curve, and the Cranes. The dream pop bands were lionized by the capricious British music press, which later took to dismissing them as "shoegazers" for their affectless stage presence.

WEB **Evan Olcott's My Bloody Valentine Page** http://sunshine.io.com/~eolcott/ ✦ WEB **My Bloody Valentine Home Page** http://www.itp.tsoa.nyu.edu/~student/brendonm/ mbv1.html

drug test Screening for drug use is increasingly required for government and corporate workers and job applicants, amateur and pro athletes, and even—following River Phoenix's death, which cost film insurers $5.7 million—big-budget movie stars. The most common test, the Emit d.a.u. (drug abuse urine), is also the least accurate, infamous for flagging Advil users as potheads. Follow-up Gas-Liquid Chromatography (GLC), Thin Layer Chromotagraphy (TLC), or Radioimmonoassay (RIA) tests are more accurate and costly, but they are often skipped. Drug testing has been a major growth business, with sales of more than $100 million in 1993. Recent years have also seen a spate of controversial home tests marketed to parents as a way of checking up on children, including a DrugAlert kit (consisting of a moist pad that is wiped across a desk or counter and then sent to the maker's New Jersey police lab for testing), a home urine test from Parent's Alert of Atlanta (accompanying instructions advise "seeking professional help" if "your child refuses" to cooperate), and a $75 RIA test from Psychemedics that can detect drug use from hair samples.

The Supreme Court has tended to favor arguments about public safety over privacy, ruling in 1989 that railroad workers should be randomly tested. (In his dissent, Justice Thurgood Marshall warned "acceptance of dragnet . . . testing ensures that the first, and worst, casualty of the war on drugs will be the precious liberties of our citizens.") In June 1995 the Supreme Court ruled that random drug tests could be given to all high-school athletes, opening the door for random tests of all students.

GOPHER **The Great Usenet Just-Say-No-to-Piss-Tests Project** gopher://gopher.well.sf.ca.us:70/00/Politics/piss.list ✦ WEB **Drug Testing** http://www.paranoia.com/drugs/drug.testing/

drumming The spectacle of the midshow drummer showcase that was always a key part of the GRATEFUL DEAD's second-set drum jams is an arcane version of RAVE's rhythmic immersion. Drum circles gradually became an integral DIY facet of the preshow parking lot scene at Dead shows, and went on to capture the attention of would-be neoprimitives and rhythmically entranced trippers. Robert Bly and the 1970s men's movement reintroduced white guys to the joy and power of drum circles (women's drumming groups can also be found). In New York's Central Park during summer, a MULTICULTURAL drum circle provides a constantly shifting beat for hundreds of ROLLERBLADERS gliding around them. The drum circle phenomenon is lastly a large part of the percussive folk music of the MTV-exposed New Jersey band Rusted Root.

USENET **rec.music.makers.percussion** ✦ MAIL LIST **Rusted Root** email jesse@eye.com

dry beer Created in 1987 by Japanese brewer Asahi, dry beer had a paradoxical appeal: it lacked basic beer-like properties such as bite and aftertaste. It was also said to not cause bad breath. (The process uses a special yeast that is later removed—along with brewing grit—using ceramic filters.) Following the heavily promoted U.S. launch of Michelob Dry in 1988, other American brewers followed suit. Sales eventually hit a plateau, however, possibly because Americans were unable to adequately grasp the concept of "dry" as it pertained to beer. Brewers largely abandoned the idea in 1994, and instead put their energy behind the new, more easily explained ICE BEER.

WEB **World-Wide Web Virtual Library: Beer & Brewing** http://www.mindspring.com/~jlock/wwwbeer.html ✦ USENET **rec.food.drink.beer, alt.beer**

DSM-IV Fourth edition of the *Diagnostic and Statistical Manual of Mental Disorders* (1994) and one of the leading indicators of America's current therapeutic mania. This shrink's bible is mainly used for diagnosis and insurance reimbursement, but its sales—more than a million copies between 1987 and 1993 for *DSM-III*, or more than 50 copies for each of the estimated 40,000 psychiatrists in the country—suggest that the manual is a best-seller for the hardcore self-help/hypochondria crowd. Compiled by the American Psychiatric Association, the 1994 edition catalogues and codes more than 300 mental disorders, opening it to criticism that it pathologizes everyday stress. (Adolescents who "defy or refuse to comply with adult's rules'" suggests the possibility of Oppositional Defiant Disorder, code number 313.81; bad writing is a leading symptom of Disorder of Written Expression, code 315.2.)

WEB **Psychiatry Online** http://www.cityscape.co.uk/users/ad88/psych.htm

dub Afro-Caribbean psychedelic music of sound subtraction. In dub, the producer becomes the center of the Jamaican reggae experience, shining an aural X-ray onto the sound to illuminate the bass and drums at its skeletal framework; vocals are sparse, other instruments drop in and out dramatically, and sound effects are added seemingly at random. By 1970, Lee "Scratch" Perry, Joe Gibbs, Bunny Lee and other producers' dub "versions" were staples of Jamaican single B-sides; King Tubby came next, raising further the level of technical sophistication. Today Adrian Sherwood, the Mad Professor, and Jah Shaka, are dub's chief practitioners, while the music's production tricks have become staples of HOUSE, TECHNO, and AMBIENT recordings.

USENET **rec.music.reggae**

E! Entertainment Television
Cable network devoted to round-the-clock entertainment coverage, usually determined by the promotional agendas of its subjects. E! was originally founded in 1987 as "Movietime," a channel sinking under heavy rotation movie trailers and stale infotainment segments; in 1989, the network was sold to a cooperative including HBO, Warner Communications, and United Artists. Lee Masters, creator of such MTV successes as REMOTE CONTROL and *The Week in Rock* was appointed to mastermind the restructuring of the network; his dedication included frequent donning of a mohawk wig shaped like the E! logo. E! was launched June 1, 1990, rolling out new long-form programming targeted primarily at a female demographic: notable shows have included the talk-show round-up TALK SOUP; *Fashion File*, a surreally paced, behind-the-seams look at the fashion industry; and *The Gossip Show*, a low-budget video syndication of the country's print columnists tinged by an air of competitive desperation. E! is one of the nation's foremost narcotainment laboratories, devoting hours of live coverage to Academy Awards preparations and stamping the O.J. Simpson murder trial with the E! logo.

Earth First! Radical environmental movement that debuted in 1981 when founder Dave Foreman (b. 1946) and others unfurled a 300-foot roll of plastic sheeting down the Glen Canyon Dam in northern Arizona. From a distance the dam appeared to have cracked.

EF!'s glory days came during the "Redwood Summer" of 1990 when hundreds of activists pounded spikes into tree trunks and sat in the limbs of redwoods to block logging in the Pacific Northwest. Its low point was a year earlier when Foreman and four others pled guilty to a reduced charge of conspiring to sabotage nuclear power plants and other facilities in Arizona, California, and Colorado. Foreman soon disavowed the eco-terrorism or "ecotage" espoused in the influential Edward Abbey novel, *The Monkey Wrench Gang*,

and in his own *Eco-Defense: A Field Guide to Monkeywrenching*. Most of the deep ecology movement in turn disavowed Foreman for welcoming AIDS and Third World starvation as antidotes to human overpopulation.

EF! picked up steam again in 1994 as a coalition of affiliated organizations rather than a single group, with local battles being waged under its banner against highway construction in Southern California, logging on national forest land in Iowa, and dam building in Quebec.

GOPHER **Earth First!** gopher://gopher.igc.apc.org/11/orgs/ef.journal ✦ WEB **Cambridge Earth First!** http://www.chu.cam.ac.uk/home/tgs1001/ef.html

Eazy-E (b. Eric Wright, 1963; d. 1995) West Coast rapper who founded his Ruthless Records label reportedly with proceeds from drug dealing. The first Ruthless release was Eazy-E's solo album *Eazy-Duz-It* (1988), a proto-GANGSTA album that sold half a million copies. Eazy traded up the following year, assembling the combustible N.W.A, HIP-HOP's most successful collection of talent. Post-N.W.A, the diminutive Eazy-E and his manager Jerry Heller were viciously lampooned in raps by the pair most often credited with N.W.A's success, ICE CUBE and DR. DRE. Although he made inexplicable gestures like befriending Officer Theodore Briseno (one of the policemen charged in the RODNEY KING beating case) and, in 1991, attending a $2,500 Republican Inner Circle fund-raising luncheon with President Bush, Eazy-E remained one of hip-hop's top entrepreneurs. His assets included a Ruthless solo album (it's on *[Dr. Dre] 187Um*

EAZY-E (right) with his N.W.A, post-ICE CUBE.

Killa—heavily influenced by Dr. Dre's production style), platinum vocal group Bone Thugs N Harmony, and a fiercely contested contract that gave him ongoing royalties participation in the careers of Dre and Cube.

On March 16, 1995, amid rumors of an N.W.A reunion, Eazy-E's attorney announced at an L.A. press conference that his friend and client had AIDS. The father of a reported seven children by six different women, Eazy-E died on March 26, 1995, from complications of the disease.

USENET **alt.rap**, **rec.music.hip-hop** ✦ WEB **HardC.O.R.E. Cubed Web Service** http://www.public.iastate.edu/~krs _one/homepage.html

ECHO Woman-run, women-friendly computer bulletin board service (BBS) with a relatively high proportion of female subscribers (some 40 percent in mid–1995). Proprietor and sysop (system operator) Stacy Horn (b. 1956) founded ECHO in March 1990 to cultivate a kind of cyber-salon: the name stands for East Coast Hang-Out. Aiming for "a virtual Algonquin Round Table," the BBS cultivated early online allegiances from a mix of New York artists and culture critics that lends cachet to email addresses bearing the "echonyc" domain name. Technical advisor Mark Abene (a.k.a. PHIBER OPTIK), who has been romantically linked to Horn, is a legendary computer HACKER.

WEB **Echo Home Page** http://www.echonyc.com

ecotourism Environmentally themed travel that aims to remake traditionally despoiling tourism into a conservation tool. Packaged trips proliferated and went mainstream in the early '90s. These often included hands-on volunteer work that condensed a two-year Peace Corps tour of duty into a vacation-friendly two-week or two-month project. As the term became debased, it included bus-bound safaris and, eventually, repackaged beachside resorts. For many environmentalists the new industry became the best hope for preserving undisturbed corners of the planet by offering local peoples a low-impact but economically viable form of development—

essentially, making the local scenery pay for itself so that it's not destroyed. Pioneers include Breakaway Adventure Travel's tours of the Amazon rain forest.

WEB **Adventure Source** http://www.halcyon.com/dclawson/ advsource.html

Ecstasy Legal in the U.S. as recently as 1985, Ecstasy (also "E," "X," "XTC" and "Adam") is the street name for MDMA (N-methyl–3,4- methyl-enedimethoxymethamphetamine), a drug invented by Parke-Davis in 1917 as an appetite suppressant. While some have jokingly suggested that "Magnanimity" would be more accurate a nickname, others swear MDMA is nothing less than "penicillin for the soul." ALEXANDER SHULGIN, the self-described "stepfather" of MDMA, has argued strenuously in favor of the therapeutic use of the drug, which is most commonly experienced as a potent "empathogen" giving the user pleasant feelings of acceptance and love. Ecstasy was also the chief catalyst behind the rise of RAVE culture in late-'80s Britain and early-'90s California.

USENET **alt.drugs.mdma** ✦ WEB **Hyperreal** http://www. hyperreal.com/drugs/mdma

Educational Testing Service Princeton, New Jersey, organization which administers the country's best-known standardized tests, including the principal arbiters of higher education admissions (e.g. SAT, CAT, GRE, LSAT). ETS has been under attack in recent years by Naderite groups bent on exposing the tests' cultural bias against women, minorities, and the poor, beginning with Ralph Nader's own 1980 *The Reign of ETS: The Corporation That Makes Up Minds* (co-author Allan Nairn) and David Owen's 1985 *None of the Above*. The latter led to the formation of FairTest, which filed a Civil Rights complaint against ETS and the College Board in February of 1994. ETS has responded in part by replacing the vocabulary section of the SAT with more reading comprehension questions, "recentering" the test around the average score of 500, allowing students to use calculators, and experimenting with COMPUTER ADAPTIVE TEST-

ING. None of these reforms addresses the fact that a pricey Stanley Kaplan, Princeton Review, or other test preparation course can quickly ramp up the supposedly objective "aptitude" score of most students.

"Cyber-Rights" symbol, created by *WIRED* magazine and downloaded from EFF's Graphics Archive (http://www.eff.org/pub/Graphics/).

EFF Electronic Frontier Foundation. Cyber-liberties non-profit organization founded and funded in 1990 by Lotus Software billionaire Mitch Kapor (with the help of other industry heavyweights including Apple co-founder Steven Wozniak) to foster Kapor's vision of an online Jeffersonian democracy. Fronted initially by John Perry Barlow, a bearded, scarf-wearing, former GRATEFUL DEAD lyricist, the group overlaps heavily with the ACLU when it comes to freedom of expression, but has brought the concerns of hardcore techies to Capitol Hill and the courtroom—to wit, the EFF's persistent efforts to guarantee citizens' high-bandwidth access to the burgeoning INTERNET. The organization is not wholly loved: phone phreak ZINE *2600* has sniped at lists of EFF's corporate contributors (including the American Petroleum Institute); and, despite a leading role in countering the government's anti-privacy Clipper Chip, the EFF helped broker a 1994 legislative compromise in the Digital Telephony Act that will use public money to ensure that phones can be tapped in the future. The compromise was opposed by smaller groups such as the Voters Telecommunications Watch (VTW) and the Computer Professionals for Social Responsibility's Electronic Privacy Information Center (EPIC). In the wake of the Digital Telephony Act, the EFF's director took much of the blame and left to found the Center for Democracy and Technology; in the summer of 1995, the EFF moved to San Francisco.

WEB **EFF** http://www.eff.org/ ✦ USENET **comp.org.eff** ✦ WEB **EPIC** http://epic.org/ ✦ WEB **Voters Telecommunications**

Watch http://www.panix.com/vtw/ ✦ MAIL LIST **ACTION (ACTIvism ONline)** email listserv@eff.org with "ADD action" in the subject

Egoyan, Atom (b. 1960) Film director born in Cairo to Armenian parents who named him after Egypt's first nuclear reactor, Atom Egoyan is the most distinctive Canadian filmmaker since David Cronenberg. Since his 1984 debut, *Next of Kin*, he has made a series of stylishly idiosyncratic movies—*Family Viewing* (1987), *Speaking Parts* (1989), *The Adjuster* (1991), *Calendar* (1993), and *Exotica* (1995)—which probe sexual and emotional secrecy with dialogue that is often overly clinical and flat. Egoyan uses banal occupations—such as censor, insurance adjuster, or stripper—to contrast the emotional damage people do one another in romantic relationships and as participants in financial transactions of dubious moral value. "The characters I find most dramatically compelling are usually dysfunctional," he told the *Los Angeles Times* in March 1995.

'80s revival When the *New York Times* heralded the '80s revival in December 1992, it signaled a phenomenon that would later be dubbed "the nostalgia gap" by Chicago journal *THE BAFFLER*. '70s FASHION nostalgia was still afoot in 1992 but had grown institutionalized and over-mediated; the '80s revival, coming before that decade was cold in its grave, marked the very idea of a revival becoming ironic. A particularly empty set of symbols were being paraded at parties like the one thrown, according to the U.K. *Guardian*, by *ROLLING STONE* journalist P. J. O'Rourke in November 1992: Reagan, conspicuous consumption, John Hughes movies, and the halcyon days of early MTV. (Oddly enough, as the '90s wore on, the '80s began to seem almost like a simpler, more innocent time.) Embracing a decade of artifice and avarice seemed like a rarefied taste, but before long the '80s revival was officially sanctioned in TV-advertised mail-order compilation albums like *Totally '80s* and VH–1's show *The Big '80s*, and

then MTV's own *It Came from the '80s.*

WEB **The '80s Server** http://cctr.umkc.edu/userx/kmwilson/80s/80s.html

88 White separatist code for Heil Hitler (*h* is the eighth letter in the alphabet), equal in significance for many racist SKINHEADS to the swastika. Keyboardists also know 88 as the number of keys on a grand piano.

Electronic Hollywood Short-lived early electronic publishing venture founded in 1991 by Jaime Levy (b. 1967), who also consulted on former pop star Billy Idol's ill-fated *Cyberpunk* album (1993) and computer disk. *Electronic Hollywood* was a small-circulation ZINE on a MACINTOSH floppy disk; its area of coverage was new media, underground film, and its style, though primitive-looking compared to then-imminent CD-ROM magazines, was an impressive, accessible melange of color graphics and ALTERNATIVE music. Although it only lasted a handful of issues (selling for $7.50 in L.A. bookstores), *E.H.* was influential in electronic publishing circles. Levy parlayed it into a New York University multi-media teaching post, a development position at IBM, and the job of creative director for the Web magazine *Word.*

WEB **Word** http://www.word.com/

Elliott, Chris (b. 1960) Discovered by David Letterman while guiding Rockefeller Center tours, the son of the radio humorist Bob Elliott (of '50s Bob and Ray fame) created some of *Late Night with David Letterman*'s more memorable characters during the '80s, including the Guy Under the Seats, the Fugitive Guy, and the world's dorkiest Marlon Brando. In 1990 Elliott spun off his ironically imbecilic onstage persona into the underappreciated series *Get a Life*, which lasted just two seasons (35 shows) on Fox in 1990–92. Elliott starred as an adult paperboy named Chris Peterson who exhibits naïveté bordering on retardation. (Peterson's favorite song is "Alley Cat," and a running joke involves him getting killed at the end of nearly a dozen episodes.)

Elliott next wrote and starred in the fitfully amusing *Cabin Boy* (1994), which, despite a charitable cameo from Letterman, ended his career as a leading man. The comedian responded by losing himself in the cast of SATURDAY NIGHT LIVE during its painful 1994–95 season.

USENET alt.fan.chris-elliott

Ellis, Brett Easton (b. 1964) Though it properly belongs to the era of pre-ironic excess known as the '80s, Brett Easton Ellis's *Less Than Zero* (1985) has become a semi-seminal document of GENERATION X culture. Set in L.A., the novel paints young adulthood as a dull, deadening existentialist void where tawdry sex and costly drugs stand in for meaningful experience. (The botched 1987 film version was notable for a RICK RUBIN soundtrack that effectively combined rap, metal, and pop.)

Ellis's second novel, *The Rules of Attraction* (1987), failed to attract readers, but in 1991 he returned to the headlines with *American Psycho.* (Fellow "brat pack" novelists Jay McInerney and Tama Janowitz achieved, respectively, literary respectability and fading relevance.) Graphically violent and relentlessly amoral, this story of a yuppie serial killer touched off a censorship furor when the original publisher, Simon & Schuster, dropped the book, forfeiting a $300,000 advance; several national chains even refused to carry it. (*Pyscho* was largely dismissed by leading reviewers as witless polemic hiding behind bad writing.)

Ellroy, James (b. 1948) When crime writer James Ellroy was ten, his mother was found strangled to death on the outskirts of L.A. After his father's death a few years later, Ellroy spent a decade as a boozing, doping, paperback-skimming transient arrested some thirty times for drinking, shoplifting, and house-breaking. In 1977 he sobered up and found work caddying at a Los Angeles golf course; two years later he sold his first crime novel, *Brown's Requiem.* Ellroy hit his stride in 1987 with *The Black Dahlia*: consciously playing out the parallels between the famous 1947 murder of would-be actress Elizabeth Short and that of his own mother, *Dahlia* kicked off the novelist's Los Angeles Quartet, stylized and violent books that interwove real characters from the Hollywood demimonde with tortured and brutal authority figures. A master of tense, telegraphed prose, Ellroy describes a world whose emotional vocabulary has been reduced to anger, revenge, paranoia, and lust. His tenth novel, 1995's *American Tabloid*, was a feverish 600-page celebration of the behind-the-scenes "bad men" who engineered Kennedy-era history.

WEB **The Mysterious Homepage** http://www.db.dk/dbaa/ jbs/homepage.htm

EMF risk Health concern about the electromagnetic fields radiating from everything electrical. Paul Brodeur's 1989 *NEW YORKER* article (and his soberly titled book, *Currents of Death*) first touched off public fears, and even conspiracy theories. Brodeur reported on epidemiological studies in Denver, Colorado, New Haven, Connecticut, and elsewhere, suggesting a "genotoxic" connection between cancer and living or working around powerlines. (The article made much of the tendency over the last fifty years to place powerlines and public schools together, reporting on schoolyard jungle gyms that vibrate at 60 hertz.) In 1993 the issue made tabloid headlines with the scare over CELLULAR PHONES, but some experts pointed out that greater radiation is emitted by electric blankets (which pregnant women are often advised to avoid) and high-wattage hair dryers. In 1994, *60 Minutes* reported on the pending lawsuits of state troopers afflicted, after years of resting radar guns in their lap, with testicular cancer. The still-contentious issue has also affected the workplace, where computer users are increasingly insisting on low-EMF video displays.

WEB **EMF Link** http://archive.xrt.upenn.edu:1000/0h/ emf/top/emf-link.html/ ✦ WEB **EMF FAQ** http://archive.xrt. upenn.edu/0h/faq/powerline_faq/

Emigre Experimental design company started as a magazine in Berkeley in 1984 by graphic designers Zuzana Licko (b. 1961) and Rudy VanderLans (b. 1955). The couple created a distinctive font foundry that exploited the freedom of desktop publishing; feeding on and diversifying the growth of MACINTOSH use in the United States, Emigre's commercial typeface success escalated after 1991. The less extreme of the Emigre fonts are now widespread, appearing in NIKE and Cadillac commercials, on McDonald's place mats and the opening titles to the movie *Batman Returns* (1995). Emigre style was partially popularized by *Beach Culture* magazine (art directed by DAVID CARSON), which gusted through the design world during its short life in 1990 and 1991. *Beach Culture* was followed by the magazine that commercialized and capitalized on the use of experimental design, *Ray Gun*.

WEB **Emigre** http://www.emigre.com/

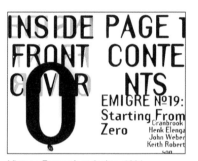

Vintage EMIGRE font design, 1991.

emoticons Online culture's foremost contribution to either the evolution of language or the death of literacy, depending on your point of view. Employed wherever people send written messages through cyberspace, emoticons (aka smileys) are essentially pictures of facial expressions made out of punctuation marks. :-) is the original smiley face, but countless variations are used to express everything from lasciviousness ;-) to angelicism 0:-). *The HACKER'S Dictionary* attributes the first smiley use to Carnegie Mellon computer scientist Scott Fahlman in 1980. Emoticons are used to alert readers that the irony, humor, or other intention of a remark (NEAL STEPHENSON, writing in *The New Republic*, bemoaned the practice as "the written equivalent of the Vegas rimshot"). Online writers also save time and reduce the risk of CARPAL TUNNEL SYNDROME by employing tortured acronyms like IMHO instead of "in my humble opinion," which serves the useful purpose of alienating "newbies" (made plain by the admonition RTFM—read the fucking manual).

WEB **The Unofficial Smiley FAQ** http://www.io.com/~zbo-ray/JumpSta/SmileyFAQ.html ✦ WEB **Welcome to Online Emoticon** http://www.emoticon.com/emoticon/

Eno, Brian (b. 1940)   Few would have suspected when he was a synth-twiddling member of early-'70s glam avatars Roxy Music that Brian Eno would go on to forge a prolific career as a conceptual-rock star. But this occasional lecturer on popular culture has managed to put scores of his ideas into practice: Eno's 1975 album *Discrete Music* and its numerous follow-ups laid the foundation for AMBIENT music (he reportedly coined the term in 1978), and he has staged over 100 video-and-music "installations" in various cities across the world. Eno has also, among countless collaborations and productions, helmed some of David Bowie and the Talking Heads' best work, and (with co-producer Daniel Lanois) untethered U2's earthbound sound over the course of four albums—not to mention conceptualizing the band's revelatory *Zoo TV* tour. In May 1995 *WIRED* magazine put Eno on the cover, bestowing upon him the dubious title of "prototypical Renaissance 2.0 artist." As such he made a perfect accessory for Microsoft's mammoth launch of its Windows 95 software. "Even if you don't know who Brian Eno is," the ad copy gushed about the start-up sound Eno created, "you'll still think the sound is cool."

WEB **The Nerve Net Page** http://140.148.1.16/eno/nerve_net.shtml ✦ WEB **The (Unofficial) EnoWeb** http://www.nwu.edu/music/eno/ ✦ WEB **Eno-related Archive** http://www.acns.nwu.edu/eno-l/archives.html ✦ USENET **alt.music.brian-eno**

ephemeral films   Term coined by film archivist Rick Prelinger (b. 1952) to designate industrial, educational, amateur, and advertising films produced to instruct viewers how to become better citizens and consumers. Tendentious and practical, they are also disposable; nothing, Prelinger suggests, is more ephemeral than a film about new 1948 Chevrolets in 1949. According to Prelinger, while such films as *Shy Guy, A Date With Your Family*, and *How to Be Popular* are frankly hilarious, they disguise a deeper level the archivist refers to as "the conspiracy," an ideological program to "manipulate the way people think and behave from the top down in order to ensure social consensus and a captive market." Voyager followed up their release of the 1994 CD-ROM anthology *Ephemeral Films* the following year with *Our Secret Century*, a twelve-CD series containing 75 of Prelinger's more than 90,000 reels.

WEB **Voyager Retail Programs** http://www.voyagerco.com/CD/gh/p.retail.html

Estep, Maggie (b. circa 1962)   Petulant, videogenic poet who was chief beneficiary of MTV's fleeting fascination with SPOKEN WORD culture. Estep's mini-tirades made perfect, pithy inter-program soundbites in the manner of DENIS LEARY; she featured prominently on the channel's 1993 "Poetry Unplugged" special and its subsequent "Spoken Wurd" tour. With her backing band I Love Everything, Estep released *No More Mr. Nice Girl* (1994; on the record label of Nuyorican Poets Café, the New York venue where she made her name in "poetry slams"), but record sales were as hard to come by as continued MTV support.

Eurotrash   Epithet originally applied to rich foreigners, usually from old families, living in the United States. Eurotrash mascot Taki Theodoracopulos, who helped disseminate the term in society columns for *Vanity Fair* and the British *Spectator*, claimed in a 1984 interview to have heard "Eurotrash" first applied in 1980 to "very rich Milanese who came here and used up everyone's drugs." The Reagan era smiled on such Euro immigrants, who, along with their virtually indistinguishable Middle Eastern and South American friends (schooled in Switzerland and outfitted in Paris), injected the New York club and social scene with plenty of fusty titles, *bon chic bon genre* sartorial style (Gucci loafers, Hermes scarves, signet rings), and ostentatious cheek- hand- and *ciao*-kissing. During the leveling 1990s, "Eurotrash" in popular parlance came to refer to just about anyone who has an accent, sports a deep tan (acquired by birth or otherwise), haunts chichi nightspots, and wears clothing too tight, tailored, or precious to appear "American" (or heterosexual, thus the homophobic variation, "Eurofag").

extreme sports Catch-all term, coined circa 1990, for a variety of athletic challenges that have virtually nothing in common except high risk and an appeal to men ages 18–34—the dream demographic for many advertisers. Many extreme sports developed as variations on previously existing non-extreme sports: SNOWBOARDING, sky-surfing, free climbing, barefoot waterskiing, street luge, etc.. After gaining popularity in fitness-obsessed locales like Colorado, extreme sports caught on with the media: magazines like *DETAILS* lavished space on these hyper-kinetic, photogenic activities, and *MTV Sports* and ESPN's *Extreme Sports* (both started in 1991) brought them to television, with a rock-video style and soundtrack. Advertisers including NIKE ("Just Do It") and Mountain Dew ("Been There,

Done That") also found the "extreme" credo to their liking. In 1993, ESPN2—"the younger, wilder brother of ESPN"—was born; in 1995, ESPN developed the $10 million, first annual Olympics-style Extreme Games, which included competitions in dozens of events from SKATEBOARDING to BUNGEE JUMPING.

WEB **Everything Extreme** http://www.duke.edu/~cperhun/
✦ WEB **AdventureTime Magazine** http://www.nauticom.net/adventuretime/

Extropians California-based, non-profit mini-cult of fewer than 500 members built on the belief that future technologies will overcome problems that today seem insoluble. Immortality through technology is a central tenet of Extropianism: fervent hopes for the future include cryogenics, time travel, and "uploading" one's consciousness to a computer. The organization, whose guiding light is an Englishman called Max More (b. Max O'Connor), also embraces libertarian thinkers such as Ayn Rand; ideas like privatizing the air are expounded in the magazine "Extropy," as are neologisms like "de-animation" (death), "disasturbation" (wishful disaster scenarios), and "smart-faced" (stoned). The Extropians' slender achievements were hymned in a lengthy 1994 *WIRED* feature.

EMAIL more@extropy.org EMAIL exi-info@extropy.org ✦ WEB
Extropian Links http://www.gsu.edu/~libndc/extro.html

Faludi, Susan (b. 1959) Author of the 1991 best-seller, *Backlash: The Undeclared War Against American Women*, which argued that women were under cultural counter-attack in retaliation for the assertiveness of the '60s and '70s women's movement. The title soon become a '90s political slogan for feminists. As the San Francisco-based Faludi later explained, the 550-plus page book was prompted by a 1986 *Newsweek* cover story on marriage which claimed that college-educated women, after reaching age 40, are "more likely to be killed by a terrorist" than find a husband. The idea for *Backlash*, much of which is devoted to debunking apocryphal studies, came from the lack of interest in follow-up articles questioning the thin scientific basis for the *Newsweek* story. As an undergraduate at Harvard in the early '80s, Faludi wrote an article for the student newspaper about sexual harassment that prompted a professor to take a leave of absence; she won a 1991 Pulitzer Prize for her *Wall Street Journal* reporting on the worker lay-offs following the leveraged buyout of Safeway supermarkets.

family values Flexible catchall term for social conservatives, generally denoting politics that are anti-abortion, anti-gay-rights, anti-feminism, anti-sex and pro-religion. (The term has effectively become the antonym for ALTERNATIVE.) Coined in 1966 to counter the rising counterculture by novelist and Catholic priest Andrew M. Greeley, family values entered the Republican Party platform by 1976. Four presidential elections later, the wholesome ideal defined the "culture war" proclaimed by candidate Patrick Buchanan, a keynote speaker at the 1992 Republican Party Convention's "Family Values Night." As part of that same campaign, Vice President Dan Quayle—whose wife once said she felt like a "single parent" thanks to his career—championed family values by condemning the titular single mom of the sitcom *Murphy Brown*.

Fantagraphics Books Beginning in 1981 with the HERNANDEZ BROTHERS' *Love and Rockets*, Seattle-based publishers Gary Groth and Kim Thompson have carried not only the flame of underground comics, but also maintained the classic tradition, publishing snazzy comics reprints of such cartoon classics as *Popeye, Li'l Abner,* and *Prince Valiant* along with modernists like Jules Feiffer, Vaughn Bode, and R. CRUMB, and alternative stars PETER BAGGE and DAN CLOWES. The Seattle-based company also publishes *The Comics Journal*, comics' most literate and cranky industry publication. In the early '90s Fantagraphics began bolstering its support of new comics talent like Roberta Gregory, Jim Woodring, Al Columbia, Chris Ware, and others with profits from its often innovative line of X-rated Eros comics.

WEB **Fantagraphics** http://www.eden.com/comics/fantagraphics.html ✦ USENET **alt.comics.alternative**

FAQ Frequency Asked Questions, the INTERNET version of a manual that reflects the grass-roots origins of much of Internet culture. Instructions and explanations on everything from starting your own USENET newsgroup to the complete video-ography of R.E.M. grow organically out of the questions that experienced participants don't feel like repeatedly answering.

Farrakhan, Louis (b. Louis Eugene Walcott, 1933) "Farrakhan's a prophet and I think you ought to listen to / What he can say to you," bellowed Chuck D. in PUBLIC ENEMY's first hit, "Bring the Noise" (1987). The bow-tied leader of the NATION OF ISLAM is both heir to MALCOLM X's fiery legacy and upholder of the Nation faith which Malcolm X was assassinated for breaking. America's best known

"Minister LOUIS FARRAKHAN Calls For A Million Man March" from THE NATION OF ISLAM's home page (www.afrinet.net/~islam).

racial separatist, he combines street credibility and black nationalism with right-wing attacks not just on homosexuals and Jews but also on abortion and welfare mothers. The son of a Barbados immigrant, Farrakhan grew up in Roxbury, Boston. He found success as Prince Charmer, a calypso star, before being introduced to the Nation in the mid-'50s by Malcolm X. He now lives in the Chicago mansion that formerly belonged to the late Nation leader Elijah Mohammed. [See also KHALLID ABDUL MUHAMMAD.]

WEB **The Nation of Islam** http://www.afrinet.net:80/~islam/

Farrell, Perry (b. Perry Bernstein, 1959) Born in Queens, New York, Perry Bernstein dropped out of college in his freshman year and worked as a dancer in a Newport Beach private club. After changing his name to Farrell (his brother's first name), the future icon made one album and an EP with the art-GOTH band Psi-Com before forming Jane's Addiction in 1986. The band's PROGRESSIVE ROCK influences and artsy take on the PUNK ethic attracted a fanatical following among those disenfranchised by the processed pop-metal bands then dominating L.A. (*The Trouser Press Record Guide* [1991], however, lists Jane's as "obnoxious glam-punk poseurs.") Then there was Farrell's persona: wailing falsetto, religious obsessions, drug-strafed lifestyle, and rambling on-stage pronouncements that were a throwback to the shamanic rock stars of the high '60s. An independently released live album led to a Warner Bros. deal and two albums, *Nothing's Shocking* (1988) and *Ritual de lo Habitual* (1990). The latter featured Farrell sleeve art—including a naked man, two naked women, and SANTERIA icons—that was distributed to some stores with the First Amendment printed on a white jacket.

Farrell ensured his 2016 induction into the ROCK AND ROLL HALL OF FAME when he founded the epoch-defining LOLLAPALOOZA tour in 1991. Jane's Addiction triumphantly headlined the initial outing, but Farrell split up the band at the height of their popularity for fear of growing formulaic. (He performed the last concert in Hawaii naked.)

Ironically, Jane's would never benefit from the ALTERNATIVE revolution they helped create. The 1993 debut album from Farrell's new band Porno For Pyros was highly anticipated, but it was a slickly produced and perplexingly esoteric set—which leaves Farrell as an icon without a significant constituency.

WEB **Jane's Addiction and Porno for Pyros** http://raptor.swarthmore.edu/jahall/JA/ ✦ MAIL LIST **Jane's Addiction List** email janes-addiction-request@ms.uky.edu with "SUBSCRIBE" in the message subject

fat grrrls Young, radical component of the 25-year-old "fat acceptance movement," as fostered and articulated by Olympia-based RIOT GRRRL Nomy Lamm (b. 1975). Lamm is the creator and writer of *I'm So Fucking Beautiful*, a confrontational ZINE which catalogues "fat-prejudice" and seeks to debunk myths about the health risks of being hefty. Where mainstream feminism has grappled, under the rubric of "body image," with the relationship between cultural attitudes and women's self-esteem, Lamm's direct approach advocates organizing and raising awareness of "sizism."

MAIL LIST **NAAFA (National Association for the Advancement of Fat Acceptance)** email naafa-members-request@world.std.com ✦ WEB **FaT GiRL** http://http.icsi.berkeley.edu/~polack/fg/

fat-free Sure-fire advertising claim for food labels that replaced '80s buzzword "lite" in the calorie-conscious lexicon. Diet soda packagers added gratuitous non-fat boasts and high-calorie cookies were marketed to dieters as fat free. Like the scientific studies showing that oat bran cuts fat, much of America's initial low-fat and fat-free marketing turned out to be too good to be true. In 1994 *New York* magazine sent muffins and frozen desserts labeled low- or non-fat out for lab tests that revealed many to contain more fat than ice cream. (Reports the same year from the Center for Science in the Public Interest that movie theater popcorn cooked in coconut oil had as much fat as eight Big Macs, dominated dietary discourse.) Meanwhile the FDA cracked down on fat free claims, telling BEN

& JERRY'S that the company's highly successful low-fat frozen yogurt wasn't slimming enough to use the two magic words, and instituting new labels recommending a healthy—and for Americans, atypical—daily ceiling of 2,000 calories and 65 grams of fat.
WEB **FATFREE FAQs** http://www.fatfree.com/faq.html ◆ WEB **Julie's Low&Fat-Free Resources List** http://www.eskimo.com/~baubo/lowfat.html

Fay, Michael (b. 1975)   American teen caned in Singapore for possessing stolen street signs and allegedly spray-painting parked cars. The May 1994 sentence, administered by a prison martial arts expert, entailed four powerful strokes of a four-foot long, half-inch wide sopping wet rattan cane to the bare buttocks—a punishment categorized as torture by AMNESTY INTERNATIONAL. Fay's father in his hometown of Dayton, Ohio, publicized his son's sentence (and coerced confession) in the months before it was meted out, believing that Americans would be appalled (most states ban corporal punishment in public schools) and press Singapore to commute it. He was mistaken. Though the Clinton administration logged a protest on Fay's behalf, tabloids and talk radio turned the errant youngster into a whipping boy for Americans fed up with crime. The case prompted public officials in Sacramento, St. Louis, and elsewhere, to propose bringing back public flogging, a punishment not seen in the U.S. since 1952.

female condom   Contraceptive device introduced in the summer of 1994 by the tiny Wisconsin Pharmacal company under the trade name "Reality." Like a male condom, the $2.50 female version is designed to prevent pregnancy and inhibit the spread of AIDS and other sexually transmitted diseases, but it is larger, with two rings that keep it open (the first remains outside the body, while the other is inserted into the vagina past the pubic bone). The product has been beset with problems: some users complain that it squeaks, others that the lubrication feels like Crisco; even worse is the 26 percent failure rate in normal use. "The female condom is better than no protection at all,"

said FDA Commissioner David A. Kessler, while recommending that couples continue using male condoms. A new version patented in January 1994 by Jane Hunnicutt, a Sebastopol, California, seamstress and inventor, eliminates some shortcomings by attaching the condom to designer underwear that is worn during intercourse. Originally developed so poor women in Third World countries (where male partners may be less willing to use condoms) would have more control over AIDS protection, the female condom is said to be especially popular with Thai prostitutes.
WEB **Latex and Condoms** http://cornelius.ucsf.edu/~troyer/safesex/condoms.html

figure engineering   After the breathtaking success of the WONDERBRA, designers responded by building push-up bras into swimsuits, evening dresses, and anything else they could think of, creating a new category of figure-engineered clothing. For his fall 1994 Chanel couture collection, Karl Lagerfeld created elaborately boned jackets that forced the wearer's figure into a perfect hour-glass shape. Ready-to-wear designers (including Gianni Versace and John Galliano) followed suit with a raft of corsets meant to be worn over, under, and instead of other clothing. In early '94 *Mirabella* declared the trend evidence of "a new take on femininity, in which woman is the master, and never dresses as a mistress." But for women too young to remember the tyranny of the panty girdle, a few minutes squeezed inside a corset gives a new, palpable meaning to the concept of women's liberation.

Film Threat   Alternative movie magazine that operates under the assumption—announced in its first photocopied issue published by founder Chris Gore when a student at Detroit's Wayne State University—that "Hollywood cinema is making an ass out of you and me." *FT* went L.A., glossy, and bi-monthly in 1991 when Gore sold it to, and went to work for, porn publisher Larry Flynt (*Hustler*). The magazine, which has enjoyed a boost from vocal INTERNET fans, stakes its punky reputation on periodic vendettas against targets ranging from

Premiere magazine ("While it's not . . . owned by the studios, it might as well be") to QUENTIN TARANTINO ("ripoff artist") and the more urbane *Movieline* magazine ("a sloppy-seconds boneyard of has-beens"). Gore still owns the underground *Film Threat Video Guide* and Film Threat Video line that keeps obscure works by the likes of RICHARD KERN in circulation.

USENET **alt.cult-movies**

Final Exit   Book equivalent of a Dr. Kevorkian suicide machine, this how-to manual reached the top of best-seller lists in the summer of 1991. Authored by Derek Humphry (b. 1930), the 1980 founder of the right-to-die Hemlock Society, *Final Exit* included instructions for the terminally ill on subjects such as cyanide poisoning, hoarding sleeping pills, "self-deliverance via the plastic bag," and even writing a farewell note. Moralists worried that the book—thoughtfully rendered in large print—would push teens and the depressed over the edge (indeed, suicides by asphyxiation, the book's recommended method, quadrupled in New York City the year following the book's publication, according to the study of a Cornell psychiatrist), but its immense sales were probably another sign of people's wish, most evident in the rise of ALTERNATIVE MEDICINE, to take control of health decisions back from orthodox medicine.

WEB **DeathNet** http://www.islandnet.com/~deathnet/

Fincher, David (b. 1962)   Former animator with George Lucas' INDUSTRIAL LIGHT AND MAGIC who founded influential video production house Propaganda in 1986. Fincher is the creator of heavy-hitting, big-budget videos for MADONNA ("Vogue," "Express Yourself," "Oh Father," "Bad Girl"), George Michael (the SUPERMODEL-fest "Freedom '90"), the Rolling Stones ("Love Is Strong," in which the band dwarfs Manhattan skyscrapers), and ads for NIKE ("Instant Karma" [1992] and "Ref" [1993, starring Dennis Hopper]) and the American Cancer Society ("Smoking Fetus," 1983). He is also is one of the few video-makers to run into trouble for plagiarizing a photographer—

reputedly settling out of court with Robert Frank because the 1989 clip for Don Henley's "The End of the Innocence" too closely resembled pages of Robert Frank's elegiac photo-book *The Americans.* Fincher made his feature film debut with 1992's *Alien 3*, which was then the highest-budget ($40 million) picture by a first-time director. His stylish follow-up *Seven* starred BRAD PITT and was one of 1995's surprise hits.

Fingerman, Bob (b. 1964)   New York comics artist and illustrator whose work first appeared in FANTAGRAPHICS BOOKS's porn line, Eros. After updating the "Tijuana bible" tradition (cheaply printed mid-century cartoon smut) in *Atomic Age Truckstop Waitresses* (1991), which parodied TWIN PEAKS and *Rocky and Bullwinkle* cartoons, Fingerman's *SKINHEADS in Love* (1992) was a naturalistic and truly erotic punk-sex document. *Skinheads* got inside a pair of POLITICALLY CORRECT skins with lives wallpapered by perfectly captured East Village anarchist graffiti and handbills for imaginary hardcore bands. Fingerman's next major project was *White Like She* (Dark Horse, 1994). In this grammatically corrected update of John Howard Griffin's *Black Like Me*, a black janitor's brain is transplanted into a white postpunk female's head. Fingerman wrote *Screwy Squirrel* (1995) for Dark Horse before completing his semiautobiographical *Minimum Wage* (1995).

USENET **rec.arts.comics.alternative, alt.comics.alternative**

First Amendment Coalition   Network of anti-POLITICAL CORRECTNESS campus activists based in Gainesville, Florida. The group invoked the '60s New Left manifesto "The Port Huron Statement" at an April 1994 conference of campus conservatives from around the country, issuing a "Cambridge Declaration" in opposition to SPEECH CODES, MULTICULTURALISM, affirmative action, and diversity seminars. The group has since de-emphasized its associations with right-wing patron Center for the Study of Popular Culture, focusing on First Amendment issues at a Columbia University conference the following fall, where it called for a

"National Free Speech Bill" that would cut off federal funds to schools with speech codes.

WEB **California First Amendment Coalition Home Page**
http://www.ccnet.com/CSNE/cfac/welc.html

Fisher, Amy (b. 1976) In 1992, Amy Fisher's affair with auto mechanic Joey Buttafuocco and her attempted murder of his wife created a new paradigm for the American media. The combination of underaged sex, violence, and working-class mores turned this Long Island couple into celebrities, further dissolving barriers between news reporting, infotainmment, and plain old sleaze. The burgeoning tabloid TV industry had a field day with the Fisher story, dragging more esteemed news sources along for the ride; one week in winter 1992-'93, three different networks aired "Long Island Lolita" TV movies, two starring authentic ingenues DREW BARRYMORE and Alyssa Milano.

Fisher was convicted and sentenced to 5 to 15 years; Joey did 6 months for statutory rape, but not before parlaying his fame into countless invitations to quasi-jet-set parties and one small film role. (He was fined in 1995 for soliciting an undercover policewoman in Hollywood.) Amy and Joey were eventually forgotten, but their legacy paved the way for the MENENDEZ BROTHERS, dangerous skater Tonya Harding, O.J. Simpson, and dozens more sordid stories.

Five Percent Nation Harlem-born offshoot of the black Muslim NATION OF ISLAM (though its adherents do not observe the strict dress or diet of NOI followers). Five Percenters, possessing "self-knowledge" of blacks' racial superiority, take their name from the central belief, articulated by the NOI's Elijah Muhammad, that enlightened followers of Islam make up a minority of the population (5 percent) charged with educating the vast, lumpen majority (85 percent), who are oppressed by corrupt "white devils" (10 percent). Five Percent "science" became, in the early '90s, a badge of political awareness for young New York rap acts who broadcast lyrical fragments of the separatist ideology to a wide audience. Rap band Brand Nubian set the standard for Five Percent philosophy on record, with 1990's *One For All* (MTV quickly banned the "Wake Up" video, which included a horned white businessman played by a black actor) and 1993's *In God We Trust*. Other affiliated groups include Poor Righteous Teachers and X-Clan; in a 1991 reply to Five Percenters, rap veteran Kool Moe Dee satirized Nation language: "pseudo science and material math / Six degrees of knowledge brother you don't know the half."

WEB **The Nation of Gods and Earths** http://sunsite.unc.edu/nge/

Flanagan, Bob (b. 1952) L.A.-based author, musician, and performance artist who elevated masochism into an art form; regarded as a pivotal figure in the MODERN PRIMITIVE movement. Flanagan was a founding member of the Society of Janus (a pioneering S/M group formed in 1981) and first gained notoriety by the publication in 1985 of the *FUCK Journals*, a graphic chronicle of S/M encounters with partner/dominatrix Sherrie Rose. Flanagan's art combines, sometimes with upbeat wit, the themes of sickness (he was born with cystic fibrosis, a usually fatal lung disease), pain, and eroticism. The 1989 AMOK-sponsored show, "Nailed"—for which a frail, whipped, pierced, and branded Flanagan sewed his scrotum and nailed it to a board—was typical of his oeuvre. He also starred as torture victim in the MTV-banned NINE INCH NAILS video, "Happiness is Slavery." Flanagan continues to make pain-inspired museum, gallery, and performance space appearances. He has written five books and was most recently the subject of the 1991 RE/SEARCH book, *Bob Flanagan: Supermasochist*.

Fleener, Mary (b. 1951) Southern California cartoonist and popular commercial artist. Fleener's comics transform otherwise banal vignettes about small-time Bay Area decadence (casual sex, party drugs, bad rock) into odd little folktales not unlike those of her hero, novelist Zora Neale Hurston, whose stories she illustrated in her 1992 comic *Hoodoo*. Fleener's magnum opus is "Tales From the Pink Coffin" in the second issue of her sporadic

Slutburger comic, in which she tones down her Picassoesque pictography to relate a compelling ghost story about life before and after AIDS.

USENET **rec.arts.comics.alternative, alt.comics.alternative**

Florida death metal Inbred relative of heavy metal exported from the Sunshine State since the mid '80s. Death metal spews forth dirgelike tirades on sex, violence, and nihilism with occasional sprinklings of SATANISM and fascism. The original exponents were Death, whose frontman Chuck Schuldiner leads a current incarnation; other practitioners have included Morbid Angel, Sadus, Deicide, and Genitorturers (whose stage act is as unpleasant as their name suggests). The appeal of this self-contained fringe scene extends only to a stoic group of international believers and to the prurient elements of the mainstream media—although it occasionally catches the eye of law enforcement officials. Alleging that death metal's "hideous, frightful, and repulsive" sentiments were liable to "inspire a sense of violence in the listener," British customs officials sought to ban the importing of an album by Swedish death metal act Dismember in 1992. Expert witness, music writer David Toop, compared death metal to Greek or Jacobean tragedy, and the case was dismissed.

WEB **death metal/black metal archive** http://bigdipper .umd.edu/index/metal.html ✦ WEB **death info** http: //www.geom.umn.edu/~bmeloon/music/bandinfo/death.html

Fluevog Vancouver, British Columbia, footwear company founded in 1970 by John Fluevog (b. 1948) and Peter Fox, the partnership split up in 1980. Since then Fox has flourished as a mainstream designer and Fluevog has found renown as, among other things, an early proponent of the platform-shoe revival. The colorful, outlandishly impractical Fluevog shoes (made in England, often with DOC MARTEN-made soles) have long been favorites with CLUB KIDS, but they reached national renown in 1991 when one scallop-heeled model was worn in videos and photo-shoots by DEEE-LITE singer Lady Miss Keir. Designers ANNA SUI, Byron Lars, and BETSEY JOHNSON have augmented their runway shows with Fluevogs, which are these days sold through boutiques and a chain of self-named stores nationwide.

Deee-Lite *World Clique* 1990 album (Elektra Records)

DEEE-LITE's Lady Miss Kier (center) brings FLUEVOG footwear to the masses, 1990.

footwear fashion mutations In the early-'90s, mid-level shoe retailers developed a penchant for street fashion, repackaging faddish styles with little regard for received good taste. Suddenly, for every two new shoe trends there was a bright entrepreneur who wanted to combine them: *faux*-TIMBERLAND pumps and cowboy boots with hefty POLECLIMBER soles were among the many fashion crimes perpetrated. In December 1992 the *New York Times* noted the advent of the cowboy boot clog by the Brooklyn's Nisal Inc. "We tried to hit all the fads at once," said company owner Sal Caserta, who had also issued a motorcycle boot with platform sole.

Fortean Times "The Journal of Strange Phenomena." Where THE SKEPTICAL INQUIRER is out to debunk and expose, the London-based *FT* (founded as a newsletter in 1973) fosters an air of suspended, tongue-in-cheek suspicion as it documents the rise of spontaneous human combustion reports and the decline of fairy sightings. The bi-monthly takes its name from New Yorker Charles Hoy Fort (1874–1932), who pioneered UFO theory and spent his life investigating and writing about the peculiar and paranormal. In 1994 *FT* raised its profile by issuing its first annual Index of Weirdness. (The Index and its press release, calculated from trends in 34 representative categories ranging from ALIEN ABDUCTIONS to crop circles, pronounced 1994 off 2.0 percent in general weirdness from 1993). The U.S. based International Fortean Organization publishes a separate but like-minded counterpart, *The Info Journal.*

Fortean Times Home Page http://alpha.mic.dundee. ac.uk/ft/credits.html

40 oz. malt liquor Libation of choice among GANGSTA rappers and their constituents, boasting a higher alcohol content than beer, as well as a sweeter taste and economical pricetag. Popular brands include St. Ides, Colt 45, Old English, and PowerMaster. St. Ides' maker, the San Francisco-based McKenzie River Brewing Co., has been the subject of criticism and federal complaints for using rap stars such as the GETO BOYS and ICE CUBE to target-market this powerful intoxicant to black youth. One Ice Cube ad boasted that the malt liquor would "get your girl in the mood quicker / Get your Jimmy thicker." Among denouncers of St. Ides is fellow rapper Chuck D of PUBLIC ENEMY, who in 1991 lodged a $5 million lawsuit against McKenzie River for SAMPLING his voice in a radio advertisement (the company settled in 1993); later in '91, Chuck D attacked the ghetto marketing of malt liquor in "1 Million Bottlebags" ("What is Colt .45, another gun to the brain"). Struggling to shake its bad-boy image, McKenzie River donated $50,000 in 1992 to a post-L.A. RIOTS program, helping finance a HIP-HOP fund-raising effort called "You Can Get the Fist." Rap stars SNOOP DOGGY DOG, Notorious B.I.G., Scarface, and Ice Cube continue to lend their names, faces, and lyrical talents to malt liquor campaigns.

Fourth Reich California SKINHEAD sect busted by the FBI in July 1993 for an elaborate plan to incite a race war in California through strategic acts of terrorism against RODNEY KING, PUBLIC ENEMY's Chuck D, and other public blacks, Latinos, and Jews. Fourth Reich also pled guilty to pipe-bomb attacks on the SPUR POSSE for "degrading the White Race." The leaders, aged 20 and 17, were sentenced to a combined total of 13 years in jail and a psychological reconditioning program dubbed "Operation Grow Hair" that forced them to watch *Schindler's List* (1993) and meet with prominent L.A. blacks and Jews.

fraternity hazing 19th century tradition increasingly threatened by POLITICAL CORRECTNESS and its own well-publicized excesses even as frat membership reached an all-time high in the '90s (up from a 1972 hippie-era low of 149,000, peaking at nearly 500,000). Thanks to groups like CHUCK (Committee to Halt Useless College Killings), more than 35 states now have anti-hazing statutes, but enforcement is often limited to after-accident punishment and civil lawsuits. With most national fraternities clamping down on school chapters (in part out of necessity to qualify for insurance purchasing collectives), initiation rites are now as likely to include DATE RAPE sensitivity training or alcohol awareness seminars as they are strippers, toxic levels of JÄGERMEISTER, or black-face slapstick. Recent hazing accidents include the May 1994 death of a pledge at the black Kappa Alpha Phi chapter of Southeast Missouri State (he was "body-slammed"), that led to a major lawsuit exposing such practices as "bringing the knowledge" (in which pledges are struck on the head with a dictionary).

Free Software Foundation Apotheosis of the HACKER "information wants to be free" ethic. Since 1985 a staff of a dozen-odd programmers, supported mainly by corporate gifts, have been writing software (the GNU Project) which can be given away. FSF programs are protected by "copyleft," a copyright license agreement that forbids people selling or otherwise distributing the software from placing further restrictions on its use. The FSF's charismatic president Richard S. Stallman, himself a programming legend, dismisses anti-piracy laws as "civic pollution," likening software to "a loaf of bread that could be eaten once, or a million times." The GNU Project aims to clone the AT&T Unix operating system which undergirds most of the INTERNET; the acronym stands partly for "Not Unix." In the early 1990s programmer Linus Torvalds stole thunder from Stallman by releasing his own free version of Unix called Linux. Ironically, Linux was based largely on GNU tools.

WEB **Free Software Foundation Home Page**

http://info.desy.de/gnu/www/gnu_bulletin_9401/gnu_bulletin_9401_3.html#SEC3

fringeware   Electronic brain tools, the most commercially accessible of which is the Synchro Energizer. Patented in 1980 by the late Cleveland bioresearcher Denis Gorges, the SE consists of a goggle lined on the inside with tiny lights, headphones that pulse with NEW AGE music and a carrier tone. The SE slips the user into a daydreamy "theta" state similar to relaxing presleep moments. Judith Hooper and Dick Teresi's *Would the Buddha Wear a Walkman?* (1990) describes a plethora of such "consciousness tech"—contraptions like the Somatron, Graham Potentializer, the Tranquilite, Binaural Signal Generator, and Cerebrex. Consciousness can also be expanded through psychological software, light and sound machines, esoteric therapies, biofeedback machinery, isolation tanks, repetitious sound, rebirthing centers, and assorted flotsam and jetsam of the new SPIRITUALITY. The "cyber ZINE" *Fringeware Review* offers an alternative shopping service for such items.
WEB **FringeWareInc.** http://www.fringeware.com/ EMAIL @fringware.com

Fruitopia   Soft drink launched by the Coca-Cola company in March 1994 to compete with SNAPPLE for the $6 billion "ALTERNATIVE" beverage market. This corn-syrup/fruit juice concoction was undistinguished, save for its advertising: much of the $30 million first-year marketing budget was spent on a series of TV/cinema ads by Chiat/Day that featured kaleidoscopic RAVE-ish graphics and music by English sprite songstress Kate Bush. The NEW AGE-y "Welcome to Fruitopian life" theme was conveyed by Forrest Gump-like slogans counseling "The apples don't fight the pineapples in Fruit Integration" (like Strawberry Passion Awareness, an initial Fruitopia flavor) and "This is what Citrus Consciousness can do to your tongue—imagine what it can do to your soul." As a result of "con-

FRUITOPIA–what the NEW AGE tastes like.

sumer engineering" two "lighter-tasting" flavors were added in November '94. In April '94 *Advertising Age* reported that former students at Ohio's Miami University claimed that they'd coined the Fruitopia name as part of a 1991 Coca-Cola-sponsored marketing project; the company, although it owns the project's ideas anyway, denied the connection.

fuck-in-law   Person who has slept with someone you have slept with, a relationship that has taken on special meaning in the age of AIDS. Alternate terms include "sex degrees of separation" and "Eskimo brother."

Fugazi   Hardcore PUNK foursome from Washington, D.C., known for its anti-commercial purism. Long before PEARL JAM took on TICKETMASTER, Fugazi refused to charge more than $5 for concerts; despite offers of lucrative deals, the band has eschewed major labels to become one of the best-selling independent act ever. Lionized as "the conscience of the American music underground" (and invoked by credibility-hungry celebrities such as KEANU REEVES and proto RIOT GRRRL Joan Jett), Fugazi has maintained its constituency with a string of powerful "harDCore" albums—*Repeater* (1991), *In on the Killtaker* (1993)—and a long tradition of pummeling live shows that double as a pulpit for admonitory sermons. Lead singer Ian MacKaye (b. 1962) is well known for his opposition to MOSHING, and rowdy audience members frequently find themselves singled out and sent packing (with a full refund, of course).
WEB **A Fugazi Homepage** http://pages.prodigy.com/VA/fessler/fugazi.html

full service network   Time Warner-coined term for the company's Orlando, Florida, experiment in interactive cable services. Although initially announced in late 1992 just before "500 channels" became a reigning buzzword, the Orlando development was delayed for years by technical glitches in coordinating the supercharged Silicon Graphics set-top boxes with the glitzy 3D, full-motion video-on-demand, HOME SHOPPING, interactive news, and network game software. By the time the first tests were unveiled in late 1994, the INTERNET was looming as the more likely venue for the interactive future. Other major joint ventures between computer, cable, and entertainment conglomerates include AT&T and Viacom's similar test in California; cable behemoth TCI's work with BMG; and the New Leaf collaboration between IBM and Viacom-owned Blockbuster, which hopes one day to replace record store inventory with in-store CD, tape, and video pressing plants.

WEB **Pathfinder** http://pathfinder.com

Futuristic family fun, from TIME WARNER.

Furlong, Edward (b. 1977) Winsome young film star catapulted to fame opposite Arnold Schwarzenegger in the 1991 blockbuster *Terminator 2*. Furlong has since alternated appearances in sci-fi/horror flicks (*Pet Sematary Two*, 1992; *Brainscan*, 1994) with a variety of well-received, low-budget dramas (*American Heart*, 1993; *Little Odessa*, 1995). A heavy-metal enthusiast, the teenager turned up as

a joy-riding rogue in an AEROSMITH video ("Livin' on the Edge," 1995) as well as experimenting briefly with a singing career (his 1992 debut album was released only in Japan). Accompanying *T2*'s success was a messy custody battle between his uncle and estranged mother. Two years later, Furlong emancipated himself from his uncle's legal guardianship over objections to his choice of girlfriend: 29 year-old Jackie Domac, his former stand-in from the *T2* set who became his private tutor and, subsequently, his lover.

fuzzy logic Branch of artificial intelligence research aiming to program computers that can analyze imprecise situations like "warm" instead of having to pick between "hot" or "cold." As with the fractals of chaos theory and game theory of ARTIFICIAL LIFE, fuzzy logic tempers the certainties of machine logic with an appreciation of vagueness, paradox, "graded memberships," and "degrees of truth." FL's most visible spokesperson, author Bart Kosko (*Fuzzy Thinking*, 1993), was an early disciple of UC Berkeley's engineering professor Lotfi Zadeh, who introduced the notion of fuzzy sets in a 1965 paper drawing upon the work of philosopher Max Black. In the '90s fuzzy logic—usually thought of as an insult—entered consumer marketing with some plausibility as common devices like dishwashers began incorporating microprocessors and sensors to determine, for instance, how much soap to use based on the dirtiness of the water in the first rinse cycle. Kosko paints a picture of U.S. children sitting at home mesmerized by VIDEOGAMES, while Japanese superscientists are developing the fuzzy future's "smart cars," novel-writing computers, molecular health soldiers, and "sex cyborgs modeled after the pop and other stars of the day."

WEB **MathWorks Home Page** http://www.mathworks.com

gabberhouse The *ne plus ultra* of brutal, uptempo electronic music. Partisans might describe gabberhouse as dance music, but few civilians would apply that label. The music first appeared in Rotterdam, Holland, circa 1992, when producers upped the beats-per-minute ante to a health-imperiling 200; "gabber" is the local name for soccer hooligan, and it was among working-class youth that this music found its supporters. Gabberhouse's assaultive roar and macho following (including a Brooklyn contingent) have brought accusations of sexism (an oft-quoted popular number is "No Woman Allowed" by Sperminator) and even fascism, but gabberhouse is more an acquired taste than a grave social problem.

MAIL LIST **Gabber** email gabbers-request@cindy.et.tudelft.nl with "Subscribe" as the subject

Gaiman, Neil (b. 1960) Alongside ALAN MOORE, Gaiman is the most influential of several young British comic book writers whose sensibility gave DC's Vertigo line of comics its thoughtful, downbeat bent. In *The Sandman* (1988–95), Gaiman created an eerie, maze-like, and, most of all, literate milieu beloved of many GOTHS. Somewhere in the realm of the Endless lives the title character, alongside other immortals including a cute girl named Death; from here Gaiman spins narrative webs into far-flung environments and styles. Gaiman's work is enhanced by the dark surrealism of his longtime design collaborator, Dave McKean; their 1994 *Mr. Punch* is graphic storytelling at its most powerful.

WEB **The Dreaming** http://www.duke.edu/~dfowlkes/sandman.html ✦ WEB **Neil Gaiman Page** http://haven.uniserve.com/~puck/sandman/ ✦ USENET **rec.arts.comics.dc.universe** ✦ WEB **Tori Amos & Sandman** http://www.mit.edu:8001/people/nocturne/tori/faq.html

Gak An inspired marketing spin-off from the NICKELODEON network's unruly kids' game show *Double Dare*, Gak, launched in the summer of 1992 by Mattel, is a malleable purple goo of uncertain composition and unlimited allure. (Scientists allege a water-based combination of acrylic/silicone.) This stretchy, bouncy substance annexed kids' imaginations in the early-'90s just as Slime and Silly Putty had done in earlier decades; approximately 8 million units (or "splats," as the Gak cartons are known) were sold in 1993, at $3 each. Bans in some schools could not halt the cult of Gak; Mattel devoted an 800 number to questions about it.

Galas, Diamanda (b. 1952) Greek-American vocalist and performance artist who reportedly spent the '70s as variously a prostitute on the streets of L.A. and a pianist for jazz legend Ornette Coleman. With her 1979 debut album *Wild Women with Steak Knives* Galas unleashed a 3 1/2-octave, operatically trained voice that, it has been said, pitches itself "between *The Exorcist* and Maria Callas." Galas' most notorious work is *Plague Mass* (1991), which the singer debuted in a New York cathedral with her naked torso drenched in gore. The piece, written after the AIDS-related death of her brother, indicts the hypocrisy of the Catholic church—who responded by labeling it "blasphemy." Galas' blues-inflected album *The Sporting Life*, produced in 1994 by former Led Zeppelin bassist John Paul Jones, was tame by comparison, but it was still off the pop scale. As indeed is Galas' penchant for the outrageous quote: she once told a journalist that "People who wear RED RIBBONS should be forcibly injected with HIV-positive blood."

gangsta Generic name, coined circa 1987, for tough-talking West Coast HIP-HOP. Some regard Philadelphia's Schoolly D as the original gangsta rapper, but the genre was fully inaugurated in ICE-T's 1987 album *Rhyme Pays*. Ice-T and N.W.A—whose March 1989 *Straight Outta Compton* album followed group-member EAZY E's solo debut the year before, *Eazy-Duz-It*—portrayed a lifestyle that further exaggerated the macho myths of '70s blaxploitation movies. Gangsta style revolved around "gats" (from the 19th century Gatling gun), gang wars, treacherous females ("bitches" and "ho's"), and

LOWRIDER car culture. Later accessories came to include blunts (fat joints) and 40-OUNCE bottles of malt liquor. For hip-hop, gangsta meant an irrevocable change of tenor, a tectonic shift away from politically aware performers like PUBLIC ENEMY and KRS-One to a music of boastful, vengeful pleasure-seeking. By 1992, both MTV and the pop charts felt the impact of self-proclaimed gangstas like former N.W.A members ICE CUBE and DR. DRE, and the latter's discovery SNOOP DOGGY DOGG. The crossover success matched ultraviolent VIDEOGAME phenomena like MORTAL KOMBAT as a measure of the culture's indulgence of (mainly white, suburban) male bloodlust.

With the likes of Dr. Dre and Oakland's TUPAC SHAKUR accumulating impressive rap sheets, and Snoop Doggy Dogg charged in an August 1993 murder, Congress staged hearings on gangsta rap in February 1994. The politicians failed to remark upon gangsta's patriotic spirit: an unrelenting emphasis on the first two Amendments of the constitution (free speech, the right to bear arms); rampant individualism; superhero persona as sales tool; and an unquestioning endorsement of capitalist gain.

WEB **Hip-hop lyrics site** http://www.brad.ac.uk/ ~ctttaylo/lyrics.html/ ✦ USENET **alt.rap, rec.music.hip-hop** ✦ WEB **Rap FAQ** http://dynamo.geof.ruu.nl:8080/~haven/ alt.rap.FAQ.html

Gap, the Mammoth clothing retailer and amorphous sign of the times. The Gap, which has chains of more than 1,500 related stores in the U.S. alone, started life in 1969 as a humble music and Levi's jeans store in San Francisco. The outlet (named after "generation gap") evolved into a slightly faceless, if hugely profitable chain of discount sportswear stores. By the end of 1994 it had 1100-plus Gap-named outlets across the country. The company found its current egalitarian-chic style after the 1983 hiring of retail savant Mickey Drexler; he upped sales by introducing designer black into the company's palette and putting a retro spin on its sensibility—the Gap was still generic, but now it was *upscale* generic.

In the late '80s/early '90s, two memorable Gap ad campaigns in particular flouted the spendthrift tenets of the time: the first draped a carefully chosen series of hip young celebrities (among them Nicholas Cage, SPIKE LEE, and HENRY ROLLINS) with the Gap's nondescript apparel. The implication of these simple, elegant portraits (by photographers like STEVEN MEISEL and Annie Leibovitz) was that fashion didn't have to be aspirational—by simply donning a pocket-T we could be like *them*. (The strategy succeeded—"The new Maoism," said *The Village Voice*.) The Gap next colonized collective nostalgia by using icons like Hemingway, Kerouac, and Monroe as models in an impeccably photo-researched ad campaign that bore the tag line "So-and-so wore khakis." Not everyone indulged this conceit: in the *Los Angeles Times*, novelist Christopher Corbett asked: "What about Benito Mussolini? And Adolf Hitler?" If further comparisons to Saddam Hussein didn't alienate the Gap, the accompanying photo of a khaki-clad Führer probably did—without comment the chain stopped advertising in the paper. Further controversy awaited a company that was burnishing its benevolent, POLITICALLY CORRECT image with high-profile charity donations and ecologically sound policies. In early 1992 there were reports about inhuman treatment of Chinese immigrants working for the Gap and other garment manufacturers in the American-Pacific territory of Saipan. The U.S. Department of Labor successfully sued the Saipan's prominent Tan family for its employment practices, but the Gap continued to farm work out to the island.

The Gap continues to prosper, adding to its 1983 purchase of the Banana Republic with GapKids, Baby Gap, Old Navy/Gap Warehouse. The chain has even dabbled in the area of street-fashion, where it is second only to URBAN OUTFITTERS as a mass-marketer of new styles like POLECLIMBERS, THIGH-HIGH stockings, and plaid mini-skirts.

Garofalo, Janeane (b. 1964) New Jersey-born actress/comedian/former BIKE MESSENGER whose curmudgeonly riffs on pop-culture won her berths on THE LARRY SANDERS SHOW (debuted 1992) and Fox TV's short-lived *The BEN STILLER Show* (1992–93). In Stiller's sketches, she showed an uncanny talent as both acute impressionist and sharp-witted actress—skills which made her an obvious candidate for SATURDAY NIGHT LIVE. She joined the ailing show at the start of the 1994–95 season, but took a leave of absence before the season's end, loudly criticizing the male-dominated writing and production staff. Garofalo's ambivalence toward success and her apparent streak of self-loathing was typified by a *Letterman* appearance where she forcefully mocked the GENERATION X-slanted marketing of *Reality Bites* (1994), the Ben Stiller film in which she outshone nominal stars ETHAN HAWKE and WINONA RYDER. A rash of 1995 projects included reporting duties on MICHAEL MOORE's *TV Nation*, hosting *Comedy Product* on Comedy Central, and starring with UMA THURMAN in *The Truth About Cats and Dogs*.

JANEANE GAROFALO shines on CONAN O'BRIEN.

WEB **Reid Fleming's Janeane Garofalo Page**
http://www.crl.com/~rfleming/Janeane/Janeane.html ✦ WEB **Janeane Garofalo Worship Page** http://www.swcp.com/synth/janeane.html

Gates, Daryl (b. 1926) Former chief of Los Angeles Police Department, forced to retire in June 1992 at the end of a stormy year that began with the videotaped beating of RODNEY KING and concluded with the L.A. RIOTS. The national attention turned the career cop into a law-and-order figure of Nixonian dimensions; his most incendiary one-liners gained wider circulation, including "casual drugs users ought to be taken out and shot," and—commenting on a controversial police chokehold—that the arteries and veins of black people "do not open up as fast as they do on normal people." In retire-

ment, Gates marketed a VIDEOGAME and proved himself a bland talk radio host and a bankable cultural icon on the right-wing lecture circuit. Heavily criticized in the Webster Commission report on the L.A. riots for withdrawing police from poor neighborhoods at the start of trouble, Gates concurred, adding: "We should have blown a few heads off."

Gates, Henry Louis, Jr. (b. 1950) Leading African-American scholar and symbol of the academic star system, having hopped from tenured positions at Yale to Cornell to Duke to Harvard. At the latter establishment Gates brought in fellow Afro-Am celebrity CORNEL WEST; the team makes for, in the words of *The Village Voice*, "formidable opposition to Eurocentrists and AFROCENTRISTS alike." Known as "Skip," Gates regularly moves in circles outside the academy, publishing HIP-HOP album reviews in *Entertainment Weekly* and political commentary in *THE NEW YORKER*, partying with black media mogul Quincy Jones and testifying at the 2 LIVE CREW trial. Gates originally made his name as a "literary archeologist" preserving forgotten writings of 19th century African-Americans, particularly slave narratives by women. He also helped repopularize Zora Neale Hurston's 1937 novel *Their Eyes Were Watching God*, in an effort to create MULTICULTURAL expansions of the Western cannon. His 1989 academic opus, *The Signifying Monkey*, finds roots in African myths for the boasting, "signifyin(g)" parody of African-American spoken and literary traditions. Gates is also a fierce defender of affirmative action, which he has credited with getting him from Piedmont, West Virginia, to Yale.

Gathering of the Tribes Eerily prescient 1990 festival organized by Ian Astbury (b. circa 1959), singer of British would-be hard-rockers The Cult. In October 1990 in Orange County, and the Bay Area, Astbury assembled Gathering of the Tribes, a dubious-looking, scene-straddling bill of acts reportedly inspired by opinion pieces by *SPIN* editor Bob Guccione Jr. and *L.A. Times* critic Robert Hilburn. Rappers QUEEN LATIFAH and ICE-

T shared a stage with a bill that included trip-pop-pers Charlatans U.K., lesbian strummers the Indigo Girls, and power GRUNGE quartet Soundgarden. Although attendance was healthy there was no repeat performance. One year later PERRY FARRELL put on his own dubious-looking, scene-straddling festival, LOLLAPALOOZA.

Gaultier, Jean-Paul (b. 1953) Excitable French *couturier* and street-fashion maven best known for designing the cone bra worn by MADONNA on her 1990 Blonde Ambition Tour. The '80s were Gaultier's prime time: the cliché *enfant terrible* could almost have been coined for the man who—at spectacularly staged, oddly located runway shows—turned underwear into outerwear, made pinstripe suits into club fashion, and persistently tried to put skirts on men. Under the weight of personal problems Gaultier waned at the turn of the decade, but returned in full force, drawing on influences from Orthodox Jews (see RELIGIOUS FASHION) and Eskimos to that old perennial, PUNK. He was installed in 1993 as the co-host of British TV's tabloid-deluxe magazine show *Eurotrash*; after his triumphant spring 1994 show in Paris, featuring Icelandic chanteuse BJÖRK, British style magazine *The Face* declared a "Gaultier renaissance." Many Americans were introduced to the designer when he, in a 1994 TV ad for his Gaultier perfume, MORPHED from an old woman into himself.

Gauntlet, The The McDonald's of PIERCING parlors, founded in 1975 by Doug Malloy and Jim Ward; the chain's flagship West Hollywood store boasts over 75,000 served. Gauntlet business—which doubled each year between 1992 and 1995 with outlets operating in San Francisco, New York, and Chicago—is one of the surest indices of piercing's spread in the era of SUPERMODEL and video-star navel rings. In a National Public Radio round-up of 1994, the New York Gauntlet reported that its top five piercings for the year were "by leaps and bounds" navel, followed by nipple, nostril, tongue, and eyebrow.

WEB **BME: The Body Modification E-Zine** http://www.io.org/~bme/ ✦ USENET **rec.arts.bodyart**

gay and lesbian teens Outreach programs for gay teens seeped into local communities nationwide in the early '90s, prompting Senator Jesse Helms to propose in 1994 banning federal money for any school district that permits school counselors to refer students to gay and lesbian support groups. As such groups proliferated on- and off-line, so did studies of the hardships faced by gay teens. One nationwide 1993 survey found that gay insults were the worst possible harassment for high school boys, dreaded even more than being beaten up. Similarly, a 1994 Children's Aid Society report estimated that: one-third of teen suicide victims are homosexual; 40 percent of homosexual youth are victims of violence from family or friends because they are gay; and half of New York City's 15,000 homeless youth are homosexual. Safe sex has also been a major issue relating to gay teens—repeated studies using attitude surveys and HIV infection rates showed that '90s teens were ignoring it more than those in the late '80s. [See also P-FLAG.]

WEB **Project 21** http://emanate.com/glwa/proj21/ ✦ WEB **soc.support.youth.gay-lesbian-bi home page** http://www.youth.org/ssyglb/ IRC **#gayteen** ✦ USENET **soc.support.youth.gay-lesbian-bi**

gay marriage Logical conclusion of the trend toward mainstreaming gay lifestyles, pushed by progressive labor unions and gay conservatives ("homo-cons"): the former looking to secure spousal benefits such as tax deductions and health insurance for "domestic partners"; the latter, such as *New Republic*

THE GAUNTLET puts PIERCING on the map.

editor Andrew Sullivan, trying to reconcile Republican and religious FAMILY VALUES with the homosexuality right-wingers increasingly define themselves against. In 1993 the Hawaii Supreme Court ruled that a refusal to grant marriage licenses to same-sex couples violated the state constitution. Two years later other states (including Utah, South Dakota and Alaska) drafted laws outlawing gay marriage (see also ANTI-GAY RIGHTS INITIATIVES). Some homosexuals argue that gay marriage is a bourgeois attempt to normalize gays and lesbians. In 1994 the Doonesbury comic strip popularized the late Yale professor John Boswell's *Same-Sex Unions in Premodern Europe*, which found evidence of church-sanctioned gay weddings in the Middle Ages.

WEB **Same-Sex Marriage Home Page** http://www.nether.net/ ~rod/html/sub/marriage.html ✦ WEB **Marriage Mailing List** http://www.nether.net/~rod/html/sub/marriage/maillist.html

gay street patrols After a 31 percent average increase in hate crimes in 1991 (according to the National Gay and Lesbian Task Force, 1992), gay safety patrols have been appearing throughout the country. New York's Pink Panthers, formed in New York City in summer 1990, were followed by groups in cities like Washington, D.C., Boston, San Francisco, and Dallas. Active groups include the Pink Angels in Chicago and the Queer Street Patrol in Seattle and Vancouver, British Columbia. Safety patrols consist of miniature armies of young volunteers, who usually don some variation of an all-black outfit that features a pink logo. In unarmed groups of five to 10 people, they march the streets of gay neighborhoods every weekend, watching for potential disturbances; police are called via a radio and dispatcher if necessary. Many groups also hold self-defense training for the community.

Generation X Canadian novelist DOUGLAS COUPLAND knew the name of his first book was damaged goods: originally the title of a British 1964 youth-pulp book, *Generation X* had also been the name of Billy Idol's '70s punk-pulp band before it appeared as a chapter in *Class* (1983) by essayist Paul Fussell. As Coupland's literary soufflé rose into a word-of-mouth phenomenon, pundits and marketers took the handy title to describe the entire post-BABY BOOM generation. The advent of Generation X (as opposed to *Generation X*) brought down an avalanche of media attention; Coupland's observations about parental divorce, diminished job expectations, and irony-rich living were amplified and distorted by a slew of think-pieces that also employed labels like "slackers" (after RICHARD LINKLATER's film), "baby busters," and "twentysomethings." Marketers quickly caught Gen X-hysteria and frantically attempted to explain the tastes and mores of the 46 million Americans between 18 to 30; youth-centric ad campaigns inevitably followed (the 46 million had *$125 billion* in spending power!), often with embarrassing results: if this "generation" ever had any common cause, it was a revulsion at egregious pitches like the now-legendary spokesboy for Subaru's Impreza sneering in 1993, "this car is like punk rock."

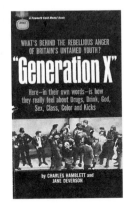

Just one of GENERATION X's many prior incarnations– UK paperback 1964.

In 1965 culture critic Renata Adler noted that "a few simple questions quickly identify a generation . . . not only from its parents and its children, but from its brothers and sisters as well." That was before the youth culture industry had cable TV, niche magazines, and mass-hip boutiques at its disposal. With the '90s proliferation of consumer choice the very idea of a "generation" taxes the credulity of everyone but the most desperate magazine feature editors. The Gen X circus was roundly ridiculed in *Generation Ecch!*, a 1994 screed by Jason Cohen and Michael Krugman; *Village Voice* critic Mike Rubin said it more simply: "Generalization X." Initial contempt for the "Gen-X" label eventually wore off, allowing it to became a mildly ironic form of self-reference. In the June 1995 issue of *DETAILS*, Douglas Coupland asserted that "X got hypermarketed right from the start," continuing, "And now I'm here to say that X is over"—just in time for his new catchphrase . . . *Microserfs*!

USENET **alt.society.generation-x**

Gertz, Alison (b. 1966; d. 1992) Straight, white, and affluent, Gertz became the "it can happen to anyone" symbol of AIDS after appearing on the cover of *People* magazine in 1990. Gertz made a tour of talk shows and college campuses warning young people about the dangers of unprotected intercourse, counseling abstinence as "the only real safe sex," and maintaining that she contracted the virus at age 16 from a one-night stand with a Studio 54 bartender whom she later learned was BISEXUAL. *Newsweek* reported that "a federal AIDS hotline received a record 180,251 calls" the day after a made for TV movie based on her life (starring Molly Ringwald) aired on ABC in March 1992. Gertz died that August 8th at her parent's summer home in the Hamptons.

Geto Boys, the HIP-HOP controversialists from Houston's notorious Fifth Ward. With the 1988 album *Making Trouble*, the Ghetto Boys' (the spelling slip came later) set a new standard in recorded violence; their raps evoked slasher-movie series like *Child's Play*, *Friday the 13th*, and *Nightmare on Elm Street* rather than one of their GANGSTA peers. National notoriety came in 1990 when the band signed to RICK RUBIN's Def American label; the resulting *Geto Boys* album (largely rehashes of old songs) was deemed so offensive by Def American's then-partner Geffen that the company refused to distribute it. The cover of the next, platinum, Geto Boys' album *We Can't Be Stopped* (1991) bore an abiding image of the group: a documentary photo in which band members push a hospital gurney bearing the fifty-four-inch frame of band member Bushwick Bill (b. Richard Shaw, circa 1967). The latter talks into a CELLULAR PHONE despite a horrific eye injury incurred after he asked his girlfriend to shoot him. Ironically, the album yielded the pop hit "Mind Playing Tricks On Me," a record whose soulful, reflective mood SCARFACE

(b. Brad Jordan, 1970) carried over into his solo career. In 1995 Bushwick Bill changed his name to Dr. Wolfgang Von Bushwickin the Barbarian Mother Funky Stay High Dollar Billstir for his album *Phantom Of The Rapra*.

WEB **Hip Hop Lyrics: The Geto Boys** http://www.brad.ac.uk/ ~ctttaylo/lyrics/geto.boys/geto.html

GHB Stimulant that started in gyms as an alternative to outlawed steroids, then crossed over to L.A. clubs. The substance, gamma hydroxy butyrate, is usually sold in powdered or capsule form, but users typically boil it into a liquid and keep it in the fridge. The FDA warned consumers in 1990 not to take the "illegally marketed drug" after widespread reports that mixed with alcohol and other drugs, it can cause nausea, life-threatening breathing problems, seizures, and comas. Sales were banned, but possession is still legal. Authorities continue to prosecute gyms and health food stores that sell GHB as a "legal psychedelic" and fat-burner. TATTOOED body builders in Atlanta call it "Georgia Home Boy"; in Hollywood, Billy Idol (who was felled by it in 1993) and others know it as "Grievous Bodily Harm" (British legal term for assault). GHB is also reportedly popular in young Hollywood; it turned up in the autopsy of RIVER PHOENIX.

WEB **ghb synthesis** http://hyperreal.com/drugs/depressants/ghb.synthesis

Gibson, William Ford (b. 1948) As indebted to Raymond Chandler's California NOIR as to traditional science fiction, Gibson's 1984 novel *Neuromancer* inaugurated the new sci-fi genre of CYBERPUNK. An American residing in Vancouver, British Columbia, Gibson wrote *Neuromancer* on a manual typewriter after publishing such stories as "Johnny Mnemonic" (source for Robert Longo's unsuccessful 1995 film) and "Burning Chrome," which were set in the *Neuromancer* universe. While the gangling, 6'6" Gibson didn't invent cyberpunk, he did coin the term "cyberspace," which he defined as a surf-able 3-D representation of all the computer data in the world. (For Gibson, this "consensual hallucination" primarily concerns the transactions of multinational capital.) Having established his finely drawn dystopia, Gibson fleshed it out in two more novels, *Count Zero* (1986) and *Mona Lisa Overdrive* (1988), becoming something of a media star in the process. (Interviewing U2 for *DETAILS* and playing a cameo in the TV series *WILD PALMS* were two of his newfound perks.) In 1990, Gibson co-authored the STEAMPUNK computer novel *The Difference Engine* with BRUCE STERLING; he edged closer to the mainstream with his 1994 novel *Virtual Light* by focusing less on technology and more on its societal effects.

WEB **William Gibson and Cyberpunk** http://sfbox.vt.edu: 10021/J/jfoley/gibson/gibson.html ✦ USENET **alt.cyberpunk, rec.arts.sf.written**

Gilbert, Sara (b. 1975) Emmy-nominated, perpetually black-clad daughter of *Roseanne*'s sitcom family (and real-life sibling of *Little House on the Prairie*'s Melissa). As Roseanne's daughter Darlene Conner, Gilbert is existential, suspicious of authority, and always with a hip quip on her lip—traits that came in handy when Gilbert voiced Bart's girlfriend on *THE SIMPSONS*. A measure of Gilbert's worth to the *Roseanne* show was the effort producers made when she enrolled as a psychology major at Yale in fall 1993: storylines were written around the absent actress, and her scenes were filmed away from the rest of the cast in an East Coast studio. It remains to be seen if Gilbert will flourish beyond the confines of the Conner household, but her low profile and occasional outside work (she smooched DREW BARRYMORE in 1992's *Poison Ivy*) bode well.

Global Positioning System Network of U.S. military satellites that relays one's location on planet earth, accurate to within inches, to increasingly miniaturized sensor devices. Handheld consumer versions began appearing for under $1,000 in 1992 that have been deliberately modified to only give readings accurate to within 100 feet. In 1994 Japan became the first country to widely market GPS devices coupled with CD-ROM roadmaps as car navigation aids, a digital cartography technology that brings to mind the Steven Wright joke, "I have

an actual size map of the United States at home. One mile equals one mile."

WEB **GPS Global Time Series** http://sideshow.jpl.nasa.gov/ mgh/series.html ✦ MAIL LIST **GPS Digest** email gps-request@tws4.si.com

Goa Indian coastal state whose endless, perfect beaches, cloudless climate, and minimal cost of living have long made it a desirable destination for multinational hippies. Since the late '60s people have arrived in Goa and stayed for months, sometimes years, just letting their hair grow and tans deepen. The advent of RAVE culture brought a new generation of sybarites to the shores of this former Portuguese colony, turning it by the early '90s into what *Option* magazine called a "bohemian Club Med." Despite the attentions of the local police force, the beaches of Baga and Cangalute still play host to thousands-strong crowds partying till dawn on to a TECHNO soundtrack provided by name-brand European Djs.

WEB **GOAWEB** http://mrlxp2.mrl.uiuc.edu/~menezes/ goa/goaweb.html

goatee Pointy, billy-goat beard often worn by nouveau bohemians like ETHAN HAWKE and PERRY FARRELL to evoke the era and aura of BEATS, bongos, and bop. Metal variations include the Mephistophelian shaved-head-and-chin-strip sported by Anthrax founding member Scott Ian. The band's 1992 appearance on *Married with Children* may have influenced son Bud Bundy (David Faustino) to take up the "full circle" beard (mustache and chin-fuzz touch). The goatee is not to be confused with the lone tuft of hair beneath the lower lip known as a "soul patch" (worn by *BEVERLY HILLS 90210*'s Luke Perry in *Buffy the Vampire Slayer* [1992].)

gold teeth Most commonly used by dentists as a non-toxic alternative to porcelain dentures, gold teeth are also valued as a status symbol by black youth. PUBLIC ENEMY rap star Flavor Flav was a pioneer in this area, sporting a mouthful of precious metal spelling "Flavor" as far back as 1988. Other dental decorations included the Mercedes Benz and

NIKE symbols. Predominantly used as a permanent operation, clip-on gold (or gold-plated) teeth slipped into the mainstream when none other than MADONNA sported one during her *Erotica* album period.

Goth   Unlikely as it may seem, this movement fostered at a London nightclub called the Batcave in 1981 has become one of the longest-enduring youth-culture tribes. The original Goths, named after the medieval Gothic era, were pale-faced, black-swathed, hair-sprayed night dwellers who valued imagery both religious and sacrilegious, consumptive poets, and all things spooky. (A mammoth 1995 Goth history in *Alternative Press* named 1969's *The Marble Index* by former Velvet Underground chanteuse Nico as the first true Goth album.) Their bands included Sex Gang Children, Specimen, and Alien Sex Fiend, were post-PUNK doom merchants who sang of horror-film imagery and transgressive sex, and hinted at forces older than rock itself. When Goth returned to the underground in Britain, it took root in a part of the world where the sun actually shined, namely California. English bands like Bauhaus, Siouxsie and the Banshees, and the Sisters of Mercy cast a powerful spell over the imaginations of suburban legions of the night, and pop-Goth variants The Cure and Depeche Mode filled stadiums. As Goths grew up they often embraced INDUSTRIAL (NINE INCH NAILS) and even NEW AGE (Dead Can Dance) variations. To this day the movement continues to replenish itself with fresh blood of new bands and fans—Goth debates thrive on the INTERNET, and nationwide there flourish club nights at which those original Batcave dwellers would not feel out of place.
WEB **VampLeStat's Gothic Server** http://www.dnx.com/vamp/Gothic/ ✦ WEB **Gothic Stuff** http://www.crg.cs.nott.ac.uk/~rji/Gothic/index.html ✦ USENET **alt.gothic** ✦ MAIL LIST **GOTHIC-TALES** email carriec@eskimo.com with "subscribe" in the subject and "subscribe gothic yourname @Host" in the message

Grad Nite   Annual all-night drug- and alcohol-free bash for graduating high school seniors.

Disneyland, for instance, has sponsored Grad Nites since 1961; at Disney World in Florida, over 100,000 students from over 700 schools bus in for the four-night event, during which the park is kept open from 11 P.M. to 5 A.M. and Top 40 pop stars are paraded before the throng. Disney enforces a strict dress code and conducts random searches to ensure appropriate behavior; however, every year cleanup workers find some evidence of impropriety, such as discarded underwear and caches of empty ZIMA bottles. Universal Studios, Sea World, and other entertainment complexes also run their own Grad Nite promotions, while many communities sponsor less elaborate versions at local pools, bowling alleys, and that old standby, the school gym.

Grateful Dead   San Francisco band whose ursine leader Jerry Garcia (b. 1942, d. 1995) died of heart failure in a drug treatment center on August 9, 1995. (His last performance with the band was in Chicago, July 9.) Before Garcia's demise cast doubt on its future, the band was described variously as the longest-running of the original San Francisco hippy bands; the richest psychedelic roots-music noodlers on the planet; and perpetual drug culture accessory. No account of this band (formed in 1965 as the Warlocks) can ignore the formidable, $50-million-plus per annum, economy it built around itself. While charging significantly less for concert tickets than other major acts, the Dead consistently topped charts of box-office earnings; their organization was reportedly used as a model at IBM management-training courses (minus, presumably, the band's profit-sharing component); Garcia himself licensed lucrative lines of ties and skis (not to mention BEN & JERRY'S "Cherry Garcia" flavor). And the Dead always encouraged taping of its three-hour-plus, ever-changing shows (see *GRAY AREAS*) while selling old concert material though its own label by the hundreds of thousands. The most remarkable part of the Grateful Dead phenomenon, however, are the thousands of DEADHEADS who trek across the country in the band's wake.
WEB **The Grateful Dead** http://www.cs.cmu.edu:8001/afs/cs.cmu.edu/user/mleone/web/dead.html

Gray Areas Periodical dedicated to such ethically debatable practices as taping live music, ticket scalping, and the pirating of film, video, and software. Launched by Alan Sheckter and Netta Gilboa in 1992, *Gray Areas* appears more or less on a quarterly basis. These consumer alternatives will likely multiply as the popular arts are increasingly digitized. Bands such as the GRATEFUL DEAD and PHISH have long acknowledged this, providing special seats for tapers at their concerts without any detectable effect on sales of their legitimate product. In another piracy custom, videotapes of Academy Award-nominated films provided to Academy of Motion Picture Arts and Sciences members are habitually bootlegged; similarly, street bootlegging of music exploded in the early '90s (see HIP-HOP BOOTLEGGING), along with bootlegged films camcorded in cinemas.

Great Grunge Hoax, The *The New York Times* accompanied a November 15, 1992 "Styles of the Times" article on "GRUNGE" with a sidebar "Lexicon of Grunge: Breaking the Code" defining the hip new "grunge speak, coming soon to a high school or mall near you." The piece translated happening new terms for ripped jeans ("wack slacks"), an uncool person ("lame stain"), and hanging out ("swingin' on the flippity-flop"). The only problem was that the glossary turned out to be a prank. As first reported *THE BAFFLER*, The Great Grunge Hoax was perpetrated by Megan Jasper, an employee of Caroline Records in Seattle who had similarly duped the British magazine *Sky*.

Green Day "Do you have the time / To listen to me whine?" sang Anglo-inflected Bay Area native Billie Joe (b. Billie Joe Armstrong, 1972) on Green Day's 1994 single "Basket Case." The answer was in the affirmative from over 4 million buyers of the band's *Dookie* album; there was apparently a post-GRUNGE appetite for bracing PUNK-pop directly descended from British acts like the Buzzcocks and The Jam. Green Day earned their success through constant touring and two modestly selling independent-label albums, the first of which, 1990's *39*

Smooth, was reportedly recorded for a mere $600.

Green Day raised its profile by bringing a blast of MANIC PANIC'd nostalgia to WOODSTOCK '94. Billy Joe downed his guitar and, to sparse bass-and-drums accompaniment, baited the crowd with a selection of rock chants; the ensuing muddy stage invasion (in which drummer Mike Dirnt [b. Michael Pritchard, 1972] had teeth broken) drew comparisons both to The Who's anarchic routine at the original Woodstock, and to Sha Na Na, the group that brought a blast of pomaded '50s nostalgia to the 1969 love-fest. (Former Sha Na Na member Elliot Cahn is one of Green Day's managers.)
USENET **alt.music.green-day**, **alt.music.green-day.sucks** ✦ WEB **Dookie Page** http://b61791.student.cwru.edu/green-day.htm ✦ WEB **Homage to Green Day** http://www.cs.caltech.edu/~adam/greenday.html

green marketing Major merchandising shift in the early '90s that used feel-good environmental claims to deflect grass-roots criticism and sell everything from deodorant and pantyhose to laundry detergent and fast food. This corporate strategy in turn prompted the Federal Trade Commission (FTC) and state legislatures to restrict deceptive promotional claims. In one typical case from 1994, the country's second-largest producer of Styrofoam, Amoco, agreed to drop the term "recyclable" from its marketing because, while the cups and plates *can* be recycled, in practice they are not. Green marketing has had its most practical impact on packaging, including the record industry's decision to drop the CD LONGBOX in 1992 and McDonald's 1990 shift from foam containers to brown paper under pressure from a national GREEN TEEN movement called Kids Against Pollution. Not to be outdone, Pepsi and other marketers "improved" the use of browns and other natural colors with CLEAR PRODUCTS.
WEB **Green Seal** http://solstice.crest.org:80/environment/GreenSeal/ ✦ WEB **Internet Green Marketplace** http://envirolink.org:80/products/allproducts.html

green teens Generic description for the type of teen environmental activism that has forced McDonald's to stop using polystyrene packaging

(1990), Star Kist to sell only dolphin-safe tuna (1989), and, most influentially, parents to reduce, reuse, and recycle. Other successes include a 1990 California law banning the mass release of balloons (birds can choke on shreds of burst balloons) and thousands of cases of schools switching, under pressure, to reusable cafeteria-ware. There are hundreds of local groups, but the three largest organizations—Kids Against Pollution (KAP), Kids For A Clean Environment (KidsFACE), and STUDENT ENVIRONMENTAL ACTION COALITION—each claim thousands of chapters nationwide. Cultural manifestations include eco-superheroes (e.g. Marvel Comics' *Captain Planet*, voiced by Tom Cruise on the TBS cable network); the bestseller *50 Simple Things Kids Can Do to Save the Earth*; and GREEN MARKETING products targeted at kids.

WEB **SEACweb: Home Page of the Student Environmental Action Coalition** http://www.seac.org/
✦ WEB **Environment – All Links** http://adams.ind.net/Environment.html

Greenpeace   Paragon of environmental activism, born as a Canadian anti-nuclear group in 1971, Greenpeace's oppositional credentials are still intact in spite of a membership numbering in the millions, offices in 30 countries, and an annual income of $50 million. The organization is still best known for its fearless guerrilla flotillas. Greenpeace ships have been rammed (November 1992, while trailing a plutonium-laden Japanese ship), shot at (October 1992 by Russian Coast Guards, while probing intro nuclear waste dumps in the Arctic Circle), and in June 1985, blown up by French secret agents. In that infamous incident, a Greenpeace photographer was killed, and the Mitterrand administration severely compromised. (Columnist Christopher Hitchens concluded, "One cannot eat enough to vomit enough at the mention of Mitterrand's name.") Among the group's more theatrical protests: wrapping the French and Italian embassies in Greece with 600 yards of fishnet to protest harmful fishing practices (1994), rappelling down the United Nations building in New York to highlight inadequate policies on global warming

(1992), and freeing a whale captured by Norwegian mariners (1994).

WEB **Greenpeace International** http://www.greenpeace.org/

Greyson, John (b. 1961)   *Urinal*, this Canadian director's 1988 feature debut, was a coruscating comedy of gay post-modernism set in a world populated by famous BISEXUAL artists (Oscar Wilde, Yukio Mishima, Gertrude Stein), and powered by angry pedantry. In 1993, Greyson upped the ante for homo po-mo with *Zero Patience*, an ambitious musical comedy based on the life of the French-Canadian flight attendant who may have introduced the AIDS virus to North America. With music by composer Glenn Schellenberg and songs by Greyson himself, the film—partly inspired by ACT-UP—attacked narrow-minded politicians, profiteering doctors, and even the entire empirical tradition in Western science. Greyson's spiteful wit will probably preclude the type of art-house success realized by gay and lesbian directors like Rose Troche (*Go Fish*), TODD HAYNES, and GREGG ARAKI.

Groundlings   L.A. improvisational and sketch comedy troupe that serves as a training grounds for TV comedy. Incorporated in 1974, the Groundlings—named after a *Hamlet* reference to the poor members of the audience ("The groundlings, who for the most part are capable of nothing but inexplicable dumb-shows and noise")—draws players from its 300-student Improv School. Famous grads include CONAN O'BRIEN, PAUL REUBENS (as Pee-Wee Herman), and *SATURDAY NIGHT LIVE* alumni such as Larraine Newman, Phil Hartman, Jon Lovitz, and Julia Sweeney. Two recent Groundlings, Cheri Oteri and Will Ferrell, were drafted for *SNL's* 1995–96 season.

grunge   Under the cumulative influences of PUNK and '70s heavy metal (not to mention year-round rain, coffee, cheap, potent beer, and, occasionally, HEROIN) a cohort of SEATTLE bands developed a soulful hard-rock variant that was instrumental to ALTERNATIVE music's early-'90s move overground. "Grunge" was originally a tongue-in-

GRUNGE
pencil set
by PETER
BAGGE.

cheek term for the pungent guitar noise propagated by cultish independent label SUB POP. When Sub Pop act NIRVANA went platinum on major label Geffen, grunge bands began to displace pop-metal acts on MTV; by 1993 the desolate anthems and crepuscular images of Soundgarden, Alice In Chains, and Candlebox (all from Seattle), and the STONE TEMPLE PILOTS would replace the tumescent choruses and perky videos of Warrant, Poison, Slaughter, and Cinderella as the station's dominant aesthetic. Numerous culture-makers embarrassed themselves in the gold rush to exploit the only vital white youth culture in years. Grunge "fashion"—the perpetual flannel shirt/COMBAT BOOTS/RIPPED JEANS uniform of suburban burnouts everywhere—was suddenly used as an exotic novelty by designers like MARC JACOBS, ANNA SUI, and Christian Francis Roth, who created their interpretations of same; department store racks groaned under the weight of these unsold, high-priced K-Mart knockoffs. The nadir of the media's grunge fixation came on November 15, 1992, with the GREAT GRUNGE HOAX in the *New York Times.*

Guerrilla Girls   Small, direct-action group of anonymous art-world feminists who don gorilla masks for demonstrations; founded in New York in 1985 with the explicit mission of increasing the visibility of women and minorities in the art world. Although membership is said to include well-known artists and gallery proprietors, identities are also hidden by assuming the names of famous women artists like Frida Kahlo or Georgia O'Keefe. New York and L.A. street-theater demonstrations and agitprop posters, akin to those of ACT-UP and WAC, often attack the artworld establishment with straightforward headcounts—one poster before the 1993 WHITNEY BIENNIAL stated plainly, "No female black painter or sculptor has been in a Whitney Biennial since 1973." Other messages use sarcasm: "The advantages of being a woman artist: working without the pressure of success, having an escape from the art world in your four freelance jobs, being reassured that whatever art you make will be labeled feminine."
WEB **Voyager: Guerrilla Girls** http://www.voyagerco.com/becca/gg.html

hackers Computer-designer or -programmer equivalents of Zen adepts, able to do hexadecimal long division mentally and subsist for days on nothing but JOLT soda and corn chips. Though almost all hackers distinguish themselves from the "crackers" or "dark side hackers" that use their often-inferior skills to vandalize computer systems, news reports rarely make the distinction. The mythology of the hacker—both master and student of all logical systems from sewer tunnels to phone networks—is nonetheless fed by the headline-getting exploits of rogue hackers like PHONE PHREAK KEVIN MITNICK and blue collar gangs such as New York's Masters of Deception (see PHIBER OPTIK). The golden rule of hacker morality, informally recognized as "the hacker ethic," is that information wants to be free—though computerization has catapulted hackers like Bill Gates into untold riches. [See also FREE SOFTWARE FOUNDATION, *2600.*]

WEB **The New Hacker's Dictionary** http://www.eps

mcgill.ca/~steeve/tnhd.html ✦ WEB **Name Hack Attack**

http://www.well.com/conf/hack/ ✦ IRQ **#hack**

hair pulling madness Disease (in Latin, *trichotillomania*) thought to afflict between two and four million Americans. The majority of sufferers are women who begin in their teens or early '20s the years-long process of follicle damage that leads to denuded scalps, eyebrows, facial hair, and pubic areas. Like overeating, bulimia, and anorexia, hair pulling is classified as an obsessive compulsive disorder and has been shown to sometimes disappear entirely under PROZAC therapy.

WEB **Obsessive Compulsive Disorders Home Page**

http://mtech.csd.uwm.edu/~fairlite/ocd.html

Hall, Arsenio (b. circa 1956) After moderate success as a stand-up comedian and actor—mainly as a movie foil to pal Eddie Murphy—Cleveland-born Arsenio Hall changed the face of late-night TV with his own syndicated talk/variety program, which debuted in January 1989. Hall's show marked the first time a black entertainer had ever hosted a late-night show. While critics sniped at Hall's obsequious interviewing style, his high-energy nightly event carved out a distinctive audience by regularly featuring such previously unthinkable guests as hardcore rappers, professional athletes, and African-American political figures. (Demographics-conscious President-to-be Bill Clinton appeared on the show in June 1992 to don sunglasses and play saxophone.) In May 1992, Jay Leno replaced Johnny Carson as the host of the *Tonight Show*, and despite Hall's widely reported vow to "kick [Leno's] ass," began to draw younger viewers away. Further doubts were raised by Hall's refusal, in February 1994, to drop controversial Muslim minister LOUIS FARRAKHAN from his show. The final *Arsenio Hall Show* aired on May 27 1994; Hall's final week drew 2.5 million viewers each night, and remained popular with national advertisers. Since the cancellation, Hall has kept a low profile, occasionally producing motion pictures (including 1993's *Bopha!*, directed by Morgan Freeman).

Hammer (b. Stanley Burrell, 1962) In March, 1992, a racehorse called Dance Floor was breaking for the lead in the Florida Derby when it suddenly began bleeding from the nostrils. Two years later its owner, bubblegum rapper Hammer, would know how that felt. M. C. Hammer's 15-million-selling *Please Hammer Don't Hurt 'Em* was the biggest album of 1990 and the biggest rap album of all time. The massive single "U Can't Touch This" was based on a sample of Rick James' oldie "Super Freak"; a lawsuit was settled out of court. Nicknamed for childhood hero Hammerin' Hank Aaron, M.C. Hammer won the hearts and allowances of preteen America with his flashy dancing, baggy pants, and Christian morals. While hawking Pepsi, Taco Bell, and KFC, M. C. Hammer stayed at the top of the charts for 21 weeks, until forced off by white bubblegum rapper Vanilla Ice. For 1991's *Too Legit To Quit*, Hammer dropped his M.C. and sales dropped to 5 million, despite Capitol Records' most expensive marketing campaign ever. Hammer dolls (part of BARBIE's

Celebrity Friends line) languished on toy store shelves and a *Hammerman* Saturday morning cartoon was canceled after one season. In 1994, the virtually forgotten Hammer was repositioned as a GANGSTA rapper, with predictably dismal results.

Hang Ten   San Diego, California-based surfwear company founded in 1960 by a surfer named Duke Boyd, and passed on to employee Doris Boeck shortly thereafter. Hang Ten's hooped T-shirts (and surfing shorts) with embroidered footprint logo— introduced 1962—achieved near ubiquity on beaches and playgrounds in the '60s and early '70s. Hang Ten underwent a thrift-store revival at the start of the '90s when those same shirts (known as Bobby Brady shirts after the *BRADY BUNCH* character) became an essential element in street fashion's growing INFANTILIZATION. The company responded by reintroducing in 1992 vintage Hang Ten reproductions alongside its current line.

hardcore (techno)   Label for the more punishing strains of TECHNO music. Although it has regional variations, "hardcore" generally denotes the uncompromising flail of frenzied breakbeats associated with the early '90s wave of club culture in which the jagged rush of speed replaced the amiable glow of ECSTASY. Hardcore is the polar opposite from AMBIENT techno; British critic Simon Reynolds, writing in *The New York Times*, compared this schism to rock's late-'60s/early-'70s class divide: then, PROGRESSIVE ROCK catered to the gentle middle class, while heavy metal attracted hard-drinking, Quaalude-damaged lumpenproletariat. In today's scenario, ambient is the domain of thoughtful, older listeners, while hardcore caters to the more thrash-happy macho element.

WEB **Casper's Jungle and Happy Hardcore Page**
http://web.mit.edu/afs/athena.mit.edu/user/j/c/jcarow/www/br eaks.html

Harrell, Andre (b. 1962)   Black entrepreneur who presides over Uptown Entertainment, a music, film and television conglomerate he founded in 1992 with a seven-year, $50 million credit line from MCA Records and Universal Pictures. The product of a Bronx housing project, Harrell started his career at 16 as the first half of the hit rap duo Dr. Jekyll and Mr. Hyde; he quit after a couple of years to study communications and business management at Lehman College in the Bronx, then dropped out to sell radio ads. In 1983 he started working for rap mogul RUSSELL SIMMONS' Rush Management, rising to a vice-president's position by 1985. Two years later Harrell founded Uptown Records, where he won an unimpeachable reputation for predicting popular taste, with a series of gold- and platinum-selling albums from artists like Jodeci, Mary J. Blige, Heavy D and the Boyz, Guy and Al B. Sure! With these artists, Harrell introduced a new, black urban sound that marries R&B's soul with HIP-HOP's groove; in 1993 Uptown became the first record label to be given its own MTV *UNPLUGGED* special.

WEB **AMP: NEXT (MCA Records)** http://www.mca.com/ mca_records/amp4/next.html

Hartley, Hal (b. 1960)   Filmmaker specializing in low-key, highly stylized comedies marked by elliptical conversations, deadpan delivery, and artfully arranged visual tableaus. Hartley's first three features, *The Unbelievable Truth* (1990), *Trust* (1991) and *Simple Men* (1992), are set in suburban Long Island, where he was raised. In four features and numerous short films, Hartley has groomed a coterie of talented actors including Adrienne Shelly, Martin Donovan, Karen Sillas, Robert Burke, and Elina Lowensohn. After seeing *Trust*, which won a screenwriting award at SUNDANCE, French star Isabelle Huppert wrote to Hartley asking to be in one of his films; she was cast in 1994's *Amateur*. (Hartley's film-school classmate Parker Posey is scheduled to star in 1996's *Flirt*.) In addition to writing, directing, editing and producing, Hartley frequently writes soundtrack music under the name Ned Rifle.

WEB **The Hal Hartley Web Page** http://www.best.com/ ~drumz/Hartley/

Harvard Lampoon Harvard College social club/humor magazine that functions as the semi-official boot camp for America's booming comedy industry. "Poonsters," most famously CONAN O'BRIEN, tend to dominate the writing teams of *DAVID LETTERMAN*, *SATURDAY NIGHT LIVE*, *THE SIMPSONS*, *THE LARRY SANDERS SHOW*, the Comedy Central network, and endless hours of network fare. Other famous alumni include *SPY* co-founder Kurt Andersen; Doug Kenney, *Animal House* and *Caddyshack* screenwriter and co-founder of the once-mighty *National Lampoon* (1971); and John Updike, Robert Benchley, and James Thurber. Housed on campus in a mock castle financed by newspaper magnate William Randolph Hearst—and further enriched by a licensing windfall from the *National Lampoon* movies—the Lampoon is also legendary for the prodigious drug decadence that rages within its walls.

hat acts Young male singers who revived country music's sex appeal in the 1990s. Building on the "neotraditionalist" sound and everyhunk good looks of pioneer hathead George Strait, artists like Clint Black and Alan Jackson sing warmhearted-working-man lyrics to solid country arrangements. Garth Brooks, of course, is the pre-eminent hat act, although he's actually more mawkish than most. A backlash against the sensitive-stud gimmick led to a "No Hats" tour in 1994 featuring Travis Tritt and Marty Stuart (no relation to the Men Without Hats of "Safety Dance" fame). As Stuart tells the ghost of Hank Williams in "This One's Gonna Hurt You" (1992), "Right now country music's got more singers than I believe I've ever seen . . . But I feel different . . . 'cause I'm a natural born cat / I'm country to the bone, but I don't wear no hat."
WEB **Clint Black Home Page** http://www.tpoint.net/ ~wallen/country/clint-black.html ✦ WEB **Garth Brooks home-page** http://www.tecc.co.uk/mparkes/garthbrooks/ ✦ USENET **rec.music.country**

Hatfield, Juliana (b. 1967) Former bass player/vocalist of shambling Boston INDIE-ROCKERS

Photo by Brooke Williams

JULIANA HATFIELD, *swinger*.

Blake Babies (1987–1992) who made her solo debut with 1992's *Hey Babe*. Hatfield, the daughter of a *Boston Globe* fashion writer, is a well-scrubbed, well-fed Berklee School of Music graduate whose example bolsters the contention that INDIE-ROCK is the folk art of the upper middle class. Her own art is not a robust thing: Hatfield's vocals are high-pitched and quavering, her lyrics awkwardly whimsical, her arrangements inchoate. Meanwhile, the singer's plentiful press coverage has politely disregarded her lack of measurable success; much of it focuses instead on Hatfield's personal charms, her ambiguous relationship with frequent collaborator EVAN DANDO, and her oft-remarked virginity. (When she bluntly told *Interview* magazine in September 1992, "I'm a virgin. I've never really gone all the way," some cynics hailed it as a brilliant marketing stroke.) Hatfield further reinforced her credibility in December 1994 with an acting-and-singing appearance as a homeless angel on TV's *MY SO-CALLED LIFE*.
WEB **Mammoth Records** http://www.nando.net/mammoth/ juliana.html

Hawke, Ethan (b. 1970) Young actor who is a confirmed member of the "success is a bitch," wanna-BEAT school. By lending his earnest, idealistic presence to films like *Dead Poet's Society* (1989), *A Midnight Clear* (1992), and *Alive* (1993), Hawke built an impressive, if low-key, body of work that hinted at great potential. Paradoxically, the actor's rise to prominence came when he stereotyped himself—apparently willingly—as an unwashed, GOA-TEED, GENERATION X poster boy in both BEN STILLER's *Reality Bites* (1994) and RICHARD LINKLATER's *Before Sunrise* (1995). This easily packaged image ran contrary to Hawke's wish to be taken seriously, whether acting with his New York-based experimental theater group Malaparte, or declaring his "addiction" to Bob Dylan in *Details* magazine.

Haynes, Todd (b. 1961) Controversy-prone director of meticulously art-directed independent movies. Haynes debuted in 1987 with *Superstar: The Karen Carpenter Story*, a 43-minute film in which BARBIE and Ken dolls play out the singer's life and eventual death from anorexia. JOHN WATERS called it "the little film from hell"—Karen Carpenter's brother Richard agreed and refused to grant music rights, thus blocking the movie's release. Hayes' next film *Poison* was an ambitious, stylistically diverse three-parter which, after winning a Grand Prize at the 1991 SUNDANCE festival, was targeted by REV. DONALD WILDMON; the Tupelo troubleshooter was dismayed that an NEA grant (for one tenth of the $250,000 budget) had funded the film's suggestive "Homo" segment (based on Jean Genet's novel *Miracle of the Rose*). Other than a 1994 TV play for PBS, Haynes was silent until 1995's *Safe*, a viral horror story set among the arid spaces, smooth surfaces, and double-car garages of the San Fernando Valley of Haynes' youth.

He Said/She Said comics Tabloid-exploiting comic book series. A newly enacted local law banning sales of SERIAL KILLER cards prompted Long Island, New York, brothers Joe and Paul Mauro (a law student, b. 1965, and English professor, b. 1963) to publish a set of "Sex Maniac" cards under the name First Amendment Publishing in 1992. They soon branched out to capitalize on another local issue, AMY FISHER, publishing a comic book based on news reports and trial records that, read one way, told Joey Buttafucco's side of the story; flip it over and upside down and it's Amy's version. A sold-out print run of 70,000 led to subsequent treatments of problem pairings such as Mia Farrow and Woody Allen, Bill Clinton and Gennifer Flowers, Tonya Harding and Jeff Gillooly, O.J. and Nicole Simpson, and as the O.J. "trial of the century" dragged on, even attorneys Marcia Clark and Robert Shapiro.

Hello Kitty Mouthless, twinkling-eyed star of a line of cartoon-ish products introduced by Japan's billion dollar Sanrio Co. (founded in 1960 with the motto, "small gifts for big smiles") in the absence of an actual cartoon. Sanrio entered the U.S. market shortly after Hello Kitty's 1974 debut with a chain of its own stores and department store boutiques. Sanrio products exude "kawaii," a type of cuteness valued by Japanese women in their teens and twenties. Hello Kitty found its foothold in the U.S. market with two other demographics: under–10s and irony-struck grown-ups. To hear the fervor with which the latter group discusses dozens of ingenious products related to Kitty (and, of course, her friends the Little Twin Stars, Tuxedo Sam, My Melody, and Keroppi the frog) is to be either enchanted or further convinced of the INFANTILIZATION of American culture. (MTV journalist TABITHA SOREN appeared in a *New York* magazine portrait wearing a Hello Kitty dress.) Sanrio briefly sold "Little Black Sambo" toys in Japan in 1988 until protests began in America.

USENET **alt.fan.hello-kitty** ✦ WEB **Sanrio Connection**
http://weber.u.washington.edu:80/~pokako/hello.htm

Hernandez brothers (Gilbert, b. 1957; Jaime, b. 1959) Creators of FANTAGRAPHICS' flagship comic *Love and Rockets* since 1982, Oxnard, California-bred Gilbert and Jaime Hernandez (aka Los Bros Hernandez) have drawn upon their Latino background to create comicdom's most sophisticated stories about race, sex, and Latino culture. Gilbert's extended magical-realist work "Human Diastrophism" (1988) concerns the citizens of the imaginary Latin American village of Palomar. Jaime's US-based work "Locas" (1982) stars an unlikely pair of mechanics, BISEXUAL Maggie Chascarillo and punkish lesbian Hopey Glass, and their extended circle of hip barrio pals. (Less knowing were the British new-wavers who appropriated the book's title for their band's name in the mid-'80s.) *Love and Rockets* has continued into the '90s, with Jaime extending his repertoire with the elegantly pornographic *Birdland* for Fantagraphics's Eros line.

high school student rights *New Jersey v. T.L.O.* was the first in a decade-long series of Supreme Court decisions spelling out the limited rights of teens in high school. The 1985 NJ ruling upheld the warrantless search of a high school locker or student bookbag on the grounds that the need to maintain order in the schools outweighs the privacy of junior citizens. The following year the Court O.K.'d the suspension of a student for making sexual double entendres in an assembly speech (*Bethel School District v. Fraser*); and, in 1988, ruled that teachers may censor the school newspaper (the case, *Hazelwood School District v. Kuhlmeier*, involved an article about student pregnancy). In 1995 the Supreme Court upheld the constitutionality of random DRUG TESTS for student athletes (*Vernonia School District v. Acton*).

Hilfiger, Tommy (b. 1952)   Clothier who

heroin

Romantic and doomed, heroin use has been cool since "cool" was invented in the Jazz Age. A noble artistic lineage from William Burroughs and John Coltrane, through the Velvet Underground and Keith Richards, leads up to '90s archetypes like PERRY FARRELL and Kurt Cobain, who both pushed smack toward fashion accessory status. By mid-decade, the drug had become a cultural signifier on a par with GRUNGE rockers, waif models, and GOATEED poets.

While hard figures on heroin use are scant, from the Drug Enforcement Administration down to police stations and rehab units, the consensus is this: There are larger amounts of the drug, more casualties, and more addicts seeking treatment in the mid-'90s than 10 years before. Imports of the drug rose, the *Washington Post* reported, from four to six tons a year in the early '80s to 20 tons a year by 1994. While the government sets the national junkie count at 400,000, the true figure is probably a lot higher. Unless users OD, get arrested, join a detox/rehab program, or, perhaps, volunteer the information on a questionnaire, they are invisible to the census takers.

Increased heroin use is not unrelated to developments in the world drug markets. Since the late '80s, street heroin in the U.S. became better, purer, and cheaper than it ever had been before. The traditional source of heroin, the Golden Triangle, was supplemented, according to the DEA, with new poppy fields in Mexico and South America. There, cocaine drug cartels eagerly diversified into heroin, a less-exacting crop with longer-term customers. One early '90s NNICC (National Narcotics Intelligence Consumer Committee) report compared the purity of present day samples of street heroin with a decade ago; it found that yesteryear's 7 percent had multiplied five-fold while maintaining the same average price of $100-$150 per gram. At this purity, it was no longer necessary to inject the drug to get high–smoking heroin off tin-foil ("chasing the dragon") became a socially acceptable activity in many influential circles, as did snorting. The clean, bloodless high greatly expanded heroin's appeal among an AIDS-wary public.

HEROIN packages, New York City 1995.

Many of heroin's new aficionados are graduates of yesterday's frantic coke crowd. These predominantly white middle and upper class users rediscovered heroin's storied euphoria–a "gentle explosion" as Matt Dillon's character had it in 1989's heroin-chic landmark, *Drugstore Cowboy*.

began in 1969 as a vendor of hippie fashions and later became a denizen of New York glam-rock mecca Max's Kansas City. Hilfiger designed for disco-era couturier Jordache before launching his eponymous line of straight-arrow PREPPY gear in 1985. The following year the relatively unknown designer launched a hubristic $3 million ad campaign which declared "The 4 Great American Designers for Men Are: R— L—, P— E—, C— K—, T— H—." (RALPH LAUREN, Perry Ellis, CALVIN KLEIN, and, of course, Hilfiger himself.) By decade's end Hilfiger's sales were at $25 million a year. "Tommy got the colors," conceded one young African-American aficionado of Ralph Lauren in Britain's *The Face* in 1992, referring to Hilfiger's penchant for regatta-bright designs. The designer's street popularity was confirmed when SNOOP DOGGY DOGG wore a red, white, and blue Hilfiger rugby shirt on *SATURDAY NIGHT LIVE* in March 1994. Hilfiger responded to increased sales by designing baggier garments, including his own ICE HOCKEY JERSEYS.

Some weekend dilettantes ("chippers") also discovered that heroin was gentler on the body than cocaine, and soon fell into a typical pattern of escalating doses that define the "maintenance relationship" of many long-term users.

The resurgence of heroin was most evident in the rock industry, where the Reagan-era, Just Say No silence was first broken, volubly, by PERRY FARRELL. The singer didn't stop at naming his band Jane's Addiction; he put a methadone bottle on the back of the 1990 album *Ritual de lo Habitual* and proselytized for junk in interviews. Kurt Cobain and COURTNEY LOVE showed a similar willingness to broach the topic with journalists, and dozens more ALTERNATIVE rockers indulged themselves in private. Most prominent among rock casualties were Hole bassist Kristen Pfaff (1994) and Andrew Wood of Mother Love Bone (1990); the Breeders' Kelley Deal and STONE TEMPLE PILOTS' Scott Weiland both had legal imbroglios in 1995 stemming from alleged use. Head DEADHEAD Jerry Garcia died the same year in heroin rehab.

Following the lead of *Drugstore Cowboy,* indie-Hollywood used heroin liberally in films that included *Pulp Fiction* (1994), *Killing Zoe* (1994), and *The Basketball Diaries* (1995). Not all of Hollywood's heroin was consumed onscreen. L.A.'s "smack pack" of young actors and musicians was a legend well before the heroin-related 1993 death of RIVER PHOENIX. Heroin's penetration of the culture even extended to the fashion world, where photographer Corinne Day was accused of promoting a junkie aesthetic with her hollowed-eyed shots of an emaciated KATE MOSS.

The drug's foremost man of letters, William Burroughs, was resurrected by rock stars Cobain and MINISTRY; and videos such as TORI AMOS's "God" and the Black Crowes' "Sometimes Salvation" wallowed in the opiate's beautiful sadness. (Heroin use wasn't the sole domain of the sensitive–it had also helped define the L.A. rock scene in the '80s, with the 1987 overdose of Motley's Crue's Nikki Sixx, the 1988 death of Red Hot Chili Peppers guitarist Hillel Slovak, and Guns 'N Roses' public in-fighting over member's habits at the height of the band's fame.)

Beyond the imagery of introspection and alienation that surrounds heroin–and which fits with the diminished expectations of other aspects of "loser culture"–the drug emerged as an authentic commitment in a time of mass-dabbling in transgressive styles such as body PIERCING and TATTOOING. But while the solemnity of heroin use seemed to mock the luxury of consumer choice, heroin perversely made those on what *The Village Voice*'s Ann Powers called "the outer edge of bohemia's outsider world" into the ultimate brand-loyal consumers.–*Mark Ehrman*

WEB **Hyperreal Drug Archive** http://hyperreal.com/drugs/opiates/ ✦ WEB **National Alliance of Methadone Advocates** http://www.interport.net/~clueless/nama1.html ✦ WEB **Paranoia Drug Information Server** http://www.paranoia.com/drugs/ ✦ FTP **Street Terms for Drugs and the Drug Trade** ftp://aspensys.com/pub/ncjrs/street.txt

Hill, Anita (b. 1956)   Law professor who ignited a storm of sexual and racial controversy during the October 1991 Senate confirmation hearings on Justice Clarence Thomas's nomination to the Supreme Court. Hill—a black woman who had worked in 1982 as Thomas's assistant at the Equal Employment Opportunity Commission—alleged that Thomas, also black, had repeatedly pressured her for dates and made lurid remarks (most famously about the penis of porn star Long Dong Silver and a "pubic hair" on his Coke can). During the three days of Democrat-chaired televised hearings, an estimated 30 million households watched as a panel of white male Senators attempted to discredit Hill, with Republicans Orrin Hatch and Arlen Specter suggesting, respectively, that Hill (a Republican) was in collusion with liberal groups and harbored erotic fantasies about Thomas. Thomas, who complained that the proceedings were a "high-tech lynching" of an "uppity" black, was confirmed. Sexual harassment subsequently became a subject of heated public debate, with *Time* magazine reporting that the EEOC logged a record 9,920 sexual harassment complaints in 1992 (a 50 percent increase over the previous year); the same year female candidates ran for Senate and House seats in record numbers, many citing Hill's ordeal as their reason for seeking office.

Photo by Sandra-Lee Phipps

ANITA HILL testifies at Senate hearings, October 1991.

himbos   Big chests and small brains became a popular combination for men in the early '90s as women got to objectify men for a change. Muscle-bound hunks were transformed into the newest sex symbol archetype: the himbo. Brawny model Lucky Vanous shot to stardom in 1994 when he removed his shirt in front of an admiring crowd of female office-workers in a Diet Coke commercial. Long-haired Italian muscle boy Fabio posed for the covers of countless heavy-breathing romance novels, and David Hasselhoff played a bare-chested lifeguard in *BAYWATCH*, the most watched television show in the world. KEANU REEVES'S near-mute SWAT-team cop Jack Traven in *Speed* (1994) represented himbos in Hollywood.

hip-hop   Common name for the culture surrounding rap music. First widely heard as word play in the Sugar Hill Gang's seminal 1979 hit "Rapper's Delight," "hip-hop" delineated a lifestyle of rap music, breakdancing, and graffiti. Latter-day hip-hop involves accouterments such as JEEPS, BEEPERS, and MARIJUANA, and has shaped American pop-culture from movies, street-fashion, and television, to soft drink ads.

WEB **The HardC.O.R.E. Cubed Web Server** http://www. public.iastate.edu/~krs_one/homepage.html/ ✦ USENET **alt.rap, rec.music.hip-hop** ✦ WEB **The Totally Unofficial Rap Dictionary** http://www.sci.kun.nl/thalia/rapdict/ dict_en.html ✦ WEB **Vibe magazine** http://www.vibe.com/ ✦ WEB **Hip-Hop Lyrics Site** http://www.brad.ac.uk/~ctttaylo/ lyrics.html

hip-hop bootlegging   Rap piracy reached epidemic levels in the early '90s, arousing the rhetorical wrath of rappers and prompting record companies to take the unusual precaution of not releasing advance cassettes of anticipated albums. On the Brand Nubians' track "In God We Trust," the group asserts that widespread bootlegging prevented their debut album from going gold. The hard men of Onyx were even arrested in 1993 for re-enacting the "beat-down" lyrics of their song "Bichasbootleguz" on a New York street vendor. Bootlegging is an ironic affliction for hip-hop culture, in which many rappers and DJs first establish their reputations through homemade tapes and street mixes—a case of rap's street credibility also being a liability. Other contributing factors include the advent of cheap color copying and a general rise in piracy manifest on city streets through BOOTLEG FASHION and the peddling of first-run movies on videotape. At the 1995 SUNDANCE Festival, the hip-hop bootlegging film *Rhythm Thief* split the Jury Prize.

hippie parents For many children of the '60s, one parental indiscretion means a lifetime laboring under a name like Dweezil, Chastity, or Justice.

The paradigm for hippie parenthood is the 1980s sitcom *Family Ties*: mom and dad mellow into nice liberals, while Michael J. Fox rebels by becoming a smartass Young Republican. The Keifer Sutherland/Dennis Hopper *Flashback* (1990) featured a similar setup, in which Keifer rejects his commune upbringing and becomes an FBI agent. As an explanation for post-'60s conservatism, both stories offer a nice bit of self-justification for BABY BOOMERS: it wasn't hippies who turned into yuppies, but their *children*. The British sitcom *ABSOLUTELY FABULOUS* offers up a more sympathetic scenario: the ex-hippie mother is now a self-obsessed fashion designer, while her resentful daughter is proper, practical, and politically far to her mom's *left*. And HAL HARTLEY's film *Simple Men* (1993) confronts boomer/buster Oedipal rivalries head on: the charismatic '60s radical dad, still on the run from the FBI, not only overshadows his son's accomplishments, but steals his girlfriend.

In reality, many families are now into their second generation of DEADHEADS, with youngsters who only have to prune the living room plants to procure some pot. While paisley-diaper babies had to face traumas like carob birthday cakes, "pink parties" to celebrate menarche, and casual parental nudity, most seem to have survived relatively unscathed. For every RIVER PHOENIX, who reportedly was initiated by his parents' commune into a sex cult at age four, there are many more WINONA RYDERS and UMA THURMANS—perfectly nice kids with weird names.

Hirst, Damien (b. 1965) British artist-impresario who defined the mid-'90s London avant-garde with the 1994 show he curated, "Some Went Mad, Some Ran Away." The show, the title of which cultivated an embattled stance towards anti-art conservatives and populists, featured Hirst's parody of JEFF KOONS's own parody of the art world, the famous basketball suspended in a fish tank: a dead but still woolly lamb floating upright in a tank of formaldehyde ("Away From the Flock"). The work capped Hirst's preoccupation with lifeless animals, including a severed pregnant cow and calf presented a year earlier, and a 14-foot tiger shark also suspended in formaldehyde ("The Physical Impossibility of Death in the Mind of Someone Living," 1992), snatched up by the world's principal collector of contemporary art, adman Charles Saatchi. Hirst himself crossed-over into advertising in 1994, producing a British ad for a series of "weird" movies on Ted Turner's TNT station that featured—what else?—a dead cow replete with maggots crashing to the floor of a darkened basement.

home AIDS testing The Confide brand of home AIDS test was made controversial in 1994 by aggressive promotion from its manufacturer, a Johnson & Johnson subsidiary, and by the concerns of many prominent AIDS groups that an absence of counseling could lead to suicides. (According to the government, more than half of all HIV-positive people go untested until they become seriously ill under the present system, in which AIDS testing is only done by trained professionals.) To take the $35 test (unapproved by the FDA as of January 1995), one simply mails a small, self-drawn blood sample to the company, and then retrieves results one week later by phone, using an anonymous i.d. number. Some of the test's biggest supporters are recipients of substantial financial largess from Johnson & Johnson, including Newt Gingrich and former Surgeon General C. Everett Koop; some of the test's biggest critics stand to lose public health money spent on AIDS testing. Ora Sure, a lollipop-stick saliva test, is less controversial because positive results still need to be confirmed by conventional tests.

home shopping The Home Shopping Network (founded 1985) and QVC (1986) started out as easy punchlines, laughable, high-number-channel, consumer alternatives to TV religion, through which to order low-quality luxuries like

china Elvis dolls and genuine cubic zirconia. But the call-in shopping companionship (frequently marked by profound pathos on the part of callers) offered by peppy hosts and celebrity guests, such as blackballed baseball legend Pete Rose, *Dallas* duende Victoria Principal, and NEW AGE, nouveau riche Ivana Trump, soon proved fantastically lucrative. TV presenter John Tesh, for instance, sold more than 200,000 copies of his orchestral tribute to the athlete's champion spirit, *Live at Red Rocks* (1994), on QVC. Home shopping emerged as one of the largest revenue-generating elements of interactive entertainment—total home shopping sales reached $3 billion in 1994, nearly half of that by QVC, which racked up $18 million in sales on one record day. MEDIA MOGUL and would-be technovisionary Barry Diller recognized this fact in late 1992, moving in on QVC, pumping up its product-shifting capacity, and dragging it upscale with an offshoot (Q2).

Also seeking a more respectable home shopping dollar was MTV Networks (MTV, VH–1, NICKELODEON) which in 1994 entered the fray with product pitches tailored for the youth-culture enthusiast: WOODSTOCK '94, BEAVIS AND BUTT-HEAD, and the Rolling Stones were successful guinea pigs for MTV/VH–1; Nickelodeon offered an Isaac Mizrahi line inspired by vintage TV shows on Nick At Nite. *THE NEW YORKER'S* John Seabrook found in Mizrahi's campy half hour "further evidence of the seepage of commerce into our amusements," adding: "It is possible that I was looking at the Devil."

WEB **QVC** http://www.qvc.com/

homeopathy Contrary to a common belief, not an ancient herbal practice but an ALTERNATIVE MEDICINE based on the tenet "like cures like." In homeopathy, illness is treated with minutes doses of poisons that in larger quantities cause the same symptoms as the illness itself. The common treatment for malaria, for instance, is quinine taken from cinchona bark (cinchona itself causes malaria-like fevers). This example is said to have inspired German physician Dr. Samuel Hahnemann, the early-19th century father of homeopathy, to search for other toxic substances. Two centuries later, the medical mechanism is still not understood—some think the infinitesimal doses stimulate the body's own natural defenses, others question whether the body can detect such minuscule amounts. Long popular in Europe, homeopathic elixirs went mainstream in early-'90s America. Homeopathy also began to arouse the grudging curiosity of the American medical establishment which had successfully banished it a century earlier.

WEB **Homeopathy Home Page** http://www.dungeon.com/home/cam/homeo.html ✦ WEB **Homepathic Internet Resource List** http://www.dungeon.com/home/cam/interlst.html

Hong Kong action movies Product of a new generation of HK moviemakers who graduated in the mid-'80s from the badly synched, "chop-socky" of the '70s. With astonishing stunt work and choreographed violence, the new movies have gained a fervent cult following in America and Europe through art house festivals and underground video stores. Hollywood powers like QUENTIN TARANTINO, Walter Hill, Martin Scorsese, and Joel Silver all regularly gush over (and "borrow" from) the stylized gunfire of JOHN WOO's gangster epics, the death-defying KUNG FU acrobatics of JACKIE CHAN and Jet Li (*Fist of Legend*), and the hallucinatory visions of Tsui Hark (*A Chinese Ghost Story, Once Upon a Time in China*). HK cinema is also notable for its strong female heroes played by the likes of Michelle Khan (*Project S*), Bridgette Lin (*Swordsman*), and the HK MADONNA, Anita Mui (*Heroic Trio*).

WEB **Hong Kong Movies Homepage** http://www.mdstud.chalmers.se/hkmovie/ ✦ WEB **Query Hong Kong Movie Database** http://egret0.stanford.edu:80/hk/hkquery.html ✦ USENET **alt.asian-movies**

hooks, bell (b. Gloria Jean Watkins, 1952) Feminist scholar, poet, and social critic. Known for her deconstructive analyses of race and gender in popular culture, as well as her ribald essays and nude photos. Early in her career, Watkins, a Kentucky native, adopted and lower-cased her nom de plume from that of her outspoken great-grand-mother, Bell Hooks. Watkins came to prominence with the 1981 book, *Ain't I a Woman: Black Women and Feminism*, ranked in 1992 among the 20 most important women's books of the last 20 years by *Publishers Weekly*. A prolific writer, Watkins was also a wildly popular Women's Studies professor at Oberlin College from 1988; in 1993 she took a tenured position in the English department of New York's City College. In a classic example of Watkins' "talking back" (the title of a 1988 essay collection), she told *VIBE* magazine in 1995 that chat show host Oprah Winfrey was evidence that "black people get to the top and stay on top only by sucking the dicks of white culture."

WEB **Excerpts from hooks' Books** http://drum.ncsc.org/ ~bowen/peeps/bhooks.html/

HORDE Horizons of Rock Developing Everywhere, a tour developed by Blues Traveler frontman John Popper to bring together bands who greet the new century by jamming, riffing, and improvising for between-tour DEADHEADS. The first HORDE tour, in 1992, featured BT, the Spin Doctors, PHISH, Widespread Panic, Aquarium Rescue Unit, and Bela Fleck and the Flecktones. The tour was distinguished by the transitions between acts, when members of one band would gradually replace their predecessors during extended jams. Popper's original notion—of a package larger than the sum of its parts—began to waver in 1994, when grizzled Southern-boogie merchants the Allman Brothers were added to ensure strong sales; in 1995 fresh-faced pop-boogie merchants the Black Crowes were brought on board.

WEB **HORDE** http://www.rockweb.com/horde/ USENET **alt.music.horde**

horrorcore GANGSTA rap subgenre, realized circa 1994, accenting the usual lyrical nihilism with the fantastical ghoulishness of slasher series like *Friday the 13th* (1980–) and *Nightmare on Elm Street* (1984–). Although such entertainments have long been alluded to in HIP-HOP (and even in Michael Jackson's 1982 *Thriller*), horrorcore's gangsta ghost stories are decidedly grimmer, shocking with vivid images of incest, rape, child murders, drug addiction, body mutilation, devil worship, grave-site vandalism, and corpse abuse—often eerily described in the first person. Musically similar to hardcore hip-hop, bands such as the Gravediggaz, the Boogeymonsters, and the Flatliners use heavy bass lines and drum patterns, rapping their lyrics quickly and intensely. Conventional wisdom suggests that horrorcore will be remembered as a bizarre, short-lived incarnation of hip-hop.

WEB **Gravediggaz** http://www.cee.hw.ac.uk/~ceeag/ Gravediggaz.html

house Electronic dance music developed in mid-'80s Chicago. Early house producers like Marshall Jefferson and Steve "Silk" Hurley took the four-on-the-four principles of disco and honed them into a form as simple and strict as the 12-bar blues: thundering, 120 beat-per-minute electronic drums, with Eurocentric sequenced synthesizers and bass, forcefully gripped the listener's pelvis; hammering piano and wailing soul voices tugged the heartstrings. For many, house's golden age was in the mid-'80s, when DJs like Larry Levan (at New York's storied Paradise Garage) and Frankie Knuckles (whose Chicago club the Warehouse gave the genre its name) whipped followers into a Dionysic frenzy at gay clubs. As the '80s ended, house spun off sub-genres such as deep house, garage, ACID HOUSE, and AMBIENT house; but house's U.S. pop crossover (exemplified by Technotronic's 1990 smash "Pump Up the Jam") further pointed up its inherent limitations.

WEB **DJTraxx** http://www.mordor.com/avery/djtraxx/

huffing Act of getting high from inhaling the toxic fumes of legal household or industrial chemicals; decried as the "cocaine of the '90s" by the AUSTIN-based National Inhalant Prevention Coalition. In 1995 the *L.A. Times* quoted figures of

more than 1,000 U.S. deaths annually, and cited studies showing that inhalants were third only to alcohol and marijuana in drug use by teens, with 20 percent of all eighth-graders having huffed. Common solvents range from glue, nail-polish remover, and freon to butane, spray paints, and gasoline. (One odd tribute to the latter substance is the name of punky Epitaph band, Gas Huffer.)

WEB **Hyperreal Inhalants** http://hyperreal.com/drugs/inhalants/

Hughes brothers (Albert b. 1972; Allen b. 1972) In the early '90s wave of gritty urban dramas by young black directors, Albert and Allen Hughes's *Menace II Society* (1993) was the grittiest. Like such films as Mario Van Peebles's *New Jack City* (1991), Matty Rich's *Straight Out of Brooklyn* (1991), and Ernest Dickerson's *Juice* (1992), the Hughes brothers offered a vision of the American inner-city full of low-income housing and high-caliber weapons, young punks and old problems. *Menace II Society* reiterated the power of "New Jack Cinema" with the supercharged nihilism of a GANGSTA rap anthem. (Ironically, much of the press coverage was reserved for a performer who did not appear in the film-rapper/actor TUPAC SHAKUR,

who attacked Allen Hughes after being fired from the project.) The Hughes brothers worked next on *Dead Presidents* (1995), a Vietnam-era heist film; the soundtrack was released on Underworld, the record company the Hugheses formed with Capitol Records.

hypertext Term coined by computer utopian Theodor Nelson in his 1974 *Computer Lib/Dream Machines* to describe electronic texts embedded with links to other texts. Such connections can break down the traditional linear narrative of the written word by encouraging readers/users/surfers to find their own paths though large amounts of information. These ideas came to fruition with the early '90s advent of the WORLD WIDE WEB, where "hypermedia" also includes sounds, pictures, and moving images. The literary arrival of hypertext was announced in a series of 1993 *New York Times Book Review* essays by novelist Robert Coover championing the "volumeless imagination" of hyperfiction.

WEB **Douglas Cooper: Delirium** http://www.pathfinder.com/twep/Features/Delirium/DelTitle.html ✦ WEB **Project Xanadu** http://www.picosof.com/850 ✦ WEB **Ted Nelson Newletter: Interesting Times** http://www.picosof.com/849

ibogaine Bitter-tasting white powder derived from the bark of a flowering West African shrub (*Tabernanthe iboga*). The hallucinogen, used ritually by the Bwiti tribe of Gabon in what one researcher calls "a chemical bar mitzvah," has earned a largely untested reputation in the West as a miracle cure for cocaine and other drug addictions—it is said to block cravings, neutralize withdrawal pains, and, owing to its psychedelic properties, even release a transformative torrent of suppressed memories. In 1962 a New Jersey HEROIN addict named Howard Lotsof tried ibogaine while looking for a new high and, goes the legend, found himself completely straight the next day. Since then Lotsof has been on a crusade (partisans include William Burroughs and Hunter S. Thompson) trying to interest governments, addiction treatment experts, and pharmaceutical companies. In 1993 the U.S. National Institute of Drug Abuse, in the peculiar position of learning of a new drug treatment from addicts, added ibogaine to a list of potential treatments for drug addiction, and began sponsoring a study to test the purported wonder drug.

WEB **The Ibogaine Story** http://204.156.22.13/love/feat/iboga/iboga.html/ ✦ WEB **The Staten Island Project** http://www.calyx.com/ibogaine/iboga.html/

ice As CRACK is to cocaine, so ice is to speed (methamphetamine)—the drug in a smokable, more potent crystal form. It was the subject of a drug scare in the early '90s as news reports from Hawaii warned of an impending "ice storm" that would eclipse the urban devastation of crack, heroin, and PCP combined. The drug's effects are dramatic—both intensifying and, unlike crack, extending the effects of the snorted form of the drug—but the "designer speed" is so potent (the high can last for a whole day) that it actually scares customers off. Widely used by male sex workers in the U.S., ice also turns up as an illicit diet aid and in RAVE subcultures. Said to be popular in Asia where it goes by the names "shabu" and "hiroppon," it was briefly used in the '60s for dieting and

before that, to boost the stamina of Japanese soldiers during WWII and North Koreans during the Korean War.

WEB **Ice** http://www.paranoia.com/drugs/stimulants/ ✦ WEB **Drugz** http://cyborganic.com/drugz/

ice beer 1993 marketing gimmick from the big beer companies looking to grab market share and cash in on the specialty markets being expanded by micro-breweries. "Coldness" and beer are supposed to be synonymous, but "ice beer" actually refers to the brewing process. The beer is cooled five to ten degrees below freezing until ice crystals form and are then filtered out. This yields a supposedly smoother taste and, like malt liquor, a higher alcoholic content (4.4 percent compared with an average 3.6 percent in regular beers). The first ice beer in the U.S. was imported from Canada by Molson, followed soon thereafter by Anheuser-Busch's Budweiser Ice Draft—the same company responsible for the 1990 introduction of the unsuccessful Bud Dry (see DRY BEER).

Ice Cube (b. O'shea Jackson, 1969) Los Angeles rapper whose self-assured solo debut *AmeriKKKa's Most Wanted* (1990) proved how easily he would thrive without former band N.W.A. Born

Photo by Sue Kwon

ICE CUBE, post-N.W.A.

of Southern parents, Cube has a rhyme style that is unhurried and country-inflected but nonetheless bluntly aggressive; his nihilism is more soulful than the scorched-earth screeds of his then-loathed ex-bandmates (though the misogyny remains the same). He can veer from unlettered GANGSTA bluster to racial cant to sentimental reflection to prodigious cultural literacy without missing a beat of his deep funk grooves. Politically, his criticism of the black community can be just as bitter as his attacks on white racism.

Ice Cube made his acting debut in John Singleton's *Boyz N The Hood* (1991), in which he evinced the same kind of *gravitas* as on record; the pair reunited on 1994's *Higher Learning*. In 1995 Ice Cube appeared in two films, low-key police drama *The Glass Shield* and the broad hit comedy *Friday*, which he co-wrote. A 1994 re-union with former N.W.A bandmate DR. DRE made the band's vocal public "feuds" look as staged as any World Wrestling Foundation grudge match.

WEB **i-Station Online – Ice Cube** http://istation.internet.net/I-Station/New.releases/Rap/Ice/index.html/ ✦ WEB **Hip-Hop Lyrics** http://www.brad.ac.uk/~ctttaylo/lyrics.html/

ice hockey jerseys With their baggy cut perfectly fitting HIP-HOP's fashion aesthetic, NHL uniform-tops became an urban staple between 1993 and 1994. *VIBE* magazine credited raw R&B star Mary J. Blige with starting the trend when she wore a hockey jersey in the video for her "Real Love" hit; hockey's new cachet was confirmed when SNOOP DOGGY DOGG slouched onto the stage of the *ARSENIO HALL Show* wearing Toronto Maple Leafs colors. The Pervert street-fashion label was among the first to cash in with an imitation hockey garment of its own, a confounding cross-over considering that there have been fewer than one hundred black hockey players in the history of the NHL.

Ice-T (b. Tracey Marrow, 1958) Rap star whose soaring media profile has been unhindered by his moderate rhyming skills. Born in Newark, New Jersey, Ice-T appeared in several early '80s rap cash-in films, but didn't record an album until 1987's *Rhyme Pays*. That record, and the following year's *Power* (with Ice-T's bikini-clad, shotgun-toting girlfriend Darlene on the cover) anticipated the West Coast's GANGSTA movement by trading in sex-and-guns imagery. Never a JEEP staple, Ice-T abandoned HIP-HOP credibility in 1991 when he took his thrash-metal combo Body Count on the first LOLLAPALOOZA tour. He struck a MULTICULTURAL vein that CYPRESS HILL would later profitably mine: the harmony between gangsta rap's cartoonish violence and heavy metal's cartoonish morbidity.

Body Count's unacclaimed, self-titled 1992 album became a *succès de scandale* when Vice President Dan Quayle and his boss George Bush singled out the song "Cop Killer" as a pressing threat to the safety of law enforcement officials. As Ice-T and gangsta rap entered the national political discourse, veteran rock critic Dave Marsh brought a modicum of perspective: "My question is, 'Where are the dead cops?'" he asked. "That's how you inject rationality into this thing." The rapper voluntarily took the track off the album and parted ways with controversy-magnet TIME WARNER.

Encouraged by the media's appetite for his Delphic wisdom, Ice-T published in 1994 *The Ice Opinion*, a widely quoted, co-written book of his *pensées*. His now muscular acting résumé includes appearances in *New Jack City* (1991), *Trespass* (1993, with ICE CUBE), and *Tank Girl* (1995).

WEB **Body Count** http://www.mca.com/winterland/products/body_count.html ✦ WEB **Ice-T Pictures** http://sashimi.wwa.com/hammers/pictures/ice.html

IKEA For first-time apartment occupants, IKEA's do-it-yourself particleboard design is one step up from milk crates and cinder blocks: furniture that gives the semblance of stability and style, without the price tag (or the long-term durability). Founded in 1947 by Swedish catalog king Ingvar Kamprad (IKEA is an acronym for his name and hometown, Elmtaryd, Agunnaryd), the chain made its successful break into the American market in 1986. By 1994, there were 125 stores in 26 countries, with total sales of $4.7 billion.

IKEA is guided by a corporate philosophy spelled out in Kamprad's quasi-religious "Testament of a Furniture Retailer." Instead of traditional stores, displays are set up at warehouses and sales help is kept to a bare minimum. IKEA is also known for its innovative marketing: it was, for instance, the first company to feature gays in a mainstream TV ad (a couple discusses their IKEA-furnished future together). The company's success has not been completely unqualified, however: in 1994 there were revelations about Kamprad's WWII-era Nazi affiliations.

WEB **i3 Home (Swedish furniture and Design Pages)**
http://www.i3.se/i3_html/i3_home.html

indie-rock Literally, music released by record labels independent of control by multinational entertainment conglomerates; more specifically, noisy guitar-bands descended from late-'70s PUNK and '80s college rock. The SST label, an early force in indie-rock, summed up the scene's raison d'être in its much-disseminated slogan "Corporate Rock Sucks"; DINOSAUR JR.-offshoot Sebadoh hymned the genre in 1991's sardonic "Gimme Indie Rock."

Indie's do-it-yourself ethic fueled the growth of a nationwide network of like-minded clubs, radio stations, labels, and record stores that laid the groundwork for the NIRVANA-led ALTERNATIVE revolution. The mid-'90s found indie-rock—or, as it's sometimes known, Amerindie—heading in two distinct directions. Larger independents such as Matador, Mammoth, and SUB POP embraced major-label distribution and backing, while other, smaller labels such as Touch and Go, Drag City, Simple Machines, Teen Beat, and K Records continued to release stubbornly unmarketable music to brand-loyal cult followings.

WEB **Drag City Records** http://www.mcs.com/~apharris/
dragcity/home.html/ ✦ WEB **Your K Homepage**
http://www.wln.com/~kpunk/ ✦ EMAIL Kempire@aol.com ✦
WEB **Touch and Go** http://kafka.southern.com:80/Southern/
labels.html

Industrial Light and Magic Movie special effects company founded in 1975 by director George Lucas. Industrial Light and Magic, based in San Rafael, northern California, has since picked up 13 Oscars and worked on eight of the 12 highest-grossing movies of all time (including *E.T.*, 1982; Lucas' own *Star Wars*, 1977; and the *Indiana Jones* series, 1981, 1984, and 1989). Standard techniques like matte backdrops and animated models were abandoned as ILM became an early leader in digital effects, creating stunning, next-generation images for James Cameron's *The Abyss* (1989) and *T2* (1991). The company consistently produces the most talked-about technical breakthroughs in cinema: JIM CARREY's infinitely malleable features in *The Mask* (1994), Tom Hanks' historical drop-ins in *Forrest Gump* (1994); and the creatures of *Jurassic Park* (1993) all came from ILM. With its tremendously successful computer games division, ILM looks set to capitalize on the imminent entertainment paradigm: VIDEOGAMES that use expansive storylines and movies that use digital technology.

WEB **LucasArts Homepage** http://www.lucasarts.com/
✦ WEB **The ILM Homepage** http://bantha.pc.cc.cmu.edu/
ILM/

industrial Music genre that originated in London in 1976 when confrontational noisemakers Throbbing Gristle founded the Industrial Records label. (TG later mutated into PSYCHIC TV.) Disappointed that PUNK rock had joined the rock 'n' roll tradition instead of destroying it, British and American fellow travelers like Leather Nun, Monte Cazzazza, and Cabaret Voltaire aligned themselves with Industrial Records, creating a broad church for (usually rhythmic) experiments with noise collage, found sounds, and extreme lyrical themes. (These post-rock musicians owed a debt to pre-rock experimentalists like the Italian Futurists, John Cage, and Karlheinz Stockhausen.)

The industrial subculture (touching on TRANSGRESSIVE FICTION, S/M, and PIERCING) spread worldwide in the following decade, flourishing with minimal media attention: Test Department (U.K.), Einstuerzende Neubaten and KMFDM (Germany), Laibach (the former Yugoslavia), and Front 242 (Belgium) have all paid lip service to industrial principles without necessarily claiming the label. Domestically, Chicago's Wax Trax label (founded 1980), with its impressive volume of monthly releases, nurtured dancefloor-friendly industrial acts like MINISTRY and Vancouver's Skinny Puppy. By the early '90s industrial was rivaling metal as the music of choice for suburban outsiders, and crossover beckoned; it came when NINE INCH NAILS and MINISTRY triumphed on successive LOLLAPALOOZA tours. Both have since moved on stylistically as industrial has fragmented beyond recognition; today's sonic terrorist is just as

likely to occupy the outer fringes of TECHNO.
WEB **Industrial Gateway** http://www.uib.no/People/henrik/
industrial/ ✦ USENET **alt.industrial** ✦ WEB **The Net Industrial
EBM Gothic Cyberculture Music Review Magazine**
http://www.synet.net/sonic-boom/

inflatable Scream   Inflatable version of
Edward Munch's *angst*-classic painting "The
Scream." The 50-inch doll and the 12-inch
Scream Junior have become a kitschy shrug of
resignation at life's overwhelming burdens in

---

infantilization

In the mid '90s American youth seem to be getting, well, younger. URBAN OUTFITTERS sells Play-Doh to its twentysomething customers. INDIE-ROCK album covers are adorned with baby pictures and childish *art trouvée*. The kinderwhore look, in the image of patron saint COURTNEY LOVE, pairs Mary Janes with frilly, empire-waisted dresses. RAVERS clutch furry pets and cute lunch boxes.

There was a time in America's recent history when newly minted adults defined themselves against the world of their parents, whether rebelling against their values or buying into them. Infantilization is a '90s counter-trend which has seen young adults behave–and decorate popular culture–as though in an arrested state of infancy, reciting too-cute paeans to the carefree years of the schoolyard. How to explain all this?

Infantilization as antidote to the uncertainties of the day. Age-regression is a protective shield in an era in which the specter of AIDS and changing gender roles make for fraught relations between the sexes. Childhood is an appealing sanctuary from such concerns. Prominent among those who've regressed from the horrors of modern adulthood are members of indie-rock's ruling caste, bands with kiddie names like Ween, Weezer, and DINOSAUR JR. EVAN DANDO, the leader of a band named after a brand of candy (Lemonheads), recorded in 1993 a childishly simple folk number called "Being Around"; it contained the immortal couplet "If I was a booger / Would you blow your nose?" Similarly, Dando's former roommate JULIANA HATFIELD sings in the tiny voice of a small girl and declared to a reporter at age 25 that she was still a virgin. (MTV personality KENNEDY similarly advertised herself as untouched.) Calvin Johnson, of the skeletal-sounding OLYMPIA band Beat Happening, writes

lyrics about ghosts and fortune cookies; Johnson's K Records labelmates, Stinky Puffs, are fronted by Simon Fair Timony, an 11-year-old boy. (Former NIRVANA members Dave Grohl and Krist Novoselic played on the Puffs' debut album; Cody Linn Ranaldo, son of SONIC YOUTH guitarist Lee Ranaldo, is also a member.) Then there is the trio Shonen Knife, three Japanese women who won ALTERNATIVE credibility by singing songs about candy bars and zoo animals in cutesy English.

Diminished expectations lead to a conscious abdication of adult responsibilities. This generation is known as one that will be financially worse off than its parents, a group for which adult trappings like raising families and owning homes tend to be a more remote prospect. Infantilization may therefore signal the young's reluctance to even compete. Opting out is not a new trend in itself: *Harper*'s magazine editor Lewis Lapham noted that the gilded '50s youth of his Hotchkiss School lived by the credo: "If you don't think you can win, make it look as if you didn't try."

A similar type of disaffection finds frequent expression in contemporary art. The 1992 album *Dirty* by the gilded SONIC YOUTH is adorned with depressing rag-doll photographs by L.A. artist MIKE KELLEY, the most renowned artist to have emerged from the 1990 "Just Pathetic" show at L.A.'s Rosamund Felsen Gallery. (Among others associated with the "pathetic aesthetic" are JIM SHAW, Raymond Pettibon, and Cady Noland; DENNIS COOPER is one literary counterpart.) Kelley's work speaks of endless hours spent trawling for suitably resonant material in dumpsters and at the same thrift stores that yield so much of today's infantile fashion. That threadbare fashion shabbily separates the wearer from the ravaging currents of consumer culture. But as Cornell professor Hal Foster pointed out in a 1994 *New York Times* editorial on "loser culture," dorms and offices across the U.S. and Japan. According to the maker, St. Louis-based On the Wall Productions, sales were boosted in 1994 while the original painting was in the news for being stolen from—and then, several months later, returned to—the National Art Museum in Oslo, Norway.

infomercials Program-length commercials posing as talk shows or dramas. While sophisti-

---

"Obviously kids in slums cannot slum in this way, and in old working-class neighborhoods resignation is hardly a pose. To be down and out in these places is not an affectation."

Generational poverty didn't spawn the impulse to childishness–the trend actually bespeaks material comfort. Just as in the '70s, suburbanites took to wearing sweatsuits in public as a outward expression of their leisure-class status, infantile fashion could be interpreted as a show of ease and aloofness. When women's thrift-store style is re-interpreted by high-ticket designers like ANNA SUI, Isaac Mizrahi, and RALPH LAUREN, its meaning transmutes–worn by actual working women, infantilized fashion can send out the confident message that the wearer need not pay lip service to the entrenched codes of the workplace. Yet again, there is a counter-theory: in the *Los Angeles Times* in October 1994, USC professor Lois Banner called the infantile trend "an attempt to contain women . . . to react to the feminist movement from a negative point of view."

Modernity causes infantilization. Some of today's technologically driven forms of pop music have altogether abandoned the sexual and emotional elements that drove rock 'n' roll, from Big Joe Turner to Jon Bon Jovi. Something such as rave culture, solipsistic and huggy, is even more infantile than indie rock, forgoing the knowing irony of bands like Sonic Youth for antics that are purely needy and child-like. A song sampling the *Sesame Street* theme was just one of TECHNO's kiddie-anthems. Participants at raves get high by way of the kid remedy VICK'S VAPO RUB and clutch Pez dispensers. At raves, lollypops and pacifiers are used to assuage that sucking reflex resulting from ECSTASY intake. This is unsurprising, perhaps, since the computer revolution that spawned techno music (fast, unnuanced, asexual) is itself the preserve of lifelong adolescents. To wit, the publisher of *WIRED* magazine, acknowledged voice of the electronic meritocracy, conceded in the *New York Times Magazine* in May 1995 that his readers, "some of the most powerful people on the planet," were "juveniles trapped in the bodies of successful businessmen."

Americans can no longer think of one another as grown-ups. When young adults insistently temper their speech with UPSPEAK or the word "like," their locutions sound to older listeners–whatever the imparted irony–no different than those of teenage girls. Self-deprecating syntax like "Should we do the coffee shop thing?" and "I have to do the work thing" cannot be blamed solely on the young, however: even President George Bush, with his fractured syntax and "vision thing," found it difficult to form adult sentences. Meanwhile, chat-show empathists like Oprah Winfrey and RICKI LAKE interpret their guests' emotions with recently coined, equally simplified phrases like "you're in a healing place / you're in a hurting place."

Young America's reluctance to grow up is particularly evident in Hollywood. Even though many 26-year-olds are powerful studio executives, few films today confer truly adult roles to actors and actresses under 35. As *Movieline* magazine observed in March 1995 "Grace Kelly was 22 when she made *High Noon*, the same age as WINONA [RYDER] in *Reality Bites*. Lauren Bacall was 19 in *To Have and Have Not*, the same age as JULIETTE LEWIS in *What's Eating Gilbert Grape* . . . Remember the days when women were women and girls were under 21?"–*Eric Konigsberg*

Teenage HOLE fans, New York 1994.

Internet

It wasn't until as recently as 1993 that "500 channels" became an information age catchphrase. Cable companies, announcing intentions to expand channel capacity ten-fold (by the end of 1994!), defined "information superhighway" as an onslaught of more thinly sliced TV channels. Back then the Internet was a 25-year-old computer network, primarily the preserve of university scientists and computer geeks–the few computer-savvy publishers aware of the new sound and graphics capabilities of personal computers were focused on the CD-ROM as an extension of book publishing. By the time in 1995 when TIME-WARNER finally debuted one of the first small-scale tests of next generation cable (see FULL SERVICE NETWORK), the "@" ("at") sign of Internet email addresses had become a conventional badge of modernity, and there weren't 500 channels on the Internet's WORLD WIDE WEB, there were 50,000 HYPERTEXT-linked pages. The Internet was the information superway.

Key to the Internet's explosive growth was its openness. Text-based computer BBS's, where computer users could leave messages for each other and exchange software, were a grassroots '80s phenomenon that was being commercialized in the '90s by the likes of AMERICA ONLINE. But these slick services charged by the hour and felt like airtight malls. In contrast, the Internet was a global street bazaar, the thousands of conversations that made up the USENET newsgroups and IRC chat channels were international and uncensored, and most access was unmetered beyond flat-rate fees whether one was talking to the other side of the planet or campus.

The unfurling social communication was even more remarkable for its peculiar origins in Cold War history. In 1969 the U.S. Defense of Department built an experimental computer network that was designed to withstand a nuclear attack. Employing a brand-new computer technology called packet-switching, the Internet's predecessor ARPANET (named for the DoD's Advanced Research Projects Agency Network) connected California research universities so that no one network node depended on any other. Such an acephalous, "peer-to-peer" architecture also guaranteed that, like the phone system, there would be no practical way to control what people said to each other. The advent of DIGITAL CASH and personal encryption (see PGP) would later add further protections against attempts to regulate free speech in cyberspace, turning Internet connectivity into a major political issue for authoritarian regimes around the world (which, *pace* CYBERSEX and PGP, have included the U.S.). By the mid-'70s researchers were puzzling in a government report over the surprising volume of electronic mail in network traffic: "one [can] write tersely and type imperfectly, even to an older person in a superior position." It appears to have been entirely unanticipated that users of the subsidized network would homestead a new society. Sci-fi writer BRUCE STERLING once enthused: "It's as if some grim fallout shelter had burst open and a full-scale Mardi Gras parade has come out."

The Internet itself was the prime example of a hothouse cyber-culture. Most of its open standards and software infrastructure had evolved over two decades on an almost weekly basis through the cooperation (and competition) of a core group of several hundred programmers. Ideas that would have taken months to disseminate in print journals circulated online in hours.

By the time the World Wide Web–a standard for using point-and-click graphics to navigate all this information–reached critical mass in 1994, the hyper-communication had spread throughout aca-

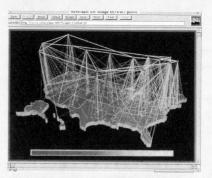

A pre-privatization 'Net staple–"the NSFNet INTERNET backbone"– downloaded from EFF's Graphics Archive (http://www.eff.org/pub/Graphics/). There is also an animated version.

alt.culture

demic discourse, fan culture, political activism, and simple social life. There were 10,000 academic disciplines, 10,000 STAR TREK discussions, and 10,000 dirty picture downloads; rapid-fire, Tocquevillian mobilizations of civil liberty coalitions and multi-user dungeon (MUD) text-worlds from which many undergraduates never emerged; trivia-obsessed micro-fan followings of pop culture obscura, and Monty Python-esque parodies such as the long-running personality cult of James "Kibo" Parry headquartered at "alt.religion.kibology." One of the most drmatic examples of new communication was the live #gayteen chat channel, which became a gathering place for isolated kids, from Manhattan to rural Texas, to socialize.

In 1995 this openness seemed irreversible, a counterweight to the elimination of decades-old rules preventing the consolidation of the country's print publishers, broadcasters, and phone and cable operators into the hands of a few giant corporations. The evolving Internet seemed to guarantee a level, accessible playing field that would make it difficult for established corporations to choke off small-time media entrepreneurs. The Internet, in spite of the final 1995 privatization of the U.S. government's National Science Foundation backbone, simply made communication too efficient to price the public out of publishing. The Web was as open to the smallest ZINE as it was to *Time* magazine.

As Web content avalanched, providing high-end Internet service began to appeal to cable operators and phone companies as a practical, here-and-now product-substitute for the movies-on-demand services that were supposed to finance the country's re-wiring (at a cost that one analyst calculated in 1994 would require every household in the country to order five movies a week). The U.S. web audience, estimated at one million at the end of 1994, was projected to increase to nine-million before the end of 1995.

The rapid reach of the Internet into everyday life has not been universally celebrated as a civic panacea—skeptics speculate about the social effects of the wired existence as people disconnect from real life—or "R.L." as the material world is sometimes dismissed online. (Not to mention the global majority left completely out-of-the-loop.)

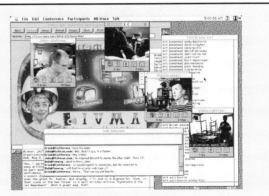

An INTERNET smorgasbord.

Harper's magazine editorialized in 1995 that "the marvel of postmodern communications" makes it so that we "recede from one another literally at the speed of light. We need never see or talk to anybody with whom we don't agree." The Internet's newsgroups, however, are notorious for both blinkered specialization and the ferocious debates of blinkered specialists. Most likely is that these expanding social spaces, already highly structured by expensive technology, will become commercialized. The twentieth century transformation of citizens into consumers is a widely noted phenomenon, but as traditional publishers and broadcasters open for business on the Internet, one successful strategy will be capturing readers and viewers as "members" of "branded" collectives, not unlike Southern California's gated suburbs, or Disney's planned communities in Florida. Time Warner's *Sports Illustrated*, for example, might endeavor to create the dominant forum for online sports talk. Once these virtual communities are established, a July 1995 Goldman-Sachs report advises "there should also be an opportunity for transaction- and advertising-related revenue streams to be introduced." For Wall Street, the open logic of the Internet dictates that community is the new commodity.—*Nathaniel Wice*

USENET **alt.culture.internet, alt.internet.media-coverage, comp.internet.net-happenings** ✦ WEB **The Center for the Study of Online Community** http://www.sscnet.ucla.edu/soc/csoc/ ✦ WEB **Zen and the Art of the Internet** http://www.cs.indiana.edu/docproject/zen/zen–1.0_toc.html

alt.culture

cated marketers like NIKE emphasize soft-sell cool, infomercials revel shamelessly in the joys of consumerism. In the early days of television, variety-show hosts and sitcom stars endorsed the products of their single-sponsor underwriters; the practice ended with regulation of broadcast marketing in the '60s and a shift to purchased advertising time. As part of Reagan-era deregulation in 1984, the Federal Communications Commission dropped the 16-minutes-per-hour limit on TV commercials. Innovative marketers like Ron Popeil ("Ronco") developed long-format ads—from ten to 60 minutes—rehearsing the manifold virtues of not-available-in-any-store products. The '80s breakup of AT&T also led to a steep drop in the price of toll-free 1–800 lines, giving direct-marketers the key to cheap, easy, and impulse-motivated sales.

In 1990, nine pioneers formed the National Infomercial Marketing Association, which established certification and guidelines for the rapidly expanding industry. Within five years infomercial sales tripled to more than $1 billion. A 1994 Gallup poll found that eight out of 10 Americans watched infomercials, and that 30 percent of those had actually purchased from them. Infomercials have revived careers—such as that of singers/psychic friends Dionne Warwick and Latoya Jackson and Suzanne "Thigh Master" Somers—and even created a few ardent new stars, most notably Susan "Stop The Insanity" Powter, Jay "The Juiceman" Kordich, and Mike "*Amazing Discoveries*" Levey. In '94 major corporations like Apple and Toyota begin experimenting with slicker "story-mercials." They were bested by the Windows 95 launch in August 1995, which used NBC stars like Jay Leno and Anthony Edwards to promote the "biggest product roll-out since New Coke." Related phenomena include HOME SHOPPING TV channels and INTERNET advertising packaged as entertainment.

WEB **cultureschlock** http://www.bitwise.net/~mk/ schlock.html/ ✦ WEB **Infomercial List** http://www.best.com/ ~dijon/tv/infomercials/info-list.html/ ✦ USENET **alt.tv.infomercials** ✦ USENET **alt.tv.infomercials**

interactive press kit Originally intended as a novelty promotional item to catch the attention of jaded music journalists and record reviewers, IPKs were soon distributed publicly to catch the attention of jaded record buyers. The floppy disk sent out to promote Billy Idol's 1993 flop disc *Cyberpunk* was first, with dozens of examples from record and movie companies soon proliferating on commercial online services for fans to download. In mid-1994 IPKs for the movie *Speed* and R.E.M.'s *Monster* were some of the flashiest uses of nascent cyberspace. The thrill of hearing, say, DINOSAUR JR. blaring through the computer speaker was at once primitive (bandwidth limits audio to a few seconds of looped music) and futuristic, with clickable info and even games hidden behind idiosyncratic graphics. IPKs hint at time when—via online services and CD-PLUS—standard album packages will include music videos and VIDEOGAMES; in the present they pose the question, why are people so eager to download commercials?

Internet See page 114.

Internet Underground Music Archive Early and ambitious WORLD WIDE WEB site that distributes the songs of unsigned bands over the INTERNET. Founded in late 1993 by two University of California, Santa Cruz, students—Jeffrey Patterson (b. 1973) and Robert Lord (b. 1970)— the Archive started with the goal of circumventing record labels, distributors, and record stores. Within a year, however, IUMA emerged as a new facet of the music industry, charging small fees for making band pictures, biographies, songs, and videos available, and doubling as the launchpad for major label forays into cyberspace. Hundreds of artists have taken advantage of the opportunity—ranging from folk to ska to INDIE-ROCK—and, through a public bulletin board component, the site has emerged as one of the principal rock communities online. The most popular songs are downloaded thousands of times—impressive, considering that a single stereo song can take half an hour to receive through a standard phone connection. IUMA competitors include Open Mike, Kaleidoscope, Planet Starchild, and Wilma (the last dedicated to live music). [See also REALAUDIO.]

WEB **IUMA** http://www.iuma.com

internship Usually an unpaid, career-building summer or single-semester position as a gofer in a glamorous-sounding big city government, media, or non-profit office. Students are actively recruited for this system by the career service departments of colleges; many schools that offer academic credit for such programs actually *charge* tuition fees for the unpaid work. The rise of unpaid internships in the early '90s is consistent with other trends in the destabilization of the workplace, such as employers' classification of full-time workers as "consultants" in order to save on medical, tax, and pension benefits.

WEB **America's Top 100 Internships** http://www.review.com/career/8104.html

intervention General term for substance abuse treatment within therapeutic circles, but also a specific confrontation orchestrated by friends, relatives, or co-workers to get an addict or alcoholic into treatment. In a typical intervention, the subject is surprised by a group of familiar but grim faces who proceed to catalogue the subject's drug problems for several hours. The successful TOUGH LOVE intervention concludes with the subject ushered directly to a pre-arranged residential treatment program. Such interventions date from the 12-step recovery movements of the 1970s, but since 1990 have become commonplace in West Coast yuppie and rock circles. Kurt Cobain went into rehab two months before his suicide, *Esquire* magazine later reported,

only after his bandmates threatened, in the midst of an intervention, to quit NIRVANA, but he escaped over a fence on the second day of treatment. Intervention guru Bob Timmins is renowned within the rock world for the at least temporary rehabilitation of Ringo Starr, AEROSMITH's Steven Tyler, RED HOT CHILI PEPPERS' Anthony Kiedis, and others. When an intervention was staged for *BEVERLY HILLS 90210* character Dylan McKay (Luke Perry) in November 1994, it was led by former substance-abusing child actress McKenzie Phillips.

WEB **National Clearing House for Alcohol and Drug Information** http://www.health.org/

IRC INTERNET Relay Chat, a program that enables users around the world to gather in "channels" and type messages to each other in real-time (as opposed to USENET, where messages are posted and read more in the manner of a public bulletin board). Channels can be formed at any time, but by 1995 there were dozens of stable ones ranging from #hottub, where users pretend they are swinging together, to #12step, where virtual 12-step meetings are held. IRC has gained fame through big early-'90s news stories, serving, for instance, as an important conduit for information to Moscow during the summer 1993 coup attempt against Boris Yeltsin. Several weddings have also taken place on IRC. The IRC program, written in Finland in 1988 by Jarkko Oikarinen, is a notorious INTERNET security hole and is widely scorned by HACKERS as a petri dish of COMPUTER VIRUSES.

WEB **Internet Chat Guide** http://www.prospero.com/globalchat/schedule.html/ ✦ WEB **The IRC Library** http://mistral.enst.fr/~pioch/IRC/IRC.html ✦ USENET **alt.irc.***

J. Crew Fashion catalogue and retail chain emphasizing preppy, pared down functionalism *sans* the actual hiking equipment offered by traditional mail-order outfits like L.L. Bean. Founded in 1983 by the owner of the Popular Club Plan to sell affordable knock-offs of RALPH LAUREN. J. Crew sales skyrocketed after the owner's then 25-year-old daughter, Emily Cinader Woods, took over as president and began perfecting the Crew catalogue's idealization of the upper-middle class's intelligent-looking collegians and young professionals. In 1994 the company mailed out 18 catalogues with an average circulation each of 4 million copies. By the end of 1993, there were 28 stores in 15 states, accounting for one-third of the company's sales, with the retail empire expanding into Japan and Europe. J. Crew has been ridiculed at times for color names such as "Dijon," "yucca," and "kelp."

Jacobs, Marc (b. 1963) A cacophony of carefully "improvised" layering, rhinestone-trimmed BIRKENSTOCKS, and chiffon versions of plaid flannel shirts, Marc Jacobs's spring 1993 collection for the Perry Ellis label was the most critically acclaimed designer interpretation of the GRUNGE look; but before it reached the stores the Ellis company shut down its designer line and Jacobs was out of a job. He made a big comeback in 1994, debuting a new collection under his own name on his 31st birthday. Jacobs's ironic take on '70s trashy luxe featured see-through shirts, laminated sequined jeans, and lots of neon rubber—perfect for disaffected rock video STYLISTS and fashion editors, who swooned over Jacobs's slightly dangerous-looking brand of glamour.

Jägermeister Thick, medicinal-tasting, 70-proof liqueur that is an established favorite among frat boys and hard-rockers alike. The umlaut could account for part of the drink's appeal, but more likely it's the legend that ingredients include some unspecified opiate. Nicknamed "liquid valium," Jägermeister ("master hunter" in the original German) has a reputation for immobilizing the most hardened drinker after just a few shots. Usually chilled for consumption, the drink is heavily promoted around colleges nationwide by a team of over 900 scantily clad "Jägerettes" (and around 100 "Jägerdudes," working gay clubs) who thrust promotional trinkets on the most enthusiastic drinkers. According to a 1994 *Wall Street Journal* article, Jägermeister's U.S. importer Sidney Frank Importing Co., which does almost no advertising, spends an impressive $6 million a year on Jägerette-related events.

The legendary JÄGERMEISTER, a.k.a. "liquid Valium."

Courtesy of Sidney Frank Importing Company

jam bands In the mid-'90s, a new generation of neo-psychedelic jam bands began to emerge in the central and northeastern parts of the country. Taking the late-'70s DIY as a given, these bands retrenched to a '60s improvising vernacular. Although they look to the GRATEFUL DEAD and FRANK ZAPPA as grandparently influences, they are more directly informed by the likes of PHISH and PRIMUS. The ranks of these ragged experimentalists include Ken Kesey collaborators Jambay, from San Diego; Leftover Salmon, the self-described "polyethnic cajun slamgrass" ensemble from Boulder; ekoostik HOOKAH, a Denver quintet elongating the Southern psychedelic boogie; New Jersey folkies Rusted Root; Binghamton, New York's Yolk; Buffalo, New York's conceptually oddball moe.; and the neofunking Moon Boot Lover from Albany, New York.

MAIL LIST **Unofficial Rusted Root Mailing List** email listproc@envirolink.org with "SUB rust-tribe firstname lastname" in message body ◆ USENET **alt.music.phish**

jeep Quintessential HIP-HOP vehicle. Developed by the U.S. Army during WWII, the name derives from the pronunciation of the military parts code, GP. In the '80s the Jeep became an inner city favorite, partly because it was ideal for mounting large speakers. Though a brand name, "jeep" is frequently used as a generic term for what the auto

industry calls sport utility vehicles, such as Range Rovers, Broncos, Pathfinders, and Troopers. In 1988 Ralph Nader and *Consumer Reports* unsuccessfully lobbied for the recall of Suzuki Samurais after revelations that the jeep tended to roll over in tight, 40 mph turns; young jeep buyers largely ignored the warnings. In the hip-hop community, the word "jeep" is perhaps most commonly used in rap criticism as an attributive noun modifying "beats."

WEB **The 4x4 Jeep Page** http://www.indirect.com/www/a4x4/jeep.html/ ◆ WEB **Jeep Showroom** http://www.chryslercorp.com/showroom/jeep/jeep.html

jellies   Soft, edible-looking fisherman-style sandals that were dragged from fashion's toy chest when the rage for INFANTILIZED fashion spread beyond pacifiers, BARRETTES, and ankle socks. Summer 1995 saw the return of the kids' and teens' seasonal sandal that had previously been popular in the mid '70s and early '80s. By employing another '90s tactic of loading a single item with as many styles as possible (see FOOTWEAR FASHION MUTATIONS), the jelly evolved beyond the simple flat heel into a chunky high heel that was sometimes flecked with glitter. Whereas this throwaway shoe could once be bought for around $5, designer versions can cost as much as $50; DKNY, PATRICK COX, and Guess? are among the labels that have touted their own versions.

Jell-o shots   Downmarket aspic. The old fraternity concoction of flavored Jell-o made with vodka and liqueurs, then slurped from a paper cup, spread from college bars to become a rowdy influence in sports bars and yuppie drinking holes in the late '80s. Because of alcohol's lower freezing point, the vodka usually congeals into a chilly slug. Typical flavors emphasize the INFANTILIZED appropriation of children's treats: Grape Crushes are commonly made out of grape Jell-o, vodka, and raspberry liqueur, while Lemon Drops mix lemon vodka with sugar. [See also BINGE DRINKING.]

Jerky Boys   Prank callers Johnny B. [Brennan] and Kamal [Ahmed] who cashed in on the decade-

old underground tape phenomenon of recorded phone pranks with two hit albums (*The Jerky Boys*, 1993, and *Jerky Boys 2*, 1994), appearances on HOWARD STERN and the WOODSTOCK '94 stage, and a 1995 Disney movie. Their name comes from the habit of dubbing hapless victims—usually inexplicably willing New York sales-, delivery-, and repairmen—"jerky." Elsewhere in the genre, Bart Simpson's prank calls to Moe's Tavern ("I'm looking for an Al Coholic") borrow heavily from the legendary Tube Bar tapes that document the habitual harassment of a hot-headed Jersey City bartender named Louis "Red" Deutsch. (Those tapes also spawned the FILM THREAT-issued 1991 "Red" video and *The Red Newsletter*.) The Benny Garrick Calls, another classic series best known in the country music world, document years in the life of a Tennessee used car salesman. "Audio verité" seems unthreatened by the advent of *69 and caller ID.

Jimmy the Cabdriver   As played by actor Donal Logue (b. 1966) and filmed by former EVAN DANDO-bandmate Jesse Peretz, this oleaginous Boston-Irish motormouth is one of MTV's cleverest innovations. Introduced in June 1994, Jimmy McBride's rabid, misinformed interpretations of the station's heavy-rotation videos are punctuated by cutaways to bored/irritated passengers in the back seat of his taxi. These ad-length outbursts (edited from

Jimmy McBride, MTV's biggest fan.

hours of improvisation) are, of course, usually followed by business-as-usual displays of the same overblown egos that Jimmy has just deflated. As with McBride's fellow deconstructionists DENIS LEARY and BEAVIS AND BUTT-HEAD, MTV manages to draw strength from its most astute critics.

WEB **mtv.com** http://www.mtv.com/

Johnson, Betsey (b. 1942)   Born a Connecticut WASP, Betsey Johnson made a name for herself in the '60s designing clear vinyl dresses, silvery motorcycle suits, and other groovy threads for the youthquakers who shopped at Paraphernalia, the trendy New York-based boutique chain. She opened her own company in 1978, and weathered countless trends by sticking to a distinctive funky, vaguely vintage sensibility, producing lighthearted, inexpensive clothes and reviving her own '60s and '70s styles as the looks resurfaced. Apt to begin her manic runway shows by cartwheeling down the catwalk in a tutu, bright red braids and hair extensions flying, Johnson thrives on spectacle, but take away her models' nose rings, platform combat boots, and ripped fishnet stockings, and many of her floral-printed BABY-DOLLS and princess-style dresses are sweet enough for a junior high school dance.

Jolt Sugary, super-caffeinated cola drink introduced in 1986 and marketed—without dramatic sales success—as a defiant statement against health-conscious consumerism. Each 12 oz. can contains 72 milligrams of caffeine, twice that of a regular Coke or Pepsi. In 1994 *Forbes* magazine attributed the cola's survival to its popularity with workaholic computer programmers, noting that Software Development magazine even awards an annual "Jolt Product Excellence Award" (the statue is a plastic-encased can of soda). In the early '90s Jolt also did well by exporting the soda (especially to the Soviet Union, where it became easier sometimes to find Jolt than Coke) and by promoting it as a mixer (a rum-and-Jolt is known as a Jumper Cable).

Jonze, Spike (b. Adam Spiegel 1969) Co-founder of the now-defunct *SASSY* sibling magazine *Dirt* (debut 1991), this former photographer with a reputation for daredevil stunts has become one of the most distinctive video directors of the '90s. After contributing jittery skateboarding footage to Sonic Youth's "100%" video, Jonze—an heir, he is loath to admit, to the Spiegel catalog fortune—directed some of the more memorable images of post-NIRVANA MTV. The Breeders, the BEASTIE BOYS, Weezer, and DINOSAUR JR. have all benefited from Jonze's eye for absurd, unforgettable images and pointed cultural references. (For "Buddy Holly"

[1994], Weezer were digitally deposited in an episode of *Happy Days*; that same year the BEASTIE BOYS were re-cast as maverick '70s TV cops in "Sabotage.") As part of the BEASTIE BOYS/SONIC YOUTH/Sofia Coppola culture-cabal, Jonze—and his unnervingly childlike public persona—are positioned to be an influential cultural force for the remainder of the decade. (Nintendo, WOODSTOCK '94, Levi's, NIKE, and Coors are some of the corporations for which he has shot ads; he filmed the opening titles for failed BIKE MESSENGER sitcom *Double Rush*.) In 1995 Jonze signed with Tristar Pictures to direct a mid-budget movie adaptation of the children's book *Harold and the Purple Crayon* (screenplay by MICHAEL TOLKIN). "It was clear to me," the president of Tristar told *The New York Times*, "that Spike was Harold."

joyriding Ghetto teens in Newark, New Jersey, hotwiring, racing, and crashing late model sports cars taken from the outlying white suburbs were a brief media sensation in 1992, quickly overshadowed by the specter of CARJACKING and a crackdown that left many of the teens shot by police or sentenced as adults under tough new laws. Favorite stunts included burning rubber "doughnuts" and "figure eights" in the pavement, "riding ghost" at night without headlights, and pulling off "backward threes" (three tight highspeed spins while in reverse). Newark barred Nick Gomez, hot from his homemade street-tough debut (*Laws of Gravity* [1992]), from filming there the Universal-financed, SPIKE LEE-produced *New Jersey Drive* (1995).

juku After-school and Saturday cram schools that put elementary and high-school-aged students through intensive math and vocabulary-building programs, primarily to help immigrant children compete with native-born peers. Juku (a Japanese word; in Chinese, *buxiban*; in Korean, *hagwon*) have long existed in Asian society, where college-bound high school students are expected to spend dozens of hours per week cramming to pass difficult standardized entry exams. Some American parents view their recent import with apprehension, wondering if they give those willing to pay the average $200 a month an unfair advantage while robbing children of youthful play; many others simply sign up their kids, as the success of the 400-plus chain of Sylvan tutoring centers shows. (Unlike its Asian counterparts, this American franchise rewards kids with plastic tokens that can be traded in for toys and movie posters.)

jungle Exotic by-product of the particle accelerator that is British club culture. The foundation for jungle was laid by dance producers who cranked up HIP-HOP drum samples to the breakneck pace of HARDCORE TECHNO; jungle added raw, booming basslines and DANCEHALL "ragamuffin" chants to the mix. (Its name comes from the Tivoli section of Kingston, Jamaica, known locally as "the jungle.") Partly as a response to its local origins, the street popularity of this distinctively British dance music was overwhelming in the U.K. in 1994, initially via underground clubs and pirate radio; in the U.S. it took root mainly in major-city clubs.

WEB **Steve Shapero's Jungle Pages**
http://polestar.facl.mcgill.ca/courses/engl378/socks/jungle/

✦ WEB **Casper's Jungle & Happy Hardcore Page**
http://www.mit.edu:8001/people/jcarow/breaks.html

Junior Vasquez (b. Donald Mattern, circa 1946)   Celebrity DJ and remix specialist, more commonly known as the co-founder of New York's SOUND FACTORY club. In 1989, Vasquez, a one-time record store clerk, teamed up with a former employee of the legendary Paradise Garage to create the Sound Factory. There, Vasquez built a cult following for his trademark DJ-ing style, an imaginative fusion of raw, baseline-rich tribal and HOUSE with a boundless repertoire of sampling and remixing techniques. The faithful would reverently groove to his selections, whether they were discs spun at incorrect speeds and barely audible volume, or out-of-nowhere SAMPLING of "The Stripper" and the "Looney Tunes" theme. Influential as a musical groundbreaker (new dance tracks are frequently debuted and monitored at the Sound Factory), Vasquez is increasingly sought out to produce, remix, and write for others, most notably for MADONNA and most bizarrely for heartland rocker John Mellencamp.

Kaelin, Brian (Kato) (b. 1959) Fifteen-minute celebrity who extended his stay. Kaelin, an aspiring actor and professional free-loader, came to prominence as the comic relief in the media meltdown that was the 1994–95 O.J. Simpson murder case. With his bleached blond hair, surfer mannerisms, slacker lifestyle, and goofy charm, Kaelin became an easy human punchline. The nickname—borrowed as a child from Bruce Lee's character in *The Green Hornet*—was also shared with the dog of victim Nicole Brown Simpson. After buoyantly addled testimony at O.J. Simpson's preliminary hearing, Kaelin parlayed his fame into a stint as guest host of E!'s *TALK SOUP*, a handful of small movie and TV roles, and a Las Vegas standup comedy gig. Kaelin—also the subject of a bare-chested portrait in *THE NEW YORKER*, a jokey running column in an issue of *Entertainment Weekly*, *GQ* and *Playgirl* photo fashion spreads, and a Larry King interview on CNN—became a regular on the Hollywood party circuit, forming a special bond with movie guy CHARLIE SHEEN. Kaelin's first celebrity appearance drew 5,000 screaming fans at an Indiana mall on April Fool's Day 1995. Before the year's end he had his own radio talk show in L.A.

Kangol Headgear beloved of '80s rappers like Run-D.M.C., Doug E. Fresh, and especially LL Cool J, whose attachment to his terrycloth Bermuda model was almost unnatural. Founded in the North of England in 1938, Kangol (the ang is for angora, the ol for wool, the K for euphony) hats had long been worn by workers, golfers, and members of the British armed forces before they caught on in the HIP-HOP world. When the aforementioned generation of rappers was superseded, Kangol's street popularity faded, but the 1991 Spitfire model (made of the angora/wool mix "furgora") restored their status. The Spitfire was usually worn backwards to highlight the hat's kangaroo logo. (According to Britain's *Independent* newspaper, the marsupial was introduced in deference to consistent mispronunciation of "Kangol" as "Kanga" by New York customers.)

Kani, Karl (b. Carl Williams 1968) Influential Brooklyn-born black sportswear entrepreneur. Kani began around 1986 by selling self-designed baggy jeans from his home and the trunk of his car; he moved to L.A. and opened Seasons Sportswear in the Crenshaw district, coming to the notice of L.A. label CROSS COLOURS, which hired him to do his own line in 1992. The partnership was dissolved in early 1994 when the latter ran into severe business difficulties; Kani set out on his own, launching the Karl Kani Infinity label in May of that year. Although he is outspoken about wanting to take market share from the likes of RALPH LAUREN, TOMMY HILFIGER, and other white designers popular among blacks, Kani himself has thrived by combining elements of PREPPY-wear with HIP-HOP's baggy look and, occasionally, AFROCENTRIC colors. Kani's solution to persistent piracy of his garb (see BOOTLEG FASHION) was to attach a difficult-to-reproduce metal patch to many items. The company launched a footwear brand in 1994 and children's and womenswear lines in 1995.

Kelley, Mike (b. 1954) Michigan-born conceptual artist who graduated in 1978 from California Institute of Arts and dabbled in performance art before finding his voice in drawing, painting, and sculpture. Kelley's most notorious works eerily recontextualize such found material as mangy, once-loved stuffed animals, hand-knitted blankets, and high school yearbooks. His obsession with the folksy detritus of American life paid off handsomely: these days his pieces sell in the low to mid-five figures; in 1993 the *Los Angeles Times* acknowledged the widely held belief that Kelley, long celebrated in Europe, is "perhaps the most influential American artist of the '90s." Although he was part of the Los Angeles Museum of Contemporary Art's definitive *Helter Skelter* exhibition, and has had a retrospective at New York's WHITNEY Museum, Kelley is known to

Sonic Youth, *Dirty* album sleeve

MIKE KELLEY's "pathetic aesthetic" via SONIC YOUTH, 1992.

many outside the art world for the cover art to SONIC YOUTH's 1992 album *Dirty*. In 1994 the band's leader Thurston Moore released a three-CD retrospective on his Ecstatic Peace! label by Destroy All Monsters, Kelley's PUNK-era band with fellow *Helter Skelter* artist JIM SHAW. The group staged a Michigan reunion in spring 1995.

Kennedy (b. Lisa Kennedy Montgomery, 1972) MTV VJ/hate-object best known for publicly declaring both her chastity and her affiliation with the Republican party. (A TATTOO of the GOP elephant decorates her pelvic region.) The Oregon native arrived at MTV via the graveyard shift at L.A. radio station KROQ (where she styled herself "the virgin Kennedy"), and she quickly became the station's most singular character—an unabashed irritant whose petulant persona earned her the "Least Favorite VJ" award in the *ROLLING STONE*'s 1993 reader poll.

Kennedy's controversy-seeking antics came to a head at MTV's September 1994 Music Video Awards, where she enthusiastically performed fellatio on a microphone while New York mayor Rudy Giuliani was being interviewed by a colleague. Although carpeted for the offense, Kennedy continues to extemporize off-color monologues with a verbal agility that makes her cohorts look like mushmouthed mannequins. In testament to Kennedy's peculiar success, the "McGovern" character in BABYBOOMER sitcom *Murphy Brown* was fashioned after her in 1995.

WEB **Kennedy Gallery** http://www.well.com/user/xkot/kennedy.htm/

Kennedy, John F. Jr. (b. 1960) Camelot's dashing Prince Charming when, on his third birthday, he saluted the casket of his murdered father, President John F. Kennedy. Romantic links for "John John" include MADONNA, Brooke Shields, Julia Roberts, Sarah Jessica Parker, and multitudes of models, but his five-year relationship with Daryl Hannah made the pair one of the country's most glamorous couples; they broke up soon after the 1994 death of Kennedy's mother, Jacqueline

Kennedy Onassis, who reputedly disapproved of the Hollywood girlfriend. Much of what's left of socialite glamour in Manhattan depends on sightings of America's Most Eligible Bachelor rollerblading or fundraising. Apparently uninterested in elected office, Kennedy worked as an assistant district attorney in New York (making headlines when he twice flunked the New York Bar exam). In 1995 he founded *George*, an apolitical political magazine under the aegis of consumer magazine corporation Hachette-Filipacchi.

kente cloth Brightly patterned African cloth traditionally worn as dresses and wraps. Genuine kente cloth is handmade—usually in Ghana and Togo—and costs hundreds of dollars per square yard; the yellow, red, green, and black combinations sold on U.S. streets tend, therefore, to be domestic (or Korean-made) imitations. Since it became identified in the late '80s with AFROCENTRIC HIP-HOP fashion, kente cloth has also become a handy shorthand for marketers, most notably L.A.'s CROSS COLOURS.

Kern, Richard (b. 1954) New York underground director who helped define the East Village and downtown Manhattan PUNK demimonde in the '80s with ritualized gore, Super–8 sleaze, Nazi biker chicks, and step-by-step nipple PIERCINGS featuring scenesters like SPOKEN WORD-pioneer Lydia Lunch (who, for example, got intimate with a gun in "Fingered"), polymorphous punk HENRY ROLLINS, and fellow soft-core porn transgressive Nick Zedd. In 1992, FILM THREAT issued two video collections of Kern's work; in 1994, Kern helped strike a note of historical continuity by cameo-ing in Bruce LaBruce's queer-centric mock-documentary *Super 8 1/2*. Kern also directed SONIC YOUTH's first video, the MANSON-esque "Death Valley '69" (1985).

Ketamine Disassociative substance championed by scientist John Lilly since his 1981 autobiography, *The Scientist*. Known on the street as K, Ket, Ketamine, Kit-Kat, Special K, and Vitamin K, ketamine hydrochloride is legitimately used to anesthetize animals and children. Available over the counter in Mexico as Kelar (it is a schedule III drug in the United States), ketamine is most effectively taken intramuscularly, but is also viable orally and nasally. While accounts of its effects range from rapture to paranoia to boredom, it commonly elicits an out-of-body experience that puts the user in touch with beings or forces of an apparently cosmic ilk (Lilly claimed to have enjoyed conversations with the "masters of the universe"). Ketamine's tendency to render the user comatose (or put him or her in a "K-hole") makes it less than ideal for party or RAVE situations, where it is frequently sold.

USENET **alt.drugs.psychedelics** ✦ WEB **Hyperreal Drug Archives** http://hyperreal.com/drugs/psychedelics

Kids in the Hall Canadian comedy troupe-turned-TV show. When Kids in the Hall lost its sole female player in 1984 (shortly after the group was formed), the remaining members were obliged to dress up in drag, giving their comedy its most distinctive component. SATURDAY NIGHT LIVE producer Lorne Michaels, a fellow Canadian, picked up on the Kids (then a core of five: Dave Foley, Mark McKinney, Kevin McDonald, Scott Thompson, Bruce McCullough) during a long-running Toronto club residency and showcased their skewed, often cruel sketch comedy in 1989 via an HBO/Candian Broadcasting Corporation series. In 1992 the program moved to an obscure late-night slot on the CBS network, where until the middle of the 1994–95 season it continued to polarize viewers with morbid preoccupations, freakish characters, blatant homosexuality, and sketches demanding athletic leaps of the imagination. McKinney went on to perform blamelessly on SNL's 1994–95 season, Foley acted in Talk Radio, a successful 1995 sitcom launch, and Thompson joined THE LARRY SANDERS SHOW. The group plans to reunite periodically for feature films.

WEB **The Kids In The Hall Show** http://www.usit.net/public/jmbell/kith/kith.html ✦ USENET **alt.tv.kids-in-hall**

King, Rodney (b. 1966) Known as Glen until reporters took "Rodney" from police reports, King became the country's most familiar symbol of American racism when George Holliday made an amateur videotape of him being beaten by four L.A. police officers on the night of March 3, 1991. In the first trial of the officers, prosecutors didn't call King to testify for fear that King's "menacing" demeanor might have justified, for jurors, the force used in the arrest. (King's police record included a robbery conviction, and there were later news reports of drunk driving and assaulting his wife.) King remained publicly silent until the L.A. RIOTS broke out. Then, Steven Lerman, King's white personal-injury lawyer, arranged the press conference at which King, dressed in a tie and soothing cardigan, pleaded for the riots to stop, "People, I just want to say, you know, can we, can we all get along?" (May 2, 1992). The symbol of the uprising was suddenly calling for the same social calm as President George Bush; five months later King's in-laws persuaded him to switch to a black lawyer, Milton Grimes, who hired tutors to raise King's "black consciousness" and limited his interviews to black reporters. In 1994 the strategy paid off to the tune of a $3.8 million jury award in a civil suit against the City of Los Angeles. The award became the subject of more lawsuits between King's two lawyers in July 1995, the same month that King was arrested for allegedly knocking a woman to the ground with his car.

USENET alt.rodney-king

Klein, Calvin (b. 1942) Designer whose self-titled firm (founded 1968) was instrumental in the late '70s-early '80s designer jeans craze. In 1979–80, TV ads shot by RICHARD AVEDON featured featherweight pubescent actress Brooke

Photo by Natsuko Utsumi

KATE MOSS not wearing CALVIN KLEIN on an L.A. billboard.

Shields purring "You know what comes between me and my Calvins? Nothing" Klein has consistently prospered through provocative advertising. In the '80s TV and print ads for his fragrance Obsession and underwear line used images that were variously pretentious and erotic, but always talked-about. In fall 1992 Klein's often homoerotic underwear billboards helped extend the career of featherweight rapper MARKY MARK, and subsequently brought to greater prominence waif model KATE MOSS. As this garnered him publicity, Klein's BRIDGE LINE CK was losing customers to cheaper purveyors of generic sportswear, such as THE GAP. In 1992 Klein's friend, MEDIA MOGUL David Geffen, eased the pressure by buying $60 million of the company's junk bond debt. The next year Klein was the subject of a biography, *Obsession*, which portrayed him as an omni-sexual drug-fiend during the Studio 54 designer-jeans years. In August 1995 a wittily tawdry CK Jeans TV and print-ad campaign shot by STEVEN MEISEL was swiftly withdrawn amid widespread accusations that the company was flirting with child pornography.

Koja, Kathe (b. 1960) Novelist who dragged hardcore horror into the '90s, reclaiming it from the hyperaggressive male splatterpunk of the '80s. Koja's *The Cipher* inaugurated Dell's Abyss imprint (which in turn launched POPPY Z. BRITE's career) and won the 1991 PHILIP K. DICK Award for best first novel originally published in paperback. The book's mopey slackertude evoked hopeless anxiety more than the genre's typical blind, brutalist rage. Subsequent novels—*Bad Brains* (1992), *Skin* (1993), and *Strange Angels* (1994)—have drifted gradually in a MODERN PRIMITIVE direction, pointedly describing cutting-edge pain culture.
USENET **alt.horror**

Koons, Jeff (b. 1955) Artist and former Wall Street commodities broker who rose to prominence in the mid-'80s, thanks to a flawless instinct for self-promotion and a healthy sense of the absurd. In Koons' best-known works—a life-sized polychromed wood replica of Michael Jackson and his

pet chimp Bubbles; vapid *fin de siècle* readymades such as a trio of basketballs floating in a fishtank; and gleefully pornographic sculptures and pictures of himself *in flagrante delicto* with Cicciolina (the Hungarian porn star/member of Parliament in Italy he married in 1991, and later divorced)—he displayed a penchant for sexuality without nuance, slogans without ideas, and inspiration without perspiration. Skilled in neither sculpture, drawing, nor painting (his notes and jottings were often executed by European craftsmen), Koons has earned both fame and lavish compensation in the same spirit as have ANDY WARHOL, Marcel Duchamp, and Milli Vanilli. But while he has persistently asserted that his work treats profound issues of populism and elitism, many critics dismiss Koons as a man void not only of substance but of conscience. Art critic Robert Hughes summed up the anti-Koonsian position: "If Jeff Koons' work is about class struggle, I am Maria of Romania."

Koresh, David (b. Vernon Howell, 1959; d. 1993) Self-styled messiah and leader of the Branch Davidian cult in Waco, Texas. Koresh was a failed rock musician on L.A.'s Sunset Strip (friends and neighbors described his music as "melodic rock," though he was also a fan of heavy metal), destined not to find fame until February 28, 1993, when the U.S. Bureau of Alcohol, Tobacco, and Firearms raided his compound on the suspicion that the cult was illegally hoarding machine guns. The Branch Davidians fought back, picking off four ATF agents, and a 51-day standoff ensued. FBI and ATF attempts to force an end included the blasting of rock music and Tibetan chants from giant speakers aimed at what the FBI dubbed Ranch Apocalypse. The name came true when a federal tank moved on the Davidians and the compound erupted in flames—an apparent suicide that killed 86 members inside, 25 of whom were children.

Though Attorney General Janet Reno had approved the tank attack largely on the grounds that the FBI had told her the cult's children were being physically abused, she later said she had "misunderstood," and in May of 1995, she called her actions "a mistake." The April 19, 1995, bombing of a federal building in Oklahoma City took place on the two-year anniversary of Waco—demonstrating that the NRA and MILITIAS had transformed Koresh into a gun ownership martyr. When the bombing prompted Republican Congress to hold hearings three months later, the subject was the government's mistakes at Waco, not, as would be expected, the militias linked to the Oklahoma City attack.

WEB **Why Waco?** http://www.neo.com/ucalpress/whywaco/

ALTERNATIVE poster boy FRANK KOZIK featured in the Addicted to Noise WEB site (www.addict.com).

Kozik, Frank (b. 1962) San Francisco-based poster artist who was reportedly inspired by a 1982 peyote trip to quit his job driving a delivery truck and start doing posters for local PUNK bands in Austin, Texas. Kozik's garishly colored work, now renowned nationwide, often promotes shows by casting cute comic book characters (Fred Flintstone, Archie and Veronica), cultural icons (Hitler, CHARLES MANSON), and big-breasted women in disturbing poses. He now produces over 100 silk-screened posters a year in his instantly recognizable style; one that is associated with the present generation of musicians as strongly as were Stanley Mouse and Rick Griffin with the bands of the San Francisco hippie era.

WEB **Frank Kozik** http://www.hooked.net/julianne/info-k19.html/

Kureishi, Hanif (b. 1954) Half-Pakistani British novelist/screenwriter/essayist and a paragon of the modern MULTICULTURAL intellectual. Kureishi made his mark with the pair of screenplays he wrote for director Stephen Frears: *My Beautiful Launderette* (1985) and *Sammy and Rosie Get Laid* (1987). Before *Launderette*, Kureishi wrote plays for fringe theaters, augmenting his income by writing pornography. His 1991 film *London Kills Me* dealt with homelessness and drugs in the country he once described as "an intolerant, racist, homophobic, narrow-minded, authoritarian rat hole." Raised on rock 'n' roll, he attended school with the future Billy Idol, on whom Kureishi based rock star Charlie Hero in his satirical 1991 novel *The Buddha of Suburbia* (adapted as a multi-part BBC mini-series the following year).

L.A. riots Week of urban mayhem ignited by the April 29, 1992, jury acquittal of four white police officers who were captured on videotape beating black motorist RODNEY KING. The angry response in South Central produced its own brutal footage, most dramatically the live broadcast from a hovering TV news helicopter of a black man striking unconscious with a brick, kicking, and then dancing over the body of, white truck driver Reginald Denny. The final three-day toll of what many community activists took to defiantly calling the uprising, revolt, rebellion, or intifada, was put at 53 dead, some $1 billion in property damage, nearly 2,000 arrests, and the job of Police Chief DARYL GATES. GANGSTA rappers, who had long expressed black rage at police brutality, took credit for anticipating the riots, with rapper ICE-T telling public radio, "I'm fucking Nostradamus, I predicted this shit" and ICE CUBE asserting "Everything . . . was on the records before the riots." White can-do Republican Peter Ueberroth headed up the post-riot economic development efforts, saying it would take $5 billion and five years to revitalize the same depressed neighborhoods that had also served as tinder for the 1965 Watts Riots. He was gone in less than a year, with all but a few token pledges having materialized. Later in 1993 two of the four police officers were convicted on federal charges, and Reginald Denny's assailant, Damian Williams, got the maximum sentence for assault of 10 years.

L7 Pulverising L.A. band instrumental in turning ROCK WOMEN from novelty to norm. Initially associated with the so-called Foxcore movement, L7 debuted with a self-titled 1988 album on Epitaph, then made *Smell The Magic* (1990) for the equally well-credentialed SUB POP. In the latter's track "Shove" L7 ('50s slang for "square") had a belligerent would-be anthem that they have struggled to equal on two subsequent major-label albums. (Career highlights include the 1994 LOLLAPALOOZA tour, the 1992 MTV mini-hit "Pretend That We're Dead," and an appearance in JOHN WATERS's *Serial Mom*.) As much as their PUNK-metal mix, the band has come to be known for an attitude once described by the *Utne Reader* as "defiantly unladylike"; at the 1992 Reading Festival in England, for instance, guitarist Donita Sparks threw her used tampon into the audience. (Later that year Sparks revealed her pubic area live on British television.) The band was also instrumental in the foundation of the ROCK FOR CHOICE organization in 1991.

WEB **Rock for Choice** http://www.mojones.com/kiosks/rock-forchoice/r4c.html ♦ USENET **alt.music.alternative.female**

Lab, The Orange Country, California, retail center targeted at hip teens and young adults and touted as an "anti-mall shopping concept" by its founder Shaheen Sadeghi, a former surf-wear executive. Opened in March 1994 with URBAN OUTFITTERS, Na Na Shoes, and a specialized TOWER RECORDS outlet called Tower Alternative as the main anchor stores, The Lab offers a theme park simulation of the hip but authentically crumbling urban neighborhoods not found in its suburban environs.

LaChapelle, David (b. 1963) Connecticut-born photographer whose artifice-obsessed work is seen mainly in magazines like *DETAILS* and Britain's *The Face*. Initially distinguished by his fixation on WHITE TRASH imagery, LaChapelle moved on to construct futuristic fashion-shoot scenarios, saturating colors and manipulating his work on computer. He is also known for placing his subjects in extravagant tableaux, whether they are Hollywood celebrities like *BEVERLY HILLS, 90210*'s Tori Spelling, or INDIE-ROCK personalities like EVAN DANDO.

Lacoste Crocodile-logo sportswear label founded in 1933 by French tennis star René "The Crocodile" Lacoste, and renowned for its piqué-cotton polo shirts. The shirts were standard-issue PREPPY-wear through the early '80s, as enshrined in *The Official Preppy Handbook* (1980), but parent company Izod took the brand progressively down market by introducing patterns and polyester blends. During the ironic preppie revival of the early '90s, original Izod shirts were a rare commodity, and became once again a fetishized label. (The ever-astute URBAN OUTFITTERS company turned the shirts into dresses by sewing them onto skirts.) As with PUMA, ADIDAS, and HANG TEN, there was a reissue of the original style, this one in February 1994; the Lacoste family bought back the license for more than $30 million and reissued its polo shirts in a deluxe $65 edition, with hand-stitched crocodiles and mother-of-pearl buttons.

Lake, Ricki (b. 1968) Originally discovered by sleaze auteur JOHN WATERS for his crossover-camp movie *Hairspray*, this beatific, big-boned actress raised herself from anticelebrity to talk TV power through sheer force of will. After reuniting with Waters on *Cry-Baby* (1990) and doing a tour of duty on TV's *China Beach*, Lake resurfaced 125 pounds lighter, in 1993, as the host of her own afternoon talk show. *The Ricki Lake Show* may have been yet another emotional small-claims court, with topics like "I'm Not the Only One Carrying His Baby" and "Get Real, Honey, Your Boyfriend is a Dog," but Lake's easy empathy cushioned the exploitation. She succeeded in the post-school slot where *SASSY* editor Jane Pratt perished, luring the elusive young demographic to talk-TV. Lake gained timely notoriety during November 1994 sweeps week when she spent a night in jail for storming the offices of fashion designer Karl Lagerfeld with other PETA members.

WEB Ricki Lake Show http://www.spe.sony.com/Pictures/ tv/rickilake/ricki.html ✦ USENET **alt.tv.talkshows.daytime**

Landers, Sean (b. 1963) Autobiographical artist who covers gallery walls with handwritten, often comic diary accounts of his poor work habits, social humiliations, and sexual fantasies. *THE NEW YORKER* and other critical voices hailed the young artist's 1990 show at the SoHo Postmasters Gallery as the post-'80s model of humility and diminished expectations. For that show, Landers—a graduate of the Philadelphia College of Art and Yale—hid his clay sculptures under plastic trash bags; in 1992 he showed a looping hour videotape of himself pro-

crastinating in his studio along with apologetic letters to his student loan officer. In his 1994 L.A. show, "Thought Bubble," the scrawl-of-consciousness moved from yellow legal paper to large, Abstract Expressionist canvases but preserved his excruciating self-doubt about premature ejaculation and painting. Also that year Landers published a—what else?—handwritten autobiographical novel, *Sic*, about his Irish Catholic childhood in a small Western Massachusetts town. The tall, pale Landers is often grouped with other "pathetic aesthetic" artists like Cary Leibowitz, MIKE KELLEY, and JIM SHAW.

Courtesy of Regan Projects

"Thought Bubble" (detail) by SEAN LANDERS, 1994.

Larry Sanders Show, The Lauded late-night talk show parody created by comedian Garry Shandling (b. 1949) and premiered in 1992 on cable network Home Box Office. The conceit of the guest star-laden *Sanders Show* is to switch between the talk show itself and the backstage back-biting of Larry (Shandling), his war-horse producer (Rip Torn), an unctuous co-host (Jeffrey Tambor), and assorted wives, agents, and staffers (including *SATURDAY NIGHT LIVE* malcontent JANEANE GAROFALO). Rarely has so much discomfort been mined in the name of comedy; and never has the show business food chain been so unmercifully traced. Shandling himself shows an admirable willingness to let himself look bad, at times taking his trademark self-deprecating shtick to almost self-immolating proportions. Shandling opted for satire over wealth when he turned down, during the early-'90s satire-friendly "talk show wars," a reported $5 million offer from NBC to be David Letterman's late-night talk show replacement. (As occasional guest host of *The Tonight Show* from 1983, Shandling had looked like Johnny Carson's heir apparent; from 1986 to 1990, he fronted the meta-sitcom *The Garry Shandling Show* on Showtime and Fox.)

WEB **The Larry Sanders Show** http://pmwww.cs.vu.nl/ service/sitcoms/LarrySanders/

Lauren, Ralph (b. Ralph Lifshitz, 1939) Bronx-born designer who has since 1967 catered astutely to the American longing for old-world, Anglophile style. In 1994, *Forbes* magazine estimated the global sales of Lauren's many-tiered pseudo-PREPPY empire at $3.9 billion, and his personal wealth at $500 million. The designer found a strange place in the youth culture pantheon in the mid-'80s when elements of his main, horse-logo'd, Polo line found favor among status-savvy B-BOYS, including Brooklyn's fabled 'Lo-Life gang. (Lauren is also a major influence on STÜSSY and on Phat Farm, the clothing label of HIP-HOP mogul RUSSELL SIMMONS.) Ironically, many fashion-conscious white kids then adopted Lauren's WASP-y clothes for the cachet bestowed upon them by their black counterparts.

Lawrence, Martin (b. 1965) As the spring-heeled, bug-eyed original MC for HBO's *DEF COMEDY JAM*, Martin Lawrence developed into one of the most magnetic performers on TV. Lawrence's uncanny rapport with the show's raucous live audience marked him as a potential successor to black superstar Eddie Murphy, with whom he co-starred in 1992's *Boomerang*. In 1992 Fox TV acknowledged the growing status of this *Star Search* alumnus and *House Party* (1990) scene-stealer by launching the sitcom *Martin*, an instantly successful star vehicle which initially ran after *THE SIMPSONS*. Lawrence drew some flak from black critics of his "unthreatening" portrayal of the titular DJ, a genial, self-deprecating fellow (plus several auxiliary characters, including DRAG favorite Sheneneh). If these voices were not stilled by Lawrence's 1993 and 1994 NAACP Image Awards, they may have paused after *You So Crazy* (1994), the lewd Lawrence concert-movie that was controversially saddled with a restrictive NC–17 rating before its eventual, unrated, release. In February 1994 the comedian spurned what many considered a good crossover opportunity by performing a puerile, apparently unrehearsed monologue as guest host of *SATURDAY NIGHT LIVE*.

Lead or Leave Inside-the-beltway, D.C.-based lobbying group that pushed deficit reduction and SOCIAL SECURITY reform as the defining youth issues of the '90s. Founded by Rob Nelson (b. 1964) and Jon Cowan (b. 1965), the organization's original pre–1992 election financial backers included conservatives Pete Peterson and Ross Perot. Arguing that current benefits for affluent senior citizens are bankrupting the country, Lead or Leave took its case to MTV, the White House, bookstores (1994's *Revolution X*), and even meetings of the AARP (American Association of Retired Persons). Short of funds and followers, the duo shut up shop in May 1995, promising to make a statement during the 1996 presidential campaign by burning social security cards—if they weren't too busy studying for the law school admissions tests. The organization is closely associated with the surviving THIRD MILLENNIUM, another self-consciously GENERATION X political group which Lead or Leave helped create.

WEB **Lead or Leave Home Page** http://www.cs.caltech.edu/ ~adam/lead.html

Leary, Denis (b. 1957) Fast-talking actor and performance monologist who came to prominence via series of bilious MTV promo spots. Leary's commercial-length outbursts riffed on pop culture phenomena like SUPERMODEL Cindy Crawford and R.E.M. while highlighting his comic persona—a charming Irish-American boor with a taste for red meat, rock music, hard liquor, and especially cigarettes. He subsequently released a one-man show, *No Cure for Cancer*, as both a CD and a book in

1992; recorded the novelty song "Asshole" (1993); filmed commercials for NIKE; and returned to acting, with roles in the urban-jungle adventure *Judgment Night* (1993), the dark comedy *The Ref* (1994), and the cutesy jungle adventure *Operation Dumbo Drop* (1995). This "acerbic blond bombshell" (per gossip veteran Liz Smith) is unusual among MTV-bred stars for forging a respectable career after leaving the channel.

Leary, Timothy (b. 1920) Legendary philosopher-showman of the '60s drug counterculture who shifted his "tune in, turn on, drop out" utopian emphasis on evolutionary consciousness from LSD and other psychoactives to silicon chips with the advent of VIRTUAL REALITY. Much of the original shtick still worked: where Leary told *Playboy* in the late '60s, "one of the great purposes of an LSD session is sexual union," in the '90s Leary titillated audiences with the double entendres of as-yet-unrealized CYBERSEX. Uncle Tim—as he was known in the glory days—continues to function as kindly guru to youthful experimentation, garnering cheers at a 1995 ZIPPIE event in London (by teleconference—Leary is banned from the U.K.) when the 74-year-old explained, "I take every form of illegal drug. I prefer illegal drugs to legal ones." Leary is said to have announced with some logic that TERENCE MCKENNA is the Timothy Leary of the '90s. Leary announced in 1995 that he was "thrilled" to learn that he was dying of prostate cancer, saying, "How you die is the most important thing you ever do. It's the exit."
WEB **The Timothy Leary and Robert Anton Wilson Show Homepage** http://www.intac.com/~dimitri/dh/learywilson.html

Leavitt, David (b. 1961) Author who in 1982 published his first short story in *THE NEW YORKER* while still an undergraduate at Yale—it was also the magazine's first openly gay fiction. Leavitt's literary reputation was cemented by a trio of finely wrought works (*Family Dancing* [1985], *The Lost Language of Cranes* [1986, adaptation shown on PBS], *Equal Affections* [1989]), many of which involved issues of homosexuality, that elevated him above many media-

celebrity contemporaries. But in 1993, Leavitt's reputation suffered severe damage when his novel *While England Sleeps*, based on Stephen Spender's 1951 memoir *World Within Word*, was withdrawn from publication after the still-living poet threatened to sue Leavitt for "plagiarizing my life." A revised edition with 17 changes had not yet been released at the time of Spender's death in July 1995.

Lee, Brandon (b. 1965; d. 1993) Actor son of martial-arts icon Bruce Lee (b. 1941; d. 1973) who, like his father, died suddenly and mysteriously from an injury sustained on the set of a movie. Lee debuted inauspiciously in a 1986 TV-movie revival of *Kung Fu* (the original series was conceived by his father but then handed to the Caucasian David Carradine). A cinematic adaptation of the underground comic *The Crow* was to be his breakthrough movie after two low-budget efforts. The reincarnation-revenge story began filming just as his father's bio-pic *Dragon: The Bruce Lee Story* (1993), with an interpretation of Bruce Lee's death as the result of a curse on the line of Lee men, was finishing production. That curse seemed to come true a second time during the filming of *The Crow* (1994), when a prop gun fired at Brandon Lee in his character's death scene turned out to be loaded with a bullet; he died hours later. The completed *Crow* succeeded in part due to the mystique of its real-life tragedy.
WEB **The Crow** http://jeffo.diamondmm.com/crow/the_crow.htm/

Lee, Spike (b. Shelton Jackson Lee, 1956) Brooklyn-born filmmaker whose independent first feature, *She's Gotta Have It* (1986), a spirited romantic comedy, had critics calling him "the black Woody Allen." (Lee reportedly despised the moniker. Both men have a child named Satchel.) With major studio backing Lee focused his talents on dramatizing race relations in films like *School Daze* (1988), *Do The Right Thing* (1989), and *Jungle Fever* (1991). (Widely considered Lee's strongest picture, *Do The Right Thing* prompted inaccurate predictions of race riots the summer of its release.) The commercial viability of these films helped pave the way for other black directors (including the HUGHES BROTHERS and JOHN SINGLETON); it also allowed Lee to open a chain of boutiques (Spike's Joint) specializing in T-shirts, hats, and other paraphernalia bearing logos of his films—even those still in production. In 1992 Lee directed *MALCOLM X*, a conventionally told bio-pic of the slain civil rights leader; he showed his penchant for PR bravura when he uttered the controversial pronouncement that "children should skip school the day *Malcolm X* opens." Lee directed two films in 1995: the phone sex saga *Girl Six*, an apparent response to ongoing criticism that he can't write female characters, and *Clockers*, an adaptation of Richard Price's 1992 crack novel.

Leguizamo, John (b. 1965) Manic Hispanic performance artist. Entering the fray in 1991 with the galvanic one-man show *Mambo Mouth* and a starring role in Joseph Vasquez's *Hangin' With the Homeboys*, Leguizamo won instant acclaim. But a second one-man show *Spic-o-rama* was followed by a disappointing forays into film, *Whispers in the Dark* (1992) and *Super Mario Brothers* (1993). Still, Leguizamo has continued to work in film, television, and on stage; in 1995, he not only got top billing in a Fox-TV comedy/variety show, *House of Buggin'*, but also starred in the transvestite drama *To Wong Foo, Thanks for Everything, Julie Newmar*.

Leigh, Jennifer Jason (b. Jennifer Leigh Morrow, 1958) When *Esquire* declared with a 1994 cover-line that "Jennifer Jason Leigh Feels Your Pain," the magazine struck the major chord of this inscrutable actress's repertoire. Films like *Last Exit To Brooklyn* (1989), *Miami Blues* (1990), and *Rush* (1991) saw Leigh putting herself through more scenes of humiliation and degradation than most actors rack up in a lifetime and helped cement her reputation as Hollywood's dark shadow. In *Single White Female* (1992) and *Mrs. Parker and the Vicious Circle* (1994), Leigh subsumed herself physically in her roles with a commitment that dwarfs the "method" posturings of many of her peers. By consistently refusing to seek out material that will cast her as sympathetic, and therefore media-friendly, she has effectively absented herself from the next level of celebrity.

Leigh, Mike (b. 1943) British filmmaker best known in the U.S. for 1993's picaresque, fiercely misanthropic *Naked*. That film came close to equaling the impact of his British television plays of the '70s and early '80s, which were released on video in America the following year. Developed, like all Leigh's work, through lengthy improvisation sessions with his actors, TV-plays like *Abigail's Party* (1976), *Nuts In May* (1976), and *Grown Ups* (1980) are unblinking accounts of mundane lives that embrace class satire, comedy of discomfort, and gut-wrenching tragedy. As a chronicler of late-century British life, this Manchester-born filmmaker's most obvious point of comparison is doom-struck singer MORRISSEY.

Lesbian Avengers Principal '90s lesbian protest group. Co-founded by ACT-UP activist and author Sarah Schulman (b. 1958) to raise lesbian visibility, the Avengers got their start in 1992, protesting ultimately successful attempts to kill the homo-tolerant Rainbow Curriculum in New York's public schools. Opting for the "zaps" of ACT-UP rather than more traditional demonstrations or speaker-centered rallies, the Lesbian Avengers have made themselves known with gleeful effrontery, spreading from New York to twenty-odd other cities, including heartland trouble spots (see ANTI-GAY RIGHTS INITIATIVES) and a particularly active chapter in London. On Valentine's Day 1994, four members of a local chapter—wearing T-shirts with the Avenger motto "We Recruit"—handed out balloons, candy, and leaflets saying "Girls who love girls and women who love women are OK" to elementary school girls in Springfield, Massachusetts. One of the group's hallmarks is fire-eating (a practice—and motto, "The Fire Will Not Consume Us"—begun after the arson double-murder of a lesbian and gay man by SKINHEADS in Oregon in 1992). Fighting marginalization of lesbian causes within the gay rights movement, the L.A.'s have, since 1993, held their own higher-energy, often bare-chested "Dyke Marches" before the annual June commemoration of the 1969 Stonewall Uprising in New York City. WEB **Lesbian Avenger Home Page** http://www.cc. columbia.edu/~vk20/lesbian/avenger.html/ ✦ WEB **The Lesbian Avengers-London Chapter** http://www.cs.ucl.ac. uk/students/zcacsst/LA.html/ ✦ WEB **International Lesbian Avenger Email List** http://www.helsinki.fi/~kris_ntk/ lezlist/la.html/

"LESBIAN CHIC," a best-selling issue for *New York* magazine.

lesbian chic 1993 was a good year for lesbians. Or, more precisely, a good year for mainstream magazines to put lesbians on their covers. *New York* did it in May, *Newsweek* in June, both best-selling issues; in August, *Vanity Fair* showed SUPER-MODEL Cindy Crawford "shaving" lesbian country crooner k.d. lang. "Lesbian Chic," as *New York* dubbed it, is the glamorous, apoliti-cal, man- and market-friendly flipside of lesbian vis-ibility (an earlier phenomenon that grew largely without the aid of corporate media). According to the received wisdom, chic lesbians are gorgeous femmes, all-American tom boys, lipstick lesbians, or androgynous enigmas rather than diesel dykes, butches, or BIRKENSTOCK-wearing folkies. Their celebrity ranks include entertainers Melissa Etheridge and SANDRA BERNHARD, athlete Martina Navratilova, and models Rachel Williams and Jenny Shimuzu. Lesbian chic has manifested itself in TV and movies: in 1994, *Roseanne* and *BEVERLY HILLS 90210* both had lesbian episodes; the surprise suc-cess of lesbian independent film *Go Fish* in 1994 led to production of similar girl-girl projects, including *The Incredible True Adventures of Two Girls in Love* (1995) and a mooted feature film re-make of Oscar-nominated short documentary *Chicks In White Satin* (1993). As an entertainment executive noted in 1994's dyke-flick *Bar Girls,* "lesbians are hot right now."

Lewis, Juliette (b.1973) Sartorially baffling actress who, at 14, successfully petitioned to be emancipated from her parents. Being legally declared an adult put Lewis clear of child labor laws, allowing her to vigorously pursue her trade. The actress's apparent hubris was justified by her Oscar-nominated portrayal of an awkwardly bloom-ing teenager in Martin Scorsese's 1991 film *Cape Fear.* (Her reputation was cemented by a single-scene tour de force of discomfort in which she sucked on the thumb of Robert De Niro's villain Max Cady.) Lewis, a devotee of SCIENTOLOGY, was effectively cast as a precocious co-ed by Woody Allen in his *Husbands and Wives* before going on to briefly specialize in WHITE TRASH wastrels in *What's Eating Gilbert Grape* (1993, with JOHNNY DEPP) and the SERIAL-KILLER CHIC movies *Kalifornia* (1993, opposite then-paramour BRAD PITT) and OLIVER STONE's *Natural Born Killers* (1994).

Leyner, Mark (b. 1956) "To speak today of a famous novelist is like speaking of a famous cabinet-maker or speedboat designer," quoth Gore Vidal. "Adjective is inappropriate to noun." *Et Tu, Babe* (1992) is Hoboken novelist Mark Leyner's 1992 Nietzschean power fantasy about how a writer ("a Mark Leyner") might redress that oxymoron. Leyner's 1983 novel debut, *I Smell Esther Williams: and Other Stories,* may be for completists only, but the white-hot textual overkill of *My Cousin, My Gastroenterologist* (1990)—which included medita-tions on the Wilford Military Academy of Beauty and self-surgery clinics—marked this chum of good taste guru Martha Stewart as a verbal slapstick spe-cialist. Many of Leyner's magazine writings for *THE NEW YORKER* and other magazines were collected in 1995 as *Tooth Imprints on a Corn Dog.*

Lifetime Learning Systems Leader, founded 1978, in the newly vibrant industry of marketing to children during school. "Kids spend 40 percent of each day in the classroom where tra-ditional advertising can't reach them," complained a late-'80s Lifetime brochure. "Now you can enter the classroom through custom-made learning materials created with your specific marketing objectives in mind." Along with Modern Talking Pictures, Scholastic, and other kid-marketing outfits, Lifetime specializes in disguising advertising as educational texts, filmstrips, and videos for the classroom. M&M/Mars sponsors a lesson plan on nutrition; Procter & Gamble sponsors "Facts about Dishwashable Surfaces," as part of their home cleaning curriculum; Georgia-Pacific, the lumber company, provides a text discussing the virtue of removing old growth trees from the forest and replacing them with new "supertrees." Cash-strapped schools get posters, quizzes, and texts loaded with information on everything from the safety of nuclear power to the thickness of spaghetti sauce. "If there's a cardinal rule in preparing sponsored material," explains Modern's Ed Swanson, "it is that it must serve the needs of the communicator first. But it also must have perceived value in the classroom." [See also CHANNEL ONE.]

like Youthful verbal tic with remarkable expressive range, capable of denoting both hesitancy and impatience, uncertainty and conviction, exaggeration and understatement. (Not to be confused with the comparative use employed by those over forty—thus the title of the 1992 MTV teen politics show *Like We Care* should properly be read "as if we care" not "this is the way in which we care.") A 1993 *New York Times* op-ed defense of the generational/grammatical hiccup, entitled "We Are Like Poets," declared, "Much more than the random misfire of a stunted mind, 'like' is actually a rhetorical device that demonstrates the speaker's heightened sensibility and offers the listener added levels of color, nuance and meaning." [See also UPSPEAK.]

WEB **MIT Linguistics Homepage**
http://web.mit.edu/afs/athena.mit.edu/org/l/linguistics/www/Homepage.html

Limbaugh, Rush (b. 1951) Ideologue one minute ("the most dangerous man in America"), entertainer the next ("I'm just a lovable little fuzzball"). Talk-show superstar Limbaugh may not be an intellectual but he plays one on the radio. The scourge of "feminazis," homosexuals, and liberals, Limbaugh is a Reagan Republican who practically kept the party together after George Bush's 1992 defeat by Bill Clinton. A free-market fanatic who occasionally punctuates his daily three-hour, five-days-a-week right-wing spiel with calls from supporters ("dittoheads"), Limbaugh has built a powerful media empire since replacing Morton Downey Jr. on a Sacramento station in 1984. Limbaugh's show took off two years after his 1988 move to New York, and by 1995 was heard by an estimated 20 million people on more than 600 stations nationwide (with his syndicated TV show seen on another 200-plus stations). In 1994 the group Fairness & Accuracy in Reporting catalogued "Limbaugh's lies" in *The Way Things Aren't* (whose title parodied 1993's *The Way Things Ought to Be*, the first of Limbaugh's two best-selling books). While Limbaugh's politics remain staunchly conservative, he has toned down his shtick in recent years, no longer performing "caller abortions" to the sound of a vacuum cleaner.

WEB **Unofficial Rush Limbaugh Home Page**
http://www.eskimo.com/~jeremyps/rush ✦ USENET **alt.fan.rush-limbaugh, alt.rush-limbaugh, alt.flame.rush-limbaugh** ✦ WEB **FAIR** http://www.igc.org/fair/limbaugh-debates-reality.html

line dancing Cross between the lambada dance fad of the late '80s and the mechanical bull-riding fad of the late '70s. First popularized with the success of Billy Ray Cyrus's 1992 country-fluff hit "Achy Breaky Heart" and the accompanying "Achy Breaky" dance, line dancing took off at nightspots across the country, even in areas not normally associated with country music. (Gay- and lesbian-bar versions have their own separate history that can be traced back to prohibitions on same-sex couple-dancing.) Highly choreographed steps involved lined-up dancers kicking and swiveling in unison with the help of a DJ's instructions and instructional videos which sold in the hundreds of thousands. An anachronistic dance craze in the age of MOSHING.

Linklater, Richard (b. 1962) Texas-born filmmaker who wandered into the cross-hairs of mass-culture with his first feature, *Slacker* (1991). Filmed in Austin, Texas, *Slacker* was a rambling, real-time affair peopled by non-aspirational types who fit 1992's favorite media trend-story: "slacker" was enthusiastically filed alongside "GENERATION X" and "twentysomething" in the '90s lexicon. (Asked in an *America Online* forum how he felt about this attention Linklater replied, "How do you feel when a Doberman humps your leg?") Link-later's next, better-funded movie *Dazed and Confused* (1993) was another sprawling, loose narrative about a day in the lives of the unambitious—this time 1976 Texas high-schoolers. With its ravishing Bicentennial detail (the pooka-shell necklaces! the French-cut T-shirts!) and merciless depiction of the high school social order, the movie struck many a generational nerve. In 1995 Linklater moved into the realm of the romantic but kept his trademark timeframe: in *Before Sunrise* Euro-traveler ETHAN HAWKE finds love with Julie Delpy over the course of one Viennese evening.

WEB **Linklater** http://www.hyperweb.com/linklater/ linklater.html

RICHARD "Slacker" LINKLATER, 1993.

Photo by Sandra-Lee Phipps

Liquid Television MTV animation program that is the main national TV outlet for the kind of independent animation previously distributed only in festival compilations shown at art houses. The show, produced by San Francisco-based Colossal Pictures, first aired in June 1991 as a natural extension of the what MTV already did best, its animated station IDs; the Emmy-winning series brought MTV grudging respect in the underground art world for showcasing avant-garde work from around the globe as the music videos rarely succeeded in doing. The show's biggest successes are its two spin-offs, *AEON FLUX* and *BEAVIS AND BUTT-HEAD* (the original "Frog Baseball" episode aired on *LT*), but also well-received were *Stick Figure Theater*, a thin excuse to replay classic movie dialogue, and CHARLES BURNS's live action *Dog Boy*.

WEB **mtv.com** http://www.mtv.com/ ✦ USENET **alt.tv.liquid-tv**

Little Luxuries Generation Term coined by Roper Group market researchers hired by *Mademoiselle* magazine in 1992 to study the shifting values of the magazine's readership. (A similar concept, Small Indulgence Syndrome, is attributed to trend watcher Faith Popcorn.) Either unable or unwilling to make traditional commitments like starting a family or buying a home (or even a car), the Roper theory contends, young adults indulge in affordable luxuries such as compact disks or cappuccinos. Variations of this consumption-friendly argument have since reassured marketers trying to reach the nettlesome GENERATION X niche—and also helped explain the resemblance of young adult apartments to consumer electronic showrooms.

lo-fi Broad-based tendency toward lower production values in rock. Lo-fi was born of necessity among INDIE-ROCK bands, who were used to recording on primitive 4- and 8-track set-ups, but recent years have seen a significant number of bands adhering to its strictures out of choice. Prime exponents of the lo-fi aesthetic are Ohio's raucously Anglophile Guided by Voices, the ultra-prolific Sebadoh (brainchild of former DINOSAUR JR. member Lou Barlow), and OLYMPIA, Washington's Beat Happening. Calvin Johnson, leader of the latter band, explained to *Guitar Player* magazine that he regards lo-fi as a shift toward "appropriate technology," an early-'70s term used by author E.F. Schumacher in relation to American foreign aid policies. Even well-compensated major label acts have lately eschewed the temptations of 24-track (and upwards) recording, among them SONIC YOUTH, PAVEMENT, and L.A. folk-PUNK ragamuffin Beck.

WEB **Way To Go Sebadoh!** http://joemama.mit.edu/ sebadoh/sebadoh.html/ ✦ WEB **Guided By Voices** http://www-dev.lexis-nexis.com/~mikesell/gbv/

lock-ins Community-sponsored slumber parties for teens held at malls, churches, and schools. Lock-ins were embraced in the 1980s by parents' groups as a way to keep all-night revelry adult-supervised and free from drugs and alcohol. (Being locked in a mall overnight is, depending on one's outlook, either a consumerist fantasy or an Orwellian nightmare.) In the '90s, lock-ins have become an increasingly popular choice for graduation festivities. [See also GRAD NITE.]

logo parodies Almost as common as '90s street-fashion labels are quick-buck merchants who emblazon T-shirts with variations on established commercial trademarks. There are scores of popular examples, including "Cocaine—enjoy the real thing" taken from the Coca-Cola logo; "Nice Trippies," after Rice Krispies; and "Awidas," which posits the ADIDAS trefoil in the shape of a pot leaf. (The latter was withdrawn in February 1994 after a threatened lawsuit). Streetwear companies even cannibalize their own in the search for a quick buck: Shawn Stüssy, the godfather of streetwear, saw his STÜSSY logo ripped off twice by upstart designers who re-wrote it as "Stüpid" and "Püssy"; and "Phillies Cunts" was fashioned after Not From Concentrate's smash-hit "Phillies Blunts" T-shirt.

One possible source of inspiration for this fashion "SAMPLING" trend might be Wacky Packages, a collectible series of stickers released by the Topps company (and created by ART SPIELGELMAN) in the late '70s. Among the products clumsily spoofed were Crest ("Crust"), Cabbage Patch Kids ("Garbage Pail Kids"), and Wonder Bread ("Blunder Bread").

Lolita bag Tiny cotton backpack from the junior line (founded 1984) of French designer label Agnès B. (founded 1976); named after the prepubescent temptress in Vladimir Nabokov's classic, once-banned novel. Its $25 price means that the Lolita bag—a precursor of the MINI-BACKPACK—achieved high visibility on the backs of young women who wouldn't have been seen dead in Agnes B.'s regular, pricier garments. At their 1993 prime,

the bags could be seen at both RAVES and INDIE-ROCK shows, usually worn in some combination with a floral print dress, suede PUMA sneakers, and BARRETTES.

Lollapalooza Movable MULTI-CULTURAL music festival established summer 1991 and fronted by wild-eyed Jane's Addiction singer PERRY FARRELL. (The idea for the venture is credited, in Gina Arnold's *Route 666: On the Road to Nirvana* (1993), to Jane's drummer Stephen Perkins and the band's then-agent Marc Geiger.) On paper Lollapalooza looked like a logistical nightmare: seven bands from clashing—if nominally ALTERNATIVE—cultures schlepping from coast to coast under the aegis of a mercurial (to say the least) ringmaster. But not only did the tour work as a recession-busting value-pack, it effected—along with NIRVANA's winter chart assault—a sea change in pop music, putting the "youth" back in youth culture.

Ticket from the first-ever LOLLAPALLOZA (via TICKETMASTER).

The premiere Lollapalooza was headlined by Jane's Addiction (their final tour), with support from ICE-T's Body Count, English GOTH-rockers Siouxsie and the Banshees, black jazz-metal fusioneers Living Colour, HENRY ROLLINS, the BUTTHOLE SURFERS, and iconoclastic scene-stealers NINE INCH NAILS. Personality clashes were few, organization was smooth, and fans of each genre reveled in their new-found, collective cultural power.

Summer 1992 saw Lollapalooza confirmed as a major commercial franchise, an official celebration of generational identity that consistently filled modest-sized stadiums. The '92 bill was led by newly minted pop stars the RED HOT CHILI PEPPERS, with ICE CUBE, PEARL JAM, DREAM POP proponents Lush, vintage mope-rockers the Jesus and Mary Chain, GRUNGE avatars Soundgarden, and iconoclastic scene-stealers MINISTRY. Perry Farrell's utopian ideal of a nomadic multi-culti village translated into political sign-up stalls, T-shirt vendors, PIERCING shacks, veggie-burger bars, SMART DRINKS tents, and occasional sideshow freaks like the Jim Rose Circus.

The third Lollapalooza waned: the line-up of female PUNK-thrash trio Babes In Toyland, DINOSAUR JR., PUNK-funk progenitors Fishbone, rural rappers Arrested Development (whom Ice-T notoriously called "slave rap"), grunge-doom merchants Alice In Chains, Belgian INDUSTRIAL troupers Front 242, unlikely headliners PRIMUS, alterna-metal giants Tool, and iconoclastic scene-stealers RAGE AGAINST THE MACHINE was a relatively pallid, if successful, package. Pointed questions were raised about whether the whole undertaking might not be further institutionalizing alternative culture.

Perry Farrell was spurred to renew his involvement in his wayward creation, making 1994 something of a comeback year for the festival: artful New York rappers A Tribe Called Quest, The Breeders, Antipodean doom-crooner Nick Cave (and the Bad Seeds), L7, GEORGE CLINTON (and the P-Funk Allstars), GREEN DAY, and Japanese noiseniks the Boredoms made for an unpredictable mix on the main stage; the village began to plug in tentatively to the INTERNET; and the increasingly prestigious second stage played host to tyros like Stereolab, Guided by Voices, the Pharcyde, and BEASTIE BOYS acolytes Luscious Jackson. The Beasties themselves stole the show, confirming their smooth move from frat-rap pariahs to arbiters of white cool; the SMASHING PUMPKINS (and occasional guest star COURTNEY LOVE) had an unenviable task following them. (That same summer Farrell played Woodstock '94 with his new band Porno For Pyros.)

Although the fourth Lollapalooza was generally well received, Farrell (one of three partners in Lollapalooza Inc.) reportedly considered selling the enterprise. He relented, announcing a less-commercial 1995 line up that comprised Courtney Love's Hole, SONIC YOUTH, PAVEMENT, Beck, punky Chicagoans Jesus Lizard, frat-house ska band the Mighty Mighty Bosstones, SINEAD O'CONNOR, and CYPRESS HILL. Perhaps predictably, Courtney Love proved the most interesting figure on an uncharismatic bill: she engaged in verbal fisticuffs with Cypress Hill (calling them

"pothead pussies"), outshone Sonic Youth onstage, and backstage punched the band's associate, RIOT GRRRL Kathleen Hanna. Sinead O'Connor left the tour prematurely owing to pregnancy.

WEB **Home Page** http://www.lollapalooza.com

longbox Cardboard packaging for CDs that was dropped by record labels in April 1993, after 13 years of service. The 6 x 12-inch longbox was originally designed to fill LP bins, two-abreast, but the industry came to value the outer shell for theft prevention and displays. Although the conversion was widely seen as the result of environmental lobbying by fans and acts such as U2, Don Henley, and Sting (discarded longboxes were said to produce 20 million pounds of garbage a year), the *Washington Post* quoted one retailer who, noting that the U.S. was the last country still using the boxes, argued that it was a financial, not environmental, decision in deference to the world-standard "jewel box." Record stores had more than a year to prepare for the switchover, but many still found themselves spending the first week that April furiously liberating millions of CDs in inventory from the extra packaging.

Loompanics Unlimited Million-dollar-a-year mail-order book publisher whose catalogue reads like an anarchist Sharper Image for freaks, geeks, and cheats. How-to best-sellers pushing the First Amendment envelope include *Complete Guide to Lock Picking* and "Uncle Fester's" *Secrets of Methamphetamine Manufacture* (which made a brief cameo on *60 Minutes* during a drug raid). In the late '80s a police search of the home of a jailed investment banker turned up a copy *How to Launder Money*. Other major "going off the grid" themes include tax protest, revenge, explosives, survivalism, and privacy. Michael Hoy, the middle-aged head of Loompanics and self-proclaimed "lunatic fringe of the libertarian movement," founded the Port Townsend, Washington, company in 1974 by enterprisingly publishing an index to the unrelated, highly collectible *National Lampoon*.

EMAIL loompanx@olympus.net ✦ GOPHER **Catalogue**
gopher://gopher.well.com/00/Business/catalog.asc

Lords, Traci (b. Nora Louise Kuzma, 1968) Reformed porn star nonpareil. A teenage runaway and aspiring model, Lords ended up (through forged ID) gracing the pages of *Penthouse* at just 15.

TRACI LORDS at "23"—February 1986 *Hustler.*

Cocaine addiction led Lords into porn movies, of which she made dozens (including compilations) before being arrested in her Redondo Beach home by the FBI in May 1986. Although Lords' agent and two producers were indicted for sexual exploitation of a minor, charges against them were dropped. *I Love You Traci* (1987), shot in France, is Lords' single legal-age film from her porn years. JOHN WATERS cast Lords in *Cry-Baby* (1990, alongside trash-icons Patty Hearst, Iggy Pop, and *Tiger Beat* refugee JOHNNY DEPP), and gave her a cameo in *Serial Mom* (1994). Thus legitimized, Lords went on to claim roles in sitcoms *Roseanne* and *Married . . . With Children*, then to command the respect of her generation as a cult member on *Melrose Place*. When Lords turned her hand to singing, her 1995 debut single "Control" (from the album *1,000 Fires*) topped the *Billboard* dance charts.

WEB **Radioactive Records** http://radioactive.net/ radioactive/BANDS/TRACI/index.shtml ✦ WEB **Traci Lords Mini-Page** http://gellersen.valpo.edu/~pmilliga/delirium/ lords/lords.html

Love, Courtney (b. 1964) Singer-leader of ALTERNATIVE rock group Hole; widow of NIRVANA's Kurt Cobain; larger-than-her-music PUNK networker and celebrity; MOSH-pit warrior. Born to HIPPIE PARENTS, Love grew up near Eugene, Oregon; much of her peripatetic adolescence—kicked off with a stint in an Oregon reformatory for shoplifting a Kiss T-shirt—was spent pursuing rock dreams in L.A., Liverpool (hanging with singer Julian Cope), San Francisco (singing with an early version of Faith No More), and Minneapolis. After winning a small part in 1986's *Sid & Nancy*, the director Alex Cox gave her the lead in the following

year's punk indulgence *Straight to Hell*. The movie bombed, returning Love to singing in bands, the most successful of which was an early version of Babes In Toyland with that group's leader Kat Bjelland and Jennifer Finch, later of L7. Hole was founded in L.A. in 1989.

Love's expansive ambitions came together with her romance of rising star Kurt Cobain in 1991. That year Hole released the debut album *Pretty on the Inside* (co-produced by SONIC YOUTH's Kim Gordon) which, despite much rock-critic fawning, sold in paltry numbers. The record was an undistinguished punky thrash, although the unstinting honesty of Love's lyrics, her "kinder-whore" style (the *L.A. Times* described it as a "paradigm of damaged slutty glamor"), and her unvarnished interview technique, made her one of INDIE ROCK's more compelling figures. In February 1992, at the height of Nirvana's era-defining success, Cobain and a with-child Love married. In a profile of the GRUNGE celebrities, *Vanity Fair* detailed her and Cobain's alleged heroin use while she was pregnant with daughter Frances Bean (named for '30s movie star Frances Farmer, who became a mythic mental patient and alcoholic); denials were fierce, but legal action was notably not forthcoming, and the couple was prohibited from seeing their daughter without supervision in the baby's first month. Later in 1992, Hole signed a deal with Nirvana's label, Geffen Records.

Cobain's overdose in Rome and his subsequent April 8, 1994 suicide moved Love to center stage in the world of alternative rock, where the propensity to see her as the era's reigning punk feminist or crass opportunist tended to break down along gender lines. When *Rolling Stone* magazine politely wondered about the use, in her "Doll Parts" video, of a Kurt-like boy (in a "Smells Like Teen Spirit" striped T-shirt, made by the same director SAMUEL BAYER), Love indignantly replied, "it was my right to reference it . . . it was tasteful." Meanwhile fellow SEATTLE band Mudhoney asked in song "Why don't you blow your brains out too?" and former Nirvana drummer Dave Grohl sang on the Foo Fighters 1995 debut, "How could it be I'm the only one

alt.culture

who sees your rehearsed insanity?" At the 1994 MTV Video Awards, Love bemoaned the disparity between her headlines (which included becoming the INTERNET's first official Rock Star by taking on all comers in AMERICA ONLINE's Hole folder) and commercial success: "I wish people would just like me for what I am, the singer of an o.k. New Wave band." 1995 highlights for Love-watchers included: in May, a cloying cover story in *Vanity Fair*; in June, her brief hospitalization for what was explained by the record company as an "adverse reaction to prescription drugs"; and in July a tempestuous outing with the LOLLAPALOOZA tour that resulted in a suspended jail sentence.

WEB **Home of the alt.fan.courtney-love FAQ** http://www.mordor.com/rcmaric/clfaq.html ✦ WEB **tHE DrOwN SoDa HoLe WeB PaGes** http://www.albany.net/~rsmith/hole.html ✦ WEB **Geffen Records** http://geffen.com/hole.html ✦ USENET **alt.fan.courtney-love**

lowriders Custom-car enthusiasts who augment their vehicles with elaborate paint jobs and hefty hydraulic systems (powered by extra batteries). Lowriding originated among Hispanics who found post-World War II employment in California's heavy industries; expressions of their newfound status included adapting the suspensions of Chevrolets and Fords, putting the cars distinctively—and perilously—close to the ground. The '60s brought improvised, heavy-duty hydraulics of the type still used to create fearsome lunging motions (hydraulic systems are now pre-packaged along with complex switching systems). Lowriders now have their own magazine (*Lowrider*, founded 1976) and a network of clubs that belies the image of lowriding as gang-banging accessory; on the circuit of well-organized, lavishly catered arena exhibition shows any number of Chevy Impalas, *bombas* (restored vintage cars), and customized minitrucks are paraded, some "dancing" to music. Lowriding is no longer the exclusive purview of Latinos (as is often proved by GANGSTA rap videos) or unique to California: there are lowrider enclaves in Miami, Atlanta, and even Japan.

LSD On April 19, 1943, Dr. Albert Hoffman dosed himself with .25 mg of d-lysergic acid diethylamide tartrate, which he had accidentally ingested a few days earlier, and took his storied bike ride through the streets of Basel, Switzerland. A generation later the substance, abbreviated as LSD, fueled a cultural revolution despite criminalization in 1965. (LSD's social history can be read in Jay Stevens's 1987 *Storming Heaven*.) The most potent of all psychedelics, LSD is usually ingested orally on blotter paper frequently festooned with cultural icons. (Examples from recent LSD resurgences include Bart Simpson and BEAVIS AND BUTT-HEAD.) While the typical late-'60s tripper probably took around 250 mg of "acid," the average strength of the hits sold in recent years, known to old-timers as "disco doses," is less than half that. LSD embodies a potentially infinite array of effects, ranging from mild sensory distortions to peak religious experiences. LSD is essentially a boundary-dissolving, experience-enhancing substance—as with most psychedelics, the effects tied to the mind set of the user and the setting in which it is ingested.

WEB **Hyperreal** http://www.hyperreal.com/drugs/psychedelics/lsd ✦ USENET **alt.drugs.psychedelics**

LUGs "Lesbians Until Graduation." Lesbian equivalent of sell-out or "oreo," used to brand college students who take advantage of their campus's tolerant environment to try out the Sapphic lifestyle, then return to the straight world upon graduation. Also called "four-year lesbians" or, after defection, "hasbians." [See also LESBIAN CHIC.]

Lynch, David (b. 1946) Deadpan filmmaker whose cult stock rose steadily in the decade between the expressionistic black and white fever-dream *Eraserhead* (1977) and *Blue Velvet* (1986). The latter film was a lush tour de force of warped sensuality that defined the Lynch style, rendering perverse the oppressive normality of the director's Pacific Northwest childhood. Intoxicated by the film's almost unanimous acclaim, ABC network executives gave Lynch unheard-of latitude to create (with partner Mark Frost) a drama series, *TWIN PEAKS*, in 1990. The show was a landmark in television history, but sustaining it overtaxed Lynch's considerable talents. At the height of *Twin Peaks* mania, Lynch's violent, disengaged road movie *Wild At Heart* (1990) was released, and taken as a portent that his obsessions might be growing tiresome. The ill-conceived movie *Twin Peaks: Fire Walk With Me* (1992) confirmed those suspicions (though he has overcome setbacks before—the disastrous 1984 sci-fi epic *Dune*, for example). Lynch's subsequent output was restricted to several high-budget TV ads, two segments of an HBO movie trilogy, and *On the Air* (1992), a short-lived sitcom about '50s television pioneers.

WEB **Your David Lynch Resource** http://www.interport.net/ ~regulus/pkd/pkd-int.html

Lynch, Jennifer (b. 1968) Filmmaker chiefly known for the furor surrounding her one movie, *Boxing Helena* (1993). Lynch (daughter of director DAVID LYNCH) originally cast MADONNA in her story of a limbless, manipulating beauty; when the singer withdrew, former Bond girl Kim Basinger took her place. When Basinger in turn bailed out, in June 1991, she was sued by Lynch and partners for damaging the film's advance sales; a March 1993 ruling awarded $8.1 million to the plaintiffs, which led Basinger to claim bankruptcy. When *Boxing Helena* was finally released later that year (with *TWIN PEAKS*' Sherilyn Fenn in the title role) it had a cursory theatrical release before appearing in video stores. (Lynch also wrote the best-selling *Twin Peaks* spin-off book *The Secret Diary of Laura Palmer* [1990].) In September 1994 the California Court of Appeal reversed the decision against Basinger.

M.A.C. Toronto-based make-up company that is credited with introducing the first "POLITICALLY CORRECT" (vegetable- not animal-based) lipstick when it was founded in 1984. Distinctive, muted-color M.A.C. (Makeup-Art Cosmetics) products, initially marketed only to make-up artists, have since found favor among an impressive array of SUPERMODELS and celebrities including Princess Diana, MADONNA (product of choice: Russian Red lipstick), and DREW BARRYMORE, who occasionally acts as an unpaid spokesperson for the company. Such attention has helped M.A.C. become an essential lifestyle accessory for many women; from 1991 to 1993 the company's revenue made leaps of roughly $10 million per annum, reaching almost $40 million in 1993. In 1995, the company signed an overseas distribution deal with Estée Lauder, and hired DRAG entertainer RUPAUL as the spokesmodel for its Viva Glam lipstick, the profits of which go to AIDS charities.

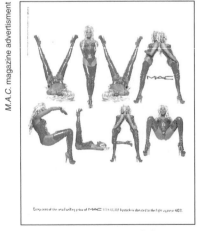

Full-service DRAG entertainer RUPAUL turns M.A.C. model, 1995.

Macintosh The first personal computer to replace typed commands with a graphical user interface (GUI), i.e., a mouse for pointing and clicking at windows and icons. (Most GUI—pronounced "gooey"—ideas were developed at Xerox by computer visionary Alan Kay and his followers in the '70s.) Apple Computer, the Macintosh's maker, has cultivated an oppositional stance for the computer since it was introduced in 1984 with the lavish, now legendary Ridley Scott commercial that equated the rival IBM company with Big Brother. Ten years later, HENRY ROLLINS tells you "what's on his PowerBook" in ads for laptop Macs. Apple has also co-opted future leaders by selling Macs at deep discounts to undergraduates. The company's mystique derives in part from its garage origins. Founder #1 Steve Wozniak lost $30 million on his two U.S. rock festivals; founder #2 Steve Jobs dated Joan Baez and developed the Next computer, an ahead-of-its-time flop. Desktop publishing, a key factor in the proliferation of ZINES and other publishing start-ups, was born on the Mac. The 1995 release of Microsoft's Windows 95 operating system brought much of the Macintosh's ease of use to Apple's rivals.

WEB **Apple Computer** http://www.apple.com

Madonna (b. Madonna Louise Veronica Ciccone, 1958) Few predicted that this one-time disco bimbo would go on to be one of the major pop icons of the late 20th century—but she has, through impressive willpower and an uncanny instinct for public taste. Madonna's consistent ability to write a durable dance-pop tune, transform her image, co-opt subcultures (VOGUING, S/M, HOUSE, SANDRA BERNHARD), overcome setbacks (her acting career, swearing at David Letterman), pick timely new collaborators (producers Dallas Austin, Nellee Hooper, and JUNIOR VASQUEZ, to name a few), and titillate the media with a new twist (the *Sex* book [1992], *Bedtime Stories* [1994], "return to romance") have put her so far ahead of the competition that there *is* no real competition. Even Madonna's detractors predict for her a bright future in marketing, which ignores the fact that marketing has been her major since she sang her first note.

WEB **Warner Records** http://www.iuma.com/Warner/html/Madonna.html USENET **alt.fan.madonna**

Madonna Studies   The former Mrs. SEAN PENN had inspired a small academic industry in Madonna-theory even before Florida State University grad student Chip Wells made headlines in 1990 with his master's project titled "Like a Thesis: A Postmodern Reading of Madonna Videos." While Madonna scholars view themselves as scholarly rebels finding high theory and radical interpretability in pop culture (unraveling clues to feminism, race, and homosexuality in Madonna's signifier-drenched work), their critics view them as pretentious, celebrity-addled dupes. The three main collections of Madonna-crit are Adam Sexton's *Desperately Seeking Madonna*, Cathy Schwichtenberg's *The Madonna Connection*, and Lisa Frank and Paul Smith's *Madonnarama* (all 1993). (Alex Keshishian, who broke into Hollywood as the director of Madonna's 1991 *Truth or Dare* "documentary," initially won her over with a videotape of his 1987 senior thesis at Harvard, a musical staging of *Wuthering Heights* using lip-synched pop songs.)

Magic: The Gathering   Phenomenally successful card-based fantasy game that is a multi-million dollar anachronism in an age of multimedia diversions. Invented by a doctoral student in mathematics at the University of Pennsylvania and first released in summer 1993, Magic requires only a pack of cards and an opponent: each "wizard" is dealt a random selection of cards that are used to cast spells and summon creatures in an effort to drain the opposing wizard's "life force." The catch is that no two packs of cards are alike; rare cards with special powers are randomly distributed in limited-edition sets, encouraging players to keep buying. The strategy works—by 1995 nearly one billion cards had been sold. This new gaming genre has attracted dozens of imitators, including an immensely successful STAR TREK line and the Spellfire series from TSR, the makers of Dungeons & Dragons. Like D&D, Magic (a.k.a. "Magic: The Addiction" and "Magic: The Money Gathering") is now a brand-name fantasy universe that has been spun off into novelizations, comic books, and computer games.

WEB **Magic: The Addiction** http://sunsite.unc.edu/ mgd/mtg.html ✦ USENET **rec.games.trading-cards.magic**

Malcolm X   (b. Malcolm Little, 1925; d. 1965)   Pre-eminent American figure of black nationalism, assassinated at Harlem's Audubon Ballroom on February 21, 1965, by the separatist NATION OF ISLAM for breaking with leader Elijah Muhammed and beginning to preach a kind of MULTICULTURAL humanism. Posthumously celebrated in the perennial best-seller *The Autobiography of Malcolm X,* in which co-author Alex Haley told the journey from street hustler to political leader as a classic American story of self-improvement. Malcolm X was revived in the 1980s as an uncompromising, populist revolutionary for blacks either impatient with the unrealized ambitions of the Civil Rights Movement or too young to appreciate its achievements, only to be claimed by the Nation of Islam's campus sensation LOUIS FARRAKHAN. In the months before SPIKE LEE's 1992 $25 million bio-epic starring Denzel Washington, the "X" decorating baseball caps, T-shirts, and jackets, became a ubiquitous urban street fashion. In May 1995, Malcolm X's widow, Dr. Betty Shabazz, met publicly with Farrakhan—whom she had long accused of playing a role in her husband's death—to denounce the federal government for charging her daughter, Qubilah Shabazz, in a plot to murder Farrakhan.

Mambosok   SNOWBOARDING apparel power that started from a shorts-as-hat novelty item invented by childhood friends Tom Bunnell and Dan Hoard during a 1989 Australian holiday. The "Mambosok" quickly sold out in the SEATTLE bar where Bunnell was working in 1991; the partners next retailed several variations for between $10 and $20, then expanded—reportedly without a business plan—into other clothes. By September 1993, they were hailed as entrepreneurs on the cover of *Inc.* magazine and projecting earnings of $3 million. Asked to define Mambosok's "outlaw" aesthetic, Bunnell told *USA Today,* "It's a rowdy person who's having fun."

alt.culture

Manchester Northern-English industrial town whose danceable guitar bands briefly threatened to invade America before the early-'90s GRUNGE revolution. Emerging in the late 1980s, groups like Inspiral Carpets, Chameleons UK, and the Happy Mondays developed a buoyant sound that strove to forge a link between the city's post-PUNK tradition and the ACID HOUSE scene in which most of the musicians were immersed. (Design-conscious record label Factory spanned both eras, with its best-selling band New Order and its ECSTASY-Mecca club, the Hacienda.) None of the bands managed to entrench themselves against the NIRVANA-led seachange, but the charismatic, relatively hard-rocking Stone Roses looked the likeliest survivors. They took an astonishing six years, between legal problems and prevarication, to deliver *The Second Coming* (1995), a placid light-boogie sophomore album that had moderate success in the U.S. college charts.

WEB **Stone Roses Newspage** http://www.best.com/~thompson/roses/ ✦ USENET **alt.music.stone-roses**

Manchurian mushrooms NEW AGE fad combining the surrogate-child appeal of the pet rock craze with chain-letter superstitions and miraculous health claims; it had millions of Americans in 1994 brewing a homemade, cure-all tea out of a white mushroom-like blob also known as "Kombucha." (Even Ronald Reagan was reportedly a believer.) The specific steps involve obtaining a starter blob by mail-order, from a health food store, or from a friend looking for a home for the offspring of his or her own blob. Then one ferments the mass for a week in sugary black tea until blob "babies" form (which many Kombucha enthusiasts then name). The leftover tea is the prized, sworn-by elixir, by now smelling like vinegar, tasting like hard cider, and containing prodigious quantities of caffeine and sugar. The mushroom—according to some researchers, a collection of easily contaminated yeasts and bacteria that may produce antibiotics—is in fact the basis of a centuries-old folk remedy widely used in China and Russia.

USENET **misc.health.alternative** ✦ WEB **Kombucha Home**

Page http://www.webcom.com/~sease/kombucha/kombucha.html

mandatory minimums Sentencing guidelines for convicted drug offenders imposed by the Reagan administration's Sentencing Reform Act of 1984. Instead of weighing each drug-related crime according to its merits, judges must apply mandatory penalties; these can only be adjusted upwards. (No such federal minimums apply to aggravated assault, child molestation, murder, or rape, however.) According to 1994 Department of Justice figures—popularized by the activist organization Families Against Mandatory Minimums—nearly a quarter of the U.S. prison population (the world's largest, per capita) consists of low-level, non-violent drug offenders. Some judges now refuse to try drug cases, arguing that the guidelines unfairly limit judicial discretion. The preponderance of young DEADHEADS in the federal prisons (where no parole is available) is due to inconsistent carrier weight laws; while 100 doses of pure LSD carries a mandatory sentence of between 10 and 16 months, the same amount on sugar cubes earns the perp between 15.5 and 19.5 years. [See also WAR ON DRUGS.]

WEB **Hyperreal** http://www.hyperreal.com/drugs/politics/misc ✦ WEB **Families Against Mandatory Minimums** http://bianca.com/lolla/politics/famm/famm.html

Mandela, Nelson (b. 1918) President of South Africa and preeminent symbol of peaceful revolution. In 1961, the African National Congress (ANC) head was charged with treason when, after decades of nonviolent protests, the group declared a guerrilla war against the white minority government. Given a life sentence in 1964, Mandela was locked up in Robben Island, the Cape Town equivalent of Alcatraz. During the next 27 years of his imprisonment, Mandela was banned from public discussion, but the blackout only further mythologized the leader. His release in February 1990 signaled the endgame for South Africa's system of racial discrimination known by the Afrikaans word for apartness, "apartheid." Four years later black South Africans voted for the first time in the country's history and Mandela was elected president. Unfortunately his wife did not share in the triumph. Separated from her jailed husband for decades, Winnie Mandela was a powerful figure in the ANC who, through a series of scandals, was estranged from her husband in 1992 and, in 1995, dismissed from her post in the Mandela cabinet.

WEB **US Institute of Peace** http://witloof.sjsu.edu/peace/s-africa.html ✦ WEB **ANC Home Page** http://www.anc.org.za/ ✦ MAIL LIST **South Africa discussion** to subscribe email listserv@csf.colorado.edu with "subscribe" in the message body ✦ USENET **soc.culture.south-africa, soc.culture. african**

manga Phone-book-sized COMIC books ubiquitous in Japan. Six billion dollars in annual sales made comic books Japan's single most powerful media entity in 1994, with circulation numbers for top-selling manga (published monthly or weekly) dwarfing those of the larger newspapers. In Japan, manga (pronounced MAN-gah) is published for a wide range of tastes and interests—from basketball-crazed schoolkids, Mah-jongg playing housewives (who perhaps read *The Lewd Mah-jongg Devil* or *No-Panty Mah-jongg With The Tables Turned*), and weary "salarymen," to freaks and fetishists of all persuasion. But as manga has begun to follow the transpacific crossover of its video cousin ANIME (the sexy, violent Japanimation usually inspired by successful manga titles), action comic titles have dominated. Translated editions of the popular manga titles *Ranma 1/2, Battle Angel Alita, Oh My Goddess!, You're Under Arrest!,* and *Akira* all became available in the early 1990s. In Japan, the most popular manga artists—such as "giant robot" auteur Go Nagai, Rumiko Takahashi (creator of the bikini-clad alien sweetheart Lum), and Astro Boy creator Osamu Tezuka—are the celebrity equivalents of rock stars, with commensurate incomes from royalties, adaptations, and endorsements.

WEB **Manga** http://ccwf.cc.utexas.edu/~susanooh/ manga.html ✦ WEB **Manga Titles** http://www.mit.edu:8001/ afs/athena.mit.edu/user/r/e/rei/WWW/Manga.html ✦ USENET **alt.manga**

Manic Panic Artificial-looking vegetable-based hair dye first imported from Britain to the U.S. in 1977 by Tish and Snooky (the Bellomo sisters), owners of the eponymous downtown New York boutique. Popular during the original PUNK era, Manic Panic had a second lease of life during the '90s punk revival—at $8 a tube it still represents one of the most egalitarian fashion statements going. PERRY FARRELL, Weiland of the STONE TEMPLE PILOTS, Mike D of the BEASTIE BOYS, and Billy Joe of GREEN DAY have been among prominent devotees of the more garish end of Manic Panic's 32-color spectrum.

Manson, Charles (b. 1935) Racial supremacist and convicted mass murderer championed for anti-establishment shock value by everyone from NINE INCH NAILS' Trent Reznor to newslady Diane Sawyer. The towering figure in SERIAL MURDER CHIC, Charles Manson is the subject of the all-time best-selling true-crime book, *Helter Skelter* (1974). A symbol of the curdled '60s, Manson was the 5' 2" ex-con founder and leader of the Family, an L.A. acid and orgy commune, which ended when, the week of Woodstock in August 1969, a group of his white middle-class followers snuck into director Roman Polanski's home and fatally stabbed Sharon Tate, his eight-months-pregnant actress wife, and four of her guests. The counterculture rhetoric of Manson and his youthful followers during the trial confirmed the country's worse fears about hippies, with one defendant shouting "Your children will turn against you" as her guilty verdict was read.

Found guilty of ordering the murders (seven in all), Manson is serving a life sentence in the California prison system, where he is prohibited from profiting from the lucrative Manson cottage industries. These range from neo-Nazi fetishists (Manson read an impending race war into the Beatles's *White Album*, from where he took the words "helter skelter") to the Christian fundamentalist Zooport Riot Gear of Newport Beach, California, which sold 20,000 shirts of Manson's face with slogans like "Charlie Don't Surf" and "The Original Punk" after Axl Rose wore one through the 1993 Guns 'N Roses tour. (The group covered a Manson song, then withdrew it from their 1993 album *The Spaghetti Incident?*) Manson has also been invoked by REDD KROSS, PSYCHIC TV, SONIC YOUTH, Lemonhead EVAN DANDO, Philip Glass protégé John Moran, GEORGE CLINTON, Nine Inch Nails protégé Marilyn Manson, and DR. DRE and ICE CUBE, who titled their planned 1995 reunion album *Helter Skelter*. In 1994 a SEATTLE record company released prison recordings by Manson.

WEB **The Family** http://underground.net/Art/Crime/ manson.html/

Marcus, Greil (b. 1945)   Former editor at *ROLLING STONE* and *Creem* whose 1975 tome *Mystery Train* re-defined the parameters of rock music criticism. The book places rock 'n' roll within the context of American cultural archetypes from Moby Dick to Jay Gatsby to Staggerlee. Marcus's "recognition of the unities in the American imagination that already exist" unleashed, for better or for worse, the fevered fancies of numberless rock scribes. His next book was equally ambitious: *Lipstick Traces: A Secret History of the 20th Century* (1989, developed from an earlier essay) stretched his trademark riffing across a millennium of Western civilization. Positing PUNK rock as a transhistorical cultural phenomenon, Marcus illuminated hidden connections between entities as diverse as the Sex Pistols, the Dadaists, and medieval heretics. *Dead Elvis*, a 1991 collection of writings about Presley, and 1993's *Ranters and Crowd Pleasers*, an examination of post-punk political pop, could not but seem earthbound in comparison. This "bespectacled Zeitgeist surfer" (the *Boston Globe*) continues to hang ten in the pages of *Artforum*.

marijuana chic   Pot renaissance wafted to pop ubiquity in 1993 on the twin updrafts of '90s natu-

ralism and rap endorsement. The distinctive green, multi-pointed marijuana leaf appeared on T-Shirts, baseball caps, TATTOOS, and album covers, updating pot fashion from hippie to HIP HOP. Most potent was DR. DRE's multi-plantinum album *The Chronic* and the Phillies Blunt phenomenon. The former took its title from the Compton, L.A. slang for killer weed; the latter is a cheap dime store cigar used to pack burly blunts, a street-association invoked in the use of the Phillies brand logo for a much copied T-shirt design by New York company Not From Concentrate. The shirts were seen all over MTV, worn by BEASTIE BOY Ad Rock and *High Times* coverstar and NORML (National Organzation for the Reform of Marijuana Laws) celebrity spokesperson B. Real of CYPRESS HILL (which saw its 1993 *Black Sunday* jump to the top of the charts on the strength of such ganja GANGSTA tunes as "Hits from the Bong").

Marketers seized the opportunity: a Disney-owned label sent out bongs to promote the latest album of its metal band Sacred Reich; and RICHARD LINKLATER's 1993 *Dazed and Confused* was pushed as a pot movie under the winking slogan "See it with a bud" (this after ratings authorities killed "Finally! A movie for everyone who did inhale"). Building on the best laugh line of the 1992 Presidential campaign (Bill Clinton's claim "I didn't inhale"), Roseanne spent half an episode of her sit-com stoned after stumbling across (and partaking from) her 20 year-old stash. Even *THE NEW YORKER* weighed in with a 1994 short profile of a scientist

"True Money" cannabis currency viewed in Hyperreal's alt.drugs archive (http://hyperreal.com/drugs/pictures).

who argued that the pot revival was reducing ghetto crime by sedating drug dealers. Cannabis also took on eco-political dimensions: Jack Herer's best-selling *The Emperor Wears No Clothes* (1985) argued that the 1937 outlawing of hemp was a petro-conspiracy to rob America of a superior, ecologically sound source of fuel oil. On Capitol Hill, the Drug Policy Foundation got a $6 million grant in 1994 from financier George Soros to advocate for "harm reduction" (diverting WAR ON DRUG resources to health care for addicts). In 1995, an annual University Michigan study of drug use among teens reported that, after 13 years of decline, pot use had increased for the third straight year.

WEB **Hemp and Related Links** http://www.linnet.ca/~catseye/hemp/links.html/ ✦ WEB **NORML (National Organization for the Reform of Marjiuana Laws)** http://www.norml.org/~norml/ ✦ WEB **Hyperreal** http://hyperreal.com:/drugs/marijuana ✦ USENET **alt.drugs.marijuana**, **alt.hemp**, **alt.hemp.politics**

Marky Mark (b. Mark Wahlberg, 1971) Having been, with brother Donny, an original member of New Kids on the Block, Marky Mark Wahlberg left before the band bloomed as a late-'80s teen-pop phenomenon. He claimed his own place in the pop pantheon in 1991 with a platinum album of unremarkable raps. Cultural icon status was bestowed upon Wahlberg by CALVIN KLEIN, who hired him as an underwear mannequin in 1992: massive billboard exposure of the star's chiseled physique (first alone, later with KATE MOSS) made Wahlberg an icon of gay culture, albeit an uneasy one. Always prone to inexplicable behavior (he dedicated a Marky Mark photo-book to his penis), Wahlberg's support of homophobic remarks by SHABBA RANKS drew gay protests against Calvin Klein in 1993; revelations about a 1988 conviction for assaulting two Vietnamese men in Dorchester, Boston (Wahlberg served half his 90-day sentence), only hastened the star's declining popularity. (Reports also surfaced about a previous attack on black elementary schoolers.) Wahlberg publicly apologized and moved on swiftly, replacing his B-BOY locutions with a normal speaking voice, and

launching himself as an actor. His debut in the unsuccessful comedy *Renaissance Man* (1994) went unnoticed, but a solid performance opposite LEONARDO DiCAPRIO in *The Basketball Diaries* (1995) brought some critical approbation and a chance at a second career.

McJob Term first coined by McDonald's in 1983 to promote an affirmative action program for handicapped employees. By the late '80s it was widely used to describe the general shift in American work from manufacturing to low-skill, low-wage service jobs, particularly those in the fast-food industry. "McJob" was famously deployed by generational commentator DOUGLAS COUPLAND in his 1991 novel *Generation X*; it was briefly, and widely, used as a buzzword by advertising copywriters and screenwriters jumping on the 1992–93 GENERATION X marketing bandwagon. The on-going elimination of skilled blue-collar work has caused the lifetime earnings gap between college and high school graduates to widen, but related cost-cutting at the managerial level also reduced the demand for college graduates in the early '90s. In 1994, the U.S. Bureau of Labor Statistics estimated that one out of five college graduates was in a job that doesn't require a college degree, twice the rate of the late '60s.

McKenna, Terence (b. 1946) Ethno-botanist, philosopher, historian, and Nabokavian know-it-all, Terence McKenna is an articulate advocate for psychedelics as a crucial part of humanity's collective birthright. In a nutshell, he believes that having relinquished our Paleolithic utopia, mankind is in a headlong rush to a millenarian apotheosis slated to occur December 21, 2012 (as determined by his TimeWave software). The best way to prepare for that date, he explains, is through the ingestion of "heroic doses" of psychedelic drugs from the tryptamine family, specifically smoked DMT and PSILOCYBIN MUSHROOMS. One of the world's great rhetorical ravers, McKenna was affiliated briefly with the early-'90s RAVE scene. The world's preeminent ethnobotanist,

Harvard emeritus Richard Evans Schulte, hailed *Food of the Gods* (1992) as a "masterpiece of research and writing," but McKenna is probably best known for *The Archaic Revival* (1991). Other works include the autobiographical science fiction *True Hallucinations* (1993) and *The Invisible Landscape* (1975), co-written with his ethnopharmocologist brother, Dennis.

WEB **Terence McKenna Land** http://www.intac.com/~dimitri/dh/mckenna.html ✦ USENET **alt.drugs, alt.drugs.psychedelics** ✦ WEB **Terence McKenna Homepage** http://www.organic.com/Music/City.o.tribes/Alien.dreamtime/mckenna.html ✦ WEB **Alien Dream Time** http://www.organic.com/Music/City.o.tribes/Alien.dreamtime/index.html

media moguls   With the imminent advent of the "information superhighway" it is expected that television programming, music, HOME SHOPPING, magazines, VIDEOGAMES, books, online services, and movies will spark an orgy of corporate cross-breeding, producing untold profits for those who can harness their "synergy." With this backdrop, the media has imputed high drama to the efforts of highly driven, middle-aged businessmen like David Geffen, Rupert Murdoch, Bill Gates, Barry Diller, Sumner Redstone, Ted Turner, and Jeffrey Katzenberg to establish powerful combinations of media properties. (Diller's long, unsuccessful struggle to buy the film studio Paramount in 1993–94 was covered as though it was a small war.) In March 1995 *Time* magazine used a *Meet the Beatles*-like cover to exalt Geffen, Katzenberg, and Steven Spielberg, the BABY BOOMER power trio behind the newly announced, highly non-specific media conglomerate DreamWorks SKG. *Newsweek* went one better on June 12th with an exhaustive cover story on C.A.A. superagent Mike Ovitz, who was expected to take over MCA, the recent acquisition of beverage corporation Seagram—the following week's magazine carried a short story on the collapse of the deal. (In August 1995 Ovitz made more legitimate headlines when he joined the Walt Disney Company as second-in-command.) [See also SILLIWOOD.]

Megadeth   Kicked out of Metallica for drug and alcohol abuse, Dave Mustaine (b. 1961) looked set to become a footnote in the history of hard rock. But Mustaine rebounded quickly, forming Megadeth and releasing the 1985 LP *Killing is My Business . . . And Business Is Good* (which included an unforgettable cover of Nancy Sinatra's "These Boots Are Made For Walkin'"). Drummer Gar Samuelson and guitarist Chris Poland didn't last, and neither did their replacements. But Megadeth's trademarks—a punishing thrash attack, Mustaine's sadistic vocals, and a skull mascot named Vic Rattlehead—have endured, powering the mainstream-leaning *Countdown to Extinction* (1992) to double-platinum status. That same year Mustaine partnered MTV's TABITHA SOREN to report on the Democratic Convention in New York City. The shorter compositions of *Youthanasia* (1995) showed a more mature Mustaine, five years sober, three years a father.

WEB **EMI Records** http://www.riv.nl/emi/heavy/mega.htm ✦ WEB **Megadeth Arizona** http://underground.net/Megadeth/megadeth.html ✦ USENET **alt.rock-n-roll.metal.megadeth**

Meisel, Steven (b. 1954)   Perpetually *chapeau*'d photographer known for striking, highly art-directed portraits of celebrities and androgynes of both sexes. Meisel routinely "samples" photographers like Brassai and Bert Stern (who reportedly threatened to sue over one Madonna-as-Marilyn Monroe "homage") and styles ('60s *Playboy* for MADONNA's October 1992 spread in *Vanity Fair*). Meisel is a drop-out from New York's Parsons School of Design, where he met occasional collaborator ANNA SUI and quintessential '80s designer Stephen Sprouse, whose career he helped launch. Meisel himself graduated through fashion magazines and ads for CALVIN KLEIN, PRADA, and the GAP to develop the kind of star-making *puissance* that anointed the late '80s SUPERMODEL trinity of Naomi Campbell, Linda Evangelista, and Christy Turlington. The photographer's highest-profile year was without doubt 1992: he lensed Madonna's photo-book *Sex* and signed a $2 million exclusive contract with magazine power Condé Nast. *New York* magazine writer Michael

Gross noted of Meisel's skill and commercial acuity: "If AVEDON and ANDY WARHOL had a baby he would be Steven Meisel."

meme   Unit of cultural meaning. Coined by Richard Dawkins—the idiosyncratic Oxford zoologist who also developed the theory of the "selfish gene"—and fleshed out by post-modern critics such as Jean Baudrillard and Arthur Kroker, memetics (the science of memes) holds that cultural ideas, whether trivial (pop songs, disaster jokes, fashion fads) or monumental (religions, languages, philosophies), replicate so rapidly and so ruthlessly that they can be compared with viruses. The idea was central to Douglas Rushkoff's *Media Virus!* (1994); Rushkoff theorized that modern media are living entities, hosts that comprise a "datasphere" that is continually compromised by the introduction of new memes, whether backwards baseball caps, political T-shirt slogans, or bumper sticker nostrums.

Menendez brothers (Joseph Lyle, b. 1968; Erik Galen, b. 1970)   Sons of wealthy Cuban-American video-business executive in L.A. who shot their parents in 1989 while the victims sat eating bowls of ice cream. The pair indulged their childhood fantasies for months while the murders were initially blamed on the mafia: Lyle bought a childhood haunt, Chuck's Spring Street Café in Princeton, NJ; Erik purchased a wardrobe of silk shirts and attempted to play on the pro tennis circuit. The brothers confessed in July 1993 (a week before trial) when their culpability was eventually discovered, but maintained that their parents had sexually abused them. As the macabre Menendez trial unfolded in tabloids and on Court TV, some jurors were slowly persuaded that the boys murdered their parents in self-defense; mistrials were declared. Having largely depleted the impressive Menendez inheritance, the two defense attorneys—Leslie Abramson and Jill Lansing—hesitated about representing the boys in their fall '95 retrials.

Mentos   Minty sugar candy from the Netherlands-based Van Melle company which doubled its U.S.

sales between 1991 and 1994 with an extensive ad campaign—originally created to reach European consumers—so inept that it became an underground preoccupation. The absurd "freshmaker" commercials—which center around young adult protagonists who overcome everyday social frustrations with quick thinking, a Mentos, and a Mentos-bearing gesture redolent of a middle-finger thrust—have provoked awed disbelief first expressed in the media by comedienne JANEANE GAROFALO. Other manifestations of Mentos' commanding "mind share" (in ad speak) include a WORLD WIDE WEB site replete with new abbreviations ("FAFOL: Fresh and full of life"), the upbeat "doo-doo, do-wah!" ABBA-esque jingles, and studious synopses of "The Broken Heel" and other ad scenarios. The Mentos campaign placed second in a *USA Today* ad industry poll of 1994's worst TV spots.
WEB **Mentos FAQ** http://www.cs.hmc.edu/people/zbaker/ mentos-faq.html ✦ USENET **alt.television.commercials**

metal detectors, in high school
Increasingly popular strategy for improving school security by screening student backpacks and bodies for firearms, knives, and other tools of aggression. A 1994 survey reports that 15 percent of high schools use a form of metal detectors—some place walk-through airport-style units at their entrances, while others have security officers roam the halls with hand-held units. In *People v. Dukes*, a New York City criminal court ruled that like airport and courthouse security measures, metal detector scans in schools are "administrative searches" which do not require "probable cause," so long as no individual student is singled out. Metal detectors in schools now have broad-based support. For example, federal funding for them was included in President Clinton's Goals 2000 education agenda. But as students find ways around the detectors (hiding razor blades under their tongues, for example), schools have begun looking at even more elaborate security devices such as VIDEO SURVEILLANCE cameras.

Metallica   Speed-metal leviathan of the '80s that metamorphosed into stadium-rock king of the '90s.

alt.culture

On albums such as *Kill 'Em All* (1983), *Ride the Lightning* (1984), and *Master of Puppets* (1986) the band (led by mustachioed vocalist/guitarist James Hetfield [b. 1963]) bore down on songs with locomotive force, earning itself the undying adulation of disenfranchised suburban burnouts everywhere. (MTV's BEAVIS, for example, permanently sports a Metallica T-shirt). Even a 1986 tour-bus accident that killed original member Cliff Burton (b. 1962) didn't derail Metallica; with a new bassist on board the band released the complex . . . *And Justice For All* (1988), which earned kudos but little airplay. In 1991, Metallica released an immensely expensive (approximately $1 million) eponymous LP that opted for shorter songs and more traditional hard-rock arrangements; extravagant videos propelled sales, despite the band's earlier opposition to the form. The LP sold eight million copies, spawning a stadium tour co-headlined by Guns N' Roses and eventually a box set of concert material entitled, with characteristic delicacy, *Live Shit: Binge and Purge* (1993).

WEB **Elektra Records** http://www.pathfinder.com/
@ @qyNokQAAAAAAQA**/elektra/artists/metallica/
metallica.html ◆ USENET **alt.rock-n-roll.metal.metallica**

metaverse.com WORLD WIDE WEB site of former MTV VJ Adam Curry. When the veteran big-hair presenter quit the network in 1994 he sparked a high-profile legal dispute over the name of the site—then mtv.com—that made it one of the first Web addresses to gain exposure in the mainstream media. After this credibility-enhancing bout with MTV, Curry rechristened his site metaverse.com, a name this time borrowed from NEAL STEPHENSON's novel *Snow Crash*. The site features include CyberSleaze, a daily gossip column, and corporate sponsorships like WOODSTOCK '94. Outflanked in 1995 by the egalitarian-minded INTERNET UNDERGROUND MUSIC ARCHIVE, the arrival of Web sites run by record and movie companies, and the advent of organized music criticism on the INTERNET, the site's highlight became Curry's Dutch-language RAVE and TECHNO radio shows (broadcast with REALAUDIO).

WEB **metaverse.com** http://www.metaverse.com

methcathinone Latest in a long line of scare-inducing designer drugs, methcathinone—or cat—is a crude, highly addictive relative of methamphetamine (speed) and the organic Somali stimulant Khat (itself the subject of a late 1992 drug scare when U.S. forces landed in Somali). A powder that can be smoked or inhaled, cat produces a sense of well-being and an energy that can reportedly last for days—as well as a come-down of similar length. The drug emerged in the Michigan area in 1989 when a pharmaceutical worker shared with friends old condemned stock from his employer, Parke-Davis. (Cat was originally intended for sale as an anti-depressant in the '50s, but never marketed due to side effects.) The actions of this chemical Johnny Appleseed are thought to be solely responsible for cat's popularity in the economically beleaguered Midwest. (Russia is one of its other strongholds.) The recipe for cat, based on (widely available) ephedrine, has been widely disseminated on the INTERNET. As of November 1994, anyone selling ephedrine is required by law to furnish the DEA with purchasers' names and addresses, with further restrictions expected.

MIDI Musical Instrument Digital Interface—a simple technical standard set in the late '70s for orchestrating computer control of keyboards, drum machines, and even stage lighting. MIDI-enabled sequencers led to an at-home revolution in music composition that has transformed face of pop song-writing and film scoring. Much of the new R&B, INDUSTRIAL music, TECHNO, and most HIP-HOP require MIDI to string together drum loops, bass lines, and whatever else is played by computers locked to time code on tape. The sequencer also made it possible to fudge playing skills by using cut-and-paste to build whole parts from mere approximations. MIDI points to the future of all-digital recording, when synthesized performances will pose the same questions as digitally edited photos or film (see NONLINEAR FILM EDITING): What is real, and how is it valued? Recent debates over SAMPLING and authorship began to include MIDI programs, as artists and publishers started arguing over whether they should be treated as performances or sheet music for purposes of copyright and royalties.

WEB **MIDILink Musician's Network**
http://www.interaccess.com/users/midilink/ ✦ WEB **Midi Links** http://www.eeb.ele.tue.nl/midi/index.html

Mighty Morphin Power Rangers Principal kiddie pop fad of the '90s, thanks to Fox-TV's instantly successful after-school show (first aired August 1993). Produced by legendary shlockmeister Haim Saban, the show consists of a squeaky clean, MULTICULTURAL group of suburban Californian teens who, in every episode, save the earth from dino-monsters dispatched by the evil witch Rita Repulsa. The Rangers are conveniently masked for battles, a fact the show uses to segue into footage recycled from several Japanese live-action *sentai* (superhero) shows. In one bizarre example of corner-cutting, the Yellow Ranger—played by a male in Japan—is represented in some American sequences as a girl named "Trini." Although none of the original Japanese sources are actually named in the show's credits, the blow-out success of *MMPR* action figures and other merchandising (some $350 million in '93 alone) cleared the path for 1995's ANIME imports *DRAGONBALL* and *SAILOR MOON*. The mediocre performance of the summer '95 *Power Rangers* movie suggested that the phenomenon might be running its course.

WEB **Sentai Page!** http://www.primenet.com/~gridman/sentai.html

militias Self-styled defensive paramilitary groups that coalesced in the early 1990s around far-right hatred of "big government." Though diverse, militias tend to agree that the U.S. is on the verge of a military takeover by United Nations forces bent on creating a global government—called the New World Order—controlled by nefarious banking and industrial interests; that all such plots to curtail citizen rights are marked by attempts to limit gun sales and ownership (see NRA); and that the bombing of an Oklahoma City federal office building (167 dead) was a Clinton administration stunt to discredit the militias. Rallying causes include the 1992 shoot-out at supremacist Randy Weaver's Idaho farm and the

1993 siege of DAVID KORESH's Branch Davidian compound in Waco, Texas, that left some 80 cult members dead (the Oklahoma bombing took place on Waco's two-year anniversary, April 19th, 1995). Militias and related "patriot" groups rally their members to arms through a homegrown network of computer bulletin boards, fax linkups, public-access cable shows, and short-wave radio broadcasts. [See also WISE USE.]

WEB site run by Don Black, former Imperial Wizard of the Knights of the Ku Klux Klan (http://stormfront.wat.com/stormfront/).

WEB **Left Side of the Web Militia Watch** http://paul.spu.edu/~sinnfein/progressive.html/ ✦ WEB **Amerikan Politics** http://www.intellinet.com/~publis/politiks.htm/ ✦ USENET **misc.activism.militias** ✦ WEB **Patriot Aims/The Militias** http://www.infi.net/nr/extra/militias/m-index.htm/ ✦ USENET **misc.survivalism**

Miller, Frank (b. 1957) Writer/cartoonist best known for the ultraviolent revisionism of *Batman: The Dark Knight Returns* (1986) which inspired the moody hues of TIM BURTON's two Batman films. Miller came to mainstream comics in 1979, fashioning film NOIR-inspired scenarios for Marvel's *Daredevil* series, where he focused the storylines on the blind superhero's intensely ambivalent relationship with the sensual Elektra (collected as *The Elektra Saga*; and later revived in 1985's *Elektra: Assassin* and 1990's *Elektra Lives Again*). In 1987 Miller transported a thirteenth-century ninja to the distant future for his most innovative work to date, *Ronin*. In the MULTICULTURAL '90s—as though to atone for his vigilante Batman—Miller and artist Dave Gibbons created a heroic black vigilante named Martha Washington (1992's *Give Me Liberty* and 1994's *Washington Goes to War*). Miller's crossover into film has produced critically derided scripts for the second and third *RoboCop* flicks. In 1992 Miller began the blunt, violent, NOIR-ish *Sin City* series.

mini-backpacks "It's like a backpack and a purse married and had a little baby," one trend analyst explained to the *Los Angeles Times* in the summer of 1994, when mini-backpacks had become a ubiquitous chic carryall of choice. Diminutive versions of the backpacks that have in recent years gone from country-hiker staple to urban accessory, mini-backpacks—some scarcely big enough to hold a wallet—were essentially useless mutations of an old utilitarian standby. Chanel made a $1,400 version of the tiny status symbol in gold or bronze metallic leather. CLUB KIDS bought theirs on the street, and wore them over baby T-shirts, another "small is beautiful" fashion trend.

MiniDisc Sony's smaller, recordable version of the CD, popular in Japan. On the MiniDisc's 1992 launch, Sony promised that it would eclipse the audio cassette as CDs had the LP, but the format's early years have been difficult. The type of audiophiles most likely to pay hundreds of dollars for MiniDisc players are unlikely to compare the sound quality favorably with competing digital DAT and DCC formats. (Sony's compression scheme sacrifices supposedly inaudible frequencies in order to fit 72 minutes of sound onto the disc.) Unbowed, Sony has undertaken aggressive promotions like stocking record stores with pre-recorded MDs (issued by its subsidiary Columbia Records—see also AUDIO HOME RECORDING ACT), polybagging a MiniDisc in subscriber copies of a June 1994 *ROLLING STONE*, and arranging for a monthly MD column in the same. The last act prompted DCC purveyor Philips to wonder in *Billboard* "if *Rolling Stone*'s editorial is for sale." In early 1995 plans were announced to adapt the MiniDisc as a storage add-on for personal computers.
WEB **Sony** http://www.sony.com/

Ministry Brainchild of Chicago record-store clerk Alain Jourgenson (b. 1958) that operates on the hard rock end of INDUSTRIAL. Having started out pushing effete synth-pop (1983's major-label album *With Sympathy*), Jourgensen took the pithier moniker "Al" when he took to denser, more threatening dance music. Ministry shifted toward a heavier guitar-driven sound on such releases as 1989's *A Mind is a Terrible Thing to Taste,* and the *Rabies* (1989) collaboration with fellow industrialists Skinny Puppy. Ministry's spot on the second LOLLAPALOOZA tour was preceded by an LP, *Psalm 69* LP (1992), which consolidated the band's aesthetic of distortion, aggression, and appropriation. When he's not administering Ministry, Jourgenson (based in AUSTIN, Texas since 1993) lets his "aggro" fantasies feed other projects, like Pigface and the intentionally sleazy Revolting Cocks.
WEB **Unofficial Ministry Home Page**
http://pulsarcs.wku.edu/~gizzard/ministry/
✦ USENET **rec.music.industrial**

Miramax New York-based film company largely responsible for the current lucrative state of American independent cinema. Formed in 1981 by burly Queens, New York-bred brothers Bob and Harvey Weinstein, Miramax prospered by distributing and marketing a long string of high-brow hits like *The Thin Blue Line* (1988), *Cinema Paradiso* (1989), *Like Water for Chocolate* (1992), *sex, lies, and videotape* (1989), *My Left Foot* (1989), *The Crying Game* (1992), *Reservoir Dogs* (1992), *The Piano* (1993), and *Clerks* (1994). Miramax's production record was unimpressive until they bankrolled QUENTIN TARANTINO's *Pulp Fiction* (1994), which helped earned them more 1995 Oscar nominations—25—than any of the major studios. (The catastrophic fashion-world satire *Ready To Wear* [1994] took the edge off their celebrations.)

Miramax's ability to capture the "cappuccino movie" dollar inspired upstart companies like Fine Line (part of New Line), Sony Classics, Gramercy Pictures (Universal/Polygram), none of which seem likely to replicate Miramax's runaway success—the Weinbergs are uniquely canny marketers whose management style is as unique as their hit-picking record. (In *Fortune* magazine one former Miramax employee described the Weinstein method as "Japanese management theory on acid"; Harvey's editing methods earned him the appellation

"Harvey Scissorhands.") In April 1993 the Weinsteins sold a majority share of their company to Disney for an estimated $60 million. One condition of the alliance was that Miramax would not distribute unrated films; the company's MARTIN LAWRENCE concert movie *You So Crazy* had to be sold off to Samuel Goldwyn (who released it unrated—see also NC–17). When LARRY CLARK's teen-sex drama *Kids* presented similar problems in 1995, the Weinsteins created a separate company, Excalibur, to distribute the movie.

Mitnick, Kevin (b. 1963) PHONE PHREAK and computer outlaw legend who managed to tap the phones of the FBI agents assigned to catch him during a two-year manhunt. Mitnick was finally caught in February 1995 after a successful INTERNET attack on one of the foremost computer security experts, Tsutomu Shimomura, provoked the Japanese sometimes-ski-bum into a full-time search for Mitnick. The story of the eight-week cyber-hunt was thrillingly told in the *New York Times* by reporter John Markoff, who had closely followed the Mitnick story since profiling the HACKER for the 1992 CYBERPUNK book he co-authored. (The reports omitted to mention, however, that Markoff and Shimomura were working together on a lucrative book and movie deal about Mitnick.) The teen exploits of Mitnick, who grew up a shy, overweight loner in the L.A. suburb of Sepulveda, included break-ins at MCI, the Manhattan phone system, and—foreshadowing 1983 hacker film *War Games*—a NORAD defense computer. Mitnick is renowned for his mastery of "social engineering"—gaining proprietary information not via computer but through interpersonal ruses such as posing as a phone company repairman.
WEB **L'affaire Kevin Mitnick** http://www.sct.fr/cyber/ mitnick.html/ ✦ WEB **Mitnick Archives** http://sfgate.com/ net/mitnick.archive.html ✦ WEB **Mitnick Voicemail Taunts** http://gnn.interpath.net/gnn/meta/imedia/resources/mitnick.ht ml ✦ USENET **alt.2600, alt.fan.kevin-mitnick**

Moby (b. Richard Melville Hall, 1965) Former DJ who became that rarest of anomalies: a name-brand TECHNO star. Raised in whitebread Darien, Connecticut, Moby (a distant descendent of *Moby-Dick* author Herman Melville) is an accomplished musician who went through a PUNK phase before working as a New York disk jockey in the mid-'80s. When Moby became a performer, a handful of inventive tracks established him as a dancefloor maverick with conceptual leanings, particularly 1992's "Go," which sampled the *TWIN PEAKS* theme, and "Thousand," a 1,000-plus beat-per-minute exercise in absurdity that made the *Guinness Book of World Records.* Moby is distinguished in the electronic dance-music world by his non-drug stance, his "nondenominational" Christianity, and a style of cathartic live performance that has been compared to Iggy Pop. Moby's 1995 major-label debut *Everything Is Wrong* was an eclectic coming-of-age record that jumped from techno to DANCEHALL reggae to AMBIENT, with even a nod to his punk roots.

TECHNO tyro Moby, August 1992.

WEB **Dan's Moby Page** http://ouray.cudenver.edu/~ decerman/moby.html ✦ WEB **Elektra Records** http://www.elektra.com ✦ USENET **alt.music.moby** ✦ WEB **Moby Discography** http://hyperreal.com:2000/ 0/music/artists/moby/discog

Mod revival Disinterring Britain's sharp-dressing mid-'60s youth culture has been a perennial occupation since it was warmed over both there and in the U.S. in 1979. Mod's next revival was in the early/mid-'80s among U.S. suburban teens who took parkas, multi-mirrored scooters, and albums by '70s Mod enthusiasts The Jam as articles of faith. Mod's summer 1995 revival in America was a more mainstream affair, started in the heights of design studio rather than the streets; '60s-influenced English bands such as Blur, Oasis, Menswear, and Supergrass set the mood at the *ateliers* of designers like ANNA SUI, CALVIN KLEIN, Gucci, and PRADA. The results were women's suits with short, boxy jackets and slim, knee-length skirts; dress-length leather coats; overcoats with velvet collars; and, for men, slim-cut trousers and deeply-vented jackets. The June and July 1995 issues of *Vogue* and *Harper's Bazaar* chronicled the fledgling fashion movement with a combined total of nineteen feature pages—thorough coverage, considering the U.K. Mod outbreak sprung from just a handful of London clubs in 1993–94.

Modern Primitive Label applied to the recent revival of such so-called primitive body modification practices as TATTOOING, PIERCING, BRANDING, and SCARIFICATION. The name was coined in 1978 by FAKIR MUSAFAR, commonly regarded as Modern Primitivism's leader-cum-shaman. MP tenets advocate a "return" to the "pre-Christian" idea of exploring spirituality through the body (which is regarded as the only unmediated avenue for experience in a media-saturated culture). The MP movement grew slowly and steadily throughout the '80s and reached critical mass in 1989 when RE/SEARCH published *Modern Primitives*, a book that combined photos of decorative and spiritual body modifications from modern and primitive cultures.

WEB **Modern Primitives** http://www.clas.ufl.edu/ anthro/Modern_Primitives.html ✦ WEB **Body Modification E-Zine** http://www.io.org/~bme/ ✦ WEB **Piercing FAQ** http://www.cis.ohio-state.edu/hypertext/faq/usenet/ bodyart/piercing-faq/top.html

THE MODERN REVIEW celebrates KEANU REEVES.

Modern Review "Lowbrow culture for highbrows" was the motto of this British bi-monthly, launched in 1992 by writer Toby Young and star newspaper columnist Julie Burchill. (U.S. distribution came in 1994.) In the minds of the *Modern Review* tyros, *Entertainment Weekly* had joined Baudrillard and Lacan as required reading for would-be cultural critics; illuminating essays on mass-culture appeared alongside baffling diatribes on mid-budget movie flops. (Who knew that *Young Guns 2* or Rob Reiner's *North* had so many layers of meaning?) The magazine folded in May 1995 after a highly public rift between Burchill and Young.

Mondo 2000 Lavishly designed CYBERPUNK glossy that has been glamorizing computer lifestyles since 1988, when it evolved from the *Reality Hackers* and *High Frontiers* ZINES. Founded by R. U. Sirius (Ken Goffman, b. 1952) and "domineditrix" Queen Mu (b. Alison Kennedy, circa 1950), the sporadically-published magazine often seemed bloated in the early '90s with "cyberwear" fashion spreads, cheery interviews with gimmicky bands, and ads flaunting premillenial snake oil in the form of SMART DRUGS. Yet beneath *Mondo's* highly ornamented, MACINTOSH-designed exterior lurked avant-garde appreciation of techno-theories and tools that have since become commonplace. (Many were collected in 1992's *Mondo 2000: A Users Guide to the New Edge*). Exerting a strong influence on subsequent like-minded titles such as *FRINGEWARE Review* and *bOING-bOING*, *Mondo* ironically prepared the ground for the competitor that all but eclipsed it in 1993: the better-financed, slicker, and more upscale cyber-mag *WIRED*.

gopher **WELL Cyberpunk & Postmodern Culture** gopher://gopher.well.sf.ca.us:70/1/Publications/MONDO

Moore, Alan (b. 1952) In the late '80s, British comic book writer Alan Moore was the hottest fanboy epiphany since FRANK MILLER. Moore set out to subvert the costume-hero mythology of his childhood in the Swamp Thing series, *Miracleman* (1985), *V for Vendetta* (1988–1989), and most effectively in his 1987 magnum opus, *Watchmen*. Moore has largely shied away from superheroics since, collaborating with Bill Sienkiewicz on the uncompleted *Big Numbers* series, and his sixteen-part, Eddie Campbell-illustrated take on Jack the Ripper, *From Hell* (1991). Outside of the comics frame, Moore has published his unproduced script for *From Hell*.

WEB **Watching the Detectives Start** http://raven.ubalt.edu/

Moulthrop/hypertexts/wm/wmstart.html ✦ WEB **Twilight Series Proposal** http://www.digimark.net/wraith/Comics/ twilight.html ✦ USENET **alt.comics**

Moore, Michael (b. 1954) Documentary filmmaker, provocateur, and the most dangerous man in a baseball cap since Roger Maris. After more than a decade of print journalism and NPR commentaries, Moore gained wide attention in 1989 with *Roger and Me*, a semi-autobiographical, unabashedly partisan piece of agit-prop which took General Motors to task for the abandonment of its Flint, Michigan, birthplace.

In the summer of 1994, Moore brought his guerrilla ethic to NBC with *TV Nation*, a crankier, hopped-up *60 Minutes* out to score laughs at the expense of the rich and the Republican. Moore's search for the Russian missile pointed at his hometown was a typical feature, as was his bite-the-hand-that-feeds decision to issue a "CEO Challenge," via bullhorn, to the president of NBC's owner General Electric (the GE head was asked to replace a burned-out light bulb for a segment in which the president of Ford changed the oil in his car). The show moved to Fox the next year, were it stood a better chance of finding a place in the regular line-up, bringing along a cast that included JANEANE GAROFALO and the Zen comedian Steven Wright. Moore's first feature, *Canadian Bacon* (1995), was the last for the late John Candy, who died during filming; for want of a Cold War enemy in the Kubrick-like satire, the U.S. arms industry picks a war with its northern neighbor.

WEB **TV Nation** http://www.teleport.com/~xwinds/ TVNation.html ✦ USENET **alt.tv.tv-nation** ✦ EMAIL TVNatn@aol.com

Moosewood Cookbook, The The bible of vegetarian cooking. Originally distributed in 1977 as a stack of mimeographs, *The Moosewood Cookbook* collected recipes from the kitchen of the Moosewood Restaurant in Ithaca, New York. Hand-lettered and illustrated by author Mollie Katzen (b. 1950), the book captured the CRUNCHY back-to-basics spirit of the vegetarian movement, inspiring

millions to live on hummus and tofu. The restaurant, in turn, became a model for co-operatively owned and run college-town veggie enclaves. *Moosewood* and its follow-ups, including *The Enchanted Broccoli Forest* (1982) and *Still Life With Menu* (1988), have sold a combined three million copies, and have recently been reissued in revised editions that trim the fat and provide more non-dairy options. Katzen's most recent project is *The Mollie Katzen Cooking Show* for PBS. [See also VEGANISM.]

WEB **Vegetarian Pages** http://catless.ncl.ac.uk/Vegetarian/ ✦ WEB **World Guide To Vegetarianism** http://catless.ncl.ac.uk/ Vegetarian/Guide/index.html/

morphing Computer-produced visual effects in which one physical object appears to metamorphosize—or morph—into another. Morphing made its Hollywood debut in the movie *Willow* (1988), when a reclining tiger smoothly transformed into a sleeping woman. The technique, also used in *Indiana Jones and the Last Crusade* (1989) and *The Abyss* (1989), became a household word with *Terminator 2* (1991), which featured a killer robot built from "liquid metal." Michael Jackson's 1991 video *"Black or White"* pushed facial (in this case, inter-racial) morphing that was later used in commercials. Hollywood's biggest morpher, INDUSTRIAL LIGHT AND MAGIC, reportedly bought $3.5 million worth of computers to produce the special effects for *Terminator 2*. Within two years morphing software became available for personal computers, leading to new amateur graphic clichés such as morphing political opponents and rival SUPERMODELS.

Morris, Mark (b.1956) SEATTLE-born dancer/ choreographer whose early fascination with flamenco and brutish disregard for ballet tradition led him to found the Mark Morris Dance Group in 1981 at the age of 24. After stepping to the likes of renowned choreographers Eliot Feld, Twyla Tharp, and Lar Lubovitch, Morris was tapped to helm the prestigious Brussels Monnaie Opera House (1988–91). In the final tumultuous year of his appointment, Morris's unconventional update of Tchaikovsky/Balanchine's standard *The Nutcracker*

Suite—re-titled *The Hard Nut*—toured internationally. Among a whirlwind of novelties in his work, Morris mixed the gender of those on their toes throughout and substituted BARBIE DOLLS and G.I. Joe's for the Christmas gifts in the original ballet. Eclectic musical and literary influences characterize Morris's repertoire, which includes a Baroque piece "One Charming Night," inspired by ANNE RICE's *Interview With the Vampire*, and a pornographic ballet, *Lovey,* set to the music of the Violent Femmes. His masterpiece is said to be 1988's *L'Allegro, Il Penseroso ed Il Moderato*, canonized at New York's Lincoln Center in 1995. The same year, when London's *Guardian* newspaper asked him to elaborate on his particular philosophy of dance, Morris answered simply: "I make it up and you watch it."

Morrison, Grant (b. 1960) After a promising stint on Vertigo's *Animal Man* from 1988 to 1990, this esoteric U.K. COMIC-book writer tilted at the conventions of superhero storytelling during his four-year stint (1990–94) at the helm of *Doom Patrol*. Quitting while ahead, he took a break to experience the world, returning for short stints at *Hellblazer, Kid Eternity, Judge Dredd, Swamp Thing,* and other U.S. and British series. In 1994 the Scottish writer's most ambitious series to date, *The Invisibles*, began charting a cosmic battle between the titular forces of psychic liberation and their dark counterparts: sleazy insectoid agents of control and repression. In the 1995 graphic novel *Kill Your Boyfriend*, Morrison told an over-the-top takeoff of OLIVER STONE's *Natural Born Killers* called "Naked Killers." ("We're going to take all your money and spend it on crap!" the rampaging couple promise their victims.) Morrison's next project was *Bizarre Boy* (1995), a bleakly humorous collaboration with writer Peter Milligan.

WEB **Wraithspace-Comixographies-Grant Morrison** http://www.digimark.net/wraith/Bibliographies/HTML/Morrison-Grant.html ✦ WEB **The Invisibles Semi-Exposed (Annotated Comics)** http://www.rt66.com/bobek/gmvlf/exposed.html ✦ WEB **Grant Morrison Voodoo Love Fetish** http://www.rt66.com/bobek/gmvlf/ ✦ USENET **alt.comics**

Morrissey (b. Stephen Patrick Morrissey, 1959) Manchester's Nabob of Sob; proud Laureate of England's decline. Morrissey started his career fronting The Smiths (1984–87), with whom he made four albums (and several compilations) of lyrical, tortured pop that attracted an almost suicidally devoted following. The band itself may have trafficked in workmanlike retro pop, but Morrissey's lyrics marked out a wholly original bailiwick, limning the lives of England's underclass with startling candor, cruel wit, and uncommon specificity. In 1994, critic Julie Burchill remarked in the London *Sunday Times* that Morrissey is the only pop singer who writes as though English is not his second language. Without his Smiths writing partner Johnny Marr, Morrissey has been a diminished power, vacillating between rockabilly thrash and Grand Guignol glam-rock gesture. Alternately lauded and lambasted in his homeland, the singer seems unwilling or unable to fully capitalize on a U.S. following whose adoration has only grown since the demise of the Smiths.

WEB **The Morrissey Internet Digest Web Site** http://copper.ucs.indiana.edu/~jstefani/ ✦ USENET **alt.music.morrissey** ✦ WEB **The Cemetery Gates** http://www.public.iastate.edu/~krajewsk/

Mortal Kombat Most popular VIDEOGAME of 1993. Together with its also huge predecessor, Street Fighter II (turned into a 1994 Jean-Claude Van Damme movie), MK established a new genre of head-to-head fighting games in which players, assuming characters based on ethnic and national stereotypes, vicariously bloody each other on the screen. The "finishing moves," in which one on-screen, photorealistic martial arts character rips out the heart of another, served as the focus for fears over videogame violence, prompting Sega and Nintendo to institute its own version of the voluntary rating system used by music and movie companies. Mortal Kombat itself was made into a summer 1995 movie.

WEB **The Best of Mortal Kombat WWW** http://www.nauticom.net/users/baraka/mk.html ftp **Mortal Kombat FAQs** ftp://ftp.netcom.com/pub/vi/vidgames/faqs/

moshing   Ritual frenzied dancing that combines the thrill of agony with the warmth of community. Moshing—a descendant of PUNK slamdancing—involves seething masses of people crashing into one another in front of the stage. In the early '90s, it became the main attraction for many concert-goers at increasingly mainstream venues. Dense crowds support bodies "surfing" overhead on raised arms; a frequent component is stage diving, in which a fan or an intrepid performer leaps from the stage into the "mosh pit." (COURTNEY LOVE delights in riling up the pit before diving.) Bloody noses and sprained ankles are common (a free clinic in San Francisco's Haight Ashbury has a Rock Medicine program devoted to such mosh ailments), but in 1994 two deaths were actually attributed to stage-diving head injuries: 21-year-old Lee O'Connor at a London Motorhead concert on June 21; and 17-year-old high school senior Christopher Mitchell at a Bensonhurst, New York, metal club on December 17. That year moshing rendered two participants quadriplegic, at a Rhode Island LOLLAPALOOZA show and at a Sepultura/Pantera/Biohazard show in Maryland. Despite such injuries, the appeal of moshing for many is its paradoxical promise of safety. Moshers tend to look out for one another, and it's not uncommon for the crowd to part to allow a participant to retrieve a lost sneaker. As one observer pointed out, "the mosh pit offer[s] the feel of an experience, but with no threat of violence or the effort of transgression." Some women disagree. Moshing is a largely (though by no means exclusively) male activity, and many women who do play say mosher boys often cross the line with their sweaty groping.

Photo by Tina Paul

HENRY ROLLINS fans MOSHING, New York 1993: "the thrill of agony, the warmth of community."

Moss, Kate (b. 1974)   South London teenager who got her start toward SUPERMODEL stardom after a July 1990 cover for Britain's *The Face,* shot by photographer Corinne Day. At 5'7" and a little over 100 pounds, the delicate-featured Moss prompted a re-evaluation of commercial beauty: '80s amazons like Rachels Williams and Hunter were replaced on the catwalks and fashion spreads by Moss-proportioned "waif" models like Amber Valetta, Emma Balfour, and Shalom Harlow. By Fall 1992, Moss had a lucrative contract with CALVIN KLEIN, for whom she posed revealingly, sometimes with beefcake rapper MARKY MARK.

Moss's reign has not been wholly untroubled: a June 1993 underwear spread for British *Vogue* drew accusations of pedophilia, and *People* magazine put her on their cover in September that year under the words "Skin and Bones." (In July 1993 *Harper's Bazaar* defended this ectomorphic public enemy no. 1; it cited Moss's great appetite and stamina in denying culpability for an increase in eating disorders among women and especially young girls.) By 1995, Moss's well-publicized relationship with actor JOHNNY DEPP drew attention away from the weight debate.

WEB **The Digital Waif Server** http://cctr.umkc.edu/user/cbjuland/kate/index.html ✦ WEB **Kate Moss Photo Archive** http://marlowe.wimsey.com/~jamacht/Kate/Pictures/

Mossimo   Orange County beachwear label that started in 1987 with a line of volleyball shorts, and grew to international prominence by dominating the EUROTRASH end of the street-wear spectrum. The company name comes from Mossimo "Moss" Giannuli (b. 1963), the son of an Orange County, California, landscape architect, and a graduate of the same high school as Shawn STÜSSY. With none of Stüssy's street credibility, Mossimo took his company to revenues of over $30 million in the early '90s thanks to a good eye for design and an uncommon appetite for merchandising—if an item is big enough to carry the Mossimo signature it will probably appear in department stores sooner or later. Sunglasses, belts, backpacks, lighters, footwear,

MTV

When MTV was launched in August 1981 the station's hidden agenda was not—despite the endless video-killed-the-radio-star bellyaching of pop-Luddites—creating a nation of drooling dotards, imaginations stunted by preheated imagery and Uzi-rapid editing. Nor was it merely introducing a sometimes-forbidden pleasure into the family living room. MTV's deepest concern was cleansing pop music of any remaining unseemly, rough elements; working in concert with abundantly funded video directors and record company marketers, the channel strove to elevate highly mediated products to iconic status and to deny admission to anything reeking of authenticity. In short, it wanted to eradicate youth culture.

After its early flirtations with quirky, glamorous, and above all *available* videos by English haircut bands subsided, MTV's mid-decade programming came to reflect America's values at the time. The channel created a rarefied ego-system for the likes of MADONNA, PRINCE, and Bruce Springsteen, entertainers who cavorted in a sublimely lit video Olympus where production values were more akin to *Dallas* or *Dynasty* than anything from rock's previous decades. For all the hyperkinetic video trickery, music hadn't been this sterile since the '50s heyday of Pat Boone and Patti Page.

More serious than MTV's neutering of youth culture was its treatment of blacks. No less than Michael Jackson, future "King of Pop" (his compulsory MTV handle in 1994), had to wait patiently for admission to this most exclusive of culture clubs, thanks to his then-skin color. It allegedly took grave threats from Columbia Records to ensure the playlisting of Jackson (whose 1983 single "Billie Jean" was a pop Number One without MTV) and the relaxing of MTV's pop apartheid to the point where it could safely accommodate black mavericks like Lionel Ritchie and DeBarge. To its credit, though, MTV pursued its exclusionary bents with a characteristic lack of conviction and consistency—the station ended up embracing HIP-HOP, the most vital youth culture of the '80s (albeit 18 months from the decade's end). The modest *Yo! MTV Raps* video show, launched in

August 1988, became a runaway MTV hit, a weekly (expanded to daily) dissemination of urban black modes of dress, speech, and music to the white suburbs; the show made L.A. Raiders gear, baggy jeans, and TIMBERLAND boots de rigueur for the racially transgressive white teens described on the talk shows of the time as "wiggers."

While it wasn't promoting the booming HIP-HOP culture, turn-of-the-decade MTV was pushing an incoherent roster of video confections that included Cher, Milli Vanilli, ZZ Top, and Wilson Phillips; the likes of Billy Joel and Sting were not an uncommon sight, among other refugees from MTV's adult-oriented sibling VH–1. The most threatening note was struck by the likes of Winger, Poison, and Trixter, pop-metal "hair bands" who were whimsically dispatched to the bargain bins after the 1991 arrival of NIRVANA, an act that MTV took much credit for breaking. When the muddy tones of the band's late-1991 video "Smells Like Teen Spirit" colonized the national teen imagination, MTV began pushing GRUNGE bands like Soundgarden, PEARL JAM, and Alice In Chains with revolutionary zeal. Wave after wave of anti-stars were welcomed with open arms as MTV imagery went from garish to downbeat.

MTV's large part in the ascent of grunge speaks of its position as the central pop medium in a country without a coherent music press or a national radio station. The fact that the channel puts post-Nirvana bands cheek by jowl with R&B crooners and GANGSTA rappers is testament to the eccentricity of the domestic wing of a franchise that reaches a quarter billion people worldwide. As such, MTV enjoys a privileged position practically unequaled in broadcasting. Video outlets like THE BOX and Black Entertainment Television cannot touch its reach; no network can match its global brand recognition. MTV is so entrenched that it has been able to sit back and watch while would-be competitors from two conglomerates (Time Warner/Sony/EMI/PolyGram and Bertelsmann Music Tele-Communications Inc.) simply gave up the ghost. The lack of competition has made MTV one of the oddest major media

Logo-centric MTV.

properties in the world: a quasi-monopoly driven by the ever-fragmenting, hormone-crazed tastes of adolescents.

Thus, even as MTV settles into its role as a linchpin of the new youth culture, the channel itself is prone to violent mood swings. For every well-meaning special on gun control, there's a scantily clad Beach House edition of *The Grind*; for every interview with Bill Clinton, there's a *Singled Out*, a thronging, hot-pants variant on the *Dating Game*. And to counter MTV's over-weening sense of self-importance, its mid-'90s sensibility even incorporates straitening doses of self-criticism from BEAVIS AND BUTT-HEAD and JIMMY THE CABDRIVER—genuine successes that have ended up being, like "soap-umentary" THE REAL WORLD, milked half to death.

Lapses of judgment are both frequent and extreme: '80s Olympian Michael Jackson has continued to enjoy the indulgence of this most capricious medium. MTV brazenly serviced the star with a bewildering range of programs, promo clips, and specials in the face of unseemly personal travails, a dwindling fan base, and public distaste that was reportedly shared even by his wife, Lisa Marie Presley. And the channel's desire to deliver viewers to advertisers for more than just a few fleeting minutes has led to numerous wrong numbers: the unwatchable dramas *Dead At 21* and *Catwalk* spring to mind, as do post-Beavis animation series like *The Maxx* and *The Brothers Grunt*; not forgetting *Road Rules*, a peripatetic REAL WORLD with less reality.

Despite such unfathomable gaffes, '90s MTV remains perennially open to experimentation. Not just through ALTERNATIVE showcases like *120 Minutes* and *Alternative Nation*, but in its fierce rotation of clever, incessant "Buzz Bin" promos for novel bands, and in the quasi-ironic attitudes of on-camera talents like KENNEDY, PAULY SHORE, and young Jake Fogelnest of SQUIRT TV. Even under the MTV News rubric, excitable tour reports and making-of-the-video exclusives co-exist with solid reporting and with *MTV News UNfiltered*, a show that puts cameras in the hands of concerned young citizens (*The* TOO *Real World*).

The early harvesting of each and every new youth fad to come down the pike is a given at the new MTV, from the bestowing of valuable *Unplugged* specials to neophyte bands, to the urban-hip fashion reporting of *House of Style,* to the instant packaging of each and every new pop micro-trend on News segments and *The Week in Rock*. By so eagerly embracing absolutely anything reeking of authenticity, the channel devalues what it touches. '90s MTV has still got it in for youth culture—only this time it's killing it with kindness.—*Steven Daly*

USENET **alt.tv.mtv** ✦ WEB **mtv.com** http://www.mtv.com/

swimwear, and cigarette lighters are available, with underwear and bedding following.

movie rides   Short movies using special effects, moving seats, and new pumped-up film standards to compete with amusement park rides and immersive VIDEOGAMES. Most pioneering examples in the early '90s have been adaptations of hit movies (like *Back to the Future*, *The Right Stuff*, and *Indiana Jones*) that play at theme parks or Vegas, but developers such as Douglas Trumbull (Ridefilms), Iwerks (TurboTour Theaters), and Sony Imax (through a joint venture with Sega) hope to soon bring the "dollar-a-minute" movies to thousands of malls and specialized movie theaters. While still more expensive to build than the standard cineplex, "software" rides are much cheaper to update than the "hardware" of traditional rollercoasters; also, because they are not actually interactive—the viewer is passive—they require far less computing power than their VIDEOGAME counterparts. Peter Gabriel has experimented with rock-driven rides, including "Mindbender," a 1993 ride-adaptation of his "Kiss That Frog" video that toured with LOLLAPALOOZA.

MTV   See page 156.

MUDs   INTERNET update of role-playing games (like the dice-and-rulebook Dungeons & Dragons), with worlds created out of text descriptions and in-character player interactions ranging from gas-lit San Francisco at the turn of the 19th century to ANIME firefights to fiction writing workshops. Variations from "Multi-user dimension," "multi-user dungeon," and "multi-user dialogue" include MUSHes ("multi-user shared hallucination"), MOOs ("MUD object oriented"). Some tend to be combat-oriented (LPMUDs & Diku MUDS), while TinyMUDS accent hanging out. While the first MUDs date to 1979, the explosive early '90s growth of the Internet has only recently led to the proliferation of hundreds of separate MUDS— some which last only a few weeks, others such as LambdaMOO and AberMUD which run for

years—and bans at many college campuses where MUDS are considered threats to computer resources and student health. Some of the most popular MUDs are based on novels and movies, leading in 1994 to the first lawsuit threats from copyright holders. MUDs are already at the forefront of multimedia experiments on the Internet.
USENET **rec.games.mud.*** ✦ WEB **Lydia Leong's MUD Resource Collection** http://www.cis.upenn.edu/~lwl/mudinfo.html/ ✦ WEB **Aragorn Server** http://aragorn.uio.no/ ✦ WEB **MUD FAQ** http://math.okstate.edu/~jds/mudfaqs.html/

Muhammad, Khallid Abdul (b. circa 1948)   Charismatic NATION OF ISLAM disciple with the delivery style of a DEF COMEDY JAM regular, turning pronouncements like "I want black coffee, no sugar, no cream," into crowd-pleasing racial epithets. Muhammad became a national figure when his anti-Semitic and anti-Catholic remarks during a November 1993 speech at New Jersey's Kean College were widely publicized and condemned (he called the Pope, for instance, "a cracker"). LOUIS FARRAKHAN, leader of the Nation, publicly admonished him while complaining at the same time that Khallid Muhammed was being persecuted for telling the truth. Farrakhan's conflicting message was widely interpreted as a sign of a power struggle between a mellowing Farrakhan (looking to move closer to mainstream Islam and form alliances with Jesse Jackson and moderate groups like the NAACP) and the Nation orthodoxy, which mobilizes young people with fiery rhetoric. Muhammad also vents his "truth terrorism" at black figures, calling SPIKE LEE "Spook Lee." In May 1994 Muhammad was shot in the foot by an ostracized Nation member at a speech in Riverside, California.
WEB **The Nation of Islam** http://www.afrinet.net:80/~islam/

mullet   Short-on-top, long-in-back haircut that combines—and yet at the same negates—both crew-cut neatness and hippie laissez-faire; the bi-level mullet can be adapted to occasions demanding either hairstyle. Sometimes called the "ape drape," a fancy-free women's version was pioneered by

Suzanne Pleshette on *The Bob Newhart Show*; in the late '70s this look gave birth to the "tail," where one strand of hair is left long in the back, sometimes braided or dyed. Since that time the mullet has become the tonsorial domain of headbanging heavy metal fans and fashion-impaired celebrities. Issue two of the BEASTIE BOYS ZINE, *Grand Royal*, afforded the fullest possible consideration to the mullet and its complex class implications.

multiculturalism Cosmopolitan philosophy arguing for the preservation of distinct ethnic, religious, and racial identities and substituting a "gorgeous mosaic" (in the words of New York City's first African-American mayor, David Dinkins) for the melting pot of earlier immigrant generations. Multiculturalism is perceived by its right-wing (and some establishment liberal) critics as a subversion of Western civilization, and by many AFROCENTRISTS as an assimilated "religion of science."

The current campus battle over multiculturalism reached critical mass in 1987. At a Stanford University march that year, nearly 500 students joined the Rev. Jesse Jackson to chant "Hey hey, ho ho, Western culture's got to go!" They were referring to an existing course, pushing for a replacement that would stress the cultural accomplishments of women and ethnic minorities. Stanford acceded, changing the course; dozens of other universities across the nation began to mandate multicultural curricula, teaching history and literature from "multiple perspectives."

As the visibility of multiculturalism increased (and some schools began instituting compulsory "sensitivity training" and SPEECH CODES), critics such as Arthur Schleschinger and Irving Kristol argued that the "ethnic cheerleading" movement was little more than a form of intellectual affirmative action, complete with minority set-asides. Kristol, writing in the *Wall Street Journal* in July 1991, derided multiculturalism as "a desperate strategy for coping with the educational deficiencies, and associated social pathologies, of young blacks." Despite these criticisms, the rise of hyphenated

middle classes (African-American, Asian-American) and the cultural cachet of ethnicity (reflected in everything from the popularity of Yiddish classes to the sales success of salsa over ketchup) has continued to flavor college curricula and pop culture.

Observing the degree to which Americans do *not* lead culturally segregated lives thanks to television and consumer culture, critic Louis Menand noted in 1993, "People in the United States still want, as people in the United States have always wanted, to be 'American.' It is just that being American is now understood to mean wearing your ethnicity, religion, gender, and sexual history . . . on your sleeve."

multiple chemical sensitivity Affliction first identified in 1985 by the Ontario Ministry of Health in which the victim becomes allergic to the manmade chemicals of modern life. Though recognized as a disability in federal law, the controversial diagnosis is still widely regarded as a psychiatric condition within the medical establishment. Many MCS experts hypothesize that the disease is actually a kind of toxic poisoning resulting from exposure to common building materials (carpets, wallboards, and plywood can give off formaldehyde and isocyanates), pesticides, or even food additives. Symptoms, which range from fatigue and rashes to asthma and vomiting, can be touched off in MCS sufferers by the slightest manmade fume, be it a whiff of perfume, cologne, or automobile exhaust. Treatments include deconditioning—as is standard for many allergies—by exposure to small doses of the offending substance, or—more unusually— seclusion in a living environment swept clean of 20th century materials. The 1995 TODD HAYNES movie, *Safe*, told the story of an MCS-stricken San Fernando Valley housewife who retreats to a NEW AGE healing colony. [See also SICK BUILDING SYNDROME.]

Musafar, Fakir (b. Roland Loomis, 1930) Onetime Silicon Valley, California, advertising executive who had begun clandestinely experimenting with pain and *National Geographic*-inspired ritualistic body modification practices at puberty (he pierced his foreskin with a nail). Today Fakir is considered to be the spiritual leader of the MODERN PRIMITIVE movement. He achieved subcultural fame in the late-'70s documentary *Dances Sacred and Profane* (directed by Charles Gatewood). In that film, he recreated the Mandan Indian Oh-Kee-Pah rite of passage ceremony by hanging from a cottonwood tree with hooks in his chest. He is currently editor and publisher of *Body Play*, a quarterly magazine for body modification enthusiasts.

WEB **Modern Primitives** http://www.clas.ufl.edu/anthro/Modern_Primitives.html

Museum of Jurassic Technology, The

Storefront L.A. meta-museum, founded 1988, specializing in artful, deadpan satires of science. Curated and staffed principally by the Denver-born David Wilson (b. 1947), a former filmmaker and Hollywood special effects worker. The 1995 show "Tell the Bees ... Belief, Knowledge and Hypersymbolic Cognition" uses a stuffed mouse suspended over a piece of bread in one display to illustrate that bed-wetting can be cured by eating mice on toast. One highlight in the permanent exhibition, discussed in a 1994 *Harper's* magazine article and elsewhere, is a stuffed Deprong Mori bat from South America that can use its radar, the exhibit explains, to fly through solid objects. Accompanying text details the great difficulty scientists encountered netting the bat.

My So-Called Life

"Lately I can't even look at my mother without wanting to stab her repeatedly," confessed Angela Chase in a tone-setting voice-over at in the first of this TV drama's 19 episodes (1994–95). *Life* was television's first halfway believable foray into the mind of a female adolescent: part Annie Hall, part *SASSY* magazine cover waif, Angela (Claire Danes, b. 1979) is a good girl gone skeptical. Her troubled and fascinating friends include Ray Anne (a morphing alco-

holic), Ricki (homosexual romantic), and Sharon (healthily sexual girl next door). If Angela's concerned parents seem wrenched from *thirtysomething*, it could be because both shows were produced by Marshall Herskovitz and Ed Zwick (and scored by one W. "Snuffy" Walden). When ABC threatened to cancel *My So-Called Life* due to anemic ratings, a massive email campaign (Operation Life Saver) was launched by Angela's fans, with the blessing of most major TV critics; MTV did its part by re-running the show daily while ABC deliberated. It was to no avail. Some fans believed that Danes's ambivalence about long shooting schedules contributed to the May 1995 cancellation. In July the actress was nominated for an Emmy—in August she signed on to film a new version of *Romeo and Juliet* opposite LEONARDO DICAPRIO.

WEB **My So-Called Life: Cast Life** http://www.umn.edu/nlhome/g564/lask0008/mscl.html

MY SO-CALLED LIFE, dead at 19 episodes.

Photo by Mark Seliger, courtesy of Capital Cities/ABC

Mystery Science Theater 3000

Comedy Central show created in 1988 by former standup comic Joel Hodgson for KTMA, a local UHF station in Minneapolis, Minnesota. (The next year the show was picked up by what was then HBO's Comedy Channel.) Hodgson played Joel Robinson, a human trapped in space and forced by mad scientists to watch a different B-movie every week with his two robot friends he built from scrap. The trio, silhouetted in front of the screen, bravely respond with a relentless running commentary of smart-ass wisecracks and off-the-wall cultural references; somehow these fourth-millennium intergalactic travelers have a set of bargain-basement obsessions that include the 1950s character actor Richard Basehart, *Police Woman* costar Earl Holliman, and the 1987 film

Mannequin starring Andrew McCarthy. After Hodgson left in 1993, head writer and accomplished actor Mike Nelson stepped in as the scientists' new experimental subject. While some fans complained that Joel's sleepy-eyed innocence was irreplaceable, the *MST3K* cult has continued to thrive, spawning fan clubs, conventions, and a ream of catch-phrases and insider jokes. The show's Minneapolis-based production company signed a deal in 1995 to produce its own low-budget movie.

WEB **Deus Ex Machina** http://sunsite.unc.edu/lunar/mst3k/mst3k.html ✦ USENET **rec.arts.tv.mst3k.announce**, **rec.arts.tv.mst3k.misc**

N.W.A (Niggaz Wit' Attitude) Short-lived band from L.A.'s Compton district who formally instigated HIP-HOP'S GANGSTA era. Bankrolled and fronted by former drug dealer turned solo rapper EAZY-E, N.W.A's original line-up featured future rap superstars ICE CUBE and producer/DJ DR. DRE, alongside MC Yella (b. Antoine Carraby circa 1967) and MC Ren (b. Lorenzo Patterson circa 1966). The group's debut *Straight Outta Compton* (1989) came as a shocking counterpoint to East Coast hip-hop's emerging AFRO-CENTRIC, politically conscious tendencies: Dre's raw production carried forth unfettered messages of street violence, crime, and misogyny which posited the revolving narrators as blaxploitation anti-heroes. The band's style, too, was an affront to hip-hop's prevalent aesthetic: they wore baggy "prison blues," the silver-and-black colors of the bad-boy L.A. Raiders, and had unfashionable Jheri-curl hairstyles that prompted critic Frank Owen to dub the band "NIGGERS With Activator."

Straight Outta Compton went platinum with minimal radio play; it gained mainstream attention only when the track "Fuck tha Police" was condemned by the 200,000-member national Fraternal Order of Police and a representative of the FBI. Shortly after *Compton*, Ice Cube exited N.W.A over a financial dispute, but the group carried on, recording the lesser *100 Miles and Runnin'* EP (1990) and album *Efil4zaggin* (1991), which entered the charts at #1 under the newly instituted SOUNDSCAN system.

Naked Guy, the UC Berkeley junior—real name Andrew Martinez (b. circa 1973)—who became a national news story in November 1992 when he was suspended for attending class sporting only a pair of sandals. The six-foot-four Martinez, who had staged a "nude-in" with more than 20 other people in September '92, was unrepentant; he was later expelled for his refusal to don apparel. "I don't want to facilitate the power structure with my conformity," he told the *Los Angeles Times*.

nanotechnology Big thinking about little atoms. This new science promises machines the size of molecules that can fashion caviar or diamonds out of the atoms of common garbage. K. Eric Drexler (a.k.a. "Captain Future"), the leading proponent of the as yet unrealized technology, is credited with first envisioning the possibilities of "nanoassembling" matter one atom at a time as a graduate student at MIT in the mid-'80s (though physicist Richard Feynman anticipated the basic ideas in a 1959 speech). Drexler's theoretical work did prefigure the scanning tunneling microscope's ability to manipulate single atoms, but the field has thus far mainly flourished in publishing, most notably NEAL STEPHENSON's science fiction novel *The Diamond Age* (1995), and a best-selling nonfiction book *Nano* (1995). The hypothetical science has already cross-pollinated, leading to visions of self-adjusting nanoplastic toilet seats, wall TVs that can create as well as display, and biochemical DNA computers operating thousands of times faster than the swiftest silicon supercomputers.
WEB **Nanotechnology** http://nano.xerox.com/nano/
✦ USENET **sci.nanotech**

Nation of Islam Black nationalist religion founded by W. D. Fard, a Detroit door-to-door salesman during the Depression. Originally built on ideas from Marcus Garvey's "Back to Africa" movement, the Nation creed urges blacks to drop the "slave religion" of Christianity and return to their ancestral Islamic faith. But the NOI has never joined Islam; the basic theology teaches that a mad black scientist named Yakub created white people 6,000 years ago as a curse and test for the superior black people. With its bow ties, detox and prison programs, manhood training, militant Fruit of Islam bodyguards, street corner sales of bean pies and the *Final Call* newspaper, the Nation has been regarded for decades by white America as a curiosity of ghetto black life. Attention has focused intermittently on the anti-white comments of charismatic leaders like MALCOLM X in the '60s, LOUIS FARRAKHAN in the '80s, and KHALLID ABDUL

MUHAMMAD in the '90s. While familiarity with Nation tenets is one measure of basic political consciousness among black campus radicals, black inmates, the urban black underclass, and rappers, the *New York Times* estimated in 1994 that the actual Nation membership could be fewer than 10,000 people and no more than 100,000.

WEB **The Nation of Islam** http://www.afrinet.net:80/~islam/

NEA Federal government program for arts funding that has been red meat for the Republican right since 1989. That year, Sen. Jesse Helms made an issue of National Endowment for the Arts funding for Robert Mapplethorpe's homoerotic photography and Andres Serrano's "Piss Christ," a photograph of a crucifix submerged in urine. Dubbed the "ayatollah of North Carolina" by art critic Robert Hughes, Helms succeeded in requiring recipients of NEA money to pledge not to create "obscene or indecent art." Many refused, but the debate moved farther to the right from whether Congress should censor art to whether it should fund it at all. The NEA's 1994 appropriation of $167 million—most of which went as matching grants to uncontroversial institutions from the Harlem Boys Choir to the Alabama Shakespeare Festival—is, its defenders noted, less than the amount the Pentagon spends on military marching bands. Later in '94, the Clinton NEA defunded the RON ATHEY theater group after press accounts incorrectly reported that HIV+ blood had been dripped on the audience at a performance.

WEB **Arts USA: UpDate** http://www.artsusa.org/action/ record.htm ✦ WEB **NEA Crisis** http://musdra.ucdavis.edu/ Documents/nea_neh_docs/nea_crisis_home.html

Pat Buchanan uses the NEA to bash Bush in a 1992 campaign ad.

National Medical Enterprises Chain of 132 for-profit psychiatric hospitals which raked in billions of dollars during the mid '80s and early '90s by systematically misdiagnosing teens for depression and holding them against their will until their insurance policies ran out. Complementary schemes, prosecuted by the government, involved paying bribes and kickbacks for referrals from social workers and doctors. (A similar Kafkaesque scam was the basis of BEASTIE BOY Adam Horowitz's 1989 movie debut in *Lost Angels*.) In an extraordinary twist, Dallas doctors who worked at the chain's most notorious hospital sued their former patients in 1994 for slander. This came after one of those patients, Banny Lyon, published accounts of a year-long imprisonment which included seven months of "chair therapy"—sitting facing a wall for as many as 12 hours a day.

National Service Program Popular plank in Bill Clinton's "Putting People First" 1992 campaign platform which proposed rewarding young people's community service with the largest federal tuition aid since the WWII G.I. Bill. The program, which sought to address middle-class anxiety about astronomical college costs (see STUDENT LOANS), was one of the strongest applause lines in Clinton's stump speech ("If you borrow four years' worth of education, you can do two years of work at reduced pay . . . doing community service, and pay off your college loan"). After the election, however, the scope of AmeriCorps—as it came to be known—was sharply limited to the point of little more than a test program, though it did call attention to worthy programs, such as one model of urban youth service, City Year, that was able to expand from Boston to other cities. In 1995 Republicans called for AmeriCorps' demise, even proposing to rescind previously appropriated funds that had not yet been spent. The series of compromises leading up the law's passage was exceptionally well documented in Steven Waldman's 1994 *The Bill: How the Adventures of Clinton's National Service Bill Reveal What Is Corrupt, Comic, Cynical—And Noble—About Washington.*

WEB **Whitehouse** http://www.whitehouse.gov/ ✦ WEB
AmeriCorps Network Northwest http://www.nwrel.org/
edwork/direct.html

NC–17   "No Children Under 17 Admitted"
movie rating created by the Motion Picture
Association of America (MPAA) in 1990 to signify
adult material without invoking the pornographic
associations of the retired "X" rating (created with
the first movie ratings system in 1968). The NC–17
reform was prompted by an unsuccessful MIRAMAX
lawsuit over the X given to PEDRO ALMODOVAR's art
film *Tie Me Up! Tie Me Down!* Although MPAA
president Jack Valenti insisted at the time that the
new child-proof rating was a guideline, not a
stigma, many theater chains refused to show
NC–17 or unrated movies. Consequently the first
NC–17 movie, *Henry and June* (1990), remained
for years the only major studio release to ever bear
the rating. Most Hollywood directors sign contracts
requiring whatever edits are necessary for an R rating; the few major films that have received NC–17
ratings are either recut, as in the case of *Basic
Instinct* (1992), or simply sold to a more suitable
distributor, as with MARTIN LAWRENCE's 1994 concert film *You So Crazy.* (The preceding reform,
PG–13, was introduced in 1984 after parent groups
complained about a beating heart ripped from a
man's chest in *Indiana Jones and the Temple of
Doom.*) In September 1995 MGM broke ranks with
the movie industry by accepting an NC–17 rating
for its stripper-movie *Showgirls* and opening the
film in multiplexes nationwide.

needle exchange programs   Public health
measure to slow the spread of AIDS by providing
intravenous drug users with clean needles so they
won't share dirty ones. Although studies since the
late '80s have repeatedly demonstrated the effective-
ness of such clean needle programs—especially in
limiting HIV's spread in the heterosexual population—WAR ON DRUGS hawks assert that needle
exchange condones and promotes drug use.
Hundreds of ACT-UP and other activists went to jail
in the early '90s for running underground syringe

programs that are still illegal in many urban centers
of IV drug use.

WEB **Hyperreal Needle Exchange FAQ**
http://hyperreal.com/drugs/politics/needle.exchange/index.ht
ml/ ✦ WEB **Adam Drug Policy** http://www.xs4all.nl/
~mlap/count/nl/adam1.html/

Negativland   "Media hacker" band who appropriate material from the airwaves and elsewhere to
provoke and provide pointed commentary on the
culture industry's machinations. With a creative
nucleus consisting of Mark Hosler, Dan Joyce, and
Chris Griegg, the group has been recording since
1980 as well as hosting *Over the Edge*, a weekly
three-hour, improvised radio show on San
Francisco's KPFA-FM. In 1988 the artistic
pranksters fabricated a Midwestern familicide
allegedly inspired by their track "Christianity Is
Stupid." The resulting media hoopla was documented on the album *Helter Stupid.* In 1991 the
legal feces hit the fan hard when Negativland
released "U2," a single that sampled both the Irish
pop stars and wholesome DJ Casey Kasem caught
in a foul-mouth moment. Negativland documented
the case—which cost their label SST a substantial
settlement—in *Fair Use: The Story of the Letter U
and the Numeral 2* (1995), which delineates the
paradoxes and pitfalls of artistic use of copyrighted
material.

WEB **word from our sponsors . . .** http://sunsite.unc.edu/
id/negativland/ ✦ WEB **Negativland/U2** http://www.eskimo.
com/~irving/negativland/u2/

new age   Broad definition of hippie-ish cultural
beliefs in the post-hippie age. SPIRITUAL enlightenment is at the core of new age-identified practices.
For women, this can span crystals, self-help books,
and goddess worship. For men, it can encompass
Iron John/men's movement literature, "primitive"
retreats, and an inner search for female intuition.
The name "new age" derives in part from the Age of
Aquarius, an astrological era that is supposedly
marked by greater peace in the world.

WEB **New-Age Directory** http://www.wholarts.com/
psychic/newage.html/ ✦ USENET **talk.religion.newage** ✦ WEB

The New Age Web Works http://www.newageinfo.com/res/
santeria.htm ✦ USENET **talk.religion.newage**

new jill swing   In the wake of the TEDDY
RILEY-inspired new jack swing boom came a distaff
version of the same late-century soul, with strident
vocals and sly innuendos laid over crisp HIP-HOP
beats. Building on the work of groups like Salt-N-
Pepa and En Vogue, the new jills went up the hill in
the early '90s; female R&B acts such as SWV, TLC,
Jade, and flinty Detroit diva Mary J. Blige were
soon making black music's domination of the singles charts near-total.

New Music Seminar   Annual industry junket
held in New York every August through 1994, now
defunct. Started in 1980, the NMS quickly became
an important means of exposure for new bands, and
served a crucial role in smoothing the path from
college radio to megaplatinum. Over a hundred acts
would show up to play clubs throughout the city
during the seminar weekend, both with record deals
and without. The seminar's panels became opportunities for artists to pontificate, which often led to
conflagrations, which often involved ICE-T. In its
later years, the seminar was criticized for becoming
too mainstream, and its finances were never exemplary; after the 1994 conference, it fell apart.
Industry interest has now shifted to Austin's slightly
more freewheeling South by Southwest conference,
while Apple Computer has stepped in to fill the
New York summer music void with the
"MACINTOSH New York Music Festival." (Smaller
such gatherings include New York's *College Music
Journal* New Music Marathon and San Francisco's
Gavin Report Convention.)

WEB **Macintosh New York Music Festival**

http://festival.inch.com/

new news   Term coined in *ROLLING STONE* by
media critic and mystery writer Jon Katz (b. 1947)
to describe the novel sources of information—"serious and trashy, print and electronic, network and
cable"—crowding out traditional mass media news
outlets like the newspaper and network news.

"Increasingly the New News is seizing the functions
of mainstream journalism," Katz argued in 1992,
"sparking conversations, and setting the country's
social and political agenda." Throughout his critique, Katz reversed the standard debate over news
versus entertainment, insisting instead that the fil-
tering role of professional journalism was largely
irrelevant in the age of talk shows, online discourse,
Court TV, and HIP-HOP. As the INTERNET bloomed
in the following years, Katz focused his attack on
newspapers, claiming that they are doomed in the
face of the raw data, immediacy, and database depth
of "digital news."

new wave of new wave   Spurious mini-
trend promoted in 1994 by a novelty-hungry
British music press. A core of young bands—
including S*M*A*S*H, Elastica, These Animal
Men, and Echobelly—were hailed as harbingers of a
return to the astringent values of late-'70s/early-'80s
power-pop. Hitherto unfashionable influences like
Blondie and XTC were suddenly legitimate in the
rush to bury the memory of DREAM POP, the amorphous style of previous seasons. Between them, the
new wave of new wave bands claimed a healthy
number of front pages and a handful of hits in their
native land, but America was largely unmoved—
most of the NWONW bands played in front of
audiences who were enjoying their own PUNK
revival. The exception was the spunky, three-quarter
female outfit Elastica, whose songs are so memorable they are obliged to pay publishing royalties to

Nouveau new wavers Elastica
at record company WEB site
(http://www.geffen.com/elastica/).

English punk-era veterans Wire and The Stranglers.
WEB **The Elastica Connection** http://www.wmin.ac.uk/~
braziej/elastica/ ◆ WEB **Geffen Records: Elastica** //www.
geffen.com/elastica/: http://www.geffen.com/elastica/

Newton, Helmut (b. 1920) Fashion photographer known for some of the most stridently sexual images this side of New York's 42nd Street. In the '60s and '70s Newton's shameless objectification of fashion models (often in sterile, pseudo sci-fi settings) flirted with pornography and misogyny, to the great chagrin of feminists everywhere. His 1971 discovery of "ring flash" lighting would help define the look of much of that decade: intense light reflected back from peripheral surfaces placed dark outlines around Newton's subjects (and those of his contemporary Guy Bourdin), and bathed them in a cruel, almost antiseptic aura. The fashion industry's 1993–94 "return to glamour" brought Newton a major resurgence of influence; in the post-waif world, ring flash was again flavor of the month among glossy magazine image-makers (among them, Schoerner and Juergen Teller). Newton showed he had lost none of sense of outrage in 1995: his dumbfounding fashion story in February's *Vogue* featured Teutonic SUPERMODEL Nadja Auermann in such accouterments as a wheelchair, a leg brace, and $1,000 Chanel pumps.

New Yorker, the Venerable weekly established 1925 as a venue for now-legendary wits like Dorothy Parker, Robert Benchley and James Thurber. The *New Yorker* went through a mere four editors in the subsequent 66 years, during which time its unimpeachable literary standards and whimsical cartoons claimed a unique place in the genteel culture of East Coast WASPs. In 1992 the magazine's editorial reins were handed to Tina Brown, the high-powered Briton who had famously salvaged the 1984 re-launch of *Vanity Fair*. Many feared that Brown's celebrity- and advertiser-friendly predilections would coarsen the *New Yorker*'s tone, and they were not reassured by the introduction of full-page photographs and the occasional omission of fiction from issues. Brown, who quickly raised the magazine's profile, circulation, and spending, claimed fidelity to the irreverent spirit of founder Harold Ross.
gopher **Electronic Newsstand: New Yorker**
gopher://gopher.enews.com:70/11/magazines/alphabetic/all/
new_yorker

Next Progressive, the Quarterly journal of liberal and Democratic Party politics and culture started in 1991 by recent Yale graduate Eric Liu (b. circa 1968), then working as an aide in the Washington D.C. office of Oklahoma Senator David Boren. Liu went on to edit *Next*, a 1994 anthology of twentysomething essays, and in 1993 became the youngest (and only Asian-American) member of President Clinton's speechwriting staff. As of 1995, the magazine is published from Cambridge, Massachusetts, where Liu attends Harvard Law School. The journal tends to aim for Clinton-like consensus, balancing most criticisms of the right with jabs at the left, and is marked by its lack of youthful idealism.

Nickelodeon Children's cable-TV channel launched in 1979 by Viacom's MTV Networks. Nickelodeon's key insight was to create kids' programming from a kid's point of view; the guiding aesthetic was raucous and rude. Early hits included the game show *Double Dare*, which featured copious amounts of purple slime (see GAK). In 1991, Nickelodeon launched *Nicktoons*, creator-driven cartoons that bucked the decade-long network trend of only basing cartoons on existing characters or, even better, toys. With quality animation and clever writing, *Rugrats, Doug* and especially REN AND STIMPY became big hits and merchandising bonanzas. Nickelodeon also won kids over with authority-questioning shows like *Clarissa Explains It All* and THE ADVENTURES OF PETE AND PETE, and launched a *SPY*-style kids' magazine in 1994. The channel's success was used as ammunition by conservative politicians bent on de-funding public television, especially after the network offered, in 1995, to pick-up *Sesame Street* and *Barney* should the shows lose funding.

Since 1985, Nickelodeon has done double duty as Nick at Night, with a gently ironic evening lineup of nostalgic television for BABY BOOMERS (*I Love Lucy*, *The Dick Van Dyke Show*) and the younger generation raised on '70s TV (*The Partridge Family*, *Welcome Back Kotter*).

WEB **Nick at Nite** http://nick-at-nite.viacom.com ✦ USENET **alt.tv.nickelodeon**

nicotine patch "Transdermal" bandage worn on the upper arm to salve the "nic fits" of cigarette quitters. The patches were a hit when first introduced in 1991, with more than four million prescriptions; demand slackened, however, amid fears about rashes, overstimulation of the heart, and other side effects. The drug companies behind Nicoderm, Habitrol, and other patch products are attempting to get FDA approval to sell them over-the-counter, as is customary in Europe. Even as part of a "comprehensive behavioral smoking-cessation program" required under the current FDA approval (a requirement met by one company that sent postcards to your home saying "Your teeth and fingernails are slowly returning to their normal color"), the patch only boasts a 20 percent success rate. Other forms include the far less popular Nicorette gum available since the mid-'80s, and a nasal spray awaiting FDA approval called Pharmacia. The spray is said to be the most effective for quitting smoking, as smokers dose themselves only when they have an urge to smoke.

USENET **alt.support.stop-smoking**, **alt.smokers** ✦ MAIL LIST **TOBACTALK** listserv@arizvm1.ccit.arizona.edu ✦ WEB **NicNet** http://www.medlib.arizona.edu/~pubhlth/tobac.html/

nigger Centuries-old racial epithet for black people. The term has enjoyed a resurgence in '90s popular culture via HIP-HOP, where it draws on the word's specialized use in black vernacular as a hard-edged term of endearment among African-Americans (e.g. "nigger, please!" for "you're too much"). Many rappers also took defiant pride in calling themselves "nigger" (as in California's N.W.A—Niggaz Wit' Attitude). Though white audiences became increasingly exposed to use of the word by blacks, its use by whites to describe blacks is still construed as racist in all but the rarest of cases. (Hate crime studies, in fact, showed that "nigger" was still the most commonly used insult in racially motivated attacks.) On Mother's Day—virtually a religious holiday in urban black communities—in 1993, the Rev. Calvin O. Butts, pastor of Harlem's Abyssinian Baptist Church, launched a largely ineffectual campaign against use of the word (along with misogynistic lyrics) in rap music, to encourage a return from "niggas," "bitches," and "ho's" to "brothers" and "sisters."

Nike World's largest sneaker company and hero factory, owing to vast advertising campaigns, relentless roll-outs of new shoe styles, and aggressive management of athlete spokesmen. The Air Jordan line bearing the name of endorsement ultrastar Michael Jordan is the best-selling sneaker ever, with new models of the putative performance-boosters released annually since his 1984 rookie debut. Named for the Greek Goddess of Victory, Nike began as a running shoe company that sped past ADIDAS in 1980 on the heels of the country's jogging craze.

Nike's dominance of the sneaker business since the late '80s has been predicated on endorsements from basketball stars; this, plus the fact that Nike's 1993 revenues equaled, according to Donald Katz's *Just Do It* (1994), "all the TV deals, tickets and paraphernalia of the NBA, NFL, and major league baseball combined," has made the company the prime symbol of the commercialization of sports. This was dramatized at the 1992 Barcelona Olympics, when Dream Team player CHARLES BARKLEY said he had "two million reasons" not to accept a gold medal while wearing a USA sweatsuit bearing the Reebok logo (it transpired that he was actually getting $4 million that year); diplomacy prevailed in the end when team leader Michael Jordan wore the jacket with a US flag draped over the enemy's logo. College basketball also operates under Nike's shadow, with players required to wear swoosh-marked socks and shoes chosen by their coaches (who often make more in sneaker endorsement deals than salary).

Although Nike's most successful ad campaign (which made the reputation of Portland, Oregon, agency Wieden & Kennedy) has implored since 1988 "Just Do It," less than half of Nikes are ever worn for their stated cross-training or sports use; within the company, this is euphemistically known as "implied performance." As with software monolith Microsoft, Nike's youthful corporate culture is defined by an informal Pacific Northwest headquarters steeped in the ethos of its products. Nike buildings on the Beaverton, Oregon, "World Campus" are named after athlete-endorsers like baseball pitcher Nolan Ryan and tennis badboy John McEnroe.

Michael Jordan returned to basketball in 1995 after a two-year hiatus following his father's 1993 death, just in time to promote the Air Jordan XI shoe.

WEB **Charlie's Sneaker Pages** http://www.neosoft.com/users/s/sneakers/ ✦ USENET **alt.clothing.sneakers** ✦ WEB **Nike** http://www.fpi.co.jp/NIKE/Welcome.html

Nine Inch Nails

Nine Inch Nails Group alias of INDUSTRIAL superstar Trent Reznor (b. 1965), a former computer engineering student whose slight build and soft speech belie his deranged stage persona. Nine Inch Nails' lyrically ghoulish debut album *Pretty Hate Machine* (1989) was a menacing dance-synth opus that brought the band a significant following; the band's gear-shredding spot on the first LOLLAPALOOZA tour sent the album platinum. There followed an enforced hiatus from recording while Reznor toured and wrangled with his record company, TVT. Interscope (TIME WARNER-linked home of DR. DRE's Death Row Records) joined with TVT to release the *Broken* EP (1992), a stormy record fueled by contractual rage. (*Broken* earned Reznor an unlikely Grammy: Best Metal Performance with Vocal.) Reznor next ensconced himself in the Benedict Canyon house where followers of CHARLES MANSON had murdered Sharon Tate and her friends. The resultant album, *Downward Spiral*, weightier than *Pretty* and less overtly "industrial," debuted at #2 on the *Billboard* charts in 1994, and installed NIN's jarring videos as MTV staples. That same year Reznor produced the collage-SOUNDTRACK for OLIVER STONE's *Natural Born Killers* (1994), and staged—for a reported $250,000 fee—a mud-spattered, gear-shredding WOODSTOCK '94 performance that converted further legions of non-believers. In fall 1995, Reznor and his band toured on the same bill as English concept-rock veteran David Bowie.

WEB **Live/ Rare Imports Homepage** http://www.csh.rit.edu/~jerry/NIN_RI/welcome.html ✦ WEB **The Unofficial Nine Inch Nails Homepage** http://ibms15.scri.fsu.edu/~patters/nin.html ✦ USENET **alt.music.nin, alt.music.nin. creative, rec.music.industrial**

924 Gilman Graffiti-decorated warehouse space in Berkeley, California, that provides a stage for the area's PUNK performers. With minimal promotion and no signage, this collective (est. 1986) only rarely makes the news: Jello Biafra was beaten up in May 1994 because he "sold out" and pop-punk band GREEN DAY incurred the clientele's wrath because they "went mainstream." (As early as February '94, the *San Francisco Chronicle* reported a "Destroy Green Day Now" graffito in the club.) 924 Gilman is adamant about its version of punk ethics: no sexist, racist, or homophobic lyrics; no skinheads; no violence; no stage-diving; no hierarchies; no derogatory symbols. Run by a core of about 20 volunteers, the club puts on two or three shows a weekend ($1 membership, $4 at the door) with up to six bands a night, ranging from STRAIGHT EDGE to art rock to RIOT GRRRLS. No alcohol is served.

Nintendo thumb Repetitive strain injury (RSI) afflicting habitual users of the basic push-button controllers that come with mass-market home VIDEOGAME systems. Can also be used as a general term for the ubiquitous calluses, but in extreme cases tendinitis may develop in the thumb, sending pain shooting up nerves into the arm (see CARPAL TUNNEL SYNDROME). Also known as numb thumb.

WEB **RSI FAQ's** http://www.cis.ohio-state.edu/hypertext/faq/usenet/typing-injury-faq/top.html

Nirvana SEATTLE trio universally credited with instigating the mainstream assimilation of ALTERNATIVE rock. Nirvana's accelerated trajectory from obscurity to superstardom to self-destruction began in Aberdeen, Washington, in 1986 when the band was formed by singer/songwriter Kurt Cobain (b. 1967; d. 1994) and bassist Krist Novaselic (b. 1965). Nirvana's pugnacious debut, *Bleach* (recorded for a little more than $600) was released in 1988 by Seattle's SUB POP records. Critical raves instigated a major-label bidding war eventually won by DGC; with the addition of drummer Dave Grohl (b. 1969), the band's final lineup was in place. *Nevermind* was released in 1991 and, bolstered by the disaffected, anthemic hit single "Smells Like Teen Spirit," went to #1. *Nevermind* combined PUNK momentum with a rare pop melodicism, setting postmodern moodiness and thrash aesthetics against a backdrop of '70s arena rock. Nirvana's lyrical sensibility combined a peculiarly modern mix of unfocused rage and wan self-deprecation, Cobain's ragged shout careening from frenetic to deadpan and back again. The platinum success of *Nevermind*—a record by an obscure band working in a genre theretofore dismissed as hopelessly uncommercial—launched the GRUNGE phenomenon and marked an era of unprecedented exposure for alternative acts. It also saddled the band—and the frail Cobain in particular—with the onus of unanticipated superstardom.

Cobain married COURTNEY LOVE, singer of the raw, confrontational band Hole, in February 1992. Later that year, a *Vanity Fair* profile of Love alleging that she used drugs during her pregnancy brought the pair overweening media attention. (The couple's daughter, Frances Bean, was born healthy that August.) Nirvana's difficult *In Utero*, less focused and more introspective than *Nevermind*, was released in late 1993. While touring in support of the album in March 1994, Cobain overdosed on tranquilizers and champagne in Rome. The tour was cut short and the singer returned to Seattle to recuperate. Cobain was found dead of a self-inflicted shotgun blast to the head on April 8—he was 27 years old. The publicity that followed

NIRVANA *UNPLUGGED*, 1993.

Cobain's death—much of it labeling him a "spokesman for his generation"—was exactly the kind of overwrought mythmaking that undid him. Love, meanwhile, engaged in very public mourning, reading from his suicide note at a Seattle memorial gathering. His death coincided with the release of Hole's album *Live Through This*, whose fatalistic lyrics seemed eerily apropos. After Cobain's death, MTV frequently screened Nirvana's *UNPLUGGED* special, an album which went to #1 on its November 1994 release; Nirvana drummer Dave Grohl formed a new band, Foo Fighters, that issued a promising debut in 1995.

WEB **Nirvana Web Archive** http://www.ludd.luth.se/misc/nirvana/ ✦ USENET **alt.music.nirvana** ✦ WEB **Verse Chorus Verse** http://www2.ecst.csuchico.edu/~jedi/nirvana.html ✦ WEB **Geffen Records** http://geffen.com/nirv.html

nitrous oxide Laughing gas; available from the dentist, Whip-It canisters, and Dead shows, as well as in tanks from medical and restaurant supply stores. (There are also even more dangerous forms of N_2O, auto-grade and homemade.) A lungful of the gas produces about thirty seconds of auditory hallucinations (likened to quickly covering and uncovering one's ears), communion with the cosmic yin-yang, and possible minor brain damage. Studies of addicted dentists and emergency room walk-ins document that larger quantities and long-term use can cause paralysis and dementia; everyday risks include frost-bite from the release of the pressurized gas and accidental asphyxiation. Recreational use usually involves the aforementioned Whip-Its used

A balloon, possibly containing NITROUS OXIDE. DEADHEADS in parking lot, 1989.

for dispensing whipped cream and sold in many grocery stores. Other devices include crackers—metal or plastic devices sold in head shops and specifically made for releasing the Whip-It into a balloon—and charging bottles similar to the kind used for seltzer.

WEB **Just Say N20** http://www.resort.com/~banshee/Info/N2O/N2O.html/ ◆ WEB **Hyperreal Inhalants** http://hyperreal.com/drugs/inhalants/

No Fear T-shirt and baseball cap logo introduced in 1990 by the same Southern California sportswear designers who created both the punky and Day-Glo "Life's A Beach" surf clothes in the '80s. The intrepid motto perfectly captured the EXTREME SPORTS ethos and made it accessible to those who didn't necessarily want to SNOWBOARD down a 45-degree incline. No Fear became so virulent among the "Just Do It" sports set that the company was able to launch its first TV ad during the 1995 Super Bowl. The brand was also one of the most heavily pirated clothes logos of the early '90s, to the point where the company estimated in 1993 that "counterfeiters are making as many T-shirts as we are." The brand's bawdy sub-slogan "Will Work for Sex" echoes the popularity of the more downmarket COED NAKED T-shirts.

noir Abbreviation of "*film noir*," a term coined by French film critics to describe a dark, cynical strain of mid-century American crime movies. As the term suggests, these pictures—typified by John Huston's *The Maltese Falcon* (1941), Billy Wilder's *Double Indemnity* (1944), and Howard Hawks's *The Big Sleep* (1946)—were more black than white, tending to dwell on characters that inhabited the underside of the American Dream. *Noir* gained renewed currency from the early '80s on with a series of direct *homages* (the most eminent being 1981's *Body Heat*) and stylistic adaptations (notably *Blade Runner* [1982] and the COEN BROTHERS' *Blood Simple* [1984]). In recent years, *noir* has become—as well as a catch-all adjective—an established, some would say stultifying, part of the vocabulary of many commercial directors, photographers, and video- and moviemakers. Apart from many unsuccessful, overly literal attempts at *noir*, 1994's *The Last Seduction* is often singled out as a laudable attempt to recapture the original spirit.

nonlinear film editing Video and film version of DESKTOP PUBLISHING's onscreen cut-and-paste, making decent film production standards affordable and accessible. Nonlinear film editing software replaces traditional film cutting (or far clumsier video duping) with clean digital edits and effects. The evolution of computerized tools began with the primitive ADO system in the '80s; the first useful software to run on personal computers appeared in the early '90s from Editing Machines Corp., and Avid. By 1994 powerhorses included the ImMIX VideoCube, Ediflex, and the Hollywood features favorite, Lightworks. The continuing price-plummet suggests a near future when the average word processor will be capable of feature film post-production work.

Noon, Jeff (b. 1957) Novelist whose heavily promoted debut *Vurt* (1994) made him the first British CYBERPUNK star to achieve U.S. renown. In the book, Noon inverts sci-fi form by projecting the future into the present rather than vice versa. The characters ramble around gray neighborhoods that resemble Noon's native Manchester, consuming the colored Vurt feathers that provide a wide variety of trips melding VIRTUAL REALITY and dreams. The book's young protagonist is on an Orpheus-like search for a sister-lover lost in Vurt purgatory. A former PUNK rocker who possesses a gleeful no-future perspective, Noon also taps into deep emotional terrain at the expense of cyberpunk's usual technofetishism. *Pollen* (1995, U.K.), the second novel in Noon's *Vurt* tetralogy, offered a somewhat lighter look at the same scene a dozen years later, when the Vurt world invades the real world with a plague of hay fever.

Norplant   Highly effective, long-term female contraceptive consisting of matchstick-sized rods that are surgically inserted into the upper arm. The rods, which release a trickle of the anti-fertility hormone progestin, are effective for five years and cost much less than a comparable supply of birth control pills. The ostensibly hassle-free Norplant was hailed as a breakthrough when it was introduced in the U.S. in 1991. By 1994 more than one million women were using it, and studies found the device far more effective than the pill in preventing teen pregnancy. Nevertheless, Norplant became embroiled in a series of political and medical controversies. Liberals were accused of genocide for encouraging Norplant use in Baltimore public high schools, while conservatives (including Louisiana Klan leader and state legislator David Duke) pushed schemes linking the implant to welfare support (thus many of the myths among poor women about Norplant's dramatic health risks). In 1994 a class action suit was filed by women who had painful experiences getting the rods extracted; that same year Norplant lost more of its luster with the arrival of the less expensive DEPO PROVERA.

WEB **Contraception Resources**
http://www.cmpharm.ucsf.edu/
~troyer/safesex/contraception.html

NRA   Founded in 1871 by Union Army veterans unnerved by the incompetence of Civil War riflemen, the National Rifle Association first became a player in national gun-control politics after the passage of the Gun Control Act of 1968. After seeing membership rise threefold from nearly a million in the '70s, the NRA spent the '80s consolidating its power as a feared legislative lobby. The modest gun control victories of the early '90s—the 1993 Brady Bill, which required a five-day waiting period for handgun purchases, and the 1994 ban on more than a dozen classes of assault weapons—shifted the NRA's base away from sportsmen, collectors, and gun-safety advocates and toward more radical pro-MILITIA and anti-government elements. In March of 1995, in the wake of the Oklahoma City bombing, the NRA sent a fundraising letter that referred to federal officials as "jackbooted government thugs." While this rhetoric alarmed several longtime members—one, former President George Bush, resigned his lifetime membership in protest—the campaign seemed designed to galvanize the NRA's new militant core. In June '95 it was revealed that the group's expanded membership (3.4 million), and immense lobbying efforts, had come at the direct expense of the group's decades-old financial health.

WEB **NRA Home Page** http://www.nra.org/

Nutrament   Sugar-laden "Energy & Fitness Drink" popular among athletes when it was launched in the early 1960s. As the nation's health awareness increased, Nutrament was left behind by more efficacious products, and sales tailed off. The *Wall Street Journal* reported in 1994 that the previous year Nutrament's manufacturer Bristol-Myers Squibb Co. started vigorously marketing the drink to the inner-city market, where its supposed aphrodisiac, medical, and nutritional properties are legendary. But despite the upscale imagery that is used to sell it, Nutrament is known, along with Yoo-Hoo, as a favorite under-$2 comfort food among CRACK addicts.

O'Brien, Conan (b. 1963)
Former *SIMPSONS* and *SATURDAY NIGHT LIVE* writer and on-camera novice given the NBC timeslot vacated by David Letterman's exhaustively reported departure. *SNL* creator and former boss Lorne Michaels brought the six-foot-four redhead in as a potential head writer and producer for the new *Late Night*, but offered him the host's chair when Gary Shandling declined to accept. The show, which has built a solid college audience despite constant rumor of cancellation (dorm-dwellers not being wired for Nielsen ratings), reflects O'Brien's writing background (including presidency of the HARVARD LAMPOON) as well as his lack of performing experience. There are prodigious quantities of labor-intensive, often brilliant sketch humor ("interviews" with newsmakers consist of moving lips seen through a cut-out photo of Ronald Reagan or President Clinton); then there is O'Brien's often tentative interview style. Round-faced sidekick Andy Richter, widely reviled in the show's early months as an overgrown frat-boy, has been key to many of the show's best routines (e.g. "In the Year 2000" and "Staring Contest").

WEB **alt.fan.conan-o'brien FAQ** http://www.cis. ohio-state.edu/hypertext/faq/usenet/conan-obrien-faq/faq.html

✦ USENET **alt.fan.conan-obrien**

O'Connor, Sinead (b. 1966)   On October 3rd, 1992, this powerful Irish singer appeared on *SATURDAY NIGHT LIVE* on the strength of her PRINCE-written #1 ballad "Nothing Compares 2U." After performing an a cappella version of the BOB MARLEY song "War," O'Connor pulled out a picture of Pope John Paul II and ripped it up, spluttering "Fight the real enemy!" A predictable wave of media outrage ensued, and when O'Connor appeared at a Bob Dylan tribute show two weeks later, she was roundly booed for her televised temerity. O'Connor's subsequent career slide cannot solely be attributed to her anti-Papal sentiments, however: this former COLLEGE RADIO favorite didn't help her situation by recording in 1993 *Am I Not Your Girl?*, an album of big-band standards. It was not until her interrupted stint on the 1995 LOLLAPALOOZA tour that O'Connor was able to take her rightful place among the new generation of female ALTERNATIVE rockers.

WEB **The Sinead O'Connor Homepage** http:// www.engr.ukans.edu/~jrussell/music/sinead/sinead.html

Oakley   Futuristic-looking, brightly hued "performance" eyewear beloved of aspiring jocks everywhere, often associated with the MULLET haircut, and marketed with the tag-line "Thermonuclear Protection." Innovative Oakley designs like the aerodynamic M Strip, V frames and the Zeroes collection (with its anti-UV "Plutonite" lenses) have much to do with the company's primacy in the "activewear" market, but one mall owner had an equally plausible explanation for the *Los Angeles Times* in 1993: "[People] come in here and try on a pair of sunglasses and say, 'Oh, now I look just like Arnold Schwarzenegger,' and they'll say it with his accent."

Offspring   Unassuming band from the unlikely PUNK bastion of Orange County, California, whose unanticipated third album *Smash* sold 4 million copies. The record, released by influential punk INDIE Epitaph in March 1994, was announced by the single "Come Out and Play (Keep 'em Separated)," a song whose novelty Arabic guitar hook and bouncy aggression tapped the same nouveau-PUNK-pop Zeitgeist that put GREEN DAY over the top. Perhaps because of their very inoffensiveness, Offspring (whose first single was released in 1987) managed to offend many of the punk faithful; their long-hair, college educations, and mainstream fans didn't help matters, nor did a pop sensibility that was further proven by the thrash-pop anthem "Self Esteem" (a close relative, like many contemporary hits, of NIRVANA'S "Smells Like Teen Spirit").

WEB **Epitaph Records** http://nebuleuse. enst-bretagne.fr:80/~lepoulti/BAD.RELIGION/EPITAPH/

OK Soda   Downbeat soft drink introduced in selected cities by Coca-Cola in mid–1994. The brainchild of Coke marketing chief Sergio Zyman (who also developed the NEW AGE "brainwater" FRUITOPIA), OK Soda targeted the GENERATION X marketing niche by packaging an off-tasting beverage in matte-gray cans featuring slackers drawn by comic book artist DAN CLOWES and CHARLES BURNS. With an advertising scheme developed by PORTLAND ad power Wieden & Kennedy, the OK Soda's launch featured offbeat slogans like "don't think there has to be a reason for everything." There was a 1–800-I-FEEL-OK hotline, where callers could record comments, listen to the cynical comments of others (ad agency plants, it transpired), and undergo a "personality test" that included such true/false statements as: "Sometimes my TV sends special messages to me." OK Soda's message failed to penetrate: lackluster sales led to its 1995 re-packaging as a "unique fruity soda."

WEB **OK Soda Home Page** http://spleen.mit.edu/ok.html

Courtesy of The Coca-Cola Company

OK Soda–what GRUNGE tastes like.

Oldham, Todd (b. 1962) Born in Corpus Christi, Texas, Todd Oldham started his design career at age 15 by sewing two K-Mart pillowcases together to make a sundress for his sister. He moved to New York in 1988 and began producing campy, lighthearted fashion inspired by everything from paint-by-numbers art to video Yule logs. With his magpie eye, POLITICALLY CORRECT NEW AGE-y attitude, and unfailingly polite, aw-shucks manner, Oldham gently thumbs his nose at the fashion establishment without being iconoclastic. "All in all, I'm not interested in this industry. I find it very vapid and silly" he told *Paper* magazine in 1994, not long before signing a lucrative part-time creative consulting contract with Escada, the German fash-

ion colossus. A regular on MTV's *House of Style*, Oldham is also a franchise-friendly creator of product lines for the MTV, VH1, and NICKELODEON group; a line of Oldham originals based on *Batman Forever* (1995) were sold in Warner Bros. Studio stores.

Olympia, Washington State capital; independent-minded musical neighbor of SEATTLE; home to the legendarily liberal Evergreen State University. The RIOT GRRRL movement was as much a part of Olympia as it was of Washington, D.C.; the town (population 33,000) is also home to K Records, an independent label of enduring, if small influence. K was founded by Candice Pedersen and Calvin Johnson (whom *L.A. Weekly* once called "the human HELLO KITTY"). Beat Happening, lead by Johnson, are proponents of "love rock," the skeletal, fey sub-genre for which the Olympia scene is otherwise known. K music tends toward a naive honesty that to its admirers sounds affecting (and detractors regard as the musical equivalent of finger-painting). In August 1991 Johnson staged the International Pop Underground Convention, a six-day series of concerts and folksy activities that has become fabled in the INDIE-ROCK community for the familial spirit that prevailed.

WEB **Your K Homepage** http://www.wln.com/~kpunk/ ✦ EMAIL KEmpire@aol.com ✦ WEB **Our Home Town** http://164.116.97.22/olympia/oly1.html/

online press conferences Celebrity cyber-appearances, at their best creating unprecedented communication between mass culture stars and their fans, at their worst, tightly moderated publicity stunts that offer little more than a radio call-in show slowed down by typing. Such events on commercial services like AMERICA ONLINE became standard tour stops in mid–1994, but—far from retrofitting fame for the 21st century—the main effect was to validate the online world, suggesting that cyberspace is a big celebrity hangout where one may land a date with a SUPERMODEL, talk about drugs with Mick Jagger, get backstage at the Oscars with Joan Rivers, play mission control to orbiting astronauts, or express one's hopes for Haitian democracy to President Jean-Bertrand Aristide.

Open Magazine Westfield, New Jersey-based pamphlet series, often timed to coincide with political events. The first edition of Greg Ruggiero (b. 1964) and Stuart Sahulka's (b. 1965) activist publishing venture was NOAM CHOMSKY's "On U.S. Gulf Policy," released just prior to the Gulf War in January 1991. Open pamphlets contain eight-to-ten-thousand word essays, lectures, and reports by social critics like Chomsky ("The New World Order"), Edward Said ("Peace in the Middle East"), and MIKE DAVIS ("The L.A. Riots"). With these and several indie bookstore best-sellers to their credit, Ruggiero and Sahulka started the Open Magazine Radio Series. The pair's Immediast Underground publications promotes "the liberation of all public space from government, corporate and business messages" with titles that include The Immediast Underground's "Seizing the Media" and Mark Dery's "Media Hackers."

Operation Rescue Anti-abortion group that radicalized the pro-life movement in the late '80s through mammoth clinic blockades and rhetoric equating abortion with murder and the Holocaust. Randall Terry (b. 1959), who founded OR in 1987 while working as a used-car salesman in upstate New York, is credited with originating anti-abortion civil disobedience and militancy. The group's protests first came to the country's attention at the 1988 Democratic National Convention in Atlanta and peaked with the 46-day shutdown of Wichita, Kansas, in 1991. Three years later OR was in splinters. In the month of May 1994, RU–486 was licensed for U.S. production, the Freedom of Access to Clinic Entrances Act was signed into law, and a Houston jury ordered OR members to pay $1 million in punitive damages for a 1992 blockade of a local Planned Parenthood clinic. The Catholic Church also began to grow wary of the sidewalk counseling, surveillance, blockade, and harassment tactics taught at the group's Melbourne, Florida, training center. After Minneapolis was selected by

OR in 1993 as one of seven "cities of refuge," the Archbishop there explicitly asked OR to stay away.

The March 1993 murder of Florida doctor David Gunn (see ABORTION CLINIC VIOLENCE) led to a split between those condoning and condemning the violence—Terry left OR for the MILITIA-affiliated United States Taxpayers Party, while some of the group's most strident leaders formed the American Coalition of Life Activists, a group that in 1995 published a "Deadly Dozen" list targeting 12 American abortion doctors for harassment.

WEB **LifeLinks** http://copper.ucs.indiana.edu/~ljray/lifelink.html/ ◆ WEB **Who's Who on the Anti-Choice Front** http://www.cais.com/agm/whoswho.htm/

Oralet Raspberry-flavored narcotic lollipop; the first sedative approved for children. The Anesta company's fentanyl candy was approved by the FDA in October 1993 for use calming kids before undergoing often traumatic preoperative anesthesia, but Abbott Labs' controlled roll-out was then delayed for a year while the FDA decided how to make sure that doctors didn't over-prescribe this highly efficacious pacifier. Studies have shown that children are chronically undermedicated for pain: many practicing doctors were educated when it was still widely believed that infants couldn't feel much with their underdeveloped nervous systems. Before Oralet, doctors who gave painkillers to kids relied on their own recipes for adult sedative cocktails such as Versed diluted with cherry Tylenol syrup.

Courtesy of Anesta Company

ORALET lollipop–pacifier by prescription.

otaku Japanese expression for an obsessive fan or hobbyist, taken from "otaku-zoku," which translates as "home tribe." Otaku mythology roughly corresponds to America's anti-social computer HACKER, but the passion for obscure trivia (often traded as databases over computer networks) also attaches to a wide variety of pop enthusiasms from VIDEOGAMES,

Ultraman, and MANGA to teen idol singers, American HIP-HOP, and HONG KONG ACTION MOVIES. Though still something of an insult in Japan along the lines of "homebody" or "fanboy," the term has gained currency, in part via the INTERNET, as a badge of honor among American ANIME devotees.

WEB **The HomePage of the Otaku Animation Association**
http://ucsu.colorado.edu/~oaa/Home.html/

outing   Practice of forcing lesbian and gay celebrities "out of the closet." The term's coinage was prompted by Michelangelo Signorile's (b. 1960) "The Secret Gay Life of Malcolm Forbes," a March 1990 *Outweek* story which appeared one month after the millionaire's death. Signorile's action—dubbed "outing" by *Time* magazine—engendered ferocious debates over journalistic ethics. Gay, closeted public figures were accused of hypocrisy, and their would-be exposers were charged with "lavender fascism." Signorile's defenders pointed out the mainstream media's own growing appetite for selectively exposing the private lives of public figures and argued that outing would help erase the prurient stigma of homosexuality.

In the "Peek-a-Boo" corner of his *OutWeek* column, the unrepentant Signorile fingered other New York, D.C., and Hollywood targets. The ACT-UP spin-off QUEER NATION, which Signorile helped found, also plastered downtown Manhattan with posters declaring the homosexuality of public figures. (Parodists followed with "exposés" of celebrity toupee-wearers.) The issue was revisited in 1995 when *Advertising Age* broke media ranks and, by reporting the details of Jann Wenner's failed marriage, unleashed its more salacious competitors on the *ROLLING STONE* founder.

USENET **alt.politics.homosexuality**

P-FLAG Parents, Families & Friends of Lesbians & Gays. A potent symbol of tolerance and support in the gay rights movement, P-FLAG often evokes tearful ovations at gay pride marches. P-FLAG began informally in San Francisco in the early '70s, was incorporated in 1981, and expanded nationally through local chapters in the '80s. Its greatest growth, however, has come in recent years as the country's culture battle over homosexual rights has extended to middle America. P-FLAG claimed 350 chapters and 30,000 member households at its 1994 annual convention. The media relies on the group for its bounty of heart-rending, human interest "I was a conservative, church-going Republican" interviewees who can talk about "coming out" as the parent of a gay or lesbian child.

WEB **P-FLAG/L.V. Homepage** http://www.geopages.com/ WestHollywood/1082/

Speed-talker CAMILLE PAGLIA strikes a pose on her 1994 essay collection.

Paglia, Camille (b. 1947) Art history academic; speed-talking, eminently quotable assassin of the feminist establishment; and fanciful, often out-of-step pop culture commentator. A self-proclaimed child of the '60s, this severe-looking, close-cropped lesbian champions its causes—sexual liberation, democratic folk art—to defend '90s cash cows like the Rolling Stones and MADONNA against "puritanic, anti-progress" cultural critics. Her academic tome *Sexual Personae* (1990)—which argued that great art derives from male lust—contained ad hominem attacks on the "weakness of those who cry DATE RAPE." But it was a *New York Times* Op-Ed essay proclaiming Madonna as a true feminist that launched Paglia's media career as a pro-porn celebrator of sexual experimentation and enemy of "that Stalinist Gloria Steinem." One sure sign of Paglia's overexposure was her 1995 *Esquire* magazine interview with Tim Allen, the affable star of the family sitcom *Home Improvement.*

WEB **The Camila Paglia Checklist** http://www.cs. tuberlin.de/~jutta/cpc/index.html

paintball High-tech game of tag for weekend warriors, corporate staff, and even a few pro competitors. Associated with camouflage draped suburban survivalists in the '80s, in the mid-'90s the sport boasts ESPN coverage and hundreds of in- and outdoor arenas in the U.S. alone, not counting unlicensed warehouse and backroad variants. The sport is said to have begun in California with cattle-marking pellets launched from slingshots; by 1992 *Action Pursuit Games* magazine estimated that five million people had played at least once and that manufacturers of the gumball-sized, paint-filled gelatin ammunition sold one billion rounds. Paintball artillery ranges from simple pump pistols up to CO_2 cartridge-driven machine guns with custom ammo bandoleers and even paintball grenades, paintball mines and paintball rocket launchers. Direct hits often leave welts or bruises. Light-based toy versions like Photon and Laser Tag have also been popular toys since the late '80s.

WEB **Warpig Paintball Home Page** http://warpig.cati. csufresno.edu/paintball/paintball.html/ ◆ USENET **rec.sport.paintball**

Palac, Lisa (b. 1964) Postfeminist cyber-entrepreneur whose *Future Sex* magazine (published quarterly since 1992) heralded a world where modems and vibrators commingle, and "non-exploitative pornography" is the order of the day. A fallen disciple of anti-porn lawyer Catharine MacKinnon, Palac moved to San Francisco from Minneapolis in 1989 to work (as Lisa LaBia) with SUSIE BRIGHT on the pioneering lesbian sex magazine, *On Our Backs. Future Sex,* in reality a rather prosaic product, brought Palac abundant attention from media makers drawn as much to her magazine's giggle and jiggle as its promises of technotopia. In 1993, with the financial support of TIME WARNER, Palac produced the first in a series of *Cyborgasm* CD's, a "virtual audio sex" experience.

Panter, Gary (b. 1950) Texas-born, New York-based artist whose career took off alongside the do-it-yourself amphetamine burst of the late-'70s Los Angeles PUNK scene. A virtuoso of scratchy drawing and painting, Panter works a fine line between "high" art and the commercial spontaneity of countless illustrations and album covers. Beginning in the pages of the L.A. proto-ZINE *Slash*, his *Jimbo* is published by *SIMPSONS* creator Matt Groening's Bongo Comics Group. Responsible in great part for the surreal visual impact of *Pee-Wee's Playhouse* (1986–1991), Panter has described his work as a conjunction of Mexican mural art and Jack Kirby's *Fantastic Four*. In addition to his many side projects, Panter edits the comic *Go Naked* and has recorded a pair of albums, *Savage Pencil Presents "One Hell Soundwich"* (1990), with longtime accomplice Jay Condom, and *Pray for Smurf* (1993).

WEB **Seconds Interview** http://www.iuma.com/ Seconds/html/issue28/Gary_Panter.html

parachute kids Teenagers, mainly of wealthy Taiwanese families, shipped off to live in America where they can benefit from the less-pressured, less-competitive educational system, establish residency, and, in many cases, avoid military service at home. Known as "xiao liu xue sheng" ("little overseas students") in Taiwan, parachute kids are simply called "unaccompanied minors" by the social workers helping pick up the pieces after "astronaut parents." A 1992 study found between 30,000 and 40,000, with the highest concentration in the posh Southern Californian towns of San Gabriel and Hacienda Heights. Though many parachute kids are indulged with money and freedom beyond the dreams of the typical high school student, other parachute kids pay their way as indentured servants for "paper aunties and uncles" who cash support checks. Parachute horror stories involving drugs and gang violence are a staple of the Korean, Hong Kong, and Taiwanese press.

Parental Advisory: Explicit Lyrics Black and white warning label adopted voluntarily by the Recording Industry Association of America, representing all major record companies, in 1990 to head off mandatory labeling bills moving through state legislatures. Many retail chains began treating stickered albums as the equivalent of R-rated movies, restricting sales to 18-year-olds and over. The first year of the new policy, a Florida clerk was arrested for selling a 2 LIVE CREW album to a minor. Follow-up efforts included a 1992 Washington State ban on lewd lyrics and, in 1994, a back-up label from Epic Records: "The lyric content contained on this album solely expresses the views of the artist." Recent furors over album lyrics—including Republican virtue-monger William Bennett's 1995 attacks on TIME WARNER and GANGSTA rap—can be traced to the Parents Music Resource Center, co-founded in 1984 by Tipper Gore, and subsequent 1985 Senate hearings featuring FRANK ZAPPA and Twisted Sister's Dee Snider (addressed by Senators as "Mr. Sister"). The PMRC's original proposal was to label records: "V" for violence, "X" for sex, "D/A" for drugs or alcohol, and "O" for occult.

WEB **General Questions (Frank Zappa and the PMRC)** http://www.fwi.uva.nl/~heederik/zappa/faq/main/main–2.html

Partnership for a Drug Free America Non-profit sponsor of public service ad campaigns to "unsell" illegal drugs by portraying drug use as both dangerous and unhip. The Partnership was founded in 1986 as the advertising industry's affirmative response to Nancy Reagan's "Just Say No" anti-drug drive. The "Drugs Don't Work" campaign (begun 1993) also urges employers to strive for "drug-free workplaces" in part through DRUG TESTING. Dozens of ads, using billions of dollars of television and print advertising space, have been donated over the years from the same media and ad agencies that depend fiscally on alcohol and tobacco advertisers. PSAs include the "This is your brain. This is your brain on drugs" fried-egg ad that has become, in parody form, a T-shirt classic; another 1987 ad supposedly depicted the brain waves of a 14-year-old smoking pot (the monitor reading was actually that of a coma patient); and a

print ad targeting parents with the image of a dissolute preteen in a jean jacket under the message "What she's going through isn't a phase. It's an ounce a week." This claim bespoke a consumption rate that would challenge the most hardened pothead (not to mention a four-figure monthly budget). Until the advent of '90s MARIJUANA CHIC, the Partnership was frequently credited as a factor in the decline of drug use among teens.

Patagonia   Sportswear company spun off in 1974 from the equipment company of French rock-climbing legend Yvon Chouinard (b. 1938). Patagonia sales topped $100 million by 1991 thanks to Chouinard's designs, which were both more practical and more colorful than those of his earth-toned rivals. (Patagonia's exotic colors and Aztec patterns are still demure compared to the prevailing neon hues of ski-wear.) In 1984 Patagonia started channeling part of its revenue to environmental charities, later catching flak for encouraging the radical EARTH FIRST! organization. (The *Los Angeles Times* called the company's catalog the "tree-hugger's *Playboy*.") At Chouinard's behest, Patagonia introduced more environmentally friendly products, notably "synchilla," the fleecy material made from recycled plastic bottles. In recent years Patagonia (called Pata*gucci* by some Northeastern preppies) has catered to a burgeoning Northwestern outdoors aesthetic that also prevails among many DEADHEADS: their zipper-jackets are the basic element of a look that commonly incorporates cut-off army pants with TEVA sandals or all-surface NIKE "lava" boots.

Pavement   Stockton, California-based exponents of slacker angst and defiant LO-FI production. Pavement became INDIE-ROCK critical favorites on the strength of two elliptical LPs, *Slanted and Enchanted* (1992) and *Crooked Rain, Crooked Rain* (1994). The band tends to deliberately corrupt winsome melodies with sketchy arrangements, cracked vocals, and snotty lyrics; "Range Life," for instance, goes from an aching soft-rock chorus to a sneering critique of GRUNGE pariahs the STONE TEMPLE

PAVEMENT rock out, elliptically, 1994.

PILOTS. *Wowee Zowee!*, Pavement's third LP, was released in the spring of 1995; while the album sounded much like its predecessors, it was a tribute to the band's inscrutability that critics scrambled to find a trajectory of development. (Some suggested that the band had sacrificed the last shreds of its ALTERNATIVE credibility to make an accessible pop record, others insisted that the LP marked a return to willful eclecticism and fragmentation.)

WEB **Mookie's Pavement Page**
http://weber.u.washington.edu/~mookie/pavement.cgi

Pearl Jam   Band formed by Stone Gossard (b. 1966) and Jeff Ament (b. 1963) of SEATTLE's Mother Love Bone after singer Andrew Wood (b. 1966; d. 1990) overdosed on HEROIN. (Gossard and Ament had previously been in seminal SUB POP band Green River.) California surfer-singer-gas-station attendant Eddie Vedder (b. Edward Louis Seversen III, 1964) was suggested as Wood's replacement by former RED HOT CHILI PEPPERS drummer Jack Irons, and was enlisted after submitting sample lyrics. The newly christened Pearl Jam released their debut album *Ten* in September 1991, just as NIRVANA unleashed *Nevermind.* Although Nirvana made the dramatic impression, the more orthodox Pearl Jam would far outstrip them in sales: their blues-rock take on GRUNGE settled alongside both classic and alternative rock radio formats, and Vedder's overwrought, publicity-shy persona fit comfortably into the rock-poet archetype of yore. (Many of their alliances reinforce this impression: they have supported Rolling Stone Keith Richards, and at the 1993 MTV awards backed NEIL YOUNG, with whom they would later record and tour; Vedder appeared at tribute concerts to Bob Dylan and Pete Townshend of The Who, and flirted with self-parody by filling in for the late Jim Morrison when the Doors were inducted to the ROCK AND ROLL HALL OF FAME in January 1993.) When their second album *Vs.* entered the *Billboard* charts at #1 in October 1993, *Ten* was a chart fixture, certified nine-times platinum; the band was now in the rare position of being able to refuse to make promo videos.

Although their stock has never been particularly high in the INDIE-ROCK community, Pearl Jam showed in May 1994 that they took the PUNK ethic as seriously as anyone, filing a complaint with the Justice Department against TICKETMASTER. A year later, Ticketmaster was found guilty of no wrongdoing, and there was an notable absence of vocal support for Pearl Jam among fellow rock stars. In June 1995 the band started, stopped, then restarted a non-Ticketmaster tour; their manager announced in *ROLLING STONE* that Pearl Jam would in future play only "about thirty shows a year."

WEB **The Official Unofficial Pearl Jam Page**
http://www.temple.edu/~rossdst/pj_link.html ✦ USENET
alt.music.pearl-jam ✦ WEB **Pearl Jam Fan Page**
http://www.engin.umich.edu/~galvin/pearljam.html/

Peltier, Leonard (b. 1944) American Indian Movement activist serving two life terms at Leavenworth Federal Penitentiary in Kansas for the June 1975 execution-style murder of two FBI agents on the Lakota Sioux's Pine Ridge Indian Reservation in South Dakota. The government's case against Peltier (pronounced Pel-TEER) has been judged harshly by the likes of filmmaker Michael Apted (1992 documentary *Incident at Oglala*), AMNESTY INTERNATIONAL (which classifies Peltier as a political prisoner), and even by the federal judge who spoke out publicly against the FBI after dismissing Peltier's appeals on technical grounds. Some 500,000 signatures supporting clemency for Peltier were delivered to the White House in 1993.

WEB **International Office of the Leonard Peltier Defense Committee** http://www.unicom.net/peltier/index.html/

Penn, Sean (b. 1960) Character-actor son of director Leo Penn and actress Eileen Ryan. Penn's first major role came in military academy drama *Taps* (1981), but his star rose with the following year's portrayal of surfer-stoner Jeff Spicoli in the hit (and enduring cult favorite) *Fast Times at Ridgemont High* (1982). In subsequent films like *The Falcon and the Snowman* (1985), *At Close Range* (1986), *Casualties of War* (1989), and *Colors* (1988), Penn's penchant for detestable characters set him apart from his good-guy, romantic lead contemporaries in terms of both acuity and talent, but created public-image problems. When he married MADONNA in August 1985 overweening paparazzi attention provoked a series of altercations that eventually led to Penn serving one month in the L.A. County jail for assaulting a photographer. (Since Penn and Madonna divorced in early 1989, he has largely avoided publicity and has had two children with actress Robin Wright, from whom he is estranged.)

After filming *State of Grace* (1990), Penn formally retired from acting (but for a brief return as a detestable coke-fiend/lawyer in *Carlito's Way*, 1993) to focus on his work as a director. Penn's elegiac debut film *The Indian Runner* (1991, based on a Bruce Springsteen song) debuted at the Cannes Film Festival and was a critical success if not a commercial hit. Penn's next directorial project, *The Crossing Guard* (reportedly completed for fall 1994 release), was rejected for the 1995 Cannes festival, then held by MIRAMAX until its late 1995 release.

WEB **Jeff Spicoli Page** http://turtle.ncsa.uiuc.edu/spicoli/

Personal Digital Assistant Handheld, pen-based sub-sub-notebook computer with the feel of a *STAR TREK* "tricorder." Apple, AT&T, Sharp, and Sony thought as late as 1993 that such devices would be in common circulation by the end of 1994. In their mildly sci-fi scenario, we would all be taking notes and phone calls, making dates, reading email, and beaming faxes and computer files at PDA-friendly, networked kiosks all over campuses, malls, and corporate offices. The handwriting-recognition shortcomings of the first widely market PDA, Apple's 1993 Newton, supplied *Doonesbury* with a week's worth of punchlines; Sony's MagicLink, launched in late '94, concentrated more successfully on basic Filofax and "communicator" functions, and was the first product to use the bally-hooed "intelligent agent" software by Apple spin-off General Magic.

WEB **Sir Isaac's Spot: The World Of Newton And Other PDAs** http://www.netaxs.com/people/bluesky/Newton.html

✦ USENET **comp.sys.palmtops**

Peruvian hats   Knitted, brightly patterned headgear (known locally as *chullos*) that achieved popularity in the '80s among the outdoors and DEADHEAD elements of PREPPY culture. The multi-cultural statement became a HIP-HOP fashion between 1991–93. With its pointy head, and draw-strings attached to an ear-piece designed to keep Peruvian Indians' ears warm miles above sea level, the hat tended to make all but the toughest non-rural wearers look ludicrous—as was amply proved by Chris Barron, the goat-bearded frontman of the Spin Doctors.

Pervitin   Cheap amphetamine with cocaine-like effects synthesized from cooking the ephedrine found in many over-the-counter cough syrups with iodine and phosphorus. Pervitin is closely associated with PRAGUE, where it became a behind-the-iron-curtain drug of choice in the '60s and '70s. As Prague emerged as a European youth capital in the '90s, small-scale use in clubs and parties turned into a major export business of "Piko" capsules to nearby Holland and Germany. The drug was supposedly invented by the Nazis to stimulate soldiers and, through sales to the Japanese military, kamikaze pilots.

PETA   People for the Ethical Treatment of Animals; best-known animal rights group of the '90s. PETA ad campaigns include the 1994 "I'd rather go naked than wear fur," for which SUPER-MODELS Cindy Crawford, Christy Turlington, and others posed in the nude. PETA opposes a wide range of animal products and uses, including leather, down, wool, silk, pets, zoos, rodeos, and any medical research which involves animal experimentation. (Not all of PETA's many celebrity support-ers—recruited by charismatic co-founder, former model Dan Mathews—are aware of the orga-nization's wider agenda, as RICKI LAKE discovered when David Letterman grilled her for showing up in leather shoes shortly after her arrest at a 1994 PETA action.) The Maryland-based group, which distributes free of charge a disturbing videotape of animals in pain, was heavily criticized in 1991 for running an $11,000 full-page ad in the *Des Moines Register* comparing SERIAL KILLER Jeffry Dahmer's drugging, murder, and dismemberment to the cor-porate treatment of animals. Official PETA policy neither "condemns nor condones" the more radical ANIMAL LIBERATION FRONT which PETA helps publicize.

WEB **PETA On-Line** http://envirolink.org/arrs/peta/home.html

PETA Catalog–Fall 1994

SUPERMODEL Cindy Crawford with fur, real and fake.

PGP   Pretty Good Privacy, a freely distributed but quasi-legal computer program that helps guarantee the privacy and authenticity of electronic messages using "public key cryptography," a form of com-puter encryption developed in the mid-'70s. First released by anti-nuclear activist Phil Zimmermann in 1991, PGP soon became the standard encryp-tion method for email on the INTERNET, to the point where CYPHERPUNKS and many cyber-liber-tarians consider it a badge of honor to include one's PGP "public key" in correspondence. (This works with the "private key" with which a user encrypts messages—in the words of the EFF's John Perry Barlow, "You can have my encryption algorithm . . . when you pry my cold dead fingers from my private key.") The program infringes on a U.S. patent held by the original commercial developers of public key cryptography, RSA Data Security, which in turn is fighting the U.S. government's attempt to limit the spread of encryption tools. The government, meanwhile, has been pursuing Zimmermann for making the program available on the INTERNET under laws prohibiting the export of munitions.

WEB **PGP Homepage** http://www.mantis.co.uk/pgp/pgp.html

✦ USENET **alt.security.pgp**

Liz PHAIR in high school, with flip–the crown jewel of the Liz Phair Gif O'Mania picture archive (http://www.armory.co m/~fisheye/gifs.html).

Phair, Liz (b. Elizabeth Clark Phair 1967)   In a 1994 interview with *Option* magazine Liz Phair called herself "an upper-middle-class cute girl with smart parents singing dirty words"—an acute self-summation from one of the smartest operators in INDIE-ROCK. This Oberlin-educated adopted daughter of Chicago professionals got her break via influential label Matador, which picked her up on the strength of the inchoate, now legendary *Girly Sound* demo tapes. Phair's first album *Exile In Guyville* was released in 1993 to almost universal critical acclaim: she titillated rock critics with some alarmingly frank writing about sex, relationships, and modern life— and with the brash (if absurd) claim that her debut was a track-by-track response to the Rolling Stones classic *Exile On Main Street*. If Phair's follow-up *Whip Smart* (1994) failed to reach its predicted gold status (500,000 sales), it certainly enhanced her reputation: again, searing subject matter ("Supernova"'s "you fuck like a volcano" was one oft-quoted line) compensated for shaky playing and uncertain pitch, and a dubious live reputation. Probably aware as anyone of her limitations as a mainstream act, Phair exerts near-total control over her output, staying resolutely humble in her production values, and even directing her own modestly budgeted videos.

WEB **LizNet: The Unofficial Liz Phair Home Page** http://cencongopher.concordia.ca/liz/

Phiber Optik (b. Mark Abene, 1972)   Master of computer and telephone technology, who led New York City's MOD (Masters of Deception) HACKER gang. The group made headlines in November, 1989 when it crashed computers at one of New York's public television stations, WNET, leaving the message, "Happy Thanksgiving you turkeys, from all of us at MOD." (Abene claims he was not involved in the stunt.) In July 1992, Abene and four other members of MOD were arrested for a mostly harmless series of computer break-ins; Abene pled guilty and served ten months of a one-year sentence in Pennsylvania's Schuylkill County Prison, where he received so many visits from journalists and TV crews that the other inmates nicknamed him CNN. Denied a computer in prison, Abene emerged as a folk hero; he was soon employed by his friend Stacy Horn of the ECHO bulletin board service. Abene's exploits were immortalized in the hacker hagiography *The Gang That Ruled Cyberspace*, by Michelle Slatalla and Joshua Quittner.

GOPHER **Phiber** gopher://gopher.well.sf.ca.us:70/00/ Publications/authors/dibbell/phiber/

Phish   From its 1985 origins as a Burlington, Vermont, bar band, this rambling, improvisational rock group has evolved into an arena-filling DEADHEAD-beloved phenomenon of eclectic American music. An instrumentally oriented, lyrically obtuse JAM BAND, Phish is as philosophically akin to the Art Ensemble of Chicago as the GRATEFUL DEAD. The band occasionally integrates audience concepts into its performances: a mail-in poll led the group to cover the entire Beatles *White Album* during a 1994 Halloween show; fan input also helped determine the content of a 1995 double live album. Phish's large online following manifests itself at live shows with the wearing of "rec.music.phish" T-shirts.

WEB **Phish.net Homepage**: http://archive.phish.net/phish ✦

WEB **Dan Hewins' Phish Page** http://www.cec.wustl.edu/
~hewins/music/phish.html ✦ USENET **rec.music.phish**

Phoenix, River (b. 1970; d. 1993) Sensitive teen idol, critically acclaimed for his openness and intensity, who strenuously advocated clean living. Phoenix died of drug-induced heart failure at L.A. celebrity hangout the VIPER ROOM on the night before Halloween, 1993.

Named for the river of life in Herman Hesse's counterculture novel, *Siddhartha*, River was raised by HIPPIE PARENTS who traveled widely with River, his brother, Leaf, and his sisters, Rain, Liberty, and Summer; born in Madras, Oregon, he spent most of his childhood in Venezuela where the parents worked as Children of God missionaries. Soon after the family's arrival in L.A., a 10-year-old Phoenix landed commercial roles that led to a TV series (*Seven Brides for Seven Brothers*, 1981) and a movie career of variable quality. He received an Oscar nomination for his supporting role in 1989's *Running On Empty*. But lauded films like *Stand By Me* (1986, made when Phoenix was 15) and GUS VAN SANT's *My Own Private Idaho* (1991) were far outnumbered by mundane teen and twentysomething fodder like *A Night in the Life of Jimmy Reardon* (1988) and the posthumously released *Thing Called Love*. Given this imbalance it is to Phoenix's credit that he was treated almost as a generational martyr; as such he foreshadowed the death, five months later, of NIRVANA's Kurt Cobain.

phone phreaks Mischievous persons who delight in exploration and manipulation of the telephone system. The vocation first developed in the '60s before computers were widely available, and the early achievements of phone phreaks dwarfed those of the crackers (SEE HACKERS) who eschewed the intricacies of the local phone switching office for those of the hardware chip and software operating system. Legends include one Cap'n Crunch, who was able to produce the 2600 hertz tone that gained control of the old phone system using a toy whistle from a box of cereal. The journal *2600* carries the phreak banner in the '90s.

WEB **Phrack Magazine** http://freeside.com/phrack.html
✦ WEB **2600** http://www.2600.com/ USENET **alt.2600**

phone sex Low-tech, billion-dollar-business which grew rapidly in the late '80s as phone companies began separate billing for 900 numbers and other pay lines. In 1989, the Supreme Court struck down a federal "dial-a-porn" law sponsored by Sen. Jesse Helms that outlawed charging for any "indecent" or "obscene" telephone talk (and was the basis for the 1995 COMMUNICATIONS DECENCY ACT). Such laws were perceived by the gay and lesbian press as an attack on safe sex, not to mention on their advertising base. Bored phone-sex workers have in recent years become common drama fodder, notably Robert Chesley's play "Jerker" (1987), JENNIFER JASON LEIGH as a weary housewife-sex worker in Robert Altman's *Short Cuts* (1993), and SPIKE LEE's *Girl 6* (1995). Not-for-profit "ear jobs" have also been portrayed, most extensively in NICHOLSON BAKER's novel *Vox* (1992). Federal prosecutors shut down TMD Enterprises, a Pennsylvania-based company, in 1994 for allegedly extorting more than $2 million by blackmailing users of phone sex lines. (The company purchased lists of phone sex deadbeats from around the country.) TMD scams, which included threatening to tell the superiors of those in the military that a caller owed money to a "gay chat line," collected as much as $100,000 a week.

WEB **The Hot Phone Sex Page** http://www.america.com/
~cruise/html/phonesex.html ✦ WEB **Complete Guide to
Internet Sex Resources** http://www.webcom.com/~
phonsex1/resorce.html

piercing Thousand-year-old practice in some Eastern countries, that arrived in America via, in order, S/M, PUNK, METAL, and SUPERMODEL subcultures. Beyond the barely-worth-mentioning earlobe, popular sites of puncture include the navel, nostril, nipple, eyebrow, and tongue. AEROSMITH's 1993 "Cryin'" video, in which ALICIA SILVERSTONE gets a navel ring and TATTOO, is credited by the GAUNTLET chain with mainstreaming what had been a West Coast underground fad.

More adventurous piercees go as far as the genitalia (one popular penis pierce is known as a "Prince Albert"). Proponents claim a well-performed pierce doesn't have to hurt much or—if capillaries are properly navigated—draw blood, and that the right pierce can provide added sexual sensitivity. Professional piercers caution to use the proper equipment—the type of piercing gun used on the earlobes is not sturdy enough to handle more resistant body parts. Poorly performed pierces, which can become infected, have led to a demand for the regulation of piercing parlors, most of which are still outgrowths of the semi-legal TATTOO trade. California governor Pete Wilson, however, vetoed such a bill in 1994, saying the health risks were minor. [See also MODERN PRIMITIVES.]

WEB **BME Piercing** http://www.io.org/~bme/bme-pirc.html ✦ WEB **Thuleboy's Body Modification** http://frank.mtsu.edu/ ~csc10004/bodmod.html ✦ WEB **An Introduction To The Scorpion** http://bronze.ucs.indiana.edu/ ~cpstone/scorp2.html ✦ WEB **Christian's Piercing Page** http://stripe.colorado.edu/~vanwoude/piercing.html ✦ WEB **Cort's Bodyart Page** http://www.halcyon.com/maelstrm/ meba.html ✦ WEB **David's Bodyart Page** http://www.rpi.edu/ ~bealsd/pierce.html ✦ WEB **Nomad Body Piercing Studio** http://web.sirius.com/~stas/NOMAD/nmdhome.html/ ✦ USENET **rec.arts.bodyart**

PIRGs   Student-run, grass-roots environmental and consumer Public Interest Research Groups, linked together in a network of state chapters (e.g. CALPIRG, NYPIRG) with a national parent, USPIRG. Founded in the early '70s and associated with consumer advocate Ralph Nader, PIRGs may be the closest thing America has to a real Green Party. But they are best known to high school and college students for the seemingly endless supply of "Jobs for the Environment" which draw the idealistic into door-to-door canvassing, less to organize communities than to collect petition signatures and earn fund-raising commissions that supplement the jobs' low pay.

WEB **Index of PIRGs** http://www.sandelman.ocunix.on.ca/ PIRGs

pit bulls   Stocky, powerful canines crossbred from bulldogs and terriers. Pit bulls were first brought to the U.S. in the late 19th century where they earned their name in pitfights on which spectators would bet. The dogs graduated from rural redneck terror to fierce urban presence with the rise of CRACK, as drug dealers began using the dogs for guard duty, dogfight gambling (depicted in the 1994 movie *Fresh*), and macho fashion statements. Gruesome reports of illegal dogfights and the training methods used to hone the animals' killer instinct regularly surface, including in 1994: the curious disappearance of people's pets in Northeast Philadelphia and their subsequent discovery as shredded carcasses in city parks; a Virginia videotape of people cheering and betting on a pitbull mauling a kitten; a Texas sheriff arrested at a dogfight whose only defense was that he showed up expecting a dogshow; and a bloody dogfighting arena, busted elsewhere in rural Texas, that was equipped with lights, bleachers, and kennels filled with 40 chained, snarling pit bulls.

WEB **Craig Foltz's Bully Archive** http://sculptor.as.arizona. edu/foltz/bullys/

Pitt, Brad (b. 1964)   When he insinuated himself into *Thelma and Louise* (1991) with washboard stomach and vagabond charm, Brad Pitt became something of a next-generation sex symbol, a HIMBO who hinted at a modicum of credibility. But the grungy blond looker lost momentum in low-profile indie-films and big-budget flops in which he seemed to bridle at the public's expectations of him. Pitt reprised the old charm with a bong-wielding cameo in the QUENTIN TARANTINO-scripted *True Romance* (1993). *Interview With the Vampire* (1994) and, especially, 1995's box office-hit *Legends of the Fall*, proved that Pitt as romantic lead could "open" a movie, and officially placed him at the locus of female desire in America. (Made official soon afterwards when *People* magazine voted Pitt the "Sexiest Man Alive.") A lesser form of notoriety came in the 1995 indie film *Living in Oblivion*, in which James LeGros performed a parody of a preening, clueless star said to be based on Pitt. The latter could take comfort in *Seven,* a box-office smash form the same year.

WEB **Brad Pitt Picture Gallery** http://www4.ncsu.edu/ eos/users/c/cajohnso/www/brad.html ✦ USENET **alt.fan.brad-pitt.**

Pixelvision   Launched as a children's toy in 1987, the Fisher-Price PXL 2000 was discontinued shortly afterwards for lack of marketshare. In its brief life the 2000—which retailed at around $100 and used fast-running audio cassettes as film stock—became a cult item among underground filmmakers. Sadie Benning (b. 1973) and Michael Almereyda (b. 1960) are its most renowned proponents of "Pixelvision": the former got a camera from her filmmmaker father when she was 15 and made a string of films, like *Welcome To Normal* (1990), about her lesbian awakening in Milwaukee, Wisconsin; the latter made the 56-minute feature *Another Girl Another Planet* (1992) entirely in Pixelvision. (Almereyda's 1995 film *Nadja* was partly filmed using the camera.) The original cameras are now reputed to fetch as much as $1,000.

Photo by David Corio

PJ HARVEY gets *jolie-laide*, in New York, 1995.

PJ Harvey (b. Polly Jean Harvey, 1969)   Singer from rural southwest England who earned acclaim for 1992's *Dry* LP, a debut which mixed brazen feminist politics with moody, minimalist rock. (To the consternation of record store rackers, Harvey called her *band* PJ Harvey.) An instant rock critics' darling, Harvey hastily recorded a follow-up: *Rid of Me* (1993), produced by STEVE ALBINI, firmed Harvey's commitment to erotics, politics,

and rock history (she covered Bob Dylan's "Highway 61 Revisited"). After disbanding her trio and releasing an album of *4-Track Demos* (1993) from the *Rid of Me* sessions, Harvey released *To Bring You My Love* (1995), a somber, high-profile LP on which she sought common ground between INDUSTRIAL rock and deep blues. Along the way, Harvey has manipulated her public image from defiant androgyny (*Dry*'s combat gear and guitar poses) to stark asexuality (on *Rid of Me* the rail-thin Harvey looks more starved child than rock star) to confident, even menacing, glamor (the cover photo of *To Bring You My Love*, all flowing SATIN and *jolie-laide* sensuality).

WEB **PJ Harvey WWW Page** http://www.louisville.edu/ ~jadour01/pjh/ ✦ MAIL LIST **PJ Harvey list** email majordomo@homer.louisville.edu with "subscribe pjh" in the message body ✦ WEB **Island Records** http://www.poly-gram.com/polygram/PJBio.html

platform sneakers   In the wake of the '70s-revival-inspired platform shoes, New York CLUB KIDS began to heighten the soles of their sneakers with add-on rubber soles. Regular sneakers, often CONVERSE or ADIDAS, would be taken to neighborhood cobblers in Manhattan who would add on the requisite levels, usually in alternating black and white levels. The trend became prominent at major-city clubs and RAVES in 1992; they were widely used in New York runway shows in November 1993, and designer Donna Karan produced her own version that year. Converse itself caught on the same year, producing its own, less outrageously lofted, line.

poleclimbers   Old-fashioned-looking lug-soled boots, also known as Georgia Boots after the name of one (Tennessee-based) manufacturer. DOC MARTENS may have taken over a decade to go from exotic cipher to mall staple, but poleclimbers—and their lower-cut relative, logger boots—seemed to do it overnight. First seen on fashionable feet around 1992, they quickly achieved ubiquity thanks to the rage for chunky footwear and for WORKWEAR generally; soon they were everywhere, from catwalk to

POLECLIMBERS–the soles that launched a thousand mutations.

Courtesy of Georgia Boot Company

MOSH pit, worn with dungarees and with SATIN SLIP DRESSES. (In May 1993 *Harper's Bazaar* quoted one flustered New York store manager as saying "people call us in a panic asking when our new shipments will be coming in.") As is now the case with most popular shoe styles, the poleclimber became a FOOTWEAR FASHION MUTATION when its sole was applied to an unlikely range of spin-offs.

political correctness See page 186.

Politically Incorrect Debate series on the Comedy Central network created and hosted by stand-up comedian Bill Maher (b. 1956). *Politically Incorrect*, which debuted in July 1993, is noted for the exotic juxtapositions within its four-guest panels: former *SASSY* editor Jane Pratt and N.R.A.-booster/former guitar hero Ted Nugent; libertarian Rush drummer Neil Peart and PROZAC celebrity Elizabeth Wurtzel; comedian Garry Shandling and human punchline KATO KAELIN; Arianna Huffington and, well, *anyone*. *P.I.*'s pan-cultural lineups breeze through the hot-button issues of the day, but contrary to its title the show has no set agenda of subversion. Quick-witted ringmaster Maher, however, often gives vent to his own knee-jerk contrarian urges in between tightly scripted tirades.
WEB **Comedy Central** http://www.comcentral.com/

Pop Eye Laguna Beach, California marketing firm that ranks alongside MTV as the most efficient processor of '90s youth culture. Founded in 1992 by former sportswear designer Suzi Chauvel (b. 1951), Pop Eye furnishes videos of the latest street fashions to a lengthy client list that includes NIKE,

Mattel, Speedo, Reebok, Pepsi, SNAPPLE, and Sony. For an annual subscription of around $3,000 these trend-hungry entities get three 90-minute tapes shot in the MTV style by Chauvel and her international agents at rock shows and cafés, SNOWBOARDING events and clubs. Subjects are interviewed and Chauvel interprets current trends, the better that the corporations might re-sell them.

poppers (amyl nitrate) Liquid inhalant drug (and inhaler paraphernalia) that has been part of gay club culture since the 1970s. Amyl nitrate was originally used by physicians in the 19th century to expand the arteries and relieve angina heart pains. The drug's brief, visceral high also tends to open up everything else, from the muscles of the anus to the experience of full orgasm—thus the poppers' popularity in the fast-sex disco era. The first article the *New York Times* ever ran about the AIDS epidemic, a July 1981 report about a mysterious "gay cancer," mentioned a pattern among those afflicted of amyl nitrite and LSD use "to heighten sexual pleasure." Ever since there has been inconclusive speculation that poppers are somehow related to the Kaposi's sarcoma of AIDS; the attention led in the '80s to state bans of over-the-counter sales of the glass ampules (which are broken—or "popped"—releasing the inhalable gas). People turned to butyl and other nitrites, leading Congress to outlaw sales of "aromas" in 1989 and 1990 for all but industrial uses (thus the subsequent classified ads in many gay magazines advertising carburetor cleansers).
WEB **rush** http://hyperreal.com/drugs/inhalants/rush ✦ WEB **Project Inform** http://www.hivnet.org/inform-www/index top.html ✦ WEB **AIDS FAQ** http://www.cis.ohio-state.edu/ hypertext/faq/usenet/aids-faq3/faq.html

Portland Lacking a Boeing to juice it up economically like its northern neighbor SEATTLE, the modest (pop. 440,000) metropolis of Portland, Oregon, is the quintessential '90s city. Too wet to attract sun-worshiping retirees or Brits, it boasts COFFEE BARS and microbreweries in good ratio, thus ensuring its populace a healthy emotional equilibrium. Home to the country's best bookstore, Powell's City of Books, Portland is neither a cultural wasteland nor an art mecca in spite of the steady stream of New York musicians who emigrate there to escape the East Coast sprawl. What will ultimately determine the city's fate, however, are the

more than half a million software and computer-assembly workers expected to flood its outlying suburbs by the end of the millennium. (Many of these will be successfully retrained loggers prohibited from working the state's environmentally protected forests.) The influence of nearby NIKE, in

political correctness

The origins of the phrase "political correctness" are lost somewhere in the rambling, clique-ridden history of the American left. Was the term first used by Depression-era Leninists to applaud vigilant party liners? Or did it migrate from China in tribute to Mao's various pronouncements on this-or-that form of rectitude? Was it a put-down of overzealous comrades? Or praise of the highest order?

Whatever the answers, by the early 1990s political correctness had transcended its sectarian origins and become a figure of everyday speech. "You're so uptight" became "You're so politically correct" as commentators of every persuasion sought the moral high ground by attaching the label to their opponents. The Comedy Central talk show *POLITICALLY INCORRECT* congratulated itself in its title for candid discussions of public issues; *PCU* (1994), a middling campus comedy, appeared briefly in movie theaters. Just about everyone agreed that it was both politically correct and fatuous to call a handicapped person "differently abled."

In part the attack on p.c. stemmed from a larger backlash against social changes, particularly in universities. As late as 1970, the University of Virginia, for example, did not admit any black students. Over the next two decades, blacks and women entered college in great numbers, and Afro-American and women's studies programs proliferated. Meanwhile, many corporations diversified their workforces, and set up "sensitivity training workshops" to make sure that the process went smoothly. Critics of political correctness— Dinesh D'Souza and Roger Kimball among them—sniped that these changes brought on a culture of intimidation. They argued that the liberal idea of "diversity" was really a very narrow one—a

diversity of skin colors but not of points of view. And they tirelessly documented incidents that suggested a climate of politically correct intolerance had settled over the land.

Some of these stories were arresting, and quickly achieved the status of national folklore; they became campus legends passed from mouth to mouth and from modem to modem. At the University of Pennsylvania, a student was investigated for hurling the insult "water buffaloes." At ANTIOCH College, students were instructed to ask for explicit consent at every stage of sexual foreplay. (In other words, sex was turned into something any college administrator would love: a negotiated exercise in conflict resolution.) And at the University of New Hampshire, a Congregationalist minister was accused of sexual harassment and suspended from his teaching job after he refused to apologize for the offense. The harassment, in this case, consisted of telling his students that writing was like sex. In time, his position was restored.

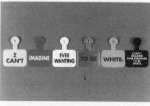

Daniel J. Martinez's "Museum Tags" distributed to visitors at the 1993 WHITNEY BIENNIAL.

Courtesy Robert Berman Gallery, Santa Monica, CA

For all their rhetorical savvy, p.c.'s conservative critics were often brazenly hypocritical. D'Souza, whose best-selling book, *Illiberal Education* (1991) excoriated campus thought control, had earlier written an admiring biography of that great free-thinker the Rev. Jerry Falwell. In a speech at the University of Michigan, President

Beavertown, is most directly felt through Wieden & Kennedy, the thriving ad agency world-renowned for "Just Do It."

Portland's current artistic community includes such cult figures as filmmaker GUS VAN SANT, novelist Katherine Dunn (*Geek Love*, 1990), personal

essayist Richard Meltzer, and infamous *Answer Me* publishers the Goads (see ZINES). (*SIMPSONS* creator Matt Groening is a native son.) In the post-GRUNGE lull, Portland was sometimes touted—notably in the *Seattle Times*—as the "next Seattle," but bands like Pond, Heatmiser, The Spinanes, and Hazel

George Bush warned that a p.c. "inquisition" was threatening the First Amendment. But Bush's own allegiance to free speech was far from absolute: among other things, he supported a constitutional amendment to ban flag burning. Still, the anti-p.c. juggernaut rolled on. With mischievous glee, young conservatives used the phrase indiscriminately to taunt their opponents. It seemed that anyone who held a strong belief, or a passionate conviction about anything, could be treated with the charge of political correctness. This was a style of political argument that suited many young Republicans, who struck the poses of the educated frat boy—a rollicking (or haughty) superiority confected out of small portions of Ayn Rand and large doses of P. J. O'Rourke.

Nonetheless, the charges of political correctness often struck home because the phenomenon they referred to, however clumsily, did exist. Denied political influence during the Reagan years, left-of-center academics often turned toward a politics that emphasized cultural identity and group enfranchisement. The result was an ironic reversal of liberal and radical aspirations. '60s radicals espoused erotic license; the Antioch rules imposed new, unenforceable regulations on the bedroom. In the '60s, Berkeley students started a free speech movement; in the '90s, administrators imposed SPEECH CODES. Traditionally, liberals and radicals had thought of high culture as a repository of critical thinking and aesthetic bliss, and had fought to make it available to more people. In the '90s, cutting-edge CULTURAL STUDIES academics taught that the canon was an instrument of power, and the literary texts were strategies of control.

At times, the radical professoriate peddled

especially unyielding brands of identity politics and MULTICULTURALISM. Group membership was taken as the cornerstone of identity, and group differences were celebrated as the essence of diversity. But this philosophy had its problems. And it's not surprising that some people objected to them. Once you start warming to groups, and group differences, where do you stop? Does every group deserve preferences of its own? And why is it all right to generalize about groups if your conclusions are flattering, but not otherwise? Absorbed in these questions, would-be reformers lost their purchase on reality. Causes that involved universal ideals and pragmatic compromises—causes like health care reform and raising the minimum wage—were largely ignored by the academic left.

In the 1994 elections, all of the attacks on political correctness–both justified and *ad hominem*–appeared to have their day. Talk show hosts exulted in the defeat of liberals, and their p.c. allies. As one Georgia congressman put it, "the politically incorrect working people of this country rose up . . . and voted for change." But the rout of p.c. was hardly complete. After all, p.c.is not really a partisan phenomenon: speech codes and didactic art derive from deep-seated aversions to pleasure and thought, and they are at least as attractive to the right as to the left. It may be that, in their escalating confidence and zeal, the new conservatives will only succeed in earning the unflattering epithet "political correctness"— or, as some suggest, "patriotic correctness"—for themselves.–*Alexander Star*

WEB **The Right Side of the Web** http://www.clark.net/pub/ jeffd/index.html ✦ WEB **AlterNet** http://www.alternet.org/an/ ✦ WEB **Links For Those With Conscience and Consciousness** http://artitude.com/links.htm ✦ USENET **alt.politics.correct** never quite made the transition from lower-division INDIE ROCK strivers to mass media trend fodder.

PowerBar   Brand-leader in new category of pricey, high tech "sports energy bars" prized by athletes for their gastro-friendly quick energy boost and by would-be athletes for their healthful, active-life aura. However, these action accessories are just as sweet and contain just as many calories as their candy cousins. The wide variety of proteins and carbs they contain—ranging from corn and rice syrups to fruit juice concentrates, oat bran, dairy proteins, and soy blends—are principally designed to supply simple carbohydrates that the body easily turns into its main energy source, glucose. (Dried fruit produces a similar fillip for a fraction of the price.) The PowerBar was first marketed by Berkeley-based marathoner Brian Maxwell (b. 1953) and his chemist wife Jennifer Biddulph in 1987; in 1993 they sold 24 million. As brands have proliferated, bars like the Clif Bar have been targeted at rock climbers and other sport subcultures.

WEB **The PowerBar Story** http://www.primenet.com/ ~krp/story.html ✦ WEB **The International Powerbar Women's Challenge** http://www.primenet.com/ ~krp/power.html ✦ WEB **Sports Nutrition** http://www.loria.fr/~washingt/bike/nutrition/nutrition.html

Prada   Italian luggage company established 1913 and run since 1979 by former communist Miuccia Prada (b. 1950), granddaughter of founder Mario. The high-profile, high-ticket cult of Prada was built on the company's 1985 introduction of tote bags and backpacks made of a black nylon woven on machines used for Italian Army parachutes. These initially unlabelled items were highly valued among the fashion cognoscenti for their anti-status properties; the introduction of a small, triangular metal label did not hinder the bags' proliferation. (As of 1995, the backpack retails at just under $400; hard-to-detect bootleg versions are profuse.) In 1988 Prada introduced an eponymous clothing line that is much praised for its modernity, clean lines, and "elegant minimalism"; the BRIDGE LINE Miu Miu

(Miuccia's nickname) came three years later. Prada's contemporary cachet was sealed in 1995 when DREW BARRYMORE appeared in ads for MIU MIU, and UMA THURMAN arrived at the Oscar ceremony in a lavender Prada gown.

WEB **The Made In Italy HomePage** http://www.flashnet.it/ made.htm

Prague   Post-Cold War youth capital for democratic idealists, film students, and German suds-guzzlers. Located in the province of Bohemia, the Czech city was the stage for Communism's most romantic overthrow, the 1989 Velvet Revolution. The overthrow took its name from the relatively peaceful transition to democracy (and, improbably enough, for the influence of the Velvet Underground on dissidents during the dark years of rule by Soviet-backed Communists). Czechoslovakia's genuinely oppositional hippie, rocker, and anarchist counterculture produced many of the country's post-Revolution leaders, including the country's president, playwright Vaclav Havel. Progress of the YAP—Young American in Prague—invasion can be followed in the pages of the twentysomething English-language *Prognosis* magazine, founded by a group of University of California, Santa Barbara, graduates.

WEB **The Prague Post** http://actrix.gen.nz/general/ prague.html ✦ WEB **Official Prague and Chech Resources** http://www.hec.unil.ch/prague/prague/cz&pragu.htm ✦ USENET **soc.culture.czecho-slovak**

PREPPY (with irony), by X-GIRL, 1994.

preppy   Aspirational style based on the crisp sartorial codes of the Eastern, WASP upper-middle class. (The term itself derives from expensive pre-college "prep" or preparatory schools.) The height of preppy was the early '80s, when Lisa Birnbach's waspish *The Official Preppy Handbook* sat astride the bestseller lists, and the country was merry on the heady draft of Reaganism. Along with many other '80s excesses the trend faded, but it had something of a renaissance in 1993–94. This time, preppy style was both a sardonic statement by B-BOYS (see RALPH LAUREN, TOMMY HILFIGER), and an ironic talisman for non-aspirational whites. The BEASTIE BOY/SONIC YOUTH-linked X-Girl clothing line concisely expressed this latter strain with a T-shirt bearing the "X-Girl Prep"; inlaid into the shirt's *faux*-heraldic crest was the word "snooty."

http://pantheon.cis.yale.edu/~burtons/prep.html

Primus Unlikely gold-selling, WHITE-TRASH purveyors of pinballing funk-metal. Led by singer/songwriter/bassist Les Claypool, Primus includes Zappa/Garcia-influenced guitarist Larry LeLonde and globally percussive drummer Tim Alexander, who debuted in 1989 with the live EP, *Suck on This* ("Primus sucks!" is their fans' love cry). They united in their enthusiasm for PROGRESSIVE ROCK icons Rush, for whom they opened in 1994. Their subsequent records include the gastronomically inviting *Sailing the Seas of Cheese* (1991), *Pork Soda* (1993), and *Tales From the Punchbowl*; the latter debuted in the Billboard Top 10 in June 1995, buoyed by the prosthetics-heavy video for the Devo-esque "Wynona's Big Brown Beaver."

WEB **Los Bastardos** http://www.csua.berkeley.edu/~savage/primus/primus.html/ ✦ USENET **alt.music.primus** ✦ USENET **alt.music.primus**

Prince, The Artist Formerly Known As

(b. 1958)   A rare bastion of pop mystique, this Minneapolis native has repeatedly earned the title "The Imp of the Perverse" (per his British biographer Barney Hoskyns). The movie and soundtrack album *Purple Rain* raised the pan-sexual, pan-ethnic singer/composer from salacious shock-rocker (most graphically on 1981's *Dirty Mind*) to pop-pheno-menon in 1984, but his career then fell into a confounding pattern. *Purple Rain* was followed, typically, by the whimsical, lightweight records *Around The World In A Day* (1985) and *Parade* (1986); he staged a bold recovery with the eclectic *Sign 'O' The Times* (1987), and the process began

anew. In 1993, Prince engaged his label Warner Bros. in a public feud when they reportedly balked at his prolific release schedule. Much of the singer's fabled energy has since gone into a range of extracurricular projects: he sanctioned a touring ballet based on 13 of his songs (*Billboards* by the Joffrey Ballet, 1993); opened Grand Slam clubs in Los Angeles, Miami, and Minneapolis; had a 13-song score dropped from the one-time musical *I'll Do Anything* (1994); wrote an erotic stage show "inspired by Homer"; and released officially *The Black Album* (1994), a 1988 bootleg of undistinguished funk work-outs. On his 35th birthday, Prince replaced his name with ♀ and "retired," threatening to release only vaulted material. (The threat, of course, proved false.) In 1994 he took to scrawling the word "SLAVE" on his cheek as a comment on his relationship with Warner Bros., for whom he made 1995's underwhelming *The Gold Experience.*

WEB **Prince Swap List** http://www.mtsu.edu/~spth0001/ ✦ FTP **Prince Lyrics List** ftp://math.montana.edu/pub/carlson/pltt/ ✦ WEB **Prince-Come** http://www.iuma.com/Warner/html/Prince.html ✦ IRC **#prince** ✦ USENET **alt.music.prince**

Processed World Launched in 1981 by disaffected Bay Area office drones Chris Carlsson and Caitlin Manning, this Situationist-inspired, triannually published magazine is dedicated to the critique of the life-negating "Cubicular World" of corporate culture. Anthologized in the 1990 collection *Bad Attitude*, the magazine is written by and for repetitively stressed, VDT-blinded information programmers, degraded office temps, burnt-out BIKE MESSENGERS, and all the other unrecognized cogs in the corporate machinery. Art and comics by Jay Kinney, Paul Mavrides, and Dan Perkins (*Tom Tomorrow*) are interspersed with articles like "A Day in the Life of Employee 85292," "The Dead-End Game of Corporate Feminism," and "Ten Ways to Wreck a Video Display Terminal," and slogans like "Sell your time to buy the time that other people sold."

product placement Time-honored Hollywood custom of using movies to subtly promote products. Product placement heated up in the '80s, most notably with the legendary Reese's Pieces placement in *E.T.* (1983); Columbia Pictures' tenure as a Coke subsidiary from 1982 to 1989; and Armani's promo-costuming in *American Gigolo* [1980]). It went supernova in the early '90s. The plug-laden dialogue of *Demolition Man* (1993) featured jokes about Taco Bell, the only restaurant chain left in 21st century America (changed to another Pepsi subsidiary, Pizza Hut, for the Japanese release), prompting trade magazine *Inside Media* to wonder in one headline, "Movie or Commercial?" Other milestones include another time-traveler joke, the RockDonald's restaurant chain in *The Flintstones* (1994); Red Stripe beer, sales of which increased 53 percent after Tom Cruise sipped it in *The Firm* (1993); and the moment in *Wayne's World* (1992) when Wayne holds up a Pizza Hut box in a "spoof" on product placement.

progressive rock Chops-*über-alles* form that blighted rock in the 1970s, largely provoking the minimalist backlash of PUNK. Originally typified by the florid, English-pastoral excesses of Yes, Genesis, Pink Floyd, and Emerson Lake and Palmer, "prog rock" expressed itself in the Americas through, among others, the furious noodlings of Rush and the pop-chart grandiosity of bands like Styx. Although it was almost ridiculed out of existence by the '80s, progressive has enjoyed something of a Nixon-like restoration in recent years: a worldwide network of bands, many of them covers-only tribute outfits, continues to enrapture an audience that seeks gentle musical complexity as a refuge from harsh contemporary sounds. Prog-rock's modern descendants are harsh, contemporary outfits like the ROLLINS Band, Helmet, and PRIMUS. (The term "progressive" has also become a sometimes synonym for ALTERNATIVE, as in the COLLEGE RAP groups PM Dawn or DE LA SOUL.)
USENET **alt.rock-n-roll.metal.progressive**, **alt.music. progressive** ✦ WEB **Gibraltar Encyclopedia of**

Progressive Rock http://www.cogsci.ed.ac.uk/~philkime /gepr.html

Project Censored Founded in 1976 by Sonoma State University Communication Studies professor Carl Jensen (b. 1929) *Project Censored* is an annual newsletter (circulation approximately 5,000) containing the "10 best censored stories" of the year. (The project was funded by Jensen himself for its first 13 years—in 1989 he received funding from a private grant foundation.) In a 1989 interview with the *Bay Area Guardian* Jensen defended the inclusion of stories which have already appeared in alternative publications; he cited a definition of "self-censorship" by the London-based international organization Article 19, as when "journalists and editors tend to overlook or under-cover or avoid issues that are going to cause trouble."
WEB **Project Censored HomePage** http://zippy.sonoma.edu/ ProjectCensored/

Proof Positive California model agency representing exclusively HIV-positive clients. Proof Positive was founded in 1994 by the Costa Mesa-based Morgan Agency in response to requests for models to represent products aimed at the HIV-positive community. Within a year the new division accounted for over 50 of Morgan's 450-plus clients, and was representing products outside of its original purview. One of Proof Positive's high-profile clients was the Ross Products Division of Chicago pharmaceutical concern Abbott Laboratories, which produces Advera, a controversial liquid diet supplement for people diagnosed as HIV-positive.

Proposition 187 California initiative making illegal immigrants ineligible for medical care and public school educations, backed by California Governor Pete Wilson and approved by 59 percent of voters in the November, 1994 elections. (The San Francisco Bay Area was the only region of the state to reject it.) The day after balloting, enforcement of the law (denying access to prenatal care and nursing homes) was blocked by state and federal courts. In the wake of 187, discrimination against nonwhites has increased and many immigrants won't seek medical help out of fear of deportation. Critics of anti-immigrant legislation contend that illegal immigrants contribute more in taxes than they receive in government services. (A 1994 Urban Institute report put the figures at $30 billion and $18.7 billion respectively, estimating that most of the latter goes to refugees from Cold War enemies.)

WEB **1994 California Voter Information**
http://www.ca94.election.digital.com/e/prop/187/home.html/
✦ USENET **misc.immigration.usa**

Prozac   Drug of the decade, chemical icon. The anti-depressant Prozac was put on the market by Eli Lilly in 1987, since which time it has been used by an estimated six million Americans. Prozac is to the neurotic '90s what Valium and Librium ("mother's little helpers") were to the '50s and '60s.

Prozac works by increasing the levels of serotonin in the neurotransmission system; for reasons that are as yet unclear, this often improves confidence, self-image, and energy levels. Proponents of Prozac—like Peter Kramer, author of the best-selling book *Listening to Prozac*—believe that these benefits outweigh the drug's known side-effects which include nausea, diarrhea, and sexual dysfunction. (The fact that it inhibits orgasm has also made it an occasional treatment for premature ejaculation.) Kramer's critics worried that "cosmetic psychopharmacology" enters a morally dubious domain where cure stops and enhancement begins.

One of the groups that has been most exposed to Prozac is college students, to whom it has been increasingly prescribed by overworked campus psychiatrists. One such student is Elizabeth Wurtzel, Harvard Class of '89. Once *SPY* magazine's favorite rock-scribe punchbag, the photogenic depressive carved herself a piece of pop culture history with the autobiographical book *Prozac Nation* (1994), an exhibitionist epic of wasted privilege and loveless sex cast as a generational parable.

WEB **alt.drugs archive** http://hyperreal.com/drugs/misc/

prozac.interactions ✦ USENET **alt.support.depression** ✦ WEB **Pharmaceutical Information Network** http://pharminfo.com/drugdb/proz_arc.html ✦ WEB **Mood Disorders Page** http://avocado.pc.helsinki.fi/%7Ejanne/mood/

psilocybin mushrooms   The most organically prevalent—and therefore, some would argue, most safe and effective—psychedelic drug. Use of mushrooms containing the psychoactive substance psilocybin is thousands of years old; modern U.S. use was popularized through ethnomycologist R. Gordon Wasson's *Soma: Divine Mushrooms of Immortality* (1971) and through the writings of TIMOTHY LEARY, who conducted experiments with prisoners and synthetic psilocybin during the late '60s. TERENCE MCKENNA, in *Food of the Gods* (1992), argues that mushrooms possibly represent the infiltration of an alien intelligence on earth, and may even have been responsible for humankind's acquisition of language. The long-acting tryptamines in *Stropharia cubensis*, the most common street mushroom (besides the dealer-doctored store-bought variety), is usually taken in doses of from one to five grams and gives a visually complex five-to-seven-hour high similar to LSD.

WEB **Mushrooms** http://hyperreal.com/drugs/psychedelics/mushrooms/ ✦ USENET **alt.drugs.psychedelics**

Psychic TV   Band formed in 1981 by INDUSTRIAL-music pioneer Genesis P-Orridge (b. Neil Megson circa 1952), formerly of Throbbing Gristle. Throughout the '80s Psychic TV occupied the outer margins of pop culture, making undistinguished modern psychedelic records; staging cacophonous multi-media events; issuing forth strangely spelled rhetoric about "abolishing all inherited belief systems"; and propagating body-PIERCING among the Temple ov Psychick Youth, their international following. On the 1990 WAX TRAX album *Towards Thee Infinite Beat* Psychic TV heartily embraced the "alpha beat" of ACID HOUSE as the music most synchronous with the band's shamanistic leanings.

In February 1992 Psychic TV were dragged

punk

In an era rife with wildfire media viruses, one of the most stubborn MEMES is one that took years, not hours, to traverse the globe. Originally a jailhouse term for a submissive homosexual, "punk" took on its youth-culture connotation as a label for a generation of miscreant mid-'60s U.S. garage bands experimenting with post-Beatles British influence and early psychedelics. These luckless "punk-rock" outfits (among them the Seeds, 13th Floor Elevators, and the Standells) produced a slew of rough-hewn pop gems that were gathered by rock journalist Lenny Kaye into the influential 1972 album *Nuggets*.

As guitarist for singer Patti Smith, Kaye would play a central role in unleashing the punk virus on the world. Smith was grande dame of CBGBS, the downtown New York club that in 1974–75 launched a multi-pronged assault on the "dinosaur" rock hegemony of bands like the Eagles and Pink Floyd. The venue housed a cadre of bands that would define the *new* punk-rock; the one common idea among acts like Patti Smith and Television (romantic poets), Blondie and the Ramones (nostalgic beat-merchants), and the Talking Heads (minimalist PREPPIES) was a rejection of rock's then-overblown values in favor of short songs, highly conceptual styles, and a fixation with themes urban and modern. "Public access rock" is how critic James Wolcott described it in a 1975 *Village Voice* review—this generation of U.S. punks was never deemed ready for prime time.

According to legend, former Television bass player Richard Hell was the first to adorn himself in the torn clothes, spiky hair, and safety pins that are today recognized as classic punk style. Hell's look was taken across the Atlantic by London-based haberdasher and pop entrepreneur Malcolm McClaren (erstwhile handler of glam-damaged visionaries the New York Dolls), who projected it upon his new protégés the Sex Pistols. The punk virus spread like wildfire in Britain: one anthemic single ("Anarchy in the U.K.") and obscenity-laden appearance by the Sex Pistols in late 1976 turned a whole nation of adults against them and mobilized a generation to their cause.

Unlike their U.S. contemporaries, U.K. upstarts like the Clash, the Buzzcocks, the Slits, Wire, and Siouxsie and the Banshees (not to mention dozens of bandwagon-jumpers) had a zealous Year Zero rhetoric that was built around a modernist, anti-rock stance. Although the British punk bands initially took The Ramones' 1976 debut album as a minimalist manifesto (augmented by the hard-to-find works of the New York Dolls, the Stooges, and the Velvet Underground), they soon ushered in a period of experimentation with music, sexual roles, fashion, and politics. Homage was paid to heady outside influences like surrealism, DUB reggae, and situationism; names like Jackson Pollock, Debussy, and anti-Nazi collage artist John Heartfield were freely bandied about.

Much of British punk's leftist politics were the affectation of guilty middle-class art students, but as many of the genre's smartest practitioners moved on to influence in other media spheres they handed the form over to the actual lumpen proletariat. The results were not pretty. At the hands of bands like the Sham 69, UK Subs, Crass, and the Exploited, punk turned artless, brutal, homogenous and extremely non-aspirational. Still, some of these bands did enjoy both populist support and, as the '80s dawned, a certain influence in America, where punk tribes were thriving outside of trend-conscious New York. Punk variants took root in other cities—tough, hyper-masculine scenes that were as untroubled by media attention as they were by stylistic development.

In L.A. the punk tradition subsisted at the SST label formed in 1978 by Black Flag members Greg Ginn and Chuck Dukowski; Bad Religion guitarist Brett Gurewitz would start Epitaph, a tentative venture that would later become a cash cow in the '90s. In Washington, D.C., Ian MacKaye of Minor Threat (later FUGAZI) fostered the hardcore scene (and its STRAIGHT EDGE sect) at Dischord, home to Youth Brigade, Bad Brains, and SOA (State of Alert). The most unlikely punk bastion of all was Southern California's lush, suburban

Orange County, where a community of surfers and SKATE-punks sustained early-'80s stoics like Suicidal Tendencies, Agent Orange, Social Distortion, T.S.O.L (True Sounds of Liberty), and the Adolescents.

In the '80s ALTERNATIVE culture "punk" was a seldom-spoken, though unimpeachable, symbol of purity, an unsullied ideal to which ALTERNATIVE bands naturally aspired; it had become a vague, hard-loud-fast sonic accord and anti-commercial stance rather than an identifiable youth-culture style. (Fashions consisted largely of the flannel shirts, ripped jeans and combat boots that would be labeled GRUNGE in the early '90s.) "Corporate Rock Sucks" snarled the legendary T-shirt from SST, which had become home to revered talents such as Hüsker Dü, DINOSAUR JR., and the Meat Puppets. Little wonder that SST alumni SONIC

Punky sneers, then and now: Pete Shelley of Buzzcocks 1977/Billie Joe of GREEN DAY 1994

YOUTH gleefully titled their 1992 documentary *1991: The Year Punk Broke*—the "breaking" was done by Sonic Youth support band NIRVANA, who carried punk spirit into the heart of the charts. As with the Sex Pistols, irresistible pop hooks were delivered by a singer with a gift for gestures both grand and absurd, and driven home by a pile-driving rhythm section.

If the alternative nation seemed smug about the triumph of the punk credo it had earned the right to do so simply by surviving a decade distinguished by the stultifying influence of MTV. What came next could not have been predicted. A brigade of bands with an extremely literal interpretation of punk soared to platinum status after building handsome cult followings in cities overlooked during SEATTLE's moment in the sun; their convictions may have been simpleminded but they rang true for millions. Leading the charge was GREEN DAY from the East Bay of San Francisco, a town whose punk heritage stretched from '70s bands like the Avengers and the Dead Kennedys through the 1986 advent of the legendary Berkeley bôite 924 GILMAN. By 1994 Green Day were twinned in MTV rotation with Orange County's (and Epitaph Records') equally punky OFFSPRING—bringing up the rear were Rancid, a Bay Area outfit (also on Epitaph) who could actually boast a former member of the U.K. Subs in their line-up.

The mid-'90s punk revival may have lacked the original's sense of absurdity, but absurdities were not in short supply: a late 1993 Milan collection by flamboyant fashion designer Gianni Versace prominently featured slashed clothes and outsize safety pins as a nod to London, 1976; a year later, MTV's dance-party show *The Grind* was given over to a "punk" special, with pneumatic teens grinding to punk, both neo and classic; in the same July 1995 issue of *DETAILS* that had Rancid's Tim Armstrong sneering from the cover with a purple mohawk, Malcolm McClaren reviewed the new punk bands and gave a uniformly blithe thumbs up to the likes of the Offspring, Rancid, and Pennywise.

Each of these ensembles churned out rough-hewn (if homogenous) pop gems that were comfortably accommodated in the rock business alongside other prevailing trends, which in 1995 meant stadium-fillers like Pink Floyd, The Eagles, and the GRATEFUL DEAD; new country superstars like Garth Brooks and Reba McEntire; and authentic, sincere-guy rockers like Hootie and the Blowfish, Live, and the Dave Matthews Band. Punk had finally found a place in a culture that rewards anything, so long as it's traditional. *—Steven Daly*
USENET **alt.punk** ✦ WEB **World Wide PUNK!**
http://wchat.on.ca/vic/wwp.htm

unceremoniously into the headlines. A British TV documentary passed off a 10-year-old Psychic TV performance-art video as an act of SATANIC child abuse. Predictably outraged authorities rushed to judgment, and British police seized P-Orridge's possessions while he was on tour in the U.S., threatening to imprison him if he or his wife Paula ever returned to the country. He has since been exiled in California, where he haunts the margins of the RAVE scene and philosophizes with fellow traveler TIMOTHY LEARY.

WEB **Thee Temple ov Psychick Youth**

http://www.topy.org/topy/topy.htm ✦ WEB **Discography**

http://www.std.com/obi/Zines/Chaos.Control/

PTVdiscography.html

Def Jam/Columbia album cover, 1990

Fear of a Black Planet, part three of PUBLIC ENEMY'S "cryptic triptych."

Public Enemy Foremost rap group of the pre-GANGSTA late '80s. Powered by the stentorian leads of Chuck D (b. Carlton Ridenhour, 1960), the court-jester counterpoints of Flavor Flav (b. William Drayton, circa 1958), and the revolutionary production techniques of the Bomb Squad (Hank Shocklee, Keith Shocklee, Bill Stephney, Eric Sadler, et al.), the Long Island, New York-based Public Enemy recorded dense, pneumatic compositions such as "Bring the Noise," (1987) "Don't Believe the Hype," (1988) and "Welcome to the Terrordome," (1990) that preached a galvanic gospel of African-American self-sufficiency while name-checking black power leaders such as Huey Newton, Marcus Garvey, and especially MALCOLM X.

The 1989 anthem "Fight the Power," featured in Spike Lee's *Do the Right Thing*, was a curious cross-over hit with white listeners, with its lyrics: "Elvis was a hero to most / But he never meant shit to me you see . . . I'm ready and hyped plus I'm amped / Most of my heroes don't appear on no stamps." In May of the same year Public Enemy made headlines when founding member Professor Griff (b. Richard Griffin, circa 1960), leader of the S1W bodyguards and PE's "minister of information," made anti-Semitic remarks in an interview with the *Washington Times*. Griff eventually left the group and recorded solo for Luther Campbell of 2 LIVE CREW. 1990's *Fear of a Black Planet* completed Public Enemy's peak period, which started with 1987's debut *Yo! Bum Rush the Show*. Even as the balance of power in the HIP-HOP world began to tilt towards L.A., PE put out the solid *Apocalypse 91: The Enemy Strikes Black* (1991), but in 1993 the band fulfilled contractual obligations with a hastily assembled greatest hits compilation, *Greatest Misses*, that was followed by 1994's poorly received *Muse Sick-n-Hour Mess Age*. In 1995 Chuck D could be seen prowling the stage of the House of Blues THEME RESTAURANT, an institution that might have served as a ripe target during the group's golden years. Meanwhile Flavor Flav, who never completed a much-anticipated 1992 solo album, was embroiled in a series of mounting legal problems that included drug and assault arrests and a three-month sentence in late 1994 for weapons possession.

A July 1995 "farewell" concert in London was canceled after Flav broke both his arms in a motorcycle accident in Italy.

WEB **Unofficial Public Enemy Homepage**

http://www.me.tut.fi/~tpaanane/pe.html

Puma Suedes Low-top, white-soled sneaker line introduced by German-founded athletic shoe manufacturer in 1968. In the 1970s suedes took on the moniker "Clydes" in deference to snappy-dressing basketball great Walt "Clyde" Frazier, who wore his team-colored (orange, blue stripes) Pumas while playing for the New York Knicks. The sneakers were discontinued in 1985, as Puma (and ADIDAS) suffered loss of market share to rivals NIKE and Reebok. (Puma founder Rudolf Dassler established the company in 1948, after a bitter split with his brother, ADIDAS founder "Adi"

Dassler.) Clydes then became sought-after among urban tastemakers, particularly in England, where a pair could fetch over $100. When Puma noticed the renewed interest in Clydes in 1993 and re-released the line, vendors had trouble keeping them in stock. The unaffected styling of Clydes appealed to SKATEBOARDERS, INDIE-ROCK fans, and surfers alike, spurring overwhelming interest in vintage and lo-tech models from the likes of Vans and CONVERSE.

Punk See page 192.

Queen Latifah (b. Dana Owens, 1970) Statuesque New Jersey rapper whose lack of chart success never prevented her from developing an enviable media profile. Latifah's thoughtful persona and MULTICULTURAL accoutrements, plus her membership in the well-respected, loosely knit Native Tongues rap clan (A Tribe Called Quest, DE LA SOUL, Jungle Brothers) suggested considerable commercial potential, but after two moderately selling albums (*All Hail the Queen*, 1989; *Nature of a Sista*, 1991) pioneer rap label Tommy Boy failed to pick up her option. A 1993 move to the more staid Motown label, and an R&B-tinged album, *Black Reign*, finally earned Latifah gold status (500,000 sales). Always portrayed as an astute businesswoman, she has hedged against the built-in obsolescence of a HIP-HOP career by founding Flavor Unit, a management company that numbers hit rap act Naughty By Nature and SMOOTHED-OUT R&B merchants Shai among its clients. Also in '93 Latifah furthered her acting ambitions (she was prominent in 1991's *House Party 2*) as the editor of Brooklyn's *Flavor* magazine in the cheery hit sitcom *Living Single* (debuted 1993).

Queer Ken Released by Mattel in 1993 under the product name Earring Magic Ken, this doll featured BARBIE's traditionally square-jawed beau in a more '90s outfit: lavender mesh top and vest, two-tone frosted blond hair, and a small silver ring on a choker. What Mattel apparently didn't realize is that the ring Ken appropriates is actually a to-scale cock ring, which some groups of gay RAVE-goers had taken to wearing around their necks. Mattel denied that they intended the look as All-American Ken's coming out, but in the summer of '93 Earring Magic Ken became an instant artifact of gay kitsch and, consequently, the best-selling Ken doll ever.

WEB **The Plastic Prince Controversy**

http://deepthought.armory.com/~zenugirl/cockringken.html ✦

WEB **Hacker Barbie Dream Basement Apartment**

http://www.catalog.com/mrm/barbe/barbe.html/

Queer Nation Aggressive gay and lesbian rights organization known for the slogan: "We're here. We're Queer. Get used to it!" QN was formed in 1990 by four members of ACT-UP, including OUTING ideologue Michaelangelo Signorile. QN has drawn criticism from more traditional gay and lesbian rights organizations for confrontational tactics, such as disrupting fundamentalist church services in dresses and nuns' habits, interfering with the filming of *Basic Instinct* (1992), staging "Queer Scout" kiss-ins to protest the Boy Scouts' restrictive policies, and plastering cities with mock advertisements outing closeted celebrities. One of QN's most radical gestures is their appropriation of "queer." Like "NIGGER," "queer" is a taunt sometimes taken by its targets as a badge of resistance. The push to add lesbian, BISEXUAL, transgender, and other causes to the Gay Rights banner has also made "Queer" a useful, "playfully non-essentialist" catchall for the movement. Queer-as-compliment has sometimes marked a generation gap in the homosexual world, where many older people associate the term exclusively with gay-bashing.

WEB **Collected Queer Information** http://www.cs.cmu.edu/ Web/People/mjw/Queer/MainPage.html ✦ MAIL LIST **QN List** email qn-request@queernet.org ✦ WEB **Queer Infoserver** http://server.berkeley.edu/queer/qis/misc.html/

queercore Broad-based network of PUNK rock bands with gay and lesbian members and sexually specific lyrics; originally known as "homocore" in the late '80s. Groups like Fifth Column (Toronto), God Is My Co-Pilot (New York), Team Dresch, and Heatmiser (both PORTLAND) may not be identifiable as musical kin, but they did share the type of sexual ambivalence that also colored part of the '70s punk movement. San Francisco is home to the thrashy female five-piece Tribe 8 and to Pansy Division, queercore's highest-profile band. Leader Jon Ginoli made three sexually non-specific albums as an Illinois post-punk struggler before forming Pansy Division and writing bouncy, sexually specific songs like "Bill and Ted's Homosexual

Adventure" and "Smells Like Queer Spirit" (a satire). When the band supported punk pop-stars GREEN DAY on a national tour in the fall of 1994, they put queercore in the crosshairs of the national media: the queer punk phenomenon was widely reported and easily packaged by the likes of MTV and *ROLLING STONE*.

MAIL LIST **QuEEr pUnk List** email muzmorph@aol.com

R.E.M. Athens, Georgia band dubbed the "ALTERNATIVE Beatles" by the *Boston Globe* in 1995. From their 1982 EP debut *Chronic Town* on, R.E.M. married '60s folk-tinged songcraft of guitarist Peter Buck (b. 1956) to the elliptical lyrics, twangy voice, and ethereal persona of singer Michael Stipe (b. 1960). Tireless touring paid off for the band in 1987 when "The One I Love" entered the Top 10; 1988's album *Green* (their first on a major label) marked a step from college-rock immortality to the Classic Rock pantheon. The band took a two-year hiatus before making its next move: led off by the yearning, buoyant single "Losing My Religion," 1991's *Out Of Time* was a #1 album heavily nominated for Grammy awards. At the MTV Video Awards that September, Stipe peeled off a series of T-shirts bearing POLITICALLY CORRECT messages from "rainforest" to "Handgun Control." (Stipe and filmmaker Jim McKay formed the C–00 company to produce short films, pop videos, documentaries, and PSAs.)

Perversely enough, R.E.M. declined to cash in on their newfound pop profile: 1992's *Automatic For the People* album was a solipsistic, downbeat affair featuring string arrangements by former Led Zeppelin member John Paul Jones and acoustic instruments. But the band's withdrawal from the touring/publicity treadmill served to create a mystique (especially around Stipe) which contrasted favorably with the promotional pandering of contemporaries. When the band returned with September 1994's *Monster* album, critics were so grateful for a "rockin'" R.E.M. album (and supporting tour) that even an underwritten, slightly generic record couldn't deter the myth-making machine. (As *Monster* came out a now-shaven-headed Stipe signed a 2-year deal with New Line Cinema to produce feature films.) On March 1, 1995, six weeks into R.E.M.'s first tour for 5 years, drummer Bill Berry (b. 1958) collapsed in Switzerland from a brain aneurysm; he recovered six weeks later to complete the U.S. leg of the tour. In July, bassist Mike Mills (b. 1958) underwent stomach surgery;

the following month Stipe broke off the band's European tour to have a hernia operation.
WEB **Bungee Bob's R.E.M. Archive** http://www.gtlug.org/~dgoodman/rem.html ✦ WEB **R.E.M. Homepage** http://www.halcyon.com/rem/ ✦ USENET **rec.music.rem**

Radakovich, Anka (b. 1957) Ribald, often participatory sex columnist for *DETAILS* whose successful collection of articles *The Wild Girls Club* (1994) was optioned as a movie by Disney. Radakovich's claim to be the sexual spokesperson for GENERATION X was dented in 1994 when it was revealed that she was, at 37 years old, demographically ineligible for the position. This revelation came uncomfortably soon after Radakovich appeared on a June cover of *Newsweek* with fellow "Generation Xers" under the headline "Seven Great Lies about 20somethings." In her defense, the columnist explained that her real age "would have seemed old to my readers"

Rage Against the Machine With its 1992 self-titled debut LP, this L.A.-based PUNK/thrash/HIP-HOP combo took on injustice, prejudice, and complacency with all the subtlety of a plane crash. The bumper-sticker rhetoric of songs such as "Know Your Enemy" and "Settle For Nothing" abated on the lyrically more agile "Freedom," a song which helped make Native American activist LEONARD PELTIER into an MTV *cause célèbre*. Rage were no less serious about their own aesthetic purity: official press releases included the solemn pledge that "no samples, keyboards, or synthesizers are used in any Rage recording." The defiantly imageless band won over thousands of converts on the 1993 LOLLAPALOOZA tour, on which they made more established acts look perfunctory. In March of 1995, the band broke up but patched up its differences some months later, recovering for release ten months of recordings.
WEB **Rage Against the Machine Homepage** http://www.engin.umich.edu/~aklink/Rage/rageout ✦ WEB **Sony Records** http://www.music.sony.com/Music/ArtistInfo/RageAgainstTheMachine_RageAgainstTheMachine.html

Raimi, Sam (b. 1959)   Shock-schlock auteur who secured cult immortality with the 1983 low-budget film *The Evil Dead*; marked by bloody excess, elegant camerawork, and loopy humor, *Evil Dead* spawned an 1987 sequel, *Evil Dead 2: Dead By Dawn*. Raimi made his major-studio debut with *Darkman* (1990). Other projects included co-writing the Coen Brothers' *The Hudsucker Proxy* (1994) and co-producing two Jean-Claude Van Damme action spectaculars (*Hard Target*, directed in 1993 by Hong Kong legend JOHN WOO, and *Time Cop* [1994]). After filming the *Evil Dead* sequel *Army of Darkness* (1993), Raimi directed *The Quick and the Dead* (1995), a flat Western with Sharon Stone and LEONARDO DICAPRIO. The director has also enjoyed success as an executive producer for small-screen projects, including *Hercules: The Legendary Journeys* (1995); and *American Gothic* (1995), created by former teen heartthrob Shaun Cassidy.

WEB **Sam Raimi's Homepage** http://lasarto.cnde.iastate.edu/Movies/CultShop/movies/raimi.html

Rainbow Family   Self-described "dis-organization of non-members" that has gathered annually on public land since first meeting in Colorado's Rocky Mountains National Park on July 4, 1972. The week-long gathering of tribes refuses to sign permits, invoking its First Amendment right to assemble peaceably. Rainbow Family of Living Light members—including "blissers" (defined in the Family FAQ as "usually middle- or upper-class people who prefer enjoyment to work"), DEADHEADS, fairies (FAQ: "usually those of male homosexual persuasion"), and "tourists"—hang out, meditate, drum, and hold council. The food is free and decisions are arrived at by consensus; one of these included introduction of the wheel to gatherings, marking the end of the Family's "stone age."

WEB **Rainbow Family Homepage**
http://welcomehome.org/rainbow.html USENET
alt.gathering.rainbow

Rainforest Action Network   San Francisco-based environmental group largely responsible for the U.S. public's concern for the destruction of the world's rainforests in other countries. Ten years after its founding in 1985, the group boasts 31,000 members and 150 grassroots "action groups" (RAGs) in North America. RAN first came to national prominence with its successful boycott of Burger King in 1987. The boycott added a new twist to fast-food criticism and forced BK to stop importing beef from Central America, where rainforests are sacrificed for cattle pasture. The Network, which also campaigns for the human rights of indigenous people threatened by rainforest clearcutting, has exerted the most direct pressure with GREEN TEEN boycotts such as the one waged since 1990 against Dixon Ticonderoga pencils (which use jelutong wood from Indonesia). In 1995 the tormented company called the boycott a "pack of lies" and began printing a green leaf and the message "Made From Sustained Yield Wood" on its boxes of Oriole-brand pencils.

gopher **RAN-Info** gopher://gopher.igc.apc.org/11/orgs/ran ✦
EMAIL ran-info@econet.apc.org

Ranks, Shabba (b. Rexton Rawlston Fernando Gordon, 1966)   King of DANCEHALL reggae who is the first Jamaican musician since Bob Marley to become an authentic star in the U.S. Ranks acheived this distinction by working a prowling Mr. Loverman persona and throaty, emphatic rasp that blurs the line between lewd "slackness" and Bible-friendly "lovemaking." Raised in Marley's impoverished Kingston neighborhood of Trenchtown, Ranks rose to the top of the Jamaican DJ (in U.S. parlance, rapper) world on the strength of risqué hits like "Wicked inna Bed" (1989). His early-'90s move on America was well plotted, eschewing a record deal with 2 LIVE CREW's Luther Campbell to pursue, on the back of tremendous street popularity, New York major labels; duets with the likes of Eddie Murphy, KRS-One, singer Maxi Priest, and QUEEN LATIFAH have helped broaden the appeal of dancehall's rugged sound. Ranks made U.S. headlines in late 1992 when he became embroiled in the controversy over Buju Banton's gay-bashing "Boom Bye Bye." Refusing to condemn

Jamaican homophobia, Ranks told British TV show *The Word* that "If you forfeit the laws of God Almighty, you deserve crucifixion." Gay activists protested Ranks' comments and, in March 1993,

Jay Leno's *Tonight Show* dropped him as a guest, citing a "human rights issue."

WEB **Sony Records Shabba Ranks Page**
http://www.sony.com/Music/ArtistInfo/ShabbaRanks.html

rebel advertising

"Join us and become unique"–it's the paradoxical cry of an over-the-counter counterculture in which corporate advertisers get down, go underground, and pass as ALTERNATIVE." One watershed in this shift to rebel-sell was NIKE's 1985 use of the Beatle's song "Revolution" in a commercial to tout the latest minor sneaker redesign; another was *Marketing Through Music*, a late '80s newsletter from ROLLING STONE, which identified bands that could be rented for corporate sponsorship. The phenomenon can be seen as an evolution of advertising's own reaction to advertising: as commercialism grows to fill every nook and cranny of existence, the distrust and distaste of it also grows. This provides advertisers with a new sentiment to tap and a new pitch to make–they, too, can't stand the world they've helped create.

Rebel advertising has still deeper roots. The urge toward acceptable individualism is a constant in America, with icons ranging from Thomas Jefferson's idealized yeoman farmer to the kooky '80s girl bouncing to the jingle "I like the Sprite in you!" Advertisers must tell people that they are special and different from the crowd . . . so that they will buy the same mass-produced products. Then consumers construct their individuality by the unique *combination* of goods and services they buy (I'm Geo, Amstel, Reebok, CompuServe; you're Ford pick-up, Budweiser, Converse, and Microsoft Network). When Nabisco ran a contest for the most eccentric way of eating an Oreo, a press release explained: "Nabisco believes the cookie's real appeal is that it brings out each person's individuality–the freedom to be 'me'–even if only briefly."

The quickest way to say alternative is to hire a rebel celebrity or symbol–almost any "underground" figure will do, even if people don't know exactly what you're talking about. William Burroughs, BEAT poet/homosexual HEROIN

addict/accidental wife-killer was chosen by NIKE to hype its new Air Max in a pair of techno-freaky ads in 1994. If most younger people to whom the spots were actually directed didn't have a clue as to who the old guy was . . . well, cool. "It's okay not to understand who he is," said Jean Rhode, the thirtyish copywriter at Nike ad agency Wieden & Kennedy. "He's more of a cult figure," and that, she said, better links Air Max "to a more underground feeling."

Sampling the hip signifiers of the past is often easier than trying to capture present-day cool. THE GAP's "So and so wore khaki's" 1993 campaign featured mid-century icons of attitude like Chet Baker, Jack Kerouac, and Miles Davis. Pepsi paid $5 million just for the right to be the only soft drink logo in attendance at WOODSTOCK '94. Likewise, psychedelia, once an aesthetic fueled by illicit drugs, now works for Coca-Cola's FRUITOPIA; and Philip Morris fashioned the yin-yang sign into an "accommodation symbol" that is supposed to stand for nonsmokers and smokers living together in harmony.

Today's younger generation is not necessarily offended by commercial use of '60s heroes. '90s icons, in fact, are often constructed around commercialism–their edge turning on how much irony they can evince while straddling life's commercial/noncommercial divide. Thus Kurt Cobain appeared on a March 1992 *Rolling Stone* cover wearing a T-shirt scrawled with the message "Corporate Magazines Still Suck."

From the marketers' point of view, GENERATION X advertising in general must convey some sense of consumer rebellion. Young people, says the ad manager for Acura, which has made ads directed to Xers, "have a much more cynical outlook–you got to hit them with a little more irreverence for the system, a little more disdain in the voice." So cans of OK SODA, a soft drink test-marketed by Coca-Cola in 1994 and

Rap Jam Volume One Not a record company compilation, or HIP-HOP BOOTLEG tape, but a 1995 Motown VIDEOGAME that is both a natural fit and a trivialization of RAP culture. The *Rap Jam* player can stage games of hip hop-soundtracked street basketball with teams drawn from synergy-minded rhymers like PUBLIC ENEMY, QUEEN LATIFAH, WARREN G, Onyx, and Naughty By

1995, featured sullen-looking teens drawn by underground comic book artists DAN CLOWES and CHARLES BURNS. Such sponsored cynicism can easily backfire, as it did most famously in Subaru's 1993 TV spot in which a CHRISTIAN SLATER-like kid likened the Subaru Impreza to "PUNK rock" while other cars were somehow "boring and corporate." (The agency for OK and Subaru? Wieden & Kennedy.)

The attitude of stylized resentment has more successfully been harnessed by Red Dog beer. A 1994-launched campaign featured a gruff, ugly bulldog who incited his tamer canine colleagues to bite loose their leashes with the slogan "Be Your Own Dog." Trade magazines judged the new brand a hit with men in their twenties.

Bold print advertisement

WOODSTOCK "plus softener" in 1995 advertisement.

Sometimes corporations go stealth. The ads for Red Dog suggested that it was a microbrew, made by the little-known Plank Road Brewery, but it was actually a new product from corporate giant Miller Brewery (itself owned by mega-giant Philip Morris). Miller wanted this middle-of-the-road beer to sound different, youthful, kick-ass. A Miller spokeswoman said, "It's very much a beer for an independent-minded individual, but I wouldn't want to put it in the cynical camp at all. It's about friendly contrariness." Join us and become unique, she explained: "It's an alternative to the mainstream, but it's in the mainstream." The not-quite-a-beer ZIMA likewise disguised its corporate parent, Coors, which is still burdened by associations with the right-wing politics of its owners. The pseudo-indie tack also works for the hippyish Fruitopia, which often neglects to mention its Coca-Cola parentage,

and Dave's Cigarettes, another folksy Philip Morris product.

The ads that seem to be the most revolutionary attack advertising itself. Sprite, for instance, practically shouts a Shining Path line on commercialism: in a TV spot a hip-hopper, surrounded by blinking TV images of pretend ads, raps about his (and our) sick relationship with soft-drink commercials: "In my 17 years on this planet they have tried everything to get me to drink their drinks. They have subjected me to an infinite number of product shots, drink shots, megasuperstars, jingles, and the kind of people I have never ever met in real life." At the end, these words flash on screen: "IMAGE IS NOTHING. THIRST IS EVERYTHING. OBEY YOUR THIRST. SPRITE." Sprite, too, is owned by Coca-Cola.

MTV, home of rebel marketing (as well as rebel HOME SHOPPING), plays the same game expertly. In-house ads even dare the viewer to turn off the TV. One 1989 spot showed nothing but these words on the screen: "[These words] will hang out for 15 seconds until it's time for another commercial / These are words that could be saying something / but they're not / they're just sitting there / LIKE YOU." The soft-sell stiffens, however, in MTV's trade advertising. In 1993, the network ran an ad in *Advertising Age* that showed another grungy dude over the headline: "Buy this 24-year-old and get all his friends absolutely free. . . . He heads up a pack. What he eats, his friends eat. What he wears, they wear. What he likes, they like. And what he's never heard of . . . well . . . you get the idea." Like all marketers who flatter consumers as rebels, MTV is really corralling conformists too passive to rebel except in the most symbolic way—that is, by buying things.—*Leslie Savan*

USENET **alt.tv.commercials** ✦ WEB **Advert Attack**
http://Snark.apana.org.au/adverts/ ✦ WEB **Alternet**
http://www.igc.apc.org/an/

Nature. (Only the Sega/Genesis version, for some reason, features N.W.A founder EAZY-E, whose own GANGSTA-flavored game, *Hittin Switchez*, was also scheduled for release by Motown before his premature death in 1995.)

raves Energetic all-night happenings fueled by TECHNO music, rampant ECSTASY use, and an Age of Aquarius-style utopian togetherness. Outlaw by nature, raves are optimally held in a vast open-air environment, the location of which is kept clandestine by the event's promoters through flyers, secret phone numbers and INTERNET mailing lists. The raver—typically a young person wearing baggy fatigues, corporate-LOGO-PARODY T-shirt, and a backpack, carrying among other things, the all-important bottled water—will show up, cash in hand, for a euphoric marathon of dancing and chemically induced soul expansion. Originally a part of Britain's late-'80s ACID HOUSE culture, raves came to America around the turn of the decade, most powerfully in the L.A. area, where entire amusement parks such as Knotts' Berry Farm would be rented for the occasion. New York's indoor outdoor traveling rave N.A.S.A. (Nocturnal Audio Sensory Awakening) was one east coast stronghold. Though the rave scene has waned somewhat in urban areas, it has caught on in middle America, where the novelty remains fresh, clubland non-existent, and open space plentiful.

WEB **Hyperreal** http://www.hyperreal.com ✦ WEB **XLR8R Magazine Online** http://www.hyperreal.com:/zines/xlr8r/ ✦ WEB **The Official alt.rave FAQ** http://www.hyperreal.com:/ raves/altraveFAQ.html ✦ USENET **alt.rave**

RE/Search Publisher of over-sized, fringe-culture paperbacks, founded in 1980 by Andrea Juno (b. 1955) and V. Vale (b. circa 1952; former editor of Bay Area punk ZINE *Search and Destroy* and member of '60s heavy rockers Blue Cheer). RE/Search soon evolved into an immensely prescient guide to marginal cultural concerns, with early editions devoted to writer J. G. BALLARD, INDUSTRIAL culture, "incredibly strange films," and

pranks. RE/Search hit its stride with an issue dedicated to the TATTOOS, PIERCING, and other bodily modifications of the so-called MODERN PRIMITIVES. A subsequent issue on "incredibly strange music" turned into two collections of thrift-store treasures turned answering-machine fodder; other issues included a volume on S/M poster boy BOB FLANAGAN, interviews with media pranksters (*Pranks!*), and the self-explanatory anthology *Angry Women*. The RE/Search Classics list has reprinted a series of "lost" books by Ballard, Charles Willeford, Octave Mirbeau, Brion Gysin, and Wanda von Sacher-Masoch. The company moved from San Francisco to New York in 1995.

Real World, The MTV's "reality"-based soap opera. Since 1992, groups of seven carefully chosen young subjects have been installed in fancy living quarters where several months of their lives are filmed by 18-hour-a-day camera crews. (In 1994, the San Francisco installment became one of MTV's most popular shows, second only to BEAVIS AND BUTT-HEAD.) *The Real World* was created in 1991 by a veteran soap-opera producer and a documentary filmmaker, inspired in part by the chance to produce a soap opera without having to pay writers.

The first season, set in New York City, set the tone for the series. The photogenic cast was disproportionately comprised of models, singers, and actors, and uniformly good-looking. Sexual, racial and general roommate tensions were the source of frequent blow-ups and crying jags, while extreme camera angles, frequent edits, and a non-stop soundtrack of overly literal pop music gave the show its MTV "edge." The second season moved the series to L.A., with predictably stultifying effect. The third season, in San Francisco, fared better. Stars were born in PEDRO ZAMORA and, especially, in BIKE MESSENGER Puck, whose vivacious lack of sanitary habits kept Americans aged 15–25 grossed out for an entire summer. In 1995, *The Real World* moved to London (25,000 people applied for seven openings), where the much ballyhooed "cultural differences" failed to yield much of a dramatic pay-load. (Later the same year, MTV's *Road Rules* put seven strangers into an R/V for episodic stunts that made *The Real World* look spontaneous.)

The artifice and imposed narrative of *The Real World* has been widely criticized, notably by revered documentarian Albert Maysles. Talent agents have been used to recruit cast members, and MTV's fun-house living quarters suggest a country club decorated by URBAN OUTFITTERS; cast members are given $2,600 for their rights, plus a generous food and entertainment account, story-enhancing paradise vacations (filmed), and, according to L.A.'s Dominic, free therapy sessions for six months afterwards.

WEB **The Unofficial MTV Real World HomePage** http://ucsu.Colorado.EDU/~burtonb/real.html ✦ WEB **mtv.com** http://www.mtv.com ✦ USENET **alt.tv.real-world**

RealAudio   Software program released April 1995 which makes it possible to listen to low-fi audio sound over the INTERNET, even through a standard phone-line connection. Sound files previously took longer to download than play (a four-minute song might take 20-minutes to retrieve), but RealAudio reduces and compresses the signal so it can play with no delay. The technology has opened up new multimedia possibilities for the WORLD WIDE WEB, got PERRY FARRELL gushing to *Billboard* about the future of "desktop broadcasting," and provided radio stations with global, radio-on-demand outlets for their product. The initial business plan of the SEATTLE-based program-maker the Progressive Network (run by the former head of Microsoft's multimedia division), is to profit by giving the "player" program away for free and charging for the "broadcast" component. Early adapters included National Public Radio, C-Span, Adam Curry's METAVERSE, and a Marina Del Rey, California-based station called Radio HK that broadcasts unsigned rock bands only over the Internet. Future versions will undoubtedly improve the music-hostile sound quality; the company has also experimented with audio codes that, for instance, can control animated baseball characters on the screen while listening to a live, play-by-play broadcast.

WEB **RealAudio** http://www.realaudio.com

rebel advertising   See page 200.

Red Hot Chili Peppers   Former L.A. PUNK rockers, trafficking since 1984 in funk-rock fueled by the red-blooded lyrics of Anthony Kiedis (b. 1962) and the rubber-band bass of Flea (b. Michael Balzary 1962). The band's athletic stage show (and occasional habit of appearing naked but for socks on their genitals) initially earned them a sterling live reputation; however, when they enlisted GEORGE CLINTON to produce their second album *Freaky Styley* (1985), the Chili Peppers were proof that athletic energy cannot be directly translated into funk. The band remained on the fringes until 1991, when they recorded *BloodSugarSexMagik* under the aegis of legendary producer RICK RUBIN. Although inconsistent, the album yielded the epic, multi-part hit ballad "Under the Bridge" (video by GUS VAN SANT), Kiedis' eulogy to his days as a HEROIN addict. The band was officially admitted to the pantheon when they headlined that year's LOLLAPALOOZA. WOODSTOCK '94 saw the Red Hot Chili Peppers wearing huge light bulbs on their heads, a return to their novelty-dressing roots.

WEB **Chili Peppers** http://wbr.com/chilipeppers

Red Hot Organization   Charity that has raised more than $5 million dollars for AIDS groups worldwide through the success of, as of mid–1995, five well-publicized compilation albums of several musical genres. Co-founded in 1989 by New York lawyer and art critic John Carlin (b. 1955) and filmmaker Leigh Blake (b. 1953), RHO first attracted attention in 1990 with the platinum sales of its first release *Red Hot + Blue*, which featured artists like U2, SINEAD O'CONNOR, and k.d. lang covering Cole Porter classics. (ABC broadcast a one-hour TV special minus sexually direct clips from rappers the Jungle Brothers and British singer

Jimmy Somerville.) Four subsequent albums on various record labels—*Red Hot + Dance* (1992), *No Alternative* (1993), *Red Hot + Country* (1994), and *Stolen Moments: Red Hot + Cool* (1994)—enhanced the organization's considerable credibility. Producer Carlin juxtaposes nascent talents with big-selling names: critical darlings Wilco abut critical pariah Billy Ray Cyrus on *Red Hot + Country*; old-school jazzers Donald Byrd and Herbie Hancock share space on *Red Hot + Cool* with upstarts US3 and Joshua Redman. Planned projects include compilations of RAVE/JUNGLE/AMBIENT/TECHNO, bossanova, and Memphis music, plus a ZINE-and-record INDIE-ROCK project.

U.S. postage stamp of the red AIDS ribbon, in circulation since December 1993

red ribbon Celebrity and grassroots symbol of AIDS awareness. The ribbons were originally conceived for the 1991 New York theater Tony Awards, when the "gold" ribbons of the Gulf War were still ubiquitous; they were devised by Visual AIDS, the same New York-based artist group responsible for DAY WITHOUT ART. Subsequently the inverted "V," scarlet swatches conquered the Emmys in August, the Grammys in February, and the Academy Awards in March. (Ironically, L.A.'s ACT-UP chapter failed, one year earlier, to persuade celebrities to wear less-ambiguous rhinestone "Silence=Death" pins at the '91 Academy Awards.) The ribbons became a badge of concern among liberal-minded urbanites and figured prominently at the Democrats' 1992 national convention. On their MTV show, social critics BEAVIS AND BUTT-HEAD decided, while watching an awards show, that the ribbons are what stars wear to let people know they're famous.
WEB **RedRibbonNEt** http://worldclass.com/redribbn/

Redd Kross Formed on a punky impulse in 1978 by brothers Steven and Jeff McDonald (b. circa 1967 and circa 1963), Red Kross would flout contemporary musical mores with melodic, harmony-drenched hymns to the then-unfashionable (later mandatory) '70s trash-aesthetic. (The band figured prominently in the presciently kitsch 1991 movie *Spirit of '76*.) As if aligning themselves with a loathed pop decade wasn't enough, the band was dogged by misfortune: the blond-tressed McDonalds could initially only play live locally due to their tender ages; later, their label Big Time went under in the late-'80s, just as the Zeitgeist was turning in their favor. In the '90s Red Kross couldn't help looking shopworn and even a little desperate. SONIC YOUTH's Thurston Moore described Red Kross to *Entertainment Weekly* in 1993 as "one of the most important bands in America," but his endorsement may have come too late for these proto-GENERATION X visionaries.
WEB **Redd Kross** http://www.nando.net/music/gm/ReddKross/

Reeves, Keanu (b. 1964) Beirut-born, Toronto-raised actor-hunk variously regarded as idiot or savant. Reeves made his movie debut in *River's Edge* (1986), an anomic tale of suburban burnouts; he first tasted success in the teen-time-travel hit *Bill and Ted's Excellent Adventure* (1989; sequel 1991), playing an unthreatening suburban burnout. For many, Keanu (the name means "cool breeze over the mountains" in Hawaiian) was thenceforth typecast as a perpetual, mumbling adolescent whose appearances in costume dramas like *Dangerous Liaisons* (1988), *Little Buddha* (1994), and *Much Ado About Nothing* (1993) had a risible incongruity. Others—particularly the actor's female followers—see in him an admirable lack of guile, an empathic honesty. Some even look deeper: Foucault and Nietzsche were both cited in a Spring 1994 course on Reeves' films at Pasadena's Art Center College of Design. Reeves' appeal was maximized in that year's blockbuster *Speed*: his doe-eyed, near-silent bomb squad detective was widely hailed as the harbinger of a new cinema archetype, the HIMBO. *Speed* raised Reeves' salary well into seven figures—after which, in January 1995, he went on to play Hamlet in a small Winnipeg theater. As the WILLIAM GIBSON-penned, Reeves-starring *Johnny*

Mnemonic was flopping at the box-office in June 1995, Reeves chose *OUT* magazine as a venue to deny rumors of his homosexuality.

WEB **Keanunet** http://www.interport.net/~eperkins/

reflective fashion   Poised for the dawn of a new millennium, fashion designers went with a space age palette in their 1994 collection. Reflective silver metallic, borrowed from CLUB KIDS, became the color of choice from everything from hoop skirts to hiking boots. ANNA SUI made glittery leather micro-minis and studded jackets; Donna Karan used polyester treated with fiberglass to create shiny rain-coats, backpacks and sneakers, while other designers experimented with high-tech fabrics made from unexpected materials like Scotchlite, polyurethane, and aluminum. LAURA WHITCOMB showed a collection frontloaded with the type of reflective fabrics usually worn only by rescue-workers. Even platinum hair made a comeback, as actresses DREW BARRY-MORE and Meg Ryan, and models Nadja Auermann and Jaime Rishar went white-blond.

religious fashion   MADONNA's blasphemous, cleavage-accenting rosaries may have inspired many wannabes in the '80s, but the fashion industry really fell for religious motifs in the collections for fall 1993, embracing SPIRITUALITY with a vengeance. In a move that supposedly signaled a rejection of '80s hedonism, designers turned to the attire of priests, nuns, rabbis, and monks to create an interfaith look of NEW AGE atonement. Crosses—in materials rang-ing from crystal to jewel-encrusted gold—became *de rigueur* among designers like Donna Karan and Richard Tyler. JEAN-PAUL GAULTIER—who devoted a collection to nuns in 1989—presented his version of chic Hasidim, infuriating the Hasidic community. CALVIN KLEIN found inspiration in the simplicity and restraint of the Amish and the austerity of priestly vestments. Menswear designer John Bartlett made rope-belted monk's coats and loose orange Hare Krishna robes. "Personally speaking, there's nothing sexier than a monk or a Hare Krishna," Bartlett told the *New York Times* in September, 1993. "They're so inaccessible." Ponytailed Chanel designer Karl Lagerfeld incensed the Muslim world in January 1994 when he sent SUPERMODEL Claudia Schiffer down the runway in a bustier dress deco-rated with Arabic script phrases from the Koran; the garment was hastily withdrawn after vocal protests from Muslims.

Remote Control   MTV show, launched December 1987, that foretold elements of what would later be identified as "GENERATION X" cul-ture. Fronted by lantern-jawed host Ken Ober (with sidekicks ADAM SANDLER, DENIS LEARY, and the redoubtable Colin Quinn), *Remote Control* was meta-entertainment at its headiest, a trashy TV game show about trash TV (part of the set decora-tion was a giant Bob Eubanks Pez dispenser). The show's college-age contestants were strapped into La-Z-Boy recliners, impotently waving TV remote-control units to choose "channels" like "The *BRADY BUNCH* Network," "Dead or Canadian?" (little-seen celebrities), and "Inside [*Family Ties* star] Tina Yothers." It would be another five years before an obsession with '70s television and third-tier celebri-ties would be certified as a generational trait.

Ren and Stimpy   Boasting a surreal wealth of fluids and gasses, of pointy threatening teeth and painfully bloodshot eyes, the animated *Ren and Stimpy Show*'s 1991 debut season rapidly whipped up a disbelieving cult following. Part of the thrill was wondering how the NICKELODEON children's network could have sanctioned such a giddily cele-bration of flatulence, shaving scum, mucal dis-charge, and mental cruelty. (The show's inane singa-

Kricfalusi-classic *Ren and Stimpy*.

long "Happy! Happy! Joy! Joy!" immediately became a *crie de coeur* among INDIE-ROCKERS.) Starring a heavily caffeinated "asthma-hound" Chihuahua named Ren Höek and the droolingly slow-witted Stimpson J. Cat, *R&S* was the brainchild of producer/director John Kricfalusi's (b. 1955) Spumco Inc. studio. Kricfalusi's unorthodox sense of humor and work habits soon began to irritate Nickelodeon, which wrenched the show away from him in 1992 and gave it to an associate, Bob Camp. Kricfalusi retreated to create Jimmy the Idiot Boy, a character whose merchandising rights he intends to keep.

WEB **Ren-n-Stimpy Page** http://www.cris.com/~lkarper/ rands.html/✦ USENET **alt.tv.ren-n-stimpy, alt.fan.ren-and-stimpy, alt.animation.spumco**

Reubens, Paul, a.k.a. Pee-Wee Herman (b. Paul Rubenfeld, 1952)

Comic made famous by his alter-ego, a quirky Jerry Lewis-like manchild instantly recognizable by his bright red lipstick, a matching mini bow tie, and a one-size-too-small gray suit with high-waters riding well above gleaming white shoes. First debuted in 1978, the popular stand-up character was such a hit on the big screen (1985's *Pee-Wee's Big Adventure*, directed by TIM BURTON) that a ground-breaking kid's show (*Pee-Wee's Playhouse*, 1986–1991) soon followed. Extending Pee-Wee's anarchic, campy antics, the show brought in playmates like Larry (now Lawrence) Fishburne as Cowboy Curtis and Phil Hartman as Kap'n Carl, with a set design and animated effects recalling both Dali and Max Fleisher. The circus imagery of Pee-Wee's second movie (*Big Top Pee-Wee*, 1988) fit the tabloid scandal spawned by the arrest of Reubens—while visiting his parents in his childhood home of Sarasota, Florida—on July 26, 1991 for exposing himself in an X-rated movie theater. Pee-Wee dolls were recalled from toy store shelves, CBS dropped plans to broadcast the remaining five *Pee-Wee's Playhouse* episodes, and Dr. Joyce Brothers counseled parents on how to explain the situation to young fans ("People touch themselves privately, not in public"). Pee-Wee's cult following rallied, greeting his surprise

public resurfacing at the September *MTV Video Music Awards* with a rousing ovation after Pee-Wee—the butt of ten thousand wisecracks—casually inquired, "Heard any good jokes lately?" Reubens has since appeared in a series of small TV and movie roles.

Rhino Records

Smartly obsessive re-issue label started out of an L.A. record shop in 1978 by USC students Harold Bronson and Richard Foos. (The first Rhino store opened in Westwood in 1973.) Rhino Records' arch, informed sensibility distinguished the company from other re-issue merchants, and Rhino grew exponentially with the CD boom. By the start of the '90s Rhino was releasing comedy albums, novelty-record compilations, and collections of historical speeches (plus videotapes) alongside single-artist compilations and labor-intensive slabs of genre-collated material. Among Rhino's long-running series were the '70s hits compilation *Have a Nice Day*, and '70s soul collection *Didn't It Blow Your Mind?* (both over 20 volumes). Rhino's multi-million-dollar distribution deal with Atlantic/ WEA in April 1992 gave them access to impressive archives of the classic rock and soul era; a 1995 deal with Turner Entertainment Co. loosed them on old soundtracks. Exhaustive sets like *Just Can't Get Enough: New Wave Hits of the '80s* (15 volumes) and *D.I.Y.* (a nine-volume PUNK *homage*) proved that Rhino's generational nerve-tweaking was not restricted to BABY BOOMERS.

WEB **Rhino Records** http://cybertimes.com/Rhino

Rice, Anne (b. 1941)

Author of *Interview With the Vampire* (1976), a story of moody, bloodsucking pansexual immortals that, along with three sequels (*The Vampire Lestat* [1985], *Queen of the Damned* [1988], and *The Tale of the Body Thief* [1992]), helped crystallize an entire GOTH literary subculture. Readers found in Rice's work a general metaphor for romantic damnation, and then a specific metaphor for love in the time of AIDS. Raven-haired and severely pale, Rice (a pseudonymous writer of erotica) is prone to public displays of truculence that only serve to secure the admiration of her fans. After years of false starts, the movie version *Interview* was made in 1994 with *The Crying Game*'s Neil Jordan directing Tom Cruise as Lestat and BRAD PITT as Louis. Before the film started shooting, Rice lambasted the casting of Cruise, insisting that he couldn't possibly inhabit her weary Aryan epicure. Eerily in synch with the film's pre-release publicity, Rice recanted and showered Cruise with praise. Although audiences largely agreed with her initial judgment, a sequel was put in the works almost immediately after the film's decent but unspectacular release.

WEB **Anne Rice Homepage** http://ucunix.san.uc.edu/~elymt/AnneRice/AnneRice.html USENET **alt.books.anne-rice**

Riley, Teddy (b. 1967) Harlem-born wunderkind producer/writer whose band Guy almost singlehandedly revitalized rhythm and blues music with their same-titled 1987 debut. Riley's production style (which also graced records by Bobby Brown and Keith Sweat, among others) defined a new black pop that vigorously mixed hip-hop beats and rapping with soulful vocals and lush synthesizers; it was labeled New Jack Swing after term for flashy young drug dealers coined by *Village Voice* journalist Barry Michael Cooper (writer of the 1991 movie *New Jack City*, for which Riley composed the title track). A new generation of black hitmakers followed in Riley's wake, most notably Dallas Austin and L.A. & Baby Face.

When Riley's half-brother (Brandon Mitchell, a member of the Riley-produced Wreckx-N-Effect) was fatally shot in 1989, the producer retreated to a base in Virginia Beach, Virginia, from which he produced part of Michael Jackson's 1991 album *Dangerous*. In 1994 Riley formed the band Blackstreet, in a reasonably successful effort to recapture the ensemble feel that launched his career.

riot grrrls Loose-knit affiliation of feminist PUNKS, formed circa 1991 in OLYMPIA, WASHINGTON and Washington, D.C. With the rallying cry, "Revolution Girl Style Now!" bands like Bikini Kill and Bratmobile forged a mini-movement to combat the male-dominance of the punk scene

and, by extension, the rest of the world. Riot grrrl activities included national conventions in D.C., the Pussystock festival in New York City, and a slew of ZINES, notably *Girl Germs, Satan Wears A Bra* and *Quit Whining*. To their horror, the riot grrrls found themselves media darlings by 1992, featured for dragging feminism into the MOSH PIT in magazines from *Seventeen* to *Newsweek*. Internal squabbling led to resignations of people like Jessica Hopper, who was at the center of the *Newsweek* coverage. Riot grrrl leader Kathleen Hanna of

Kathleen Hannah of RIOT GRRRL band Bikini Kill, 1992.

Bikini Kill called that year for "a press block" and reporters from papers like the *Seattle Times*, *Washington Post*, and *Houston Chronicle* found themselves fleshing out riot grrrl articles by describing exactly the way in which various scenesters hung up on them.

While the riot grrrl label was soon being fixed on any aggressive or overtly sexual girl-band—including major label bands like L7 and Babes In Toyland—most actual riot grrrl bands stuck doggedly to independent record labels—especially Olympia's K—and maintained a commitment to cheap, all-ages shows. A defining moment for the riot grrrls, especially the Seattle branch, came with the tragic rape and murder of the Gits' Mia Zapata in 1993. The crime became the subject of a number of songs, including "Go Home" by proto-riot grrrl Joan Jett, who teamed up with Hanna in 1994. Riot grrrls made headlines again in 1995 when COURTNEY LOVE punched Hanna in the head backstage at LOLLAPALOOZA.

MAIL LIST **Riot Grrrl Mailing List** email trooper@stein2.u.washington.edu

robodosing High-school high from doses of over-the-counter bottles of cough syrups such as Robutussin DM or Vicks 44D. Cough syrups laced with the narcotic codeine—available only by prescription in the U.S.—are also often widely abused, especially in Hong Kong where authorities regularly decry school girl use of Madame Pearls and Cocodrine. (Some enthusiasts claim that the active ingredient dextromethorpan causes hallucinations when combined with PROZAC; some swear that Prozac isn't necessary.) Cough syrups have long been the delivery agent of powerful depressants, dating back to the late 19th century when Bayer marketed a cough syrup featuring the wonder drug HEROIN. The ephedrine found in many cough syrups can also serve as a basis for the cheap and dirty synthesis of PERVITIN and other methamphetamines.

WEB **The Dextromethorphan Page**

http://oucsace.cs.ohiou.edu/personal/bwhite/p0.html

rock women

The late '80s and early '90s saw the emergence of a remarkable number of high-profile female rock performers. The mainstream exposure of ALTERNATIVE rock brought many of these artists a visibility they might not have experienced ten years before, while the appearance of numerous bands with explicitly feminist agendas focused increased attention on rock's gender politics. Yet the most mundane explanation for this surge of female musicians is probably the most accurate: There were more women in the workplace than ever before, and the music business was no exception. Female electricians, surgeons, and actuaries, however, are somewhat less likely to find themselves the subjects of intense media scrutiny.

It's a self-evident but infrequently acknowledged fact that the history of women in rock 'n' roll runs parallel to the history of the women's movement. Not surprisingly, women's entry into the male-dominated realm of rock music provoked many of the same responses as their entry into a male-dominated work force. Those responses were often patronizing, or hostile, and the complaints of contemporary female musicians are, in essence, the same as those of other women who experience discrimination on the job. (The record industry had a spate of sexual harassment suits in the early '90s. In the most prominent of these, Geffen Records secretary Penny Much was dubbed the "ANITA HILL of the music business" in 1992 after bringing charges against her boss, executive Marko Babineau; Geffen fired him and settled for a reported $500,000.) In 1995, a flurry of critical works appeared that addressed sexism in both the recording industry and the music itself—most notably Simon Reynolds and Joy Press's book *The Sex Revolts*, which went so far as to define rock's disaffection as inherently misogynist.

As might be expected during a period labeled the "postfeminist" era, the '90s were a time when old-school feminism was struggling to redefine itself. COURTNEY LOVE, the most talked-about—and reviled—female artist of the mid-'90s, engaged in a simultaneous rebellion against, and embrace of, traditional femininity. Love refused to discuss the issue of "women in rock" for fear of ghettoizing female artists, yet also sported a hybrid of elementary-school and streetwalker fashions that she termed the "kinderwhore" look. She was a walking contradiction, and as such a fitting personification of society's mixed messages to, and about, women.

As long as women artists have taken femaleness as their subject, they have manipulated feminine imagery to political ends, from the painter Georgia O'Keefe to the bra-burning feminists of the '60s. Female rock performers have sometimes adopted cartoonish stylistic exaggerations of femininity, while others have rejected cultural proscriptions for female appearance by embracing punk's determinedly unpretty aesthetic. In a cultural environment characterized by a hyper-awareness of gender, simply being female often seemed to constitute a political act. Rock journalists spent a great deal of time trying to establish a dubious commonality between groups like SMASHING PUMPKINS and the Cranberries that had little in common except success and a female member.

During the late '80s/early '90s, there was a surge of woman hard-rock and hardcore bands who reconfigured the genre's aggression as a

alt.culture

Rock and Roll Hall of Fame Depending on one's ideological stance (and birth date), the Rock and Roll Hall of Fame is either a worthy attempt to ennoble an underregarded art form or a desperate grab for cultural cachet by aging BABY BOOMERS. Each January since 1986, rock-world dignitaries have attended annual induction ceremonies (in 1995, paying over $1,200 each) honoring voted-in artists whose body of work dates back at least 25 years; which, to date, has meant the somber enshrining of rock's most un-self-conscious years. The ceremony's pre-programmed emotional reunions and crowded "jam" sessions function both as glorified photo opportunities and a brilliant marketing strategy to jump-start becalmed careers. In defense of the enterprise, it can be said that the '60s retrospectives

vehicle for the expression of a specifically female rage. (As if women in the realm of hard rock didn't have enough trouble being taken seriously, they had SONIC YOUTH's Thurston Moore to thank for coining in 1990 the term "foxcore," the briefly voguish tag for hardcore music by women.) Bands like L7 and Babes In Toyland played no less aggressively than their male counterparts, but without the lyrical and literal posturing generally associated with hard rock. The RIOT GRRRLS, a loosely defined grass-roots movement dedicated to feminist political action and challenging male punk hege-

Photo by Sandra-Lee Phipps

COURTNEY LOVE, Roseland, New York, 1994.

mony, were born in the INDIE-ROCK communities of OLYMPIA, Washington, and Washington, D.C. The group—its relatively small number grossly over-inflated by a media titillated by the notion of a teenage girl army—did its proselytizing via fanzines and through grrrl-identified bands like Bikini Kill and Huggy Bear (who sometimes insisted on the literal meaning of "women's music," playing shows in England from which male spectators were banned.)

Not all women rock musicians set out to conquer the genre by co-opting the belligerent, over-the-top behavior that's traditionally the province of male rock stars. More often, women simply challenged traditional gender roles. SINEAD O'CONNOR told interviewers that she shaved her head in response to male record company executives who were urging her to adopt a sexier image. LIZ PHAIR got considerable mileage out of the fact that people don't expect to hear a woman sing lines like "I want to fuck you like a dog / Take you home and make you like it." Like the Slits before them, Hole, and the Muffs, defused a slang term for female genitalia by adopting it as a band name. Female and co-ed bands like the Breeders and Belly chose names that directly alluded to women's reproductive capacity. Women also routinely reclaimed rock's swaggering anthems: both Two Nice Girls and Lunachicks, for example, did covers of Bad Company's quintessentially macho '70s hit "Feel Like Makin' Love."

Despite the social change wrought by the women's movement of the '60s and '70s, sexism remained encoded in almost all aspects of American culture—not least rock 'n' roll. The mid-'90s has been a time when even outspoken female artists like Phair and PJ HARVEY appeared on the covers of national rock magazines in their underwear. An August 1994 *Time* article headlined "Rock Goes Coed" included the observation that girls these days "not only sing but play instruments and write songs, too." Rote survey stories like this exemplified the kind of marginalization contemporary female musicians deride. ("Droning on about some gender-based rock theory" appears on Hole's official Geffen biography under the heading "Cheap ways to endear yourself to the rock band Hole.") If there was anything that united the disparate women artists of the '90s it was unwillingness to accept novelty status.—*Nicole Arthur*
USENET **alt.music.alternative.female** ✦ MAIL LIST **Laddykillerz**
email ladykillerz-request@arastar.com with subject "asdf" and "subscribe ladykillerz Your Name" in the message body

evince a healthy racial mix (around 50–50) than will be bequeathed by the ALTERNATIVE rock era. (The Hall was without a physical home until the 1995 opening of its Cleveland museum site, an $80 million-plus, six-story multi-media complex designed by fashionable architect I. M. Pei.)

WEB **Rock and Roll Hall of Fame** http://www.rocknroll.org/

Rock For Choice Abortion rights organization founded by L.A. band L7 in October 1991; NIRVANA, HOLE, PEARL JAM, and the RED HOT CHILI PEPPERS are among those who have contributed their services to the cause. Proceeds of benefit concerts go to the Feminist Majority Foundation, which in turn supports the National Clinic Defense Project and campaigns against the likes of the 1977 Hyde Amendment (which withholds federal funding from women who can't afford an abortion) and consent laws (which require women under 18 to get parental permission for an abortion). A 1995 benefit album, *Spirit of '73*, featured current female artists covering songs performed (and/or written) by women in the '70s.

WEB **Rock For Choice** http://bianca.com/lolla/politics/ rockforchoice/r4c.html ✦ WEB **Rock for Choice** http://www.mojones.com/kiosks/rockforchoice/r4c.html

Rock the Vote Nonpartisan music industry campaign to raise voter registration and turnout among young adults, launched as a rearguard action in 1990 at the height of the record-labeling mania in state legislatures. Celebrity endorsers of the radical direct action known as voting included MADONNA and Iggy Pop, both of whom, it was revealed by *ROLLING STONE*, had never bothered to register. MTV, which ran the group's public service announcements round the clock, liked the Rock the Vote idea so much that it copied it, dubbing its coverage of the 1992 presidential race, "Choose or Lose." (Comedy Central's parody of the paternalistic attempt to "make voting hip" was called "Vote or Die.") While the youth vote did not actually rise as a percentage of all votes cast in the 1992 election, Rock the Vote was instrumental in rallying support for the Motor Voter Bill which gives drivers the chance to register to vote when applying for a license. The bill passed once a clause fot welfare recipients was dropped.

WEB **Rock the Vote Homepage** http://www.iuma.com/RTV/

rock women See page 208.

Rodman, Dennis (b. 1961) Tattooed and pierced 6' 8" basketball forward (Detroit Pistons, San Antonio Spurs, Chicago Bulls) also known as "The Worm." Rodman's on-court prowess contrasts with a disciplinary record that makes him less than ideal franchise-fodder. This tonsorially colorful African-American maverick has a penchant for outrageous behavior that shames most of the NBA's putative "bad boys"—in the first weeks of the 1993–94 season, for instance, he was suspended for three games for throwing ice at a referee and missing team practice; he lead the league in technical fouls in the 1994 season. Extracurricular highlights have included a March 1995 motorcycle crash that put him out of action for a month weeks consistent allusions to sexual ambiguity—"I visualize being with a man," he told *Sports Illustrated* (which called him "the best rebounding forward in NBA history"). It took an even stranger proclivity, however, to put Rodman in the cross-hairs of the tabloids—dating MADONNA.

WEB **The Official Dennis Rodman Fan Club Homepage** http://www.texas.net/users/pmagal/

Rodriguez, Robert (b. 1968) University of Texas film student who won the Audience Award at the 1993 SUNDANCE Film Festival with his $7,000 feature debut *El Mariachi*. The film (directed, co-written, produced and photographed by the Mexican-American Rodriguez) was a sanguineous, understandably raw tale of a mix-up between a musician and a hit-man; although intended as a straight-to-video calling card for the major studios, *El Mariachi* was bought in its original form by Columbia Pictures, making it the lowest-budget major-studio movie ever. Rodriguez used *El Mariachi* as a springboard to fully funded projects, including a segment alongside those of QUENTIN TARANTINO, ALLISON ANDERS, and Alexandre

Rockwell in *Four Rooms* (1995); a feature-length vampire-biker movie, *From Dusk 'til Dawn* (1995), starring JULIETTE LEWIS, TV hunk George Clooney (*E.R.*), and Tarantino, who provided the script; and *Desperado*, a $5 million sequel to *El Mariachi*, with the requisite Tarantino cameo.

rogue traders   Epithet fixed to Nicholas Leeson, the 28-year-old futures trader in Singapore who in February 1995 bankrupted a 227-year-old British investment bank, Barings, by losing $1 billion on bets that Japanese stocks would go up and bonds go down. Only one-third as magnificent was the case of Joseph Jett, a 36 year-old Kidder Peabody bond trader who was accused of racking up $350 million in profits until his bosses began to suspect in April 1994 that the brilliant trades he entered in the company computer might never have actually never taken place. (The corrected books are said to have helped a dismayed General Electric decide to unload Kidder Peabody, its Wall Street subsidiary.) Many of the worst rogue trader cases are characterized by a generation gap: senior managers don't question the profits generated by cocky, young, go-go traders who deal in derivatives and other new-fangled financial instruments.

Rollerblading   Rollerskating fad created by replacing traditional "quad" wheel design with hockey-style boots and "in-line" wheels to give the acceleration and maneuverability of ice skates. Rollerblade design patents date back to 19th century Holland, but it was Minneapolis hockey player Scott Olson and his Rollerblade company (founded 1980) that turned America on to a new national pastime. (Tragically for Olson, he sold the company before profits peaked.) 'Blading exploded in the late '80s and early '90s, appealing both to ex-joggers looking for low-impact workouts and death-defying speed freaks (not to mention LITTLE LUXURY-types who shell out up to $250 for a quality pair of skates). Skateboard culture heavily colors rollerblading's EXTREME SPORTS applications, with the half-pipe adapted for "vert" aerial stunt-work and specialized forms of "stair-bashing" on the street. Other

manifestations include a struggling in-line hockey league and an *American Gladiators* spin-off called *Blade Warriors* (1994), in which the regular series of preposterous games are all played on rollerblades.
USENET **rec.skate**, **rec.sport.skating.inline** WEB **Inline Online Magazine**
http://coyote.mcc.com:8000/galaxy/Leisure-and-Recreation/Sports/daniel-chick/io_org.html ◆ IRC **#inline**

Rolling Stone   Granddaddy of rock culture magazines, founded in 1967 by San Francisco student Jann Wenner (b. 1946). *RS* was originally a broadsheet distributed from the back of Wenner's car, but quickly grew into a national enterprise: the young editor established it as a leading countercultural voice and home to major young writers of the era, including gonzo avatar Hunter S. Thompson. Some considered the magazine's 1977 move to plush New York offices to be a sell-out, but *Rolling Stone* didn't actually become a cash cow until the successful 1985 "Perception/Reality" ad campaign, which juxtaposed common perceptions about the magazine's BABY BOOM readers (e.g. some loose change) against the reality of their spending power (credit cards). At the same time, *RS* began feeding more on celebrity culture, with movie star covers; this era's star writer was P. J. O'Rourke, a reformed *National Lampoon* editor who spun best-selling books from his dyspeptic, neo-conservative humor essays. In the early '90s *RS* reconnected with youth culture in the form of the GRUNGE generation of bands, who vied for cover space with venerable elders like Eric Clapton and the GRATEFUL DEAD's Jerry Garcia.

Rollins, Henry (b. Henry Garfield, 1961) One-man PUNK franchise spanning the MOSH-friendly Rollins Band, poetry installments of MTV's *UNPLUGGED*, a book publishing house, and pitch-man roles for the GAP and MACINTOSH Powerbook. A seminal figure in the early days of both the HARDCORE and SPOKEN-WORD scenes, Rollins was a childhood friend in D.C. of FUGAZI's Ian MacKaye; he moved to L.A. to become the lyricist and frontman for anger-mongers Black Flag (1979–1986), only to release an album of sensitive prose perfor-

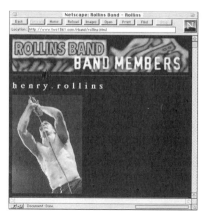

mances (*Big Ugly Mouth*, 1987) the year after the band's break-up. Equally at home stirring the mosh pit with ferocious, vein-bulging screams or meaningfully cocking a self-deprecating eyebrow at a spoken-word performance, Rollins is full of contradictions which are either character-building or deeply repressed. He's a punk icon who preaches STRAIGHT EDGE abstinence from drugs and alcohol; a hardworking '90s poet with the heavily tattooed physique, Marine buzz-cut, and Nietzschean preoccupation with power. Other projects include an alternative book publishing house, 2.13.61 (named for his birthdate), that operates out of his Hollywood Boulevard home; a nascent film acting career (*The Chase*, 1994; *Johnny Mnemonic*, 1995); and an atonal, avant-garde, some would say unlistenable direction for the Rollins Band that leaves rock and metal conventions behind in a swirl of polyrythmic intellectualism.

WEB **Henry Rollins Stuff**

http://www.st.nepean.uws.edu.au/~alf/rollins/

Romanek, Mark (b. 1959)   Director of the NINE INCH NAILS' notorious "Closer" video (1994), an indirect homage to photographer JOEL-PETER WITKIN. Romanek insisted on taking his name off the clip when MTV began screening a version with "scene missing" title-cards at strategic points: among the lost footage was a monkey on a crucifix and a 19th century photograph of a vagina. While not shocking the *bourgeoisie*, Romanek is entertain-

ing them with high-production-value videos like kd lang's "Constant Craving," En Vogue's "Free Your Mind," and MADONNA's "Rain." In 1995 Romanek helmed Madonna's "Bedtime Story," a work that merged high art references with dazzling computer-treated images for a shockingly high $2 million. Shocking, that is, until that summer's Romanek-directed "Scream," a futuristic $7 million landmark of video extravagance from Michael Jackson.

USENET **rec.music.video**

Rome, Jim (b. 1964)   Host of *Talk2*, a nightly sports-talk show on ESPN's GRUNGE spin-off, ESPN2. The program, which launched with the network in October 1993, extended a cult that had already rivaled the less analytically inclined RUSH LIMBAUGH and HOWARD STERN in the world of Southern-California radio, where Rome hosts a daily radio show. Fans revel in the frat-boy cadences and gonzo recklessness of Rome-speak, a dialect born of three years on the radio "banging calls," cataloging "scrubs who tanked," and making sure that "whining cheese-heads are bagged but good with facts, not rhetoric." "Talking smack"—defined by the 5' 9" Rome as "cockiness, candor, trash . . . bold statements that you attempt to back up"—is the central activity on both the radio show and the ESPN2 program. Rome got a lesson in "smack" in April 1994 when New Orleans Saints quarterback Jim Everett overturned a table and pushed him to the ground on air for persistently referring to Everett by the name of women's tennis champion Chris Evert. After the channel heavily promoted the incident, Rome spent the subsequent weeks denying that the event had been a staged publicity stunt.

WEB **ESPNET SportZone** http://ESPNET.SportsZone.com/

Ross, Andrew (b. 1956)   Perennially quotable, youthfully accoutred Scottish professor tenured in 1993 as director of American Studies at New York University. Ross has achieved notoriety as a trailblazer for the field of CULTURAL STUDIES (a spin-off of which is the dubious area of "MADONNA STUDIES"); he presents himself as an implacable enemy of literature and an enthusiastic banner-waver for subcultural styles. An author, editor of cultural studies periodical *Social Text*, and columnist at *Artforum*, Ross taught for eight years at Princeton before going to NYU, where he made perhaps the most notorious statement of a provocative career: he said he was teaching there "to have access to the minds of the children of the ruling classes."

WEB **Post Modern Culture** http://jefferson.village. virginia.edu/pmc/

RU–486   Abortion pill developed in 1982 and widely used in France and China since the mid-'80s. FDA-approval for use in America was not sought by Roussel-Uclaf, the German pharmaceutical megaconglomerate which owns the drug, for fear of subjecting other products to a pro-life boycott. (The existence of such a pill would make abortion as accessible as a visit to the doctor.) But soon after the pro-choice Clinton was elected in 1992, the company licensed the U.S. patent for $1 to the non-profit Population Council for clinical trials (the drug is also thought to be useful in the treatment of ulcers and glaucoma). When a Brookline, Massachusetts, Planned Parenthood clinic was attacked by a machine-gun toting fanatic in January, 1995 (see ABORTION CLINIC VIOLENCE), it was one of only twenty clinics in the country testing RU–486. Not actually a contraceptive, RU–486 is a contragestive that works by inducing the pregnant woman to menstruate. (RU–486, which is also known as the steroid mifepristone, specifically blocks the action of the hormone progesterone that is essential for maintaining a pregnancy.)

USENET **us.politics.abortion, talk.abortion** ✦ MAIL LIST

Choice-Net Report to subscribe email drv@well.sf.ca.us

Rubin, Rick (b. Frederick Jay Rubin, 1963) Long-Island, New York-born co-founder, with RUSSELL SIMMONS, of rap label Def Jam in 1984. As a producer—originally working from his New York University dorm room—Rubin lent his rap-metal aesthetic to many of the company's mid-'80s hits. When the pair fell out in 1987, the burly, bearded Rubin started Def American to indulge his unrepentantly suburban tastes: pottymouth comedian

RICK RUBIN welcomes comers to his company home page (http://american. recordings.com/).

Andrew Dice Clay, freakish GANGSTA rappers the GETO BOYS, and speed-metal act Slayer were among his early signings. When Def American distributor, Geffen, refused to distribute the *Geto Boys* album in 1990, Def American moved under the roof of Warner Bros.; Rubin himself stayed in demand as a producer, helming among other projects the RED HOT CHILI PEPPERS' 1991 commercial breakthrough *BloodSugarSexMagik*. (Mick Jagger's bomb *Wandering Spirit* was a less decorous assignment.) In August 1993 Rubin simplified his company's name to American; he continues to successfully embrace the crassly mainstream, the stoically traditional, and the avant-garde. While he produces and releases records by Johnny Cash, Tom Petty, and the Black Crowes, Rubin is licensing European TECHNO acts to his Whte Lbls imprint and starting a punk re-issue label, Infinite Zero, with HENRY ROLLINS. Rubin also owns a pro wrestling circuit in the South.

WEB **American Recordings Homepage** http://american. recordings.com/

RuPaul (b. RuPaul Andre Charles, 1960) DRAG culture's first full-service entertainer. This 6'7" (sans high heels and blond bouffant) entertainer dabbled in PUNK as a youth in Atlanta before percolating through the New York club scene into a record deal with influential HIP-HOP/dance label Tommy Boy. The 1993 "bubblegum HOUSE" anthem "SUPERMODEL" (with its hearty refrain of

"You better work!") was a video-driven hit; enchanted by the singer's showbiz chutzpah and beatific persona, Hollywood awarded him a string of movie roles both in and out of drag, notably *The Brady Bunch* (1995) and *To Wong Foo, Thanks for Everything, Julie Newmar* (1995). Defiantly dodging the one-hit wonder tag, RuPaul took his act to Las Vegas's Sahara Congo Room in late 1994; he was named spokesmodel for Canadian makeup company M.A.C. in March 1995, and three months later published an autobiography, *Lettin' It All Hang Out.*

WEB **Our Lady RuPaul** http://copper.ucs.indiana.edu/ ~jfleming/rupaul.html ✦ WEB **Unofficial RuPaul Homepage** http://www.cyber-dyne.com/~tprebble/rupaul/index.html ✦ USENET **alt.music.rupaul** ✦ MAIL LIST **The RuPaul E-Mail List** email rupaul-request@sephiroth.org with the word "subscribe" in the body

Rushdie, Salman (b. 1947)   On February 14, 1989, after days of riots in England, Pakistan, and India left several dead and hundreds wounded, the Ayatollah Khomeini of Iran issued an Islamic death sentence (fatwa) for British novelist Salman Rushdie, offering a reward that was eventually raised to more than $5 million. Rushdie's crime, and the reason for the disturbances, was to have allegedly blasphemed the Muslim religion in *The Satanic Verses* (1988). The death sentence, which technically extends to anyone who even *owns* the best-seller, cost the life of the novel's Japanese translator, who was stabbed to death in 1991; its Italian translator was wounded during a *Verses*-related knife attack that same year. (The Indian-born and Muslim-raised author had regarded Islam critically in two of his two earlier magical-realist novels about India and Pakistan: *Shame* [1981] and *Children of Midnight* [1983].) Rushdie went underground following the fatwa—emerging in brief public appearances including a 1993 U2 concert and May 1995 reading of "The Top Ten List" during the London visit of the *The David Letterman Show*—and has

since published the ostensible children's book *Haroun and the Sea of Stories* (1990) and *East, West: Stories* (1995).

WEB **Islam and the Middle East: Rushdie Links** http://www.pol.umu.se/html/ac/islam.htm

Ryder, Winona (b. Winona Laura Horowitz, 1971)   Winsome, 5'4" moviestar enthroned as a generational icon, primarily for her role as the existentially flip narrator of the high school satire *Heathers* (1989). In the '90s Ryder has chiefly chosen to appear in Hollywood period pieces (she played porcelain dolls in *The Age of Innocence* [1993] and *Bram Stoker's Dracula* [1992]; and also starred in *Little Women* [1994]). This low-key star ("Noni" to family and friends) tends to be seen in public only rarely: three such instances were the search for Polly Klaas, a 12-year-old abducted in her hometown of Petaluma, California; her paparazzi-bait relationship with JOHNNY DEPP; and her more recent domicile in lower Manhattan with Soul Asylum singer Dave Pirner. (This union, plus Ryder's earlier, reputed flirtations with her musical hero, Paul Westerberg of the Replacements, prompted *SASSY* magazine to wonder whether "Boys start bands so they can get famous enough to attract Winona Ryder.") Like RIVER PHOENIX, once a member of her Hollywood star circle, Ryder had a counterculture childhood— TIMOTHY LEARY is her godfather, and her parents edited *Moksha*, a collection of Aldous Huxley essays about the psychedelic experience.

Photo by Sandra-Lee Phipps

WINONA RYDER at ALTERNATIVE WOODSTOCK festival 1994, with boyfriend Dave Pirner and singer Victoria Williams.

WEB **Winona Ryder** http://www.sch.bme.hu/~joker /winona.html ✦ WEB **Winona Ryder** http://www.duc.auburn.edu/~harshec/WWW/Winona.html/

S/M Term for sado-masochism, preferred by practitioners to the older S&M (Sadism and Masochism), but not as current as D/S for the less overtly sexual Dominance and Submission. Once the purview of decadent upper classes (named for literary figures, the French Marquis de Sade and Austrian Leopold von Sacher-Masoch) and earlier in this century a gay subculture, S/M has been both democratized into the cultural mainstream and claimed by ALTERNATIVE subcultures in the decades following the sexual revolution, as evidenced by the widespread appropriation of its latex, body PIERCING, TATTOO, SCARFICATION, GOTH, and leather trappings. Both straight businessmen and feminists revel in the opportunity for "role reversal" that scripted, rule-oriented, and mutually consenting S/M sex offers. The fun can take place at home, with a private dominatrix, or at clubs like the Vault in New York City.

Harness bodices, dog collars, and studded leather skirts became proper attire for socialites in the fall of 1992, after Gianni Versace devoted his spring 1992 collection to the whip-lady dominatrix look. (BETSEY JOHNSON and JEAN-PAUL GAULTIER were other dabblers.) The fall release of *Sex*, MADONNA's photo fantasy book, partly shot in the Vault, helped whip up an enthusiasm for bondage wear and kinky sex, propelling fetishism into the mainstream. (The singer also used S/M in the earlier "Express Yourself" and MTV-banned "Justify My Love" videos, and in 1995's "Human Nature.") S/M fashion paid aesthetic homage to zipped-up Avenger Emma Peel, prime-time leather queen Catwoman, and the graphic sexuality of photographer HELMUT NEWTON—what, to some critics, was demeaning, others found empowering. By 1994, when Gary Marshall directed an ill-fated S/M comedy, *Exit to Eden* (putatively based on ANNE RICE's 1985 book, under the pen name Anne Rampling) starring Dana Delany and Dan Aykroyd, sadomasochism had gone from shocking to ho-hum. Handcuff-play even figured in teen TV like *Beverly Hills, 90210* and *MY SO-CALLED LIFE*.

Among the sexual intellegentsia, there is debate over whether the S/M surge is symbolic of a more violent culture or a more integrated one, since part of S/M's appeal is that it is exciting "safe" sex. It is often non-penetrative and no bodily fluids need be exchanged, yet it feels dangerous—or at least daring. Latex Versace dresses and lingerie shops branching into handcuffs are one thing, but it remains to be seen if "slave" terminology and "edge play" such as force-feeding, electric shocks, and cutting can also find a place in the country's dating habits.

WEB **Prometheus Home Page (The Eulenspiegel Society)**
http://www.mcsp.com/tes/welcome.html

Sailor Moon Japan's most popular superhero, a "cyber-BARBIE" with long blond pigtails, skintight schoolgirl sailor-frock, and tiny miniskirt who, with her friends, activates her special powers with the cry, "Moon Power . . . MAKE UP!" Created by a young woman, Naoko Takeuchi (b. circa 1967), Sailor Moon (also known as "Bishojo Senshi" or "Pretty Soldier Sailor Moon") first appeared in a monthly comics magazine for girls in 1992 before being turned into a hit (and surprisingly sexy) daily cartoon TV show by Toei, one of the companies that supplies action sequences for the MIGHTY MORPHIN POWER RANGERS. Bandai, the same firm that handles Power Ranger merchandising, parlayed Sailor Moon cosmetic kits, snack foods, and other products into unparalleled retail sales of more than $1.5 billion in the show's first three years. Such sales, combined with the show's success in France, led to the fall 1995 debut of a slightly toned down version in American prime-time and toystores—the naked costume MORPHs were cut and Moon's secret identity was changed from "Usagi" ("Bunny") to the marginally less-ludicrous "Victoria."

WEB **Sailor Moon Site** http://www2.infolink.net/~chimo/smss/

sampling Musical practice closely identified with HIP-HOP that has in recent years occasioned key rulings about the future of intellectual property rights and freedom of expression. Rap sampling—a logical extension of the disk-jockey skills which inspired the form—took off in the late '80s when cheap samplers dropped in price to as little as $100. Initially used for the perfect capture of breakbeats, sampling developed into a tool of complex sonic collage, as vigorously practiced by the likes of PUBLIC ENEMY producer Hank Shocklee. Soon albums were regularly delayed by record company efforts to research and clear the rights to "quoted" material. Among those who became embroiled in copyright disputes were DE LA SOUL and Biz Markie, whose 1992 *I Need a Haircut* contained a lengthy section of '70s crooner Gilbert O'Sullivan's "Alone Again (Naturally)." (The record was recalled under court order.) Meanwhile, sonic outlaws such as NEGATIVLAND argue for "fair use" of existing works as an appropriate artistic technique.

Sandler, Adam (b. 1966) "The most talentless, juvenile and offensive member of the current cast." That's how one irate *L.A. Times* reader described SATURDAY NIGHT LIVE's Adam Sandler after the paper ran a profile on him—and many would agree. Sandler's repeat-until-funny comedy perpetually teeters on the verge of collapse; if you laugh, it's probably because, like Sandler himself, you can't quite believe that he's actually getting away with it. Recruited from the stand-up world (via MTV's *REMOTE CONTROL*) to be an *SNL* writer, Sandler rose up to become a "featured performer" in the show's 1993–94 season. Aside from competent impressions of pompous rockers like U2's Bono and AEROSMITH's Steven Tyler, Sandler developed a roster of marginal, one-joke characters like Canteen Boy, Cajun Man, Opera Man, and Shaky-Lipped Guy. It spoke well for Sandler's charm that his leading-man movie debut, the "dumb trend" comedy *Billy Madison* (1995, directed by TAMRA DAVIS) was a big, albeit short-lived, hit. He did not return to *Saturday Night Live*'s 1995–96 season.
USENET **alt.tv.snl**

Santeria Syncretic Cuban folk religion combining African spirit worship and Roman Catholicism. Castro has supposedly supported Santeria to counter the Church's influence in Cuba, where the religion—like Haiti's Vodun (often called Voodoo)—

has deep roots in the country's history of slavery. In the U.S., the Supreme Court ruled in 1993 that Hialeah, Florida, could not outlaw the ritual animal sacrifices of Santeria. (In contrast, three years earlier, the Court said Oregon's Native American Church did not have a right to ingest peyote as part of an ancient ceremony.) In the early '90s Santeria became a dark, baleful fashion in certain rock circles already drawn to the mystical significance of astrology, tarot, and hard drugs. PERRY FARRELL's HEROIN movie-saga *Gift* (1993) included real-life footage of the Santeria blood-sharing ritual from his Mexico wedding.
WEB **Santeria: From Cuba to New York, and back . . .**
http://www.nando.net/prof/caribe/santeria.html

Sassy Teenage girls' magazine launched March 1988 (on the blueprint of Australia's raunchy *Dolly*) into a marketplace dominated by pristine perennials *Teen, YM,* and *Seventeen. Sassy* dispensed earthy, big-sisterly advice on the traumas of teen life and kept its readers up to date on the fringes of ALTERNATIVE culture ("Cute Band Alert," "Fanzine of the Month"). A

SASSY, before the fall.

highly personal approach (staffers referred to each other by first names) deconstructed magazine forms as *SPY* was doing for older readers. Although *Sassy's* familiarity and POLITICAL CORRECTNESS could be cloying, the magazine provided a welcome clubhouse for teenage girls whose lives didn't necessarily revolve around the junior prom. One of the few INDIE-ROCK arbiters that was immune to *Sassy's* charms was *THE BAFFLER*, which accused *Sassy* of pandering to advertisers in its ceaseless promotion of youth-culture fashion. (Initially *Sassy* weathered a year-long boycott by several major advertisers that was triggered by the Moral Majority and the REV. DONALD WILDMON's American Family Association.) Despite a circulation of around 800,000 *Sassy* was never a financial success, and it was sold in late 1994 to Peterson (owners of *Teen*), who moved the magazine from New York and re-launched it from L.A. as a more upbeat, generic entity. Founding editor Jane

Pratt went on to become a twice-failed talk show host, a TV infotainment reporter, and a youth guru at TIME WARNER's magazine wing, where she planned for the launch of *Jane* magazine.

Satanism   Thriving pseudo-religion born in 1966, when Anton Szandor LaVey (b. 1930) founded his Church of Satan to celebrate the power and pleasures of the flesh. Satanism has little to do with the Christian Devil, and instead worships the individual as ultimately responsible for his or her own actions. The Temple of Set, which spun off from the Church of Satan in 1975, is the largest of many smaller Satanic institutions, including The Worldwide Church of Satanic Liberation, Order of the Evil Eye, and The Luciferian Light Group. These subtleties are lost, however, on born-again Christians who claim that America is in the grips of a brutal "Satanic Underground" that practices "ritual abuse" on as many as 100,000 child victims. Often relying on memories of childhood abuse "recovered" by therapists, anti-Devil crusaders have made life a living hell for thousands of innocent witch-hunt victims, as documented in Laurence Wright's harrowing book, *Remembering Satan* (1994).

USENET **alt.satanism** ✦ WEB **Hell—The Online Guide to Satanism** http://www.marshall.edu/~allen12/index.html

satin   As the cut of clothing continued to simplify in the first half of the '90s, designers turned to fabrics to provide visual interest. Inspired by Helmut Lang's slippery-looking bias-cut SLIP DRESSES, the fashion establishment jumped on satin as the trendy fabric of choice in a mania for "shine" and "glamor" that peaked in the collections for spring 1995. Besides the predictable lingerie and evening gowns, satin showed up everywhere from ravers' polyester satin T-shirts to silk satin suits for men. The effect was elegantly tacky or tackily elegant, depending on your point of view—a very '90s splicing of synthetic '70s glam and '30s Hollywood luxe.

Saturday Night Live   One-time bastion of innovative TV comedy that fell on hard times in the '90s. Originally a late-counterculture institution and cultural watchdog, *SNL* lost its satirical teeth and was reduced to protracted catchphrase-routines. (David Spade's sarcastic air steward wishing flyers "bu-bye" was particularly loathed.) The cable-driven glut of sketch comedy (*Kids In the Hall*, *In Living Color*, MTV's *The State*) only seemed to cramp *SNL*'s style. The arrival of considerable talents like JANEANE GAROFALO and CHRIS ELLIOTT couldn't stop the rot in the all-time low 1994–95 season during which the show's demise was widely predicted. A singular embarrassment was a mammoth March 1995 article in *New York* magazine that portrayed a staff rent apart by pettiness, insecurity, and the dwindling comic powers of male veterans. (Garofalo took an extended sabbatical around this time.)

Whereas *SNL* was once the launching pad for successful film careers of reasonable longevity (Dan Aykroyd, John Belushi, Chevy Chase, Eddie Murphy, Bill Murray), this power had all but evaporated by the '90s. The success of (the now-departed) Mike Meyers' and Dana Carvey's sketch spin-off *Wayne's World* (1992) encouraged Hollywood and *SNL* producer Lorne Michaels to confidently roll into production several movies based on *SNL* sketches, some long-deceased. The underwhelming performance of *Wayne's World 2* (1993) hinted that all was not well and, although ferociously-marketed, *Coneheads* (Aykroyd, 1993) bombed at the box office, while Julia Sweeney's *It's Pat* (1994) did not even make six figures in its mercifully brief release; Warner Bros. bailed on *Coffee Talk* after reportedly paying Meyers $500,000 for the rights; Carvey and Kevin Nealon's *Hanz and Franz* was also ditched, by Columbia. Despite some positive reviews, *Stuart Smalley Saves His Family* (1995, starring Al Franken) was another catastrophe that was somewhat ameliorated by the same year's modest lowbrow successes: ADAM SANDLER's *Billy Madison* and *Tommy Boy* starring Chris Farley and David Spade. Farley and Sandler left before the 1995–96 season, and many other cast members were fired in anticipation of a direct challenge from Fox's *Mad TV* and the threat of MTV's CBS-adopted *The State*.

WEB **SNL Archives** http://www.best.com:80/~dijon/tv/snl/ ◆
USENET **alt.tv.snl**

Savage Love Rough-talking sex-advice column started by Dan Savage (b. circa 1963) in the 1991 debut issue of SEATTLE alternative weekly, *The Stranger*. (Now syndicated to nine other weeklies including New York's *Village Voice*.) Savage, a gay man, has received flak from the Gay and Lesbian Anti-Defamation League for encouraging readers to greet him with the salutation "Hey, faggot," but in the *San Francisco Chronicle* in 1994 he argued that by calling straights "breeders" he "shows up this sort of name calling by wallowing in it." His outrageous, tongue-in-cheek advice inflamed fellow-columnist, San Francisco-based Isadora Alman ("Ask Isadora"); 12-step groups criticized him for telling people to get drunk; and Mattel was not amused when he announced that the "rave" Ken doll had a cock ring around its neck (see QUEER KEN). "Savage Love Live," a radio counterpart to the *Savage Love* column, debuted on Seattle's KCMU-FM in September 1994.

scarification Flesh marking akin to TATTOOS or BRANDING. As a counterculture statement—as opposed to an ancient tribal ritual—scarification is associated with the MODERN PRIMITIVE movement and S/M, and prized both for the painful process, the trophy-like scar, and "blood prints" taken on paper from the fresh wound. Thoroughly cleansed skin is cut with a scalpel, and, if the recipient is fair-skinned, tattoo ink is rubbed into the open wound. For darker skin, an ash alkaloid is used, irritating the skin and leaving a raised scar. Some prefer a heated knife that cauterizes as it cuts. Scarification is sometimes incorporated into S/M "scenes."

In 1994, concerns about AIDS and hepatitis led outreach workers from San Francisco hospitals to offer workshops on "safe 'blood sports' sex techniques." Raelyn Gallina, one of the area's best known "cutters," told the *San Francisco Examiner*, "It's more fad proportion now . . . So you're getting people who are going crazy and not doing it for the deeper (spiritual) reasons. They're the ones who are going to go home and cut themselves to the bone." The medical establishment has started to recognize "deliberate self-harm syndrome" as a psychiatric illness akin to anorexia and bulimia, estimating from preliminary studies that seven in 1,000 people mutilate themselves. There is a Manhattan 12-step program, Self-Mutilators Anonymous, founded in 1987; and a Chicago program SAFE (Self Abuse Finally Ends), founded in 1984. For fans, *The Cutting Edge* is the best known newsletter.

WEB **BME: Scarification** http://www.io.org/~bme/bme-scar.html/ ◆ WEB **Sabina's Homepage** http://renoir.psych.nyu.edu:9999/~thebin/ ◆ USENET **rec.arts.bodyart**

Schwa Developer of conspiracy and superstition satires including an Alien Defense Kit that comes complete with a wallet-sized alien detector card and an alien invasion keychain. The Reno, Nevada, company is the brainchild of commercial and conceptual artist Bill Barker (b. circa 1956), who says UFO lore is "the only really exciting myth we have" (see ALIEN ABDUCTIONS and *X-FILES*). The company's name refers to the inverted "e" phonetic symbol which denotes the sound "uh." Schwa ad copy promises " a complete line of actual objects you can own that will end your doubts about the unknown, right now, forever!"

WEB **Schwa Fan Club** http://kzsu.stanford.edu/uwi/schwa/schwa.html ◆ WEB **Schwa** http://fringeware.com/SchwaRoot/Schwa.html

Sci-Fi Channel Cable channel rolled out in the early '90s with a pedigree (USA Networks, and USA's corporate parents MCA and Paramount) that guaranteed access to both content and cable systems. The Sci-Fi Channel's small roster of television classics (*The Twilight Zone*) and quasi-classics (*The Six Million Dollar Man*) was eventually elevated by the SF Holy Grail, STAR TREK (first movies, later the TV series). By 1995, the channel was available in a respectable but hardly impressive 22 million households; that same year the company launched a flurry of promotional efforts, including a line of merchandise (beginning, inevitably, with a CD-ROM), a tie-in with Spencer Gifts, and a substantial

WORLD WIDE WEB site. Perhaps inspired by Comedy Central's *MYSTERY SCIENCE THEATER 3000*, the channel also developed a way for fans to post on screen comments via email (ruining tapings of the '60s British cult series *The Prisoner*).

WEB **Sci-Fi Channel** http://www.scifi.com/

Scientology, Church of Self-help, anti-psychiatric religion founded in the '50s by sci-fi pulp novelist L. Ron Hubbard. His *Dianetics* (1950) is a key Scientology text. The Church's many celebrity followers include Tom Cruise, JOHN TRAVOLTA, JULIETTE LEWIS, Kirstie Alley, and the voice of Bart SIMPSON, Nancy Cartwright. Scientology claims to heal psychic traumas through "auditing" therapy that uses a simplified "E-meter" lie detector. The Church has a long history of intimidating critics through lawsuits, including groundbreaking pursuit of individuals who anonymously distributed internal Church documents via the INTERNET.

WEB **F.A.C.T.net- Information About Scientology**
http://www.xs4all.nl/~fonss/ ◆ USENET **alt.religion.scientology**

screenplay seminars Scriptwriting classes pushing tricks of the trade have grown into a thriving cottage industry, as the aspirations of young writers shifted from the great American novel to the great million-dollar "spec" script (see SHANE BLACK). Robert McKee, who himself has never had a movie screenplay made, runs the best known of all the screenplay seminars, some of which can cost upwards of $1,000. McKee's three-day *Story Structure* formalizes such script tech-talk as "the hook," the "set-up," and "the quest," and famously concludes with a scene-by-scene dissection of *Casablanca*'s legendary plotting.

Seattle Rainy Northwestern metropolis which combines the boho-liberalism of Northen California with considerable industrial clout, equally defined by corporate behemoths (Boeing, Microsoft), universities (University of Washington), and trendy gourmet companies (Starbuck's Coffee and several prominent microbreweries). When NIRVANA's "Smells Like Teen Spirit" became, in late 1991, a generational anthem, Seattle vaulted into the cultural spotlight, as had to a lesser degree Minneapolis and Athens, Georgia, in the '80s. Within months, Seattle became the geographic signifier for GRUNGE counterculture that was already flourishing in youth enclaves around the country. The city's flannel-clad underground scene itself was a prominent character in Cameron Crowe's 1992 film *Singles*, which featured members of PEARL JAM.

An October 1993 story in *Time* magazine (with Pearl Jam's Eddie Vedder on the cover) formalized Seattle's pop-culture ascendancy, and also served notice that it might be short-lived; the magazine referred to the search for the "next Seattle," considering the youth-culture scenes in cities such as Chicago and San Diego. Oddly, the next Seattle turned out to be Seattle itself; the suicide of Nirvana leader Kurt Cobain added a hagiographic dimension to the city's rock scene; Starbuck's COFFEE BARS started appearing on streetcorners nationwide; and new films and television shows—from the hit romantic comedy *Sleepless in Seattle* (1993) to *Frasier*, the sitcom spin-off of Boston-based *Cheers*—solidified Seattle's credentials as a definitively '90s milieu.

WEB **Seattle Web** http://www.seattleweb.com/ ◆ WEB **Seattle Links** http://weber.u.washington.edu/~mosaic/seattle.html/

Seattle's six-letter corporate giants face off on the Web: SUB POP (http://www.subpop.com) and Boeing (http://www.boeing/com).

Secondary Virginity Campaign to make pre-marital abstinence hip among teens, led by the religious right's organization True Love Waits. Over half a million pledge cards have been signed since the campaign was launched in 1993, many solicited through 1–800-LUV-WAIT. The program also sometimes involves a marriage-like ceremony in which parents place a "pledge ring" on a teen's finger that is not to come off until the wedding night. Secondary Virginity is much slicker than other "Just Say No"-style efforts such as Sex Respect, known as much for its slogan "Control your urgin'—be a virgin" as the school board controversies it engendered over the separation of church and state. In addition, 1993–94 saw a micro-trend of celebrity celibacy, with proud announcements from JULIANA HATFIELD, KENNEDY, and Tori Spelling's Donna on *BEVERLY HILLS 90210*.

secondary smoke Term for cigarette exhaust that connotes health risks for non-smokers. A 1993 EPA report deemed the smoke to be a carcinogen responsible for some 3,000 lung-cancer deaths per year in non-smokers, squarely shifting the issue in anti-smoking ordinances from personal freedom to public health. Although nonsmokers in smoky environs may inhale only one percent as much smoke as people dragging on a cigarette, the health effects are still dramatic: a 1994 OSHA study further calculated that some 47,000 people a year die from heart disease caused by secondhand smoke, with 150,000 more suffering non-fatal heart attacks.
WEB **Medical Sciences Bulletin** http://pharminfo.com/ pubs/msb/msbmnu.html/ ✦ WEB **Non-Smoker's Rights Society** http://www.xmission.com/~seer/AIRSPACE/ airspace.html/

Sega Channel Joint venture between computer-game juggernaut SEGA Enterprises, entertainment juggernaut TIME WARNER, and cable juggernaut Tele-Communications, Inc., that could mark the beginning of interactive TV, after a few false starts (see FULL-SERVICE NETWORK). Aimed at boys six to 15, this advertising-free service was launched in 1995 with hopes of delivering Sega games via cable-adapter cartridge to a million-plus customers in the first year. The service, costing between $12 and $15 a month, will offer playing time on any of 50-odd games as well as news, coaching help, and previews of new games. (Sega does not expect the channel to impact unfavorably on its video-game sales, since games will only be briefly available through the channel months after retail release.) One Sega executive told *Advertising Age* that the service's 12-city test in 1994 went so well that kids were "running out of adjectives to describe it."
WEB **Stop Just Watching TV** http://www.segaoa.com/ othercool/segachan.html

serial killer chic Fashion transforming deranged murderers into objects of fascination and celebration. "Somehow," wrote novelist Joyce Carol Oates in the *New York Review of Books* in 1994, "serial killers have become our . . . eerily glorified Noble Savage, the vestiges of the frontier spirit." The same year saw the long-standing strain in popular culture reach critical mass: a spate of serial killer movies (including OLIVER STONE's *Natural Born Killers* (1994), JOHN WATERS' *Serial Mom* (1994), and Nick Broomfield's 1992 documentary *Aileen Wuornos: The Selling of a Serial Killer*) followed the success of Anthony Hopkins as a suave cannibal in 1991's *Silence of the Lambs*; lawyers auctioned off real-life cannibal Jeffrey Dahmer's plates and cutlery to raise money for his victims' families; and '80s killer John Wayne Gacy, on death row, was featured in a "rare interview" in the *NEW YORKER*, and saw his clown paintings re-sell at auction for $20,000 to patrons of *art brut*. Such higher culture celebration rested on a foundation of serial killer groupies writing fan letters and trading photos; sales of serial killer shirts, COMIC books, and trading cards; and nihilistic echoes of CHARLES MANSON's notoriety struck a deep chord among rebellious rockers. In 1994 *Time* magazine reported FBI estimates that "75 per cent of the 160 or so repeat killers captured or identified in the past 20 years were in the U.S."
WEB **Internet Crime Archive: Serial Killer Hit List** http://underground.net/Art/Crime/serial.html

serial monogamy Go steady, meet each other's parents, be faithful, move in together, break up; repeat with someone new. Combining fidelity with an avoidance of long-term commitment, serial monogamy is both a result of, and a reaction against, freedoms unleashed by the sexual revolution. The condition, which tends to be marked by break-ups rather than adulterous lapses, is consistent with ever-declining rates of marriage among recent college graduates. (The term was much devalued after its appearance in the dialogue of MELROSE PLACE and 1993's *Four Weddings and a Funeral.*)

SETI   Search for ExtraTerrestrial Intelligence, a ten-year, $100 million NASA program which amounts to the world's largest channel-surfing project. Launched on Columbus Day, 1992, the name was changed to the more sober sounding High Resolution Microwave Survey, in part to protect it from congressional mockery and cost-cutting. An earlier version of SETI was originally founded in 1984 by the radio astronomer Frank Drake (who has published books describing the extraterrestrials he believes exist), and funded with help from Carl Sagan and Steven Spielberg. The much larger NASA program consists of two main components: an "All-Sky Survey" that uses computers to scan billions of radio channels at once, and a "Targeted Search" of some 1,000 star systems calculated most likely to produce life.

WEB **SETI Institute Home Page** http://www.metrolink.com/seti/SETI.html

'70s fashion   The warm spot in America's heart for wide cords, platform shoes and velour V-neck sweaters began to grow in the late-'80s and early-'90s as thrift-store shopping moved from the fringes to the masses, HIP-HOP artists SAMPLED '70s tunes, and the *Real Live BRADY BUNCH* began performing in Chicago. Celebration of 1970s kitsch with apartment parties in cities and college towns represented nostalgia for the styles and feelings that young people witnessed, but were too young to partake in while growing up. Categorizations tended to be loose, discordantly sampling anything that can be

described as retro: jump suits and daisy earrings with Jackie O glasses, the Carpenters with the Bee Gees, *Charlie's Angels* with *Welcome Back Kotter*, patch-patterned long skirts and micro-minis.

Seventies dance-music compilations were sold on late-night television, and a flurry of bars and clubs in across America had '70s nights and revival bands (like ABBA *homagistes* Bjorn Again) playing. *Good Times* T-shirts, clogs, polyester, suede fringe vests and hot pants became *de rigueur* with both small-town high schoolers and European designers. Afros returned: during production of *Crooklyn* (1994), SPIKE LEE grew one, as did—briefly—trend-setters SNOOP DOGGY DOGG and ICE CUBE. '70s fashion nostalgia serves many purposes: evoking drug culture and the sexual revolution, self-consciously embracing disposability and un-self-consciousness, and flouting the tyranny of good taste as represented today by the GAP.

USENET **alt.culture.us.1970s**

sexual aversion therapy   Controversial treatment for reprogramming the sex drive of sex offenders, problem teens, and, voluntarily, self-hating homosexuals; considered by its critics to be a form of torture and abuse. Like something out of *A Clockwork Orange* (1971), the patient is shown pornography while a penile or vaginal plethismagraph attached to a computer measures the patient's sexual arousal. In later stages of treatment, the patient is punished for becoming "inappropriately" aroused at the sight of the same images through exposure to smelling salts, ammonia odors, or electric shocks. In other forms of the therapy, the patient writes out or records a sexual fantasy "script" that is repeatedly replayed while taking some form of punishment.

shag haircut   First popular in the early '70s, the shag was both glamorous mane (Warren Beatty, David Cassidy) and sexless bonnet (Florence Henderson of THE BRADY BUNCH). In 1993 shags returned, this time as a feathery cap of layers which favored the angular faces of waif models like Lucie de la Falaise and Amber Valetta. Pronouncing a "call to arms for short hair" that year, *Harper's Bazaar* magazine even instructed its readers on how to give themselves a sweetly chic, untidy version at home. Although well-sculpted crops appeared on everyone from Annette Bening (Mrs. Warren Beatty) to *BEVERLY HILLS 90210* starlet Tori Spelling, it was the scruffy, kiddy-cut version of the shag that became the insignia of knowing, urban fashion tribes.

TUPAC SHAKUR on *VIBE* cover, February 1994—still crazy after all these years.

Shakur, Tupac (b. 1971) Son of BLACK PANTHER Afeni Shakur, who, under the name 2Pac, made his musical debut with Bay Area rap pranksters Digital Underground. In 1991, he recorded the gold-selling GANGSTA rap album *2Pacalypse Now.* (Then-Vice President Dan Quayle publicly claimed that the album's inflammatory lyrics had influenced the killer of a Texas policeman.)

Shakur launched his screen-acting with the 1992 HIP-HOP movie *Juice*, then performed creditably in JOHN SINGLETON's *Poetic Justice* (1993), and the basketball drama *Above the Rim* (1994). As Shakur's acting potential became apparent, his legal woes mounted. A 1992 fistfight with *Menace II Society* director Allen HUGHES resulted in Shakur's March '94 assault conviction, and a sentence which included 15 days in an L.A. jail; in November 1993 Shakur was arrested in Atlanta after two off-duty policemen were shot—charges were eventually dropped. That same month the rapper was picked up in New York and charged with sodomy and sexual abuse of a female fan, and weapons offenses. On the day before the verdict was delivered on the last case, three gunmen robbed Shakur in midtown Manhattan of over $30,000 worth of jewelry and shot him four times. He appeared in court the next day in a wheelchair and was sentenced to one-and-a-half to four-and-a-half years for sexual abuse. While in jail, Shakur saw his *Me Against the World*

(1995) reach No. 1 on the *Billboard* charts on the back of the soulful, reflective single "Dear Mama"; he married his long-time girlfriend in New York's Clinton Correctional facility in April 1995.

USENET **alt.rap, rec.music.hip-hop**

shaved heads Post-haircut popular in the '90s among sportsmen, celebrities, and urban youth. On the basketball court the look was pioneered by black superstars like Michael Jordan, CHARLES BARKLEY, Shaquille O'Neal, and at the 1995 NBA playoffs, all of the Indiana Pacers; entertainers like Michael Stipe and Bruce Willis used shaved heads to confront their receding hair lines; rap stars like TUPAC SHAKUR and ICE CUBE used it to heighten their fierce demeanors. (SINEAD O'CONNOR's cut was a statement of another kind.) More pointedly, gays claimed shaved heads as street-fashion, and stripped them of some of their SKINHEAD stigma.

Shaw, Jim (b. 1952) Los Angeles artist known for "Thrift Store Paintings," a collection of "naïve" art, found by Shaw and friends, that turned into his 1990 book. Shaw's thrift store finds jibed with his use of pop detritus in his magnum opus, "My Mirage," first shown in 1989 and included in the 1991 WHITNEY BIENNIAL. "Mirage" tells the story of Billy, a Midwestern adolescent, through some 170 individual video, drawing, painting, sculpture, and print components that draw on sources that span pulp novels, rock posters, comic books, Mad stickers, *Boy's Life* covers, records, and plastic toy soldiers. The *Los Angeles Times* later described the work as "a complete upchucking of the first 20 years of the life of a middle-class American boy born in the '50s." Like MIKE KELLEY, a decades-old friend, and Raymond Pettibon, Shaw is a product of California Institute of the Arts. He has gone on to a series of "dream drawings" and experiments with the video special effects that supported him in the early '80s.

Shore, Pauly (b. 1968) Southern California comedian who, as the son of Comedy Store owner Mitzi Shore, grew up absorbing enthusiasm if not talent from the likes of Richard Pryor, Sam Kinison, and Robin Williams. Shore was hired by MTV in June 1990 to host the freeform show *Totally Pauly*. His on-air persona—almost indistinguishable from his real-life one—was "the Weasel," a nerdy, lusty surfer dude; his shtick was a combination of coined Valley-ish words (grindage, fresh nugs, etc.), inappropriate pau-ses, and sweetly obnoxious man-in-the-street interviews. Shore tearfully left MTV in 1992, (at which time he was dating ill-fated porn star Savannah) and brought his Weasel act to the hit movie *Encino Man*. Over the next three years he starred in low-budget fish-out-of-water comedies (*The Son In Law*, 1993; *In the Army Now*, 1994; and *Jury Duty*, 1995), with diminishing, if respectable, box office. "Every movie I've done was awful," he told the *Washington Post* in 1995, the same year he proclaimed his growth as an actor and began searching for meatier roles.

Shulgin, Alexander (b. 1925) The CALVIN KLEIN of designer drugs. A self-described "manic libertarian psychedelic chemist," "Sasha" Shulgin began his career at Dow Chemical in the '50s. In 1963 he took mescaline and never looked back. Known as the "stepfather" of ECSTASY, Shulgin specializes in drugs chemically related to mescaline and Ecstasy. Shulgin's book *PIHKAL: A Chemical Love Story* ("Phenethylamines I Have Known and Loved," co-authored with wife Ann) is a fictionalized account of his career with reviews of 179 variations, including the eros-enhancing 2CB, Euphoria, and the long-lasting psychedelic STP. (Shulgin unwittingly unleashed the latter on the '60s when his formula was copied off a chalkboard at Johns Hopkins University.) A teacher, expert witness, and outspoken proponent of legalization, Shulgin had many friends in the law-enforcement community and long held a license to analyze scheduled compounds. A 1994 visit by the DEA and local EPA brought an end to that era of his research, although the Shulgins' continued work on their follow-up volume about tryptamines, *TIKHAL*.

WEB **Hypertext PiHKAL** http://hyperreal.com/drugs/pihkal/

Sick Building Syndrome During the office building boom of the mid-'80s, pockets of workers started complaining of a wide range of health problems when moving to their new, often airtight surroundings: persistent coughs, headaches, dizziness, and colds that wouldn't quit. Sometimes there were straightforward explanations—serious design flaws like fresh air ducts located next to loading docks—other times the culprits were more nebulous—new carpets or office furniture giving off noxious fumes, tobacco smoke, asbestos from old insulation, formaldehyde from particle board and insulation, benzene from cleaners, or random fungi and bacteria. Indoor air quality increasingly caused headaches for commercial landlords also, as the number of worker lawsuits spread in the early '90s. The EPA's own landlord was sued by 19 employees working in the agency's new D.C. headquarters (ventilation ducts had gone more than 15 years without cleaning). In 1993 the EPA estimated that SBS costs American businesses some $60 billion annually in illness and lost productivity. [See also MULTIPLE CHEMICAL SENSITIVITY SYNDROME.]

WEB **Environmental Illness** http://www.orbital.net/~jmay/enviro.html

Silliwood Combination of Silicon Valley and Hollywood, coined circa 1994 to describe the special effects and VIDEOGAME-propelled interactive rights gold rush bringing together the disparate cultures of the world's center of computer innovation in Northern California and the world's center of glamor in Southern California. Realignments began in earnest in 1993, the year that videogames first out-grossed U.S. movie box office; Michael Crichton sold the interactive rights to his novel *Jurassic Park* (1990) for $4 million, twice what he got for the cinematic rights. While Hollywood agents began educating themselves on the intricacies of electronic licensing, computer companies started dabbling in show business, most dramatically in 1995 when Microsoft co-founder Paul Allen invested $500 million in Dreamworks (see MEDIA MOGULS), saying "I always wanted to be in the entertainment business."

Silverstone, Alicia (b. 1977) MTV-bred virtual star whose pouting countenance and jail-bait allure substituted for AEROSMITH's haggard features in three of the band's most popular videos ("Crazy," "Amazin'," and "Cryin'"). Silverstone's movie debut in the low-rent Lolita wanna-be *The Crush* (1993) was scarcely any improvement on the video-mannequin status she publicly disdained; the film did, however, earn her "Best Villain" and "Best Breakthrough Performance" trophies at the 1994 *MTV Movie Awards*. After a handful more throwaway roles, Silverstone acheived legitimate fame in 1995 with Amy (*Fast Times at Ridgemont High*) Heckerling's summer-hit teen comedy *Clueless*. Shortly after the movie's opening grosses were published, Columbia pictures shocked the rest of the industry by giving this 18-year-old a two-picture deal worth almost $10 million.

WEB **Alicia Silverstone Homepage**
http://rampages.onramp.net/~dan/Alicia/Alicia.html

ALICIA SILVERSTONE is ... *Clueless* (1995)!

Sim, Dave (b. 1957) Feisty creator of the fairly inscrutable *Cerebus*, a long-running COMIC novel (aiming for 300 issues over 26 years, approaching 200 in 1995) chronicling the adventures of a barbaric, sentient aardvark blundering his couthless way through a dense, ideologically confused imaginary world. With formally elegant backgrounds provide by his partner, Gerhard (who joined Sim in the late-'80s), Sim's self-published magnum opus has arrived since 1978 in more or less monthly installments which are periodically bound into thick "phone book" collections. Sim draws on such overarching themes as money, power, sexual politics, and popular culture in the book, reserving its letters

column and "Notes From the President" for random acts of misogyny and extended rants on creators' rights, distribution problems, and integrity.
WEB **Cerebus the Page, OPERATION: Crazed Ferret**
http://www.digimark.net/wraith/cerebus.html ◆ MAIL LIST
Cerebus List email majordomo@erzo.berkeley.edu with "subscribe cerebi (your e-mail address)" in the message body ◆ USENET **rec.comics.alternative**

Simmons, Russell (b. 1958) Founder, along with RICK RUBIN, of Def Jam Records, the pre-eminent rap record label of the '80s. Among early Def Jam triumphs (it was formed 1983) were records by L.L. Cool J, Run-DMC (featuring Simmons' brother Joseph), Slick Rick, PUBLIC ENEMY, and THE BEASTIE BOYS. Rubin's departure did not significantly slow down the growth of Simmons' $40 million empire, which also encompasses a clutch of sub-labels, Rush Management, and TV and film production divisions. Simmons has not yet arrived as a fully fledged MEDIA MOGUL, but *Russell Simmons' Def Comedy Jam*, his production for the HBO cable channel (debut March 1992) is a long-running moneyspinner, having helped launch the career of MARTIN LAWRENCE. The entrepreneur's Phat Farm clothing line (debut March 1993), with its flagship store in SoHo, New York, has also been a notable success, retailing a PREPPY/collegiate-via-street look with the same marketing genius that brought HIP-HOP to suburban America in the '80s. Often seen around with a model on each arm, Simmons has long been rumored to be interested in starting his own agency.

Simpsons, The Cartoon TV series originally created by *Life In Hell* cartoonist Matt Groening (b. 1954) as bumpers for Fox's *Tracey Ullman Show*. When that show was canceled in 1990, the Simpsons got their own Christmas special and then, in January 1990, a regular series. The family— Marge, Lisa, Homer, Bart and Maggie—became a Fox centerpiece and an important cultural deconstruction site. When Marge Simpson told her daughter she didn't get the appeal of Saturday morning cartoons, Lisa responded, "If cartoons were meant for adults they'd be on in primetime." Such self-referential jokes, riding a gusher of pop-culture allusions, black humor, and merciless social satire, have earned *The Simpsons* a reputation as the best-written show on television.

Bart's catchphrases—"Don't have a cow, man," "Aye Carumba"—entered the lexicon, and the spike-haired wastrel was soon adorning dozens of popular T-shirts, including the notorious "Black Bart" bootleg. In 1991, several schools banned the shirts, particularly one that said, "Underachiever and proud of it," as a bad influence. *The Simpsons* frequently features A-list guest stars playing themselves (AEROSMITH), playing other characters (Dustin Hoffman, WINONA RYDER) or playing other characters who think they're the celebrity who is playing them (Michael Jackson). In 1994, the show became the first regular series in the U.S. to be simulcast in Spanish.

WEB **The Simpsons Archive** http://www.digimark.net/ TheSimpsons/index.html ✦ USENET **alt.tv.simpsons**, **alt.tv.simpsons.itchy-scratchy** ✦ WEB **Dave Hall's Simpsons Page** http://www.mbnet.mb.ca/~davehall/

Singleton, John (b. 1968) Self-described black film brat who signed on with the (then) all-powerful Creative Artists Agency while still in USC film school. Upon his graduation Tri-Star gave Singleton a $6 million budget to make *Boyz N the Hood* (1991), a powerful coming-of-age tale set in gang-ravaged South Central L.A., and featuring an arresting acting debut from GANGSTA rapper ICE CUBE. Consequently Singleton found himself usurping Orson Welles as the youngest director to be nominated for an Oscar (Singleton's script was also nominated). Although impressive on any level, *Boyz* revealed Singleton's tendency to moralize, a trait that would mar his next two movies. *Poetic Justice* starred diva-lite Janet Jackson as a poet called . . . Justice. (Again, Singleton got a bravura performance from a rapper, TUPAC SHAKUR.) The 1995 success *Higher Learning* placed Ice Cube as one of the central characters in a racially divided college campus.

Sir Mix-a-Lot Critically unloved HIP-HOP star who first appeared on the cultural landscape with the 1985 novelty hit "Square Dance Rap." After two unremarked (though platinum and gold) albums, Sir Mix-a-lot signed a distribution deal with master vulgarian RICK RUBIN's Def American Recordings; the pact gave the world *Mack Daddy*, a platinum album boosted by the frantic frat-rap single "Baby Got Back" (sales 2.5 million) and its leering, fleshy video (withdrawn from MTV rotation). Still there was no respect for Mix-a-Lot, whose supposed artistic shortcomings were made more egregious by his residency in the GRUNGE bastion of SEATTLE. He began 1995 by acting in *The Watcher*, a quickly canceled supernatural series on the Paramount "semi-network."

WEB **Sir Mix-A-Lot Homepage** http://american.recordings. com/American_Artists/Sir_Mix-A-Lot/mix_home.html

✦ USENET **alt.rap**, **rec.music.hip-hop**

Sister Souljah (b. Lisa Williamson, 1964) Self-described "raptivist" and one-time PUBLIC ENEMY associate who came to national notoriety in June 1992. Candidate Bill Clinton scolded Souljah in front of a gathering of Jesse Jackson's Rainbow Coalition in Washington, D.C.; playing to white voters, he condemned as racist a remark the rapper made in a *Washington Post* interview while promoting her album *360 Degrees of Power*. "If black people kill black people every day," Souljah said, in the wake of the L.A. RIOTS, "why not have a week and kill white people?" Controversy proved a boon to the career of ICE-T, but it did not transform that of Sister Souljah, a shrill rapper of modest skills and sales who spent time as a community activist growing up on welfare in New York and New Jersey. Other than occasional chat show appearances she was little heard from until early 1995 when she resurfaced with a book, *No Disrespect*, which dealt with the relationship between black men and women.

skateboarding '70s sidewalk subculture replenished by successive waves of teenagers (the average skater's age is usually estimated by the industry to be

around 14 years old) reinventing what can be done with a board, four wheels, and some asphalt. Invented in the 1950s when two frustrated California surfers nailed their roller skates to a plank and discovered they could surf the sidewalk, the sport didn't catch on until the development of the urethane wheel in 1973 provided new speed and maneuverability. By the late '70s, skateboarding was on par with other august cultural institutions such as roller disco and CB radio—it was boosted by Alan "Ollie" Gelfand's invention of a new move, dubbed the "ollie," which made it possible to jump curbs. But the new style of "street skating" led to a rash of injuries; skateboarding was denounced as dangerous, antisocial, and, most significantly, uninsurable—leading to the closing of many skateboard parks.

As the fad waned, the subculture blossomed. *Thrasher* magazine, launched in 1979, became the bible of skate style in the 1980s. Skate fashion moved from surf-derived "radwear" and shiny plastic padding to B-BOY inspired baggy pants and oversize shirts with enough give for mid-air maneuvers and enough strength to stand a few scrapes on the pavement. Musically, there's never been one single skater groove; although post-hardcore bands like the OFFSPRING are sometimes lumped into a "skatepunk" sound, *Thrasher* is just as likely to cover CYPRESS HILL, NINE INCH NAILS, PRIMUS, and even TORI AMOS. In the mid-'90s, skateboarding is America's sixth largest participant sport, and professional skateboarders tour the world, making a living off their endorsement deals. Nonetheless, skaters are still the target of police attention, as cities upset by the damage the boards' wheels can do to walls, benches, and the occasional passerby have begun passing anti-skating ordinances. The rise of "extreme sports," however, may give skaters a new respectability; as ALICIA SILVERSTONE in *Clueless* (1995) marvels after watching her stoner classmate light up a skateboard competition, "I never knew you were so motivated!"

WEB **Enternet Skateboarding** http://www.enternet.com/skate/skate.html/ ✦ WEB **DansWORLD Skateboarding** http://www.cps.msu.edu/~dunhamda/dw/dansworld.html/ ✦ USENET **alt.skate-board**

Skeptical Inquirer   Quarterly journal which debunks NEW AGE fads, religious miracles, and widely held superstitions. Published since 1977 by the Committee for the Scientific Investigation of Claims of the Paranormal, *SI* strikes an earnest, unfashionable, often humorless note of dissent from sensational and pseudo-scientific claims often disseminated by the media. A long-standing editorial position even takes newspapers and magazines to task for printing horoscope columns. Other regular targets include lie detector tests, subliminal training tapes, and ALIEN ABDUCTION reports.

WEB **CSICOP Home Page** http://iquest.com/~fitz/csicop/ ✦ USENET **sci.skeptic**

skinhead   British working-class street style of the mid/late-'60s, turned international youth-cult fixture. The original skinheads, named after their fear-inspiring shorn craniums, were as style-conscious as the MODS they succeeded: tailored Crombie coats, crisp Ben Sherman shirts from America, and DOC MARTEN boots comprised a suave but brutal-looking uniform; the soundtrack was Jamaican ska music and American soul. But when skinheads' ranks swelled to mass proportions the cult established the thuggish reputation that persists today.

Skinheads resurfaced in the late '70s as a backlash against PUNK's increasingly MULTICULTURAL tendencies. Fashion requirements were cut back to the basics of haircut, boots, and American MA–1 flight jacket as many skinheads aligned themselves with ultra-right-wing, anti-immigrant political parties like the National Front and the British Movement. Skinhead has been a virulent strain of fascist youth culture ever since, both in Europe and in the U.S., where it's associated with groups like California's FOURTH REICH—an extensive 1995 Anti-Defamation League report put fascist "Skinhead International" affiliation at 70,000 people. Ironically, recent years have seen the growth of skinhead anti-fascist organizations like Skinheads Against Racial Prejudice (SHARP).

WEB **Skinheads on the Internet** http://www.ksu.edu/~lashout/skns.html ✦ USENET **alt.skinheads**

Skoal Bandits   Chewing tobacco popular among the white teenage truck set since the early '80s; the only tobacco product for which per capita consumption has increased in recent years. A 1993 government study found that 20 percent of male high school seniors had used chewing tobacco during the previous month. (Another government study concluded that long-term users of spit tobacco were 48 times more likely than non-users to develop gum or cheek cancer.) Internal memos were leaked from the U.S. Tobacco company, and revealed during 1994 congressional testimony. They detail that teens avoid the mildest brand, Happy Days, not wishing to look like novices, but explain how other entry level lines (Skoal Bandits and mint- and cherry-flavored Skoal Long Cut) "fuel the new user base to assure graduation to our priority moist brands" such as the high nicotine Copenhagen.

Actress DREW BARRYMORE turns SKOAL spokesmodel, 1994.

WEB **Tobacco BBS** http://tt.dx.com/tobacco/

Skyy Vodka   When it was launched in 1992, Skyy Vodka had two things that made it instantly attractive to the notoriously elusive tastes of younger drinkers: a cobalt blue bottle, and a promise—a strong suggestion, anyway—that it was hangover-free. Skyy's gimmick was a four-step distillation process that creator Maurice Kanbar said eliminated congeners, the natural impurities in alcohol that may (or may not) be the cause of morning-after headaches and queasiness. Kanbar, a San Francisco inventor whose greatest prior accomplishment was a sweater de-fuzzer, targeted the GENERATION X market with well-placed magazine ads and carefully nurtured word-of-mouth. By the time scrutiny from the Bureau of Alcohol Tobacco and Firearms forced Kanbar to edge away from his hangover-free claim (he now says only that sensitive drinkers will notice the difference), the product had made a small but noticeable dent in the market.

WEB **Skyy Vodka Web Site**

http://gladstone.uoregon.edu/~sjr/skyy.html

slash lit   Once exclusively the work of female *STAR TREK* devotees, slash creations began as fan-produced stories, drawing, and poetry focusing on homosexual fantasies involving Captain James T. Kirk and Lieutenant Spock—or K/S as these works are known, taking their name from the "slash." (The male leads of *Miami Vice* [M/V] and *Starsky and Hutch* [S/H] have also been popular subjects over the course of the slash's history since the mid-'70s.) K/S fiction is collected in ZINES like *On the Double* and *As I Do Thee* that are sold in such fandom catalogs as *Datazine*. Fans meet at annual conventions to discuss issues stemming from their popcult passion for this "romantic pornography." Constance Penley, professor of film and women's studies at the University of California, Santa Barbara, wrote about the phenomenon in 1991's *Technoculture* (edited with husband ANDREW ROSS), calling slash lit "one of the most fascinating appropriations and manipulations of popular culture by women that I've ever seen." When the form reached the INTERNET in the early '90s, it become dominated there by males. [See also CULTURAL STUDIES.]

USENET **alt.sex.fetish.startrek** ✦ USENET

alt.sex.fetish.startrek ftp **alt.sex.fetish.startrek Archive**

ftp://ftp.netcom.com/pub/ev/evansc

Slater, Christian (b. 1969)   Former child actor who, with co-star WINONA RYDER, leapt to renown with the 1989 teen satire *Heathers*. Slater became a teen magazine regular with his sly, Jack Nicholson–inspired portrayal of the film's ur-rebel J.D.; he consolidated his image by playing the ur-rebel DJ in *Pump Up the Volume* (1990). He has since struggled to inhabit credible adult roles, but these have been hard to come by for the star of such bombs as *Kuffs* (1992), *Murder in the First* (1995), and *Mobsters* (1991).

Slater's bouts with the law are almost as interesting as his body of work to date: he was arrested in December 1989 after a car chase with L.A. police, with whom he fought. (He spent ten days in jail.) The actor was arrested again in December, 1994, when he walked through a metal detector at New York's J.F.K. airport with an unloaded .32

Beretta in his luggage. Shortly after getting three days' community service, he was sued for palimony by his long-time girlfriend Nina Huang.

Slick Rick (b. Ricky Walters, 1964) English-born, Bronx-raised rapper who, as MC Ricky D, made one of HIP-HOP's breakthrough records, 1985's "The Show"/"La-Di-Da-Di" with Doug E. Fresh and the Get Fresh Crew. The jewelry-laden, eyepatch-wearing Ricky D had a novel rapping style—sing-song with an arch English accent—and prodigious lyrical skills that augured well for his solo launch as Slick Rick. His 1988 solo debut *The Further Adventures of Slick Rick* was a platinum hit, but Rick's life was changed by an incident that closely mirrored the plot of his track "Children's Story." He shot his cousin on a Bronx street corner on July 3, 1990, and crashed his car after a police chase. A sentence of three-and-a-half to ten years for attempted murder in the second degree didn't dim the rapper's commercial instincts, however: while out on three weeks bail he hastily chopped out two albums worth of material and five videos. The records—1991's *The Ruler's Back* and 1994's *Behind Bars*—sold moderately well. In 1995 when the imprisoned Rick was threatened with deportation, the "Free Slick Rick" campaign was publicized in *VIBE* magazine.

WEB **Free Slick Rick Campaign** http://www.timeinc.com/vibe/theroom/docs/freerick.html

slip dresses Satiny, bias-cut slip dresses wafted down the runways of the designer collections for spring 1994, an extension of the "innerwear-as-outerwear" trend popularized by MADONNA and her vampy black lace bustiers. Seen from a distance, these fragile, usually pastel-hued dresses often looked suspiciously insubstantial for life beyond the boudoir. To minimize their transparency, CALVIN KLEIN presented slip dresses layered one on top of the other. Minimalist designer Helmut Lang showed his satin slips with body-hugging little sweaters on top, prompting more than a few double takes on the streets as passersby wondered if woman were leaving home in a hurry and forgetting to put on their skirts.

smart drinks and drugs The "nootropics" fad (from the Greek "noos," for mind) can be traced to the 1990 publication of a book called *Smart Drugs and Nutrients: How to Improve Your Memory and Increase Your Intelligence Using the Latest Discoveries in Neuroscience*, by gerontologist Ward Dean and science writer John Morgenthaler. The authors claimed that substances like hydergine, choline, perecetam, vasopressin, and ephedra have the potential to rejuvenate memory, kick-start the intellect, spark the sex drive, and even turn back the mental aging process. Entrepreneurs quickly began blending smart drugs with juices and amino acids, selling them in drink form ($3-$6) at clubs and raves under such evocative names as Energy Elicksure, Memory Fuel, Fast Blast, and Mind Mix. Many smart drinks and drugs provide a caffeine-like rush, plus whatever placebo effects consumers themselves bring to the experience. "Smart drugs," claimed Dr. James McGaugh, director of the Center for the Neurobiology of Learning and Memory at the University of California at Irvine, "are a Hula-Hoop for the mind."

WEB **Smart Drink Sites** http://www.uta.fi/~samu/nootropics_resources.html ✦ WEB **Smart Drug/Nootropic Info** http://www.damicon.fi/sd/ ✦ WEB **Herbal Ecstacy Smart Bar** http://www.he.tdl.com/~holistic/herbal.html

Smashing Pumpkins Chicago band known for grandiose rock and intra-band dramas. Despite their '90s glam-freak image, the Smashing Pumpkins are as musically generic as any major band of their generation. The Pumpkins' more energetic moments bear the clear influence of such quotidian rock-greats as Queen and The Who; the band's portentous passages of non-specific, heavy rock would not be out of place alongside '70s pomp-rockers like Styx and Journey. Singer/song-writer Billy Corgan (b. 1967) evinces many rock star traits of that benighted era: he is unabashedly pretentious and perfectionist, and reportedly autocratic

Photo by Brooke Williams

SMASHING PUMPKINS' Billy Corgan gets bombastic, 1994.

and egomaniacal. These traits were, many felt, justified by the band's platinum-selling second album *Siamese Dream* (1993), a collection of lavishly self-pitying anthems-to-be.

WEB **Smashing Pumpkins Main Page**

http://www.muohio.edu/~carmance/sp.html ✦ USENET **alt.music.smash-pumpkins**

Smith, Kevin (b. 1970) Film school dropout whose 1994 debut *Clerks* contained, in almost laughably correct proportion, the elements of credible indie cinema. Directly inspired by RICHARD LINKLATER's *Slacker* (1991), the film was shot in black and white on a budget of $27,575, which was raised by maxing out CREDIT CARDS and selling a COMICS collection. After awards at Cannes and SUNDANCE there was a distribution deal with MIRAMAX and a tacked-on SOUNDTRACK (Soul Asylum, Jesus Lizard, Bad Religion); *Clerks* even acquired a successfully challenged NC–17 rating thanks to an extensive discussion of blowjobs. The movie grossed more than $6 million and Gramercy Pictures gave Smith $5 million to make his second feature, 1995's *Mallrats,* which starred SHANNEN DOHERTY.

Smith, Will (b. 1968) Aggressively genial crossover from pop-rapper to sitcom star to action movie hero. West Philadelphia teenagers Smith (The Fresh Prince) and Jeff Townes (DJ Jazzy Jeff) first scored with a 1986 HIP-HOP novelty "Girls Ain't Nothing but Trouble" that set the stage for the Grammy-winning pop hit "Parents Just Don't Understand" (1988). The hammy "Parents" video helped ease hip-hop onto MTV, and in 1990 was cloned for the opening credits to Smith's hit Quincy Jones-produced *Fresh Prince of Bel Air* (1990) sitcom. Smith played a gay conman in the 1993 movie adaptation of John Guare's play *Six Degrees of Separation*, but reportedly refused to kiss Anthony Michael Hall on camera for fear of jeopardizing his marginal hip-hop credibility (he has continued to release moderately successful albums). In 1995's *Bad Boys* Smith looked much more at home with MARTIN LAWRENCE; a formulaic action movie, *Bad Boys* was originally supposed to star SATURDAY NIGHT LIVE alumni Dana Carvey and Jon Lovitz.

smoothed-out R&B When Boyz II Men's "End of the Road" spent a record 14 weeks atop the *Billboard* chart in late 1994 (displaced by the band's follow-up single), it marked the apex of one of the '90's most formidable pop trends: the return of R&B vocal harmonizing. Clean-cut, gospel-trained, and outfitted in PREPPY basics, B II M blend the purity of '50s doo-wop and the schmaltz of '70s soul with just enough contemporary beats to avoid sounding like a nostalgia act. A slew of soundalikes, such as Shai, 4PM, and All 4 One, have made the sound of black men's voices united in harmony a ubiquitous radio counterpoint to the era's technology-heavy pop. The often-saccharine style of these groups may seem an implicit rebuke to GANGSTA aggression, but in-between the extremes there's plenty of room for compromise, as acts like Jodeci mix Quiet Storm smoothness with shirtless macho posturing, Silk and H-Town get sexually explicit, and EAZY-E protégés Bone Thugs N Harmony claim four-part euphony for gangsta rap.

WEB **WRNB The Web's R&B Music Source**

http://www.csua.berkeley.edu/~lingo/music.html ✦ WEB **The Motown Boys II Men Page** http://www.musicbase.co.uk/music/motown/motown/motobtm.html/

snapping Long-standing African-American tradition of trading escalating insults, usually of the "your mama" variety. ("If ugliness were bricks, your mother would be a housing project"; "Your family is so poor, they go to Kentucky Fried Chicken to lick other people's fingers!") Also known as "the dozens," snapping is a cornerstone of black comedy that was also part of early HIP-HOP's braggadocio; "answer records" between feuding rappers, once frequent, are today only sporadic. A pair of snapping book collections were published in 1994; the most successful, *Snaps,* was written by a SATURDAY NIGHT LIVE producer, a PBS host, and an entertainment attorney, and led in 1995 to *Double Snaps* and an HBO comedy special.

WEB **Yo Mama Jokes** http://www.cs.miami.edu/~ldouglas/yomama.html

Snapple Fruit juice and iced tea purveyor which capitalized on the '90s shift away from soda to non-carbonated drinks. Snapple's wholesome, mom-and-pop deli image—cultivated in homey TV ads—reflects its history if not its present: in November 1994, the Quaker Oats corporation bought the company for $1.7 billion. Snapple was started by three friends—Lower East Side New York health-food store owner Arnold Greenberg and window washers Leonard Marsh and Hyman Golden—who sold fizzy apple juice to health food stores beginning in 1972. They changed the name from Unadulterated Food Products to Snapple in 1980, adding other natural juices and sodas along the way, but it was their 1987 introduction of the first hot-brewed iced-tea in bottles that brought the company consumer affection and astronomical growth. In 1993 the company weathered widespread but unfounded rumors that it supported OPERATION RESCUE, the Ku Klux Klan, and even a race war; more threatening is competition from Coke's FRUITOPIA and Pepsi's Lipton. The three founders pocketed $130 million each in the 1994 buy out.

WEB **The Official Snapple Home Page**
http://www.snapple.com/ ✦ WEB **Made from the Best Stuff on Earth** http://ernie.bgsu.edu/~jdolsk2/snapple/

Snoop Doggy Dogg (b. Calvin Broadus, 1971) Rapper-protégé of former N.W.A producer/member DR. DRE, first heard on the Dre-produced title track from the 1992 film *Deep Cover*. In the accompanying video clip, Snoop Doggy Dogg lurched onto the screen, his eyes heavy-lidded, melodically including the song's hook "187 [murder] on an undercover cop." As Snoop's history became known, that threat gained weight: it transpired that this unknown newcomer was a member of the Long Beach Insane Crips gang and had done jail time for selling cocaine and subsequent probation violations. The rapper was next heard on Dr. Dre's 1993 album *The Chronic*, guest-starring on the trio of hit singles; Snoop's seductive rhyme style and charismatic on-screen persona instantly established him as one of the most distinctive voices in hip-hop. Such was the anticipation surrounding his Dre-pro-

duced solo debut *Doggystyle* that the record's December 1993 debut at #1 (the first such performance by a new artist) and quadruple-platinum sales were entirely predictable. (The record itself was somewhat predictable, from its smutty cartoon cover to its incessant self-reference and *Chronic*-derived tracks. In the video for "What's My Name?" Snoop MORPHED into . . . a dog.)

On August 25th, 1993, an argument started in front of Snoop's new home in Woodbine Park, L.A., between the rapper, two associates, and Philip Woldemariam, a 20-year-old Ethiopian immigrant who had just been released from a year in jail. Woldemariam was allegedly pursued into a nearby park and shot from a vehicle by McKinley Lee, Snoop's bodyguard. Lee claimed self-defense, but it was widely reported that the victim's fatal wound was in his back. Snoop, who was on $10,000 bail for a gun possession charge at the time of the incident, handed himself in to police after appearing at a September 2nd MTV awards show in L.A.—his bail was set at $1 million. Snoop had another #1 album in November 1994 with *Murder Was the Case*, the multi-artist SOUNDTRACK to an 18-minute film directed by Dr. Dre and based on a *Doggystyle* track. In April 1995 it was ruled that, although key evidence had accidentally been destroyed, Snoop Doggy Dogg's murder trial would proceed that October.

WEB **The Snoop Doggy Dogg LyricsPage**
http://www.brad.ac.uk/~ctttaylo/lyrics/snoop.doggy.dog/snoo p.html/ ✦ USENET **alt.rap, rec.music.hip-hop**

snowboarding EXTREME SPORT featuring a fiberglass plank strapped to the feet; reputedly easier to master than skiing. Freestyle snowboarding stunts offer two kinds of air-time: one to adrenaline-junkie 'boarders, and another to ad makers looking to halt channel surfers in their tracks. Snowboarding owes much to SKATEBOARD culture (including slang like half-pipe and shredding), and has a rock-world following that includes members of the BEASTIE BOYS and Anthrax. The world's largest snowboard companies, Burton and Sims, each lay claim to the sport in the early '80s (when the boards were first mass-mar-

"Easier to master than skiing"?

keted). Founder Jake Burton's designs were, however, based on the Snurfer, a primitive wood snowboard developed by Michigan inventor Sherman Poppin in the '60s. It was Tom Sims, an established name in skateboards, who added the foot bindings essential to the mid-flight "boned tweaks," "stalefish," and back flips that today adorn McDonald's commercials and ESPN2.

WEB **Cyberboarder!** http://www. cyberboarder.com/

Sonic Youth   Drawing on Eastern tonal scales, the brute power of guitar noise, and the junk-PUNK culture of downtown New York, Sonic Youth has become one of the most influential and respected forces in INDIE-ROCK. From their 1982, self-titled EP debut, the band (led by guitarist/singer Thurston Moore [b. 1958] and his bassist wife Kim Gordon [b. 1953]) plied unorthodox song structures and discordant tunings (some achieved by sticking screwdrivers and drumsticks between guitar strings) to create a hypnotic, menacing effect. Sonic Youth embraced more traditional pop song structure on 1987's *Sister* and *Daydream Nation* (1988), and in 1990 they made their major-label debut *Goo* on Geffen. This album and 1992's *Dirty* showcased Gordon, whose commentaries on gender ("Kool Thing," with cameo by PUBLIC ENEMY's Chuck D, "Swimsuit Model") marked her as a voice in her own right. In the early '90s the band's venerated status gave them the opportunity to exchange cachet with fashion arbiters like ANNA SUI and MARC JACOBS; in 1993 Kim Gordon co-founded her own clothing line, X-GIRL.

Like MADONNA (whose songs they mauled on *The Whitey Album EP* and LP [1988, 1989], recorded as Ciccone Youth) and their friends the BEASTIE BOYS, Sonic Youth are as much culture-makers as musicians, consistently giving prescient exposure to trends like CYBERPUNK, ANIME, and SERIAL KILLER CHIC, and artists like MIKE KELLEY and Raymond Pettibon. Musically, Sonic Youth's patron-

age of NIRVANA (seen in the 1992 documentary, *1991: The Year Punk Broke*) helped bring that band to Geffen, thus altering the ecosystem of American rock. Although Sonic Youth seemed poised to capitalize on the ALTERNATIVE boom subsequent records have failed to yield the kind of anthemic song that might bring the band major league status. 1994's *Experimental Jet Set, Trash and No Star* was a sleepy LP whose oblique title encapsulated the band's mid-'90s identity. In the summer of 1994, Gordon and Moore, who've been married since 1984, had a daughter named Coco; the following year the band co-headlined the fifth LOLLAPALOOZA festival.

WEB **Sonic Youth Fan Page** http://www.itp.tsoa.nyu.edu/ ~student/brendonm/sonic.html ✦ WEB **Sonic Youth Page** http://geffen.com/sonic.html ✦ WEB **Sonic Youth IUMA Page** http://www.iuma.com/IUMA/band_html/Sonic_Youth.html ✦ USENET **alt.music.sonic-youth**

Soren, Tabitha (b. Tabitha Sornberger, 1967)   Red-headed co-anchor of *MTV News*, who peppily counterbalances the avuncular stoner-figure Kurt Loder. Where *ROLLING STONE* certified its counterculture credentials by unleashing gonzo leftie Hunter Thompson on the 1972 presidential campaign, MTV shored up its non-music programming with Soren's earnest coverage of the 1992 presidential race (though CNN's Catherine Crier was brought in to baby-sit for Clinton's first appearance on the network). Thanks in part to the candidates' avoidance of traditional journalists, Soren scored one of the campaign's most revealing moments, interviewing a curt, down-in-the-polls President Bush on the back of his campaign train. The attention, which coincided with the apex of GENERATION X marketing hype, led to part-time Soren reports on NBC's *Today Show* and a syndicated "youth issues" newspaper column entitled "Something to Think About" for the country's most recognizable under–30 journalist.

WEB **MTV News: The Week in Rock** http://mtv.com/cgi-bin/htimage/MTVNEWS/

Sound Factory   Legendary dance club in Manhattan's Chelsea district which, during its six-year dominion over the after-hours circuit, inspired an almost messianic devotion. Presided over by DJ JUNIOR VASQUEZ, the Sound Factory offered a frenzied melange of tribal rhythms, trance music, and hard HOUSE to its largely gay crowd, who paid $20 a head to dance until noon on Sundays. The lack of alcohol and a formal guest list did not deter the celebrity likes of MADONNA (a Vasquez collaborator and friend), David Geffen, MARKY MARK, SUPERMODEL Linda Evangelista, LEONARDO DiCAPRIO, and JULIETTE LEWIS. The Sound Factory's mythic status was cemented by its February, 1995 swan song—a 16-hour blow out after community-board complaints and extra police attention forced its closure. The scene took temporary refuge at the venerable Roseland, with the prospect of Sound Factory re-opening.

Working it at Manhattan's fabled SOUND FACTORY.

SoundScan

Computerized system for tracking music sales at medium- to large-sized retail outlets. Pre-SoundScan, the most authoritative charts for hit records, the Billboard Charts, were compiled from the subjective reports of bribable radio programmers and store managers. The switch to SoundScan in 1991 turned the world of pop music on its ear. Initially the charts became at once more volatile and more conservative: splashy, unsustained opening week performances jostled with perennial back-catalogue sellers. Populist genres like HIP-HOP, country, metal, and R&B scored on the new, more-level playing field, especially as smaller record stores were incorporated into the point-of-sale tallies.

WEB **The Charts** http://www.webb.com/concrete/charts.html

soundtrack albums

The days of pop-phenomena movie-to-album spin-offs like *Saturday Night Fever* (1977) and *Flashdance* (1983) have passed, but the form itself is burgeoning. The renaissance in black film making has yielded numerous lucrative HIP-HOP and R&B compilation soundtracks (*Above the Rim* [1994], *Boomerang* [1992]), and the ALTERNATIVE rock marketplace has created another opportunity: by assembling a palatable mix of known names and newcomers, marketers can extend a picture's franchise (via music video, record sales, and radio airplay) regardless of its eventual fate. Thus, even box-office failures can yield hit records: Cameron Crowe's SEATTLE-based comedy *Singles* (1992) flopped horribly, but the movie's soundtrack, featuring local acts like Alice In Chains, PEARL JAM, and the Screaming Trees, went platinum; BEN STILLER's unsuccessful *Reality Bites* spun off a #1 single for the then-unsigned singer Lisa Loeb. *The Crow* (1994, starring BRANDON LEE), on the other hand, was a sleeper hit enhanced by a soundtrack featuring RAGE AGAINST THE MACHINE, STONE TEMPLE PILOTS, NINE INCH NAILS, and the ROLLINS Band. In the mid-'90s, as film studios and record companies acknowledged their shared demographic target, films became increasingly front-loaded with alternative acts, regardless of cultural compatability. The bands' names are prominently featured in movie trailers, and, often, their clip-laden videos are vigorously pushed by MTV.

USENET **rec.music.movies**

South Beach

Drawn by memories of *Miami Vice* and the promise of eternal summer, '80s trend-seekers flocked to the square mile of white sands and Art Deco buildings known as Miami's South Beach, transforming the former haven for retirees and Marielitos (Cuban immigrants from the 1980 Mariel boat lift) into a hip pastel playground. Racks filled with fashion-shoot clothes jostled for space on chic Ocean Drive with camera crews shooting TV commercials; ROLLERBLADING models navigated swarms of European tourists. Undaunted by Dade County's astronomically high crime rate, celebrities such as MADONNA, Sly Stallone, and Gianni Versace ensconced themselves in opulent estates, while Mickey Rourke and SEAN PENN invested in nightclubs. Some thought of South Beach as the

American Riviera; others called it Hollywood II, or SoHo by the sea. But by the summer of 1993, no less an authority than *USA Today* announced that the fickle fabulous were moving on, and taking the party with them. "It's just begun and it's already over!" one resident wailed.

WEB **A Week In South Beach** http://www.sobe.com/ sobe/sbmc/index.html

Space Ghost Coast-to-Coast The muscle-bound star of the Cartoon Network's animated talk show is sampled from original episodes of a cut-rate Hanna Barbera character. The brainchild of program director Mike Lazlo, *SGC2C* debuted quietly on the cable channel in 1994 to parody the prior season's talk-show wars. Guests have included weight-conscious INFOMERCIAL queen Susan Powter, rapper Schoolly D, comedian/burnout Bobcat Goldthwaite, and '80s art-rock guy David Byrne. *SGC2C* combines televisual maximalism (rapid-fire editing, stock footage, phony self-importance, and TV's most stereophonically enhanced soundtrack) with some of the cheapest animation since *Johnny Quest.*

EMAIL sgc2c@aol.com ✦ WEB **Original Series** http://iquest.com/~cshuffle/sghost/

Spade, Kate (b. Katy Brosnahan, 1962) Former fashion editor/stylist at *Mademoiselle* magazine who started her eponymous accessory-design company in 1991. Along with her now-husband Andy Spade (brother of SATURDAY NIGHT LIVE sprite-comic David Spade) and another partner, Spade began by pairing classic handbag shapes with witty details like peacoat buttons and whimsical fabrics such as raffia, as well as her signature patent leather. Initially sold only locally in New York, the line soon turned up in major department stores such as Saks Fifth Avenue and Neiman Marcus. (The company created the bags for TODD OLDHAM's spring 1994 runway show.) Kate Spade's small, black fabric label sewn on the outside of her big-selling nylon totes and rounded, zip-up handbags became as recognizable to young fashion-watchers as the PRADA logo to those with slightly heftier checkbooks.

speech codes Prohibitions against "hate speech" designed to promote tolerance for minorities, women, and gays at many college campuses in the early '90s. Most speech codes have since been dropped as an affront to civil liberties. Courts deemed the expression restrictions of the University of Michigan, University of Wisconsin, and other state schools to be in violation of the First Amendment, while tending to uphold "hate-crime" laws that attach extra punishment to an offense if it is found to have been bigoted. Private colleges had their own problems with speech codes, particularly the University of Pennsylvania, which discarded its policy in 1993 after freshman Eden Jacobowitz became a national symbol of POLITICALLY CORRECT victimhood. Jacobowitz, an Israeli-born Orthodox Jew, shouted "shut up, you water buffalo" from his dorm window at five black sorority sisters who then called the campus police. He was threatened with suspension despite his protests that the epithet is a straight translation for *behemah*, the Hebrew slang for fool.

GOPHER **ACLU** gopher://aclu.org:6601/

Spheeris, Penelope (b. 1945) Director of *Wayne's World* (1992), now deeply implicated in Hollywood's risk-averse recycling of TV reruns into multiplex mulch (*The Beverly Hillbillies* [1993]; and *The Little Rascals* [1995]). Previously, Spheeris made the definitive documentaries on PUNK and metal. The former, *The Decline of Western Civilization* (1981), features the Germs, X, and Black Flag; the latter, *The Decline of Western Civilization, Part II* (1988), juxtaposes decadent in situ interviews with the likes of Ozzy Ozbourne and KISS against the debauched fantasies of metal fans.

Spiegelman, Art (b. 1948) Best-selling author of *Maus* (1986), the graphic-novel depiction of the artist's troubled relationship with his father, a Jewish survivor of Hitler's death camps. (In 1991, he published *Maus II*, the story of how his father survived Auschwitz, which led to a Pulitzer Prize for the two volumes.) A veteran of the '60s underground comix scene, Spiegelman realigned "serious" car-

tooning with *RAW* (1980–91), a sporadically published anthology of cutting-edge COMICS, cartooning, and graphic experimentalism. Co-edited with his wife, Francoise Mouly, *RAW* was a bi-continental experiment that introduced such artists as GARY PANTER, Joost Swarte, Kaz, Mark Beyer, Jacques Tardi, CHARLES BURNS, Bruno Richard, Sue Coe, and many others to a more uptown readership than they might otherwise have enjoyed. When Mouly became design director of the *NEW YORKER* magazine in 1993, Spiegelman tagged along as a consultant, shepherding several of the *RAW* artists into the magazine's relatively tony pages and producing a number of controversial covers.

WEB **Spiegelman on Maus** http://www.voyagerco.com/ CD/gh/inside/p.art.html ✦ USENET **alt.comics**

Spin   New-music magazine founded in 1985 by *Penthouse* owner Bob Guccione and his son, fellow First Amendment enthusiast Bob Jr. (b. 1955). *Spin* originally thrived in the demographic space vacated when *ROLLING STONE* outgrew its counterculture roots. The new arrival initially had an irreverence that clearly dissented from BABY BOOMER attempts to ease rock 'n' roll into a dignified middle age— *Spin* was one of the few national media outlets for the thriving college-rock/ALTERNATIVE culture. On the downside, *Spin* was a success-by-default, sloppily defining its identity by what it was not. The advent of NIRVANA, LOLLAPALOOZA, and GENERATION X-marketing boosted *Spin* (as it did *Rolling Stone* and *DETAILS*), giving the magazine an obvious cultural agenda and an audience easily defined for advertisers.

GOPHER **Spin on Electronic Newsstand** gopher:// gopher.enews.com:70/11/magazines/alphabetic/all/spin

Spinal Tap   Rock-parody brainchild of Michael McKean—latterly of *SATURDAY NIGHT LIVE*—and *SNL* alumni Christopher Guest and Harry Shearer. First seen on the ABC's *The TV Show* in 1978, Tap rose to fame with an eponymous 1984 movie— directed by Rob Reiner—that used legends of British hard-rock outlaws on tour in the U.S. to deflate bloated rock mythologies. So painfully accu-

rate was *Tap*'s detail that any musician worth his union card can quote entire slabs of the script; MTV has even absorbed the term "rockumentary" (originally from *The Last Waltz*, 1978) into its own lexicon, and phrases like "it's a fine line between stupid and clever" and "this [amplifier] goes to 11" have gone into everyday usage. (Post-*Spinal Tap*, when bands destroy hotel rooms, they do it with *irony*.) Spinal Tap's creators actually toured after the film's release, but they tainted its memory in 1992 by gigging again—and staging an NBC special—to promote a putatively funny, non-SOUNDTRACK record, *Break Like The Wind*.

WEB **Spinal Tap Homepage** http://rhino.harvard.edu/elwin/ SpinalTap/home.html

spirituality   See page 236.

spoken word   "Pointlessly stiff term for poetry read aloud with stand-up comic timing and aggression," said the *New York Times* in 1994. Renewed interest in THE BEATS during the early '90s mobilized young poets to display their verbal acuity at COFFEE BARS nationwide. From Venice's Beyond Baroque to New York City's Nuyorican Poets Café and Fez, hungry "wannabeats" entered game-show-like "poetry slams" where audience popularity determines the victor. (Chicago's Green Mill is credited with originating the form in 1986.) The GAP was among the first corporate entities to invoke spoken word, making a minor celebrity out of Max Blagg, the English-born poet featured in a $10 million TV ad campaign in 1992. (*Adweek* later proclaimed the commercials "a raving flop.") Among other spoken word mini-celebs were Reg E. Gaines and MAGGIE ESTEP, surly stars of MTV's inter-program "Fightin' Wordz" segments; in 1993 the station staged poetry specials and a tours. There was a boom in spoken word CD releases both old and new, including a three-disk collection by long-time practitioner HENRY ROLLINS; in 1994, LOLLAPALOOZA upgraded from spoken-word videos to a dedicated tent.

WEB **Best-Quality Audio Web Poems** http://www.cs.brown.edu/fun/bawp/

Spur Posse High school gang from the L.A. county of Lakeview—once affluent from Cold War military contracts—that achieved national notoriety in March, 1993, when the members' competition to see who could sleep with the most girls led nine of them to be accused of rape. The steroid-enhanced members postured as defiant womanizers for *20/20, Dateline NBC,* and a host of talkshows (Oprah and Donahue each refused to pay, citing objections to "checkbook journalism," but not Maury Povich, Jenny Jones, or Jane Whitney). Typically, they told *Rolling Stone,* "whores you just nut and leave; good girls that are fine and respectable, you give them the all night thing . . . you just romance them and eat them out and shit." Meanwhile the accusers went on MTV to speak out about DATE RAPE. The district attorney ended up prosecuting only two of the 17 cases presented. In a separate case, Posse member Dana Bellman, 20, received a 10-year sentence for burglary in January 1994; fellow member Christopher Albert was shot to death during a Fourth of July celebration in 1995. He was 21.

Spy Magazine phenomenon of the '80s, still influential today. From 1986 on, *Spy*'s satirists (led by editor-founders Graydon Carter and Kurt Andersen) administered an emetic to the horde of public figures gorging themselves on the spoils of Reaganism. With the fall of so many '80s villains,

SPY pairs porn enthusiasts PEE-WEE HERMAN and Clarence Thomas.

Spy lost some of its vitality, but the magazine's investigative reporting, cultural criticism, and labor-intensive charts consistently shamed the rest of the print media. Most of the original staff had left by the time the final issue (March 1994) was printed; circulation was a respectable 200,000 but advertising had been a problem, since *Spy* had managed to offend so many influential citizens. (*Inside Media* reported that the repercussions from an article about fashion publisher Michael Coady cost the magazine about $200,000 in lost ad revenue.) Although a August

1994 relaunch sullied the *Spy* name, the original spirit lives on as a media virus: the original magazine's ironic attitude is now standard-issue for aspiring journalists and many *Spy* staffers now occupy prominent positions in magazine publishing. (As *Spy* ran aground, Graydon Carter put *Spy* hate object Donald Trump on the cover of *Vanity Fair,* after attending his wedding; Kurt Andersen went on to edit former *Spy* rival *New York.*)

Squirt TV Attitude-heavy public access TV show produced, featuring, and taped in the Manhattan bedroom of precocious, 5'1" (as of 1995) INDIE teen Jake Fogelnest (b. 1979). Fogelnest's matter-of-fact commentaries on pop culture effluvia earned him a following that includes the BEASTIE BOYS, Weezer, and WEEN—all of whom have been interviewed on the show—and led to work directing music videos under the mentorship of SPIKE JONZE. (Wax and the Funk Junkies were early clients.) Other work includes reports for MTV's 1995 Spring Break and Comedy Central (with JANEANE GAROFALO, another fan).

*69 Relationship-altering phone feature, also a 1994 song by R.E.M ("Star 69"). In certain areas dialing *69 will call back the most recent caller. The service uses new "caller ID" phone technology which identifies the phone number of a caller. At the urging of suicide hotlines and privacy advocates, state laws authorizing caller ID have also set off an escalation of "call blocking" privacy features (like *67) for canceling the transmittal of one's number. First widely available to consumers in 1993, a commercial variant called ANI (automatic number identification) has long logged the calls of 800-number callers without any compensating "call blocking" option. Coming next, caller ID which will reveal the number responsible for a CALL-WAITING beep.

WEB **AT&T Home Page** http://www.att.com/

Star Trek Unstoppable cultural phenomenon and lucrative entertainment franchise. Despite all the media attention paid to the baffling subculture

spirituality

With the third millennium looming on the horizon, alternative spiritual currents spread through an increasingly fragmented cultural arena. Traditional religions enjoyed a surge of popularity among the younger generation, as did other MULTI-CULTURAL affirmations of time-honored ethnic identities. At the same time, fringe pop styles began invoking religious imagery to blur the distinction between cult and culture, whether in the name of GOTH, Gaia, or Elvis worship. (The latter a reminder that the word "fan" comes from fanaticus, Latin for temple zealots.)

The most ecstatic strain of pop spirituality in the '90s was spawned by the RAVE movement. Dance cultures have always been driven by a kind of transcendent hedonism, but raves injected the heftiest dose of spiritual, pagan, and paranormal desires into popular music culture since the heyday of '60s psychedelia. Rather than hunting for individual sexual encounters, most ravers sought trance-like states and a polymorphous sense of communion. DJs were treated as "digital shamans," while Hindu gods, numinous extraterrestrials, and computer-generated, hallucinogenic eye-candy appeared on record covers, posters, T-shirts, and the walls of clubs (via light shows). Many raves were tinged with a tribal fever not dissimilar from the previous generation's Happenings. The British act the Spiral Tribe and the much-hyped ZIPPIES were both overtly apocalyptic and psychedelic, while the TECHNO star MOBY became one of pop music's most outspoken, if idiosyncratic, Christians.

The rave scene never revolutionized club culture in America as it did in Britain, though it fostered numerous smaller scenes, a few of which were strongly psychedelic. Meanwhile, chill-out rooms carved out space for the soundscapes of AMBIENT music to grow and develop. The aural equivalent of incense (moody and vaporous), ambient music drew from DUB, SF soundtracks and BRIAN ENO, and spread in popularity well beyond the clubs. The ambient scene enjoyed a love-hate relationship with NEW AGE music and thought: mirroring the continued popularity of the new age's eclectic sci-fi millennialism, some ambi-ent and rave scenesters pondered prophecies, crop circles, and communal states of altered consciousness.

As feel-good products like Crystal Pepsi and Coke's FRUITOPIA began to claim significant shelf space, the wider consumer culture reflected this surge in spiritual weirdness. The feel-good mysticism of 1993's The Celestine Prophecy (following on the heels of the TV-canonization of mythology scholar Joseph Campbell) kept the book on the best-seller lists for months. Monk music CDs like Chant (1993) graced record charts. Primetime TV shows like Touched by an Angel and Aaron Spelling's Heaven Help Us (both 1994) also reflected the mainstream's growing obsession with angels, a fixation that produced several best-selling books. As middle America's Christian equivalent of extraterrestrials, angels gave rise to sightings, spontaneous healings, and paranormal interventions. Meanwhile, the self-help industry became increasingly spiritualized, with therapists MORPHING into spirit guides (like Marianne Williamson of 1991's A Course In Miracles), and child

IBM and Lotus in spiritual harmony.

IBM dons the robes of the new SPIRITUALITY (TV ad)

abuse imagined as a vast SATANIC conspiracy. RELIGIOUS FASHIONS graced the world's catwalks while New Age "empowerment technologies" entered corporate management seminars, and Taoist classics were devoured on Wall Street. The hollowness of much of this entrepreneurial spirituality was skewered by MICHAEL TOLKIN in his film The New Age (1994).

Today's younger seekers perceive spiritual narcissism, self-seriousness, and est-like authoritarian escapades as the New Age pitfalls of the BABY BOOM generation. Instead, they pride themselves on a more anarchic and diffuse world view, one that refuses distinctions between spirit and body, between the sacred and the pop profane. (One rave T-shirt is exemplary: an ADIDAS rip-off that reads Adonai—a Hebrew euphemism for God.) Compared to the hippie generation's serious embrace of the *I Ching*, the *Upanishads*, and mantra, they seem less interested in teachings or traditional practices than in raw experience: altered states, ritual, ECSTASY. The mushroom-munching spiritual tour guide replaces the disciplined yogi as the charged figure of wisdom.

Refusing the quietude of contemplative traditions, Neo-Pagan and Goddess movements like WICCA sought a creative and performative expression of the Old Ways cobbled from European and Neolithic folklore. The occult world witnessed the rise of chaos magick, an intense, turbulent and quasi-scientific supernatural theory. The rise of apocalyptic thought and imagery in both the religious fringe (from DAVID KORESH's Branch Davidians to less-threatening new age strains) and popular culture (Las Vegas' Luxor casino complex has a millennialist theme) evoked the sense that only intense and spectacular events could provide meaning at a time when everything solid, familiar, and traditional was melting into air.

The '90s hosted a grand return of psychedelics to alternative culture. The GRATEFUL DEAD's traveling tripster carnival grew in popularity, while ravers and others explored so-called entheogens (literally, "god-inducers") like ECSTASY. The liquid-tongued trip-bard TERENCE MCKENNA replaced TIMOTHY LEARY as the ideological spearhead of psychedelia, and McKenna's strange and apocalyptic rhapsodies of tryptamine space turned DMT—an obscure, fast-acting and powerful substance—into a veritable icon. New designer drugs like 2CB and DOB hit the market, while underground researchers discovered domestic analogs for ahayuasca, the powerful psychedelic brew of actual Amazonian shamans. With the rise of MARI-JUANA CHIC, and suburban high schools awash with blotter ACID, drug culture took on organic, ritual, and visionary connotations it had lost in the coke-fueled '80s.

The exploration of music- and drug-induced trance states was only one element of what Terrence McKenna called the "archaic revival." This widespread pagan and romantic impulse sought to strip away social constructs and pack-

aged identities in order to discover a primal realm of ecstatic intensity and tribal identification. Stretching from popular trends (the men's movement; goddess movements in Christian churches) to the anarchic fringe (full-moon desert raves; the pagan performance rites of the San Francisco band Crash Worship), the archaic revival also crossed-over with scenes devoted to PIERCING, TATTOOS, and S/M. Though not overtly religious, these subcultures—frequently tinged with the dark mythology of the Goth aesthetic—nonetheless speak to a desire for intense rites of passage, secret practices, and inventive, primitivist allegiance. The body was opened up not only as a surface for transgression, but for exploration of new identities and communities.

The archaic revival paradoxically shared the stage with increasingly futuristic technology. The promise of VIRTUAL REALITY occasioned mythic imaginings, while FRINGEWARE, ARTIFICIAL LIFE, and even the INTERNET gave rise to gnostic and science-fiction speculations about the digital re-creation of consciousness. Brain machines like the Syncho-Energizer—and associated chemicals, electronic beats, and ambient frequencies—demonstrated one of the powerful paradoxes of this postmodern strain of spirituality: though intended to produce the equivalent of mystical or trance states, the technology uses science and the quick-fix logic of consumer technology. The point became less to raise consciousness than to tweak it and see where it went.

This potent alchemy of science and mysticism also drove a renewed interest in UFO and extraterrestrial phenomena—most notably in rave, psychedelic and conspiracy-fringe cultures. Between the surge in ALIEN ABDUCTION reports, the popularity of apocalyptic channeled ET material, and the cult status of shows like the *X-FILES*, the living mythology of UFOs was reborn as a folk-religion (the almond-shaped alien "Greys" in Bill Barker's SCHWA art are at once pop icons, political cartoons, and harbingers of apocalypse). By fusing the "true stories" of contemporary fables with government conspiracy theories and a wholesale assault on consensus reality, the alien phenomena suggested the collapse of humanist, scientific and traditional religious authority. At the same time, it fed an anxious spiritual desire for numinous experience, awesome encounters with non-human consciousness, and a cosmic sense of scale. A kinder and gentler version of this phenomenon also hit the talk shows and best-seller lists, as the aforementioned angels and cherubim became the average American's loving ET.

Along with the explosion of interest in the spiritual psycho-dynamics of ALTERNATIVE MEDICINE (HOMEOPATHY, Ayurveda, Chinese acupuncture and herbalism), Buddhism became the most dynamic of the non-Western traditions operating in the First World. Tibetan Buddhism was particularly attractive, given an unbeatable combination of exoticism, pragmatism, a compelling political cause, and celebrity figureheads. *The Tibetan Book of Living and Dying* was a bestseller, while the Dalai Lama grew into an unsullied global icon. However, a cadre of entertainer-Bhuddists (among them film stars Harrison Ford and Richard Gere, and rock stars COURTNEY LOVE and BEASTIE BOY Mike D) raised the specter of the '60s rockers who flocked to India seeking transcendental bliss at the feet of gurus whose devotional cults strangely resembled the adoration that those very same pop stars received at home.–*Erik Davis*

WEB **Finding God in Cyberspace** http://www.dur.ac.uk/ ~dth3maf/gresham.html ✦ WEB **Pagan Resources** http:// www.ssc.org/~athomps/pagan/paganres.html ✦ WEB **New-Age Directory** http://www.wholarts.com/psychic/newage.html/ ✦ USENET **alt.religion**, **talk.religion**, **soc.religion** ✦ WEB **Journal of Buddhist Ethics** http://www.psu.edu/jbe/jbe.html

---

of TREKKERS, it is overlooked that *Star Trek* itself is a very mainstream, very profitable product. Although low ratings led to the cancellation of the original *Star Trek* television series (1966–1969), in syndication the show attracted a hardcore group of fans and became an unqualified hit. In 1979, Paramount Pictures reunited the original cast for a feature film. Over the next dozen years they returned for five sequels that grossed a total of $500 million. In 1987, a new TV series, *Star Trek: The Next Generation*, was launched. It became the highest-rated first-run syndicated show in history; in 1994 it went off the air and re-appeared in movie theaters. A third series, *Star Trek: Deep Space Nine*, was launched in 1992; and in 1995, Paramount chose a fourth Star Trek series, *Voyager*, as the flagship of its new network, UPN. The choice was astute: *Voyager* was the only success of UPN's first season. Other Star Trek media include novels (released twice a month, often straight to the bestseller lists), COMIC books, and, of course, CD-ROMs.

WEB **Star Trek WWW Links** http://www-iwi.unisg.ch/~ sambucci/scifi/startrek/www.html ✦ USENET **rec.arts.startrek**, **alt.tv.star-trek**

steampunk In the words of journalist Douglas Fetherling, steampunk science fiction imagines "how the past would have been different if the future had happened sooner." Usually set in Victorian England, steampunk's anachronistic imagery includes steam-powered flame throwers, analog computers, and gargantuan magnetic devices capable of manipulating lunar orbits. Although K. W. Jeter's *Morlock Night* (1979)—in which the Morlocks of H. G. Wells's *The Time Machine* steal the invention and return to Victorian London—is probably the first steampunk novel, James Blaylock exclusively works the subgenre (*Homunculus*, 1986; *Lord Kelvin's Machine*, 1992). The most widely known steampunk novel is WILLIAM GIBSON and BRUCE STERLING's *The Difference Engine* (1991). Other examples of the CYBERPUNK niche include Paul Di Filippo's *The Steampunk Trilogy* (1995) and Paul J. McAuley's *Pasquale's Angel* (1995).

WEB **FLEX: A Science Fiction Page** http://cs.sci.csupomona .edu/~ndang/sf.html ✦ USENET **alt.cyberpunk**

Stephenson, Neal (b. 1959) CYBERPUNK's latecomer apotheosis, second only to WILLIAM GIBSON in the genre's pecking order. Originally intended as a MACINTOSH game, Stephenson's novel *Snow Crash* (1992) replaced Gibson's *Neuromancer* as the standard-issue text for new Silicon Valley employees. Set in a near-future when America has lost its leadership in everything but "movies, microcode (software), and high-speed pizza delivery," *Snow Crash* owes much to the literature's pulp-NOIR and paperback-thriller tradition. Though Stephenson's novels are marked by abrupt conclusions that neatly tie disparate plot lines together, he is still one of science fiction's singular storytellers.

Where *Snow Crash* reverse-engineered WILLIAM GIBSON's pristine "cyberspace" into the bustling, sociable "metaverse," the sophisticated but no less entertaining *Diamond Age* (1995) spins a neo-Dickensian, STEAMPUNK tapestry based on the promise of HYPERTEXT and NANOTECHNOLOGY. Stephenson's earlier books—*The Big U* (1984) and *Zodiac: The Eco-thriller* (1988)—were tightly plotted kinetic thrillers, as was the politically juiced *Interface* (1994), which Stephenson co-wrote with his uncle under the pseudonym Stephen Bury.

GOPHER **Well Cyberpunk Archive** gopher://gopher.well.sf. ca.us:70/11/cyberpunk ✦ USENET **alt.cyberpunk.chatsubo**

Sterling, Bruce (b. 1954) Once the preeminent ideologue of the CYBERPUNK movement, Austin, Texas science fiction novelist Bruce Sterling has settled down to become one of the genre's most dependably thought-provoking figures. After writing a pair of raw, idiosyncratic novels—*Involution Ocean* (1977) and *The Artificial Kid* (1980)—that coincided with PUNK rock, Sterling launched an uppity SF fanzine called *Cheap Truth* in 1982, which he wrote and edited pseudonymously. The polemics gelled in his introduction to *Mirrorshades: The Cyberpunk Anthology* (1986). Genetically altered "Shapers" vied with cybernetic "Mechanists" in the pages of *Schismatrix* (1985), while *Islands in the Net* (1988) may be the most cogent novel to date on the implications of the then-imminent WORLD WIDE WEB. After co-authoring *The Difference Engine* (1992) with WILLIAM GIBSON, Sterling wrote about computer culture in the non-fiction quickie *The Hacker Crackdown: Law and Disorder on the Electronic Frontier* (1992, later published in full-text online), and tornado hackers in the novel *Heavy Weather* (1994). He was, appropriately, coverstar of *WIRED*'s first issue, and has continued to write non-fiction features for the magazine.

WEB **Bruce Sterling Texts on the Net** http://riceinfo.rice.edu :80/projects/RDA/VirtualCity/Sterling/sterling_res.html ✦ WEB **The Hacker Crackdown** http://www.lysator.liu. se/etexts/hacker/ ✦ USENET **alt.cyberpunk**

Stern, Howard (b. 1954) Lanky, big-haired "shock jock" whose well-documented radio exploits have earned him legions of rabid fans and appalled detractors. A deft combination of crass juvenilia, enthusiastically offensive claptrap, and hectoring social satire, Stern's humor has landed him in hot water with the FCC, DONALD WILDMON, and other media watchdogs. He typically responds to fines and boycotts by turning up the invective ("I pray for his death," said Stern upon learning that FCC chairman Alfred Sykes had prostate cancer), and has only twice apologized for his words: once to his wife for joking about her miscarriage and once to fans of slain Tejano singer Selena, whom he compared unfavorably to Alvin and the Chipmunks.

Stern's side projects are usually either dismal failures (a syndicated TV show and an abandoned "Fartman" movie) or heady triumphs (his best-selling 1993 autobiography *Private Parts*, a bawdy 1994 New Year's special that was the among the highest-grossing pay-per-view programs ever). Somewhere in between lies his nightly no-budget show on E! CHANNEL, crudely edited from video footage of the radio show. Although Stern likes to say that no topic is off limits, he studiously refuses to discuss his finances, even dropping out of a New York State gubernatorial run rather than open his books. In private, Stern is said to be a decent family man.

WEB **King of All Media Fans' Web Page!** http://krishna.cs. umd.edu/stern/

Stiller, Ben (b. 1965) Comedian-actor son of veteran comedy team Ann Meara and Jerry Stiller. After a brief *SATURDAY NIGHT LIVE* stint and a cursory acting career, Stiller was given a self-titled—and short-lived—1990 MTV sketch show which led to a similar effort for Fox TV in 1992. The pointed, media-centric satire of Stiller and his tal-

The BEN STILLER Show refuses to leave Tom Cruise, alone

ented troupe (including JANEANE GAROFALO) won over dozens of critics and about as many viewers. Stiller's apparent discomfort with his good looks was expressed in verité loser shtick, and impressions of hunks like U2's Bono and Tom Cruise. (The latter was a repeated Stiller target, most memorably portrayed in a one-man musical revue reprising his star turns in middle age.) *The Ben Stiller Show* won an Emmy for writing, and was canceled after one season; it was rerun on Comedy Central in 1995.

Stiller's feature-directing debut *Reality Bites* (1994, starring WINONA RYDER and ETHAN HAWKE) was promising, but ill-fated: the film's love-in-the-service-industry conceit was freighted with GENERATION X significance by critics and resented by its target audience. Stiller next flirted with the unfortunate idea of doing a Rolling Stones tour film before accepting roles in the comedies *If Lucy Fell* and *Flirting With Disaster* (both 1995). Stiller's talent for skewering unctuous Hollywood players explained his strenuous efforts to acquire film rights to the mythical Hollywood venality tale, *What Makes Sammy Run?* (1941). Only one thing could explain his decision to direct megabuck buffoon JIM CARREY in *The Cable Guy*—a reported $2.5 million fee.

Stillman, Whit (b. John Whitney Stillman, 1952) Well-bred independent filmmaker and former journalist whose low-budget debut *Metropolitan* (1990) chronicled the coming-of-age rituals of Manhattan debutantes and their tuxedoed escorts. The droll, talky movie showed the flip side of America's social mobility—what cultural critic Barbara Ehrenreich called *The Fear of Falling*

(1989). The movie (sold under the tag-line "Doomed. Bourgeois. In Love.") restored some Salinger-esque literary cachet to PREPPY-dom (then under the shadow of the syntax-challenged George Bush and '80s excess)—and also proposed a new acronym UHB (urban haute bourgeoisie, pronounced "ub") to replace WASP, a term that was actually coined by Stillman's godfather, historian Digby Balzell. Married to a Spanish reporter, Stillman mined more autobiographical material for his second, similarly toned movie, *Barcelona* (1994). His next planned movie is an elegy to New York's Studio 54, titled *The Last Days of Disco*.

Stone Temple Pilots The most hated quintuple-platinum rock act in America. Shortly after MTV declared itself the epicenter of GRUNGE, Southern California's Stone Temple Pilots appeared with *Core* (1993), their own entirely generic version. MANIC PANIC-ed front man Scott Weiland's troubled vibrato was so redolent of PEARL JAM's Eddie Vedder that it earned STP the nicknames Clone Temple Pilots and Stone Temple Pirates. The band's disapproval rating soared after the "Plush" video, in which Weiland even appropriated Vedder's distinctive facial tics. Vedder was moved to remark in *ROLLING STONE*, "Get your own trip, man." Stone Temple Pilots' new trip, the *Purple* album, was not exactly their own (the Beatles and Led Zeppelin were added references this time), but it entered the *Billboard* charts at #1 and proving that no one likes them except the public. In May 1995 Weiland, who had reportedly checked into the Betty Ford clinic, was arrested for possession of cocaine and heroin; COURTNEY LOVE phoned in his grave apology ("I have a disease. It's a disease called drug addiction, and I really want to say that I'm sorry . . . ") to fans on L.A.'s KROQ radio station.

USENET **alt.music.stone-temple** ✦ WEB **Pilots**
http://thoth.stetson.edu/music/pilots/

Stone, Oliver (b. 1946) In one sketch from the ill-starred TV series *The BEN STILLER Show*, a prosthetically enhanced Stiller played this writer/direc-

alt**culture**

tor/producer as proprietor of his very own Disney-land variant, "Oliver Stoneland." Exhibits included "Platunes" (ROLLERBLADING musical), "Mr. Morrison's Wild Ride" (a *Doors*-themed ghost train), "Born On the Fourth of July" wheelchair-bumper cars, and a *J.F.K.*-based shooting range. (In his portrayal of Stone as self-aggrandizing BABY BOOMER moralist, Stiller might as well have also acknowledged the director's reputation as an unreconstructed misogynist.) Nonetheless, Stone's ability to move a camera to stirring effect is undeniable; since the 1986 gonzo war movie *Salvador* through gonzo greed saga *Wall Street* (1987) and gonzo conspiracy tale *J.F.K.* (1991), he has proved himself one of American cinema's few remaining wild cards.

In between pursuing pet '90s projects like biopics of disgraced President Richard Nixon, San Francisco supervisor Harvey Milk, and *Hustler* pornographer Larry Flynt, as well as a film of MOR musical *Evita*, Stone preserves enough energy to be a production force in the '90s (*The New Age* [1994], *Zebrahead* [1993], *WILD PALMS* [1993]). And as was proved by 1994's extravagantly misguided SERIAL KILLER CHIC-satire *Natural Born Killers* (story by QUENTIN TARANTINO; collage-soundtrack by NINE INCH NAILS' Trent Reznor), he has canny taste in collaborators.

STRAIGHT EDGE lives, on the WORLD WIDE WEB (http://www.ios.com/~juergen/sXe.html).

straight edge PUNK creed of abstinence from drugs, meat, alcohol, cigarettes, and—in some variants—sex. The anti-commercial movement takes its name from the 1982 Minor Threat song in which a pre-FUGAZI Ian MacKaye announced "I've got better things to do . . . Laugh at the thought of eating 'ludes / Laugh at the thought of sniffing glue . . . I've got the straight edge." That band and song led to a clean-living hardcore (or in reference to its capital origins, harDCore) subculture that continues today mainly among white, male teenagers. '90s straight edge morality places an added emphasis on animal rights and VEGANISM; its styled include SHAVED HEADS and black "x"'s on the back of the hand (sometimes explained as an ironic reference to the mark made by bar bouncers validating drinking-age patrons).

WEB **more than you'd care to know about straight edge** http://www.ios.com/~juergen/sXe.html ◆ USENET **alt.punk.straight-edge**

Student Environmental Action Coalition

National network for some 1,500 grassroots campus environmental groups. SEAC ("seek") was founded 1988 in CHAPEL HILL, North Carolina, to promote recycling and other conservation causes, but by 1993 it had taken on a range of progressive and MULTICULTURAL "environmental justice" issues and begun connecting with GREEN TEEN high school groups and local labor and community activists. ASEED, SEAC's international offshoot, links youth environmental movements around the world. SEAC was at the center of 1994 student protests that helped block the construction of a dam, Hydro Quebec II, that would have flooded Cree Nation lands.

WEB **SEAC** http://bianca.com/lolla/politics/seac/seac.html

student loans College tuition debt that, according to critic David Lipsky, helped add up to $10,000 of liabilities for the average graduate in 1990. Defaults on these loans approach $3 billion a year, but banks—which collect interest on loans—continue to participate because the government reimburses all losses. President Clinton's Student Loan Reform Act of 1993 began to repeal the bankers' risk-free profits but did little to curtail widespread "tuition-mill" practices at barely certified trade schools and unscrupulous name brand colleges. The 1965 Guaranteed Student Loan Act originally limited government help to students who couldn't otherwise afford college. The '90s state of affairs—saddling college graduates with an unprecedented level of debt, fueling tuition growth (roughly twice that of the inflation rate), and enriching banks and schools at taxpayer expense—can be traced back to Reagan-era cost-cutting at the agency responsible for overseeing the loans, the Department of Education, and President Carter's 1978 extension of the loans to potential scholars irregardless of parental tax bracket.

WEB **Student Services, Inc.** http://web.studentservices.com/

student-faculty sex bans Restrictions on romantic relationships between students and teachers promulgated by college administrators in the early '90s, apparently in response to the sexual harassment awareness raised by the 1991 ANITA HILL-Clarence Thomas hearings. "Asymmetrical" relationships—in which the professor is teaching, grading, or advising the student—were singled out for prohibition at most schools; some, like Oberlin, also advised—to use Harvard's delicate phrasing—"amorous relationships between members of the faculty and students that occur outside the instructional context can also lead to difficulties." William Kerrigan, a University of Massachusetts English professor, unwittingly found himself the symbol of opposition to such rules when, speaking about the subject in a September 1993 *Harper's* magazine feature, he made the widely quoted assertion that students often benefit from specialized one-on-one tutoring: "There is a kind of student I've come across in my career who was working through something that only a professor could help her with. I'm talking about a female student who . . . has unnaturally prolonged her virginity."

GOPHER **Yale Policy**

gopher://yaleinfo.yale.edu:7700/ORO–3021-Acad-Fac Handbook/Other/sex

Studs Lusty late-night dating game show phenomenon that aired on Fox TV from March 1991 until its abrupt cancellation two years later. The rules were simple: two concupiscent young men contestants date three women, then come on the show with host Mark DeCarlo to identify the women's descriptions of the dates. (One such contestant was Ronald Goldman, one of the two murder victims in the O.J. Simpson case.) The show's innovation was bawdy, improbable, and highly scripted double entendres and insults such as "He has a butt like a Twinkie just bursting with cream" and "His hair is greasier than a grilled-cheese sandwich." *Studs* was the last Fox TV hit for Stephen Chao, the programmer also responsible for *America's Most Wanted* and *Cops*, before being fired for hiring a male stripper to undress at a June 1992 Fox executive retreat. The show was canceled several months later in spite of stellar ratings to make room for the short-lived *Chevy Chase Show* debacle. MTV staged its own chaotic and saucy variation, *Singled Out*, in 1995.

Stüssy The most influential street-fashion label of the '90s. Founded by Shawn Stüssy (b. 1954) in 1982, Stüssy was originally a surfboard-design imprint. Soon after the company expanded into apparel in 1985, its designs (bearing Stüssy's calligraphic signature) became the unofficial uniform of SoCal surfers. In subsequent years Stüssy has consistently set the tenor for street-fashion, introducing skate-wear, WORKWEAR, military chic, and even PREPPY elements to his impeccably-executed collections.

Stüssy's appeal grew with each new tribe it embraced. By the time of the first LOLLAPALOOZA tour in the summer of 1991, the company was clothing a generation. An avalanche of new streetwear labels followed: FRESH JIVE, Fuct, Phat Farm, X-LARGE and countless others owe their existence to Stüssy. As his gear has achieved worldwide renown and revenues have exceeded $20 million, Shawn Stüssy himself has remained a low-key, dignified figure who described his philosophy in musical terms to New York's *Paper* magazine: "I'm not ready to come out with the big hit single . . . I'm just looking for those five jazz albums year after year."

stylists Once discreet fashion world functionaries who interpreted a season's mood, usually for magazines, stylists have emerged as a kind of new media celebrity. Freelance field reporters for an industry heavily reliant on street culture for material, they are prized for their keen eye, dogged pursuit of the new, and secret-weapon style Rolodexes of sources. Well-paid practitioners of this volatile art, such as Lori Goldstein, Victoria Bartlett, and Joe McKenna, scatter across the world's fashion capitals cherry-picking and sometimes inventing the clothes they feel are necessary for the moment. By modifying existing articles (through, for example, ripping or dying) or appropriating clothes meant for other purposes (whether gas station uniforms or tennis skirts), stylists reorder the fashion food chain and knock designers out of the picture. Among stylists who have turned *modistes* themselves, two of the best-known are Daisy von Furth (X-GIRL) and LAURA WHITCOMB (Label).

Sub Pop SEATTLE independent label that was instrumental in turning the Northwest into the center of the '90s youth-culture boom. Sub Pop was founded by Bruce Pavitt (b. 1958) and Jonathan Poneman (b. 1959). Pavitt was a graduate of OLYMPIA's Evergreen State College (where he'd DJ'd on the college radio station) and the editor of the Sub Pop fanzine/compilation cassette series; Poneman was a radio DJ and club booker. Their label cultivated an identity based on the local breed of heavy, PUNK-influenced rock that would come to be known as GRUNGE. In November 1988, the duo exploited INDIE-ROCKERS' penchant for the hard-to-find with the Sub Pop Singles Club, releasing limited-edition 45s monthly, starting with NIRVANA's first-ever single "Love Buzz/Big Cheese." The single sold-out in a flash, creating a mystique around the label that was bolstered by *Sub Pop 200*, a 5,000-edition, three-EP box set which defined the thriving Seattle music scene for the first time with 16 pages of Charles Peterson's live black-and-white photos of sweat-drenched, long-haired mayhem.

Despite the fact that they would shortly look like cultural visionaries, with Nirvana and Soundgarden sitting astride the charts, Pavitt and Poneman were struggling so badly in 1991 that they created a notorious T-shirt that demanded "WHAT PART OF 'WE HAVE NO MONEY' DON'T YOU UNDERSTAND?" Had it not been for a two-album contract with Nirvana at the insistence of drunken bass player Krist Novoselic, the debt-ridden label would have simply gone broke. (When Nirvana signed to Geffen, the major label bought Sub Pop out of their contract for $72,000 and awarded the indie 2 percent profits of the soon-to-be multi platinum *Nevermind*.) In 1995, the P+P music factory sold 49 percent of Sub Pop for $20 million to the Warner Music Group; Pavitt justified the move to *SPIN* magazine by explaining that "the history of indie-rock is the history of failure."

WEB **Sub Pop Homepage** http://www.subpop.com/

Sui, Anna (b. 1955) Culturally omnivorous, celebrity-beloved Chinese-American clothing designer. Raised in Detroit, Sui went to New York's Parsons School of Design, where she was a contemporary of photographer STEVEN MEISEL, a fellow late bloomer for whom she worked as a STYLIST. Sui made her mark in April 1991 with a debut collection described by the *New York Times* with the observation: "Sly and the Family Stone crashed into Coco Chanel and then got rear-ended by Christian Lacroix." The designer has come to be renowned as a "sampler" of styles from Chanel suits to Haight Ashbury hippie to '70s glam-rock. While COURTNEY LOVE loudly staked her claim to the appropriation of the BABY-DOLL dress it was Anna Sui who cashed in commercially, including it in her spring 1994 collection (shown November 1993). Subse-quently, Sui has both moved in synch with the fashion world's "return to glamour" and dabbled in '60s MOD styles.

Sundance Film Festival Premier U.S. showcase for independent movies, instrumental since being founded (1984, by Robert Redford) in helping establish indie movies as a viable artistic and financial alternative to Hollywood. This annual Park City, Utah, event launched such movies as Steven Soderbergh's *sex, lies, & videotape* (1989),

RICHARD LINKLATER's *Slackers* (1991), Matty Rich's *Straight Out of Brooklyn* (1992), ROB WEISS's *Amongst Friends* (1993), KEVIN SMITH's *Clerks* (1994), Boaz Yakim's *Fresh* (1994), and LARRY CLARK's *Kids* (1995)—successes which in turn transformed Sundance into something of a minor league meat market for MIRAMAX and the rest of Hollywood. Despite—or inspired by—Sundance's self-described commitment to diversity, a nearby alternative festival Slam Dance, was mounted in 1995 to show movies that didn't make Sundance's increasingly competitive cut. In January '95 Sundance and the Showtime cable channel announced a joint venture called the Sundance Film Channel that will compete for programming and cable space with the Independent Film Channel, a separate service launched the previous year by the owners of the Bravo channel.

WEB **Official Sundance Homepage** http://cybermart.com/sundance/institute/institute.html ✦ WEB **Sundance Festival** http://interport.net/festival/intro.html

supermodels   This century, there has never been a shortage of product-hawking, name-brand fashion mannequins on the cultural landscape, but never have they been so intimately presented as they are in the '90s. Thanks to a compliant media the whole nation is on first-name terms with the top tier of "girls," sometimes übermodels: Cindy (Crawford), Linda (Evangelista), Claudia (Schiffer), Christy (Turlington), and Naomi (Campbell). Helena Christiansen, Elle McPherson, and waif KATE MOSS are not far behind, and each season brings a new crop: Nadja Auermann, Amber Valetta, and Tyra Banks were the next-tier supermodels-in-waiting, young women who may one day have their own restaurant or cable TV show or line of HOME-SHOPPING products to bolster them against old age.

Supermodels, conventional wisdom had it, were replacing rock stars and movie stars as the screens upon which the public projects its dreams and aspirations, a glamorous, distant echo of silent movie stars. The supermodels' undeniable allure has cer-

tainly brought them untold opportunities to expand their own franchises (as well as those of their fashion-industry paymasters): Cindy Crawford, the most enterprising, has been fronting MTV's *House of Style* since 1989; a slew of model-related media products followed, from the photo-driven *Top Model* magazine (launched March 1994) to *Models Inc.* (1994; a short-lived creation of Aaron "*BEVERLY HILLS 90210*" Spelling) to endless E! CHANNEL specials. The trend reached its apogee in April 1994 when the McPherson-Campbell-Schiffer troika opened Fashion Cafe, a THEME RESTAURANT in midtown New York. In 1995 Crawford starred in the risible thriller *Dangerous Game*, following in the footsteps of McPherson, whose role in *Sirens* (1994) had brought her a multi-picture deal with MIRAMAX.

WEB **Pit's Page of Beautiful Women** http://www.cen.uiuc.edu/~morrise/girls.html ✦ WEB **Supermodel Homepage** http://www.supermodel.com/ ✦ WEB **Elite Model Management, Milan** http://www.triple.fr/elite/milan/alt.supermodels ✦ WEB **alt.supermodels Homepage** http://www-stud.enst.fr/~legru/models.html ✦ USENET **alt.supermodels**, **alt.fashion**, **alt.binaries.pictures.supermodels**

Surfrider Foundation   Nonprofit environmental group formed by Malibu, California surfers in August 1984. Initially, the Surfrider Foundation opposed oceanside developments that would compromise the structural integrity of beaches, but as beach pollution worsened the organization shifted its focus. In 1991 the foundation scored its most notable success to date, suing two California pulp mills which were fined a total of almost $6 million for, the *L. A. Times* reported, 40,000 violations of the Clean Water Act. (It later got the city of San Diego fined $830,000 for a 1992–93 sewage pipeline leak.) Now based in San Clemente, California, Surfrider reached its 10th anniversary with 25,000 members and over 20 chapters worldwide; it continues to co-ordinate public protests and enlist students for their Blue Water Task Force to test seawater samples for pollution.

WEB **Surfrider Online** http://www.sdsc.edu/surfrider.html/

Survival Research Laboratory Named by founding member Mark Pauline (b. 1954) after an advertisement in *Soldier of Fortune* magazine, SRL builds monstrous machines that are set upon each other in loud, threatening outdoor spectacles. Employing a critical sensitivity for image manipulation and advertising, Pauline began his media hacking career defacing Bay Area billboards. SRL launched its first performance, "Machine Sex," in 1979. Subsequent performances included "Extremely Cruel Practices: A Series of Events Designed to Instruct Those Interested in Policies That Correct or Punish" and 1989's "Illusions of Shameless Abundance Degenerating Into an Uninterrupted Sequence of Hostile Encounters." "I make weapons to tell stories about weapons," Pauline said in 1992. "SRL shows are a satire of kill technology, an absurd parody of the military-industrial complex." A 1992 performance to mark the San Francisco Museum of Modern Art's groundbreaking featured a flame-throwing cannon, sonic boom gun, giant metallic pincers, and a mortar-like contraption that spat molten metal. In 1993 RICK RUBIN's Def American released the videotape *Survival Research Laboratories: The Will To Provoke.*
WEB **SRL Homepage** http://robotics.eecs.berkeley.edu/SRL/

Swatch Disposable Swiss timepieces that have become the best-selling watches in the world and the objects of a fanatic collectors' cult. Invented in 1983, the cheaply made, efficiently designed watches were integral to '80s MTV culture, thanks in part to commercials featuring the Fat Boys, and designs by artists like Keith Haring. Swatch stayed current by constantly changing their designs: over a hundred new models are introduced every year. As a result, many limited editions have become collectors' items; one 1985 model designed by French painter Christian Chapiron was sold at auction in 1991 for $45,000. Swatch manufacturer SMH has become a model for European business success. Recent projects include a collaboration with Mercedes-Benz; an electric powered "Swatchmobile" is due off the assembly lines in 1997.
WEB **art to swatch** http://www.musicwest.com/Sponsors/Swatch/art.html ✦ WEB **The Unofficial Swatch WWW** http://www.flashnet.it/swatch.htm

Tailhook   U.S. Navy's biggest embarrassment since Pearl Harbor. At the 1991 annual convention of the Tailhook Association (named after an aircraft-carrier landing device), dozens of drunken male naval aviators rechristened the third-floor hallway of a Las Vegas Hilton "the gauntlet" and grabbed, groped, and poked 30-year-old Navy Lt. Paula Coughlin and twenty-five other unsuspecting women, of whom fourteen were officers. Although the Navy Secretary resigned shortly after the scandal hit a country already primed by the ANITA HILL-Clarence Thomas hearings, the Navy was later excoriated in a Pentagon report for shielding top brass from the investigation. Nightly readings from the report on the Comedy Central channel posed the question "should heterosexuals be allowed in the military," with tales of liquor served from the penis of a papier-mâché rhinoceros and a lookout who would yell "decks afoul" (for women judged not attractive enough to attack) and "decks awash" (for those considered worthy targets).

Talk Soup   December 1991-launched television show that rounds up daily the reliably outré "nuts and sluts" talk show circuit. *Talk Soup*'s original host Greg Kinnear was a wholesome looker with a deft sense of cruelty; his ironically square-jawed demeanor was a piquant riposte to the endless footage of racial confrontations, ALIEN ABDUCTIONS, and luridly humiliated spouses. Although some talk shows refused to submit clips (and others withdrew permission), there was still plenty of material to make *Talk Soup* one of the most reliably entertaining half hours on television, and a godsend to its home channel, E! ENTERTAINMENT TELEVISION, which has been known to run it as many as fifty times a week. Kinnear left *Talk Soup* in 1994 to concentrate on his own late night NBC one-on-one interview show and a nascent film career. The show did not waver from its mission in the hands of the boyish John Henson.

WEB **The Talk Soup Unofficial Homepage**
http://tvnet.com/cgi-bin/delphi.com

Tank Girl   Spunky heroine of the long-running British comic strip, which debuted September 1988 in Britain's *Deadline* magazine. Created by artist Jamie Hewlett and writer Alan Martin, Tank Girl survives in a postapocalyptic 21st century with wit and grit; the character has become something of a lesbian folk hero in Britain, where her ragged, eclectic fashion sense both borrows from and leads street fashion trends. The 1995 movie version, directed by former JOHN WATERS producer Rachel Talalay, made some key changes to Tank Girl lore: the location was switched from Australia to the U.S., and any hint of bestiality with her half-kangaroo companion Booga was removed. *Tank Girl* tanked despite a strenuous marketing effort that included a COURTNEY LOVE-compiled alt-rock SOUNDTRACK and a chain of Macy's Tank Girl boutiques.

WEB **Deadline Magazine** http://www.sonnet.co.uk/tank-girl/

Tarantino, Quentin (b. 1963)   Boyish, hyperactive ringleader of '90s Hollywood cool. Raised in L.A., Tarantino dropped out of high school to study acting but ended up immersing himself in film history while working for four years as a video store clerk. It was during this period that Tarantino wrote the scripts for *Reservoir Dogs* (1992), *True Romance* (1993), and *Natural Born Killers* (1994). Completed in three weeks and successfully pitched to arthouse anti-star Harvey Keitel by aspiring producer Lawrence Bender, *Reservoir Dogs* became an instant cult classic with baroque tough-guy dialogue and unapologetic violence that

From Jon Bonne's TarantinoWorld
(http://www.phantom.com/~jbonne/tarantinoworld/).

was heightened by a retro-bubblegum soundtrack. (Some of the film's strongest elements were a checklist of Tarantino's inspirations, including the 1987 HONG KONG ACTION MOVIE *City on Fire*—in 1995 a 12-minute video comparison of the two movies entitled "Who Do You Think You're Fooling?" attracted attention when it was abruptly withdrawn from the New York Underground Film Festival).

Tarantino's stock was somewhat enhanced by his script credit on the exuberant, uneven 1993 outlaw movie *True Romance*, starring CHRISTIAN SLATER and Patricia Arquette. A manic cameo in *Sleep With Me* (1994), deconstructing the homoerotic subtext of *Top Gun* (1986), jibed with Tarantino's growing reputation as the all-seeing arbiter of cinema taste and references for a new generation. The heavily anticipated *Pulp Fiction* (directed by Tarantino and co-written with Roger Avary), saw Tarantino anointed as the most vital figure in '90s film, and the most dynamic cultural force since the emergence of NIRVANA's Kurt Cobain. Another time-fractured story of profoundly moral outlaws, unforgettable dialogue ("I'm gonna get medieval on your ass"), and a powerful ensemble (JOHN TRAVOLTA, Bruce Willis, Samuel L. Jackson, and UMA THURMAN), *Pulp* was a box-office juggernaut and critical sensation. (Nominated for seven Oscars, it won Best Screenplay.)

In 1995 Tarantino spent some of his accumulated goodwill on causes worthy and not, propping up the strenuously ironic flop *Destiny Turns on the Radio* with another cameo, doctoring without credit the scripts for SATURDAY NIGHT LIVE spin-off megaflop *It's Pat* (1994) (for a reported $350,000 fee) and anachronistic Cold War thriller *Crimson Tide*. While deciding on his next directorial project, Tarantino also directed an episode of TV hospital drama *E.R.* and co-starred with that show's resident hunk George Clooney in vampire road movie *From Dusk Till Dawn* (1995), and directed one segment of *Four Rooms* (1995). The summer of 1995 saw Tarantino announcing plans to extend his franchise by forming, with MIRAMAX and Lawrence Bender, a movie distribution company and a commercial production house. [See also REBEL ADVERTISING.]

WEB **Church of Tarantino** http://sunserver2.aston.ac.uk/ ~smallmj/ ✦ USENET **alt.fan.tarantino**

Tarsem (b. Tarsem Dhandwar Singh, 1962) Indian director whose dream-like, quasi-religious video for R.E.M's 1991 single "Losing My Religion" brought the influence of Russian filmmaker Andrei Tarkovsky and Italian painter Caravaggio to MTV. The station rewarded him with six Video Music Awards. Tarsem, a Harvard MBA dropout, chiefly earns his living filming advertisements for clients like Smirnoff, Anne Klein, and Lee and Levi's jeans; one of his few post-R.E.M. pop promos was Deep Forest's world music-tinged "Sweet Lullaby" (1993), filmed on several continents inside of one month.
USENET **rec.music.video**

Tartt, Donna (b. circa 1964) Diminutive novelist whose debut, *The Secret History* (1992), garnered as much attention for its advance (with foreign rights, an estimated $950,000) as for its literary merits. (Such was the promotional effort and media attention bestowed upon Tartt that *Newsweek* ran a story called "Anatomy of a Hype.") Bennington College, where Tartt was a classmate of early bloomer BRETT EASTON ELLIS, served as the unnamed Northeast campus for this collegiate gothic steeped in classicist mumbo-jumbo. Ostensibly about a cliquish murder among Greek scholars—*Lord of the Flies* interleaved with *The Bacchae*—*Secret History* was really a case study in stultifying pretension, with occasional moments of genuine emotion buried under layers of gratuitous allusion and stilted dialogue. While working on her second novel, Tartt published several pieces of writing, including an essay on basketball in a sports writing collection and a short story in THE NEW YORKER.

tattoo Ancient art which takes its name from the Polynesian word for SCARIFICATION, *tautau*. Tattoos have been sustained in the West for the past several decades by bikers, sailors, prison inmates, gang members, rock'n'rollers, and ex-Secretary of State George Schultz. In the late 1980s, tattoos became a common celebrity accessory. Frequently, high-profile romances—including those of Roseanne, JOHNNY DEPP, Julia Roberts, and SEAN PENN—proved less permanent than the tattoos inscribed to celebrate them. For the less daring, BETSEY JOHNSON showed fashions based on the tattoo art of Mark Mahoney in 1990, and by 1993, high-quality temporary tattoos had became a million dollar business. In 1995, spurred by improvements in tattoo removal technology (see YAG LASER), a reconsideration of the trend appeared to be starting: SUPERMODEL Christy Turlington, for example, had her body restored to its original state.

WEB **Tattoos** http://ziris.syr.edu/dj/dj.tatoos/tatoos.html/ ✦ WEB **David's Bodyart Page** http://www.rpi.edu/~bealsd/ pierce.html/ ✦ WEB **Thuleboy's Body** Modification:http:// frank.mtsu.edu/~csc10004/bodmod.html ✦ WEB **Cort's Bodyart Page** http://www.halcyon.com/maelstrm/meba.html/ ✦ USENET **rec.arts.bodyart**

Teach for America Ambitious Peace Corps-like program to recruit ambitious college grads for public school teaching jobs they might not otherwise consider. By 1995, some 3,000 had been placed. Founded in 1990 by Wendy Kopp (b. 1967), who dreamed the program up in her undergraduate thesis at Princeton, TFA matched the 1,000-points of light political mood of the times and was heartily embraced by corporate underwriters and the media. At the same time, many long-term observers of passing fads in school reform took issue with the suggestion that the arrival of barely trained, if well-educated, do-gooders would save the public schools. *U.S. News and World Report* reported in late 1994 that corporate donors were beginning to take such criticisms seriously, threatening the program.

techno Electronic dance music created by black Detroit musicians in the early '80s. Producers Derrick May, Kevin Saunderson (whose band Big Life was a 1988 crossover success), and Juan Atkins (Cybotron) stripped HOUSE of its emotive elements, and fashioned a speedy, spartan, dancefloor-friendly groove that owed less to any rhythm blues tradition than to the proto-robotics of Kraftwerk. In the tradition of much black American music, techno was quickly embraced by Europe, which became the central point of what culture critic Jon Savage called an "international electronic grid." By the early '90s the grid included white American RAVE and club culture. As digital music hardware got more accessible, the number of techno releases increased exponentially; successive mini-generations spawned fanciful subgenres from airy AMBIENT and trance to the high-impact HARDCORE, with its sheer aggression and white suburban following. Frequent comparisons to PUNK may sound farfetched, as they did with ACID HOUSE, but techno has in many ways realized punk's egalitarian, anti-star rhetoric.

WEB **Techno Labels Sites & Pages** http://www.techno.de/ arena/LinksMusikSite.html ✦ WEB **Rare Groove** http://rg.media.mit.edu/RG/RG.html ✦ WEB **Hyperreal Rave & Techno Archives** http://hyperreal.com ✦ USENET **alt.music.techno**

technoshamanism High tech meets ancient belief systems. The intersection of computers, designer drugs, electronic dance music, and cultural idealism has reawakened interest in what used to be called "techniques of ecstasy" by hippie anthropologists. Repetitious TECHNO and AMBIENT music, accompanied by computer-generated fractal designs, produces trance states arguably similar to those induced by shamanic chants, drums, and dances that still exist in so-called primitive peoples.

WEB **Technopagans and Technoshamans** http://www.clas.ufl.edu/anthro/technoshaman.html ✦ USENET **alt.rave**, **alt.shamanism**

Teva In 1982, whitewater rafting guide and former African-oil explorer Mark Thatcher (b. 1954) came up with a simple innovation that created a new footwear category worth over $150 million for him and his copyists: he attached an ankle strap to sandals. Thatcher's "sport sandals," marketed the following year under the brand name Teva (Hebrew for "nature"), were made of nylon webbing with neoprene rubber thongs and Velcro fixings. They were embraced first by serious outdoor types, then by the wider population, from DEADHEADS to suburban moms. Now associated with the Northwestern, PATAGONIA lifestyle, Teva sandals come in a variety of styles tailored for every manner of outdoor activity. Thatcher himself apparently sees Tevas as leading some kind of American movement toward informality: in 1994 he told the *Philadelphia Inquirer* that the idea of closed footwear (shoes) is "a fashion hangover from Europe. It's ridiculous, like ties are ridiculous."

WEB **TEVA History** http://web2.starwave.com/ outside/online/outsidestore/manufact/tevahist.html

theme restaurants The Hard Rock Café—where walls are adorned by authentic rock and roll memorabilia—was the quintessential tourist phenomenon of the '80s. Its T-shirts, both licensed and bootlegged, were ubiquitous; by 1995, there were 45 branches around the world. Planet Hollywood—where walls are adorned by authentic movie memorabilia—opened its first outlet across the street from the Hard Rock's 57th Street flagship in New York City in 1984. Following the Hard Rock method (a little too closely, according to a $1.5 billion lawsuit still pending in mid–1995), Planet Hollywood and its celebrity "owners"—Arnold Schwarzenegger, Bruce Willis and Sylvester Stallone—soon found its own international success. In 1995, it had fourteen branches.

In 1993, the Harley Davidson Café—displaying authentic motorcycles owned by Jay Leno and Billy Joel—opened around the corner from the other two, making theme restaurants an official '90s trend. By 1995, nascent chains included the SUPERMODEL-themed Fashion Café (fronted by Claudia Schiffer, Naomi Campbell and Elle McPherson), the underwater-themed Dive (partially inspired by the struggling Steven Spielberg TV show *seaQuest DSV* and fronted by Spielberg and Jeffery Katzenberg), the blues-themed House of Blues (fronted by former funnyman Dan Ackroyd), and the horror-themed Jekyll and Hyde. Television and sports restaurants on the drawing board include a BAYWATCH franchise.

Hallmarks of theme restaurants are: locations in places heavily trafficked by tourists; an eye-catching logo that decorates products from $3.50 key chains to $325 motorcycle jackets; diner-style food dressed up with cutesy names and hefty price tags; museum-like artifacts; TV monitors showing celebrities wearing the restaurant's eye-catching logo; and dubious claims of "interactivity" intended to out-dazzle competing chains. At the Harley Davidson this entailed a mock-up bike that makes engine noise and spits smoke; in Jekyll and Hyde, waiters dressed as mummies; and at the Fashion Café, audioanimatronic paparazzi.

WEB **House of Blues** http://www.ddv.com/HOB/index.html

thigh-highs RALPH LAUREN claimed credit for popularizing thigh-high stockings in his spring 1994 Ralph collection, but style-conscious types were sporting them long before that. Usually worn with very short skirts, the garterless stockings are held up by a band of elastic, exposing a band of flesh on the upper leg to create a heretofore unidentified erogenous zone—it is part naughty schoolgirl, part Varga girl. While some critics complained that designers were making fun of women by dressing them like children, thigh-highs also evoke images of streetwalkers and porn layouts. *Newsweek* declared the fad, as it was peaking in the fall of 1994, "an attempt to look as tarty as possible in an impossibly safe-sex world."

Third Millennium New York-based 1993 spin-off of D.C.'s LEAD OR LEAVE intended to broaden generational activism about the federal deficit to college campuses. Third Millennium announced its arrival with a declaration self-consciously styled after the legendary SDS (Students for a Democratic Society) *Port Huron Statement* that heralded the student movements of the '60s. Where the New Left text began "We are people of this generation, bred in at least modest comfort, looking uncomfortably to the world we inherit," the '90s lite version opened, "Like Wile E. Coyote waiting for a 20-ton Acme anvil to fall on his head our generation labors in the expanding shadow of a monstrous national debt." *Time* magazine tagged the group as GENERATION X opportunists, saying "Third Millennium is a case study of how to use the new-generation craze to grab the spotlight," but by 1995 the group had emerged as respected critics of community-rated health care and the current social security system, which transfers wealth from entry level workers to affluent retirees.

EMAIL thirdmil@reach.com

Third Wave Small organization of young multi-cultural feminists founded in 1992 by Rebecca Walker (b. 1969) and Shannon Liss (b. 1969) as a GENERATION X alternative to NOW (National Organization for Women). Walker, daughter of novelist Alice Walker and goddaughter of *Ms.* founder Gloria Steinem, is an eloquent spokeswoman and tireless self-promoter. The organization's name refers to '90s feminism—invoking the eras of Susan B. Anthony and Steinem as waves one and two—and is not to be confused with the better-known "Knowledge Age" Third Wave promoted by Alvin and Heidi TOFFLER. Thus far Third Wave's activism consists of a single event—a successful (though internally divisive) 1992 voter registration drive called Freedom Summer (meant to evoke the civil rights freedom rides of the '60s). A popular campus speaker and outspoken BISEXUAL, Walker is frequently sought out for lively quotes about the state of feminism among young women.

Thurman, Uma (b. 1970) America's #1 art-house sex symbol, thanks to roles in *Pulp Fiction* (1994), *Even Cowgirls Get the Blues* (1993), *Henry & June* (1990), and *Dangerous Liaisons* (1988), and a short-lived 1990 marriage to self-styled brooding actor-genius Gary Oldman. Thurman's full name, Uma Karuma, is that of a Hindu goddess: her father is a professor of Asian religion at Columbia University and a former Buddhist monk. Filling out the hippie pedigree, her mom was once married to TIMOTHY LEARY—Uma rebelled by becoming a cheerleader and model in high school before breaking into movies at 17. Before her wig-enhanced star turn in *Pulp Fiction*, she'd rarely been given more to do than look luminous—for many, the archetypal

Thurman scene remains Uma as Venus, emerging naked from an oyster, in *The Adventures of Baron Munchausen* (1989).

WEB **Uma Thurman Homepage** http://www.csv.warwick. ac.uk:80/~esrlj/Uma/ MAIL LIST **The Uma Thurman Internet Digest** email uma-request@arastar.com with body message "subscribe uma firstname lastname"

Ticketmaster Exclusive outside phone and retail sales agent for two-thirds of the nation's 10 million seats at major entertainment and sports arenas. Armed with Public Interest Research Group (PIRG) statistics that showed that Ticketmaster fees added almost 30 percent in "convenience charges" to the face value of an average ticket, PEARL JAM filed a civil complaint with the U.S. Justice Department in May 1994 (and later testified before Congress), accusing the company of being a monopoly, and canceling their summer tour for lack of alternative ways of selling tickets. (Even accepting TM's figure of a 14 percent margin, the markup is still the biggest in the business.) Ticketmaster rose to dominance over its main competitor Ticketron in the late '80s through innovative software and by kicking back service-charge revenue to concert halls that committed to long-term exclusive contracts. Ticketmaster was acquired in 1993 by Microsoft co-founder Paul Allen, someone already familiar with the profitability of virtual monopoly. In 1995 the Justice Department dropped its investigation of the company and Ticketmaster introduced the Tickets First co-promotion with VH–1, the mature sibling of music-video monopolist, MTV.

WEB **TicketMaster Online** http://www.ticketmaster.com/

Timberland New Hampshire-based manufacturer (founded 1973) of outdoor gear whose apparel—most notably its heavy-duty waterproof work boots—was on the leading edge of HIP-HOP culture's early-'90s move toward WORKWEAR and outdoor wear. According to *The New York Times,* sales increased by over 50 percent between 1992 and 1993 alone, to $140 million. Timberland, previously known for its clean-cut, WASPy image, was reportedly uncomfortable with the inner-city demographic that had adopted its deluxe woodsman look and tree logo; the company maintained, however, that this was a matter of marketing, not race—Timberland did not wish to be seen as a fashion (i.e. transitory) label. In 1992 it launched an extensive advertising campaign featuring the slogan "Give racism the boot."

Time Warner as target   Armed with documentation provided by the Parents Music Resource Center (PMRC), an alliance of church and state joined forces against Time Warner, Inc. on the eve of the megamedia corporation's May 1995 stockholders meeting. Empower America, the current bully-pulpit of ex-education secretary and drug czar William Bennett, teamed up with National Political Congress of Black Women president C. DeLores Tucker to target the company for distributing the horrific visions of NINE INCH NAILS and GANGSTA rap by such notables as TUPAC SHAKUR and SNOOP DOGGY DOGG. (Time Warner responded to a similar media firestorm in 1992 by withdrawing ICE-T's "Cop Killer.") The groups took credit for the May ousting of Warner Music U.S. Chairman-CEO Doug Morris, who was responsible for setting up the company's distribution deal with the gangsta-packed Interscope label, licensee of DR. DRE'S Death Row label. Presidential hopeful Sen. Bob Dole jumped on the FAMILY VALUES bandwagon, decrying the violence of gangsta rap and singling out 1993's *True Romance* and 1994's *Natural Born Killers*—both, as Dole later admitted, unseen by him. In fall 1995 Time Warner announced that it was selling its share in Interscope.

WEB **Pathfinder** http://pathfinder.com

tinnitus   Buzzing or ringing in the ears unrelated to outside noise; often caused by the damaging effects of loud noise on the eardrum. Tinnitus caused the Walkman to be viewed as a public health problem in the '80s, leading to redesigns that included open-air earphones and even a reduction of the loudest possible volume. MTV ran public service ads warning people of the dangers of loud concerts (which typically surpass 110 decibels) in 1989,

after Pete Townshend and others began to publicize their own cumulative hearing loss and the occupational hazards of regular concert attendance. By 1992, soft foam ear plugs began to approach social respectability among music industry veterans; fans, on the other hand, tended to take them as a sign—along with backstage Evian and fruit plates—of the rock business's increasing sanitization.

WEB **Tinnitus FAQ** http://www.cccd.edu/faq/tinnitus.html ✦
USENET **alt.support.tinnitus**

TLC   They may have sounded like just another pre-programmed NEW JILL SWING act on their 1992 platinum debut *Ooooooohhh . . . On the TLC Tip*, but this Atlanta girl group declared their originality by using CONDOMS as fashion accessories. TLC's Lisa "Left Eye" Lopes (b. circa 1971) made further claim to eccentricity in the wee hours of June 9, 1994, when she torched the five-bedroom suburban home of her boyfriend, Atlanta Falcons receiver Andre Rison. (The pair's tempestuous relationship had reportedly led to gunplay the previous year.) Defense attorneys used Lopes' drinking as a mitigating factor, and the diminutive singer-rapper avoided a possible 20-year sentence. TLC's late–1994 sophomore album *Crazysexycool* was a grown-up, PRINCE-influenced affair accompanied by slickly styled imaging and little overt display of birth control devices. The band filed for bankruptcy in July 1995, as their "Waterfalls" single (with accompanying $2 million video) was at #1 on the Billboard chart. Their liabilities were said to total $3 million, including $1.3 million to Lloyd's of London, the insurer of Rison's house.

WEB **TLC** http://www.csua.berkeley.edu/~lingo/music/ profiles/tlc.html

toad licking   Periodically recycled, semi-apocryphal drug fad. The story was revived in 1994 with the arrest of two Sonoma, California, teachers for possession of bufotenine, the LSD-like hallucinogen found in the venom of the Bufo marinus and Bufo alvarius (a.k.a. desert toad, cane toad, Colorado River toad). Despite the fact that the 20-minute super-trip comes from *smoking* the crystalline residue that remains after drying out the toad's milky, mucous-like secretion, the "toad *licking*" story prompted interest among both police and high-seekers, especially in Arizona, where the leathery two-pound toads are common. Drug culture fascination with toad licking dates to the late '60s when the DEA raised possession of bufotenine (which contains a variation of DMT) to the same felony status as LSD and heroin; in the late '80s, reports from Australia of previous toad overpopulation and overdoses (bufotenine can be lethally toxic even in small doses), sparked the story in the U.S. media.

WEB **Controlled Substances—Uses and Effects** http://www.wellesley.edu/Personnel/AdminHandbook/drugch art.html ✦ USENET **alt.drugs** ✦ WEB http://www.cs.cmu.edu/~mleone/dead.html

Toffler, Alvin (b. 1928) Futurist author and spokesman for Newt Gingrich's Progress & Freedom Foundation. Toffler is best known for *Future Shock* (1970), co-written with his wife Heidi (b. 1929), which looked beyond the then-raging Cold War to make a historical argument championing new consumer possibilities (paper clothes you wear once and through away, cable TV). The subsequent *Third Wave* (1980) celebrated the role of computers, communications, and modernity itself in forging a "Knowledge Age" in which information is more prized than material resources like oil or iron.

Decades-old friends with part-time sci-fi novelist and Republican Congressman Newt Gingrich, the Tofflers emerged as gurus in the wake of the 1994 Republican takeover of Congress. Though self-proclaimed liberals, the Tofflers' principal policy recommendation—forwarded by the Progress and Freedom Foundation (founded after the election and run by Jeffrey Eisenach, who previously ran Gingrich's political action committee, GOPAC)—is to clear the way for Third Wave info-age citizens and entrepreneurs by dismantling Second Wave institutions. Many of these institutions turn out to be the government antitrust regulations which reign in phone and cable monopolies. The Tofflers' INTERNET-friendly pop

sociology provides an intellectual argument for the expansion plans of Gingrich's corporate patrons, at the same time helping Gingrich's politics seem, in the words of *The Nation*, "progressive, forward-looking—and inevitable."

WEB **The Progress and Freedom Foundation WWW Home Pages** http://www.townhall.com/townhall/PFF/ ✦ USENET **alt.books.toffler**

Tolkin, Michael (b. 1950) Novelist and screenwriter who is, along with Bruce Wagner (*WILD PALMS*), a natural heir to Nathanael West as chief accountant of L.A.'s spiritual bankruptcy. With his 1988 novel *The Player*, former journalist Tolkin skewered Hollywood far more adroitly than did Robert Altman's highly praised 1992 movie adaptation. Tolkin also wrote the wicked *policier Deep Cover* (1992) and wrote/directed *The Rapture* (1991), which traced the morally lax Mimi Rogers's desperate plunge into Christian fundamentalism. *The NEW AGE* (1994) put writer-director Tolkin's preoccupations front and center once more: a well-heeled couple flirt with faddish SPIRITUALITY as they slip ineluctably down the social ladder. In the 1995 novel *Among the Dead* Tolkin's disengaged lead character tries to "create his grief for public consumption" after losing his wife and child in an air crash.

ToughLove National system of parental support groups which counsels a hard line against teenage misbehavior. The organization was founded in the mid-'70s by therapists Phyllis and David York after their own daughter was arrested for mugging a cocaine dealer. ToughLove flourished in the "Just Say No" era, becoming a byword for the renewal of discipline and punishment. In the '90s the organization has grown to over 500 chapters in all 50 states and several foreign countries. ToughLove advises desperate parents to shock their children into responsibility: parents of troubled teens are instructed to refuse to allow runaways home unless they agree to negotiate conditions for return, to decline to bail arrested kids out of jail, and to take the doors off their children's bedrooms so that the kids can't take drugs in private. [See also NATIONAL MEDICAL ENTERPRISES.]

WEB **ToughLove Home Page** http://www.io.com/ ~owen/tlove/tlove.html

Tower Records North America's first music superstore chain and, with more than 120 stores, one of the most mass of the retailers of hip styles in music, books, and, since late 1993, street fashion. The chain was founded and is still owned by Russ Solomon, who started selling Glenn Miller and Elvis hits out of his father's Tower Drugstore in Sacramento, California, in the '50s. The first large store opened in San Francisco in 1968, but it wasn't until the '80s that Tower expanded across the country, propelled in part by the higher margins on CDs. By dint of its size, Tower has become the largest single retailer of ZINES; it casts a long, but by most accounts benign shadow over the hundreds of titles for which it is the main distributor. Tower "Outpost," a special section of its bookstores, is also one of the best-stocked outlets for TRANSGRESSIVE FICTION.

WEB **Tower Records Home Page** http://www.singnet.com.sg/~skyeo/tower.html ✦ WEB **Shopping 2000** http://www.shopping2000.com/ shopping2000/tower/

toys for guns Exchange started in New York City, December 1993, by Dominican-born carpet-business magnate Fernando Mateo (b. 1958), on the premise that cash-starved crooks would give up their guns to get Christmas gifts for their loved ones. Over the next year, more than 3,000 New Yorkers exchanged firearms for Toys "R" Us gift certificates. Riding the success, Mateo founded Goods for Guns at the behest of Foot Locker and other non-toy companies wishing to participate, and attracted more than $150,000 in corporate donations. The idea spread to other big cities, but as the novelty wore off, collections slowed down. "Bitterly disappointed" by the lower returns in the weeks before Christmas 1994 (New Yorkers had only turned in 313 guns), the can-do crusader went on a brief hunger strike and emerged an advocate for stricter gun control. (U.S. citizens possess an estimated 67 million handguns.)

WEB **Goods for Guns** http://www.riverhope.org/gfguns/

transgressive fiction Contemporary fiction-writing trend that prowls the pyscho-narco-sexual frontiers and "dysfunctional" relationships of the Marquis de Sade, WILLIAM BURROUGHS, and SERIAL KILLERS. (The term was formalized for the mainstream book world in a 1993 *Los Angeles Times* essay by radio commentator Michael Silverblatt.) Examples include DENNIS COOPER, Kathy Acker, Mark Amerika, Gary Indiana, Catherine Texier, and BRETT EASTON ELLIS. These are books that, accord to one critic, can be judged by their covers—slickly packaged and target-marketed as upscale pulp. Publishers include Serpent's Tail/High Risk and Grove Press. The category has grown so fast that in 1994 New York's TOWER Books created its own "Outpost" section in the image of underground book stores such as L.A.'s AMOK.

WEB **Alternative-X** http://www.altx.com/ ✦ WEB **William S. Burroughs** http://www.charm.net/~brooklyn/ People/WilliamSBurroughs.html/

trash talking Boastful, humiliating playground poetry which, along with HIP-HOP, formed the soundtrack for much of early-'90s college and pro basketball. In a 1992 response, the NCAA instructed referees to punish "woofing" with personal fouls; the following year, after a hockey-like season of on-court fist fights, the NBA also revised its rules so that refs could call b-ball braggarts with technical fouls if they deemed particular SNAPS to be "taunting." (One trash talking example, according to a handy *Sports Illustrated* sidebar: "Man, you're ugly. And I bet if I follow you home, someone ugly will open the door.") These measures came years after the NFL outlawed excessively demonstrative end-zone celebrations (spiking the football, in particular, was judged unsportsmanlike). At the same time that league administrators bemoaned the spread of this street-inflected braggadocio, it was regularly invoked by the ad campaigns of NIKE, other sports sponsors, and even the leagues' own promotions.

travellers Combining hippie liberationism with BEATNIK wanderlust, these peripatetic gypsies roam the British Isles (mainly southern England) in gaily decorated bus and truck caravans. Tribal meetings at free rock festivals were highlighted by the annual summer solstice celebration at Stonehenge, until Margaret Thatcher banned such congregations in 1985 following the June 1 "Battle of Beanfield," at which 1,000 police smashed traveller vehicles, made hundreds of arrests and took children into custody. Former PUNK squatters attached themselves to the travellers after the Camden Town evictions of the late-'70s, which ultimately led to ever stranger conglomerations of hippie, punk, Rasta, RAVER, and, most recently, ZIPPIE subcultures. Official harassment of the travellers continues; in 1994 the Caravan Sites Act, set up in 1968 to guarantee official sites for nomadic peoples after a rash of vigilante attacks on Gypsies, was reversed.

Travolta, John (b. 1954) Once the biggest box-office name in the world (*Saturday Night Fever* [1977], *Grease* [1978], *Urban Cowboy* [1980]) and a respected actor (Pauline Kael compared him to a young Brando in Brian De Palma's 1981 *Blow Out*), this former icon and sitcom star (*Welcome Back, Kotter*, debut 1975) was languishing in the lucrative kiddie-pic franchise *Look Who's Talking* (1989, sequels 1990 and 1993) when QUENTIN TARANTINO tapped him for *Pulp Fiction* (1994). In Tarantino's movie, Travolta, a disciple of the CHURCH OF SCIENTOLOGY, was reborn: his affecting turn as blissed-out junkie hitman Vincent Vega

Courtesy of MGM/UA

Reborn gangster specialist JOHN TRAVOLTA in *Get Shorty* (1995).

brought him an Oscar nomination and took his reputation back to its *Blow Out* peak. There followed a slew of high-profile roles (*White Man's Burden, Get Shorty*, and JOHN WOO's *Broken Arrow*, all 1995) which allowed him to comfortably maintain a lifestyle which includes three aircraft and two opulent homes.

Trekkers *Star Trek* fans; the term replaced Trekkies, which is now used only ignorantly or derisively. Trekkers exist in the public mind as the quintessential nerds, an image immortalized in the classic *SATURDAY NIGHT LIVE* skit in which *Trek* deity William Shatner told Trekkers to "get a life." In many ways, however, Trekkers are pop-culture innovators: they were ZINE pioneers in the 1970s; in the '80s they were among the first homesteaders on the INTERNET (documented in 1995's *Net Trek* book). (Celebrity adherents include actor Tom Hanks, model Paulina Porizkova, scientist-superstar Stephen Hawking, and TOFFLER-ite Newt Gingrich.) Trekker activities include convention-going, writing and trading *Trek* fiction, including erotica (called SLASH), and playing drinking games. The most lively subgroup of Trekkers are Klingons, people who feel deep affinity with the warrior aliens and hold religious ceremonies in full costume, including sculpted latex foreheads. Klingon language skills are learned through books, tapes, correspondence courses, and even a four-day language camp; advanced Klingon linguists have translated much of the Bible and Shakespeare.

WEB **Kira Home Page (Star Trek Fan Links)**
http://rainbow.rmii.com/~blanche/DS9/kira.html ✦ USENET
rec.arts.startrek, alt.tv.star-trek ✦ WEB **Star Trek Sites**
http://www-iwi.unisg.ch/~sambucci/scifi/startrek/st-www.html

tribute albums Cover song compilations of a single band or artist; these albums proliferated in the '90s, in service of two music business functions: launching new artists and canonizing back catalogue. Phil Spector was an influential honoree, when in 1977 producer Don Tiven loosed PUNK and new wave youngbloods on Spector's classic '60s pop songs for *Bionic Gold*. More influential was *The Bridge,* a 1987 Neil Young tribute that included INDIE-ROCK powers SONIC YOUTH and DINOSAUR JR. Subsequent honorees have included Elton John, the Carpenters, the GRATEFUL DEAD, Leonard Cohen, Shonen Knife, Lynyrd Skynrd, Merle Haggard, R.E.M., Daniel Johnston, Black Sabbath, and Sonic Youth themselves. Deranged Texas rocker Roky Erikson has two tributes under his belt; Led Zeppelin has three. The Rolling Stones have been subjected to a symphonic tribute, and PRINCE has been covered by soft-jazz artists. The Beatles have been feted countless times (including a '60s country album). Only a few tribute albums sell well—1993's Eagles tribute album *Common Thread* topped the 3 million mark, but most tributes don't even break 50,000.

trustafarian Mocking term for affluent young DEADHEADS or other hippie revivalists marked by various permutations of PATAGONIA, MARIJUANA, and (usually white) DREADLOCKS. In spite of the dirt and nature aesthetic, other cultural signifiers include expensive consumer electronics, cyber-literacy, or sports equipment. Trustafarian has a separate meaning in '90s London, where it denotes the equally endowed and idle but more stylish denizens of the once West Indian Notting Hill section.

21 minimum drinking age Laws enacted at state level but required by the federal government since the mid-'80 as a condition of receiving federal highway construction funds. While some critics argue that the higher drinking age actually increases drunk driving by pushing underage tippling out of the bar and into the backseat, statistics show a 55 percent drop in 16–20-year-old alcohol-related fatal auto crashes from 1984 to 1994, saving approximately 1,000 lives a year. (Other critics wonder why 18-year-olds can't buy a beer, but are still subjected to DRAFT REGISTRATION.) The 21-minimum has led to a virtual prohibition movement among college administrators forced by the simple fact that when the drinking age is 18, most college undergrads are

legal; at 21, most are not. House Republicans, euphoric over their 1994 takeover of Congress, proposed eliminating all federal requirements covering highway funds (which also include safety measures such as the national speed limit and motorcycle helmet and seat belt laws).

2600 PHONE PHREAK and computer HACKER quarterly ZINE, named after the easily reproduced audio frequency that phone company repair staff once used to gain outside access to lines. Typical features range from instructions on how to pick the Simplex push-button locks on Federal Express drop-off boxes to schematics for modifying a Radio Shack phone dialer to simulate coin deposits at a pay phone. Edited and published from Long Island, New York, by Eric Corley who takes his hacker alias, Emmanuel Goldstein, from the renegade free thinker in *1984*, the George Orwell novel (and year of *2600*'s launch). The magazine's animus includes a hippie hostility for Ma Bell (and her corporate relatives) and a techie adolescent's preoccupation with intelligence (clueless cops are "as bright as unplugged dumb terminals"). Since the early '90s Eric Corley has been an oft-heard defender of hacker pranks and culture, appearing on *Nightline* and even before Congress to distinguish "nonprofit acts of intellectual exploration and mastery" from the crimes of white collar lawbreakers and foreign spies.

WEB **The 2600 Magazine Home Page** http://www.2600.com/
✦ IRQ **#hack** ✦ USENET **alt.2600**

2600 says it loud on its home page (http://www.2600.com/).

Twin Peaks April 1990-June '91 cult TV series created by filmmaker DAVID LYNCH. *Twin Peaks* introduced American primetime to surrealism, kinky sex, grotesquely fascinating characters, and oblique, glacially paced narrative. Such was the impact of Lynch's vision that the show quickly became a genuine cultural phenomenon, inspiring endless think pieces and water-cooler conversations, and making mini-stars of some of Lynch's handsome cast of young unknowns (among them Sherilyn Fenn, Madchen Amick, and James Marshall). Unable to survive under the weight of outlandish expectations fueled by its initial impact, *Twin Peaks* was canceled by ABC in 1991.

Even as *Twin Peaks* ended in America it was reborn in Japan; refracted through alien perceptions, the show's surreal sensibility was the objective of obsessive OTAKU attention. Spin-offs included fanzines, books, mock-funerals for pivotal character Laura Palmer, and tours to the show's former location in Snowqualmie, Washington. (In a Lynch-worthy scenario, the domestically despised *Twin Peaks: Fire Walk With Me* [1992] was a massive Japanese hit.) The *Twin Peaks* legacy also lives on in U.S. television, albeit in a mild form; fanciful shows like *Picket Fences* and *Northern Exposure* would have likely been impossible without David Lynch's groundbreaking efforts.

WEB **The Black Lodge** http://www.city.ac.uk/~cb192/twin-peaks.html ✦ WEB **Twin Peaks Cast** http://www.sal.wisc.edu/~boardman/TwinPeaks/table/ ✦ USENET **alt.tv.twin-peaks**

2C-B Hallucinogen (4-bromo–2,5-dimethoxyphenethylamine) first isolated by ALEXANDER SHULGIN. Street names include "Nexus," "Herox," and "Synergy." 2C-B is a bitter white crystalline substance that readily dissolves in water or alcohol. Typical doses are 20–40 milligrams taken orally; the initial onset of mild confusion, stupor, and childlike-interest in visual phenomena comes 90 minutes later and lasts some five hours. 2C-B produces minor perceptual distortions: objects appear to be covered with colored tiles, while relative sizes of objects seems to change, but without LSD's mind-bending distortions. (High doses, however, are said to produce out-of-body experiences.) Shulgin recommends taking 2C-B "at or just before" recovery from an ECSTASY trip. While availability was once limited to chemists and their friends of, mid-'90s use is said to be spreading out from San Francisco.

2 Live Crew Unlikely free-speech crusaders led by Luther "Luke Skyywalker" Campbell (b. 1960), gap-toothed Miami mini-mogul. The Crew inaugurated the uptempo Miami Bass sound with 1984's refreshingly blunt if not altogether funky "Throw the D" (as in "dick"). But what brought the band national renown was the June 1990 declaration by a Broward County judge that their third album, *As Nasty As They Want to Be* (1989, including the single "Me So Horny"), was legally obscene. (The record went on to sell three million copies, and the ruling was overturned on appeal, thanks in part to the testimony of expert witnesses such as HENRY LOUIS GATES.) Campbell and his band have been court regulars ever since: in September 1990 their label Luke Skyywalker (Campbell's stage name) Records paid director George Lucas a $300,000 out of court settlement for taking in vain the name of his "moral, wholesome" *Star Wars* character. The following month the band were acquitted of obscene performance in Hollywood, Florida. ("I wish they'd respect me for the joker that I am," Campbell told the *L.A. Times* in 1992.) In 1994 the Supreme Court ruled that 2 Live Crew's parody of Roy Orbison's "Pretty Woman" was not plagiarism. After the band's demise Campbell continued as a solo entity (with bikini-filled clips beloved on THE BOX) for his own Luke label; in 1991 he was ordered to pay Luke artist MC Shy D $1.6 million after a dispute over royalties. In June 1995 Campbell filed for bankruptcy.

Tyson, Mike (b. 1966) The youngest boxer ever to win a heavyweight crown, in 1986. At the time of his 1992 incarceration for rape, Tyson dominated the sport as no one had done since Muhammed Ali, with a 41–1 record (including 36 knockouts). The boxer's DATE RAPE victim was

TV advertising for MIKE TYSON's post-prison, pay-per-view comeback fight, summer 1995.

Desiree Washington, the Rhode Island representative at the 1991 Miss Black America Pageant. Tyson's supporters during the trial included his fight promoter Don King, prominent Baptist ministers (the head of the National Baptist Convention was taped allegedly offering Washington's father $1 million if she would drop charges against Tyson, a major church contributor), '80s millionaire Donald Trump, and defiant wearers of "Free Mike Tyson" and "I'll Be Back" T-shirts who saw Tyson as the latest in a line of celebrated black men brought down by white justice. Once a 13-year-old Brooklyn mugger, "Iron Mike" began his career under famed trainer and strategist Cus D'Amato, but his fighting style regressed to wild knockout swings after his '88 defeat of Michael Spinks. His brief marriage to PREPPY black actress Robin Givens also made headlines that year, ending amid accusations of violence. In March 1995 Tyson was paroled from his Indiana jail, having served half of his six-year sentence. A Harlem "welcome home" parade held in his honor was protested by women's groups from that community, followed by the first of a series of lopsided pay-per-view bouts planned by Don King.

USENET **rec.sport.boxing**

U2 Exhaustively touring Irish band which was among the first post-PUNK acts to successfully cross the Atlantic in the early '80s. With their impassioned update on classic rock—and the socially conscious lyrics of singer Bono (b. Paul Hewson, 1960)—U2 installed themselves as stadium, chart, and MTV fixtures by decade's end. In the process these grizzled road warriors fell in love with America, and set out to capture the mythical roots of rock with the movie and album *Rattle and Hum* (1988). Ridiculed in some quarters for clumsily appropriating roots-music influences and Levi's-ad imagery, the band withdrew to retool their image. Returning producer BRIAN ENO took the band to Berlin to make *Achtung Baby* (1991); under his stewardship they discovered decadence, dance music, CYBERPUNK, lamé suits, and, most importantly, a sense of irony that helped them pass off past sins. The spectacularly-staged Zoo TV tour (launched February 1992) became the mammoth Zooropa tour, a break from which yielded the sketchy, experimental *Zooropa* LP. After a period of overseeing business investments in their native Dublin the band recorded once more with Eno in 1995, on several film music pieces and a straightforward "rock 'n' roll" album.

WEB **U2 Links** http://www.blkbox.com/~dustin/u2links.html ◆
USENET **alt.fan.u2**

undergraduate credit card offers Faced with saturated markets among working adults already paying high interest rates on credit card debt, in the late '80s credit card companies began aggressively marketing their cards to college students. Potential customers were targeted through mass mailings and on-campus promotions which treated college enrollment as a substitute for standard income requirements. This was not, as it would seem, a vote of confidence in the job prospects of college graduates so much as the result of research showing that parents of college students are more likely to make good on their children's debt than is the population at large. Undergrad credit casualties became a widespread problem, prompting many schools to introduce credit counseling services; meanwhile credit card companies eye the teen markets.

Unplugged MTV special-turned-rockbiz institution. When *Unplugged* debuted on November 26th 1989 the format was cozy, informal: singer-songwriter Jules Shear and friends in loose, folksy sessions *sans* amplification for an intimate studio audience. Before long *Unplugged* became an MTV tradition, a handy way of presenting MTV hard rock journeyman like Great White, Damn Yankees, and Poison in a kinder, gentler (and often inappropriate) setting. (Amplification rules were relaxed to the point of being nominal.)

As the *Unplugged* format gathered steam, it became an important music industry tool: single-artist shows can bestow the stamp of respectability upon young comers like Hole, the Cranberries, and Live. These showcases are also a marketing godsend for big guns like Led Zeppelin, Rod Stewart, NEIL YOUNG, and Eric Clapton, all of whom have derived from the program career-refreshing albums and filled MTV's coffers (one inspiration for the channel's plans to start its own record label).

WEB **mtv.com** http://www.mtv.com/

upscale strip clubs Self-consciously "classy" bars and restaurants which gussied up the seedy image of strip clubs in the early '90s by introducing dress codes, yuppie amenities like credit card charges, and posh steakhouse or fernbar decor. Dallas' Cabaret Royale is often mentioned as the first example, but Peter Stringfellow turned the idea into a successful nationwide chain with Goldfingers and Stringfellows franchises that spawned imitators (such as Atlanta's Cheetah Club). In 1994, *Playboy* estimated that 5 percent of the nation's 1,500 strip clubs fit the new model. Along with the VCR-induced glut of porn videos, the new clubs altered porn economics, making live dancing a big payoff in a porn actress's career. Feminist SUSAN FALUDI has compared the appearance of the clubs, coinciding with stricter enforcement of sexual harassment laws, to "the backlash of the 19th century [against the first women's suffrage movements] when a lot of bourgeois men . . . retreated to upscale bordellos."

WEB **Ultimate Strip Club List** http://www.paranoia.com/~express/strip.html ✦ USENET **alt.sex.strip-clubs**

upspeak Declarative statement made with rising into-*nation*? L.A. valley-speak is its exaggerated form and possible source, but upspeak (a.k.a. uptalk) emerged as a widespread teen practice in the mid '80s. In recent years its distinctive "intonation contour" has threatened to become a genuine dialect shift. Although the questioning tone can connote indecision, deference, or apathy, a 1992 linguistic study of a Texas sorority found that up-speak was used most commonly by group leaders, suggesting that the tentative sound can serve as a way of getting attention, involving listeners, and enforcing con-*sensus*?

WEB **MIT Linguistics Homepage** http://web.mit.edu/afs/athena.mit.edu/org/l/linguistics/www/Homepage.html

Urb Los Angeles "urban alternative" magazine founded in December 1990 for $3,000 by Bahamas-born Raymond Leon Roker (b. 1968). *Urb*'s initial focus was HIP-HOP and dance music, and its 3,000 first issue print run was distributed for free by hand by the publishers on L.A.'s Melrose Avenue. As RAVE came to dominate the city, *Urb* became the central locus for that culture, with detailed (if often raw) reports on club life, and swirling, computer-generated ads for club events. In 1994 the magazine began nationwide distribution; as of 1995 it had a 50,000 print run.

Urban Outfitters Subculture retailer supreme, with a chain of nearly two dozen highly influential near-campus stores nationwide, often carved out of architecturally novel spaces such as a converted auto dealership, mansion, or bank. Started as a hippie head shop called the Free People's Store at the edge of the University of Pennsylvania in 1970, the Philadelphia-based Urban Outfitters had grown, by 1995, to annual sales of $110 million by merchandising underground fashion trends—BABY DOLL DRESSES, POLECLIMBER BOOTS, baby T-shirts, and

platform sneakers—to "Young Urban Bourgeois Bohemians" within months of their advent. With its funky housewares, UO also functions as kind of ALTERNATIVE IKEA. In 1994 *Investor's Business Daily* dubbed the publicly traded company the "GRUNGE KING," noting that its "sales per square foot" topped even the GAP. In 1992 the company launched a suburban NEW AGE-inflected variant aimed at older, more upscale customers called Anthropologie.

Courtesy of The Lab

Subculture retailer supreme URBAN OUTFITTERS at THE LAB "anti-mall."

Urban Plunge Program in which college students pretend to be homeless for a day in order to gain empathy for society's less fortunate. Founded in the Reagan era by the National Coalition for the Homeless, Urban Plunge is the most popular of several such well-meaning liberal outfits, which together have put thousands of people on the streets over the years. Not to be confused with unrelated programs of the same name that place students in volunteer positions, Urban Plunge aims to help young people understand homelessness, but Plungers do not actually help homeless people themselves, except perhaps to pass on the profits from one day of simulated panhandling. [See also NATIONAL SERVICE PROGRAM.]

Urge Overkill Chicago band that seeks to combine the strident pop of Cheap Trick with—under the loving art-direction of frontman Nash Kato (b. Nathan Katruud, 1965)—the suave hedonism of Frank Sinatra's Rat Pack. Launched in Chicago in 1986, Urge Overkill recorded a string of records with name INDIE-ROCK producers like STEVE ALBINI (with whom they later became sworn enemies) and Butch Vig (later of NIRVANA's *Nevermind*); given their tirelessly stated taste for deluxe trappings like medallions, velvet suits, and cocktails, it's perhaps surprising that the band did not sign to a major, Geffen, until 1992 (at the suggestion of their most famous fan, NIRVANA's Kurt Cobain). Urge's Geffen debut *Saturation* (1992)—produced by Philadelphia's "Butcher Brothers," Joe and Phil Nicolo (CYPRESS HILL, Schooly D)—fell short of the band's lofty ideals. Although the record bristled with retro power chords and witty words ("Heaven 90210"; the soap-opera tribute "Erika Kane"), it was sonically underweight and the widely predicted mainstream breakthrough never came. QUENTIN TARANTINO gave the band a much-needed break in 1994 by including their cover of Neil Diamond's "Girl, You'll Be a Woman Soon" on the soundtrack of *Pulp Fiction*. The band's 1995 follow-up *Exit the Dragon* (working titles *100% Not Guilty*, *White Chocolate*) was also produced by the Butcher Brothers.

WEB **URGE-o-FONIC** http://www.mcs.net/~alester/urge/uo-home.htm ✦ WEB **Geffen Records** http://www.geffen.com

used CDs Cottage industry among small chains and independent record stores that is driven by the durability and shimmering appeal of CD's—the same attributes which, along with high margins, helped them revitalize the sagging record industry of the early '80s. Eminently resell-able, CDs represent a kind of crude, large coin currency for the financially challenged. The total trade in used CDs approaches 5 percent of the $9 billion total U.S. recorded music business. When the 315-store West Coast Wherehouse chain began experimenting with used CDs in 1993, the four largest distributors lashed out to protect the three quarters of the market they control, refusing to engage with the chain in "co-op" advertising deals that subsidize the marketing budgets of many retail record chains; the chain desisted. In late 1992, record companies began sealing new CDs with silver, irritatingly hard-to-remove adhesive labels known as "dog bones" (for their shape) in anticipation of the LONGBOX's phase-out the following spring.

Usenet Global collection of more than 10,000 text-based "newsgroup" discussions which principally take place over the INTERENT, ranging from rec.pets.cats and rec.aviation.hang-gliding to alt.conspiracy.abe-lincoln, alt.drugs.pot, and alt.sex. first-time. As with the Internet itself, there is no central headquarters for Usenet; new messages ripple out across the network, passed along from one machine to the next, reaching some distant "host" computers in a matter of minutes while others can take days. Before commercial services like AMERICA ONLINE offered Usenet access in 1994, the discussions (dating from 1983) were dominated by computer hobbyists, the military, and those at universities and computer companies. Usenet culture has spawned such terms as "lurking" (reading but not posting) and "flame war" (acrimonious debate). The creation of new discussion groups follow a strict voting process established in the late '80s, except for those groups beginning with the "alt" prefix. Legend has it that Brian Reid, the co-creator of the free-wheeling "alt" hierarchy, was prompted in 1987 by the insistence of others that his recipe group "gourmand" be listed under "rec.food.gourmand." (See also ALT.BINARIES.PICTURES.EROTICA and CYBERSEX.)

WEB **List of USENET FAQs** http://www.cis.ohio-state.edu/hypertext/faq/usenet/ ✦ WEB **How to Receive Banned Newsgroups** http://www.cen.uiuc.edu/~jg11772/banned-groups-faq.html

v-chip "Violence chip" designed to provide parents with a way to "lock out" television programs. The technical standards for such a system were discussed at 1992 meetings of the Electronic Industries Association, which represents most TV set manufacturers, only to be shot down by broadcasters wary of any controls that might limit audiences or advertising revenue. Democratic congressman Ed Markey of Massachusetts revived the issue, proposing that the technology—essentially a specialized use of the same "vertical blanking interval" that carries captions for the hearing impaired—be required in all new TV sets and broadcasts. In 1994 the same industry group agreed to begin including the device (which can easily be reprogrammed for other ratings such as "N" for nudity or, as some wags have had it, "P" for politics) in high-end televisions, while it seems increasingly likely that the networks and cable systems will adopt some voluntary or compulsory system in the near future. HBO and cable TV companies have tended to support the Clinton-endorsed v-chip, reasoning that parents would feel more comfortable taking premium services if they can control access to them. 1995 furors over CYBERSEX prompted many INTERNET authorities—under the aegis of the newly created Information Highway Parental Empowerment Group—to consider implementing a similar rating systems for the WORLD WIDE WEB.

WEB **National Association of Broadcasters**
http://www.nab.org/on-line/files/july12.htm/

van Sant, Gus (b. 1952) PORTLAND, Oregon-based writer-director who established himself as a major voice in gay cinema with 1985's *Mala Noche*, a melancholic black and white adaptation of a Portland street poet's novel made for only $25,000. This former advertising man leapt to mainstream prominence in 1989 with *Drugstore Cowboy*, an unflinching, nuanced account of 1970s junkie life that derived much of its impact from the presence of former teen idol Matt Dillon as a user. (Junkie royalty William Burroughs cameoed as a defrocked priest.) Van Sant's next movie, the highly antici-

pated *My Own Private Idaho* (1991) starred then-current teen idols RIVER PHOENIX and KEANU REEVES as a pair of gay hustlers. *Idaho*, however, confounded many of van Sant's supporters with its oblique plot, jarring editing, and whimsical Shakespearean allusions; his stock fell further with *Even Cowgirls Get the Blues* (1994), a calamitous adaptation of Tom Robbins's quintessentially '70s novel. In 1995 van Sant made a more successful adaptation of another '70s novel, Joyce Maynard's *To Die For*, starring Matt Dillon, Nicole Kidman, and Joaquin Phoenix, River's younger brother.

veganism Strict plant-based diet in which observers avoid foods derived from animals. (Not to be confused with people who are "ovo-lacto," who eat eggs, milk, cheese and other dairy products, or "lacto" individuals, who eat some dairy and no eggs.) While *Vegetarian Times* magazine reported that more than 12 million Americans consider themselves vegetarian (and Teen-age Resource Unlimited says that 25 percent of American teens are vegetarian) fewer than 10 percent of vegetarians say they are completely vegan. The practice is often associated with animal-rights groups like PETA, of whose members the *Los Angeles Times* said in June 1995: "They are vegans; compared with them, conventional vegetarians seem like cannibals." Vegan parents have been criticized for depriving their children a balanced diet: doctors say that vegan children are prone to rickets and other nutritional deficiencies. Food manufacturers, recognizing the demand for meatless food, have begun to make what are called "meat analog products" with names like "Foney Baloney" and "Fakin' Bacon."

WEB **Vegan-Vegetarian Node** http://www.dsi.unimi.it/ Users/Students/maresa/Veget/english/Veget.html/ ✦ USENET **rec.food.veg, rec.food.veg.cooking** ✦ WEB **Vegan Action** http://envirolink.org/arrs/va/home.html

viatical settlement Early payout of life insurance to a terminally ill policyholder in exchange for being named as the beneficiary of the policy. The novel financial transaction—which takes its name from *viaticum*, the Latin name of the Eucharist given to the dying, and translates literally as the financial provisions of a journey—was pioneered for people with AIDS in 1989 by a New Mexico company called Living Benefits. The morbid business of profiting from death remained surprisingly free of scandal and criticism within the world of AIDS advocacy as it expanded to dozens of firms and cancer patients. Prudential and other established life insurers moved quickly in the early '90s to capitalize on the trend with accelerated benefits options.

WEB **DeathNet** http://www.IslandNet.com:80/~deathnet/

Vibe   Black culture magazine launched lavishly in 1993 by Time Inc. and Quincy Jones, jazz composer-turned-music, TV, and movie producer. With its broad purview, thoughtful writing (incongruous, given Time's mass-market aims), and elegant design, *Vibe* more resembled a European-style magazine than it did its U.S. contemporaries. The 1994 departure of original editor Jonathan Van Meter signaled a shift from MULTICULTURAL concerns to a focus on black entertainment. (*Vibe*'s older, scrappier rival *The Source* stoically and successfully sticks to its coverage of street HIP-HOP). Initial speculation that *Vibe* might enjoy too cozy a relationship with the celebrity industry was revived in May 1995: a cover story on some-time Quincy Jones client Michael Jackson omitted to mention the accusations of child molestation that were leveled at the star—and jeopardized his career—the previous year.

WEB **Vibe On-Line** http://www.timeinc.com/vibe/

Vick's VapoRub   Decongestant popular on the RAVE scene for its alleged heightening of the effects of ECSTASY. VapoRub became a staple of British raves around 1989-'90 when it was rubbed into the face or body; face masks later became a common way of concentrating the fumes. By 1991 English TECHNO group Altern–8 were wearing the masks on stage, and appeared on national TV with jars of VapoRub on their keyboards. Procter and Gamble, the product's maker since the 1920s, declined a suggested sponsorship deal; the lack of official promotion did not inhibit the spread of VapoRub's leisure application to American ravers.

videogames   See page 264.

video store auteurs   An influential cadre of young '90s filmmakers found a more expeditious route into the Hollywood director's chair than film school at USC, UCLA, or NYU—serving behind a video store counter. The most notorious was QUENTIN TARANTINO, who worked at the mythical Video Archives store in Manhattan Beach, California (1984–89), along with Roger Avary, director of the 1994 hemo-fest *Killing Zoe* (executive produced by Tarantino). KEVIN SMITH, director of 1994's no-budget, high-profit feature *Clerks*, actually dropped out of film school before doing *his* time between the aisles. Whereas '70s "film brats" (and film school grads) like Coppola and Scorsese had to trawl the art houses for rare showings of key cinematic *textes*, Tarantino and co. could absorb a massive range of influences in between swiping membership cards. The question remains whether this has enriched their art or rendered it soullessly referential.

video surveillance   Corporate voyeurism, increasing the likelihood that one is being photographed or videotaped while working, shopping, banking, driving, or—under some aggressive interpretations of "inventory control"—trying on clothes in a changing room. Video surveillance can be seen on television, where earthquakes are captured on convenience store security camera (known as sec-cams) and video undercover work has become a staple of tabloid TV exposés. Bow-tied senator Paul Simon has proposed ACLU legislation that would guarantee the right to know when one is being watched, but it is opposed by industry groups marketing such anti-privacy devices as miniaturized remote control cameras and VCRs capable of recording for 200 hours straight. The POLITICALLY CORRECT dystopia of the movie *Demolition Man* (1993) had Big Brother cameras monitoring L.A. sidewalks, but the fact is that many urban streets are already mechanically monitored for traffic management. (This could be seen as the flipside of the advent of the video vigilantism of camcorder citizens.)

WEB **San Diego Real-time Traffic Report**

http://www.scubed.com/caltrans/sd/sd_transnet.html/ ✦ WEB
InPhoto Surveillance http://www.interaccess.com/
inphotowww/ ✦ WEB **Stupid Remote Control Tricks**
http://www.jungle.com/msattler/sci-tech/comp/misc/remote-
control.html

vinyl   Scratch-prone, dust-attracting recording
medium that refuses to die. CD sales outpaced vinyl
in 1988 and CDs' higher profit margins sealed the
older medium's fate; by 1990 most labels had
stopped producing it. Vinyl's adherents, however,
insist that digital recording can't capture musical
warmth the way analog can. "Probably the biggest
catastrophe that has happened in the recording of
music in the last ten years," Neil Young said in *CD
Review* in 1992. The analog resistance movement
can be heard on INDIE-ROCK 7-inch singles, 12-inch
dance remixes, and a booming secondhand business.
Vinyl even hit the charts in 1994 when Pearl Jam
released its album *Vitalogy* on the format two weeks
before the CD version; PAVEMENT, GREEN DAY, the
BEASTIE BOYS, and SONIC YOUTH are among other
high-profile bands who've released short runs of
albums on vinyl. Turntable sales increased by 50 percent in 1993 and LP sales jumped by more than 60
percent the following year, but vinyl still represented
less than one percent of music sold.

Matchbox from the
VIPER ROOM, L.A.

Viper Room   Small club on L.A.'s
Sunset Strip co-owned by actor
JOHNNY DEPP. Opened in August
1993, the Viper Room was a low-key
hangout for young actors and musicians; bands who performed there
included Depp's sometime band P. The
club, which still exists, passed into
mythology on October 31st, 1993,
when RIVER PHOENIX collapsed on the
sidewalk from a drug overdose and
later died.

WEB **LA Venues** http://www.primenet.com/
~sk8boy/venues.html#viper/

virtual office   Nothing personal except computers in this workspace of the future, where staff either
stay home and "telecommute" or show up to temporarily claim space in open-air common areas
equipped with basic furniture and jacks for access to
phone, power, and computer networks. The non-ter-
ritorial notion is most closely associated with the
Chiat/Day ad agency, which adopted a far-reaching
system of unassigned carrels and personal lockers for
some 450 employees in 1993. Though many critics
wondered about its depersonalizing effects (especially in an era of "down-sizing" and temporary
workers), the experiment has been largely hailed as a
success, with C/D touting a new software program
called Oxygen that supposedly reproduces office
camaraderie over computer networks. Other pioneering attempts include IBM's 1993 "productivity
centers" and the 1992 "hoteling" desk-reservation
system of accounting firm Ernst & Young. Far more
widespread is telecommuting—seen by many environmentalists and urban planners as a solution to
car-clogged highways—with some 1995 predictions
putting the away-from-office population at three
million, set to double every three years.

WEB **Home Office Association of America (SoHo Central)**
http://www.hoaa.com/ ✦ WEB **Chiat/Day Idea Factory**
http://www.chiatday.com/web/

virtual reality   Originally used by early-'80s
computer programmers to
describe any interactive
technology, virtual reality
became a hot term in 1989,
when musician Jaron
Lanier designed a head-
mounted display screen
and special "Data-gloves"
that allowed users to
immerse themselves—and
participate in—computer-
created simulations. Known
as much for his trademark
blond dreadlocks as for his
relentless proselytizing, Lanier promoted the new
technology through his company, VPL Research (a
company he would lose control of in 1992, when all

From the home page of virtual
star Jaron Lanier
(http://www.well.com/user/jaron/).

patents were assumed by French conglomerate Thomsom CSF). Lanier's tireless advocacy came at the end of a decade full of TV shows and films about high-tech altered states, including *Tron* (1982), *Automan* (1983), *Brainstorm* (1985), and *Lawn-* *mower Man* (1992). After an early groundswell of enthusiasm, virtual reality failed to evolve as quickly as its prophets had predicted, in part because manufacturers were slow to develop miniaturized hardware and sophisticated graphic software. Of the more than

videogames

"Cyberspace," according to WILLIAM GIBSON, the science fiction writer who coined the term in his 1984 novel *Neuromancer*, was inspired by the sight of Vancouver teenagers playing videogames in an arcade–"I could see in the physical intensity of their postures how rapt these kids were . . . You had this feedback loop, with photons coming off the screen into the kids' eyes, the neurons moving through their bodies, electrons moving through the computer. And these kids clearly believed in the space these games projected." Gibson went on, in his fiction, to envision wide, gravity-free expanses dotted with sparkling, crystalline towers of pure information. But when he finally leaned over one of the kids' shoulders to see what was holding them hypnotized, he was, he reports, utterly disappointed by the crude, pixelated graphics he found.

After more than a decade of innovations that were supposed to revolutionize computer interfaces (the mouse, on-screen graphic icons and windows), videogames remain the gold standard for human-machine interaction, as social intercourse (and most of the economy) migrates to computer networks. Videogames have emerged as the principal expression of male adolescence, first in the arcades that a century ago hosted the earliest motion pictures, and later in the home where '90s cartridge systems have rendered the fast-cut graphics of MTV a model of sober contemplation by comparsion.

Videogames are also setting the pace for research and development within the computer industry–by the end of 1994, consumer electronics business had replaced the military as the largest single investor in computer innovation, with makers of personal computers re-positioning themselves to avoid becoming the kind of dinosaurs that mini-computers became a decade ago. Microsoft made a deliberate push to establish Windows 95 as a game platform (remedying Apple Computer's mistake of several years earlier when game development for the MACINTOSH was discouraged, for fear that it would make the machine seem less "serious"). By the 1995 Christmas toy season, the processing power of machines by Sony, Sega, et al will have surpassed that of personal computers selling for five times as much.

Propelled by home consoles from Nintendo and then Sega, that finally had colorful palettes, the latest videogame boom has brought fame to maze-runners Mario and Sonic the Hedgehog that movie and TV stars could only dream about. (By late 1993, Sony's game division

Six generations of the Pac Man family on display in a virtual tour of the St. Louis Coin-Op and Video Game Museum (http://sharkie.psych.indiana.edu/).

was reading every script bought by its corporate sibling Columbia Pictures.) But the most attention has gone to MORTAL KOMBAT. MK stands as the apotheosis of the martial arts game genre that swept arcades in the early '90s. Street Fighter II was the first hit, substituting hand-to-hand pummeling for the classic shooting and bombing. While the game's graphics were cartoonish, its controls included complicated combination moves that could take even seasoned players weeks to perfect. Street Fighter also resurrected the type of player-against-player competition that had largely laid dormant since the days of two-person Pong in the early '70s. Mortal Kombat followed with photo-realistic effects that included, most famously, bloody "finishing moves" which sometimes

$115 million generated by the VR industry in 1993, less than $40 million was attributable to home systems. In 1994, the emerging, accessible marvel of a global computer network (the INTERNET) pushed VR to the margins of techno-hype. Despite the techno-

logical limits circumscribing virtual reality, Hollywood continues to pursue the VR grail; by 1994, there was even a TV show devoted exclusively to the phenomenon, the short-lived Fox drama *VR5*.
USENET **sci.virtual-worlds** WEB **Internet Resources in**

---

included ripping out an opponent's heart.

The September '93 home cartridge release of Mortal Kombat occasioned a moral panic over videogame violence that echoed similar public hand-wringing over TV mayhem, music lyrics, and, in simpler times, COMIC books and pinball. It was a sign that videogames had finally climbed back to the cultural position they occupied during the golden age of Atari in the early '80s, when home computing first took off and Americans last spent more money on videogames than going to the movies. (With some 14 million Atari 2600 game machines in homes then, the cartridge version of Pac-Man pulled in more money than *Raiders of the Lost Ark*.)

Overlooked in most worries about videogame violence was the far bloodier DOOM, which escaped scrutiny because it debuted on business computers where it presumably would have no claim on impressionable children, desensitizing only corporate America to the value of human life. Videogames were also instrumental in breaking down barriers separating juvenile and adult pleasures [see INFANTILIZATION], leaving grown people free to finger Tetris Game Boys in public. Some defended "mature" gaming as a new art form, citing projectile-free puzzle adventures like the Myst CD-ROM, the acceptance of '80s design classics like Defender and Robotron in museum shows, and pinball's VINYL-like resurgence.

Doom pushed the bleeding-edge, creating a kind of cyber-PAINTBALL arena for combatants to blast each other over computer networks in one of the first playable 3D environments. VIRTUAL REAL-

Ratings were widely-adopted by the software industry in 1995.

ITY had finally found a viable commercial form. (Progress had reduced sports injuries to NINTENDO THUMB and social discontent to raging against the machine–as opposed to, say, the boss.)

The head-to-head competition of the bludgeon games and the network play of Doom are putting videogame narcotainment in a key position (along with HOME SHOPPING and the INTERNET) in commercial plans for interactive TV. (Largest of the early ventures is THE SEGA CHANNEL, launched in 1995 to rent game software over cable lines and experiment with networked play.) The continued use of the most powerful desktop business computers for high-end games–Doom was famously banned from the local network at blue-chip computer firm Intel–also points to the inter-relationship between videogames and the evolution of computer systems. Scratch the surface of the latest operating system upgrade or spreadsheet program and one is likely to find an arcade ideal only imperfectly realized as putative info-tool. The *real* goal, as any hardcore computer type will attest, is a good game of Space Invaders with its joystick and fire-button control of reality.

This overwhelmingly male agenda has its critics–design magazine *I.D.* asserted in 1994 that "There is something about the design of the inter-action in these games that attracts boys and repels girls," reporting on one unfortunate early-'90s attempt at marketing to girls called *Girl's Club* that centered around a slot machine that paid off with cute boys. Perhaps, the magazine wondered, girls would be more interested if software did not involve "one long fight." Perhaps, too, the future being fashioned in the image of videogames would look a lot better.–*Nathaniel Wice*
USENET **alt.games.video, rec.games.video** ✦ WEB **Cardiff's Video Game Database Browser** http://www.cm.cf.ac.uk/ Games/ ✦ WEB **Classic Video Games Homepage** http://www2.ecst.csuchico.edu/~gchance/ ✦ WEB **Video Arcade Preservation Society** http://www.vaps.org/

Virtual Reality http://www.hitl.washington
.edu/projects/knowledge_base/onthenet.html ◆ WEB **Jaron
Lanier Homepage** http://www.well.com/community/
Jaron.Lanier/index.html

vitamin labeling scare   "Don't let the FDA
take your vitamins away!" screamed a call to arms
that appeared in health food stores and magazines
across the country in late 1993, prompting one of
the largest letter-writing campaigns to Congress in
U.S. history. The only problem was that the FDA
didn't want to take anyone's vitamins away—or
their echinacea, amino acids, or shark cartilage—
merely prevent sellers from making miraculous
health claims about them. The industry's
Nutritional Health Alliance campaign worked,
weakening the eventual 1994 law so that manufacturers could make "structure and function" claims
like "Vitamin C and E are antioxidants, which are
essential for the immune system." It is still illegal,
however, to make snake-oil health claims about cur-
ing AIDS or growing hair on a billiard ball—unless
there is "significant scientific agreement."

WEB **Food and Drug Administration Home Page**
http://www.fda.gov/ ◆ USENET **misc.health.alternative**

voguing   Fleetingly known as an early-'90s dance
style, voguing also encompassed a performance-ori-
ented culture which grew out of the gay Afro-
American and Hispanic DRAG balls held in Harlem,
New York since at least the '50s. A stylized appropriation of the *hauteur* and posturing of the fashion
world, voguing (after *Vogue* magazine; sometimes
"vogueing") mirrored high society with its own lexicon of affectations, including "throwing shade" (giving attitude), "putting on a face" (same, but with
facial expression) and "runway" (sashaying on an
invisible fashion-show runway). At a typical competition, rival "houses" (loyalty-driven voguing teams)
vie in various categories, with "realness"—the ability
to successfully imitate another gender, persona or
culture—often deciding the contest (in the "banjy
boys" category, participants are judged on their
resemblance to street hoods).

Voguing entered the public consciousness in
1990 when MADONNA's dance track, "Vogue"
climbed the charts; the culture reached its real
apotheosis, however, with the widely acclaimed
Paris Is Burning, Jennie Livingston's exuberant 1991
documentary of the Harlem drag balls. Four years
later, many of the house elders—or "mothers"—
interviewed for *Paris* have passed on. As of 1995, a
younger cadre of house members can still be found
strutting their stuff in such clubs as New York City's
Palladium.

Vollmann, William T. (b. 1959) Metafictional
novelist and near-suicidal journalist. Vollman's prodigious body of work explores the harrowing lives of
the world's underclasses. To write his fiction, Vollman
immerses himself in his subjects' lives; he has lived
among prostitutes and street people—smoking
CRACK, having unprotected sex and getting burned
by lit cigarettes—in San Francisco, New York and
Southeast Asia. Occasionally he feels compelled to
act as well as report: in Thailand he abducted a child
prostitute from a brothel, purchased her from her
father, and enrolled her in a vocational school in
Bangkok. For *Fathers and Crows,* the second volume
of his acclaimed *Seven Dreams* series (1992), Vollman
spent two weeks alone in the North Pole the better to
empathize with an ill-fated 19th century explorer.
On May 1st 1994, while Vollmann was on assignment for *SPIN* in Bosnia, the car he was in drove over
a mine—the driver, Francis Tomasik, a friend who
was acting as a photographer and interpreter, was
killed. Vollmann writes obsessively, often 16 hours a
day, subsisting on candy bars; a resulting case of
CARPAL-TUNNEL SYNDROME forced him off computers and into notebooks.

Photo by Ben Pax, courtesy of Viking

WILLIAM T. VOLLMAN, chilling.

WAC Feminist activist group which came together in the wake of the October 1991 ANITA HILL-Clarence Thomas hearings. Adapting the direct action and media-guerrilla tactics of ACT-UP, the Women's Action Coalition's membership quickly swelled an initial art world concentration to some 2,000 members by mid-1992, with chapters in dozens of cities operating under the group's symbol, a giant eye, and credo, "WAC is Watching. We Will Take Action." In the heady days of the group's first year, WAC protested defense tactics in rape trials ("We Are Women, Hear Us Wail, Glen Ridge Rapists Go to Jail!"), shouted down a New York demonstration of OPERATION RESCUE, joined with the GUERRILLA GIRLS to rail against art world sexism, jeered the lack of leading roles for Hollywood women, marked the first anniversary of TAILHOOK, and, on Mother's Day, took over Grand Central Station to target American men who owe an estimated $30 billion in child support ("Off our backs! On our feet! We refuse to be discreet!"). Demonstrations often feature the WAC drum corps. In 1995, WAC began the process of "dying with dignity," as the handful of remaining members archived Coalition records for the New York Public Library. [See also LESBIAN AVENGERS.]

War on Drugs Although nearly every President since World War II has declared a "War on Drugs" the federal government's current prohibition movement was officially launched with a series of laws passed under Richard Nixon—and originally prompted by a HEROIN epidemic—which culminated with the 1973 creation of the Drug Enforcement Agency (DEA). Under Reagan and Bush, federal spending on drug control expanded from $1.1 billion in 1980 to $12 billion in 1992 (although most of these increases came from Congress). Petite First Lady Nancy Reagan made a drug-free America her personal cause, prompting such spectacles as her lapdance with *A-Team* behemoth Mr. T at a "Just Say No" Christmas event.

Stepped-up enforcement of drug laws has led to prison overcrowding (see MANDATORY MINIMUMS) and a shift to domestic production of cheap, potent substances like CRACK. Framed as a crime epidemic rather than a public health crisis, the drug war has also taken a toll on civil liberties: dealer "profiles" peg non-whites for police suspicion, property seizures provide police with luxury vehicles sometimes employed in the war itself, and DRUG TESTS are on their way to becoming a basic fact of school and work life. In the '90s the War on Drugs has continued to be waged (with penalties regularly increased in election years) even as other national issues have eclipsed it. In 1994 Clinton administration Surgeon General Jocelyn Elders was censured for suggesting that legalization might be studied; in 1995 Thomas A. Constantine, chief of the DEA, frustrated with the U.S.'s ongoing failure to slow cocaine smuggling from Central America, impoliticly declared that the U.S. was losing the War on Drugs.

WEB **WARSTOP** http://sunsite.unc.edu/warstop/warstop.html/ ✦ WEB **Marijuana and the War on Drugs** http://www.calyx .net/marijuana.html/ ✦ WEB **End the Drug War** http://web.kaleida.com/u/hopkins/prohibition/ ✦ USENET **talk.politics.drugs** ✦ WEB **Drug Enforcement Administration** http://gopher.usdoj.gov/bureaus/dea.html/ ✦ WEB **The National Institute of Justice** http://ncjrs.aspensys.com:81/aboutnij.html/

Warhol, Andy (b. 1927; d. 1987) Former commercial illustrator who became one of the leading figures of the Pop Art movement, along with artists such as Roy Lichtenstein, Jasper Johns, and Robert Rauschenberg. More than any of his contemporaries, Andy Warhol was known for dissolving the boundaries between high and low culture: the most famous of his pop artworks used silkscreening techniques to mechanically reproduce consumer images such as Brillo boxes and Campbell's soup cans. Warhol's art also involved a more general contemplation of celebrity, not only in his paintings of Elvis Presley and Marilyn Monroe, but in his involvement with the Velvet Underground and avant-garde films featuring such mock-stars ("superstars") as Billy Name, Holly

Woodlawn, and Ultra Violet. Warhol himself became a public figure, his shock of white hair and blank expression internationally recognized as symbols of modern art. He died during routine surgery in 1985, at which time his artistic output was counterweighed by a rise in iconic power.

Warhol's presence looms over contemporary culture, and is evoked in three mid-decade movies: a biopic of Jean-Michel Basquiat by '80s artist Julian Schnabel features musician David Bowie as Warhol; *A Low Life in High Heels* essays the life of Factory DRAG queen Holly Woodlawn; and *I Shot Andy Warhol*, is about about feminist Valerie Solanas, who did just that.

WEB **The Andy Warhol Museum Home Page**
http://www.usaor.net:80/warhol/

Warren G (b. Warren Griffin III, circa 1971) Honey-throated stepbrother of GANGSTA rap progenitor DR. DRE and boyhood partner of SNOOP DOGGY DOGG. Warren G's cautionary gangsta tale "Regulate" (based on a soft-rock sample from former Doobie Brother Michael McDonald) was integral to 1994's street soundtrack; the album that yielded it, *Regulate: The G Funk Era*, was a double-platinum smash that confirmed the ascendancy of the Long Beach G-funk (gangsta funk) sound and realized the potential the former shipyard mechanic and gang member had shown as a producer/guest on Dre's Epochal album *The Chronic*, and as a producer on the soundtrack to JOHN SINGLETON's *Poetic Justice*.

WEB **The Producer's Archive** http://www.dsi.unimi.it/ Users/Students/barbieri/awrrng.html/

Waters, John (b. 1946) Although he screened a handful of films in his native Baltimore in the '60s, it was between 1971's *Multiple Maniacs* and 1981's *Polyester* (released in "Smell-o-Vision") that this writer-director became American cinema's doyen of the truly tasteless. Waters' reputation for camp outrage was sealed forever by the harrowing scene in 1974's *Pink Flamingos* in which hefty transvestite lead Divine consumed a handful of fresh dog shit on camera. (In 1975 the film earned Waters a

$5,000 obscenity fine in Hicksville, New York.) As Waters' following grew beyond its underground beginnings, the director acceded to offers of beefed-up budgets and indulged his desire to infect the multiplexes with his brand of celluloid sin. After the successful cross-over *Hairspray* (1988), mainstream Waters projects like *Cry-Baby* (1990) and *Serial Mom* (1994) reflected many of his old obsessions, but they yielded diminishing returns for his hardcore followers.

Wayans family Described half-jokingly by sister Kim as the black Osmond family, the Wayans helped define African-American comedy for the 1990s. Led by brother Keenan Ivory Wayans (b. circa 1958), a standup comic who wrote, directed and starred in the 1988 blaxploitation spoof *I'm Gonna Git You Sucka*, the family teamed up two years later for the groundbreaking Fox TV HIP-HOP variety show, *In Living Color*. Created by and starring Keenan, the relentlessly low-brow series also featured Kim (b. circa 1966), Dwayne (b. circa 1957), Damon (b. 1961), Shawn (b. circa 1971) and later Marlon (b. 1972) Wayans. The show's break-out star, JIM CARREY, was not related. Notoriously difficult to work with, Keenan reportedly had fits of paranoia in which he believed he was being spied on by both SATURDAY NIGHT LIVE and the CIA. In 1992, Keenan feuded with Fox over creative and financial issues and quit the show, which lasted for one more season. In 1994 he returned to movies with the action-comedy *Low Down Dirty Shame*. Damon, who created some memorable *In Living Color* skits (including "Homey the Clown" and "Men on Film") went on to star in low-brow movies like *Mo' Money* (1992) and *Blankman* (1994). In 1995, Shawn and Marlon were recruited by the Warner Bros. television network, where *The Wayans Bros.* show consistently placed in the bottom five of the ratings.

Ween Duo of solipsistic studio savants from New Hope, Pennsylvania. Dean and Gene Ween (b. Mickey Melchiondo, 1970; and Aaron Freeman, 1970) don't just approximate the musical styles they

parody; they nail them with uncanny precision. Like fellow postmodern artiste SANDRA BERNHARD, Ween get inside a cliché—whether cock-rock, Philly soul, or spaghetti western balladeering (their tastes are frighteningly eclectic)—and play it out for all it's worth. The band's concerts can be like entering an alternate universe where Dean and Gene are unquestioned rock Gods who strut across club stages as though they were headlining Madison Square Garden. (This—reportedly—in between NITROUS OXIDE breaks.) The band got their biggest exposure when their single "Push the Little Daisies" (1992), a catchy bossa-nova complemented by Gene's allegedly helium-enhanced vocals, got major airplay from a disbelieving BEAVIS AND BUTT-HEAD.

WEB **Ween Website** http://nox.cs.du.edu:8001/~kkoller/ Ween/ ✦ WEB **Grand Royal Ween** http://www.nando.net/ music/gm/GrandRoyal/Bands/Ween/

Weiss, Rob (b. 1967) Long Island, New York-born filmmaker whose powerful debut *Amongst Friends* explored the lives of young, Jewish wanna-be mobsters in his native suburbs. When *Amongst Friends* was released in 1993, Weiss impressed many interviewers with his own braggadocio, and tales of how his travel agent father had helped raise $100,000 of the film's $900,000 budget via his colorful gambler friends. Weiss senior, who'd even been profiled in his own right by the *New York Times*, was charged in January 1995 with defrauding more than 300 elderly customers of over an apparently unrelated $250,000. Rob Weiss, briefly linked to the mooted big-screen adaptation of BRETT EASTON ELLIS' *American Psycho*, was dating SHANNEN DOHERTY at the time.

WELL Sausalito-based computer bulletin board (BBS) and INTERNET service. Established in 1985 by Whole Earth Catalog founder Stewart Brand, the WELL (Whole Earth 'Lectronic Link) expanded from a couple of hundred Bay Area hippies, tech freaks, and DEADHEADS to a thriving virtual community of approximately 10,000 international users. An anarchic experiment in self-government— and for many, *the* model electronic village—the WELL consists of some 200 public and private conferences subdivided into topics. Apart from the expected cultural and social terrain, the WELL's topology includes media-centric discussions, the surreal landscape of the Weird conference, and the ceaseless self-analysis of Metawell. In September 1994 the WELL was taken over by the commercially-oriented co-founder of Rockport Shoes, Bruce Katz, whose vision for his acquisition includes the establishment of linked mini-WELLs around the world. In early 1995 some 300 WELL members left to form The River to "develop an on-line community that is owned and governed by the users, the people that create the value."

WEB **WELL** http://www.well.com

West, Cornel (b. 1953) "Preeminent African-American intellectual of our time" according to HENRY LOUIS GATES, JR.; author of the best-selling collection of race relations commentary, *Race Matters* (1993); honorary co-chair of the Democratic Socialists of America; Harvard philosophy of religion professor. Though Cornel West has influenced an extensive network of academic disciples, he cuts a

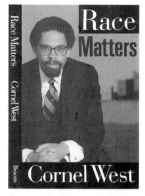

CORNEL WEST's essay collection brought socialism to the bestseller lists.

singular presence in public life with his Afro, three-piece suits, and folksy no-nonsense mix of class analysis and preacherly gospel. Alternately calling himself a "prophetic pragmatist" and "prophetic Marxist" in *Race Matters*, West heavily criticized middle-class blacks as "decadent" and pleaded with whites to stop "ignoring the psychic pain that racism has inflicted on the urban poor." West's social criticism often touches on popular culture: in HIP-HOP he sees the hopelessness and materialism of the black underclass ("black nihilism"); in its suburban popularity West reads the "Afro-Americanization of American Youth" and the closely related "commodification of black rage."

wet T-shirt contest Softcore, R-rated beach and bar promotion devolved from beauty pageants. Wet T-shirt contests were raised to a semi-professional circuit, with low-rent video and pay-per-view spin-offs in the early '90s by silicon-enhanced women at seasonal youth and business resorts around the country. Live show variants include bikini, hot legs, hot body, tight fittin' jeans, and calendar girl contests. It is customary for the winner to be chosen by the popular acclaim of the male audience. Best known of these events is MTV's annual Spring Break-fest, *Beauty & the Beach* (which had to leave its Daytona Beach, Florida, location when concerns were raised about the show's bountiful displays of flesh), and Hawaiian Tropic's annual contest.

Whitcomb, Laura (b. 1970) Los Angeles fashion designer and former STYLIST who first gained notoriety in 1993 when she launched a line of long stretch-fabric dresses adorned with the three-stripe motif of ADIDAS, under an arrangement with the German sportswear icon. Whitcomb's label, Label, received mainstream exposure when the dresses (priced at around $250) were worn by MADONNA, JULIETTE LEWIS, and WINONA RYDER. The designer next made an attention-getting deal with Playboy, gaining partial financing for her collection and permission to incorporate the soft-porn icon's bunny logo in designs. The Playboy collection, shown in April 1994, was not well received by the fashion press (some of whom found Whitcomb's new playmate unpalatable). In fall '94 Whitcomb unveiled, to lukewarm response, a collection inspired by Cold War spy icon James Bond.

white trash Socially acceptable slur originally referring to a largely Southern white underclass. In the early '90s white trash culture has spawned endless characters for tabloid TV and talk shows, from temporary penis donor JOHN WAYNE BOBBITT to figure-skating thug Tonya Harding to chief-executive sibling Roger Clinton to sitcom diva Roseanne (formerly Barr and Arnold). As illegitimacy and illiteracy rates rose, movies like *True Romance* (1993), *Natural Born Killers* (1994), *Guncrazy* (1992), *Gas Food Lodging* (1992), and *Kalifornia* (1993) rendered glamorous the white trash *milieu* for GENERATION X moviegoers. The class's bold disregard for social convention is envied by many well-born INDIE-ROCK types, most visible among them singer COURTNEY LOVE and actress DREW BARRYMORE, with their slatternly make-up and dimestore gladrags. Less obvious is indie-rock's fetish for working-class accoutrements: young adults who'd never be seen sporting the logo of a major sports franchise or entertainment product, can often be seen wrapped in authentic garage attendant jackets or a baseball cap advertising fish bait.

Whitney Biennial Politically charged art show, held in odd-numbered years at New York's Whitney Museum, spotlighting the contemporary American art scene. (The first Whitney show was held in 1932, when Gertrude Vanderbilt Whitney called attention to the Continental bias of the Museum of Modern Art by featuring the work of American artists.) The 1993 Biennial helped define the frontlines of battles over POLITICAL CORRECTNESS: metal admission badges sold to visitors were inscribed with the message "I Can't Imagine Ever Wanting To Be White." Installations included Cindy Sherman's photo posters of sex dolls and Janine Antoni's "Gnaw," a 600-pound block of chocolate and an equal-sized 500-pound block of lard, each partially chewed by the artist. The 1995 show, put under the care of a single curator rather than a committee, muffled the number of overt political messages, but still showcased pieces like Nicole Eisenman's mural of the Whitney demolished.

WEB **Whitney Museum of American Art** http://mosaic. echonyc.com/%7Ewhitney/WMAA/ ✦ WEB **Whitney Museum** http://www.uky.edu/Artsource/whitneyhome.html

Wicca Pagan, pre-Christian religion repopularized in the '70s and '80s primarily as a feminist expression of SPIRITUALITY. (The feminine form wicce and "witch" share Old English etymologies.) Occult supply stores, covens, solstice celebrations, Sabbaths, and New Year's observances of Samhain (Celtic feast of the dead) on Halloweeen be-came increasingly common around college campuses and women's centers in the early '90s. Wiccan (or "Wiccean" or "witchy") beliefs are unstructured, but usually involve an explicit rejection of a monotheistic "God the Father," as well as an environmental bent marked by ritual worship of the earth and the changing seasons. While feminist witchcraft is occult, Wiccans take pains to distinguish their worship from SATANISM and "black magic"—Wiccan newspaper editorials took Disney's 1993 *Hocus Pocus* to task for stereotyping witches, and have bemoaned reports of "skyclad" (naked) worshippers engaging in ritual sex. Gathering in covens, usually composed of thirteen women, witches may "cast a circle" (create sacred space), and perform spells, pray, sing, feast, or otherwise commune with their sisters, nature, and the goddess. Wiccan estimates tend to put U.S. participation in the hundreds of thousands, but a 1993 statistical survey of American religion (*One Nation Under God*) estimated just 8,000 "out of the broom closet," to use a pagan expression. The 300th anniversary of the Salem witch trials, commemorated there by pagans in 1992, marked a watershed in contemporary celebrations of pre-Christian folk magic.

"Out of the broom closet" at #Wicca home page (http://prod1.satelnet.org/ fuchsia/wiccahp.html).

WEB **#wicca Home Page** http://prod1.satelnet.org/ fuchsia/wiccahp.html ✦ IRQ **#wicca** ✦ WEB **#wicca Charter** http://www.eden.com/~aggedor/wicca.html ✦ WEB **Covenant of the Goddess** http://www.crc.ricoh.com/ ~rowanf/COG/iabout.html ✦ USENET **alt.religion.wicca**

Wicker Park Formerly rundown blue-collar neighborhood on Chicago's Near North Side that was colonized by hard-up artistic types in the late '80s. As often happens, the penniless *arrivistes* brought a certain scruffy gentrification, and Wicker Park became home to a music scene that would foster such successful acts as URGE OVERKILL, LIZ PHAIR, and well-compensated alterna-poppers Veruca Salt. Studios and clubs flourished alongside influential record labels like Drag City and Touch and Go. (The Wax Trax INDUSTRIAL label also now calls Wicker Park home.) In 1992 Humboldt Park residents Urge Overkill recorded "Goodbye To Guyville," a sardonic kiss-off to Wicker Park's male-dominated indie-rock scene; Liz Phair embellished the gag, titling her debut album *Exile In Guyville* (1993). Chicago's burgeoning scene was documented in a 1993 *Billboard* story (replete with neighborhood map) that declared the city "the new capital of the cutting edge." Visits from SEATTLE-addled record company executives became more frequent, and Wicker Park bars were beset with suburbanites on weekends.

WEB **Chicago Soundweb—Shmicago Links** http://www.soundweb.com/SoundLinks/shmicago.html/

Wigstock Labor Day DRAG festival held in New York since 1984. Originally centered around the East Village's Tompkins Square Park, Wigstock (sometimes called "the Super Bowl of drag") has spread to the West Village, attracting up to 20,000 celebrants of the glamorous life, many of whom manage to outdo the assembled performers in terms of garish accoutrements. Encouraged by the art-house success of several DRAG movies, Samuel Goldwyn released in 1995 the fluffy documentary *Wigstock: The Movie*, featuring such downtown divinities as Joey Arias, RUPAUL, Lypsinka, and Wigstock creator the Lady Bunny.

Wild Palms As post-*TWIN PEAKS* event television, *Wild Palms* had it all: VIRTUAL REALITY, mind control, religio-political conspiracy, psychotropic drugs, media manipulation, OLIVER STONE as executive producer, impeccable '60s soundtrack, archly retro clothing design, Angie Dickinson, and a cameo from WILLIAM GIBSON. The only thing the show lacked was viewers. The glacial pacing of this three-part May 1993 mini-series turned off all but the brave few who'd followed it as a comic strip in *DETAILS* magazine. There, as a collaboration between writer Bruce Wagner and artist Julian Allen, *Wild Palms* was a lurid, elliptical meditation on marginal Hollywood; its themes were expanded upon in Wagner's 1991 novel *Force Majeure*. History will mark *Wild Palms* down as either an underappreciated classic or consummate '90s kitsch.

Wildmon, Rev. Donald (b. 1938) America's best known anti-obscenity, anti-gay, and anti-art fundraiser. Protest campaigns by his Tupelo, Missouri, American Family Association have been waged against numerous NEA grant recipients and the very idea of government arts spending. TV targets include female hygiene-product ads, the 1993 premiere of *NYPD Blue* and, the next year, the PBS series adapted from Armistead Maupin's *Tales of the City* novels (set in gay San Francisco during the '70s). A Wildmon lawsuit temporarily blocked the U.S. distribution of *Damned in the U.S.A.*, a self-fulfilling documentary about American censorship, because it contained an unflattering interview with him. The film won an International Emmy in 1991.

Williams, Robert (b. 1945) Art school dropout who went to work for car customizer and "Rat Fink" creator Ed "Big Daddy" Roth in the mid '60s. Williams later drifted into the underground COMIX scene, appearing in *Zap Comix* in 1968, and later in such notorious works as "Snatch" and "Felch." A militantly "lowbrow" painter, Williams went onto become of the pivotal artists of the synthesis of art and hot rod culture known as Kustom Kulture. His painting "Appetite for Destruction" appeared on the cover of the same-titled Guns 'N Roses album. Williams's proclivity for painting "nekkid" ladies on tacos, hamburgers, and ice cream cones has provoked the ire of feminist groups. His work is compiled in three annotated books *Zombie Mystery Paintings*, *Visual Addiction*, and *Tales from a Tortured Libido*. In 1994, he launched *Juxtapoz*, an art magazine dedicated to lowbrow art.

Wilson, Brian (b. 1942) As the leader of the Beach Boys, Brian Wilson conjured up rococo arrangements and otherworldly harmonies that represented the first major shift away from rock's guitar-bass-drums beginnings. With in-studio skills that outshone even the Beatles, Wilson was fond of remarking that all he was doing was transcribing the voices he heard in his head. No one knew how serious he was. In the '70s, bloated almost beyond recognition, Wilson broke apart and sank into a madness that was later ascribed to drug use and childhood abuse. While the Beach Boys toured the oldies circuit, Wilson placed himself in the care of Dr. Eugene Landy, a domineering psychologist who took co-writing credit for five of the eleven songs on Wilson's 1988 solo debut. Wilson is now regarded as a fragile patron saint of the romantic loser-pop plied by so many ALTERNATIVE-rock acts. He was officially canonized in 1995 by *I Just Wasn't Made For These Times*, an astute, if sometimes dewy-eyed documentary by A-list rock producer Don Was.

USENET **rec.music.artists.beach-boys** ✦ WEB **Heroes and Villains Online** http://www.iglou.com/scm/bb/hvo.html ✦ USENET **alt.music.beach-boys**

Wired San Francisco-based magazine phenomenon that struck pay dirt on its independent launch in 1992 by tapping into computer techno-lust and the new INTERNET culture. Just as a generation earlier *Playboy* profitably teased its readers with news of the nascent sexual revolution, *Wired* successfully sold itself as "mouthpiece for the digital revolution." With a lavish look that owed much to the American design magazine *I.D.*, *Wired* forged a "cyber-yuppie"

chic for the flip-phoning info-affluent: it combined business reporting and "deductible junket" listings with electronic privacy activism and paeans to the Internet's democratic potential. On its covers, business stars like TCI cable chief John Malone (and his political ally, Newt Gingrich) trade off with CYBERPUNK authors like WILLIAM GIBSON and NEAL STEPHENSON. Whereas its Dutch predecessor *Electronic Word*—also edited by Louis Rosetto— tended to intellectualize, *Wired* emphasizes a mainstream "You Will" optimism about the future. ("Renaissance 2.0" is its wishful comparison of the Enlightenment with computer-enhanced arts.) New York publishing giant Condé Nast is the principal post-launch investor. In October 1994 *Wired* launched one of the WORLD WIDE WEB's first genuine publishing ventures, *HotWired*.

WEB **HotWired** http://www.wired.com ✦ USENET **alt.wired**

Wise Use Anti-environmental movement which takes its name but not its cause from an early 20th century conservationist, Gifford Pinchot, who worked to limit private development of federal forests in the West. The modern coalition dates from a loose confederation of far-right groups in the 1970s opposed to federal management of public lands (e.g. limits on mining and lumbering or enforcement of the Endangered Species Act). The movement has gained legitimacy with the Republican sweep of Congress in 1994 (and financial support from mining interests and the NRA) even as its MILITIA-linked fringe has grown more violent. Arguing that federal lands properly belong to localities, some members have taken up arms against "trespassers" like the U.S. Forest Service (its Carson City, Nevada, office was bombed in 1994, as was a nearby Bureau of Land Management building in Reno). In the wake of the 1995 Oklahoma City bombing, identifying logos were removed from many Washington State Department of Ecology vehicles for fear of anti-government attacks.

WEB **Bureau of Land Management Home Page**

http://info.er.usgs.gov/doi/bureau-land-management.html/

✦ WEB **National Park Service Home Page**

http://www.nps.gov/

Witkin, Joel-Peter (b. 1939) Creator of monstrous art photographs. Witkin, whose brother Jerome is a respected painter, uses dwarfs, hermaphrodites, deformed individuals ("unusual people"), cadavers, body parts both animal and human (obtained from morgues) in tableaux larded with references to religious icons and images from art history. Lovingly shot and processed by Witkin in a style suggestive of vintage photography (in an average year he produces around ten pieces), these images typically produce an unnerving mix of attraction and revulsion. As Witkin explained to the *Seattle Times* in January 1994, "My work shows my journey to become a more loving, unselfish person." Among those unconvinced by this line of reasoning was the Christian Action Coalition: in 1993 it used his photograph "Testicle Stretch With the Possibility of a Crushed Face" as part of an anti-NEA protest in the Capitol. (Witkin received a grant of $20,000 from the NEA in 1992.)

WEB **Nurse's Home Pages** http://www.tezcat.com/ ~nurse/home.shtml/

Wojnarowicz, David (b. 1954, d. 1992) Angry AIDS-casualty artist whose painted photocollages earned him the title of "visionary genius" in the Fall 1994 issue of the respected photography magazine *Aperture*, dedicated entirely to his work. In two book-length memoirs, *Close to the Knife* (1991) and *Memories that Smell Like Gasoline* (1992), Wojnarowicz described his journey from teenage, Times Square street hustler, to successful downtown artist (via New York street graffiti collaborations with Keith Haring). In 1990 Wojnarowicz successfully sued THE REV. DONALD WILDMON's American Family Association for "misrepresenting" his art in an early anti-NEA mailing; Wojnarowicz also tangled with the NEA himself: an art exhibition focused on AIDS was briefly denied federal support after Wojanrowicz called New York's Cardinal John O'Connor a "fat cannibal" in the show's catalogue copy. In 1992 Wojnarowicz's black and white photo of buffaloes heading over a cliff was used for the single cover and a video for U2's "One."

Wolf, Naomi (b.1962)   Rhodes Scholar and Yale graduate who emerged as a *grande dame* of young feminism, second only to SUSAN FALUDI, with the publication and promotion of her 1991 *The Beauty Myth*. Citing examples such as the high price of palliative skin creams and the tendency in TV news to pair older men anchors with younger women, the book argued—in a style later summed up as "breathlessly melodramatic" by the *New York Times*—that modern society's notion of beauty has less to do with aesthetics than malevolent social control of women. In her 1993 follow-up, *Fire with Fire*, the strikingly made-up Wolf championed a softer redefinition of feminism: using the non-ideological rhetoric of a seasoned politician to urge activists to forsake "victim feminism" for "power feminism," and inviting all women—even those opposed to abortion—to join the movement. Exploring what she called her "radical heterosexuality," Wolf declared in one passage, "The male body is ground and shelter to me . . . When it is maligned categorically, I feel as if my homeland is maligned." Wolf's own examples of being a woman brave enough to use her power have included her 1993 white wedding, colorfully reported in some of the same fashion magazines implicated in the Beauty Myth conspiracy, and the CULTURE BABES women's group.

Courtesy of Anchor Books

NAOMI WOLF exposes the Beauty Myth, 1992.

WEB **Spotlight on Women's Issues** http://www.best.com/ ~dsiegel/women/women_home.html ✦ WEB **inforM Women's Studies Database** http://inform.umd.edu:86/ Educational_Resources/AcademicResourcesByTopic/ WomensStudies

WOMAD   Created in large part by British pop star Peter Gabriel (b. 1950) in 1980, the World of Music, Arts and Dance (WOMAD) foundation has presented dozens of MULTICULTURAL festivals in England since its first in 1982, as well as several other countries, including the United States. These ambitious ethno-paloozas juxtapose traditional, folk, popular, and modern styles, and musicians from around the globe. The WOMAD program and a 1986 meeting of eleven UK-based independent record distributors facilitated acceptance of the marketing category "world music," which replaced "African" music to more generally signify popular music of the non-Western world. As loosely defined as it is, world music has generated its own stars—including Senegal's Youssou N'Dour, Zaire's Papa Wemba, and Tex-Mex accordion virtuoso Flaco Jimenez—who have been anthologized in WOMAD's series of "Talking Book" record albums. Gabriel's own Real World record label is also an active outlet for world music.

WEB **Global Music Centre** http://www.eunet.fi/womad/ ✦ USENET **alt.music.world** ✦ MAIL LIST **Peter Gabriel mailing list** email "majordomo@ufsia.ac.be" with "subscribe gabriel" in the message body

Women's Wire   San Francisco-based online service for women launched January 1994 as a haven in male-dominated cyberspace. Inverting the usual ratio, more than 90 percent of the 1,300 subscribers as of Spring 1995 were female. Online databases and discussions emphasize women's health, politics, and other issues in a kind of computer version of the female-targeted Lifetime cable network. The name of the West Coast ECHO-equivalent was changed from Wire (Women's Information Resources and Exchange) soon after its debut when *WIRED* magazine threatened legal action and then offered free ads. The two founders, Nancy Rhine (b. 1952) and Ellen Pack (b. 1966), met on the WELL trading information on a good women's doctor. In mid-'95 WW announced plans to expand its forums to the CompuServe online service and the imminent Microsoft Network.

WEB **Women's Wire Home Page** http://www.women.com/

Wonderbra   Bosom-boosting engineering marvel that made its U.S. debut in early 1994 after a fierce licensing battle between British manufacturer Gossard and its American rival, Sara Lee. Gossard lost, then retaliated by introducing a competing line of Super-Uplift bras, intricately crafted from 46 different pieces of material. *Newsweek* dubbed the fracas a "tempest in a D cup," and Victoria's Secret joined the fray, unveiling the Miracle Bra. By lifting the breasts and enlarging the outer edges with pockets of padding (used by U.K. club goers to conceal drugs), the new bras defied both gravity and sales predictions, revitalizing the push-up bra business. (Saks Fifth Avenue's flagship New York store sold 20,000 Super-Uplift bras in the first two months.) Some saw the new bust-enhancing brassiere as a cheap, safe alternative to BREAST IMPLANTS; others dismissed it as an overpriced alternative to Kleenex-stuffing.

Woo, John (b. Wu Yusen, 1948) First HONG KONG ACTION MOVIE director to successfully convert worship by Hollywood insiders into a transPacific career move. (SAM RAIMI once enthused, "I'd peel the tape off his splices with my teeth.") It remains to be seen, though, whether the American movie industry loves him for more than just the violence into which his stylish, soulful, and exquisitely choreographed dramas usually explode. Woo's best work includes his last Chinese-language movie, *Hard Boiled* (1992, starring his own Cary Grant, Chow Yun-Fat) and *Bullet in the Head* (1990), a point-blank cousin to *The Deer Hunter* that HK audiences found too depressing. First time out in the U.S., Woo ended up publicly disavowing Universal's cut—made partly to avoid an NC–17 rating for violence—of the Jean-Claude Van Damme bloodletting he directed (*Hard Target* [1993]). Woo's second U.S. feature, *Broken Arrow* (1995), has CHRISTIAN SLATER (reunited with *Pump Up the Volume* co-star Samantha Mathis) squaring off against JOHN TRAVOLTA in a nuclear action-thriller scripted by Graham Yost, the screenwriter of *Speed* (1994).

WEB **Hong Kong Movies Homepage**
http://www.mdstud.chalmers.se/hkmovie/ ✦ WEB **Query Hong Kong Movie Database** http://egret0.stanford
.edu:80/hk/hkquery.html ✦ USENET **alt.asian-movies**

Woodstock '94 This 25th anniversary restaging of the hippie era's epochal gathering was an

Hong Kong legend JOHN WOO directs his favorite star, Chow Yun-Fat.

incongruous notion pushed towards absurdity by the presence of MTV HOME SHOPPING, a doggedly hedonistic frat-boy element, and the presence of sponsors. (According to *Advertising Age* magazine, PepsiCola paid the three original Woodstock promoters $5 million to be the festival's soft drink, while electronics chain Nobody Beats the Wiz paid $2 million for a similar privilege; $1 million each came from Häagen-Dazs, Gibson Guitar Corp., Continental Airlines, and Vermont Pure Spring Water for on-site signage. See also REBEL ADVERTISING.) The $135 ticket was available only in blocks of four, car pass included; the $200 single ticket included a bus ride from New York. No outside beer, alcohol, or food were permitted.

The three-day, Polygram-underwritten festival (held August 12–14) featured contemporary acts like GREEN DAY, Soundgarden, and PERRY FARRELL's Porno For Pyros alongside '60s survivors like Santana, and Crosby, Stills, & Nash. (NEIL YOUNG, one-time bandmate of the latter, reportedly had "Greedstock" hats made, replacing the '60s dove logo with a vulture.) Although a perfunctory re-enactment of 1969's mud-soaked frolics was one of Woodstock '94's very few memorable images, pay-per-view revenues (at $50 per household) totaled $12 million, and album and video tie-ins performed respectably. Financial problems delayed the release of the movie of the event well past its scheduled mid–1995 date; at that point, however, there were reports of an imminent chain of "Woodstock Cafés" (see THEME RESTAURANTS).

WEB **WoodStock Home Page** http://www.woodstock.com/ ✦
WEB **The Official Woodstock–94 Internet Site**
http://www.woodstock.com/

workwear Key element in an early mid-'90s move toward proletarian chic that has also been interpreted as a rejection of the '80s designer obsession. An early example of workwear-as-fashion was the baggy, overstitched denim look sported by proto-GANGSTAs N.W.A; reportedly influenced by the uniform of the California prison system, the group's look stoked demand for CARHARTT's blue canvas jackets. The perennially fashionable TIMBERLAND workboots became a standard part of the workwear look, sometimes replaced by Redwing models. Other unlikely manufacturers to benefit as the trend came to dominate HIP-HOP culture—and by extension most streetwear in general—were San Francisco's BEN DAVIS (whose line became a signature of the BEASTIE BOYS' L.A. store X-LARGE), Dickies (work jeans), and Woolrich (nylon-lined plaid shirts).

World Wide Web   Point-and-click graphical interface for the INTERNET that emerged in 1994 and 1995 as the world's largest example of HYPER-TEXT and the electronic publishing medium of choice. The ground rules of the Web (a.k.a. WWW and W3) were first developed by Tim Berners-Lee for astronomers at Switzerland's CERN (the European Laboratory for Particle Physics) between 1989 and 1992, so they could exchange photographs and illustrations along with text. Just as DESKTOP PUBLISHING democratized high quality print production in the late '80s, the Web has the potential to equalize distribution. (Entertainment conglomerates are predicated on their ability to dominate limited record store, bookshelf, and newsstand space—commodities that are, in theory, infinite in cyberspace.) This potential was recognized on Wall Street in August, 1995, when Netscape, the leading yet profitless provider of Web "browsing" software, went public and made 24-year-old co-founder Marc Andreesen worth some $50 million. For all its uncensorable, open-ended vitality, though, the

delays in many connections and the as-yet limited ability to include sound and moving pictures mean that the Web is far from threatening TV for couch-potato appeal. This may change as the programming language (HTML) for the Web evolves to incorporate multimedia enhancements (such as Sun Microsystem's much-discussed HotJava "applets").

WEB **The World Wide Web Consortium**
http://www.w3.org/hypertext/WWW/Consortium/

Wu-Tang Clan   State-of-the-art East Coast HIP-HOP oufit consisting of nine kung-fu-obsessed conspiracy theorists from Shao Lin (otherwise known as Staten Island, New York). Eschewing the fuller grooves and more melodic hooks that have helped West Coast artists from MC HAMMER to DR. DRE cross over to a pop audience, hard-core East Coast rappers like Wu-Tang (plus Nas and Jeru the Damaja) favor a more spartan sound in the tradition of local heroes like EPMD and Eric B. and Rakim, the better to concentrate the listener's attention on each rapper's rhyme skills. The result has been the virtual remarginalization of East Coast hip-hop in the '90s. (New York artists like Run-DMC, LL Cool J, and the BEASTIE BOYS had been rap's original crossover acts in the '80s.) Wu-Tang, building on the stuttering styles of early '90s stars DasEFX and Onyx, have become such a juggernaut that they're in actually danger of crossing over. Following the platinum sales of the 1994 debut, *Enter the Wu-Tang (36 Chambers)*, band members Method Man (b. Clifford Smith, 1968) and Ol' Dirty Bastard (b. Russel Jones, circa 1969) quickly put out their own solo projects—the latter proves his nickname by flouting a decade of safe sex wisdom on 1995's vibrato-voiced hit, "I Like It Raw."

WEB **Unofficial Wu-Tang Clan Homepage**
http://www.voicenet.com:80/1/voicenet/homepages/ebonie/
wu_tang/wutang.html ✦ USENET **alt.rap, rec.music.hip-hop**

X-Files, The Supernatural, UFO-minded detective series which debuted to little fanfare in fall 1993, then quietly built a fanatical following. Languidly paced, hazily lit, often open-ended, and dolorously soundtracked, *The X-Files* has prospered by ignoring many of TV's commonly held tenets. The protagonists, a charismatic pair of wayward FBI agents named Fox Mulder (David Duchovny) and Dana Scully (Gillian Anderson), view their paranormal beat with varying degrees of skepticism (he's open-minded, she's less so)—which provides one old TV reliable, Unresolved Sexual Tension. *The X-Files* was one of the first shows to flourish on the INTERNET: self-styled "X-Philes" accrue mountains of data about the show, discuss it live online, and write e-mail to the producers, who carefully note their comments. (In 1995 Fox began sponsoring *X-File* conventions in attempts to create *STAR TREK*–like longevity and fan following.) The show's progress from obscurity to cult favorite is in pointed contrast to that of 1990–91's ill-starred *TWIN PEAKS*.

WEB **Hack (Official Fox X-Files Page)** http://www.delphi.com/XFiles/ WEB **The X-Files** http://www.rutgers.edu/x-files.html WEB **The X-Files Episode Guide** http://www.seas.upenn.edu/~cliff/xfiles-ep-guide.html USENET **alt.tv.x-files**

X-Girl Women's branch of skate-couture line X-LARGE, sold in its own shops in L.A. and New York. Designed by STYLIST Daisy von Furth and SONIC YOUTH's Kim Gordon, X-Girl was introduced in the spring of 1994 at a commando-style fashion show in the streets of SoHo in New York City. The label's first collection was based on trim PREPPY totems such as chinos, polo shirts, and tennis clothes, in what seemed a stylistic clearing-of-the-decks after the mess of GRUNGE. Sporty and clean, the line was embraced by youthful celebrity patrons such as Donovan Leitch, Ione Skye, Zoe Cassevetes, and Sofia Coppola; unwilling GENERATION X actress JANEANE GAROFALO appeared on *THE CONAN O'BRIEN SHOW* and self-consciously name-checked her X-Girl creation (worn with BARRETTES), a short cotton dress reminiscent of a dental hygenist's uniform.

WEB **X-Girl On-Line** http://www.cinenet.net/XGirl/

Kim Gordon of SONIC YOUTH sporting X-GIRL'S take on Agnes B's logo, 1993.

X-Large Clothing line established in L.A., late 1991. In X-Large's flagship store, the company's T-shirts, often emblazoned with '70s black-culture icons, were carefully augmented by other brands new to a town still swathed in ACID HOUSE couture. CARHARTT, BEN DAVIS, and old-school PUMA and ADIDAS sneakers rounded out a well-conceived HIP-HOP/SKATEPUNK aesthetic that was an instant hit with young Angelonos. (Although X-Large is often credited to the the BEASTIE BOYS, only Mike Diamond is one of its four partners.)

In 1993, with its own range expanding rapidly, X-Large spun off the X-GIRL collection for women, with a dedicated store next door on North Vermont. (X-Fuct, on Beverly Boulevard, was a joint venture with the smaller Fuct label.) The following year, after successfully opening stores in Portland, Oregon, New York, Chicago, and Tokyo, X-Large ushered in a smarter look, with ironic PREPPY themes, and MOD-centric gear from English labels Fred Perry and Lonsdale. Logically enough, the company's next move, for fall 1995, was to design suits under the X-Ecutive label.

WEB **X-Large Inte[r]network** http://www.cinenet.net:80/XLarge

YAG laser Skin grafts costing tens of thousands of dollars or disfiguring home remedies involving battery acid or flame-heated spoons were once the only means of removing TATTOOS. Such hazards were eliminated in the early '90s, helping ease tattoos further into the mainstream. The breakthrough was the advent of an $80,000 "ytterbium aluminum garnet" (YAG) laser that made tattoo removal a simple medical procedure costing a few hundred dollars. Where earlier laser treatments burned the tattoo away, the YAG laser is calibrated to break up ink particles one color at a time into smaller units that the body's own immune system can dispose of. The YAG laser has inspired campaigns in L.A., Chicago, and other cities to offer free removal of gang markings.

WEB **BME: Tattooing** http://www.io.org/~bme/bme-tatt.html/

Yahoo Directory service for the INTERNET, started in April, 1994, by two Standford electrical engineering graduate students (David Filo, b. 1966; Jerry Yang, b. 1968) to track their favorite sites on the mushrooming WORLD WIDE WEB. Yahoo, which sometimes stands for Yet Another Hierarchical Officious Oracle, grew exponentially in its first six months to become the unofficial starting place for exploring the Internet. The two left Stanford in early 1995 to become full-time online entrepreneurs, raising a reported $1 million in venture capital to hire a staff and go after paying advertisers.

WEB **Yahoo** http://www.yahoo.com/

Yoshimoto, Banana (b. Mahoko Yoshimoto, 1964) Young Japanese novelist who became a literary sensation when her debut *Kitchen* was first published in Japan, 1988. A collection of naive and sometimes absurd short stories, Yoshimoto's collection sold two million copies and earned her mention alongside Haruki Murakami (*A Wild Sheep Chase*) as one of the premier Japanese novelists of the decade. For the U.S. edition of *Kitchen* (1992), Yoshimoto herself was heavily marketed by publisher Grove Press—urban areas were postered with a drawing of the author by *SPY* car-

toonist Drew Friedman. (Contrary to popular belief, the winsome young Japanese cover model is not the author.) Dissenters from "Bananamania" pointed to Yoshimoto's banal, two-dimensional characters, but many nay-sayers were silenced by the publication of *NP* in 1993 (her second U.S. novel, and fifth in Japan). Using common metaliterary devices (translators, a book within a book), Yoshimoto wove a gripping and visceral story about sex, love, literature, and suicide.

Young, Neil (b. 1945) "Godfather of GRUNGE," slacker emeritus; Neil Young has aged more gracefully than any other rocker of his generation, offering a model of integrity, artistry, and fashion sense for bands like PEARL JAM, DINOSAUR JR., and SONIC YOUTH. Born in Canada, Young got his start in the California folk-rock scene of the 1960s, making pop hits with Buffalo Springfield, then playing only his second show as a member of soft-rock supergroup Crosby, Stills, Nash & Young at Woodstock. But it is the sound he established in the '70s with his backing band Crazy Horse that's chiefly responsible for his longevity: simple, keening melodies and plodding rhythms, out of which Young's guitar flares in discordant bursts; his vocal stylings, both tossed off and heartfelt, anticipated the sensitive-loser ethos of the coming INDIE-ROCK generation. In the 1980s, Young often lapsed into odd stylistic experiments—most egregiously the electro-voiced *Trans* in 1982, and the following year's rockabilly-tinged effort *Everybody's Rockin'*—not to mention his 1984 endorsement of Ronald Reagan. But since 1989's "Keep on Rockin' in the Free World," Young has emerged as rock's shaggy elder statesman. In 1993, he performed the song with PEARL JAM at the MTV Video awards; subsequent collaborations led to the 1995 release of *Mirror Ball*, with Pearl Jam replacing Crazy Horse as Young's backing band.

WEB **HyperRust** http://www.uta.fi/~trkisa/hyperrust.html/ ◆ WEB **Neil Young Reprise Page** http://www.repriserec.com/ NeilYoung/ ◆ WEB **IUMA/Warner Neil Young And Crazy Horse** http://www.iuma.com/Warner/html/Young,_Neil.html

alt**culture**

Zamora, Pedro (b. 1972; d. 1994) AIDS activist and openly gay member of MTV's third *REAL WORLD* ensemble, Zamora became for many viewers AIDS' most visible casualty when he passed away on November 11, 1994, shortly after the series first ran. Born in Cuba, Zamora came to the U.S. in 1980 on the Mariel boat lift. At 17, he discovered he had contracted the HIV virus from unprotected sex, and became a tireless AIDS activist and educator. Zamora was the *RW* cast member who most closely resembled an adult, educating MTV's audience on safe sex and gay romance (all while getting Puck evicted). While the episodes aired and Zamora grew sicker, MTV briefly became the subject of heavy viewer criticism for letting Zamora go without health insurance before setting up a fund for donations. Which points out the fact that *Real World* "cast members"—stars of a hit show and on call 24 hours a day for their network—do not qualify as employees earning regular health benefits.
WEB **The Unofficial MTV Real World HomePage** http://ucsu.Colorado.EDU/~burtonb/real.html ✦ USENET **alt.tv.real-world**

Zappa, Frank (b. 1940; d. 1993) Prolific art-rocker, satirist, and composer whose career spanned almost 30 years before he died of prostate cancer on December 4th, 1993. Zappa and his band the Mothers (later the ever-changing Mothers of Invention) debuted in 1966 with *Freak Out!* (rock's first double album), the opening salvo in an often-confounding career. Zappa would stake out a unique bailiwick, perversely baiting both the counterculture and the straight world with complex, theatrical works of almost ridiculously eclectic scope. Although his tireless, unpredictable output brought him an enviably loyal cult following, Zappa (who scored occasional novelty hits like "Dancin' Fool" [1979] and "Valley Girl" [1982]) attained his greatest visibility as an implacable foe of the PMRC. (He testified in front of a 1985 Senate subcommittee on rock lyrics.) Zappa's daughter Moon Unit (sometime VH–1 VJ) and his guitarist son Dweezil, publicly announced Zappa's illness in 1991, but he continued to pursue many projects until his death.
USENET **alt.fan.frank-zappa** ✦ WEB **Zappa Quote of the Day** http://www.fwi.uva.nl/~heederik/zappa/quote/ ✦ GOPHER **Zappa Discography** gopher://wiretap.spies.com/00/Library/Music/Disc/zappa.dis/ ✦WEB **St. Alphonzo's Pancake Homepage** http://www.fwi.uva.nl/~heederik/zappa/index.html/

Zima "Clearmalt beverage" launched by Coors in 1992 at the tail-end of the brief CLEAR PRODUCTS fad. Zima, distributed nationally by 1994, is essentially beer filtered through charcoal to remove all "beer cues"—i.e., color and flavor—and then injected with flavorings that make it taste something like a flat, metallic gin and tonic. Zima aggressively targeted young drinkers via promotional CDs and an INTERNET presence that included sponsorship of *WIRED* magazine's WORLD WIDE WEB site. It broke into the top 20 U.S. beer brands by 1995, but Coors was perturbed that Zima was largely considered a "girls' drink" (most popular with women aged 21–34). To entice the heavier drinking under-34 men, Coors launched Zima Gold in 1995; tasting something like a flat, metallic rum and Coke, this variant was advertised as more "bold" than Zima, meaning in part that it had an alcohol content of 5.4 percent to Zima's 4.7 percent. Despite a $14 million push, the initial response to Zima Gold was less than sparkling.
WEB **Zima Home Page** http://www.zima.com/ ✦ USENET **alt.zima**

zines See page 280.

Zippies Unencumbered by memories of America's own Zeitgeist International Party, the underground version of the Vietnam-era yippie insurgency, the U.K. Zippies launched an American "Pronoia" tour the summer of 1994. Led by Fraser Clark (b. 1943), editor of *Encyclopedia Psychedelica* and manager of the London RAVE club Megatripolis where the movement flourished in 1993, the moniker condenses "Zen-inspired professional pagans." Under the umbrella of its "pronoiac" philosophy (the nagging suspicion that someone is conspiring to *help* you), the Zippies brought together a unique and unlikely melange of New Age TRAVELLERS, CYBERPUNKS, crusties, SMART DRUG-takers, pagan spiritualists, hippies, and free-floating entrepreneurs. A 1994 foray to America was a benign yet naive attempt—blessed by TIMOTHY LEARY, TERENCE McKENNA, and a *WIRED* cover story—to connect Brit technopaganism to the relatively Luddite-oriented RAINBOW FAMILY; it concluded with an aborted jamboree at the World Unity

zines

Since 1993 Paul Lukas has published *Beer Frame: The Journal of Inconspicuous Consumption*, a digest-sized, photocopied and stapled, research report and review of downscale delights such as kraut juice, Band Aids, and tan M&M's (which *Beer Frame* unsuccessfully campaigned to preserve). Lukas is one of tens of thousands of participants effecting a publishing revolution that spans MILITIA activism, relationship diaries, and television obsession. These idiosyncratic, self-published titles can be traced to the small literary magazines and artsy chapbooks of the 1940s and '50s—as well as political dissension expressed in Soviet samizdat publications—but the name "zine" comes from an abbreviation of the PUNK-era "fanzine" (itself a corruption of "magazine," which itself dates from post-war Hollywood).

The same do-it-yourself impulse that inspired untold numbers of punk bands, also spawned numerous photocopied punk titles. Some—such as *Flipside*, *Maximumrocknroll*, *Punk*, and *Slash*—evolved into "prozines" that managed to turn small profits. The first two survived as nostalgic icons of an earlier, angrier era; the latter pair represented the form at its professional cusp. John Holmstrom and Legs McNeil's mid-'70s *Punk* combined cartoons with attitude; contributing artists such as PETER BAGGE and J. D. KING are now respectable commercial art figures. *Slash* became even more influential in its demise, having provided early developmental space for artists like GARY PANTER, before becoming a record label subsidiary of Warner Bros. Veteran zines like *Forced Exposure*, *Kicks*, and *Motorbooty* are pillars of the rock underground, enforcing strict codes of aesthetic correctness with withering satire and willful obscurity. (*Your Flesh*, *Chemical Imbalance*, *Cake*, and *Chickfactor* are part of a substratum of modern-day rock zines that tend to follow the established mix of interviews, reviews, and left-field cogitations.)

Zine culture hit its stride in the mid-'80s with the mushrooming of thousands of tiny-edition photocopied publications distributed by mail, usually to other zine publishers. Many of these small, idiosyncratic hand-crafted publications no longer emphasized the idolized object of "fan action," but rather the zine creators themselves. They were proud amateurs— they loved what they did, even if few other readers (ranging from a couple of dozen to a couple of thousand) would ever appreciate their obsessive devotion to, for example, the respective subjects of *Eraser Carver's Quarterly* or *Thrift Shop News*.

"Withering satire and willful obscurity"–Detroit's *Motorbooty*.

Anyone with a strong, obsessive personality and access to a photocopy machine (preferably an employer's or school's, although Kinko's would do at a pinch) could carve out a nook in the ranks of zinedom. Personal computers and the simplicity of desktop publishing only accelerated a process already in motion.

The zine revolution thus turned into a frantically in-breeding paraliterary space, largely through the appearance of a noteworthy zine about zines. *Factsheet Five* (along with *Alternative Press Review* and *Asylum for Shutins*), attempted to review titles as they appeared, and under different management remains the primary clearinghouse for the Sisyphean task of tracking these publications, which notoriously in-breed through bartering. (It's not unusual for a large chunk of any zine to consist of reviews of other zines.) By 1995, *Fachsheet Five*'s R. Seth

Festival in Arizona's Grand Canyon National Park that attracted more journalists than Zippies. Clark moved to San Francisco, and transcontinental recriminations were acted out in the WELL's *Wired* conference.

WEB **Megatripolis Information Node** http://www.megatripolis.org/info.html USENET **alt.culture.zippie**

Zone Books Publishing company created in 1984 by a quartet of Columbia University *habitués*

Friedman was estimating the zine universe between 20,000 and 50,000 titles.

Representing niche marketing at its most precise, zines appeal to particular and often peculiarly intimate tastes. A smattering of contemporary examples from the what-you-see-is-what-you-get department include *Asian Girls Are Rad, Fat Girl, Baseball and the 1,000 Things, Balloon Animals, Flag 'n Gun, European Trash Cinema*, and *Muppetzine*. Defiantly personal creations (one definition characterizes them as "magazines published by someone with an ego bigger than a budget"), many zines energetically chronicle their publishers' ever-shifting obsessions. RIOT GRRRLS read *Aim Your Dick* and *Womyn Who Masturbate*, computer HACKERS hunker down with *The Iron Feather Journal*, and *Seinfeld* fanatics curl up with the latest issue of *Nothing*. Other popular fields of zine expression are SPIRITUALITY (*Green Egg, Impious*), COMICS (*Boom Boom, Monkey Spuzz, Flaubert's Introduction to Art*), and poetry (*Driver's Side Airbag, Milk, Face the Demon*). A plethora of zines is of course dedicated to an impressively wide-ranging array of sexual predilections.

Pathetic Life: Diary of a Fat Slob is one state of the art "perzine," Doug Holland's account of his lonely San Francisco existence that is punctuated by vicarious, testosterone-crazed HONG KONG MOVIE interludes. Both Lisa Suckdog and Dame Darcy's *Rollerderby* and Darby Romeo's *Ben Is Dead* began as music zines before

venturing into the murkier waters of sex, death, and random obsessions. John Marr's *Murder Can Be Fun* chronicles serial and mass killing activity.

No rant zine has made more of an impact then the infamous 1994 rape issue of Mr. and Mrs. Jim Goad's self-proclaimed "hate literature," *ANSWER Me!*. The Goads' transgressive publication juxtaposed horrific real-life rape stories with hoaxes, graphic graphics, and a collection of rape jokes. The centerfold "Rape Game" is illustrated by BOILED ANGEL artist Mike Diana, the first zine creator to be found guilty of obscenity. Authors of the right-wing hate zines *Crusade Against Corruption* and *Revisionist Researcher* no doubt sympathized with his First Amendment cause.

The zine phenomenon has been documented in the 1992 book guide *The World of Zines,* written by former *Factsheet Five* editors, and fostered (and to an extent, institutionalized) by the proliferation of zine-watch columns in above-ground youth culture publications. Zines were instrumental in effecting the shift to highly personalized culture (or the "micro-politics of identity") that now thrives on the INTERNET. The WORLD WIDE WEB's home pages–the reigning playground of self-publishing and ego-gratification–may eventually render the zine medium obsolete, or at least a nostalgic remnant of print culture. As of 1994, an electronic version of *Factsheet Five* functions as one of the principal online clearing-houses for hundreds of e-zines (electronic zines, some derived from print versions) such as *BUST, Exploit Alien Technology* ("they built it, we steal it"), *Obscure Electronics, Popular Anarchy, Terror Profile Weekly*, and *Die, EVAN DANDO, Die.—Richard Gehr*

WEB **Zine Net** http://www.zine.net ✦ WEB **John Labovitz's E-Zine List** http://www.meer.net/~johnl/e-zine-list/index.html ✦ WEB **Factsheet Five–Electric** http://www.well.com/conf/f5/f5index2.html ✦ USENET **alt.zines, alt.etext, rec.mag**

Murder Can Be Fun

Murder Can Be **Fun**

No. 14 —— $1.50

Please Mr. Postman

TIE TIE TIE

Don't Shoot!

Special postal edition of John Marr's *Murder Can Be Fun*.

dismayed by the stodgy nature of academic publishing in the United States. A high-design, multidisciplinary hybrid of book and journal, *Zone 1/2: The Contemporary City* (1986) combined European and American meditations on modern urban existence. Zone's next three volumes, *Fragments for a History of the Human Body* (1989), combined essays and photo dossiers to study the body's relationship to divinity, bestiality, and the machine. *Incorporations* (1992), the most recent edition, studies the increasing overlap of humans and machines. Zone Books also publishes such philosophers and scholars as Henri Bergson, Georges Bataille, J. G. BALLARD, Michel Foucault, Gilles Deleuze, and GUY DEBORD.

EMAIL URZONE@aol.com

Index

Steven Daly (b. 1960) has written for *The Face, New Musical Express, Rolling Stone,* and American *GQ.* Born in Glasgow, he is the New York culture correspondent for BBC radio's award-winning *Mark Radcliffe Show,* and a former Music Editor at *Spin* magazine. He wrote *alt.culture* on his first computer.

Nathaniel Wice (b. 1968) has written for magazines such as *Esquire, Vibe,* and *Spin* (where he was an editor). A native of Philadelphia, he has co-authored several books, including *Net Games* and *Net Chat* (both Random House 1994). He is also a 1992 recipient of the *ASCAP Deems Taylor Award* for Music Journalism. Nathaniel's computer wrote *alt.culture.*

alt.artforum

Absolutely Fabulous	Todd Haynes	Nine Inch Nails	South Beach
ACT-UP	Pee Wee Herman	Nirvana	Art Spiegelman
Art Club 2000	Anita Hill	Camille Paglia	*Star Trek*
B-Boys	hip-hop	Pearl Jam	Oliver Stone
Barbie art	bell hooks	Liz Phair	Anna Sui
Matthew Barney	Hughes brothers	PJ Harvey	Sundance Film Festival
Beavis and Butt-head	Ice-T	platform sneakers	supermodels
Sandra Bernhard	IKEA	Prada	Swatch
The Brady Bunch	indie rock	Prince	*Tank Girl*
Tim Burton	Mike Kelley	Prozac	Quentin Tarantino
Judith Butler	Jeff Koons	Public Enemy	Timberland
Larry Clark	L.A. riots	punk	John Travolta
combat boots	Sean Landers	Queen Latifah	*2600*
Dennis Cooper	Spike Lee	R.E.M.	*Twin Peaks*
Douglas Coupland	Mike Leigh	raves	2 Live Crew
R. Crumb	Lesbian Avengers	RE/Search	U2
cyberpunk	Mark Leyner	Rhino Records	*Unplugged*
date rape	Richard Linklater	Riot Grrrls	Gus Van Sant
Mike Davis	Lollapalooza	Andrew Ross	voguing
DMT	Courtney Love	RuPaul	WAC
Doc Martens	David Lynch	S/M	Andy Warhol
drag	Madonna	Santeria	John Waters
dream pop	Greil Marcus	*Sassy*	Cornel West
Ecstasy	Marky Mark	Satanism	white trash
Brian Eno	Steven Meisel	serial killer chic	Whitney Biennial
Susan Faludi	Menendez brothers	'70s fashion	Rev. Donald Wildmon
gangsta	Miramax	Jim Shaw	*Wired*
Jean-Paul Gaultier	Modern Primitive	*The Simpsons*	Naomi Wolf
Generation X	*Mondo 2000*	slip dresses	*The X-Files*
William Gibson	NEA	Snapple	zines
Guerilla Girls	Nike	Sonic Youth	Zone Books

the culture of

THE WORLD'S MOST INFLUENTIAL ART MAGAZINE. SUBSCRIBE 1 800 966 2783

WARNING:

IN ENGLAND, MORE PEOPLE HAVE *GRANTA* STOLEN FROM THEIR HOMES THAN ANY OTHER MAGAZINE

TEN REASONS TO STEAL *GRANTA*:

1. FICTION

T. Coraghessan Boyle, Martin Amis, Louise Erdrich, Richard Ford, Isabel Allende, Allan Gurganus, Jayne Anne Phillips, Italo Calvino, Margaret Atwood, Don DeLillo, Kazuo Ishiguro, Paul Auster, Tim O'Brien.

2. POLEMIC

Germaine Greer on Cuban women, Günter Grass on the German character, Gore Vidal on God, Martha Gellhorn on why she will never return to Germany, Neil Steinberg on the tragedy of spelling bees.

3. AUTOBIOGRAPHY

Ivan Klíma on his childhood—in a Nazi concentration camp, John Updike on his stutter, Richard Rayner on his former life as a petty thief, Mary Karr's horrifying 'Grandma Moore', two murderers on what it's like to kill.

4. FIRSTS

Salman Rushdie's first statement after going into hiding; the first, and only, publication of Sappho Durrell's diaries revealing the dark side of her relationship with her famous father, Lawrence.

5. REPORTAGE

James Fenton on the fall of Saigon, Jonathan Raban on the flooded Mississippi, Amitav Ghosh on dancing in Cambodia, Helen Epstein on Aids in Africa, Nuha Al-Radi in Baghdad during the Allied bombing.

6. PHOTOGRAPHY

Gilles Peress in former Yugoslavia and Rwanda, Eugene Richards in a Denver emergency room, Mary Ellen Mark on Spring Break at Daytona Beach, Steve Pyke's portraits of the very, very rich.

7. TRAVEL WRITING

Bruce Chatwin's unpublished notebooks, Bill Bryson with fat girls in Des Moines, Redmond O'Hanlon in the Congo in search of the last dinosaur, Paul Theroux in the New York subways and in a Malawi leper colony.

8. REVELATIONS

James Ellroy on the sexed-up, drugged-out world of LA in the fifties, Ian Buruma on memory and forgetting at Buchenwald, Mikal Gilmore's story of growing up with a homicidal brother—Gary.

9. PRIZE WINNERS

Nadine Gordimer, Ben Okri, Gabriel García Márquez, Saul Bellow, William Boyd, Jeanette Winterson, Mario Vargas Llosa, Tobias Wolff, Tracy Kidder, Heinrich Böll.

10. DURABILITY

Ninety-two percent of our 100,000 readers never throw a single issue away, ever. That's why we print each 256-page issue of *Granta* on high quality, acid free paper with a striking full-colour cover—it's meant to last.

SUBSCRIBING TO OUR PRINCIPLES ISN'T ENOUGH.

You should be subscribing to our magazine, too.

Because week in and week out *The Nation* brings you the likes of Katha Pollitt, Alexander Cockburn, Barbara Ehrenreich and Christopher Hitchens in every issue.

They're not only some of the best writers around—they do their best work for us.

The Nation.
Since 1865.

Welcome to New York. Now Get Out.

The weekly magazine that tells you where to go and what to do.

http://www.prodigy.com